SPORTS WEB ENCYCLOPEDIA

SPORTS WEB ENCYCLOPEDIA

(In Two Volumes)
(Volume - 1)

Dr. C. Ashok

KALPAZ PUBLICATIONS
Delhi-110052

Sports Web Encyclopedia

ISBN: 81-7835-335-0 (set)
81-7835-336-9 (Vol. 1)

Published in 2005 in India by
Kalpaz Publications,
C-30, Satyawati Nagar, Delhi-110052
E-mail : Kalpaz@hotmail.com

Laser Typesetting at : Shiva Infosystem, Delhi
Printed at : Salasar Imaging Systems, Delhi

Dedicated to my friends who are out of the field and reach
R. Subramanian,
Sadaiyandi Cloth Stores, Andipatti.
and
M. Arulraj
S/o Y.M.S. Manickam Ambalam, Panankudi

Contents

	Preface	09
1.	Aerobics	11
2.	Archery	23
3.	Asian Games	39
4.	Athletics	55
5.	Atya Patya	71
6.	Badminton	73
7.	Baseball	85
8.	Basketball	99
9.	Beachvolleyball	119
10.	Billiards	123
11.	Boxing	135
12.	Calisthenics	151
13.	Canoeing, Kayaking, and Camping	165
14.	Carrom	179
15.	Chess	191
16.	Common Wealth Games	203
17.	Cricket	215
18.	Diving	233
19.	Equestrian	243
20.	Fencing	253
21.	Football	261
22.	Golf	283
23.	Gymnastics	299
24.	Handball	311
25.	Hiking	321
26.	Hockey	329

Preface

This book entitled "Sports Web Encyclopedia", is designed for esteemed sports lovers who aspire sports information through internet. Although a number of web sites are available, we, sports lovers, are not aware of those web sites. I have tried to cover most of the dimensions a sports lover wishes to know through inter-net. Of course, it is mandatory for an user to know how to browse information through inter-net prior to using these directions. This book is primarily intended to enable a reader to have access to the desired information quickly and so it does not cover the aspect of how to access information through inter-net. The author is wholeheartedly thankful to our Correspondent and Principal fortheir invaluable help and support rendered to me in completing this academic venture successfully. The author is also indebted to Dr. S. Sivaramakrishnan, Principal, Dr. Sivanthi Aditanar College of Physical Education, Thiruchendur, Dr. S. Bevinson Perinbaraj, Reader, Alagappa College of Physical Education, Alagappa University, Karaikudi, Dr. J. Sathiah, Director of Physical Education, Madurai Kamaraj University, Madurai, Dr. A.S. Nageshwaran, Lecturer, The H.H. Raja's College, Pudukottai and Mr. G. John Anand, P.G. Department of Computer Science, Ayya Nadar Janaki Ammal College, Sivakasi for their constant encouragement and help in preparing this book. All the suggestions and criticisms for the improvement of the book are thankfully accepted.

C. Ashok
phs_ashok@yahoo.co.in

1
Aerobics

1. **Aerobics at www.turnstep.com!**

   The Aerobics Page has a growing list of thousands of aerobic patterns from instructors all over the world! Browse through them, and submit your own. Aerobics patterns for browsing, submit yours. Has the misc.fitness.aerobic FAQ, music.

   www.turnstep.com/

2. **Aerobics Frequently Asked Questions**

   Aerobics Frequently Asked Questions. This is the html version. Step Aerobics. What is step aerobics; What are the proper stepping techniques? ...

   www.turnstep.com/Faq/faq.html

3. **AFAA-Aerobics and Fitness Education and Certification**

   As the world's largest fitness and TeleFitness® educator™, Aerobics and Fitness Association of America (AFAA) has issued more than 155,000 certifications to ...

   www.afaa.com/

4. **The Cooper Institute**

   Nonprofit research and education organization dedicated to preventive medicine. Information on training,...

   www.cooperinst.org/

5. **WebAerobics - Your Global Destination for Aerobics**

   WebAerobics - Your Global Destination for Aerobics. We provide the aerobics community a resource for categorizing aerobics related web sites. Offers free homepages for aerobics instructors, also on-line fitness shopping capabilities.

   www.webaerobics.com/

6. **Bush Aerobics - Miniclip.com**

Miniclip.com - free online games, multiplayer games and online tournaments.

www.miniclip.com/bushaerobics.htm

7. **The Cooper Aerobics Center - Dallas, Texas**

... Fitness Center health club & spa, Cooper Wellness Program for lifestyle change, The Guest Lodge hotel, and non-profit Cooper Institute for Aerobics Research. Includes clinic, spa, hotel, in a 30 acre resort-like setting. Dallas Texas. www.cooperaerobics.com/

8. **FitnessZone International - Aerobics Page**

... Aerobics The growing popularity ... know it. Nowadays health clubs and fitness centres usually offer a range of 'aerobics' classes. The ...

www.fitnesszone.co.za/aerobics.htm

9. **Old English Aerobics Workout Room**

Note: Old English Aerobics is being reorganized and rewritten to accompany Peter S. Baker, Introduction to Old English

www.engl.virginia.edu/OE/OEA/

10. **Aerobics And Your Feet: Information From The APMA**

Information on aerobics and your feet from the American Podiatric Medical Association.. ... Aerobics Advice From The APMA. What is Aerobic Dancing? ...

www.apma.org/sports/aerobics.html

11. **Aerobics - Suite101.com**

Aerobics for Fitness Enthusiasts can be your path to get an idea about anything Aerobics. Learn about your heart and your cardio...

www.suite101.com/welcome.cfm/aerobics

12. **PuNk RoCk AeRoBiCs**

enter site Offers punk-rock based aerobics classes in Cambridge and Jamaica Plain. Includes a class schedule,...

www.punkrockaerobics.com/

13. **Creative Aerobics Homepage**

... Learn more about Allen Bukoff's. Creative Aerobics Consulting Practice. Creative Aerobics® Techniques. ...

www.nutscape.com/creativity/html/indexx.htm

14. **Open Directory - Health: Fitness: Aerobics**

    ... Jazzercise (9). See also: Shopping: Sports: Fitness: Aerobics (8); Sports (109,637). ... AquaFun Fitness - Offer courses in water aerobics, fitness, and training. ...

    dmoz.org/Health/Fitness/Aerobics/

15. **Therapy Directory - aerobics**

    aerobics. Everything you need to know about aerobics. Free aerobics related downloads. Links to aerobics related pages. Chakra Tuning. ... aerobics. ...

    www.worldofalternatives.com/UKHomeopathylinksaerobics. html

16. **Amazon.com: Video: Karate Aerobics (1993)**

    www.amazon.com/exec/obidos/tg/ detail/-/6303358918?v= glance

17. **Amazon.com: Video: Gilad Step Aerobics - On the Beach at Waikiki ...**

    www.amazon.com/exec/obidos/tg/ detail/-/B00000I1PT?v= glance

18. **Click Here To Reserve Your Instructors Course**

    Courses are run over one day and usually conducted on weekends, weekdays can be arranged on request. Courses are certified by official ...

    www.allcomm.co.uk/~boxerfit/

19. **How to Become an Aerobics Instructor, A Step-by-Step Guide**

    NOTICE: THIS BOOK IS OUT OF print due to escalating costs—

    hikers.home.mindspring.com/book.html

20. **Old English Aerobics**

    Old English Aerobics. Follow this link to the main Old English Aerobics page. You will need a browser capable of running Java version ...

    www.engl.virginia.edu/OE/OEAerobics/about.html

21. **designboom.com / design-aerobics education courses**

    design-aerobics, ... — design-aerobics every year design-aerobics centers on a single theme developed over 5 sessions, each of which lasts for 2 months... ...

    www.designboom.com/aerobics/

22. **Online Ad**

    adserver1.harvestadsdepot.com/newbedfordma/ 968054 968054.shtml

23. **Step Aerobics Videos**

... Secure on-line shopping! A Great selection of Step Aerobics Videos. ... Step Aerobics Videos. ... Workout #1: warm-up 10 min., step aerobics 38 min., cool down 3 min....

www.activevideos.com/stepaerobics.htm

24. **Fitness Instructional Videos**

A great selection of Aerobics and Workout Videos! ... 60 mins. Extra Lite Beginner's Aerobics with Denise Austin $14.99 Add Qty: Just what the doctor ordered! ...

www.activevideos.com/fitness.htm

25. **Sports, Exercise, and Fitness for Senior Citizens**

Aerobics To improve life in the second 50 years! AEROBICS The most beneficial forms of exercise are aerobic exercises. Some activities...

seniors-site.com/sports/aerobics.html

26. **Cal Aerobics - Schedule**

The Cal Aerobics program offers you quality, professional instruction for all levels from the Bay Area's leading certified and experienced instructors. ...

calbears.berkeley.edu/calaerobics/aerschedule.asp

27. **Aerobics/Fitness Unit**

AEROBICS/FITNESS UNIT. Jennifer South. ... Daily evaluation on effort and attitude; Oral questioning of important material learned. FOLLOW-UP AEROBICS CIRCUIT. ...

www.usask.ca/education/ideas/tplan/pedlp/aerobics.htm

28. **NOVINKY / aerobics.cz**

World > Czech > Zdravi > Fitness > Aerobik

www.aerobics.cz/

29. **IFA Kickboxing Aerobics Moves**

Online certifications for Kickboxing Aerobics, Fitness Instructor, Personal Trainer and Sports Nutritionist. ... Please come inside! Kickboxing Aerobics Moves. ...

www.ifafitness.com/kmoves/

30. **Cybercise!: Aerobics Page**

Aerobics/Fitness: "A ship in a harbor is safe, but that is not what ships are built for.". The following ... Smile! Water Aerobics. - Aquatic...

www.cybercise.com/aerobics.html

31. **Allexperts Aerobics Q&A**
... Internet. Category: Aerobics, Sort By: None. Name, Expertise, Status. ...
www.allexperts.com/getExpert.asp?Category=2267

32. **Aerobics exercise 2**
Aerobics exercise videos. ... 60 mins. Extra Lite Beginner's Aerobics with Denise Austin $14.99. Enter Qty: Just what the doctor ordered!...
www.centralhome.com/ballroomcountry/workout_videos.htm

33. **PuNk RoCk AeRoBiCs**
Punk Rock Aerobics: The work out that rocks out. No more sucky classes full of braindead bimbos in spandex thongs. PRA is for fun people with discerning taste. ...
www.punkrockaerobics.com/index1.html

34. **Pacemaster**
For over 30 years, Aerobics Inc. ... Aerobics, Inc. Our Treadmills Technical Support Dealer Locator Contact Us. PaceMaster, © 2002, Aerobics, Inc. ...
www.pacemaster.com/

35. **WebAerobics - Your Global Destination for Aerobics**
Sorry, your requested page is no longer available. We will redirect you to the main page. WebAerobics.com.
www.webaerobics.com/aerobics.html

36. **Cardio Karaticise - safe weight loss through our soft style kung...**
... Most aerobics have a high degree of impact, putting a dangerous strain on your joints, especially if you are overweight Cardio Karaticise is the first of the ...
www.kungfuaerobics.com/

37. **FitnessZone Article - Water Aerobics**
... Aerobics: Water Aerobics by Dr Jeremy Sims If you are looking for a good all-around form of aerobic exercise, why not try water aerobics? ...
www.fitnesszone.co.za/aerobics1.htm

38. **ED347484 1992-12-00 School Children and Fitness: Aerobics for Life ...**
... School Children and Fitness: Aerobics for Life. ERIC Digest. ... Title: School Children and Fitness: Aerobics for Life. ERIC Digest. ...
www.ericfacility.net/databases/ ERIC_Digests/ed347484.html

39. **Ivy pulling is weeding and aerobics in one**
... Thursday, January 15, 2004. Ivy pulling is weeding and aerobics in one. By ANN LOVEJOY SPECIAL TO THE POST INTELLIGENCER. Last week ...
seattlepi.nwsource.com/nwgardens/156570_lovejoy15.html

40. **Aerobics: Aerobics at iVillage.com**
Aerobics: Aerobics information, advice and support for women at iVillage.com. You'll find interactive tools, friendly message ... aerobics, ...
www.ivillage.com/topics/fitness/0,,165554,00.html

41. **Yahoo! Member Directory: Aerobic**
View My Profiles Advanced Member Search, Aerobics (3383 members). Home > Health & Wellness > Fitness and Nutrition.Members: New, Join ...
members.yahoo.com/interests/Aerobics-1600162395

42. **BBC NEWS | Asia-Pacific | Thais aim for new aerobics record**
Tens of thousands of people in Thailand are preparing to take part in what could be the biggest aerobics workout ever. ... Thaisaim for new aerobics record. ...
news.bbc.co.uk/2/hi/asia-pacific/3230588.stm

43. **Ascii Aerobics™ - the ultimate online workout**
www.ourmachine.com/ascii/

44. **Aerobics**
Aerobics. ... Aerobics at QEII Park. AEROBICS. Time / Date, Monday, Tuesday, Wednesday, Thursday, Friday, Saturday, Sunday. 9.00 - 9.55am, Aerobic Circuit, ...
www.ccc.govt.nz/LeisureCentres/aerobics.asp

45. **Aerobics Certification**
American Muscle & Fitness. Aerobics Certification. ... It is a must for any serious aerobics instructor. 3 credit hours (3 CECs). Aerobics Certification $39.95. ...
gregladd.bizland.com/amfpt22/id3.html

46. **Kickboxing Aerobics Certification**
American Muscle & Fitness. Kickboxing Aerobics Certification. ickboxing Aerobics Instructor Certification. Become...
gregladd.bizland.com/amfpt22/id11.html

47. **online education. what is design-aerobics?**
design-aerobics, ... — what is design-aerobics what is design-aerobics? ... — who canparticipate? design-aerobics is here for people seeking knowledge and fun. ...
www.designboom.com/aerobics/what.html

48. **attemp**
SAY Homepage, Checkout variety of classes offered! Current Quarter's schedule, Venue, Frequently Asked Questions,
www.stanford.edu/group/aerobics/

49. **Physiologicly Optimized Total Body Fitness Program.**
Combining the benefits of Cardiovascular Training (aerobics) & Resistance Training (anaerobics or weight lifting) into one synergistic program. ...
www.csmngt.com/Aerobics.htm

50. **Rhythm aerobics**
... FITNESS BOUND Rhythm aerobics West African dance workouts put a cardio twist on an ancient rite. ...
www.latimes.com/features/health/fitness/la-he-dance3nov03,1,1342117.story?coll=la-health-fitness-news

51. **Gamezone 2001jeux : Bush aerobics**
gamezone.2001jeux.com/bush_aerobics.php

52. **Open Directory - Shopping: Sports: Fitness: Aerobics**
Gin Miller Fitness
Tour schedule, workshop presentations, and work-out products from the creator of step aerobics. ...
dmoz.org/Shopping/Sports/Fitness/Aerobics/

53. **Creative Aerobics: HEROES**
Print these instructions. CREATIVE AEROBICS®. Print these instructions. Preparation. ... Return to list of Creative Aerobics® Techniques. ...
www.nutscape.com/creativity/heroes.htm

54. **International Aerobics Meetup Day**
International Aerobics Meetup Day. in 7 Days. ... Join other Aerobics Lovers near you!Aerobics Meetups can happen in up to 612 cities worldwide on the same day. ...
aerobics.meetup.com/

55. **Online Sports Directory: Browse Sports: Aerobics**
Directory of Sports Products and Services, Online Sports Directory : Browse Sports : Aerobics. Order Line 800-856-2638. Enter keywords ...
www.onlinesports.com/pages/top,sprt,aero.html

56. **Water Aerobics - Aqua Aerobics**
... Advertisement. Water Aerobics - Aqua Aerobics Guide picks. Links to Water Aerobics and other types of Aquatic Exercise. Aerobics and ...
swimming.about.com/cs/wateraerobics/

57. **DOACS - Consumer Protection**
Health Studios, Consumer Protection. The Bureau of Consumer Protection is responsible for administering programs established to implement ...
www.doacs.state.fl.us/onestop/cs/healthstudio.html

58. **MathsNet Aerobi-graphs**
mathsnet.net, ...
www.mathsnet.net/aerobics/aerobics.html

59. **Aerobic videos for exercise and dance**
... Step Aerobics Fun moves by the 2001 IDEA Instructor of the Year. Floor Aerobics Latin and African dance moves with great drum music. ...
www.collagevideo.com/Aerobics/default.asp

60. **Karate Aerobics**
Karate Aerobics. ... It's known by several different names, including aerobic self-defense, karate aerobics and martial art aerobics. ...
www.blackbeltmag.com/archives/kki/1986/apr86/ karateaerobics/karateaerobics.html

61. **Ananova - Instructor develops air guitar aerobics work-out**
... Instructor develops air guitar aerobics work-out. ... The instructor says the work-out has been modelled on Punk Rock Aerobics which has become popular in New York....
www.ananova.com/news/story/sm_860582.html?menu=

62. **Water aerobics exercise**
Water aerobics exercise. Aerobics can be defined ... to our full terms. Review the full terms by clicking here. water aerobics exercise.
va.essortment.com/wateraerobicse_rewg.htm

63. **Aerobics Courses**

... Aerobics Courses. Aerobics. ... Aqua Aerobics. Aquatic-aerobics simply means water aerobics and the classes take place in the shallow end of the swimming pool. ...

www.liv.ac.uk/sports/sc/aerob1.htm

64. **Aerobics workout and fitness videos from Collage**

96 aerobics workout programs completely described. Ideal to lose weight and strengthen your heart. ... Aerobics workout videos really work! ...

www.collagevideo.com/aerobics/aerobics1.asp

65. **aerobics on Encyclopedia.com**

aerobics click here to track this topic Related: Sport. ... Variations include aerobic dance, jazz dance exercise, step aerobics, and low-impact aerobics. ...

www.encyclopedia.com/html/a1/aerobics.asp

66. **FITNESS.START**

Startpagina met fitness-links waaronder apparatuur, winkels, tijdschriften en evenementen.

fitness.start.nu/

67. **Fitness Tips, Tutorials: Aerobics, yoga, exercise routines...**

Free fitness tips & tutorials for a wide range of topics: yoga, bodybuilding, walking, aerobics, running and more. Fitness Tips, Tutorials ... AEROBICS. ...

www.knowledgehound.com/topics/fitness.htm

68. **Water Aerobics Products - Aqua Fitness Dumbbells, Kickboards, wave ...**

Water aerobics equipment, water dumbbells, belts, ankle cuffs and kickboards - aqua aerobic products. Burn fat and get fit with...

www.shapeupshop.com/aqua/

69. **Kickboxing Aerobics Personal Trainer Sports Nutrtitonist ...**

Online certifications for Kickboxing Aerobics, Fitness Instructor, Personal Trainer and Sports Nutritionist. ... Kickboxing Aerobics Video. Free Course Includes: ...

www.ifafitness.com/mainpage.htm

70. **Forbes.com: The Case Of The Fat Aerobics Instructor**

... Law The Case Of The Fat Aerobics Instructor Dan Ackman, 05.09.02, 2:10 PM ET NEW YORK - The idea of a fitness company being sued for refusing to hire a fat ...

www.forbes.com/2002/05/09/0509portnick.html

71. **How do I schedule aerobics, weight lifting and yoga?**

How do I schedule aerobics, weight lifting and yoga? Some people like to do yoga first to warm up and stretch the body out, making...
www.yogabasics.com/yogaQandA/g01.html

72. **Projo.com | Providence | Theater**

... Theater. Aerobics, dreams, humor: It's a real circus on stage 01:00 AM EST on Monday, January 19, 2004. BY JODY FEINBERG The (Quincy) Patriot Ledger. .

www.projo.com/theat contentprojo_20040119_cirque. 15268b.html

73. **Group Details**

Group Name: NUDAR: Aerobics. Group Description: Our fitness program providesactivities designed to help you work toward your optimal level of fitness. ...

aquavite.northwestern.edu/cal/pp/groupd.cgi?g=336

74. **Cal Aerobics - Home Page**

The goal of Cal Aerobics is to provide participants with professional instruction in a safe, effective, well balanced, and fun workout environment. ...

calbears.berkeley.edu/calaerobics/default.asp

75. **Nine months - A to Z of exercises in pregnancy**

... the UK. Price: £10.99. Back. Aerobics. If you must, low impact aerobicsare a better alternative to high impact aerobics. Exercising smart and healthy from prenatal to beyond. Information and article resources.

www.mothersbliss.co.uk/nine/exersafeornot.htm

76. **parrot, abbreviations, aerobics, un-weaned, ghana, cameroon ...**

... Introducing Your Parrot to Aerobics Written by Joanie Doss This article first appeared in the November/December 1992 issue of Parrot World, the publication of ...
www.parrothouse.com/Misc.html

77. **Recreation and Fitness Workers**

... People spend much of their leisure time participating in a wide variety of organized recreational activities, such as aerobics, arts and crafts, the performing ...

www.bls.gov/oco/ocos058.htm

78. **WHO: 70,000 Strong aerobics Session to highlight Health Benefits...**

... 70,000 Strong aerobics Session to highlight Health Benefits of physical Activity and gain entry in Guinness Book of Records. Thailand ...

www.who.int/entity/mediacentre/releases/pr88/en

79. **Aerobics - Step Aerobic, Cardio Kick, Cross-Training**

Links to Aerobics web sites (step, spinning, kick boxing, cardio), aerobics & exercisevideos, aerobic exercise equipment, and athletic clothing to hit the ...

www.netsweat.com/aerobics.htm

80. **Aerobics Articles - Suite101.com**

Articles at Suite101 relating to Aerobics for Fitness Enthusiasts can be your path to get an idea about anything Aerobics. Learn ...
www.suite101.com/articles.cfm/aerobics

81. **Fitness Aerobics - Books - MegaFitness**

... Home > Books > Fitness Aerobics. Fitness Aerobics ... It shows you how to create an effective yet fun aerobics program and add variety to your workouts. ...

www.megafitness.com/ hkp0009-fitness-aerobics087322471x. html

82. **The Jerusalem Report Magazine: Arts : Arts Article**

... Art or Aerobics? Ina Friedman. Catchy tunes and techno steps are turning the fond and familiar world of Israeli folk dancing upside down. ...

www.jrep.com/Arts/Article-9.html

83. **Recreational Sports**

Recreational Sports @ Sonoma State University, SSU Home. Aerobics, ...

www.sonoma.edu/recsports/aerobics/

84. **Recreational Sports**

... Aerobics/Group Fitness. The Aerobics/Group Fitness Program offers fitness classesto UNT students, faculty, staff, alumni and retirees. ... Aerobics/Group Fitness. ...
www.unt.edu/recsports/aerobics/

85. **URMC Fitness and Wellness Center - Aerobics Classes**

... People Club Hours and Schedules Club Membership Home People Schedule Membership Fitness Services Fitness Assessments Personal Training Aerobics Strength Training ...
www.urmc.rochester.edu/wellness/aerobics.html

86. **University of Bristol Sport | Aerobics**
[title]. You are here » Home » Exercise Classes » Class Listings » Aerobics. Switch to Flash-Enabled. ... Aerobics. TERM TIME ONLY - Please ...
www.bris.ac.uk/sport/classes/listing/aerobics

87. **Boston College Flynn Recreation Complex**
Boston College offers a variety of aerobics classes for every fitness level. ... Aerobics and yoga are not just for women, so men please do not be shy! ...
www.bc.edu/bc_org/ath/plex/aerobics/

88. **Fitness and Wellness @ The University of Georgia**
AEROBICS. Aerobics, The Department of Recreational Sports offers noncredit aerobics classes for students, faculty and staff. ... Cardio Box, PROGRAM Aerobics. ...
www.recsports.uga.edu/fitness/aerobic.php

2
Archery

1. **FITA Website of the International Archery Federation**
   Official website of the International Archery Federation (FITA).... World Field Archery Champ. Training tips English/ Francaise. Information on world archery records and all-time bests, a history of the association, rules for all...
   www.archery.org/
2. **USA Archery**
   The Development of Psychological Talent in US Olympic Champions. Download Adobe Acrobat Reader. USA Archery. Home page of the US national governing body for archery in the Olympic Games.
   www.usarchery.org/
3. **Martin Archery Home**
   Martin Archery, Traditional. Accessories. DealersHistory.Photos. Makers of Martin Bows and Accessories
   www.martinarchery.com/
4. **PSE: Precision Shooting Equipment**
   FEATURED BOW. FEATURED REST. FEATURED ACCESSORY. Jeff Dobbins Colorado Mule Deer Hunt PLAY THE RADIAL X-WEAVE™ FLASH MOVIE. 2003 PSE
   www.pse-archery.com/
5. **EastonArchery.com**
   Easton - Expect It Click here, Talk with other archers, learn about the latest trends in archery, speak your mind, all at the Easton Archery Outdoors Forums. ...
   www.eastonarchery.com/

6. **Archery dot Net - The leading site for bowhunting and archery...**
A list of other archery shops near you ? -view our completelist. An ezine of archery and bow hunting equipment and information.
www.archery.net/

7. **SCA Archery Homepage**SCA Archery Homepage. What's New? There are several archery email ... Rules, regulations, events andlinks for Inter-kingdom Archery.
www.pbm.com/~lindahl/archery.html

8. **The Grand National Archery Society**
The Grand National Archery Society - Governing body for the Olympic sport of archery in the UK. Governing body for the Olympic sport of archery in the UK.www.gnas.org/

9. **Quicks, the Archery Specialists - Welcome**
Quicks, the Archery Specialists. An unrivalled range of quality archery equipment. Worldwide Mail Order. Help and advice fromour staff of keen shooters. ...
www.quicks.com/

10. **National Field Archery Association**
Find contact information for the NFAA director in your homestate; Tournaments:Schedule of tournaments and details about the famous World Archery Festival 3 ...
www.nfaa-archery.org/

11. **Archery Network Tournament Archery and Bowhunting**
The Archery Network... Since 1994 The Archery Network has been providing online archery and bowhunting information. We...
www.archerynetwork.com/

12 **.3Rivers, Archery Supplies, Recurve Bows, Longbows, Arrows, Broadheads**
ThreeRiversArchery, TraditionalArchery, ArcherySupplies, Recurves, Longbows, Bows and Arrows, Arrows, Primitive Archery, Bow Fishing, Free Catalog, Archery Books
www.3riversarchery.com/

13. **BestWeb**
The requested page has not been found on this server BestWeb Home Page.
www.jfsowa.com/misc/mathw.htm

14. **Darton Archery**

    Darton Archery, the home of the Hybrid Cam. Breaking news on new innovations by Darton, technical info indexed by bow...

    www.dartonarchery.com/

15. **Archery articles**

    Articles about various aspects of Archery. Some from the ... ascientific intention). (Sagittarius Twente Archery). Archery articles. ...

    www.student.utwente.nl/~sagi/artikel/

16. **California Archery**

    CALIFORNIAARCHERY.

    www.archeryweb.com/archery/

17. **ASA Archery Shooters Association The leader in 3d Tournament ...**

    Description: Cabela's club for archers. Includes classifieds, forums, information about the Pro ASA and Federation...

    www.asaarchery.com/

18. **Archery Focus Magazine - The Official Publication of the NAA...**

    Archery Focus Magazine - The Official Publication of the NAA - Traditional and Modern Archery, Tournament Archery and Bow Hunting - Tips and Techniques for long ..

    www.archeryfocus.com/

19. **Archery Information Network - Tournament Archery and Bowhunting**

    Devoted to tournament archery and bowhunting. ... Fletcher, The Archery Dawg!".Want to write for Archery-Digest? and maybe win a new Bow!! ...

    www.archery-info.com/

20. **Myriad Stuff**

    Myriad Stuff I have been a part of.... Looking for the oldest and most outdated Kyudo page on the Web? Here it is.

    www.negia.net/~pdarden/

21. **Saunders Archery USA - Columbus, Nebraska**

    Saunders Archery USA, Columbus, Nebraska. Manufacturer ... slingshot.

    www.sausa.com/

22. **University Archery Club: Sagittarius Twente**
Information about Sagittarius, archery in Holland, (scientific) articles about archery,a collection archery links, pictures, anarchery blackboard and more! ...
www.student.utwente.nl/~sagi/

23. **Amazon.com: Books: Zen in the Art of Archery**
Archery Equipment Shopping for archery made easy!
www.amazon.com/exec/obidos/tg/ detail/-0375705090?v=glance

24. **Jackson_'s Archery and Hunting Page**
Steve Jackson's Personal Web Portal, Jackson's Archery Hunting Page, Javascript Ballistic Calculator, Kinetic Energy, MessageBoard, Archery Hunting Books ...
home.att.net/~sajackson/archery.html

25. **Bownet and Bow International Archery Magazine**
International archery news, information, resource centre and shopping section from the publishers of BOW International archery magazine. ...
www.bownet.com/

26. **High Country Archery....An Innovator in Compound Bows and Archery**
High Country Archery has been an innovator in Compound Bows and Archery Equipment From Our Very Beginning. Offering carbon crossbows and otherarcheryequipment.Alsooffersdealers lists, sweepstakes and
www.highcountryarchery.com/

27. **Alpine Archery - Innovators in Bow Hunting, Archery Equipment...**
Alpine Archery, located in Lewiston, Idaho, manufactures high quality, low priced archery equipment for worldwide distribution.... View Alpine Archery parts in 3D. Manufactures compound bows and accessories.
www.alpinearchery.com/

28. **archery.start4all.com**
This is Archery link page. On here, you will find all national and regional archery organisations worlswide. ... The archery sport is a sport for all ages. A guide to archery sites by country, including clubs and organisations.
archery.start4all.com/

29. **The Junior Archery Homepage**
The Junior Archery Web Page. . Welcome to the Junior Archery Homepage, Includes championship details, photos, and tournament information.
www.aasinfo.demon.co.uk/

30. **Splash**
New Archery Products. New Archery Products is committed to providing the bow hunter and target shooter with archery accessories ...
www.newarchery.com/

31. **SUAC INDEX PAGE**
How do I join? Welcome friends to the Southampton University Archery Club Web page. Hotter than a steel workers jock-strap. News, information, events, records, history, and links. England.
www.soton.ac.uk/~archclub/

32. **Hoyt USA - Innovation Since 1931**
» Hoyt's Innovative Triax Pocket Stabilization System! » The Elite Series Line of Shoot-Thru Bows are Here! » Our New 3D Ribbing ...
www.hoytusa.com/

33. **Archery Canada Home Page**
Includes gallery, news, records, results, rankings, rules and policies, and related links. Also provides...
www.fca.ca/

34. **Mathews Inc: Catch us if you can!**
Photos and specifications of compound bows, archery accessories and apparel.
www.mathewsinc.com/

35. **Kyudo: Japanese Archery**
The Art of Japanese Archery. ... This style found great favor with the general public and he is generally credited with saving Japanese Archery from oblivion. ...
www.negia.net/~pdarden/kyudo/

36. **IFAA**
The International Field Archery Association (IFAA), represents the Sport of Field Archery at International level. Through its site...
www.archery-ifaa.com/

37. **WandW Sports**

Korean manufacturer of bows and accessories. [English/Korean]
www.win-archery.com/

38. **CWRU Archery Club - Events**

Case Western Reserve University. Events. Archery Club. The club welcomes any student who want's to give archery a try. News, information, events, and links. Case Western Reserve University, Cleveland, Ohio.
www.cwru.edu/orgs/archery/archery.html

39. **University of Toronto Archery Club**

ARCHERY CLUB. U of T ARCHERY CLUB This club's purpose is to make information regarding target archery readily available through this web site. ...
www.utoronto.ca/archery/

40. **Archery Merit Badge**

The archery safety rules. Tell about the local and state laws on ownership, use, and registration of archertackle...
www.meritbadge.com/bsa/mb/019.htm

41. **Lancaster Archery Supply**

Lancaster Archery Supply Site designed, hosted and maintainedby GlobaWeb.Offers an on-line catalog with images andpricingonitemsforthecompetitiveandrecreationalarcher.
www.lancasterarchery.com/

42. **IFAF**

IFAF Irish Field Archery Federation. Click to Enter "This Federationis dedicated to the promotion of field archery in the whole ...
homepage.tinet.ie/~goto/archery/

43. **The BowMan's Archery Solutions. Bringing The World of Archery To**

Bringing The World of Archery To You. Archery Equipment for Competition Target Archery, 3D Archery and Bow Hunting. ...
www.thebowman.com/

44. **Archery History**

A Brief History of Archery.
www.centenaryarchers.gil.com.au/history.htm

45. **Archery Society of Tasmania**
Archery Society of Tasmania. which is the official governing body of Archery in Tasmania, Australia. ...
www.tased.edu.au/tasonline/archery/archery.htm

46. **Columbia Archery**
Women's Varsity Archery Team Archery Club.: Men's and women's sections. Official team site with a description of the program and contact information,...
www.columbia.edu/cu/archery/

47. **FS Discount Archery**
Archery supplier of thousands of Archers and Bowhunters in the past 40 years. ...
www.fsdiscountarchery.com/

48. **Ten Basic Steps in Archery: Index**
Ten Basic Steps in Archery. The following ... mental fitness. Fitness Fundamentals of course, for archery very strong legs are not the main concern. ...
margo.student.utwente.nl/sagi/artikel/steps/

49. **Archery, Archery Supplies, Alternative Sporting Services**
Archery supplies from Alternative Sporting Services Archery Shop. High quality archery equipment at low prices. Unique shopping ...
www.altservices.co.uk/

50. **The Bowsite (Bowsite.com) - Bowhunting and Archery Supersite**
If you like to bowhunt deer, elk, moose, sheep, or just plain shoot your bow, if you love archery, bows and arrows, traditional archery, or modern archery.
www.bowsite.com/

51. **Archery Outdoor World Championship 2003**
Organizers Website 42nd Target Archery World Championship.
www.archery.org/NewYork2003/wc2003ny.html

52. **Season's Greetings**
Create a bookmark and watch us grow! The plan is to entertain and inform... Promotional information on archery in NYC area. Includes many links to non profit and business sites.
home.earthlink.net/~kenarcher96/

53. **Browning_s Official Worldwide Web Site**
Offers a full line of firearms, archery, clothing, footwear, shooting accessories, gun safes, knives,...
www.browning.com/

54. **LVIV Archery Federation**
Lviv Archery Federation. Lviv, as the phenomenon in archery does not belong to any state, it belongs to a history of a sports archery. ...
www.archery.lviv.net/

55. **Cavalier Archery Equipment Inc**
Sellers of archery accessories for bowhunters and target archers.
cavalier.safeshopper.com/

56. **TSAA - Texas State Archery Association**
FUN and INTERESTING Archery Related Photos Use this link to upload tourney pictures. Caution and Disclaimer. Central source of information on all aspects of archery in Texas. Includes tournaments, sites, ranges,...
www.texasarchery.org/

57. **Scott Archery - The Recognized Leader in Release Innovation**
Designers and manufacturers of archery releases; features company history, product listing, pictures...
www.scottarchery.com/

58. **NYC Archery Championships**
Come and watch Olympic and World Champions compete for the gold in the 42nd World Archery Championships. For the first time ever ...
www.nyc2012.com/archeryworlds/

59. **Harrelson Traditional Archery, Inc., Montgomery, Alabama ...**
Custom crafted traditional bows. All of our bows are designed by bowyer Lynn Harrelsonan dare handcrafte...
www.mindspring.com/~bowyer/

60. **Archery and Bowhunting Equipment and Supplies Gold Tip Arrow**
Mountain Archery is your #1 Source for archery and bowhunting equipment and supplies.Featuring the Gold Tip Arrow! The Gold Tip Arrow Is Our Best Selling Arrow.
ebiz.netopia.com/mtnarcherysales

61. **MICKS ARCHERY**

Target Archery is an Olympic sport. There are clubs in these centres,

www.ozemail.com.au/~mmehono/

62. **Sure-Loc Archery Products, Sights, and Accessories for Fita, 3d ...**

Designs and manufactures archery and bowhunting products for the professional and amateur archer....

www.sureloc.com/

63. **Where to Shoot**

A page from wheretoshoot.org offering a brief outline of the different forms of outdoor archery and...

www.wheretoshoot.org/specialty/outdarch.html

64. **The Medieval Archery Site**

A first part is focused on medieval Archery; a second part on the history of Archery throughout the world; a third part concerns various information about ...

www.ping.be/olivier_picard/

65. **University of Strathclyde Archery Club - Main**

Home, University of Strathclyde Archery Club. - Archery, the sport of the stars!! (Well, Geena Davis and Blue Peter). ... Archery, the sport of kings!! ...

www.strath.ac.uk/Students/Archery/

66. **Pocket PCFITA Archery LogBook Software**Pocket PCWorld > Español > Deportes > Arqueríaperso. wanadoo.esfernandodediego/

67. **AMO**

The site you were trying to reach does not currentlyhave a default page. It may be in the process of being upgraded. ...

www.amo-archery.org/

68. **Archery Club, HKUSU**

www.hku.hk/archery/

69. **Archery Experts - Online Archery and Bowhunting Pro Shop**

Information about new archery products, bowhunting tips, and an online pro shop.

www.archeryexperts.com/

70. **ArcheryWeb**

Southern California Archery Web, with links to shops and competitions.

www.archeryweb.com/

71. **Archery Summit Winery**

Founded by Gary and Nancy Andrus, owners of sister winery Pine Ridge in Napa Valley, Archery Summit enjoyed the first crush in Oregon in 1995. New Releases! ...

www.archerysummit.com/

72. **Archery City**

The summary for this Japanese page contains characters that cannot be correctly displayed in this language/character set. www.usiwakamaru.or.jp/~doraemon/

73. **Stickbow.com - Traditional Archery and Traditional Bowhunting**

... Timeless Bowhunting - Book - By noted archery and bowhunting author, Roy Marlow - A comprehensive guide to contemporary bowhunting equipment and technique. ... www.stickbow.com/

74. **Google Directory - Sports > Archery**

Archery, ... AZ of Archery - http://www.archeryfor.me.ukProvides a comprehensive list of archery terminology anddiagrams for novice and experienced archers. ...directory.google.com/Top Sports/Archery/

75. **We have an Error Condition**

A range of archery products and accessories including low light sights, sighting pins and other aiming...

www.timberline-archery.com/

76. **Swansea University Archery Club**

News, information, training times, social events, photographs, and links.

www.swan.ac.uk/AU/archery/

77. **Paris Archery Club - Archery in France**

An archery club focused on learning and practicing archery. www.chez.com/parisarcclub/english.htm

78. **Archery New Zealand**

Website of Archery New Zealand Inc. An incorporated society affiliated to FITA (Federation Internationale de Tir al'Arc), promoting and...

www.archerynz.co.nz/

79. **Sussex Bowmen - The University of Sussex Archery Club (USAC)**

Information, meeting times, activities, contacts, competition results, and photographs. England.

www.ussu.net/usac/

80. **Alan_s Archery Pages - technical and coaching information covering ...**

Technical and coaching information covering all aspects of archery, concentrating on Field Archery and shooting compound bows with a release aid. Technical and coaching information covering many aspects of archery, but concentrating on shooting...

www.alansarchery.pwp.blueyonder.co.uk/

81. **Traditional Archery Supply of Whitman, MA USA**

Traditional Archery Supply sells new and used wooden Longbows and Recurve bows and makes custom arrows for target and hunting archery.

... oldbow.com/

82. **The Kyudo Project Incorporated: A California 501.3 (c) non-profit ...**

A California 501.3 (c) non-profit corporation dedicated to spreading timely and accurate information about Kyudo (Japanese Archery). Featuring active kyudoka outside Japan, dedicated to "timely and accurate information". Worldwide...

www.netwiz.net/~eclay/

83. **Ben Pearson!**

Archery and bowhunting Industry news. Also sweepstakes, pro shops, Chat, bulletin

board, extensive archery and bowhunting information. Forums and Hunter Gallery.

www.benpearson.com/

84. **NIAS Home Page**

Home of the Northern Ireland Archery Society and all things archery related in Northern Ireland. ... Affiliated to the. Grand National Archery Society. Provides information on all aspects and styles of archery, from how to do it, to where you can try it out.

www.ni-archery.co.uk/

85. **ArcheryWorld.com**

Just some of what you'll find here: One source for archery news. ... There are currently 40178 Postings. Check out the latest My Archery Profiles! ...

www.archeryworld.com/

86. **SAA website**

Official website of the Scottish Archery Association SAA The Scottish Archery Association (SAA) is affiliated to the national governing body ...

www.scottisharchery.org.uk/

87. **SHFAC Home**

Information, directions, shoots, and clubs. Devon, England. atschool.eduweb.co.uk/cite/staff/ moorechr/shfac/shfac000.htm

88. **Archery Club - University of Toronto - Hart House**

Welcome to the Hart House Archery Club web site. The Hart House Archery Club is located in the range at Hart House on the St. George ...

www.utoronto.ca/hharcher/

89. **edersbow.com eders bowhunting and archery source**

eders.com Best Sellers, NEW:Compound Bows for 2003 See which bows are selling the best and have the highest customer approval ratings.

www.edersbow.com/

90. **ATARN Home Page**

An organization providing for mutual exchange and support among the different archery traditions of...

www.atarn.org/frameindex.htm

91. **Grand National Archery Society**

Archery, a resource for gnas field archery, diary of events, results, records, criteria, latest news, field clubs. ... 10th Mar, FITA field archery, judging. ...

www.summersvere.freeserve.co.uk/gnas%20field.htm

92. **Specialty Archery**

Specialty Archery Products. Scopes || Stabilizers|| Releases || Peep Sights. And More. ENTER. Makers of archery sights including the Super D, Super Scope, andSuper Stixst abilizers.

www.specialtyarch.com/

93. **Moorabbin Archery Club**

Moorabbin Archery Club's home page. Victoria's Aust. Premier archery club providing member information. Information on the club and its history, famous members, facilities, competitions and results, safety...

www.mac.asn.au/

94. **Washington State Archery Association**

he purpose of the Washington State Archery Association is to foster, expand and perpetuate the practice of archery in cooperation with the National ...

www.crispie.com/wsaa/

95. **Bowtech Online**

Inventor of one of the most original compound bows.www.bowtecharchery.com/

96. **Kyudo - Meditation Archery**

Kyudo is traditional Japanese archery — the 'Zen Art of Archery.' Miyako Kyudojo in Washington, DC area. ... Kyudo Meditation Archery. Miyako Kyudojo. ...

www.erols.com/kenrawie/kyudo.html

97. **Williamson County Archery Club - Texas**

The Williamson County Archery Club now belongs to the Hill Country Bowhunters. Family oriented archery club and range near Georgetown, Texas, and features an event calendar, range...

www.osweb.com/wcac/

98. **Tenzone Home page**

The Tenzone website. This site is mostly based around Target Archery, and since the author is a Recurve archer, there's a bias that way too. ...

www.tenzone.u-net.com/

99. **Rocky Mountain Broadheads - Barrie Archery**

Broadheads, Barrie Archery, Rocky Mountain Broadheads, the Assassin, Ironhead 125, Rocky's Advantage, Titanium 100, Bator, Razor, Ultra and Fastflite broadheads. ...

www.bowhunting.net/barrie/

100. **Double Bull Archery Ground Blinds**

At Double Bull Archery Blinds dedicated to offering only the highest quality ground blinds available. Welcome to Double Bull Archery. ...

www.doublebullarchery.com/

101. **Northamptonshire County Archery Society (NCAS)**
Shooting Programme to see all other forthcoming NCAS shoots. Chairman: John Wilson. Why Not Give Archery a Try ? ...
www.birchdj.freeserve.co.uk/ncas/

102. **Centenary Archers Club**
Details of a target archery club including events, results,equipmentinformation,bowtuning,
www.centenaryarchers.gil.com.au/

103. **Online Archery Stores; Archery Equipment, Archery Supply and Bow ...**
Shop and Buy Archery equipment, Archery Supplies, Bowhunting supplies, arrows, targest, longbows, vanes, releases, arrow rests, broadheads, bow sights and more ...
www.tgoemall.com/mallarchery.htm

104. **bowyers redirect**
This site has been reorganized, please update your bookmark. http://geocities.com/ewmyers/bowyers/.
www.geocities.com/Yosemite/6802/bowyers.htm

105. **Bowhunting Net, the home of bowhunters and bowhunting, archers**
Updated daily. Archery and bowhunting company web sites and numerous columns by notable archers and bowhunters. Onlineshopping. ... Archery and bowhunting Industry news.
www.bowhunting.net/

106. **Parker Bows...Archery Equipment**
Photos and descriptions of Parker compound bows and accessories incorporating Force Multiplier technology.
www.parkerbows.com/

107. **Western PA 3-D Calendar**
Western PA 3-D Calendar.
www.lmariana.com/3dshoots.htm.
If you are not automatically sent to the new page within ...
lmariana.wso.net/3dshoots.htm

108. **Traditional Archery and Bowyers**
Traditional Archery Resources. This site is my tribute to those who love traditional archery. Whether you're an admirer of Fred Bear ...
www.women-outdoors.com/traditional/

109. **Cavalier Archery Equipment**
Cavalier Archery Equipment Inc. Click to go directly to Cavalier Archery.
www.cavalier-archery.com/

110. **Cherwell Archery Club - University of Oxford**
The Cherwell Archery Club is an active and popular archery club that meets on Mondayevenings during the summer at 17h30 at the Mansfield Road sports grounds ...
www.club.ox.ac.uk/Archery/

111. **Bowhunting and Archery Society**
The Internet Archery Society. ... He is the author of books and has appeared before Congress on how to quit smoking. Free from the Archery Society.
... www.archerysociety.org/

112. **Archery and Marksmanship Ranges in the Regional Parks**
Archery and Shooting Ranges in the Regional Parks. There are two archery ranges within the East Bay Regional Park District:The Briones ...
www.ebparks.org/dropdown/marksman.htm

113. **Online Sales: Archery Links for Hunting and Shooting**
Archery Guide picks. ... Archery and Bowhunting Links This is a listing of links to archery and bowhunting sites. ... hunting.about.com/cs/salearch/

114. **Fogdog Sports - Hunting/Archery**
Accessories Spotting Scopes Target Throwers Accessories TREESTANDS Accessories Climbing Treestands Hang-On Treestands Ladder Treestands ARCHERY Arrows/Bolts...
www.fogdog.com/category/index.jsp?categoryId=977002

115. **Yahoo! Directory Sports > Archery**
Sports > Archery Directory > Recreation > Sports > Archery, Search the Web justthis category. ... INSIDE YAHOO! Shopping: buy Archery Equipment on Yahoo! Shopping.
dir.yahoo.com/Recreation/Sports/Archery/

116. **Yahoo! Groups**
Yahoo! Groups. Top > Recreation and Sports > Sports > Archery. Start a Archery Group. View Archery Groups. Archery Groups.
dir.groups.yahoo.com/dir/Recreation___Sports/SportsArchery

117. **MIT Archery Club**

MIT Archery Club. Welcome to the MIT Archery club homepage. What is the MIT Archery Club? We are a group of MIT affiliated people ...

web.mit.edu/archery/

118. **Society Marshal - Combat - Archery**

Combat - Archery. Target Archery, Thrown Weapons, and Missile Combat Rules, APD(Anti Penetration Devices), Regulations and Policies. ... Target Archery Rules. ...

www.sca.org/officers/marshal/combat/archery/

119. **Google Directory - Shopping > Sports > Archery**

Archery, ... Shavano Archery - http://www.shavanoarchery.com PSE, Oneida, SKY and Great Plains retailer with archery rangeand pro shop located in Central Colorado. ...

directory.google.com Top/Shopping/Sports/Archery/

120. **The Manchester Museum - Archery**

The Manchester Museum - Archery. Events / Information / Collections and research/ Exhibitions / Education. Index. Historyof the Collection - Page _1_ _2_. ...

museum.man.ac.uk/archery/

3
Asian Games

1. **Asian Games.** A brief history.
   www.internationalgames.net/asian.htm
2. **South East Asian Games**
   South East Asian Games. A brief history
   www.internationalgames.net/seagames.htm
3. **XIII Asian Games, Bangkok (ASIAD 98) from Sadec Online**
   The XIII Asian Games Bangkok Asiad 98 coverage of all Games Sports Event day by day. Full event results, medal winners and Asian Games records set.
   www.sadec.com/Asiad98/Pages/Index.htm
4. **Welcome to the Official Website of Afro-Asian Games 2003**
   afro asian games 2003 will be held in Hyderabad, India from 24th of October to 1st of november. ... The official website of afroasian games.
   www.afroasiangames.org/
5. **Asian Games**
   The summary for this Korean page contains characters that cannot be correctly displayed in this language/character set.
   www.pusanasiad.org/
6. **14th Asian Games BUSAN 2002**
   SOUTH KOREA WINS BADMINTON WOMEN'S DOUBLES TITLE AT ASIAN GAMES (14:41). - CHINA WINS WOMEN'S BASKETBALL TITLE AT ASIAN GAMES (13:41).
   www.xinhuanet.com/asiangames/english/
7. **Macau 2005, 4th East Asian Games**
   ... EAGA. Past East Asian Games. Macau 2005, 4 th East Asian Games. The 4 th Macao East Asian Games Organisation. - About Our Organisation. ... East Asian Games and Teenager.
   ... www.east-asian-games2005.com/en/

8. **15th Asian Games - Doha 2006**
www.dohasiangames.org/

9. **HindustanTimes.com - Asian Games**
Fireworks explode during closing ceremony at the 14th Asian Games More Pictures, Badminton, Athletics. Hockey, Karatedo. Eqestrain, Taekwondo.
www.hindustantimes.com/news/5821_0,0034.htm

10. **Channelnewsasia.com: Asian Games**
The Asian Games ends with China in the lead wth exactly 150 golds, making it total of 308 medals. It has already exceeded...
www.channelnewsasia.com/cna/asiangames/

11. **Asian Games XIII Football Competition, Bangkok 1998 (English...**
If you can read traditional Chinese (Big5), you can go to the Chinese versionof this site. Like the Olympics, the Asian Games is held every 4 years.
members.tripod.com/~footballasia/asiangames/

12. **The 5th Winter Asian Games AOMORI 2003 .**
www.net.pref.aomori.jp/awagoc/index_e.html

13. **2005**
The summary for this Chinese (Traditional) page contains characters that cannot be correctly displayed in this language/character set.
www.east-asian-games2005.com/

14. **South China city soliciting ideas for Asian Games bid**
PDO — China's southern metropolis Guangzhou is inviting the public to contribute opinions and views on the city's bid for hosting the 2010 Asian Games. ...english.peopledaily.com.cn/20040125eng20040125_133290.shtml

15. **Hong Kong to host 2009 East Asian Games**
Hong Kong to host 2009 East Asian Games. The East Asian Games Associationannounced in Macau that Hong Kong had won the bid for hosting ...
www.lcsd.gov.hk/specials/e-asian/

16. **The 14th Busan Asian Games**
www.korea.net/learnaboutkorea/sportsandtourism/ busan2002/main.html

17. **22nd SEA Games Vietnam 2003**

    News. HOME. ABOUT SEA GAMES 22. SEA Games Solidarity, Cooperation and Development. Viet Nam - The Country - The People.

    ..Records.Latestnews about SEA Games22

    ..english.seagames22.com.vn/

18. **PusanwebAsianGamesGuideforBusanKorea**

    www.pusanweb.com/asiangames/

19. **Google Directory - Sports > Events > Asian Games**

    Asian Games, ... Asian Games - http://www.hiroshima-cu.ac.jpC/ASIA [Hiroshima,1994]Backgroundandhistory,programs,venues, information, events, and results. ...

    directory.google.com/Top/Sports/Events/Asian_Games/

20. **Doha 2006 15th Asian Games ::**

    Welcome to Doha 2006 Asian Games. (QSi) Expo Showcases ... friendly page. Doha Asian Games Organizing Committee launch new logo. DAGOC News Doha ...

    www.dohasiangames.org/english/

21. **Asian Games in Iran in 1974 Stamp Collection - Persian Stamps...**

    Asian Games in Iran in 1974 Stamp Collection - Persian Stamps - Asian Games History- Winners of Soccer Match in Asian Games- Iranian Stamps - Stamp Swap Club. ...

    www.farsinet.com/tambr/asiangames74.html

22. **SAMSUNG's Digital World - Sports Sponsorship -The Asian Games...**

    Home > About SAMSUNG > Sports and Sponsorships > The Asian Games Busan 2002. ...

    www.samsung.com/AboutSAMSUNG/SportsSponsorship/ The Asian Games Busan 2002/

23. **Yahoo! Directory Asia > Sporting Events > Asian Games...**

    CATEGORIES. Asian Games 2002 (7). SITE LISTINGS. ...

    www.amazon.com. Asian Games on eBay Find asian games at low prices. With over 5 million items for sale ... ...

    dir.yahoo.com/Regional/Regions/Asia/Recreation_and_Sports/ Sports/Events/International_Games/Asian_Games/

24. **Indiainfo.com -> News -> Spotlight -> Busan Asian Games ->**
The 14th Asian Games to be held at Busan from September 29 is seen as another unifying stage for South and North Korea - bitter enemies over the past five ...
newsarchives.indiainfo.com/spotlight/asiad/

25. **Asian Board Games at Board Game Central**
Information about Asian Board Games such as Go, Gomoku, Mah Jongg, Renju, Shogi, and more, from Board Game Central. ... More Info...FeaturedAsianBoardGames. ...
www.boardgamecentral.com/games/asian.html

26. **rediff.com: Sports: Afro-Asian Games 2003**
Home > Sports > Afro-Asian Games Feedback ... Bhupathi-Sania win mixed doubles gold The triumph gave Sania her fourth gold medal at the Afro-Asian Games. ...
www.rediff.com/sports/aag03.htm

27. **Thaifootball.Com (Asian Games Football Tournament)**
www.thaifootball.com/tournaments/ asiangames/ag-2002.html

28. **The Hindu : Afro-Asian Games in Hyderabad**
... National Printer Friendly Page Send this Article to a Friend Afro-Asian Games in Hyderabad. By Our Special Correspondent. New Delhi AUG. 23. ...
www.hinduonnet.com/thehindu/2003/08/24/stories
2003082405080800.htm

29. **Afro Asian Games 2003**
Afro-Asian Games. Athletics. Boxing. Football. Hockey. Shooting. Swimming. Tennis ...Weather.SiteMap.Search. Afro Asian Games, Venue.Period.LogoMascot.Organizers.
www.afroasiangames.orgafroasiangames.html

30. **14th Asian Games-Busan 2002 - china.org.cn**
... The closing ceremony of the 14th Asian Games starts in Busan Asiad Main Stadium Oct.14,2002. ... Uproar at Asian Games as Badminton and Boxing Teams Cry Foul. More....
www.china.org.cn/english/features/44487.htm

31. **Afro-Asian Games 2003**
Afro-Asian Games 2003. The Afro-Asian Games are a multi-sports event, not connected with the discontinued Afro-Asian Cup of Nations. ...
www.rsssf.com/tablesa/asafrgam01.html

32. **Atos Origin Major Events Experience | Asian Games '98**
Path: Home > Major Events > Experience > Asian Games '98.Asian Games '98, The 13th Asian Games were held in the capital of Thailand ...
www.sema.atosorigin.com/majorevents/ experience asiangames98.htm

33. **14th Asian Games BUSAN 2002**
Canon Technical Support 14th Asian Games BUSAN 2002. During Asian Game Canon Broadcast will provide Technical Support in Korea as below. Period. September. ...
www.canon.com/bctv/topics/0209_asiangames.html

34. **Faustino Grabs Gold At Southeast Asian Games :: UIC junior gymnast ...**
... Faustino Grabs Gold At Southeast Asian Games. UIC junior gymnast ties for first in rings during international competition this past weekend. ...
uicflames.ocsn.com/sports/m-gym/ spec-rel/120803aaa.html

35. **Kyrgyzstan won gold at Busan Asian Games on high-jump - Kyrgyzstan ...**
On October 12, a sportswoman from Kyrgyzstan Tatiana Efimenko won gold medal at the 14th Asian Games in Busan (Korea).... Style:SmallLarge....
eng.gateway.kg/cgi-binpage.pl?id=28and story_name=doc3437.shtml

36. **14th Asian Games BUSAN 2002**
The summary for this Korean page contains characters that cannot be correctly displayed in this language/character set
.rki.kbs.co.kr/agame/main.asp?lang=R

37. **== 14th Asian Games BUSAN 2002 ==**
-Upacara penutupan Asian Games Busan "Bertemu lagi di Doha, Qatar" Upacara penutupan Asian Games ke-14, di kota Busan, Korea Selatan ...
rki.kbs.co.kr/agame/main.asp?lang=I

38. **Guangzhou to bid for 2010 Asian Games**
... Guangzhou to bid for 2010 Asian Games (2003-12-22 15:44) (Xinhua) ... Officials said the current facilities updated would be sufficient for an Asian Games. ..
www1chinadaily.com.cn/en/doc/2003-12/22 content_292508.htm

39. **Amazon.com: Music: Asian Games**

www.amazon.com/exec/obidos/tg/ detail/-/B0000046PX?v=glance

40. **S. Korea Clinches Asiad Marathon Gold**

... Samsung Group Ranks 4th in Gold Medal Standings of Asian Games, [10/16]. ... Athletes Bid Farewell to Busan as Asian Games Clóse,[10/14]....for.yna.co.kr/Agame/E/default.asp

41. **Asian Games Hockey**

Asian Games Hockey. Asian Games Hockey. The Birth of the Asian Games. ... It was decided to hold the first Asian Games in 1951inNewDelhi, the capital of India. ...

www.bharatiyahockey.org/asiad/asiad.htm

42. **Asian Games 2002**

Asian Games 2002 (South Korea). South Korea, September 27 to October 13, 2002 Group A 27 Sep Busan South Korea 4-0 Maldives www.rsssf.com/tablesa/asgames02.html

43. **Yahoo! Directory Asia > Events > Asian Games 2002**

... email this category to a friend. SITE LISTINGS. 14th Busan Asian Games - official site. ...

www.amazon.com. Asian Games on eBay Find asian games at low prices. ... dir.yahoo.com/.../Asia/Recreation_and_Sports/Sports/ Events/International_Games

Asian_GamesAsian_Games_2002/

44. **Newindpress.com - Asian Games 2002**

...Drug fiasco mars India's decent show'BUSAN: Despite having put up their best showin nearly two decades at the 14th Asian Games, which concluded here on Monday...

www.newindpress.com/sports/asiangames2002/

45. **2002 Busan Asian Games**

2002 Busan Asian Games. Hong Kong and the Asian Games. Hong Kong Delegation.Results. OCA - Olympic Council of Asia. 14th Asian Games BUSAN 2002.

www.hksdb.org.hk/hksdb/html/et_rr1_arc2_2002ag3.html

46. **AndhraNews.Net - Afro Asian Games 2003, Hyderabad**

AndhraNews.net - Sports and Sporting Events in Andhra Pradesh – Afro Asian Games 2003, Hyderabad. ... Welcome toAfro Asian Games 2003. ...

www.andhranews.net/state/sports/afas03/default.asp

47. **The 12th Asian Games Hiroshima 94 Result**

The 12th Asian Games Hiroshima 94 (1-16, Oct.). Group League. Japan 1 - 1 UAE.Japan 1 - 1 Qatar. Japan 5 - 0 Myanmar.Quarterfinal Match. Japan 2 - 3 Korea. ...

www.st.rim.or.jp/~hajima/j-league/ japan/94/asia94/results.html

48. **Taipei Times - archives**

... Locals light a torch for Asian Games. ... Taiwan lit its torch for the Busan Asian Games in Nantou County amid much fanfare yesterday. ... www.taipeitimes.com/News/sport/ archives/2002/09/13/167949

49. **The 13th Asian Games**

The 13th Asian Games at Thailand : @SunSITe Thailand, including the description of Transportation to Stadiums, Map to stadiums, Ticket Distribution, and so on ...

sunsite.au.ac.th/asiangames/

50. **Asian Games Squash 2002 Busan Korea**

... 2002 Asian Games Squash Center at Yangsan College, Yang Mountain Busan, Korea

www.squashtalk.com/asiangames/

51. **ASIAN GAMES**

ASIAN GAMES. 14th Asian Games - 2002.

www.sports.gov.pk/html/Asian_Games_Index.htm

52. **14th Asian Games - Busan 2002**

14TH ASIAN GAMES - 2002. The 14th Asian Games held at Busan (South Korea)from 29th September to 14th October, 2002. Pakistanparticipated...

www.sports.gov.pk/html/14th_AsianGames_2002.htm

53. **SchlumbergerSema | Major Events Experience | Asian Games '98**Path: SchlumbergerSema > Major Events > Experience > Asian Games '98. Asian Games '98, The 13th Asian Games were held in the capital ...

www.schlumbergersema.com/majorevents/ experience asiangames98.htm

54. **FalunInfo.Net - Silver Medal Winner at the Asian Games for the ...**

Silver Medal Winner at the Asian Games for the Disabled is Sentenced to 8 Years (By a Falun Gong Practitioner in China 2/17/ 2004 4:30)....

www.faluninfo.net/displayAnArticle.asp?ID=8361

55. **Busan Asian Games 2002**

ASIAN GAMES 2006 The next Asian Games will be December 1 - 15 2006 and will be held in Doha, Qatar and will have Squash. In mid ...
www.geocities.com/asfsquash/index3.htm

56. **Guangzhou to bid for 2010 Asian Games**

PDO — China's southern metropolis of Guangzhou plans to bid for the 2010 Asian Games with the approval from the central government,localmediareportedMonday...english.peopledaily.com.cn/200312/23 eng20031223_131005.shtml

57. **Soccer: Asian Games**

Asian Games Soccer Almanac: Asian Games Asian Games ...
Asian Games. Year, Champion, Runner-up, Score, Third Place,Fourth Place, Host Country. ...
www.soccertimes.com/facts/international/asiangames.htm

58. **Li Binghua meets delegation of Macao East Asian Games Organizing ...**

Li Binghua meets delegation of Macao East Asian Games Organizing Committee(photoattached). Li Binghua, vice president of the Beijing ...
en.beijing-2008.org/68/68/article211616868.shtml

59. **13th Asian Games Scientific Congress**

13th Asian Games Scientific Congress. "Modern way of Sports". Nov. 30-Dec. 3, 1998. Bangkok, Thailand. ...
www.sportsci.com/topics2/Asian_Games_Congress/

60. **Channelnewsasia.com: Asian Games**

Team Singapore in the Asian Games. Ninety-two sportsman and women representedSingapore in the 14th Asian Games in Busan. They competed ...
www.channelnewsasia.com/cna/asiangames/sgteam.htm

61. **The Swiss Watch Industry - 2002 Asian Games: Swiss Timekeeping**

Swiss Watch News 2002. 2002 Asian Games: Swiss Timekeeping. (August 29, 2002). ... The 14th Asian Games attracted nearly 7,000 athletes representing 42 countries. ...
www.fhs.ch/english/news/2002/ejeux.php

62. **Hong Kong to host 2009 East Asian Games**

Hong Kong to host 2009 East Asian Games. Hong Kong has won its bid to host the 5th East Asian Games in 2009. The announcement was ...
www.info.gov.hk/gia/general/brandhk/1103241.htm

63. **Monday 'd-day' for East Asian Games bid**

Monday 'd-day' for East Asian Games bid. Hong Kong is making thefinal push in its bid to host the 5th East Asian Games in 2009... www.info.gov.hk/gia/general/brandhk/1029255.htm

64. **Afro-Asian Games 2003 - presented by indianfootball.com**

www.indianfootball.com/specials/aag2003/index2.html

65. **13th ASIAN GAMES BANGKOK 1998**

13th ASIAN GAMES BANGKOK 1998, 6-20 December 1998, Bangkok, Thailand.Emblem : 13th ASIAN GAMES BANGKOK 1998. Mascot : CHAI-YO ELEPHANT. ...

www.geocities.com/RainForest/7153/asian13.htm

66. **2002 Busan Asian Games**

2002 Busan Asian Games. Hong Kong and the Asian Games. Asian Games. Date. Host.No. of countries. No. of events. HKathletes. Medals won by HK. Gold. Silver.Bronze....

www.hksdb.org.hk/hksdb/htmlet_rr1_arc2_2002ag3_intro4.html

67. **Asian Games 1998**

<Asian Games 1998. Finals Score Board. Team, Goals, Win. India,4, win. South Korea, 2, -. Semi Finals. Team, Goals, Win. SouthKorea,3, win. Pakistan, 2, -. ...

pin.net.pk/hockey/asian_games_98/sb-ag98.htm

68. **BBC Sport | Football | African | Cameroon for Afro-Asian Games**

Afro-Asian Games. ... Cameroon for Afro-Asian Games. African champions ...

news.bbc.co.uk/go/click/rss/1.0/-/sport1/ hi/football/africa 3145585.stm

69. **Faustino To Participate In Southeast Asian Games :: Junior all....**

.. Faustino To Participate In Southeast Asian Games. Junior all-arounder will travel to Vietnam this week for his first international competition. ...

uicflames.ocsn.com/sports/m-gym/ spec-rel/112603aab.html

70. **SINGSOC [SINGSOC MEMBERS] Mini-Asian Games 2003**

Singapore in Asean • Singapore • Facts and Figures Government • A Taste of Singapore. President's Message • About SingSoc ... www.soton.ac.uk/~singsoc/singsocmem_03mag01.htm

71. **Pakistan Hockey Federation**

The Birth of the Asian Games. Pandit ... It was decided to hold the first Asian Games in 1951 in New Delhi, the capital of India. Held ... www.phf.com.pk/asianhistory.php

72. **South East Asian Games Federation**

South East Asian Games Federation. SEAGF / SEA Games. ... [South East Asian Games Federation flag] Located by Erik Bell, December 31, 2002. ... flagspot.net/flags/int@seag.html

73. **The Indian Women's National Team at the Asian Games**

The Indian Women's National Team at the Asian Games: I. Asian Games (New Delhi,India; 1951) not known II. Asian Games (Manila, Philipines; 1954) not known ...
www.indianfootball.com/data/wasiangames.html

74. **The Hindu News Update Service**

... Asian Games Chess and triathlon in next Asian games. Hyderabad Oct. 29. Chess ... event. Hyderabad is hosting thefirst ever Afro-Asian Games. ...
www.hinduonnet.com/thehindu/holnus/00729100089.htm

75. **Pictures of asian games**

Nejlepší odkazy ke slovu "asian games", ... AFC U20Championship.14th Asian Games- Busan 2002 Football Tournament: Men | Women. AFC Futsal 2002. ... .
.. words.elf.cz/2002_40_3150/asian+games.html

76. **Busan Asian Games**

www.korea.net/menu/taegeukgi.html

77. **RPGET SBIGBOOSTASDOHAASIAN GAMES OKAYSCHESS, TRIATHLON**RP GETS BIG BOOST AS DOHA ASIAN GAMES OKAYS CHESS, TRIATHLON. HYDERABAD

... These will be further renovatedto host the Asian Games. The
www.newsflash.org/2003/05/sp/sp002891.htm

78. **Pravda.RU Politics of the Busan Asian Games**

11:30 2002-10-15 Politics of the Busan Asian Games. PRAVDA.Ru recently reported on the trouble the South Korean military structures experienced when North Korea ...
english.pravda.ru/sport/2002/10/15/38144.html

79. **Kyrgyz athletes couldn't take part in winter Asian games which...**

... Kyrgyz athletes couldn't take part in winter Asian gameswhich will pass from February 1 till February 8 in Japanese prefecture Aomori....eng.gateway.kg/cgi-bin page .pl?id =28andstory _name =doc3838.shtml

80. **The 5th Winter Asian Games AOMORI 2003**

home, President Message, AWAGOC, General Information, Venues, Schedule,Public Data, Link, E-mail
www.net.pref.aomori.jp/awagoc/frame/left_e.html

81. **XIII Asian Games, Bangkok (ASIAD 98) from Sadec Online**
The XIII Asian Games Bangkok Asiad 98 coverage of all Games Sports Event. Full event results, medal winners and Asian Games records set. ...
www.sadec.com/Asiad98/Pages/Event7.htm

82. **game girl advance: E3 Panel on Asian Games**
... E3 Panel on Asian Games Following the crash and burn of American video game pioneer Atari, Japan took over the worldwide videogamemarket....
www.gamegirladvance.com/archives/2003/ 04/05 e3_panel _on_asian_games.html

83. **Permias - Asian Games '98**
... Global Festival. WEATHER. Click for East Lansing, Michigan Forecast. Photo Gallery - Asian Games '98. Photo Bareng, GayaDulu, Lagi Mejeng. Sport Activity. ...
www.msu.edu/~permias/gallery/asiangames98.html

84. **1st Afro-Asian Games 2003 - Result Main Page**
... Powered by Games Management System, CMC Limited, India.
aag2003.cmcltd.com:8080/

85. **Al-Azraq (Asian Games 1994)**
... Asian Games - 1994 Hiroshima, Japan 1 to 17 October 1994. ...
www.alazraq.com/soccer/asian_games/1994/index.shtml

86. **Al-Azraq (Asian Games 1998)**... Asian Games 1998 Thailand 30-Nov. to 19-Dec 1998, First Round ...
www.alazraq.com/soccer/asian_games/1998/index.shtml

87. **Indiantelevision.com's Breaking News : Afro-Asian Games lends....**
.. Afro-Asian Games lend strength to India's Commonwealth Games bid. Indiantelevision.com Team. (5 November 2003 2:00pm). ... The Afro Asian Games aired on DD Sports....
www.indiantelevision.com/headlines/y2k3/nov/nov32.htm

88. **Website chinh thuc cua Uy ban Olympic Viet Nam**
Thursday, February 19, 2004, VIETNAMESE VERSION. The medalists in SEAGames, Asian Games and Olympic Games: Please customize your search.
www.voc.org.vn/medalist.asp?lang=ta

89. **Gold Medal Predictions for the 14th Asian Games**
... Gold Medal Predictions for the 14th Asian Games. The sacred flame of the 14th Asian Games will be lit at Busan City in the Republic...
www.china.org.cn/english/2002/Sep/43788.htm

90. **JVC-Badminton.com > News > Category**
NEWS. Korea claims three individual Asian Games golds amid protests. October 14, 2002 - 0:00 AM - Source : IBF. Korea completed a clean ...
www.jvc-badminton.com/news/category.cfm?id=23

91. **WTGF Asian Games Ciang-Mai Thailand 3-9 November 2002**
World Transplant Games Federation, WORLD TRANSPLANT GAMES FEDERATION
First Asian Transplant Games Chiang Mai Thailand 3-9 November 2002. ...
www.wtgf.org/asiangames.htm

92. **Asian Games Results for Uzbek team**
Asian Games Results for Uzbek team (Saturday). ... Kim Min-suk won the 50-meter freestyle and gave his country its first goldmedal in the pool at the Asian Games. ...
www.uzland.uz/2002/october/05/16.htm

93. **14th Asian Games concludes**
Payvand's Iran News ... 14th Asian Games concludes. Pusan ... Following is the final medals table from the 2002 Asian Games: GOLD ...
www.payvand.com/news/02/oct/1049.html

94. **ASIAN GAMES: MATAN PROPELS ARCHERS TO TOP POST**
ASIAN GAMES: MATAN PROPELS ARCHERS TO TOP POST. HANOI, December 3,2003 (STAR) Florante Matan kept his fine form to finish second ...
www.newsflash.org/2003/05/sp/sp002942.htm

95. **Foot.dk - Fodboldstatistik website**
... Wales. Østrig. Udskriftsvenlig version. Samtlige vindere af Asian Games. År. Vinder. 2002, Iran. ... AFC. Adresse. Asian Cup. Asian Games. Asiens Bedste. Champions Teams Cup...
www.foot.dk/AsianGames.asp

96. **The 12th Asain Games, HIROSHIMA 1994 —soft-tennis—**
The summary for this Japanese page contains characters that cannot be correctly displayed in this language/character set.
www.cypress.ne.jp/kenichi/soft-tennis/ record/asian-games/1994.htm

97. **Asian Games Hockey - A Statistical Survey**
Asian Games Hockey. Asian Games Hockey - A Statistical Survey. Arun Arnaw Jabalpur, Madhya Pradesh. ... Top Five Countries in Asian Games Men's Hockey. ...
www.bharatiyahockey.org/asiad/statistics1.htm

98. **The Ist ever Afro-Asian Games were held in Hyderabad**
The Ist ever Afro-Asian Games were held in Hyderabad HRH Sheikh Ahmad Al-Fahad Al-Sabah, President OCA presiding over the Opening Ceremony of the Ist Afro ...
www.ocasia.org/new1.asp
99. **International 420 Class - Asian Games**
www.420sailing.org. International Sailing News. 14th ASIAN GAMES Busan Yachting Centre 3-9 October 2002. ... 43 nations participated in the Asian Games. ...
www.420sailing.org/asiagames02.htm
100. **The 13th Asian Games**
... athletes from 43 countries and regions in Asia will be arriving in Bangkok to competein Asia's greatest sports spectacular, the 13th Asian Games
sunsite.au.ac.th/asiangames/asiang.html
101. **All time results of Asian Games**
All time results of Asian Games. Busan Asian Games. 2002. sep. BangkokAsian Games synchronized swimming. 1998.
www.synchrokorea.co.kr/eng/results/asaid_e.htm
102. **Asian Games**
Bodybuilding selected for the 15th Asian Games By Rob Wilkins Special Assistant to the IFBB "Advocate of fair play in sportsand a strong believe that sports ...
www.femalemuscle.com/wilkins/asian_games.html
103. **International Hockey Federation : The Busan Asian Games 2002...**
... The Busan Asian Games 2002 Review. By Paul Lissek. The Asian Games 2002 in Busan/Korea ended with a surprising ranking considering two facts;. ...
www.fihockey.org/ vsite/vcontent/page/custom/0,8510,1181-136719-138027-24868-91862-custom-item,00.html
104. **Busan Asian Games**
www.kois.go.kr/menu/taegeukgi.html
105. **China Gathers More Medals at Asian Games**
... China Gathers More Medals at Asian Games. China Gathers More Medals at Asian Games. VOA Sports 12 Oct 2002, 23:04 UTC AP Sun Yingjie. ...
www.putclub.com/lastestnews/china.htm
106. **US Field Hockey: International events - 2002 Asian Games**
2002 Asian Games, Sept. 30-Oct. 12 | Pusan, Korea, Group A GP W L DPts GF GA Dif Korea 3 2 0 1 7 18 2 16 India 3 2 0 1 7 9 2 Japan...
www.usfieldhockey.com/results/ men/worldasian_games02.htm

107. **Results of Asian Games for Uzbekistan**
Results of Asian Games for Uzbekistan. UzLand.Uz October 4 Following are the Friday results Uzbekistan National Team in the Busan Asian Games. BASKETBALL. ...
www.uzland.uz/2002/october/05/06.htm

108. **Asian Games - Great Wall Commune a-matter - architecture and ...**
Cantilever House, Bamboo Wall, Club House, The new villa estate in Badaling next to the Great Wall of China Hardly ...
www.a-matter.com/ eng/projects/Great-Wall-Commune-pr066-01-p.asp

109. **2001 OSAKA The 3rd East Asian Games**
2001 OSAKA The 3rd East Asian Games. Team Kazakhstan...
www.yegorova.com/a/01eag/

110. **The Straits Times Interactive - 14th Asian Games**... MARATHON MAN: South Korean Lee Bong Ju takes the gold in the last trackand field event of the Asian Games on Monday, the men's marathon. ...
www.straitstimes.asia1.com.sg/mnt/ html/webspecial/asiangames/

111. **The 8th Asian Gaelic Games, Hong Kong 2003**
The official website of the Asian Gaelic Games
www.irelandhk.com/gaa/games2003/

112. **12 Iranian sportswomen to compete in Asian Games**
... Payvand's Iran News ... 9/24/02. 12 Iranian sportswomen to compete in Asian Games. Tehran, Sept 24, IRNA — Iran is dispatching 12 ...
www.payvand.com/news/02/sep/1087.html

113. **Gajah Emas -Asian Games 98**
Gajah Emas - Photo Gallery -. Singapore's Shamon Sabtu (right) tries to block a shot by Malaysia's Zabidi Sharif (left) during th...
www.gajahmas.com/as98.htm

114. **AstroTurf Named Official Supplier for Afro-Asian Games - Field...**
... AstroTurf® Chosen for Field Hockey Competition at First-Ever Afro-Asian Games! August, 2003. Africa and Asia's top field hockey ...
www.srisports.com/international/news hockey 030826 _afroasian games.htm

115. **SINGSOC [SINGSOC MEMBERS] Mini Asian Games 2003**
Mini Asian Games 2003. ... 2003 Mini Asian Games pic 01, Singapore in Asean • Singapore • Facts and Figures Government • A Taste of Singapore. ...
www.soton.ac.uk/~singsoc/singsocmem_03mag03.htm

116. **MASUJIMA STADIUM | ASIAN GAMES 98**
The summary for this Japanese page contains characters that cannot be correctly displayed in this language/character set. www.asahi-net.or.jp/~MU2M-MSJM/stadium/feature/asiangames98/asian.html

117. **Asian Games XIII**
... Advertisement. Asian Games XIII. Dateline: 12/06/98. The 13th Asian Games opened on Dec. 6 and closed on Dec. 20, 1998 in Bangkok, Thailand. ...
chineseculture.about.com/library/weekly/aa120698.htm

118. **Asian Games Village - Raj Rewal - Great Buildings Online**
Asian Games Village by Raj Rewal architect, at New Delhi, India, 1980 to 1982, in the Great Buildings Online. ... Asian Games Village...
www.greatbuildings.com/buildings/ Asian_Games_Village.html

119. **Asian Games XIII Football Competition, Bangkok 1998 (English...**
... Uzbekistan 1 1 China 0 1 Israel 0 1 Kuwait 0 1 Saudi Arabia 0 1 14 24 1997 Asian Games Site. Support the women raped in Indonesia. No Hate. ...
members.tripod.com/~footballasia/ asiangames/history.htm

120. **US Field Hockey: International events - 2002 Asian Games**
2002 Asian Games, Sept. 30-Oct. 12 | Busan, Korea, Group A GP W L D Pts GF GA Dif Korea 3 2 1 0 6 8 4 4 China 3 2 1 0 6 5 2 3 Japan ...
www.usfieldhockey.com/results/ women/world asian _games 02.htm

121. **14th Asain Games**
The 14th Asian Games. September 29, 2002 - October 14, 2002. in Korea. (Busan Metropolitan City, Ulsan Metropolitan City, Changwon ...
www.eventsworldwide.com/busan.htm

122. **Vietnamese Games Site - Play Tien Len, Domino, Chinese Poker**
... This server hosts some of the most popular asian games such as chinese poker, tienlen, gomoku, big2, domino, catte, xidach. They ...
www.vinagames.com/

123. **[pairsonice] Asian Games Results**
... Asian Games Results. Year. Champions. 1999. Xue Shen / Hongbo Zhao.CHN. Related Information. View Results by Season 2003 ...
www.pairsonice.net/competitions.php?event=Asian+Games

124. **Thaifootball.Com (Asian Games 2002)**
Team: - U23 ASIAN GAMES NATIONAL TEAM 2002. - WOMEN NATIONAL TEAM 2002. WARM UP. 12 JULY 2002, THAILAND (AG) 3:0 THAILAND (U20). 12 JUNE ...
www.thaifootball.com/tournaments/ asiangames/t-ag-2002.html

125. **Asian Games Squash 2002 Busan Korea**
SquashTalk>Asian Games Squash 2002. ...
www.squashtalk.com/asiangames/report4.htm

126. **Afghanland.com Afghanistan Football National Soccer Team Asian**
2002 Asian Games in Busan South Korea. ... The first round of the Asian Games 2002 football tournament began with a match between Afghanistan and Iran. ...
www.afghanland.com/entertainment/ soccerasiangames02.html

127. **Korea Now !!!-Sports**
2002 Asian Games Mascot. The mascot of the 14th Asian Games is a sea gull, thecity bird of Busan, which emphasizes the dynamic image of Busan. ... kn.koreaherald.co.kr/SITE/data/html_dir/ 2001/07/28/200107280035.asp

128. **Asian Games — Encyclopædia Britannica**
... Visit Britannica Store, Encyclopædia Britannica, Asian Games Encyclopædia Britannica Article. ... MLA style: "Asian Games." Encyclopædia Britannica. 2004. ...
www.britannica.com/eb/article?eu=9984

4

Athletics

1. **IAAF International Association of Athletics Federations**

   The official web of the world governing body for track and field.Latest news and live results from...

   www.iaaf.org/

2. **Oakland Athletics : The Official Site**

   ATHLETICS' PHOTO GALLERIES. ... Oakland Athletics....

   www.oaklandathletics.com/

3. **www.NAIA.org**

   NAIA - collegiate athletics, sports, collegiate sports, football, basketball, character,volleyball, baseball, softball, soccer, cross country, track & field ... National governing body for approximately 350 small-college athletics programs in the UnitedStates....

   www.naia.org/

4. **Athletics Australia**

   Get up-to-date athletics results, photos, news and follow the triumphs of your favourite athletes online. Area teams, related links, pictures, upcoming events and coaching information for individuals interested...

   www.athletics.org.au/

5. **British Athletics Home Page**

   The British Athletics Message Board. Lists forthcoming events, results and information concerning British Athletics. Comprehensive listing...

   www.british-athletics.co.uk/

6. **uka : Homepage**

   Governing body for UK athletics (track and field): events, results, features, profiles and live chats.

   www.ukathletics.net/

7. **Athletics**
Official website of the University of Michigan Athletic Department
www.mgoblue.com/

8. **Athletics New Zealand Home Page**
Athletics New Zealand aims to promote participation and facilitate excellence in the sport in New Zealand. ... Christmas Holidays - Athletics NZ Office Hours. ...
www.athletics.org.nz/

9. **Florida State Seminoles Official Athletic Site**
Official ACC Athletic Site. E-MAIL@ SEMINOLES.COM
www.seminoles.com/

10. **UWBadgers.com : The Official Badger Athletics Web Site** Badgers information including news, roster, schedule, and statistics. Instructional camps for boys...
www.uwbadgers.com/

11. **ohiostatebuckeyes.com - Ohio State University Official Athletic...**
ATHLETICSDEPARTMENT. ...
www.ohiostatebuckeyes.com/

12. **www.TexasSports.com** Official site of Texas athletics.
www.texassports.com/

13. **Oakland Athletics : The Official Site**
Offers news, scores, player roster, 2002 schedule, and ticket information.oakland.athletics.mlb.com/NASApp/mlb/ oak/ homepage/oak_homepage.jsp

14. **Michigan State University Spartans, Official Athletic Sit e**
Official College Sports Network. The most comprehensive coverage of Michigan State University Athletics on the internet...
www.msuspartans.com/

15. **Athletics Canada - Athlétisme Canada**
www.athleticscanada.com/

16. **University of Kansas Athletics**
Official site for Jayhawk Athletics. Official team pages, news, audio-video, tickets, schedule, traditi...
www.kuathletics.com/

17. **Advantage Athletics**
Improve your technique and efficiency viewing sequence photos, reading articles and using products found in Advantage Athletics. ... Advantage Athletics...
www.advantageathletics.com/

18. **EAA european-athletics.org**
    EAA European-Athletics.org
    www.european-athletics.org/
19. **UKAthletics.com | The Official Site of University of Kentucky...**
    UK Women Close Out 2003 With Austin Peay. The Kentucky women's basketball team returns to the friendly confines of Memorial Coliseum on Tuesday, Dec. ...
    www.ukathletics.com/
20. **BBC SPORT | Athletics**
    Low Graphics version | Change Edition. | Help. Sport Homepage. Athletics. World Results. UK Results. Calendar. London Marathon.
    news.bbc.co.uk/sport/hi/english/athletics/default.stm
21. **UConn Huskies Athletics**
    Complete and continuously updated coverage of all University of Connecticut sports, plus cybercasts,...
    www.uconnhuskies.com/
22. **Oakland Athletics : The Official Site**
    Team news, statistics, ballpark information, and general information from the official source.
    athletics.mlb.com/
23. **SUathletics.com - The Official Website of Syracuse University...**
    Official site for SU athletics. Scores, news, statistics, and history.
    www.suathletics.com/
24. **RollTide.com | University of Alabama Official Athletic Site**
    Asked Questions | Site Map | Feedback | Advertisers | Privacy Policy RollTide.comis the official web site of University of Alabama Intercollegiate Athletics. Official web site of Crimson Tide athletics
    www.rolltide.com/
25. **GOPack.com The Official Athletic Site for NC State University...**
    The official home page of Wolfpack Athletics at North Carolina State University.
    athletics.ncsu.edu/
26. **University of Virginia Cavaliers Official Athletic Site**
    TOP STORY. W Basketball Virginia Hosts Clemson in ACC Opener on Friday The Virginia women's basketball team opens the 2004 ACC season on Friday, Jan...
    www.virginiasports.com/

27. **California Golden Bears - Official Athletic Site**
Insight Bowl Champs. W Basketball Cal Edged By Oregon State,70-67 California saw its five-game winning streak snapped ...
calbears.ocsn.com/

28. **Official Athletic Site, San Diego State University Aztecs**
San Diego State University Athletics Site: complete coverage of all Aztecs NCAA sportsincluding basketball, football, baseball, soccer, volleyball, Sailing & ...
www.goaztecs.com/

29. **Athletics-online**
http://athletics-online.co.uk/. Provider of results and exclusively produced news of international track and field athletics since...
www.athletics-online.co.uk/

30. **HawkeyeSports.com - University of Iowa Official Athletic Site**
Official site of the University of Iowa Hawkeyes.
www.hawkeyesports.com/

31. **National Association of Collegiate Directors of Athletics ...**
The 31 winners of the Sixth Annual Division I-AA Athletics Directors AssociationAcademic All-Star Team were announced this weekend by the Division I-AA...
www.nacda.com/

32. **University of Hawaii Office of Intercollegiate Athletics**
The official site of the Wahine and the Warriors with news items, pictures, rosters, game schedules...
uhathletics.hawaii.edu/

33. **AUBURNATHLETIC DEPARTMENT**
Auburn's New Athletic Department Web Site is Located at: http://www.auburntigers.com.
www.auburntigers.com.
www.auburn.edu/athletics/

34. **Vanderbilt Commodores | Official Site for Vanderbilt Athletics**
Freshman Carla Thomas provided a spark off the bench for the Black and Gold witha career-high 18 points and eight rebounds. Vanderbilt Falls to Miami 79-57. ...
www.vucommodores.com/

35. **AggieAthletics.com**

    Director of Athletics Bill Byrne publishes a message to fans each Wednesday. ... Signup now to receive our newsletter covering Aggie Athletics. Official site of the Texas A&M Athletic Department. Schedules and ticket information for all sporting...
    sports.tamu.edu/

36. **University of Missouri, Official Athletic Site of the Mizzou ...**

    Director of Athletics Monthly Column Mizzou AD Discusses Process of NCAA Investigation ... Support Mizzou Athletics! • Truman Club! ...
    www.mutigers.com/

37. **UofLsports.com : The Official Web Site of Louisville Athletics**

    Baseball Team Releases 2004 Schedule LOUISVILLE, KY - The Universityof Louisville baseball team has released its 2004 schedule....
    uoflsports.fansonly.com/

38. **Oakland Athletics : The Official Site**

    ... A's Quick Stats. AVG, HR, RBI, SB. Wins, ERA, SV, SO. Oakland Athletics.SelectTimeframe.
    athletics.mlb.com/NASApp/mlb/oak/ homepage/oak_homepage.jsp

39. **Indiana University Athletics - Home Page**

    IU Athletics. DeMuth Recognized By Big Ten .
    www.iuhoosiers.com/

40. **scottishathletics | Front Page**

    Scottish Athletics Indoor Leagueath.
    demonhosting.co.uk/

41. **BC Athletics - Track and Field, Road Running, Cross Country, Race ...**

    BC Athletics "Faster! Higher! Further!" BC Athletics is a non-profit amateur sport organization whose purpose is to promote, encourage ...
    www.bcathletics.org/

42. **Official Athletic Site of the University of California, Los ...**

    UCLA Bruins Tournament Center. 2003 Silicon Valley Football Classic UCLA vs. Fresno
    www.uclabruins.com/

43. **The Athletics Site**

    Results around the world, news, Greek and International Athletics Statistics
    www.athletix.org/

44. **SLV FSA - www.swiss-athletics.ch - index.**
Swiss Athletics Flash Ausgabe 32/03 Zur Aktuellen Ausgabe www.swiss-athletics.ch/

45. **UCSD Athletics**Men's Sports. Official site of University of California, San Diego athletics.
athletics.ucsd.edu/

46. **University of Pennsylvania :: The Official Athletic Site** University of Pennsylvania, a member of the FANSonly Network. The most comprehensive coverage of Quaker Athletics on the internet.
pennathletics.fansonly.com/

47. **Harvard University Crimson, Official Athletic Site**
The most comprehensive coverage of Harvard Athletics on the internet. ... Who was the MVP of the fall athletics season? Je...
www.fas.harvard.edu/~athletic/

48. **University of Massachusetts - Official Athletic Site** University of Massachusetts Athletics Site: complete coverage of all Minutemen NCAA sports including basketball, football, baseball, soccer, volleyball ...
www.umassathletics.com/

49. **Personal trainer certification, fitness certification, aerobic ...** American Fitness Training of Athletics Nationally Recognized. AFTA offers online and home study fitness courses. www.aftacertification.com/

50. **Gill Athletics, Inc. - Track & Field, Training, and Conditioning** ...Offers a full line of track and field equipment. www.gillathletics.com/

51. **Chuck Taylor**
Speciali zingin Converse shoes and apparel.
www.americanathletics.com/

52. **Official Athletic Site of University of Louisiana at Monroe** Indian Territory Now on Sale Bob Anderson's book on Indian athletics is available.
... www.ulmathletics.com/

53. **The Official Athletic Site for Florida Atlantic University ...** The Official College Sports Network. The most comprehensive coverage of Florida Atlantic Athletics on the internet. ... www.fausports.com/

54. **Platform Tennis | Viking Apparel | Accessories | Product ...**
Platform Tennis | Viking Apparel | Accessories | Product Registration Platform Tennis equiptment manufacturer of Paddles, Balls and Accessories
www.vikingathletics.com/

55. **World Masters Athletics**
... for the club Vfl Sindelfingen WMA General Assembly in Carolina in July Pictures>>Signing of contract for 1st WMA World Masters Athletics Championships Indoors ...
www.world-masters-athletics.org/

56. **Commission On Athletics (COA) Online**
California Community College Commission on Athletics, the governing body for intercollegiate athletics...
www.coasports.org/

57. **Athletics South Afrca**
New heights for SA athletics SA's athletics reached new heights in 2003. ... international. - More controversy for US athletics...
www.athletics.org.za/

58. **Welsh Athletics - Official Website Gateway**
Official Website of the Athletics Association of Wales. Cymdeithas Athletau Cymru. Click Logo To Enter. Site best viewed ... Records, results and contact details for the governing body of athletics in Wales.
www.welshathletics.org/

59. **Athletics Alberta: Home Page**
Athletics is often mistaken to mean a variety of sports. It is actually ... affiliated disciplines. Athletics is both a summer and winter sport.
www.athleticsalberta.com/

60. **University of New Mexico Lobos - Official Athletic Site**
Official site of New Mexico athletics.
www.golobos.com/

61. **SMUMUSTANGS.COM :: THE OFFICIAL SITE OF SMU ATHLETICS**
Sports team information, schedules, tickets, Mustang Band and SMU Sprint Squads, photos, coach and ...
www.smumustangs.com/

62. **GoPSUsports.com - Official Home of Penn State Athletics**
Official home of the Penn State Athletics program, Joe Paterno, and the Nittany Lions. Includes intercoll...
www.gopsusports.com/

63. **Northeastern University Athletics Official Website**
Official Website of Northeastern Athletics. Official site of the Huskies. Info about the Varsity Club, intramurals, and varsity teams, plus tickets,...
www.gonu.com/

64. **Redbird Athletics - Home of Champions @ Illinois State**
Official site of the Redbirds. Team, tickets, and merchandise information, as well as campus fitness...
www.redbirds.org/

65. **University of Washington - Official Athletic Site**
Official site of the Huskies. News, merchandise, audio/video, tickets, schedules, traditions and campus...
www.gohuskies.com/

66. **Official Athletic Site of the Princeton University Tigers**
Men's Sports, Official home of the Tigers. Sportsfinder, tickets, traditions,and merch andise available online,...
www.goprincetontigers.com/

67. **Texas Tech Red Raiders :: The Official Athletic Site**
The Official Athletic Site for Texas Tech University, a member of the FANSonly Network. The most comprehensive coverage of Raider Athletics on the internet. ...
www.texastech.com/

68. **Iowa State University - Official Athletic Site**
The Official College Sports Network. The most comprehensive coverage of Iowa State University Athletics on the internet. ...
www.cyclones.com/

69. **Doorway**
Custom pads made of a patented medical-grade triblock polymer to insulate against friction, shearing, ...
www.bungapads.com/

70. **allAfrica.com:Athletics**
East African Standard.
allafrica.com/athletics/

71. **Yale University Bulldogs, Official Athletic Site**
Member of the Official College Sports Network. The most comprehensive coverage of Yale University Athletics on the internet....
www.goyalebulldogs.com/

72. **Big Green Sports - Dartmouth Athletics**
Member of the Official College Sports Network. The most comprehensive coverage of Dartmouth College Athletics on the internet. ...
athletics.dartmouth.edu/

73. **Arizona State University-Official Athletic Site**
Girls and Women in Sports Week. Maroon and Gold A History of SunDevil Athletics by seven-time Arizona Sportswriter of the Year Bob Eger. ...
www.thesundevils.com/

74. **Villanova University Wildcats - Official Athletic Site**
Official site of Villanova University athletics.
www.villanova.com/

75. **UC Irvine Athletics**
Official site of UC Irvine athletics.
www.athletics.uci.edu/

76. **Clemson University :: The Official Athletics Site**
The official Clemson Sports website, ClemsonTigers.com is the best source for information on anything...
www.clemsontigers.com/

77. **IUPUI Athletics Home Page**
Official site of the Jaguars with news items, scores, player rosters and highlights
www.iupui.edu/~jagsport/

78. **Athletics Performance**
Athletics Performance. Which is the best world record? ... Athletics world recordscan be used to compare athletic performances, at all levels. ...
www.personal.rdg.ac.uk/~snsgrubb/athletics/

79. **Official Athletic Site of the University of Memphis**
New Orleans Bowl Champions! W Basketball Women's BasketballFalls in Championship Game The University of Montana went ...
www.gotigersgo.com/

80. **Boston University Athletics**
Official site of the Terriers with news items, scores, player rosters and a schedule of games.
www.bu.edu/athletics/

81. **California Golden Bears - Official Athletic Site**
Official athletic site for University of California Golden Bears. News, reviews and ticket information.
www.calbears.com/

82. **The Official Athletic Site for The University of Toledo Athletics**
University of Toledo, member of the Official College Sports Network. The most comprehensive coverage of Toledo Athletics on the internet. ...
utrockets.fansonly.com/

83. **University of Oklahoma Sooners Athletics**
Official site of Universityof Oklahomaathletics.
www.soonersports.com/

84. **Georgetown University - Official Athletic Site**
Official site. Complete coverage of all Hoya NCAA sports plusscores, stats, news, trivia, chats,...
www.guhoyas.com/

85. **WMU Broncos - The Official Site of WMU Athletics**
Official site of Western Michiganathletics
www.wmubroncos.com/

86. **Athletics**
Athletics. ... smoking facility. In addition, Athletics has implemented a new pass-out/return policy for home football games. Register ...
www.utexas.edu/athletics/

87. **University of Illinois Fighting Illini - Official Athletic Site**
University of Illinois Division of Intercollegiate Athletics. Mission Statement To have the highest quality athletic program in all sports that allows the ...
www.fightingillini.com/

88. **Spinning.Com**
Education, apparel, forums, advice and accessories. Venice, California
www.spinning.com/

89. **College of the Holy Cross | Athletics**
Scoreboard showing up to date sports scores, and links to all men's and women's Crusaders sports sites....
www.holycross.edu/departments/athletics/website/

90. **Oregon State University, Official Athletic Site**
Las Vegas Bowl Champs Derek Potter has started the last two games at center.
www.osubeavers.com/

91. **GBRATHLETICS.COM - UK and International Athletics Records and ...**
Reference site containing deep UK athletics all-time lists, archive of British and international (including Olympic) championship medallists, British and ...
www.gbrathletics.com/

92. **UTEP Athletics: Official Site**
UTEP Receives Votes in AP Top 25 Miners recognized in national poll for the first time in nearly three years.
www.utepathletics.com/

93. **BSU Athletics Intro**
Official site of the Broncos with pictures, scores, statistics, rosters, and game schedules.
www.broncosports.com/

94. **University of Arizona :: Official Athletic Site**
Arizona Athletics Launched New Website The University of Arizona Department of Intercollegiate Athletics has launched a new design for its website produced by ...
www.arizcats.com/

95. **Boston College Official Athletic Site**
Men's Basketball and Hockey Traffic/Parking Advisory!! Yawkey Athletics CenterCheck the live webcam for construction progress!
www.bceagles.com/

96. **Official Internet Home of the University of Central Florida Golden ...**
Official web site of the Golden Knights with player highlights, scores, game summaries and rosters.
www.ucfathletics.com/

97. **LSUsports.net**

The official web site of LSU athletics with news articles, chat rooms, current standings, championships...

www.lsusports.net/

98. **WVU :: Athletics**

WVU Athletics Mountaineer athletic history ...

www.wvu.edu/~sports/

99. **ECU Athletics**

Men's and Women's track and field information is incorporated into the official athletics site

www.ecupirates.com/

100. **GoBison.com**

Official site. Features current news, tickets and merchandise, and team rosters, stats and rankings,...

www.gobison.com/

101. **MSTATEATHLETICS**

The official web site of Mississippi State athletics.

www.mstateathletics.com/

102. **The Official Internet Home of San Jose State Spartans Athletics**

Official site of San Jose State athletics

www.sjsuspartans.com/

103. **Colorado College } Athletics**

Official site of the Tigers with news items, scores, statistics, pictures, and player listings.

www.coloradocollege.edu/Athletics/

104. **University of North Carolina - Official Athletic Site**

The Award is presented annually to the college athlete who best exemplifies excellence in athletics and academics. [continue], Jordan Walker. ...

www.tarheelblue.com/

105. **Athletics Department: Home**

The Official Site of Mercer Athletics. Porter Gym. For More Mercer Athletics News, Visit:

www2.mercer.edu/athletics

106. **Eastern Michigan University - Official Athletic Site**
The official home page for EMU Athletics. Learn ... EMU 2003. This is the official web page of Eastern Michigan University Athletics. News releases, teams and schedules, facilities, and information for donors and recruits. Plus links...
www.emich.edu/goeagles/

107. **Athletics News**
The triumphant look on his face was a familiar one(Getty Images)... Full Story Sports Soccer Athletics Celebrity Photos....
www.athleticsnews.com/

108. **Ontario University Athletics: Welcome**
The official website of Ontario University Athletics, providing schedules, results, statistics, and up to date stories on all 24 OUA sports. ...
www.oua.org/

109. **UAlbany Athletics - Home Page**
... UAlbany Athletics • 1400 Washington Avenue • Albany, NY 12222 • Phone:(518) 442-2562 Copyright © 2003 University at Albany Athletics. ...
www.albany.edu/sports/

110. **Huskers.com**
University of Nebraska Athletics official site
.www.huskers.com/

111. **Southern Miss Official Athletic Web Site**
The Official Site of Southern Miss Athletics. Men's Sports Women's Sports Schedules Tickets Audio / Video Eagl...
www.southernmiss.com/

112. **NCAA Online**
Complete information about NCAA regulations (including eligibility requirements), statistics, links...
www.ncaa.org/

113. **Athletics Department**
The Jumbos' official web site.
ase.tufts.edu/athletics/

114. **University of North Dakota Official Athletic Website**
North Dakota women's basketball team showed why they ar...
www.fightingsioux.com/

115. **Philadelphia Athletics Historical Society's Official Website and...**
Official Website of the Philadelphia Athletics Historical Society...
philadelphiaathletics.org/

116. **Wofford College Athletics**
Official site of Wofford athletics.
www.wofford.edu/athletics/

117. **The Official Athletics Website of the University of Tennessee at...**
Official site of University of Tennessee - Chattanooga athletics.
www.gomocs.com/

118. **Michigan Tech Athletics**
Official site of Michigan Tech athletics.
www.athletics.mtu.edu/

119. **The University of Southern California Trojans - Official Athletic...**
Official College Sports Network. The most comprehensive coverage of University of Southern California Athletics on the internet. ...
www.usctrojans.com/

120. **Western Washington University Vikings, Official Athletic Site**
The most comprehensive coverage of Western Washington Athletics on the internet. ... Listen Live to Western Athletics! Official site of the Vikings. Includes athletic department contacts, team information, events, recruiting...
www.wwuvikings.com/

121. **University of Dayton Flyers**
The University of Dayton's baseball program is gearing up for its annual Holiday Baseball Camp, to be held at the Frericks Athletics and Convocation ...
www.daytonflyers.com/

122. **Rensselaer Polytechnic Institute Athletics**
Athletics Weekly Review & Preview Full Story Read the latest news on Rensselaer's athletic teams. Official site of the RPI Engineers. Offers news, team information, photo gallery, hall of fame, and..
www.rpi.edu/dept/athletics/

123. **Georgia State Athletics**
Official site of Georgia State athletics
www.georgiastate.com/

124. **BYUCougars.com - Official Home of BYU Athletics**
Official site of the BYU Cougars
www.byucougars.com/

125. **Gophersports.com**

The answers to previous coaches. Equity in Athletics Disclosure Act U of M Report (2002 Report), Sponsored by.

www.gophersports.com/

126. **The University of British Columbia Thunderbirds**

Official site of the Thunderbirds. Includes schedules, information, recruiting, and news for all...

www.athletics.ubc.ca/

5
Atya Patya

1. **Beneficiaries:National Sports Federations**
   Archery Association of India, Atya Patya Federation of India
   yas.nic.in/yasroot/beneficiaries/federations.htm
2. **Sheriar Books**
   Sport, Cricket. Games, Ping-Pong, Seven Tiles, Marbles, Kites, Atya-Patya, Carom, Gili-Danda. ... sheriarbooks.org/kids/favorites.shtml
3. **Sheriar Books**
   Atya-Patya (also called Nighttime in the Moonlight), Baba explained that this game represented spirituality and was invented many centuries ago in India by ...
   www.sheriarbooks.org/kids/games.shtml
4. **The Tribune, Chandigarh, India - NCR stories**
   The Atya Patya Association has offered to host the Games in Karnataka.
   www.tribuneindia.com/2003/20030617/ncr3.htm
5. **MATHORIGINS.COM_G**
   Peculiar games not seen anywhere else in the world, such as Khabbadi, Kho-Kho,Atya- Patya, Yogasanas.
   http:www.dixitfamily.com/chitpavan10.html.
   www.mathorigins.com/G.htm
6. **The Games**
   The well0known major Indian games are;Atya-Patya, kabaddi Kho-Kho, Langadi, Lagorya and viti-dandud....
   www.nagpuronline.com/people/games.html

7. **khojhyderabad.com Summer Camp**

   Aerobics, athletics, atya patya, archery, acrobatics, basketball, shuttle badminton, ball badminton, bodybuilding, baseball, boxing, cricket for boys and girls ...

   www.khojhyderabad.com/summer/

8. **MH-CET2003**

   Athletics, Atya-Patya, Badminton, Ball-Badminton, Basket-Ball, Contract Bridge, Cricket,Foot-Ball, Hockey, Hu-Tu-Tu , Kabbadi, kho-kho, Mountaineering, Rowing

   www.dmer.org/mhcet/annexure-g.html

9. **Chapter - 20**

   1. Archery. Athletics (including Track and Field events). Atya-Patya; Badminton;Ball-Badminton; Basketball; Billiards and Snooker; Boxing; Bridge;

   persmin.nic.in/doptChapter% 2015%20-%20Sports%20Quota.html

10. **Physical Education ELIGIBILITY CONDITIONS FOR ...**

    Lead up games : (i) Atya Patya (ii) Three Deep (iii) Sanjeevani (Giving life or Vish Amrit) Scheme of Grading: 50% marks will be awarded on the basis of

    www.education.nic.in/htmlweb/cbse_curri_05 phyedu_curri_xii_05.pdf

11. **ACTIVITIES**

    Tenikoit National Coaching Camp was organized in the Year 1998.

    www.geocities.com/aju123in/acttx.htm

12. **Sports Publications - Khel Sahitya**

    About the Book:- Aerobatics, Aikido, Angling, Archery, Athletics, Atya-Patya, AustBall, Automobile Racing,

    Backgammon, Badminton, Ballooning, Bandy, Baseball

    www.sportsbookshouse.com/books_of_games.htm

6
Badminton

1. **USA BADMINTON**
   Offers news, registry, tournament and competition schedules, membership information, rankings, merchandis...
   www.usabadminton.org/
2. **World Badminton**
   Provides information about the sport including history, how to run a competition, training and coaching,...
   www.worldbadminton.com/
3. **Badminton Central**
   Includes news, product reviews, events, technique tips, articles, message boards, and related links.
   www.badmintoncentral.com/badminton-central/
4. **Badminton Canada_'s Home Page**
   Home of Badminton Canada, with up-to-date information on the Canadian BadmintonScene, national rankings, athlete profiles, news, tournament results, junior ...
   www.badminton.ca/
5. **Mitsubishi Motors Badminton Horse Trials 2004**
   Mitsubishi Motors Badminton Horse Trials Sorry, This page uses frames, but your browser doesn't support them. One of the premier international 4 star CCI events. Includes information and history of the trials,...
   www.badminton-horse.co.uk/
6. **The Badminton Association of England Ltd.**
   Badminton Association of England. Welcome to the Badminton Association of England (BAofE) web site. Official site for the governing body for badminton in England. Includes news, rankings, events, club...
   www.baofe.co.uk/

7. **European Badminton Union**

   Founded in 1967, with 47 member countries.

   www.eurobadminton.org/

8. **Timeout Error**

   Error Occurred While Processing Request. Error Diagnostic Information. Timeout waiting for request to execute. The server is unable ...

   www.jvc-abc.com/

9. **Badminton.de**

   Website mit aktuellen Informationen über die nationale und internationale Badmintonszene

   www.badminton.de/

10. **Fédération Française de Badminton**

    World > Français > ... > Sports et loisirs > Sports > Badminton

    www.ffba.org/

11. **Das Schweizer Badminton Online-Magazin - Badminton, badminton**

    World > Deutsch > Sport > Ballsport > Badminton

    www.badminton.ch/

12. **Anita's Badminton Information Site**

    Starting point for the Badminton player. Features general information about badminton, tournaments, videos, players, photos, equipment, directory

    www.anitavandijk.nl/badminton/

13. **badminto**

    World > Deutsch > Sport > Ballsport > Badminton > Verbände

    www.badminton.at/

14. **JVC-Badminton.com > Asian badminton championship tournament in ...**

    The JVC Badminton website Your official source of Asian Badminton activities, news, games and players. Asian player rankings, quiz with prizes, sport entertainment, and results.

    www.jvc-badminton.com/

15. **DBF's officielle boldleverandør**

    World > Dansk > Sport > Badminton

    www.badminton.dk/

16. **Nederlandse Badminton Bond**
    World > Nederlands > Sport > Badminton
    www.badminton.nl/
17. **badminton.org**
    Badminton.org mission: To provide information to the badminton community across the world through the use of internet. Web Construction ...
    www.badminton.org/
18. **Svenska Badmintonförbundet**
    World > Svenska > Sport > Badminton > Förbund
    www.badminton.nu/
19. **world's most dynamic racquet sport....**
    Governing body for badminton in Australia. Includes general information, athlete profiles, related...
    www.badminton.org.au/
20. **Search Pad**
    Homepage. Browse our site and see many interesting articles, information and links to other Badminton sites on the World Wide Web. Governing body for badminton in Scotland. Includes events, affiliated clubs, press releases, results,...
    www.scotbadminton.demon.co.uk/
21. **La page québécoise de badminton**
    World > Français > ... > Sports et loisirs > Sports > Badminton
    www.volant.qc.ca/
22. **Badminton Alley Store - Providing quality badminton racket ...**
    Badminton Alley offers quality badminton racket, shuttlecocks and other equipment at low price to help badminton players play their best. Offers racquets, shuttlecocks, strings and accessories for badminton.
    www.badmintonalley.com/
23. **badminton racket warehouse**
    Badminton Warehouse supplies professional and recreational quality badminton racket, racquet, shuttlecock and accessories.
    www.badmintonwarehouse.com/
24. **federación española de bádminton**
    World > Español > Deportes > Bádminton > España
    www.fesba.com/

25. **SportingPulse Homepage for Badminton New Zealand**
Badminton New Zealand. Badminton NZ is the national body responsible for ...
www.badminton.org.nz/
26. **Official Website of swiss badminton**
World > Deutsch > Sport > Ballsport > Badminton > Verbände
www.swiss-badminton.ch/
27. **France Badminton**
World > Français > Sports > Raquettes > Badminton
francebadminton.online.fr/
28. **BadmintonSport.nl - de nationale badmintonsite**
World > Nederlands > Sport > Badminton
www.badmintonsport.nl/
29. **badminton-online**
World > Deutsch > Sport > Ballsport > Badminton
www.badminton-online.de/
30. **San Diego Badminton Supply**
San Diego Badminton Supply offers quality badminton racket, shuttlecocks and other equipment at low price.
www.badminton.net/
31. **Deutscher Badminton Verband eV (DBV)**
World > Deutsch > Sport > Ballsport > Badminton > Verbände
www.badmintonverband.de/
32. **Worldwide Badminton Ladder**
Badminton ladder that is now forming. Free for all players and helps find opponents, track results, post/review classifieds, and find quality badminton links. Free badminton ladder that helps players find opponents locally and abroad. Offers badminton classifieds...
www.sportsladders.com/badminton/
33. **Badminton.no - Badmintonforbund på Internett**
World > Norsk > Sport > Badminton
www.badminton.no/
34. **Ontario Badminton Association**
Exists to provide an organized, structured environment for the activity of competitive badminton in Ontario.
www.ontariobadminton.on.ca/

35. **SportsDigest.com/Badminton**
Badminton Bulletin Board; Badminton Canada; Badminton Central; Badminton in Italy; Badminton in Metropolitan Area of New York A directory of sites related to badminton.
is portsdigest.tripod.com/badminton/main.html

36. **Badminton Club Milano**
World > Italiano > Sport > Badminton
www.badminton.it/

37. **Badminton.com**
Popular badminton equipment sites. Your browser does not support inline frames or is currently ... 2003 badminton.com terms of use.
www.badminton.com/

38. **Biella Badminton**
World > Italiano > Sport > Badmintonutenti.lycos.it
BIELLABADMINTON/

39. **Badminton Fördergemeinschaft Oberbayern e. V.**
World > Deutsch > ... > Regierungsbezirke > Oberbayern > Sport
www.bafo.de/

40. **BadmintonUK**
BadmintonUK.
www.badmintonuk.ndo.co.uk/

41. **Badminton**
Badminton. A shuttlecock is hit and returned with rackets over an approximately 1.55 m-high net, fixed at the center of a 13.4 m...
www.hiroshima-cu.ac.jp/C/ASIA/Sports/badminton.html

42. **Badminton Academy**
The summary for this Japanese page contains characters that cannot be correctly displayed in this language/character set.
www.badminton.ac/

43. **Badminton Ireland**
The Badminton Union of Ireland is the governing body of the sport of Badminton in Ireland. Governing body for badminton in Ireland. Includes search feature for Irish clubs, news, events, rankings,...
www.badmintonireland.com/

44. **BadmintonOnline.net - The Ultimate Badminton Web Site**
BadmintonOnline.net Todays Badminton News Announcements. Next IBF Event Thomas & Uber Cup First and Semi-Final Stages Men's and Women's World Team....
www.badminton.online.ukgateway.net/

45. **Federazione Italiana Badminton**
World > Italiano > Sport > Badminton
www.badminton-italia.com/

46. **Badminton BC**
Organizes badminton in the province of British Columbia. Features news, schedule, resources, rankings,..
www.badmintonbc.com/

47. **Badminton Composites`**
www.asahi-net.or.jp/~zt8s-oon/badminton.htm

48. **Hi-Qua Badminton Equipments - online wholesale and retailer**
Badminton equipments direct from our factory. Badminton Shuttlecock, Badminton Racquet, Apparel, Shoes, Bag, String and Net etc. ... badminton equipment supplies.
www.hiquasports.com/badminton/

49. **SBA**
Providing Badminton information for Alabama, Florida, Georgia, Louisiana, North Carolina, Oklahoma, South Carolina, Tennessee, Texas, the Caribbean, and South
www.sbabadminton.org/

50. **Corvin's World of Badminton**
Badminton Online Guide Your source for the articles, news, links, tips , equipmentand much more! ... Current News Browse through latest badminton news.
www.credit-land.com/badminton/

51. **Badminton Meda**
World > Italiano > Sport > Badminton
mbers.xoom.virgilio.it/mbc/

52. **HTPBB redirect**
How to Play Better Badminton has moved! Redirecting you to the new site, please update your links. If you are not automatically ...
www26.brinkster.com/playbadminton/

53. **Celebrating 75 years throughout 2003**
Celebrating 75 years throughout 2003. ENTER.
www.badmintonalberta.ca/

54. **Laws of Badminton**
The LAWS of Badminton. The Laws of Badminton. As amended and adopted by ... or direct from IBF Website. Index to The Laws of Badminton.
www.worldbadminton.com/ibf_laws.html

55. **Harvard Badminton Club**
Home of the Harvard Badminton Club, with information about play times, programs, pictures and stories over the years. HARVARD BADMINTON CLUB NON EST PICNICUM....
hcs.harvard.edu/~badmintn/hbc.html

56. **ÝSTANBULBADMÝNTON TEMSÝLCÝLÝÐÝ**
Free Web space and hosting
www.badminton.bz.tc/

57. **Badminton-Turniere**
World > Deutsch > Sport > Ballsport > Badminton
www.badminton-turniere.de/

58. **Duocomputers.nl**
International Badminton Association for the Disabled IBAD A Non-discriminatory Organization. ISOD and CP Sport logo use...
www.ibad.nl/

59. **Badminton Club of Greater Buffalo**
Badminton Club of Greater Buffalo.
www.cgicafe.com/~bt829/wwwboard/wwwboard.html

60. **ActiveKarma: Sports for beginners and experts**
Basic Rules and Regulations You have heard the referee call out love-all before the game of badminton begins. Offers articles and information about the sport of badminton, from basic tips to precise improvement...
www.activekarma.com/activekarma/categories
category.asp?catid=28

61. **Genova Badminton Club**
World > Italiano > Sport > Badminton
www.genovabadminton.it/

62. **Southern California Badminton Association**
The Southern California Badminton Association. Servicing the Southern California Badminton Player.
www.scbabadminton.org/

63. **Badminton Szene im Internet, Verein, Software, Link**
Windows.
members.aol.com/okbonn/bad/

64. **Badminton Foto, Fotos, Photo, Photos - Michael Schüppel**
World > Deutsch > Sport > Ballsport > Badminton
www.badminton-fotos.de/

65. **Delta Badminton Trento**
Delta Badminton Trento's web site
www.geocities.com/deltabad/

66. **Welsh Badminton Union**
www.welshbadminton.net/

67. **www.badminton.ru**
The summary for this Russian page contains characters that cannot be correctly displayed in this language/character set.
www.badminton.ru/

68. **Badminton Warszawski**
World > Polska > Sport > Sporty pilki i siatki > Badmington
www.badmintonwawa.pl/

69. **HickokSports.com - History - Badminton**
This document is a history of badminton, with a list of all United States and Olympic champions. ... Badminton History. Table of Contents. ...
www.hickoksports.com/history/badmintn.shtml

70. **Official Website of the Badminton Swiss Open 2003**
Official site includes event highlights, services, and team information.
www.swissopen.com/

71. **Amazon.com: Books: Badminton**
Customers interested in Badminton may also be interested in: Sponsored Links (What's this?) Feedback: ...
www.amazon.com/exec/obidos/tg/ detail/0811724875?v=glance

72. **Confederação Brasileira de Badminton**
CONFEDERAÇÃO BRASILEIRA DE BADMINTON
www.badmintonconfbrasil.com.br/

73. **Malaysia Boleh !**
The Unofficial Home Page for Malaysia Badminton Team Netword : Malaysia Badminton ... Some bad news for all Malaysian badminton fans Unofficial news and information for the Malaysia Badminton Team.
www.geocities.com/Colosseum/Stadium/4696/

74. **Badders - The Badminton Community Network**
Interactive community for badminton enthusiasts. The independent voice for the badminton community. Interactive community for all badminton enthusiasts. News, discussion and league management for your...
www.badders.com/

75. **Open Directory - Sports: Badminton**
Offers badminton classifieds and player-related links section.
dmoz.org/Sports/Badminton/

76. **Singapore Badminton Association**
Public Service Badminton Tournament 2004 09/02/2004 - 05/03/2004 Civil Service Club. Singapore Badminton Association.
www.singaporebadminton.org.sg/

77. **Sluzbene stranice HRVATSKOGA BADMINTONSKOG SAVEZA**
Governing body for badminton in Croatia. Includes news, member unions and clubs, calendar, scoreboard,...
www.cba.hr/

78. **The Northeast Badminton Association**
The Northeast Badminton Association. Region one of USA Badminton. Member of the International Badminton Federation. Region 1 of the United States Badminton Association; offers links and information.
members.tripod.com/~laxman36/neast.html

79. **Yahoo! Directory Badminton**
A great selection of your favorite lawn games, including badminton. ...
hrd.yahoo.com/link/krdir/dir/us/153108

80. **Cub Scout Sports - Badminton**
Cub Scout Sports Badminton. ... Earn the Badminton belt loop, and complete five of the following requirements: Compete in a pack or community badminton tournament. ...
www.usscouts.org/advance/cubscout/ sports/badminton.html

81. **The official homepage of the Auckland Badminton Association...**
Auckland Badminton Association official website, full of information, timetables, internet bookings, coaching...
www.auckbad.co.nz/

82. **Sydney Badminton Association**
Sydney Badminton Association. SBA has a new website! Click on the link below. WWW.SYDNEYBADMINTON.COM.
www.ozemail.com.au/~sydba

83. **Badminton in Metropolitan Area of New York**
Badminton in Metropolitan Area of New York. Brooklyn Bridge and Lower Manhattan. Those ... I learned Badminton in India where I grew up. After ...
www.angelfire.com/ny/jonleif/

84. **Barton Badminton Club**
Barton Badminton Club is based in the Staffordshire village of Barton-under-Needwood. Offers details about upcoming matches, membership and location.
website.lineone.net/~barton_badminton/

85. **Badminton**
Australian Sports Commision Logo, Badminton. Australian Sports Commision Logo, ... Badminton Australia. Athlete profiles - maintained by Badminton Australia.Contains player profiles, related links, and past Olympics results.
www.ausport.gov.au/info/badminton.htm

86. **Farum Badminton**
World > Dansk > Sport > Badminton > Klubber
www.farumbadminton.dk/

87. **ringsted-badminton**
World > Dansk > Sport > Badminton > Klubber
www.ringsted-badminton.dk/

88. **Badminton Victoria Website**
Badminton Victoria Website! ... design by Bigblue Planet Productions Inc. © 2001 Badminton Victoria.
www.badmintonvictoria.com/

89. **Nova Scotia Badminton Association**
Enter the NSBA logo If you are not on the NSBA subscription list and would like to be, simply fill out the form below. Dedicated to promotion and regulation of the sport, and training and certification of coaches. Lists...
www.accesswave.ca/~gerrymar/nsba/nsba.html

90. Buckley Badminton Club - playing in North East Wales with teams in Flintshire and Chester badminton leagues. The site is about Buckley Badminton Club, for badminton players in and around North Wales especially...
www.buckleybc.org.uk/ - 9k - 5 Jan 2004

91. **Midwest Badminton Association**
The Web Site of the Midwest Badminton Association. Information about badminton in the midwest, tournaments, membership, and related information. Badminton in the Midwest, tournaments, membership, and related information.
www.midwestbadminton.com/

92. **EngholmBadminton.dk - Badminton - Siden hvor der springes over...**
World > Dansk > Sport > Badminton
www.engholmbadminton.dk/

93. **Badminton clubs, product reviews, news and message boards**
Cornwall County Badminton Association includes product reviews, news, newsletters, tournament information, club searches, match results and links. Includes product reviews, news, newsletters, tournament information, club searches, match results and links.
www.cornwallbadmintonassociation.co.uk/

94. **KIF Badminton - Hovedside**
World > Dansk > Sport > Badminton > Klubber
www.kifbadminton.dk/

95. **Leeuwarder Badminton Club te Leeuwarden**
World > Nederlands > Sport > Badminton > Verenigingen > Nederland
home.hetnet.nl/~leeuwarderbc/

96. **smash - badminton site**
Badminton Archive of results from international Badminton events.
members.tripod.com/~tangkis/

97. **MIT Badminton Club**
MIT Badminton Club. Happy New Year! January Dates: Sun 1/4, Sun ... MIT-Only Badminton Tournament
web.mit.edu/mitbac/www/

98. **Redhill Badminton Club - Worcester (UK) - Home , A Worcester...**
A club in the Worcestershire league. Members, directions, map, fixtures, and history.
www.redhillbadminton.itgo.com/

99. **Badmintonportal für Hamburg**
World > Deutsch > Sport > Ballsport > Badminton
www.christineselchow.de/

100. **Badminton in Hamburg und Umgebung - Ein Service vom Hamburger**
World > Deutsch > Sport > Ballsport > Badminton > Verbände
www.hamburg-badminton.de/

101. **Castleford Badminton League**
Castleford and District Badminton League. Founded 1952. Welcome to the Castleford and District Badminton League's Web Site. League Tables.
www.casbadminton.co.uk/

7
Baseball

1. **Major League Baseball (MLB)**
   Official site featuring links to all of the major league teams' official sites, stats, news, schedules, online broadcast links, and more.
   www.mlb.com
2. **Minor League Baseball**
   Official site, oversees all of minor league baseball.
   www.minorleaguebaseball.com
3. **Little League Baseball**
   Official site features rules, history, structure, teams, and more.
   www.littleleague.org
4. **Yahoo! Sports: Fantasy Baseball**
   Free and pay games offering live drafts, custom leagues, multiple scoring options and more.
   baseball.fantasysports.yahoo.com/baseball
5. **NCAA Baseball**
   Official site with scores, team and player stats, brackets, a game schedule, and more. Offers Division I, II, and III coverage.
   www.ncaasports.com/baseball/mens
6. **National Baseball Hall of Fame and Museum**
   Official site presents the exciting history of baseball through the display of artifacts, photographs, and memorabilia.
   www.baseballhalloffame.org
7. **WorldSeries.com**
   Official postseason site of Major League Baseball.www.worldseries.com
8. **ESPN.com: Fantasy Baseball**
   Fee based games with news, injury reports and stats provided foreveryone.games.espn.go.com/cgi/flb Request.dll?FRONTPAGE

9. **Baseball-Reference.com**
Statistics for MLB players, teams, and leagues. Includes batting, pitching, and fielding stats.
www.baseball-reference.com

10. **NCAA College World Series**
Official site with news, scores, a photo gallery, trivia, and more.
www.ncaasports.com/baseball/mens/championship-info

11. **Baseball Almanac**
Provides statistical information about awards, records, and feats.
www.baseball-almanac.com –

12. **ESPN.com - Baseball Index**
FANTASY BASEBALL. Shrink | Out of Box. Most Added/Dropped. Player Rater. Classic Fantasy. Fantasy Baseball Coverage The season's over, but not forgotten... ...
baseball.espn.go.com/mlb/index

13. **Sporting News - Baseball**
Provides feature articles, player profiles, team rosters, schedules, and stats.
www.sportingnews.com/baseball

14. **Baseball.com**
Scores, news, standings, recaps, and more.
www.baseball.com

15. **Ballparks by Munsey & Suppes**
Past, present and future baseball parks. Also includes sections on football, hockey, and basketball venues and golf courses.
www.ballparks.com

16. **John Skilton's Baseball Links**
Comprehensive source for baseball resources.
www.baseball-links.com

17. **Baseball Canada**
Governing body for amateur baseball in Canada, as recognized by the provincial baseball associations, Sport Canada and the International Baseball Association.
www.baseball.ca

18. **Baseball Archive, The**
Home of the Online Baseball Encyclopedia. Archive of information, including stats from 1871-present, awards, records, feats, almanac, attendance, sabermetrics, and more.
www.baseball1.com

19. **USA Today: Baseball**
    Offers league news, team pages, schedules, rosters, and more.
    www.usatoday.com/sports/mlb.htm
20. **Science of Baseball**
    See what makes a home run, learn how a curve ball curves, and check your fastball reaction time.
    www.exploratorium.edu/baseball
21. **Baseball**
    Home of the Online Baseball Encyclopedia. Archive of information, including stats from 1871-present, awards, records/feats, almanac, attendance, sabermetrics, and more.
    www.baseball1.com/
22. **USA Baseball**
    NOVEMBER 2003. 2003 USA BASEBALL OLYMPIC QUALIFYING TEAM Next faces Colombia Tuesday at 10:00 am EST Horacio Ramirez slated to take the mound for the Americans...
    www.usabaseball.com/
23. **Yahoo! Sports: MLB**
    Scores, news, standings, stats, and schedules.
    sports.yahoo.com/mlb
24. **Open Directory - Sports: Baseball**
    Baseball, Description. ... Russian (2), Spanish (79), Swedish (32). Usenet rec.sport.baseball - news: - Google Groups. ...
    dmoz.org/Sports/Baseball/
25. **I.B.A. International Baseball Association**
    International and Olympic Baseball.
    www.baseball.ch/
26. **Baseball: The Game and Beyond**
    The Game and Beyond! You are ... more. You can learn how to score a game and study the physics behind baseball. You ...
    library.thinkquest.org/11902/
27. **Collegiate Baseball Newspaper** College baseball newspaper - Amateur Baseball - Polls - High School - Youth - And More! ... I and High School) as selected by Collegiate Baseball. ...
    www.baseballnews.com/

28. **Black Baseball's Negro Baseball Leagues**

The award-winning Black Baseball Negro Baseball Leagues website features photos, RealAudio soundclips and extensive profiles and information on players and ...
www.blackbaseball.com/

29. **Negro League Baseball**

News, feature articles, player and team profiles, and more.
www.negroleaguebaseball.com/

30. **Baseball Express/Softball Express**

Large selection of baseball sports equipment including bats, balls, gloves, mitts, and more. Full onlineordering
www.baseballexp.com/

31. **Sporting News**

Sports weekly covering college and pro football, baseball, hockey, and college and pro basketball
www.sportingnews.com/

32. **The Baseball Scorecard - A Scoring Tutorial**

This site is geared towards teaching the casual fan how to score a baseball game. ... You can find baseball news, and weather for Major League Baseball cities.
www.baseballscorecard.com/

33. **Professional Baseball (Japan)**

Yearly results and stats since Japan Professional Baseball launched in 1936. Includes all-time leaders.
www.inter.co.jp/Baseball/

34. **Fantasy Baseball Cafe**

Offers strategy advice, player rankings, sleepers and forums.
www.fantasybaseballcafe.com/

35. **Baseball Cards: 1887-1914**

A Library of Congress treasure of 2,100 early baseball cards.
memory.loc.gov/ammem/bbhtml/bbhome.html

36. **PONY Baseball/Softball**

Announces 2004 rule changes for Baseball and Softball-check the News Section! ... copyright © 2002, PONY Baseball/Softball, Inc. ...
www.pony.org/

37. **The BASEBALL Page**

The Baseball Page has original baseball commentary, with a perspective on baseball history. Baseball player pages, all-time teams...
www.thebaseballpage.com/

38. **Baseball Musings**
Weblog with news and commentary from David Pinto.
www.baseballmusings.com/

39. **High School Baseball Web**
Offering information for players, parents, and coaches including message board, articles, team sites, camps, and showcase listings.
www.hsbaseballweb.com/

40. **Baseball Excellence**
Newsletter for players, parents and coaches. Instructions and major league tips on pitching, hitting, fielding, base running by big league players and experienced youth coaches.
www.baseball-excellence.com/

41. **Junior League Baseball Magazine**
Devoted to kids and parents who play and love baseball.
www.juniorbaseball.com/

42. **Baseball HQ: Fantasy baseball analysis, player projections**
Fantasy baseball players have been coming to Baseball HQ since 1986 for cutting-edge baseball analysis, player projections and all the tools they need to win ...
www.baseballhq.com/

43. **PureBaseball.com**
Fantasy baseball, fantasy sports, gaming, stats Inc., statistics, baseball stats, baseball statistics, perpetual leagues, gamesite, major league baseball, MLB ...
www.purebaseball.com/

44. **This Date in Baseball History**
Daily updates.
www.nationalpastime.com/

45. **Negro Leagues Baseball Museum**
Preserves the history of Negro League baseball from the 1920s to the early 1960s. Located in Kansas City, Missouri.
www.nlbm.com/

46. **ESPN.com: Major League Baseball Scoreboard**
Offers inning-by-inning scores, updated frequently.
sports.espn.go.com/mlb/scoreboard

47. **Baseball Parent Newsletter**

Newsletter written exclusively for the parents and coaches of youth baseball players.

www.baseball-parent.com/

48. **Atlanta Braves**

Official site. Features up-to-date stats and results, player bios, minor league information, ticket and merchandise ordering info, player photos, and audio highlights.

www.atlantabraves.com/

49. **Baseball Ontario**

Offers information updates for baseball associations and events across the province.

www.baseballontario.com/

50. **Heavy Hitter_s Baseball Central**

Maker of deep carved bats and other commemorative items.

www.heavyhitter.com/

51. **Baseball Newsstand**

Offers links to team coverage and columnists for every major league team.

www.baseballnewsstand.com

52. **Baseball News**

With news and commentary from a variety of sources.

baseballnews.blogspot.com/

53. **Historic Baseball**

Profiles of players, teams and leagues with a special section dedicated to players with ties to South Carolina.

www.historicbaseball.com/

54. **NCAA Division III Baseball**

NCAA Division III Baseball. ... 10. Carthage, 35-8, 165. Summaries of Past NCAA Division III Baseball Seasons. Summaries of the Division III Championship Series. ...

odac.bridgewater.edu/div3base/baseball.htm

55. **Baseball**

Get player information, team pages, results, predictions and more from About Guide to baseball - Michael B. Dowd. ... Baseball. Baseball. ...

baseball.about.com/mbody.htm

56. **Baseball Immortals**

Offers extensive statistics on the greats of the game.
www.baseballimmortals.net/

57. **Federazione Italiana Baseball Softball**

Federazione Italiana Baseball Softball - Viale Tiziano 74 - 00196 - ROMA - Tel.+39 0636858376 - Fax. ... 31 ottobre 2003
NAZIONALE PRE OLIMPICA BASEBALL. ...
www.baseball-softball.it/

58. **The Baseball Guru - A World of Baseball!**

Vast baseball resource. Data archive. Famous baseball web tour. Free games. Trivia, bookstore and research help. Fun for kids. Questions? Ask the Guru! ...
baseballguru.com/

59. **Baseball Corner**

Offers baseball bats, gloves, and equipment from Mizuno, Easton, Rawlings, and other brands.
www.baseballcorner.com/

60. **ThinkQuest USA Library Entry**

ThinkQuest USA Library. Index Baseball... and Math. ... We accomplished this by providing mathematical problems that were related to baseball. ...
tqjunior.thinkquest.org/6082/5stm.html

61. **Baseball & Softball Portal**

NEWS. Major League Baseball Roadshow Trainer/-innen gesucht. ... | © Deutscher Baseball & Softball Verband eV 2002 Alle Rechte vorbehalten - HINWEIS |.
www.dbvnet.de/

62. **Fantasy Baseball Central**

Collection of links and advice for fantasy baseball players.
www.fantasybaseballcentral.com/

63. **Baseball World: Baseball World Series, Mark McGwire and Sammy**

Baseball World Series is here, baseball playoffs everywhere! ... Baseball World Series fever is here, baseball playoffs everywhere...
www.geocities.com/Colosseum/Park/1138/

64. **Mr. Baseball**

Headquarters for history and memorabilia.
www.mrbaseball.com/

65. **Oyez Baseball**

Comparing the greatness and mediocrity of baseball players and Supreme Court Justices. baseball.oyez.org/

66. **Baseball Notebook**

Forecasts the performance of major league baseball players and teams and offers tips for fantasy baseball or rotisserie owners and fans interested in player forecasting.
www.baseballnotebook.com/

67. **TBS Radio - the baseball -**

The summary for this Japanese page contains characters that cannot be correctly displayed in this language/character set.
www.tbs.co.jp/baseball/

68. **Scottsdale Baseball Cards**

Baseball, basketball, football, hockey, boxing, non-sports cards and more.
www.scottsdalecards.com/

69. **The Baseball Reliquary Inc. - Home**

The Baseball Reliquary is dedicated to fostering an appreciation of the historical development of baseball and its interaction with American culture. ...
www.baseballreliquary.org/Default.htm

70. **Baseball Crank**

Blogging on baseball, war, politics, and more.
www.baseballcrank.com/

71. **Texas Rangers**

Official site. Features up-to-date stats and results, player bios, minor league information, ticket and merchandise ordering info, player photos, and audio highlights.
texas.rangers.mlb.com/NASApp/mlb/index.jsp?c_id=tex

72. **BaseballLibrary.com**

NOVEMBER 3 IN BASEBALL HISTORY. ... Red Barber (10/3) » Barber was New York City's first baseball radio broadcaster, and the first baseball telecaster anywhere... ...
www.pubdim.net/baseballlibrary/

73. **www.baseball.de - Promotion-Website des Deutschen Baseball und**

Baseball.de - Die Promotion-Website des Deutschen Baseball und Softball Verbandes. Informationen über Baseball und Softball. ...
www.baseball.de/

74. **Sports-Wired.Com - The Baseball Cube, The Hockey Cube**
The Baseball Cube The best baseball statistics web site on the net! Complete historical minor league ...
www.sports-wired.com/

75. **Texas Rangers**
Official site. Features up-to-date stats and results, player bios, minor league information, ticket and merchandise ordering info, player photos, and audio highlights.
www.texasrangers.com/

76. **Ballparks of Baseball**
Information and pictures of stadia from the past to the future.
www.ballparksofbaseball.com/

77. **ABCA - Home**
American Baseball Coaches Association. Proudly serving Amateur Baseball for over 55 years. Contact Information: National ...
www.abca.org/

78. **Nederlandse Honkbal en Softbal site, YOUR BASEBALL SITE**
Your Baseball Site, Nederlands internationale Honkbal en Softbal linkpagina, De World Wide Web's meest uitgebreide verzameling van Honbal en softball ...
members.lycos.nl/YourBaseballSite/

79. **Baseball Tips**
Offers pitching machines, radar guns, batting cages, training equipment and videos, baseball gloves, bats, and other equipment, plus free baseball tips and instruction.
www.baseballtips.com/

80. **Math, Baseball & the San Francisco Giants**
Problems and activities based on many aspects of baseball.
www.kn.pacbell.com/wired/baseball/

81. **Batter's Up Baseball (Math Games)**
Macromedia. Play, Batter's Up Baseball (math game). Tell your friends about this page! Select which game you want to play...
www.prongo.com/math/

82. **SLAM! Baseball**
Major League baseball news from Canada.
www.canoe.ca/Baseball/home.html

83. **West Michigan Whitecaps**
Official site.
www.whitecaps-baseball.com/

84. **Big Bad Baseball**
Provides sabermetric analysis and articles on minor and major league baseball statistics.
www.bigbadbaseball.com/

85. **Diamond Mind Baseball**
Providing realistic strategy-oriented baseball simulation games for use on home computers and the Internet.
www.diamond-mind.com/

86. **The Physics of Baseball**
The Physics of Baseball. Welcome to my site devoted to the physics of baseball. I have ... Vibrational Analysis of a baseball bat.
www.npl.uiuc.edu/~a-nathan/pob/

87. **RDS - Baseball Québec**
RDS.CA offre une couverture complète du Baseball Majeur et des Expos, incluant les nouvelles, éditoriaux, résultats, statistiques, calendrier, alignement ...
www.rds.ca/baseballquebec/

88. **American Legion Baseball**
Nationwide youth baseball program sponsored by the American Legion.
www.baseball.legion.org/

89. **WebBall**
Free drills, skill tips, and strategy ideas to help coaches and players improve their baseball performance.
www.webball.com/

90. **Baseball Manager**
Fantasy baseball game with real stats, players, and ulcers.
www.baseballmanager.com/

91. **Baseball B.C.**
Governing body for amateur baseball in British Columbia.
www.baseball.bc.ca/

92. **ESPN.com: Fantasy Baseball**
Fee based games with news, injury reports and stats provided for everyone.
games.espn.go.com/cgi/flb/Request.dll?FRONTPAGE

93. **Durham Bulls**
    Oficial site.
    www.dbulls.com/

94. **Baseball Direct**
    Sells baseball gift items such as videos and calendars through direct marketing.
    www.baseballdirect.com/

95. **Dixie Youth Baseball**
    Includes information on the Dixie Youth World Series.
    www.dixie.org/

96. **Colorado Rockies**
    Official site. Features up-to-date stats and results, player bios, minor league information, ticket and merchandise ordering info, player photos, and audio highlights.
    www.coloradorockies.com/

97. **Baseball Junkie**
    News, stats, analysis, weblogs, links, and more.
    www.baseballjunkie.net/

98. **St. Louis Cardinals**
    Official site. Features up-to-date stats and results, player bios, minor league information, ticket and merchandise ordering info, player photos, and audio highlights.
    www.stlcardinals.com/

99. **Baseball Heckle Depot**
    One-liners, humor, and heckles.
    www.heckledepot.com/

100. **Baseball Softball UK**
    Runs youth, men's, and women's leagues throughout the U.K.
    www.baseballsoftballuk.com/

101. **Babe Ruth League**
    Amateur youth baseball and softball program.
    www.baberuthleague.org/

102. **American Women's Baseball (AWB)**
    Nonprofit, sports organization that promotes female amateur baseball competitions nationally and internationally.
    www.womenplayingbaseball.com/

103. **Major League Baseball : Official Info : Baseball Basics**
Baseball Basics: On the Field. ... Search Entire Site for. ...
mlb.mlb.com/NASApp/mlb/mlb/baseball_basics
mlb_basics_on_the_field.jsp

104. **The Amateur Baseball Umpire Home Page**
The authoritative web site for information on baseball umpiring and officiating. Welcome to www.AmateurUmpire.com. This educational ...
www.amateurumpire.com/

105. **Canadian Baseball League**
Some of CBL?s best still performing Although the Canadian Baseball League has suspended play until the summer of 2004 several of its best players are still ...
www.canadianbaseballleague.com/

106. **ctnow.com: BASEBALL**
BASEBALL, November 2, 2003 Valentine In Japan To Discuss Job - Hartford Courant Former Mets manager Bobby Valentine arrived in Tokyo ...
www.ctnow.com/sports/baseball/

107. **Baseball Musings**
Baseball Musings Has Moved! That's right, I now own Baseball Musings.com. .... Nothing To Do With Baseball: Well, just a little. ...
pages.map.com/pinto/blogger.html

108. **Baseball Information Network**
Subscription service providing information on youth baseball tournaments, teams, coaches, national organizations and NCAA recruiting regulations and guidelines.
www.baseballinfo.com/

109. **Only Baseball Matters**
Archives << current Digits.com. Only Baseball Matters First visit? Drop me an email @ John J Perricone, or pin my Guest Map. Only Baseball Matters has moved! ...
onlybaseball.blogspot.com/

110. **Yahooligans! - Sports and Recreation:Baseball**
Inside Yahooligans! Big Picture: check out baseball and other sports news on Yahooligans! Big Picture Ask Earl: learn about baseball with Yahooligans! Ask Earl. ...
www.yahooligans.com/sports_and_recreation/Baseball/

111. **MSNBC: Baseball**

Provides team pages, scores, and standings.

www.msnbc.com/news/mlb_front.asp

112. **Interactive Baseball Rules**

Includes quiz generator and rules resources.

www.macroweb.com/ibrules/

113. **Australian Baseball Home Page**

Baseball Australian Baseball Home Page, Season 2003. ... Australian Baseball Federation. Where can I find things? ... Ross Straw [Australian Baseball], ...

www.isport.com.au/baseball/abf/

114. **Aaron's Baseball Links**

Links to the official websites of professional teams and more.

www.aaronslinks.com/

115. **Why I Like Baseball, by Cecilia Tan**

Bravenet Services. Most Recent Entries: October 21: The Women's Baseball Marathon. ... October 14: Baseball Is Not Life. "I have the urge to break things right now. ...

www.ceciliatan.com/baseball.html

116. **Dansk Baseball Softball Forbund**

Denne Web-side bruger rammer, og din browser understøtter ikke rammer.

www.softball.dk/

117. **Ripken Baseball.com**

Official site of Hall of Famer Cal Ripken, Jr., and the Aberdeen Iron Birds.

www.ripkenbaseball.com/

118. **Baseball Ink - A variety magazine about baseball**

A baseball magazine - variety, stories, history, nostalgia, memories, fiction, poetry, etc. Baseball the way it was meant to be

www.codelikethewind.com/bbi/

119. **Ballparks by Munsey and Suppes**

Facts, figures and photos about past, present and future baseball parks

www.ballparks.com/baseball/

120. **Rochester Red Wings**

Official site. Includes schedules, player profiles, ticket info, and stadium updates.

www.redwingsbaseball.com/

121. **Baseball Planet Sportscards**

Live online sportscard and memorabilia auctions.

www.baseballplanet.com/

122. **Major League Baseball Canada**

Features news, stats, and player profiles of all Canadian players in the majors and prospects in the minors and college ball.

www.majorleaguebaseball.ca/

123. **Cape Cod Baseball League**

Summer league featuring the best college players.

www.capecodbaseball.org/

124. **Baseball Sim Central : The Definitive Site For Baseball Gaming**

Baseball Sim Central: For all you baseball gaming needs spanning the PC, PSX, PS2 and DC. ... MVP Baseball 2003 Review Posted On 04-28-2003 by Scott Jeffries, ...

baseball.simcentral.net/index/

125. **InfoSports - Youth Baseball on the Web**

Youth Baseball on the Web. InfoSports is a nice resource for youth baseball. On this youth sports site you will find baseball tournments ...

infosports.net/baseball/

126. **Baseball Factory**

Hands-on marketing approach for select high school juniors and seniors who have the ability to play college baseball.

www.baseballfactory.com/

127. **Fantasy Baseball - Free fantasy and rotisserie baseball**

Fantasy Baseball Headquarters 2003, Quick Hits: FBH Homepage.

www.fantasybaseballheadquarters.com/

128. **Amateur Athletic Union Baseball**

Official site.

www.aaubaseball.org/

8
Basketball

1. **NBA.com**

   The official site of the National Basketball Association. Includes news, features, multimedia, player...

   www.nba.com/

2. **Basketball.com**

   Basketball! College basketball, Pro basketball, highschool, NBA, schedules, daily news, statistics, more! ... more... Top-25 College Basketball Game Capsules. Ezine with scores, picks, teams, players, leagues, schedules, news and statistics.

   www.basketball.com/

3. **The Official Site of USA Basketball**

   Deron Williams (left) and Daniel Brown (right) not only play major roles in the backcourt for Illinois, but the duo has done so for USA Basketball the past two ...

   www.usabasketball.com/

4. **FIBA - FLASH**

   Site for FIBA including press releases, rules and regulations, promotions and FIBA partners, latest...

   www.fiba.com/

5. **The Basketball Highway**

   A community that allows a coach to search for relevant information and resources. Features articles,...

   www.bbhighway.com/

6. **The Official Web Site of the Naismith Memorial Basketball Hall of...**

   Entertaining and educational exhibits celebrating the game of basketball. Located in Springfield,...

   www.hoophall.com/

7. **Open Directory - Sports: Basketball**

   Top: Sports: Basketball (8,412), Description. ... Bankshot Basketball (3); Beach Basketball (6); Deaf Basketball (6); Maxi-Basketball (2);...

   dmoz.org/Sports/Basketball/

8. **Power Basketball, coaching youth basketball resource**

   Coaching youth basketball - the coaching staff offers tips on offense and defense - also purchase products, books, and videos for the basketball coach. A resource providing information for youth basketball coaching and player development. Features drills,...

   www.powerbasketball.com/

9. **Basketball.ca - Official Site of Canada Basketball**

   Basketball.ca - Official Site of Canada Basketball Canada Basketball. Provides national representation for all Canadian Basketball associations. Many links.

   www.basketball.ca/

10. **SI.com - NBA**

    www.cnnsi.com/basketball/

11. **Basketball Australia**

    Basketball Australia. Features news, results, statistics, tournaments, information and player recruitment classifieds.

    www.basketball.net.au/

12. **The Official Site of the Dallas Mavericks**

    Official site containing news, scores, audio and video files, player statistics, schedules, and roster.

    www.nba.com/mavericks/

13. **basketball.de: Bundesliga, Europaliga, Pokale, NBA, CollegeWorld_>_Deutsch_>_..._>_Basketball_>_Verzeichnisse_und_Portale**

    www.basketball.de/

14. **ESPN.com: NBA**

    Daily NBA news from ESPN Sports Zone television.

    sports.espn.go.com/nba/index

15. **1-On-1 Free Basketball Game**

    A Free 1-On-1 Basketball game/simulation played over the Internet! Create a player and Take on the World! Free online game/simulation played over the Internet

    basketball-game.com/

16. **Google Directory - Sports > Basketball**

    Google, Directory Help Search only in Basketball Search the Web. Basketball, Sports > Basketball, Go to Directory Home. Categories. Bankshot ...

    directory.google.com/Top/Sports/Basketball/

17. **Basket Math Interactive Learning**

    Science Academy Software developes educational software including interactive online software for applying technology in the classroom, at work, or at home. Interactive learning application that spans grade levels 4-10.

    www.scienceacademy.com/BI/

18. **National Wheelchair Basketball Association The Official Website**

    The Official Website of the National Wheelchair Basketball Associationwheelchair, wheelchair basketball, basketball, NWBA, nwba, sports, disabled sports, nba ...

    www.nwba.org/

19. **Journal of Basketball Studies**

    Journal of Basketball Studies looks at basketball like no one else can. ... Applying Math & Science to Basketball, In Defense, The Scheme's The Thing. Clearinghouse of research about basketball. Primarily statistical studies as tools to analyze teams...

    www.rawbw.com/~deano/

20. **ESPN.com: College Basketball**

    Getting Tech-nical. Isma'il Muhammad and Tech are a little low in the polls. Sure, the coaches and media may have agreed this week ...

    sports.espn.go.com/ncb/index

21. **NCAAsports.com - The Official Site for NCAA Sports** Division I Women's Basketball. Coke Counts the Days to the Women's Final Four. ... Continue. Division I Men's Basketball. Official site of the NCAA Women's and Men's Basketball Championships. News, scores, brackets, venues,...

    www.finalfour.net/

22. **Canadian Wheelchair Basketball Association Web Site**

    The Canadian Wheelchair Basketball Association (CWBA) is the National Sports Governing Body responsible for the organization of wheelchair basketball in Canada. ...

    www.cwba.ca/

23. **Basketball in Europa / Basketball in Europe**

Basketball in Europa / Basketball in Europe. Country-by-country listing of international basketball-related links. Bilingual site in English and German.

www.uni-giessen.de/~gl23/club/europa.html

24. **BBL - Basketball Bundesliga**

www.basketball-bundesliga.de/

25. **NBL > Home**

Game results, news, fixtures, current and historic statistics, and team information. Includes newsletter...

www.nbl.com.au/

26. **WBHOF**

Located in Knoxville, TN. Information about the inductees and for visitors, timeline, programs, merchandi...

www.wbhof.com/

27. **WBCA.org "The Address for Women's Basketball!"**

Basketball, coaching, Women's basketball, College basketball, girls basketball, women's sports, coaching association, Final Four, Wade Trophy, Title IX. Homepage of the WBCA dedicated to women's basketball at all levels. News, awards, membership information...

www.wbca.org/

28. **SLAM! Sports - Basketball**

Canada, Sports news, scores, stats, features and more in Canada and abroad from SLAM! Sports

www.canoe.ca/Basketball/home.html

29. **Basketball Daily**

Basketball Daily provides latest Sports World News from the most comprehensive global news network on the internet. ...Basketball Alberta". AAU Girls' Basketball....

www.basketballdaily.com/

30. **Bet On NBA And NCAA Basketball At Select Online Sportsbooks**

Bet On Basketball. Click to Visit. Bet on Basketball At Select Online Sportsbooks Offering A Great New Player Sign Up Bonus...

www.betonbasketball.ws/

31. **basketballscotland - the official website for the scottish ...**

Basketballscotland - online Sponsors Page National Teams. [CEO'S REPORT].

www.size10design.co.uk/basketballscotland/

32. **USATODAY.com**
    NBA features and news coverage of the popular "USA Today" daily newspaper.
    www.usatoday.com/sports/nba.htm
33. **AAU Girls' Basketball**
    The AAU Girls' Basketball Program was established in 1972 as part of the AAU Junior Olympic program. Amateur Athletic Union girls basketball official web site.
    www.aaugirlsbasketball.org/
34. **D3hoops.com: The definitive Internet resource for Division III...**
    Features news, scores, message board, and related links.
    www.d3hoops.com/
35. **Basketball.com**
    Basketball! College basketball, Pro basketball, highschool, NBA, schedules, daily news, statistics, more! ...
    www.basketball.com/database.shtml
36. **Outdoor Basketball Initiative**
    The English Basketball Association created the Outdoor Basketball Initiative (OBI) with the aim of providing BASKETBALL FOR ALL.
    www.basketballengland.org.uk/
37. **USBL - United States Basketball League**
    Official site of USBL covers teams, league, scores, store, invest, chat and fan clubs.
    www.usbl.com/
38. **BBhighway**
    This document contains frames.
    bbhighway.telebasket.com/
39. **NBA Pro Basketball NBA**
    About.com's Pro Basketball Guide brings you the most insightful and informative NBA resources on the Internet. NBA ... Hoops. Pro Basketball.
    probasketball.about.com/
40. **Basketball Ontario**
    Membership, championships, coaching information, officials, 3-on-3.
    www.basketball.on.ca/

41. **ENGLAND BASKETBALL**
England Basketball National Cup Finals. Senior Basketball Results.
www.englandbasketball.co.uk/

42. **MassLive.com: Hooptown**
HOOP HALL ESSENTIALS. » Basketball is born » Hoop Hall facts » Hours & directions » List of inductees, NBA COVERAGE...
www.hooptown.com/

43. **Duke Basketball Report**
Detailed news and resources for Duke fans.
www.dukebasketballreport.com/

44. **Basketball Glossary**
Interactive Basketball Glossary: terms and phrases with definitions for Basketball, as they appear in Basketball Made Simple: A Spectator's Guide, published by ...
www.firstbasesports.com/basketball_glossary.html

45. **The official website of the British Basketball League**
Official site. Information about news, teams, games, competitions, players and statistics. Also includes...
www.bbl.org.uk/

46. **National Association of Basketball Coaches, Official Athletic Site**
National Association of Basketball Coaches Official Athletic Site: complete coverage of all Wildcat NCAA sports including basketball, football, baseball, soccer ...
www.nabc.com/

47. **NCAA Division II Men's Basketball Home Page**
Scores, schedules, national and regional rankings, conference standings, information on tournaments...
www.umr.edu/~sports/bbindex.html

48. **Basketball BC**
Happy Holidays from the Board of Directors and Staff of Basketball BC.
www.basketball.bc.ca/

49. **YBOA Home Page**
Youth Basketball of America, Inc. ... All Natural Capri Sun, the "Official Beverage of YBOA", is proud to join the Youth Basketball of America family. International governing body for youth sports which promotes youth basketball worldwide. Offering...
www.yboa.org/

50. **The IWBF website!**
Member countries, tournament results, latest news and future events for the IWBF.
www.iwbf.org/

51. **Basketball Explorations**
Basketball is a game that involves many disciplines, including math, physics, and art, along with many others. The purpose of this ...
library.thinkquest.org/12006/

52. **About Basketball**
Basketball has become an universal game enjoyed by millions. Learn new facts here, and explore neat basketball stuff. Basketball Shoes best selection and price. General basketball news, trivia, players, fantasy, shopping, links.
www.about-basketball.com/

53. **CBS.SportsLine.com - NCAA Basketball Home**
College Basketball coverage including NCAA news, scores, standings, stats, schedules, injuries, polls, team and player news, NCAA Tournament, NCAA Hoops, NCAA ...
cbs.sportsline.com/collegebasketball/

54. **Michael Wells Basketball Coaching Information Web Page**
Basketball coaching information web page. Basketball offenses, defenses, drills and strategy. ... MICHAEL WELLS. BASKETBALL COACHING INFORMATION. WEB PAGE. Coach Michael Wells offers a complete list of links to other sites containing basketball coaching...
members.aol.com/coachmjw/pp22.htm

55. **FédérationbasketballQuébec World > Français > ... > Sports et loisirs > Sports > Basketball**
www.basketball.qc.ca/

56. **Indexhttp://www.basketball.vuurwerk.nl World_>_Nederlands_>_Sport_>_Basketbal**
www.basketball.vuurwerk.nl/

57. **"_Basketball Alberta"_**
anada Basketball.gif (43200 bytes) Canada Basketball STRATEGIC PLAN AVAILABLE ONLINE.Association profile, calendar, programs, results, tournaments, services.
www.basketballalberta.ab.ca/

58. **Nike Basketball**
www.nikebasketball.com/

59. **BASKETBALL ZINE**
www.basketball-zine.com/

60. **NJB**
California-based national youth organization with over 25000 participants in 6 states.
www.njbl.org/

61. **Basketball Plays, Basketball Drills and Coaching Software**
Online basketball plays and basketball drills, in an easy to use plays and drill database. With playbook software to make your own ...
www.jes-soft.com/playbook/

62. **www.lkl.lt**
The official Lithuanian Basketball League site keeps You informed about the basketball action in Lithuania
www.lkl.lt/

63. **ctnow.com: BASKETBALL**
BASKETBALL, December 30, 2003 Pierce Leads Celtics On Road – Hartford Courant Paul Pierce had 21 points, seven rebounds, six assists ...
www.ctnow.com/sports/basketball/

64. **ThinkQuest : Library : Basketball Mania!**
Basketball Mania! ... including the trivia questions. They hope to get other people excited about the game of basketball. The history of basketball, fundamentals, and how to play the game. Test your knowledge with basketball...
tqjunior.thinkquest.org/3952/

65. **Dutch Basketball World_>_Nederlands_>_Sport_>_Basketbal**
home.hetnet.nl/~sylvia68/

66. **Basketball Ireland - New Website**
Christmas Greetings from President of Basketball Ireland. Strategic Plan - Connecting Basketball in Ireland. Scholarship. Basketball Ireland Noticeboard. Governing body of basketball in Ireland, includes news of the ESB leagues, national cup, and national team.
www.iba.ie/

67. **The Official Website of the Philippine Basketball Association**
The Official Site of the Philippine Basketball Association.News and information on the league, teams, players and coaches, along with game schedules, standings,...
www.pba.com.ph/

68. **Basketball Times — The Nation's Top College Basketball ...**
Web version of the magazine with informative articles and stories.
www.basketballtimes.com/

69. **BCI Basketball**
BCI Basketball National Office Mailing Address PO Box 1388 Addison, TX 75001 Physical Address 12660 Coit Rd, Suite 200 Dallas. Offers national, state and local tournaments and organized league play.
www.bcibasketball.org/ - 13k - **Cached - Similar pages**

70. **Yahoo! Directory Basketball**
Basketball Items for Sale on eBay Great deals and amazing selection on basketball items. ... The Better Basketball Videos Looking to improve your game?
dir.yahoo.com/Recreation Sports/Basketball/

71. **Men's Basketball - University of North Carolina - Official ...**
MEN'S SPORTS. • Baseball • Basketball • Cross Country Basketball, FedEx Air & Ground Stats. ...
www.fansonly.com/schools/unc/sports/ m-baskbl/unc-m baskbl-body.html

72. **Basketball New Zealand**
Official site. NZ "Caught in the Net" resources, teams, the NBL (new Zealand Basketball League)
www.bbnz.org.nz/

73. **Association for Professional Basketball Research**
DO I HAVE DO BE SOME KIND OF BASKETBALL EXPERT? ... A TRIBUTE TO ARMED FORCES BASKETBALL 1941 - 1969" AVAILABLE NOW!!!!! Basketball ...
hometown.aol.com/bradleyrd/apbr.html

74. **Basketball mania**
The summary for this Japanese page contains characters that cannot be correctly displayed in this language/character set.
mk.sakura.ne.jp/~fixx02/BSK/BSK.html

75. **bij de basketball site van Nederland**
World > Nederlands > Sport > Basketbal
www.debasketballsitevannederland.nl/

76. **This Is Basketball World > Nederlands > Sport > Basketbal**
www.thisisbasketball.be/

77. **ESPN.com: NCB**
espn.go.com/ncb/

78. **Patricia's Various Basketball Stuff**
Includes news and links for the NBA and and the Dallas Mavericks.
www.dfw.net/~patricia/

79. **Basketball Rules!**
Basketball Rules! is a great place to go for all your basketball needs. Combined with references for other sports, Basketball Rules! ... Basketball Rules! ...
www.angelfire.com/ca6/gbfgbfgbf/

80. **Indiana Basketball Hall of Fame - New Castle, Indiana**
Website of the Indiana Basketball Hall of Fame, located in New Castle, Indiana. Featuring complete online database of Inductees, information ...
www.hoopshall.com/

81. **USA Basketball Women's Programs**
Team Player USA Basketball.com catches up with 2003 World Championship For Young Women gold medal winner Lindsay Whalen, who tells us she learned to be a team ...
www.usabasketball.com/women/

82. **WomensBasketballOnline.Com**
Where women's basketball meets the internet. Fan site with players pages, teams/leagues, various basketba...
womensbasketballonline.com/

83. **Indiana Basketball News - News In Indiana, High School Hoops**
Monthly basketball newsletter and online resource
www.inbnews.com/

84. **Yahooligans! - Sports and Recreation:Basketball**
How Does a Basketball Bounce? ...
www.yahooligans.com/Sports_and_Recreation/Basketball/

85. **Robert Vyklicky**
News, articles, rules, photos. Bilingual site by Sonja Pavlikova (English and Czech)
vyklicky.tripod.com/

86. **the Basketball Portal.com - The Best Basketball Sites!**
Comprehensive portal to Basketball sites on the Web. Features popular Basketballsearches, best of the Web, and a full directory of Basketballsites. ...
www.thebasketballportal.com/

87. **World Beach Basketball**

World Beach Basketball®. ... What is Beach Basketball®? World's Fastest Growing Beach Sport. Played on a Circular Court. With No Backboard on the Goal....

www.beachbasketball.com/Default.htm

88. **Kansascity.com - Your Kansas City Everything Guide**

Police on the trail of Orlando Magic jersey thief Someone snatched a framed 10 ...

www.kansascity.com/mld/kansascity/sports/basketball/

89. **Women_s Division II Basketball Page**

NCAA Division II Tournament Scores, Etc. Links. NCAA Division II Site. DII Women's Basketball Links by School, Conference. Division II Men's Basketball Page.

www.ndsu.nodak.edu/ndsu/wschwart/wbbd2/

90. **ESPN.com: Womens College Basketball**

Loree Moore benefited from a summer with USA Basketball . ... Voepel: Top Ten There's a lot of good basketball being played by a lot of people in the Big Ten.

espn.go.com/ncw/

91. **Small College Basketball Homepage**

Want to play small college basketball? Visit www.hoophelp.com for a complete list of every Division II and Division III program. Web site to promote Division II and II print newsletters.

www.teleport.com/~gsr/

92. **Basketball**

News and information on men and women play, including national teams, Superleague, High League, and...The summary for this Russian page contains characters that cannot be correctly displayed in this language/character set.

www.basket.ru/

93. **Centre Sport Statistics. Basketball**

Basketball. National Basketball Association (NBA) 1949-2002. National Basketball League (NBL) 1937-1949. Basketball Association of America (BAA) 1946-1949. All statistics of league, teams and players (1937-2002). NBA, ABA, BAA, NBL.

www.sport.km.ru/basketball/index.php

94. **Search Tips About Basketball Life Home Health Family**
Basketball.LifeTips.com offers Guru tips about the game of basketball with free basketball tips, links, weekly newsletters.
www.basketball-tips.com/

95. **fanzam.com Basketball**
Basketball information guide that includes list of popular NBA sites, and news.
www.fanzam.com/basketball.html

96. **NBA Basketball Trade Rumors - Forums, Speculation and Daily...**
Lebron James becomes rookie of the year, that will be an insult to the game of Basketball. " Posted by NothingButNets ..
www.wowbasketball.com/

97. **basketball 365: united kingdom**
Basketball 365: United Kingdom - The ultimate on-line experience for Basketball players and fans in England, Scotland, Wales and Northern Ireland. ...
www.basketball365.co.uk/

98. **NBA Basketball Tickets and NBA Finals Tickets**
NBA-Basketball-Tickets.com is your #1 source for all NBA tickets....
www.nba-basketball-tickets.com/ - 7k - **Cached - Similar pages**

99. **The History of Women's Basketball**
The History of Women's Basketball. Regarding John Molina's work..the history of womens basketball "It is one of the finest collections ...
www.womensbasketballmuseum.com/

100. **Nitty-Gritty Basketball Series Website- Books, Clinics, Video...**
The Nitty-Gritty Basketball Series website offers freebies, discounts, tips, articles, advice, and clinics. clinics as well as Phil ...
www.mrbasketball.net/

101. **Pro Basketball**
NBA championships, All-Star Game results, annual awards, ABA, CBA, ABL and WNBA.
www.infoplease.com/ipsa/A0003691.html

102. **RecSupply.com Pool Shot Water Basketball**
Site of Recreation Supply Company selling pool shot water basketball products.
www.recsupply.com/myweb/products/poolshot.htm

103. **VL of Sport - Basketball**

A virtual web library on all basketball-related sites

sportsvl.com/ball/basketball.htm

104. **Mini Baskett Ball**

National governing body. Includes information on mini basketball, MBE publications, upcoming workshops,...

www.mini-basketball.org.uk/

105. **International Basketball Directory**

INTERNATIONAL. BASKETBALL. DIRECTORY. ... BASKETBALL IS LIFE. LIFE IS BASKETBALL. Extensive list of links sorted by country.

www.geocities.com/internationalbasketballdirectory/

106. **Women_s Sports Page - Women in Basketball**

Women In Basketball. Women's Basketball newsgroup American Basketball League ... the ABL. Women's National Basketball Association. USA ...

www.gslis.utexas.edu/~lewisa/basketball.html

107. **Nike Basketball**

www.nike.com/nikebasketball/

108. **2003 CAAD Basketball Tournament**

2003 CAAD Basketball Tournament. Updated 29 Jun 2003. ... Central Athletic Association of the Deaf 58th Annual Basketball Tournament. Deaf basketball coverage from Central Athletic Association of the Deaf (CAAD)

www.wi-deafsports.org/Special/2003CAAD/caad2003.htm

109. **hoopsjunkie.net: where HoopHeads get their fix!**

Analysis and opinions on the latest developments in the world of professional and college basketball.

www.hoopsjunkie.net/

110. **GoDuke.com - The Official Site of Duke University Athletics**

Duke University's Official Athletic Site: complete coverage of all Blue Devil NCAA sports including basketball, football, baseball, soccer, volleyball, & ...

www.goduke.com/

111. **Asian Basketball Confederation**

News, press releases, tournament calendar, training programmes, gallery, players and links.

www.asianbasketball.com/

112. **Street Basketball Association**

Dedicated to bringing the game of street ball to the world. Teams throughout the United States.

www.streetbasketballassociation.net/

113. **Basketball talk - Ramblings and Babblings and Everything Under**

This site is all about Basketball, professional or amateur, men's or ladies', local or international, frontyard or schoolyard; its stars, players and coaches ...

bballtalk.com/

114. **USATODAY.com**

Football. Football matchups. Football injuries. Basketball (M). Basketball matchups. Basketball injuries. Basketball (W). Baseball. Ice hockey. Other sports.Life.

www.usatoday.com/sports/basketba/skm/skcm.htm

115. **Mr. Basketball and Miss Basketball Youth and High School ...**

Mr. Basketball and Miss Basketball Tournaments

www.misterbasketball.com/

116. **CBA - Continental Basketball Association**

Official league site; offers news and press releases, composite schedule, standings, league leaders,...

www.cbahoopsonline.com/

117. **Women's Basketball Magazine**

Women's Basketball is published six times a year by Ashton International Media, Inc. All contents of this web site copyright© 2003 ...

www.wbmagazine.com/

118. **Hoop Hall History Page**

The game of basketball began in 1891. ... Basketball's history is long and storied, so remember to check this section often for updates. ...

www.hoophall.com/history/history.htm

119. **Orange Europe Basketball Directory**

Provides links to English language basketball web sites related to Europe. The links are arranged by country. Orange Europe. Basketball Directory....

www.ael-limassol.net/basketball_directory.html

120. **Sport! Science - Basketball**

Sport Science. Basketball -Last updated May 13, 1997. Books, Articles, Brancazio, Peter. ... Classroom activities related to basketball and basketball shoe design. ...

www.exploratorium.edu/sports/biblo/SSBasket.htm

121. **HomepageNew.gif**

A non-profit grade based summer developmental youth basketball program currently operating within 15 states.

www.aybtour.com/

122. **Basketball drills and coaching - På̲l Degerstrø̲m**

The complete site for basketball coaches, with hundreds of free drills, a discussion forum, and downloadable tools. Basketball drills. ...

www.degerstrom.com/basketball/drills/

123. **Web Hosting**

Contains basketball recruiting, merchandise, news, courts, members, t-shirts, and calendar of events.

cherrypickin.com/

124. **BASKETBALL WORLD - Camps, Clinics, Books, Videos, Apparel**

BASKETBALL WORLD: SHOOT IT BETTER Mini Camps, Basketball Day Camps, Basketball Books, Basketball Videos, and Basketball Apparel. ...

www.basketballworld.com/

125. **Basket ball - Actus et infos sur le basket**

World_>_Français_>_Sports_>_Balles_et_ballons_>_Basketball

www.basketball-news.com/

126. **moviebkb**

Basketball Movies. ... He also was voted the second most influential basketball player (behind George Mikan) in the first half of the 20th century. List of recommended titles on this theme, giving the stars, brief plot summary and release date for...

www.sandlotshrink.com/moviebkb.htm

127. **Coaching Basketball Links**

Coaching Basketball Links. What's On This Web Page: Basketball Links. Coaching Basketball Websites/Links. ...

www.angelfire.com/ks2/basketball1/

128. **2000 Beach Basketball**
Beach basketball sports apparel and game pieces
www.beachbasketball.com/catalog.htm

129. **University of Kansas Athletics**
Official site of the Jayhawks with news items, scores, statistics, pictures, and a roster.
www.kuathletics.com/mensbasketball/

130. **RALPH MILLER'S PRESSURE BASKETBALL SYSTEM**
Diagrams from defense to offense, the breaking game, drills, conditioning, the Golden Era of Basketball and much more.
www.pressurebasketball.com/

131. **Olympic Basketball Links**
Links to news, history and other information about the Basketball events at the Olympic Games.
www.sirlinksalot.net/2000basketball.html

132. **Planet Basketball**
Search engine for professional and amateur information, also includes a forum and news updates.
www.planetbasketball.net/

133. **Basketball-Goals.com- Best Quality Residential & Institutional...**
We sell the best quality basketball systems and equipment accessories. For residential & institutional use in schools, gymnasiums ...
www.basketball-goals.com/

134. **AllExperts.com**
Professional Basketball. Atlanta Hawks, Miami Heat. Basketball Instruction, Minnesota Timberwolves. Basketball Trivia (general), New Jersey Nets. ...
www.allexperts.com/sports/basketball.shtml

135. **Yahoo! Sports Fantasy NBA**
Our free game gives you the chance to run your own team of real National Basketball Association players from the season's opening tip right through to the ...
basketball.fantasysports.yahoo.com/nba

136. **Basketball Australia**
Basketball Australia. Announcements, :: Leading News Stories, One Basketball Sponsors. ...
www.basketball.net.au/fs_home.asp

137. **Basketball Coaching- In Search of Excellence**

Coaching youth basketball site featuring basketball coaching tips, drills, plays, practice plan, weight training, playbook, and team building tips. ...

coachlikeapro.tripod.com/basketball/

138. **Eurobasket - European Basketball**

... EUROBASKET Eurobasket is a network of 6 web sites (eurobasket.com, usbasket.com, etc.), which provide complete coverage of international basketball. ...

www.eurobasket.com/

139. **NBA Players Association — Home Page**

National Basketball Players Association Powered by Switch Technologies. Official Site of the association of NBA players. Calendar of events and details of the collective...

www.nbpa.com/

140. **iSportsDigest.com/Youth Sports/Basketball**

Directory containing hundreds of youth basketball sites and resources.

isportsdigest.tripod.com/youth/basketball/main.html

141. **sunspot.net | pro basketball**

Scoring life lessons, fun Basketball: A Baltimore nonprofit's tournament is aimed at teaching youths sportsman- ship and teamwork — all while having a good ...

www.sunspot.net/sports/basketball/

142. **Scarborough Basketball Association**

Train and teach basketball fundamentals to all age levels.

www.scarboroughbasketball.com/

143. **Compare Prices and Read Reviews on Basketball at Epinions.com**

Epinions has the best comparison shopping information on Basketball. ... Basketball. Find and Compare, Browse categories in Basketball. Consumer-generated reviews, buying tips and advice, ratings, price information, and searchable...

www.epinions.com/sprt-All-Basketball

144. **NCAA Basketball**

Men's Basketball, Women's Basketball. All-Season. NCAA Basketball Rules Committees Delay Changes (News Release); Official Web site (www.ncaasports.com); ...

www.ncaa.org/sports/basketball/

145. **Men's Athletic: Basketball Shoes**

Men's Athletic: Basketball Shoes; Browse through our selection of Men's Athletic: Basketball Shoes such as: adidas The T-Mac III, adidas Promodel 2G Patent...

www.zappos.com/n/es/d/722000061.html

146. **Basketball Software, Basketball Stat Software, All Stats ...**

Basketball Software that is loaded with features that any basketball coach will benefit from. Create schedules, phone lists, rosters and track player, team, and league stats.

www.allstats.com/basketball/

147. **InfoSport, Inc.**

Comprehensive directory of basketball information includes coaching, professional, and collegiate links.

www.infosportinc.com/h-links.html

148. **Africa: African Sports: Basketball**

An E-Community for Africa, Africa: African Sports: Basketball. ... FIBA - International Basketball Organisation. TeleBasket - BasketBall news from Africa. Congo DR. ...

www.clickafrique.com/sports/basketball.asp

149. **Lucas' Basketball Site**

Personal pages with pictures, clips, quizzes, Vince Carter, Allen Iverson and links.

basketballsportsfan.tripod.com/basketball/

150. **United States Basketball Writers Association**

Official basketball journalists' organization.

www.sportswriters.net/usbwa/

151. **Basketball Rules**

Links to sites about basketball rules, basketball in general and current basketball news. ... Basketball Rules. Blog about Basketball.

basketballrules.blogspot.com/

152. **Basketball in Indiana**

Indiana high school basketball scores, stats, records, game of the week, and polls.. SEASON'S GREETINGS THANK YOU - We just turned ...

www.basketballinindiana.com/

153. **Using Mean, Median, Mode, and Range through Basketball**
Using Mean, Median, Mode, and Range through Basketball. Grade level: 8th grade. Materials: paper, pencil, sports section during basketball season. ...
euclid.barry.edu/~marinas/mat476/bball/kup319fr.html

154. **Basketball Coaching Magazine - Basketball Sense**
Basketball Sense Magazine is packed with of expert coaching advice, providing the best information on basketball coaching available today. ...
www.basketballsense.com/

155. **The Official Site of the Lebanese Basketball Federation**
The official site of the Lebanese Basketball Federation (FLB) - flbb.com – from Lebanon. ... more... The Lebanese Basketball Federation. ...
www.flbb.com/

156. **Basketball Digest Magazine**
Basketball Digest Table of Contents. COVER STORY. Basketball Digest Interview: Steve Francis. By Brett Ballantini. ...
www.centurysports.net/basketball/

157. **Basketball WA Homepage**
BASKETBALL WA (The Western Australian Basketball Federation Inc.). ... Basketbal WA Poll. Currently there is no opinion poll available...
www.basketballwa.asn.au/

158. **Basketball Sports Betting Lines : NBA Sports Betting**
Basketball Betting Lines: NBA betting lines at Basketball Sports Betting is your information central for up-to-the-minute NBA lines for the 2004 championship ...
www.basketballsportsbetting.com/

159. **University of Michigan Men_s Basketball Wolverines**
Official University of Michigan Wolverines Athletics department site. Tickets, merchandise, facilities,...
www.mgoblue.com/basketball-m/

160. **FreezeTagBasketball (invented by Phil Anker & Dave Fisher)**
A form of basketball where select players can "freeze" other players. Contains a listing of rules...
freezetagbasketball.tripod.com/

161. **The answers to the IAABO Refresher Test**

... print out a price list and order form for great training videos on Block/Charge, Game Management, Traveling and other topics concerning basketball officiating. ...

www.iaabo.org/

162. **Fan Draft - Fantasy Basketball Draft Software**

Fantasy software to enhance leagues live drafts.

www.fandraftbasketball.com/

163. **Basketball Traveler_s Inc.**

Organizes basketball tours and tournaments for college and high school teams.

www.basketballtravelers.com/

164. **GBWBA Web Site**

Great Britain Wheelchair Basketball Association. official governing body for wheelchair basketball in the UK. Club and division listings, results,...

www.gbwba.org.uk/

165. **Havenport basketball links page**

Havenport Prize Money Basketball Shooting Accuracy Skill Championships for women and men in free throws and three point shots, Shooting skill could win cash ...

www.havenport.com/hosa/btlinks.html

9
Beachvolleyball

1. **European Beachvolleyball Foundation ebf**
   World > Deutsch > ... > Ballsport > Volleyball > Beachvolleyball
   www.ebf.li/
2. **Beachvolleyball Aargau**
   www.beachvolleyball.ch/
3. **Ostbeachland.de - Die Site der ostfriesischen Beachscene.**
   World > Deutsch > ... > Ballsport > Volleyball > Beachvolleyball
   www.ostbeachland.de/
4. **beachvolleyball - beach-volleyball 2b, Beachvolleyball, Beach**
   www.beach-volleyball2b.com/
5. **Beach Volleyball**
   Sponsors, profiles, and results for the team of Kerri Pottharst and Natalie Cook.
   www.beachvolleyball.com.au/
6. **volley.de - Volleyball**
   www.volley.de/
7. **volley.de - Volleyball**
   ww.volley-beachvolleyball.de/
8. **beach volleyball - beach-volleyball 2b, Beachvolleyball, Beach**
   www.beach-volleyball.de/
9. **Beach- Volleyball - Berlin**
   Beachvolleyball Berlin
   www.beachvolleyball-berlin.de/
10. **Jever - Was läuft?**
    World > Deutsch > ... > Ballsport > Volleyball > Beachvolleyball
    www.jever.de/was/beachvolleyball/beach_frame.htm

11. **Sport1 - Mehr Sport | Beachvolleyball **
www.sport1.at/coremedia/generator/id=2026454.html
12. **Volleyball, Beachvolleyball, Strandvolleyball, Sportalen med guide**
www.sportalen.no/volley.htm
13. **BEACHLUTSCHER**
wwwstud.uni-leipzig.de/~mai00bhf/
14. **Beachvolleyball-Navigator.de - Beachvolleyball Linkdatenbank**
www.beachvolleyball-navigator.de/
15. **eachvolleyball.de - Ihr Beach-Volleyball und Volleyball - Shop**
www.beachvolleyball.de/
16. **Kaffeesud: Beachvolleyball**
Beachvolleyball. Austrians best beachvolleyball team Berger-Doppler starts as number 2 (worldranking) into the grand slam tournament in Berlin.
www.paumann.org/blog/archives/000066.php
17. **alleskIar - größter deutscher Webkatalog**
www.alleskIar.de/ surftipps.php?surftipp=Beachvolleyball
18. **Beach-Volleyball in Schule und Verein mit Übungen, Übungsreihen**
Special Beachvolleyball.
www.volleyball-training.de/special_beach.htm
19. **SVZ online: Beachvolleyball**
www.svz.de/sport/trendbeachvolleyball/
20. **Pfronten im Allgäu**
www.pfronten.de/index.shtml?infosys&infosys=Beachvolleyball
21. **Yahoo! Sport - Beachvolleyball**
de.sports.yahoo.com/b
22. **Beachvolleyball**
zeh-server.sport.uni-oldenburg.de/sportarten/170.html
23. **Beachvolleyball**
www.beachvolleyball.at/deutsch/news.php
24. **Vereine-Online.cc - Sportvereine im Internet**
www.vereine-online.cc/start.php?sport=3
25. **Beachvolleyball**
www.fabasoft-steg.at/fabasoftstegwebsite/volley-links/beachvolleyball.htm
26. **Volley-Shop**
www.volley-shop.de/index.php3?ud=&ushop=14

27. **BSC Obfelden Beachvolleyball**
    www.bsc-obfelden.ch/beachvolleyball/index.php
28. **beachvolleyball online spielen computer c64 Spiele Freeware Games**
    www.freegame4all.de/beachvolleyball-online-spielen.htm
29. **Beachvolleyball - SSK Feldkirch**
    members.vol.at/ssk.feldkirch/beach.htm
30. **beachvolleyball - Tips zum Thema**
    www.link-tips.com/beachvolleyball.html
31. **SALZBURG.INDOOR.BEACHVOLLEYBALL**
    www.indoor-beachvolleyball.at/
32. **Beachvolleyball World Tour Gstaad 2003**
    www.post.ch/SiteOnLine/DE/Accueil/ 1,1727,7724-195,00.html

10
Billiards

1. **Billiards Digest.com On-line Billiards Magazine featuring live...**
The on-line complement of the most comprehensive magazine in billiards. The premier place on the Web...
www.billiardsdigest.com/

2. **Billiards.com**
Offers pool cues and cases, balls and ball racks and gameroom furniture.
www.billiards.com/

3. **Play Pool Online - 8 Ball Billiards**
Play pool online, 8-ball billiards, 9-ball billiards, straight pool, high score contest pool. Great free games at Candystand. Play Online Billiards, ...
www.candystand.com/games/cs_shock_cspl.htm

4. **Billiard Congress of America**
Your one-stop source for The Business of Billiards: BCA Expo updates, billiard marketplace and business membership information. Calling all players! ...
www.bca-pool.com/start.shtml

5. **Brunswick Billiards. Billiards tables and accessories since 1845.**
Billiards Sponsorships, Promotions and Events, Business Opportunities, Rules and How to Play, ...
www.brunswickbilliards.com/

6. **Billiards - Be good at billiards**
Be good at Billiards is the web site reference for all billiard and snooker players. ... Billiards is one of the most complex games to play. Basic, informative direction for the beginner by Canadian billiard enthusiast. Includes animated pictures...
www3.sympatico.ca/eric.perreault/default.html

7. **About Billiards**

See what's happening in the exciting world of 9-ball, 8-ball, Straight pool, Three-cushion and Snooker....

billiardspool.about.com/

8. **AzBilliards.com**

Jason Miller wins Derby Bank Pool. Jason 'Killer' Miller from Dayton Ohio put on a bank-shot exhibition to win this year's Derby ...

www.azbilliards.com/

9. **Pool and Billiard Magazine**

Watch Entire Derby City Live Broadcast for only $9.95 - For Immediate Release – DIAMOND GUARANTEES AFFORDABLE LIVE BROADCAST - Diamond Billiards Products, Inc. ...

www.poolmag.com/

10. **Megasoft2000.com**

Palm OS utilities. Palm OS games. Pocket PC games. Billiards. Overview. Benefits. System Requirements.

ww.megasoft2000.com/palm_division/billiards.htm

11. **Billiards and Chaos Theory**

The Billiards Simulation. Polygon Table. Circle Table. Stadium Table. Ellipse Table. Documentation. Derya Davis, Mathematics and Physics; Carin Ewing, Philosophy;. ...

serendip.brynmawr.edu/chaos/home.html

12. **Barb's Billiards Art**

Free Billiards Art for link Exchange - Please use picture below for links. Barb's Billiards Art. ...

www.proaxis.com/~cbiz/

13. **Billiards and Physics**

Billiards and Physics. ... > The law of reflection can only be used in billiards to > approximate the angle of reflection for a billiard ball.

www.phy.ntnu.edu.tw/~hwang/billiards/billiards.html

14. **Billiards, Snooker, Pool. Rules and more!**

Life's short, play pool! Billiards, Snooker, Pool is maintained by Sjoerd Arlman Made:

www.arlman.demon.nl/pool/

15. **Shooters Pool Cues, Cue Cases and Billiards Accessories**
Shooters Billiards Supplies Discount Pool Cues and Pool Tables ! As a leader in online pool cues and billiards supplies, we hope that you visit often!
www.shootersbilliards.com/

16. **Olhausen Billiards pool tables**
Manufacturer of slate pool tables, with a showroom in Kearny Mesa. Includes photos of pool tables
www.olhausenbilliards.com/

17. **WPBA.com | Home**
Official site for the WPBA, providing membership information, television and tour schedules, tournament
www.wpba.com/

18. **Cornwall Billiards and Snooker Association's Home Page**
The latest updated and improved website of the Cornwall Amateur Billiards and Snooker Association.
www.cornwallbilliardssnooker.fsnet.co.uk/

19. **World Standardized Rules**
GENERAL RULES OF POCKET BILLIARDS ... SUPPLEMENTAL RULES. The following are rules that are referred to within the General Rules of Pocket Billiards above.
www.bca-pool.com/play/tournaments/rules/rls_gen.shtml

20. **The Illustrated Principles of Pool and Billiards**
Book and online resources for learning the principles and techniques of pool and billiards. ... The Illustrated Principles of Pool and Billiards.
www.engr.colostate.edu/~dga/pool/

21. **Viewing list of forums - Forums powered by UBB.threads™**
Message board with on-line with experts, players and enthusiasts of the sport.
www.billiardsdigest.com/ccboard/

22. **Billiards**
The summary for this Japanese page contains characters that cannot be correctly displayed in this language/character set.
www10.big.or.jp/~south-w/billiards/

23. **Scratcho?billiards?**
The summary for this Japanese page contains characters that cannot be correctly displayed in this language/character set.
scratcho.s22.xrea.com/

24. **World Snooker Association**

The official website of the world governing body featuring the latest snooker news and results, plus

www.worldsnooker.com/

25. **Triangle Billiards: Pool Tables, Cues, Lighting, Barstools ...**

Retailer of cues, cases and furnishing.

www.tribilliards.com/

26. **Pool and Billiard Cues - Hawleys Billiards On-Line - Billiards and ...**

Offers cue sticks, pool cues, cue cases, table lights, and accessories.

www.billiardstore.com/

27. **Billiards - Pool - Snooker - Links - A categorised directory of ...**

The following links will take you deep into the world of Billiards, Pool and Snooker across the continents in the following categories. A mammoth site of categorized Billiard, Pool and Snooker links worldwide.

www.blackball.org.uk/

28. **Pool Cues and Billiards Supplies**

Offers billiard balls, sticks, cue cases and accessories.

www.cuesight.com/

29. **Four Great Pool and Billiards Webrings**

A webring for sites that offer pool instruction, news, and supplies and equipment. home.earthlink.net/~acetoscano

gpbsotwhome.html

30. **CBSA - The Canadian Billiards and Snooker Association**

www.CBSA.ca, the official web site of the The Canadian Billiards and Snooker Association. The premiere source ... Canadian cue sports. ...

www.cbsa.ca/

31. **Ivars Peterson's MathLand**

Billiards in the Round. ... One mathematician who thought of playing billiards on a circular table was Charles L. Dodgson, better known as Lewis Carroll. ...

www.maa.org/mathland/mathland_3_3.html

32. **Billiards, The DandD Family Billiard Room in Downingtown Pa. 610-269 ...**

The family billiards room with weekly 8 and 9 ball tournaments.

www.thebilliardstour.com/

33. **Multiplayer Billiards Straight Pool - Candystand Billiards**
Play multiplayer billiards straight pool. Free multi player pool online at Candystand.Multiplayer Pool Game, Multiplayer Billiards Straight Pool. ...
www.candystand.com/games/cs_shock_csmps.htm

34. **On The Wire Billiards News Supplies Instruction**
Online version of "On The Wire" newspaper, a publication dedicated to promoting billiard sports. Informat...
www.onthewirebilliards.com/

35. **Jim Loy's Billiards/Pool Page**
Features billiards and pool articles, essays, and fiction, including many with how-to diagrams and graphics.
www.jimloy.com/billiard/billiard.htm

36. **Compare Prices and Read Reviews on Backstreet Billiards for...**
Epinions has the best comparison shopping information on Backstreet Billiards for Playstation 1. Compare prices from across the web and read reviews from other ...
www.epinions.com/ game-Titles-Consoles-SonyPlaystation-All-Backstreet_Billiards

37. **Northern Ireland Billiards and Snooker Association**
The latest news, results, rankings and competitions from the Northern Ireland Billiards and Snooker Association. Enter button, Enter, ...
homepage.ntlworld.com/snooker.nibsa/

38. **Esnuka - freeware game of billiards, snooker and pool**
Freeware video game of Billiards, Pool and Snooker. Contest and computerized multiplayers option. ... Shoot pool on your computer with this billiards program! ...
www.versee.com/esnuka/ae0-2-billiardspoolsnooker.html

39. **Pool, Billiards and Snooker: Rules, tips, tutorials**
Links to a wide variety of how-to guides covering topics from rules to form.
www.knowledgehound.com/topics/pool.htm

40. **147 Snooker Billiards Pool**
coname=147 Snooker Billiards Pool snooker billiards pool biljart billard Belgium europe europa hasselt limburg sport peradon bce cuecraft craftsman boxxer ...
www.freewebs.com/147mjm/

41. **Cleveland Billiards and Snooker League**
The league run ten KO competitions with awards or trophies provided for winners and runners-up in...
homepage.ntlworld.com/ian.whittle/cbsl1.htm

42. **Free Pool Lessons, Billiards Instructions and Snooker Tips online ...**
News and articles about pool, billiards and snooker. ... Learn how to play pool and billiards. Username: Password: [Create an account]. ...
www.easypooltutor.com/

43. **Yahoo! Directory Games > Billiards**
Games > Billiards Directory > Recreation > Games > Billiards, Search the Web just this category. ... INSIDE YAHOO! Games: play Billiards with your friends on Yahoo! ...
dir.yahoo.com/Recreation/Games/Billiards/

44. **Reference for billiard links, web sites, pool magazines and rules.**
Personal and commercial billiard sites, magazines, professional players, tournaments and leagues....
free-reference.com/billiards.htm

45. **Coming Soon!**
An interactive site with forums and many educational articles by its visitors.
www.wbom.com/

46. **playpool.com**
Find pool rooms and pool tournaments anywhere in the USA. Single and double elimination tournament
www.playpool.com/

47. **Google Directory - Sports > Billiards**
Billiards, ... OnTheCheese.Com Billiards - http:
www.onthecheese.com/ Includes news, stories, cartoons and links. Raleigh, NC and South Eastern United States...
directory.google.com/Top/Sports/Billiards/

48. **McDermott Pool Cues: Pool Cues for Billiards; Two Piece Cues and Cue ...** McDermott pool cues are two piece, quick release pool cues for billiards.
www.mcdermottcue.com/

49. **BILLIARD WORLD**

Published by Pat in loving memory of Jim Meador. The links below will take you to Jim's earliest work on Billiard World.

www.billiardworld.com/

50. **Queen's University Belfast Snooker, Billiards and Pool Club**

The site includes information on the latest competitions. Belfast, Northern Ireland.

quis.qub.ac.uk/snooker/welcome.htm

51. **EASB | English Association for Snooker and Billiards**

The official website of the governing body for snooker and Billiards in England, providing tournaments,...

www.easb.co.uk/

52. **Billiards Zone - The Finest Billiard and Pool Supplies on The...**

Offers a complete selection of accessories including cues, cue cases and decorations.

www.billiard-zone.com/

53. **Live Billiards - play 3D Billiards game :: Virtual Online Pool ...**

Live Billiards - play 3D Billiards game, Virtual Online Pool Club, free 3d billiard game, free download, demo version, Straight Pool, 8ball, 9ball, 14.1, 3ball ...

www.terragame.com/lbclub.shtml

54. **Open Directory - Sports: Billiards**

About Billiards - See what's happening in the exciting world of 9-ball, 8-ball, Straight pool, Three-cushion and Snooker. ... Boulevard Billiards - Allentown, PA. ...

dmoz.org/Sports/Billiards/

55. **Michigan Union Billiards and Games Room**

... pool. 2nd Place: Mike H. $35 gift card + Michigan Billiards T-shirt + Jeanette Lee poster + BCA Goody bag + 1 week free pool. 3rd ...

www.umich.edu/~billiard/

56. **OnTheCheese.Com Billiards: Pool Sport Resources for Raleigh NC...**

Includes news, stories, cartoons and links. Raleigh, NC and South Eastern United States.

www.onthecheese.com/

57. **Emory Billiards Club (EBC) - shooting pool at Emory University in ...**
Emory University's pool club! Holds regular billiards tournaments and promotes pool on campus. ... Offers access to national billiards competitions. ...
www.emory.edu/STUDENTS/POOL/

58. **Yahoo! Groups**
Yahoo! Groups. Top > Games > Billiards. Start a Billiards Group. View Billiards Groups. Billiards Groups (457). Browse for more specialized Groups. ...
dir.groups.yahoo.com/dir/Games/Billiards

59. **Fantastic Game Billiards**
The summary for this Japanese page contains characters that cannot be correctly displayed in this language/character set.
billiards.jp.gentei.org/~yuuji/

60. **Google Directory - Shopping > Sports > Billiards**
Billiards, ... Alkar Billiards - http://www.alkarbilliards.com Online shopping for billiard supplies, balls and racks, cloth, cues, cases, books and videos. ...
directory.google.com/Top/Shopping/Sports/Billiards/

61. **The Sports Authority - More Sports: Billiards**
SEARCH BY Keyword or Online Item #. Browse the Store. ...
www.thesportsauthority.com/category
index.jsp?categoryId=711741andcp=717754

62. **Pool and Billiards Frequently Asked Questions**
Pool and Billiards Frequently Asked Questions. There are reader questions on this topic! ... None of these are Billiards Congress of America (BCA) rules. ...
www.faqs.org/faqs/sports/billiards/faq/

63. **Billiards Rules**
3x3 Basic Billiards Parameters 1) Elimination Tournament. ... See below for the detailed Rules of Play Detailed Billiards Rules of Play 14.1 Continuous. ...
www.stanford.edu/group/Intramurals/billiardsrules.html

64. **Memorial Union Games Area - BILLIARDS**
The discount card can be purchased at the Games Area for a fee. The card entitles the holder to a 50% discount on billiards. The ...
gamesarea.ucdavis.edu/billiards.htm

65. **Union Underground: Billiards**
Union Underground: Billiards. The Underground has 12 regulation billiards tables. Table rental varies depending upon day and time. ...
www.utexas.edu/student/txunion/ae/ undergroun ?under=billiards

66. **K-State Student Union » Billiards**
Thirteen full-size Pocket tables and one Snooker table are available for your leisure enjoyment! Billiard leagues are also offered ...
www.union.ksu.edu/index.php?ID=17

67. **Open Directory - Games: Video Games: Sports: Billiards**
... Top: Games: Video Games: Sports: Billiards (8), Description. Backstreet Billiards (1); Expert Pool (0); Virtual Pool Series (7). ...
dmoz.org/Games/Video_Games/Sports/Billiards/

68. **Ace's Discount Billiards and Pool Cues - Pool Table Lights - Pool ...**
Remember This Site;. Ace's Discount Pool and Billiards Cues - Lights – Tables - Supplies - Accessories ... Gifts for pool players. Pool and billiards gifts. ...
home.earthlink.net/~acetoscano/cuesandsupplies.html

69. **Kmart.com - Billiards**
... Billiards, Homepage, Billiards, Accessories Balls/Racks Books and Videos Cue Racks Tables Cue Sticks/Accessories Game Room Furniture. ...
www.bluelight.com/category/index.jsp?categoryId=711741

70. **Women's Sports Foundation Billiards**
This is not simply a game of pool, this is billiards. We all wish when we played with friends that we had the skill set of thes...
www.womenssportsfoundation.org/cgi-bin/ iowa/auction/billiards/

71. **CRS Intramurals**
intramurals.binghamton.edu/billiards.htm

72. **Billiards, Indoor Games, Sports, Outdoors, More Categories...**
Billiards , Indoor Games , Sports , Outdoors , More Categories - The NexTag shopping guide has prices, reviews from stores all over the web. ... Billiards. ...
www.nextag.com/Billiards~2701042z0zBwzmainz5-htm

73. **CAROM CAFE Billiards - The new mecca for 3-Cushion Billiards, Pool ...**
Sang Chun Lee and Michael Kang welcomes you to Carom Cafe Billiards, the new center for 3-Cushion Billiards in the USA! Full description ...
www.caromcafe.com/frameset.html

74. **NBC.com > Fear Factor**
Fear Factor Billiards Chances are most people will go through life never having to eat a combination of live ants, fermented squid guts and burning hot ...
www.nbc.com/Fear_Factor/stunts/ stunt_213_billiards.shtml

75. **Buy Billiards, Sporting Goods, Sports, Cues on eBay**
Buy Billiards on eBay including Tables, Other Items, Accessories, Cues, Sports, and Sporting Goods. ... (115). See all matching Stores, Billiards, 5645 items found, ...
listings.ebay.com/aw/plistings/list/ all/category21209/?from=R4

76. **York Faber Shield Snooker and Billiards Home Page**
Offers news, resources, fixtures and results for a variety of leagues and tournaments in the United...
freespace.virgin.net/r.stroughair/

77. **Union Online Billiards**Billiards Area. There are several billiards tables located in room 158 (next the copy center) on the first floor of the Union. ... Billiards Pricing (per hour). ...
www.union.utah.edu/recreation/billiards/

78. **Buy all DVD Snooker / Pool / Billiards at the best price with ...**
Buy Snooker / Pool / Billiards Buy DVDs at the best shops online. Select a DVD title below or use our search form to find best prices for all DVDs. ... Billiards. ...
films.kelkoo.co.uk/b/a/cpc_149201_gs_15483622_category.html

79. **We have used bowling balls and bags for sale! Equipment is sold" ...**
For individual activities.
www.uusa.vt.edu/recreation/BreakZONE/bowling.htm

80. **Billiards — from MathWorld**
Billiards, The game of billiards is played on a rectangular table (known as a billiard table) upon which balls are placed. ...
Tabachnikov, S. Billiards. ...
mathworld.wolfram.com/Billiards.html

81. **Billiards, Pool and Snooker Additional Sports - Prices and Reviews ...**

    Compare shop for Billiards Pool and Snooker Additional Sports at DealTime.co.uk - read reviews and compare prices from stores all across the Web. ...

    www.dealtime.co.uk/ xDN-Additional_Sports _billiards__pool___snooker

82. **Billiards and Snooker - Online guide**

    The Billiards Family. Origins - Ground Billiards. The .... However, records do show one game that is related to Billiards. Sometime...

    www.tradgames.org.uk/games/Billiard-Family.htm

83. **Bar Billiards - Online Guide**

    Bar Billiards - History and Useful Information. ... History of Bar Billiards. The similarity of ... Pool. Italian Bar Billiards. This famil...

    www.tradgames.org.uk/games/Bar-Billiards.htm

84. **Live Billiards download page. Live Billiards by TerraGame ...**

    Live Billiards is a comprehensive 3D pool simulator, giving you full reality sensation.

    www.globalshareware.com/GamesSimulations/ Live-Billiards.htm

85. **Brunswick Billiards: Billiards Sponsorships**

    Billiards Sponsorships. Brunswick Billiards is the official table, rack, and ball sponsor for the WPBA Classic Tour in 2003. ... Brunswick Billiards US Open. ...

    www.brunswickbilliards.com/sponsor/sponsor.html

86. **Billiards, Games, Toys, More Categories - compare prices ..**

    Billiards , Games , Toys , More Categories - The NexTag shopping guide has prices, reviews from stores all over the web. ... Billiards.

    www.nextag.com/Billiards~2700638z0zBwzmainz5-htm

87. **Illinois State University - Bowling and Billiards Center**

    The BBC provides entertainment for students, faculty/staff, and the general public in the form of: bowling, billiards, popular video and pinball games. ...

    www.bsc.ilstu.edu/bbc/index.shtml

88. **WBS Events**

    Based out of the University of Western Ontario. The Western Billiards Society has been this university's...

    www.usc.uwo.ca/clubs/billiards/

89. **Live Billiards Deluxe**

The BEST SITE for Live Billiards Deluxe cheats, Live Billiards Deluxe codes and Live Billiards Deluxe walkthroughs, previews, reviews, videos and screenshots.

play.ign.com/objects/617/617632.html

11
Boxing

1. **Boxing**
   www.boxing.com/
2. **HBO: Boxing**
   HBO's boxing website: previews of upcoming fights, fight results and analyses, fight schedule, latest rankings by weight class, expert columns, a boxing bbs ...
   www.hbo.com/boxing/
3. **ESPN.com - Boxing**
   Schedules, champions, previews of upcoming ESPN fight cards and boxing newswire service. Includes...
   espn.go.com/boxing/
4. **Boxing Times Online**
   Hard-core insider's coverage of boxing including columns, world rankings, knockout photography, fight breakdowns and anaylsis, television schedules and ...
   www.boxingtimes.com/
5. **USA Boxing**
   The official website of USA Boxing, the national governing body of amateur boxing.
   www.usaboxing.org/
6. **flash_detection**
   www.boxingonline.com/
7. **BOXING MONTHLY - The Worldwide Sports Magazine Homepage**
   BOXING MONTHLY - the essential sports magazine for serious followers of the boxing world. Complete site for online articles, rankings ...
   www.boxing-monthly.co.uk/

8. **BoxingInsider.com : Insider Boxing News, Boxing Results, Schedule ...**

   Boxing News, Results, Boxing Rumors, Odds, Forum, and more. Get The Inside Dirt On Boxing. ... Fantasy Boxing Betting Leagues - Play FREE!! KNOCKOUT Your Debt! ...

   www.boxinginsider.com/

9. **Boxing News And Views - East Side Boxing**

   Boxing news and inside coverage of boxing including interviews, international boxing news, previews of upcoming fights, post fight boxing results and analyses ...

   www.eastsideboxing.com/

10. **World Boxing Association**

    The Russian described his style as scientific and speedy boxing, with which he is planning to dethrone the WBC 115-pound champ Masamori Tokuyama, who is ...

    www.wbaonline.com/

11. **Boxing News For The Serious Boxing Fan**

    Boxing news and content updated everyday. Get boxing news, rankings, schedules, boxer profiles, results, and predictions. ... More Real Boxing Buzz: ...

    www.boxingtalk.net/

12. **Boxing Canada**

    BOXING CANADA 2003. "The Official Website". ... IND E X. About Boxing Canada. Directories. Boxing Canada, Prov., Clubs. News Bulletin (Announcements, Events

    www.boxing.ca

13. **IBHOF.com /International Boxing Hall of Fame Homepage**

    Boxing: The International Boxing Hall of Fame in Canastota, New York.

    ww.ibhof.com/ibhfhome.htm

14. **Boxing News and Video Coverage at MaxBoxing.com broadcast and ...**

    Providers of boxing news, articles and photos.

    www.maxboxing.com/

15. **Boxing - Home Page**

    Help you find what you need to know about Boxing. Boxing. with Andrew ...

    boxing.about.com/mbody.htm

16. **Boxing News 24 hours/day — the #1 resource in boxing — following ...**

    Boxing news, results, rankings, schedule — follow Muhammad Ali, Mike Tyson, Sugar Ray, Oscar De La Hoya and all your boxing favorites. Provider of boxing interviews, rumors, results, schedules and a directory of links.

    www.fightnews.com/

17. **IBF-USBA-Boxing.com**

    Official site of the International Boxing Federation. The IBF is a voluntary association organized...

    www.ibf-usba-boxing.com/

18. **CBS Sportsline - Boxing**

    Results, rankings, schedules and interviews. Includes exclusive content from the CBS media library...

    cbs.sportsline.com/u/boxing/

19. **AIBA -**

    AIBA Boxing. Newsletter: Latest AIBA Newsletter. NATIONAL BOXING FEDERATIONS, Use the map to locate a National Boxing Federation. fficial site of the International Amateur Boxing Association. Includes rules,
    medical handbook, director...

    www.aiba.net/

20. **Cat Boxing.com! - Video and Pictures Of Feline Fighting!**

    Blow by blow, swap by swap and growl after growl! Round after round of feline fighting! In no way...

    www.catboxing.com/

21. **Boxing.de - Universum Box-Promotion**

    Offer Articles, records, profiles, video and audio features of the Klitschko brothers and other world...

    www.boxing.de/

22. **Forum Boxing Inc, legendary USA boxing promoter**

    Forum Boxing's history fight dates results news press releases television video Miss Ringsider Contest and boxer profiles. Viewing

    www.forumboxing.com/

23. **WBC**

    Official site of the World Boxing Council. An interactive site with opportunities for fan feedback....

    www.wbcboxing.com/

24. **Boxing Betting- Bet On Boxing At Select Online Sportsbooks**
BOXING BETTING. Find The Best Place Online To Bet On Boxing At Select Online Sportsbooks! Featured Sportsbooks. ... Boxing Betting. Sports Interaction Sportbook. ...
www.boxingbetting.org/

25. **BritishBoxing.Com**
The premier site dedicated to British Boxing Profiles, Records, News, Discussion, Tickets. ...
www.britishboxing.com/

26. **Women's Boxing**
Women's Boxing Top Coverage of the Sport with the latest boxing news in the world of women's boxing! ... So What does "PU ALI" mean on Jeffries Boxing Trunks?! ...
www.womenboxing.com/

27. **The Cyber Boxing Zone: Home Page**
An online boxing magazine devoted to current news, opinions, a boxing encyclopedia, and book reviews.
www.cyberboxingzone.com/boxing/cyber.htm

28. **USATODAY.com**
Maintains USA Today Ratings in each weight class as a counterpoint to the world sanctioning bodies,...
www.usatoday.com/sports/boxing/news.htm

29. **Boxing Central**
Resource for boxer records, ratings, schedules as well as regular articles on the sport.
www.boxing-central.com/

30. **Boxing News Results Website**
Boxing site - News, Chat forum, Boxers emails, Fight Schedules, Rankings and more... ... Boxing News. Click here to make Saddo Boxing.com your homepage. ...
www.saddoboxing.com/

31. **The Cyber Boxing Zone**
A online boxing magazine with extensive content.
www.cyberboxingzone.com/

32. **WeBL - The Web Boxing League**
A boxing management game played over the Internet. Each player ... A free boxing game from the creator of EKO. Boxing\ Photo. Sign Up...
www.vivi.com/

33. **Bet on Boxing - Wager online on boxing matches**
Bet on Boxing Here are the top online sportsbooks to bet on boxing.
www.betonboxing.ws/

34. **Title Boxing - Boxing equipment discount prices: Punching bags ...**
Title Boxing, View Cart, ... Check out our specials page for great deals on boxing gloves, punching bags, kickboxing gear and more!!! The Title Boxing Newsletter, ...
www.titleboxing.com/

35. **FOX Broadcasting Company: Celebrity Boxing II**
FOX.com, Trademark and Copyright Notice: TM and © FOX and its related entities. All rights reserved. Use of this Web site assumes ...
www.fox.com/boxing/

36. **Boxing Records Archive**
Database of boxing records with an online search facility.
www.boxrec.com/

37. **BBC SPORT | Boxing**
Low Graphics version | Change Edition. | Help. Sport Homepage. Boxing. Results and Schedule. Champions List. Have Your Say. Photo Galleries. ...
news.bbc.co.uk/sport/hi/english/boxing/default.stm

38. **WBO**
Official site of the World Boxing Organization. Site includes real time news updates, world rankings,...
www.wbo-int.com/

39. **The Pugilist - Inside Boxing**
Providers of boxing information, news and interviews.
www.insideboxing.com/

40. **Women's Boxing Page**
Comprehensive coverage of news, issues and personalities in women's boxing.
www.geocities.com/Colosseum/Field/6251/

41. **Melanie Ley's Amateur Boxing Home Page**
Fight news, schedules, articles and ratings for amateur boxing.
www.amateur-boxing.com/

42. **Showtime - Boxing Home Page**
Offer upcoming schedules and results for the television network.
www.sho.com/boxing/

43. **TBG Boxing Game - Web Browser Based Boxing Game**

Boxing simulation game run over the Internet. You create fictional fighters and manage their careers....

www.boxinggame.com/

44. **Boxing Day at Web Holidays**

Discover the origin Boxing Day and currently how it is celebrated.

www.web-holidays.com/boxing/

45. **Urban Legends Reference Pages: Holidays (Boxing Day)**

Boxing Day, Advertisement. Claim: The name of Boxing Day comes from the need to rid the house of empty boxes the day after Christmas. Tells what is known about the origins of Boxing Day. Also includes several legends about the day's origins.

www.snopes2.com/holidays/christmas/boxing.htm

46. **netboxe.com**

www.net-boxing.com/

47. **Boxing Top Rank inc.**

Visit toprank for all your boxing , boxing training, boxing equipment Mike Tyson boxing news Oscar De La Hoya, Lennox Lewis, Prince Naseem Hamed, Floyd ...

www.toprank.com/

48. **BoxingHelp.com - Ultimate Boxing Address List (boxing addresses ...**

BoxingHelp.com is home of the Ultimate Boxing Address list, an extensive directory of addresses for boxers, managers, trainers, coaches, promoters, gyms, etc. ...

www.boxinghelp.com/

49. **ChessBase.com - Chess News - You thought we were making it up**?

Chess boxing? Putting players in a boxing ring for chess and boxing? ... Chess Boxing World Championship. This is the real thing, no holds barred. ...

www.chessbase.com/newsdetail.asp?newsid=1348

50. **flash_detection**

Einer der zwei großen Boxställe stellt sich vor. Sehr hoher Informationsgehalt, stets aktuell, mit...

www.boxing-online.de/

51. **Balazs Boxing Online**

    Supplier of boxing and martial arts equipment for home fitness and professionals.

    www.balazsboxing.com/

52. **Showtime - Boxing Home Page**

    www.sho.com/site/boxing/

53. **WOB - World of Boxing.com.au**

    World of Boxing.com.au. ... To be the best, you have to fight the best, Hopkins needs a big fight, I believe, more than anyone currently in boxing. Australian and international boxing news, profiles, rankings, memorabilia and forum.

    www.worldofboxing.com.au/

54. **Boxing's Finest, LLC. Your Premiere Online Magazine, Entertainment ...**

    Contains news, interviews, upcoming fight schedules and ring card girls.

    www.boxingsfinest.com/

55. **The Boxing Wise Website: Dedicated to the Sweet Science of Boxing.**

    Boxing Wise has been issued the 10 count. A massive server error or hacker has irretrievably destroyed all files associated with Boxing Wise. ...

    members.tripod.com/~fivedogs/

56. **Boxing - Heavyweight News**

    Boxing news from the heavyweight division - Mike Tyson, Lennox Lewis, Holyfield, Klitschko and more!! boxing ...

    www.heavyweights.co.uk/

57. **BCN homepage**

    Offers tips on spotting original items and a subscription newsletter devoted to collecting boxing...

    www.boxingcollectors.com/

58. **Oriental Boxing**

    Oriental Boxing by JOE KOIZUMI. 2003/12. ... Oriental Boxing in 2001 Oriental Boxing in 2000 Oriental Boxing in 1999 Oriental Boxing in 1998 Oriental Boxing in 1997. ...

    www.ring-japan.com/oriental.htm

59. **Boxingranks.com**
Oscar De La Hoya in what will surely be the biggest fight of his life for if he loses that night his time as a major revenue earner in boxing will have come to ...
www.boxingranks.com/

60. **Boxing**
Los Angeles-based indie rock band. Includes news, MP3s, pictures and contact information.
www.boxingtheband.com/

61. **Boxing Memorabilia**
Boxing Memorabilia, Largest Selection of Muhammad Ali Autograph items and Boxing Autographs from pugilists past and present. Boxing ...
www.boxing-memorabilia.com/

62. **The International Boxing Organization**
Official site of the International Boxing Organization and their regional body, the USBO. The IBO...
www.iboboxing.com/

63. **Boxing-Pics.com - Home**
Providers of photography of many big fights, available for purchase online.
www.boxing-pics.com/

64. **Herald.com - Your Miami Everything Guide**
... Football | Dolphins. • Hockey | Panthers. • Boxing. • Colleges. •FAU. • FIU. • FSU. ... Back to Home > Sports >, Tuesday, Dec 30, 2003. Boxing,BOXING, ...
www.miami.com/mld/miamiherald/sports/boxing/

65. **Boxing**
Provides articles covering all weight divisions.
www.allsports.com/boxing/

66. **Canadian Professional Boxing Federation**
The official site of the Canadian Professional Boxing Federation. Up-to-date results, ratings, boxing cards, profiles, rules and safety code. Enter. ...
www.canadianboxing.com/

67. **Boxing Closeouts .com - Discount and Close Out Boxing Supplies and ...**
www.boxingcloseouts.com/

68. **Boxing Equipment and Punching Bags**

www.boxingdepot.com/

69. **Las Vegas boxing news upcoming Las Vegas boxing schedule...**

Offers Las Vegas boxing news, upcoming fight schedule, and venue reviews.

www.lvboxing.com/

70. **Cougar Boxing, Edmonton, Canada**

Information about Cougar Boxing Club, events, results, photos, athletes, links, etc. Edmonton, Alberta, Canada 9425 109a Ave. (entrance ...

www.cougarboxing.com/

71. **Boxing Day**

Boxing Day. The day after Christmas, the Feast of St. Stephen, the first Christian martyr, is better known as Boxing Day. The term ...

www.pch.gc.ca/progs/cpsc-ccsp/jfa-ha/boxing_e.cfm

72. **Amazon.com: Books: On Boxing**

On Boxing by Joyce Carol Oates (Author). List Price: $14.95. ... Customers interested in On Boxing may also be interested in: Sponsored Links (What's this?) Feedback: ...

www.amazon.com/exec/obidos/tg/ detail/-0880013850?v=glance

73. **Ringside boxing,THE source for boxing equipment online**

The internet's premier source for quality boxing equipment. ... Looking for the latest adidas boxing equipment styles and apparel?...

www.ringside.com/

74. **and World Boxing**

World Boxing Association Champions, Titlebouts, General Info. Provides boxing championship results from a broad range of the sports governing bodies.

www.andworldboxing.com/

75. **ELAINE'S BOXING DAY PAGE**

Boxing Day is a holiday celebrated in Britain, Australia, New Zealand, and Canada. It falls on December 26th, which is also St. Stephen's Day. St. ...

homepages.tesco.net/~derek.berger/ holidays/boxingday.html

76. **Yahoo! Sport - Boxing**
Latest News. Photo View Photo (AP). Roy Jones Jr. More Photos - Boxing. ... My Yahoo!
•, Add Boxing news to My Yahoo! Fantasy football. Fantasy football. Yahoo! Games. ...
uk.sports.yahoo.com/boxi/

77. **Boxing and Martial Arts Gear**
Quality Boxing equipment,martial arts,boxing gear, exercise equipment, sports equipment, and accessories at catalog prices. Offers Everlast gear, gloves, bags, and training equipment.
www.boxing-gear.com/

78. **SLAM! Sports - Boxing**
... Hopkins, Spinks want Mosley, De La Hoya A long night of boxing had turned into morning by the time Bernard Hopkins finally entered the ring. FULL STORY. ...
www.canoe.ca/Boxing/

79. **Sporting Life - Boxing**
... Home, Boxing, News, Fanzine, Competitions, Diary, Calendar, Results, About Us, Contact Us, BOXING NEWS. ALL OR NOTHING ...
www.sportinglife.com/boxing/news/

80. **Everlast Boxing Equipment - Punching Bag, Speed Bag, Heavy Bag and**
... available today. Everlast Boxing Monthly Boxing Equipment Specials,... Everlast Boxing Feedback We love hearing from you! Feedback from ...
www.everlastboxing.com/

81. **Boxing.cz**
MAGAZIN EXTRALIGA WOMEN PROFI SHOP FORUM CALENDAR LINKS.
www.boxing.cz/

82. **Stack Boxing Equipment Sales [ORDER GLOVES HERE]**
-Boxing gym list and more Margaret Sidoroff 3 time world champion Windsor, Ontario"These gloves are sweet...". Buy top quality boxing gear at our online store! ...
www.stackboxing.com/

83. **Boxing News 24/7: Mike Tyson, Lennox Lewis, Muhammad Ali, Roy ...**
... Pictured Above: Kid Gavilan. Doghouse Boxing Fun Audio (We don't Archive FUN Audio. ... Doghouse Boxing Team Join Our Team. Owner/ Webmaster: E-mail: iCheehuahua. ...
www.doghouseboxing.com/

84. **Doghouse Boxin**
Doghouse Boxing, Top rate site for boxing news. Updated boxing news every hour. Doghouse Boxing since 1998. Your Fun resort for the Sport of Boxing. ...
pages.zdnet.com/icheehuahua/

85. **MrBoxing is closed**
... this website. I will from now on concentrate on my first passion and which brought me 21 years ago to boxing: refereeing. I will ...
users.pandora.be/mrboxing/

86. **BOXING DAY**
BOXING DAY. A sermon by. James Ishmael Ford. ... She wanted to start picking hymns and noted that the title, "Boxing Day," didn't mean a lot to her. ...
www.vuu.org/jford/ss991226.htm

87. **EFF Response to Barney Legal Threat (July 6, 2001)**
EFF Response to "Barney" Legal Threat. E-zine Parody Is Protected Expression
www.eff.org/IP/IP_SLAPP/20010706_eff_barney_response.html

88. **Blue Square - Interactive Betting - Bluesq.com**
... Other Sports, Boxing, Boxing Coupon The top forthcoming bouts in coupon form. Artur Grigorian v Acelino Freitas WBO Lightweight Title Fight. ...
www.bluesq.com/bet?action=go_typesandclass_id=11

89. **THE GURU'S CIGAR PAGE**
The Boxing Guru's REALM: The Guru's BOXING MUSEUM; The Guru's BOXING LINKS PAGE; Boxing on Videotape: THE 8-COUNT BOXING HOUR. ... BOXING FANS MUST SEE: ...
www.angelfire.com/nm/allbox/

90. **Boxingphotographs.com**
Boxingphotographs.com.
www.boxingphotographs.com/

91. **Boxing orange - convergent Technologies**

Boxing Orange are trusted providers of leading security products and managed securit services which can be managed and monitored from our Security Operations ...

www.boxingorange.com/

92. **Boxing - www.SecondsOut.com Home Page**

USA Boxing - Click Here! UKBoxing - Click Here! World Boxing - Click Here! Ringside and Training Principles

www.secondsout.com/

93. **CBS.SportsLine.com**

... Boxing Home, Results; Champions; Schedules; WBC Rankings; WBA Rankings; IBF Rankings; NABF Rankings, Boxing. » Sports Store. ... MESSAGE BOARDS. » Boxing. ...

cbs.sportsline.com/boxing

94. **Las Vegas SUN Sports: Boxing**

... back to sports. Stories | Schedule. Boxing stories. Monshipour Defends Bantamweight Title 16 Dec. 13:46:47; Cory Spinks Shines in Mayorga Upset 15 Dec. ...

www.lasvegassun.com/sports/boxing/

95. **World Heavyweight Boxing**

... It's time for the sixth annual World Heavyweight Boxing Awards. ... RATINGS. - World Heavyweight Boxing top 100. - World Heavyweight Boxing continental ratings. ...

www.world-heavyweight-boxing.com/

96. **www.boxingfanatics.com**

... The Brawl at the Hall II San Diego - The Brawl at the Hall II turned out to be another exciting night of boxing for San Diego residents.....

www.boxingfanatics.com/

97. **Annie's Boxing Day Page**

Annie's Boxing Day Page Celebrated on December 26th (the day after Christmas)each year. ... The Dictionary tells us this about"Boxing Day". ...

www.annieshomepage.com/boxingday.html

98. **New Mexico Boxing - Main page**

... Friday's Column Lots of fights, but few contenders: It was a year of unanswered questions for the sport of boxing in New Mexico. Who will succeed Johnny Tapia? ...

www.newmexicoboxing.com/

99. **Boxing Saskatchewan - Who we are:**

Who we are | How to start a Boxing Club, Who we are: Boxing Saskatchewan is a non-profit society which regulates the sport of amateur boxing in Saskatchewan. ...

www.saskboxing.com/

100. **Ukrainian boxing**

Choose your language. UA Zone.net Ukrainian Internet Information Project, Sport Digest, Dynamo Kyiv from Shurik! Sokil Kyiv and the ...

boxing.uazone.net/

101. **World Cup of Boxing**

A new and revolutionary competition system for men's professional boxing. Consisting of two main rankings: the Total Ranking and the World Cup Ranking. ...

www.worldcupofboxing.com/

102. **The Boxing Fan Site about The Fight Game**

BOXING FAN UPDATE Bob' Philly CheeseTakes I am not generally moved to write about fights themselves. ...

www.geocities.com/fightgame/boxing.html

103. **All Coupons**

Home All Sports Antepost Dogs Baseball Basketball Boxing Cricket Darts Football Golf Horse Racing Ice Hockey Motor Racing Politics Rugby UnionSnooker Specials ...

www.willhill.com/iibs/en/ allsportsandcoupons.asp?sport=BX

104. **Powerhouse Boxing: Boxing Gloves, Punchbags**

... Powerhouse Boxing Equipment: boxing gloves, punchbags, headguards, gumshields boxing equipment, punchbags, boxing gloves, boxing products, punch bags. ...

www.powerhouse-boxing.co.uk/

105. **Online Sportsbook and Casino - Sportsbook Rules**

... Motorsport/Auto Racing. Boxing. Baseball. ... Boxing. A full round is only considered for wagering purposes when the bell sounds signifying the end of said round....

www.delugeonline.com/sportsbook_rules.html

106. **wreck**

Wrecking Crew Boxing would like to acknowledge our own Lenny DeJesus who was an integral part of team Pacquiao serving as both cutman and adviser. ...

www.wreckingcrewboxing.com/

107. **Hot Boxing News: Boxing**

Boxing news, upcoming events, fight results, Ali, Lennox, De La Hoya, Mosley, Trinidad. ... Minnesota boxing great seeks return of state commission (DEC 26) ST. ...

www.hotboxingnews.com/

108. **Cambridge Boxing Club**

Cambridge Boxing Club. Your browser does not support frames, and thuscannot view this website correctly. If you wish to view this ...

www.cambridgeabc.co.uk/

109. **Boxing Forum - Index - Boxing Chat**

Boxing Forum - Index - Boxing Forum - Message Board - Chat, Welcome, Guest. ... Boxing Forum News: Join my mailing list... http://www.saddoboxing.com/mailing-list/. ...

www.saddoboxing.com/boxing_forum/index.php

110. **Boxing .host.sk - Boxing News and Headlines**

Boxing. Google News Google News search results by Grouper: boxing news Boxing News — 24 hours/day - Reload often! By David L. Hudson, Jr. ...

boxing.host.sk/

111. **Boxing Videos on VHS and DVD**

A page devoted to mostly Mike Tyson and other boxing news and fighters. A place to buy and trade boxing videos. A must for all boxing fans. ...

silversurfer91.homestead.com/tyson.html

112. **boxinggifts2**

... Fres Oquendo (22-1) vs. George Arias (31-4) (no US TV) Lamon Brewster (27-2) vs. Tommy Martin (23-2) The Fight Fans Boxing Schedule. ...

www.esecure.co.uk/boxinggiftsshop/

113. **irishboxingnews.com - Boxing - Web Site For SALE**

Dedicated to boxing in Ireland and includes boxing news, results, rankings, records, boxing clubs...

www.irishboxingnews.com/

114. **Open Directory - Sports: Boxing**

... Top: Sports: Boxing (292), Description. Boxers ... 5). Russian (7), Spanish (7), Swedish (9). Usenet rec.sport.boxing - news: - Google Groups. ...

dmoz.org/Sports/Boxing/

115. **Online Betting sports - Online Boxing sites, stats, results, odds...** Betting on Boxing.com offers gambling information for sports betting.Reviewed sportsbooks and Schedules.Boxing Links, Gambling Links and Webmasters Information.
www.betting-on-boxing.com/

12
Calisthenics

1. **Calisthenics Victoria Inc**
   CVICVI Solo / Duo ItemsSolo / Duo Items ASCA - VicASCA - Vic What is Calisthenics? What is Calısthenics? Guide to Calisthenic Clubs An Australian artistic sport, combining gymnastics,marching, singing, simplified ballet, folk and modern...
   www.calisthenics.asn.au/

2 **Calisthenics**
   Action Calishtenics is a Canberra based Club which promotes the sport of calisthenics. ...
   www.mycala.com/action/

3. **Iggy's Mental Calisthenics**
   iggy-on-edge.blogspot.com/

4. **Keyboard Yoga: Learning to Breathe**
   ... These eye calisthenics will not only make you feel better, they'll make you look better, too. benefits. Physical. •, Helps prevent eye strain. ...
   www.ivillage.com/fitness/tools/yoga/eye.html

5. **Online Sports Directory: Browse Sports: Calisthenics**
   Directory of Sports Products and Services, Online Sports Directory : Browse Sports : Calisthenics. Order Line 800-856-2638. Enter keywords ...
   www.onlinesports.com/pages/top,sprt,exer.html

6. **calisthenics**
   calisthenics. This is about calisthenics. Callistus Cabrillo National Monument Caledonian Canal Cambodia calendula Cambon Pierre Paul ...
   www.lifeinafrica.org/calisthenics.html

7. **Cubicle Calisthenics**

   ... more. Learn more. Education > Exercises > Cubicle Calisthenics. Cubicle Calisthenics. C. Schurman for Sports Etc. Jan. 2002 issue. When ...

   www.bodyresults.com/E2CubicleCalisthenics.asp

8. **calisthenics on Encyclopedia.com**

   calisthenics click here to track this topic Related: Education. see aerobics . ... Related Premium Content from eLibrary. Magazines and Newspapers for: calisthenics. ...

   www.encyclopedia.com/html/X/X-calisthe.asp

9. **about Calisthenics**

   Calisthenics is widely practiced in Australia and is recognised as a fun and healthy way to keep fit for girls of all ages. ... WHAT IS CALISTHENICS? ...

   members.ozemail.com.au/~casainc/about.html

10. **Crag Hill's poetry scorecard: Political Calisthenics**

    Political Calisthenics. She doesn't hate the man. ... Listed below are links to weblogs that reference Political Calisthenics: Comments. Crag,. ...

    scorecard.typepad.com/crag_hills_poetry_score/ 2004/01 political_calis.html

11. **CALISTHENICS - Definition by HyperDictionary.com**

    ... Search Dictionary: CALISTHENICS. Pronunciation: 'kalis' theniks. Matching Terms: calisthenic, calisthenic exercise. Medical Dictionary. ...

    www.hyperdictionary.com/medical/calisthenics

12. **CALISTHENICS - Definition by HyperDictionary.com**

    ... Search Dictionary: CALISTHENICS. Pronunciation: 'kalis'theniks. MatchingTerms: calisthenic, calisthenic exercise. WordNet Dictionary. ...

    www.hyperdictionary.com/dictionary/calisthenics

13. **Outside Online - Bodywork**

    ... Why modern calisthenics can bridge the gap between gym and field ... Indeed, a calisthenics program can be the perfect bridge to the sports of spring and summer. ...

    outside.away.com/magazine/0499/9904body.html

14. **Chi machine - effortless aerobic exercise**

... NEW CALISTHENICS AEROBIC EXERCISE. by DR. Wei-Penu Zhao Based on human physiological function, a human being might have a life span of 150 years. ...

www.7essentials.com/calisthenics.shtml

15. **Calisthenics**

Calisthenics is a widely practiced sport and art form in Australia and is recognised as a fun and healthy way to keep fit for girls of all ages. ... Calisthenics. ...

www.girl.com.au/calisthenics.htm

16. **History_Links**

HISTORY OF CALISTHENICS. Although originating in England and Europe, Calisthenics came to prominence in the Victorian Gold Rush. ... WHAT IS CALISTHENICS? ...

www.mycala.com/action/History.html

17. **Oriental Secrets: Ancient Calisthenics for Outer Strength - Yi...**

Oriental Secrets: Ancient Calisthenics for Outer Strength - Yi Chin Ching. ... Purchase Oriental Secrets: Ancient Calisthenics for Outer Strength - Yi Chin Ching. ...

www.goldhil.com/ catalog/oriental-secrets—ancient calisthenics-for-outer-strength—yi-chin-ching.htm

18. **yoga at work, relax and stretch: ivillage keyboard yoga**

... These eye calisthenics will not only make you feel better, they'll make you look better, too. benefits. Physical. ·, Helps prevent eye strain. ...

www.ivillage.com/diet/tools/yoga/ pages/0,,218471_414766,00.

19. **calisthenics definition of calisthenics. What is calisthenics?...**

Definition of calisthenics in the Dictionary and Thesaurus. ... Provides examples from classic literature, search by definition of calisthenics. ...

www.thefreedictionary.com/calisthenics

20. **Calisthenics @ calisthenics.us - Fundamental Calisthenics ...**

Calisthenics @ calisthenics.us - Sports Directory Online. Find Information on Sports Products and Services @ calisthenics.us.

www.calisthenics.us/

21. **Not Just Calisthenics 1**

    Not Just Calisthenics. Physical Education is not just push-ups, jumping jacks, chin-ups, or sit-ups any more. It's a combination...
    www.lfelem.lfc.edu/tech/DuBose/webquest/nellessen NOTJUS~1.HTM

22. **Definition of calisthenics - WordReference.com Dictionary**

    Word Reference .com. Source: The Collins English Dictionary © 2000 HarperCollinsPublishers: calisthenics [?kælis'??niks] noun a variant spelling (esp. ...

    www.wordreference.com/englishdefinition.asp?en=calisthenics

23. **calisthenics. The American Heritage® Dictionary of the English...**

    calisthenics. The American Heritage® Dictionary of the English Language: Fourth Edition. 2000. ... 2000. calisthenics.

    SYLLABICATION: cal·is·then·ics. ...

    www.bartleby.com/61/70/C0037000.html

24. **BOOK TRAIL - Power Stretching Calisthenics And Warm-Up**

    ... Self Defense Fitness - Power Stretching Calisthenics And Warm-Up Approx. ... 20 minutes stretching, 20 minutes calisthenics, 20 minutes warm-up. ...

    www.booktrail.com

    Video_SelfDefensePower%20Stretching%20Calisthenics%20 And%20Warm-Up.asp

25. **USATODAY.com - Lizards communicate with calisthenics**

    10/26/2001 - Updated 03:14 PM ET. Lizards communicate with calisthenics.Q: Why do lizards do pushups? [© D Williams, California State U. ...

    www.usatoday.com/news/science/wonderquest/ 2001-10-24-lizards.htm

26. **Ballarat Calisthenics College**

    Calisthenics is one of the fastest growing artistic sports – unique to Australia. ... Calisthenics combines the best aspects of sport and art. ...

    www.bcc.goldlinksweb.com/

27. **Calisthenics**

    Calisthenics combines fitness, teamwork, poise, flexibility, and graceful movement. It can be undertaken on a competitive or non ...
    home.vicnet.net.au/~cgcc/calisthenics.html

28. **AYCC**

    Altona Youth Club Calisthenics Inc. Updated: 17th October, 2003. Home. ... E-mail. Other calisthenics and related links. Academy Calisthenics; Action Calisthenics Inc. ...

    www.geocities.com/ayccmel/links.html

29. **SUNSET CALISTHENICS - CaliLinks**

    <B>Sunset Calisthenics</B> is a calisthenics club located in Palmerston, Northern Territory, Australia. CaliLinks More Calisthenics ...

    www.geocities.com/ozichikki/sunset-calilinks.html

30. **Article: Putting Business Calisthenics To Work**

    PUTTING B USINESS CALISTHENICS TO WORK by Alan J. Zell, Ambassador of Selling. ... It is suggested the Business Calisthenics be inaugurated in the following order:

    www.sellingselling.com/articles/buscal-2.html

31. **Googlism : what is calisthenics**

    ... http://www.247tobacco.com Buy discount cigarettes online at 247Tobacco. 247Tobacco offers a large ran ... calisthenics. calisthenics ...

    www.googlism.com/what_is/c/calisthenics/

32. **Chemical Calisthenics - Blackalicious mp3 - Free mp3 music...**

    Chemical Calisthenics - Blackalicious mp3 - free mp3 music download. Commend certain sites ...

    www.alwaysmusic.net/mp3/download27/318811.htm

33. **HumanaNatura.org > Calisthenics Program > Calisthenics Guidelines**

    ... Walking. - Calisthenics. Natural Living. Our Future. ... Unlike walking, many people are unfamiliar with calisthenics, so each exercise is described in detail below. ...

    www.humananatura.org/Calisthenics%20Program%20Pg3.asp

34. **WDVL: Calendar Calisthenics**

    ... indexOf("2.")>=0)) {document.write(' ');. Calendar Calisthenics. Aaron Weiss. December 13, 1999. Much earlier in this article ...

    www.wdvl.com/Authoring/Languages/ Perl/PerlfortheWeb/calendar.html

35. **Verbal Calisthenics**

    Verbal Calisthenics. My love for you is more athletic than a verb, Agile as a star The tents of sun absorb. Treading circus tight...

    www.angelfire.com/tn/plath/vc.html

36. **WebMD Anatomy**
... System Health Topics. Click on a part of the image below. Exercise Results. Exercise Results. Calisthenics. Calisthenics Number of calories ...
www.mythos.com/webmd/Content.aspx?P=CALEXCandE=4

37. **The Open Video Project :: Video Details**
Video Details, Lathrop School, calisthenics. A group of preadolescent boys and girls is standing in a row facing the camera position. ...
www.open-video.org/details.php?videoid=4669

38. **Cultural Calisthenics**
... Cultural Calisthenics. By Karen King. ... That company, Delgadiallo says, has the highest turnover rate in Juarez because it makes employees do morning calisthenics. ...
www.bizsites.com/1997/MJ97/insitecalistahenics.html

39. **Welcome to the Gateless Gate**
... Morning Calisthenics. (Variations on the Arica gym). 1. Standing: Integration Breath—legs wider than shoulders, outsides of feet ...
www.gatelessgate.org/prison/spanish morning_calisthenics.html

40. **HumanaNatura.org > Calisthenics Program > Understanding.....**
Walking. - Calisthenics. Natural Living. Our Future. Contact Us. ... There are a total of seventeen exercises in the calisthenics program, divided into three groups: ...
www.humananatura.org/Calisthenics%20Program%20Pg2.asp

41. **Article: Business Calisthenics**
BUSINESS CALISTHENICS—EXERCISES IN BUSINESS TO KEEP BUSINESS HEALTHY by Alan J. Zell, Ambassador of Selling. BUSINESS CALISTHENICS ...
www.sellingselling.com/articles/buscal-1.html

42. **AllRefer Encyclopedia - calisthenics (Education: Terms And ...**
AllRefer.com reference and encyclopedia resource provides complete information on calisthenics, Education: Terms And Concepts. ... calisthenics: see aerobics. ...
reference.allrefer.com/encyclopedia/X/X-calisthe.html

43. **Callisthenics**
What is Calisthenics ???? The word calisthenics comes from the Greek words 'kallos' for beauty and 'thenos' for strength. Indeed ...
www.scelva.univ-rennes1.fr/site/pages_langues/ anglais/grammaire/b/Divers/Calisthenics.htm

44. **Gawler Calisthenics Club**

    Gawler Calisthenics Club. Home Page of the Gawler Calisthenics Club.

    home.primus.com.au/pallen/gcc/

45. **calisthenics**

    ... calisthenics, Calisthenics@groups.msn.com, What's New Calisthenics. *Friendship*Fun*Fitness*. To find your local Calisthenics Club/College,. ...

    groups.msn.com/Calisthenics/calisthenicsgroup.msnw

46. **Matt Furey - Superior Conditioning with Bodyweight Calisthenics**

    #1 Fitness and Conditioning Website in the World! Politically Incorrect Fitness and Fighting Instruction, Matt Furey has five FREE...

    www.mattfurey.com/products.html

47. **Cowboy Bob's Cowboy Calisthenics**

    Cowboy Bob's Cowboy Calisthenics: Tired of expensive equipment, health clubs, and exercise programs that only work for a while? You've come to theright place! ...

    www.lemen.com/ex01.html

48. **Calisthenics - InfoSearchPoint.com**

    Calisthenics. United States Usage. Calisthenics is a type ... own body for resistance. The history of Calisthenics is linked to gymnastics. ...

    www.infosearchpoint.com/display/Calisthenics

49. **calisthenics — Dictionary Definition**

    Dictionary Definitions, Dictionary Definition of "calisthenics". The noun "calisthenics" has 1 senses. 1. calisthenics, callisthenics ...

    www.yourdictionary.net/calisthenics.html

50. **Unit 2 : The English Renaissance (1485–1660) : Brain ...**

    ... Return to book index, Unit 2 : The English Renaissance (1485–1660) Brain Calisthenics. from Essays Brain Calisthenics (p. 448). Use ...

    www.classzone.com/books/language_of_lit_gr12 page_build.cfm?content=links_rs_brainandu=2

51. **calisthenics. The Columbia Encyclopedia, Sixth Edition. 2001**
The Columbia Encyclopedia, Sixth Edition. 2001. calisthenics. see aerobics. The Columbia Encyclopedia, Sixth Edition. Copyright © 2003 ...
www.bartleby.com/65/x-/X-calisthe.html

52. **Moreland Community Portal - Community Information Database...**
This site requires the use of frames. Please upgrade to the latest versions of Netscape Communicator or Microsoft Internet Explorer.
www.moreland.vic.gov.au/communityportal
1searchsportscalisthenicsfr.htm

53. **Keyboard Yoga: eye calisthenics**
Our eyes are constantly being irritated y pollutants, germs, dust and screen glare. Try these eye calisthenics to feel and look better. ... Eye calisthenics. ...
www.ivillage.co.uk/dietandfitness/experts/ keyyoga/articles/ 0,,280_165508,00.html

54. **OverSpeed Training - Books: Calisthenics**
BOOKS: CALISTHENICS. Tai Chi Chuan: A Simplified Method of Calisthenics for Health No Synopsis Available. Price: $8.96. If you can ...
www.overspeedtraining.com/Books/Calisthenics.htm

55. **Calisthenics, a self-publishing testimonial**
A Self-Publishing Testimonial. By Lynne Hayward, Australia, author of "CALISTHENICS:A unique Australian Sport". Published by Hayward and Wootton, 1995. ...
www.cunepress.com/cunemagazine/ news/article
calisthenics.htm

56. **Calisthenics**
Calisthenics. Subject Categories: 651 Health Historical note: 1973.
www.ibe.unesco.org/International/DocServices/ Thesaurus/ 00002003.htm

57. **Calisthenics**
img0046p.jpg is a 1024x656 JPEG image, 122.49k.
www.grfx.com/brnin2k1/img0046p.htm

58. **alaina is: sweet and sour: chemical calisthenics**
... chemical calisthenics. This pretty well summarizes my summer thus far: Blackalicious' Chemical Calisthenics. July 18, 2003 in personal | Permalink. TrackBack. ...
www.alaina.org/tigerbunny/2003/07/chemical_calist.html

59. **Blackalicious - Chemical Calisthenics Lyrics**
Chemical Calisthenics Lyrics. ... Blackalicious - Chemical Calisthenics Lyrics. [Gift of Gab] I can do anything Neutron, proton, mass ...
www.seeklyrics.com/lyrics/Blackalicious/ Chemica Calisthenics.html

60. **Calisthenics and Stretching for Older Adults Aims and Objectives...**
Page 1. CALISTHENICS AND STRETCHING FOR OLDER ADULTS AIMS AND OBJECTIVES: 1. To provide a warm-up period in preparation for aerobic activity. ...
www.zajko.org/CALISTHENICS.pdf

61. **William Hodgson ~ Vocal Calisthenics**
<< Back to Chris Bell-Pearson. VOCAL CALISTHENICS A New Approach to the Teaching of Singing. In the world of musical performance the ...
www.chrisbellart.co.nz/vocal.html

62. **Health and Healing Products Oriental Secrets Ancient Calisthenics ...**
... Oriental Secrets Ancient Calisthenics for Outer Strength: Yi Chin Ching Price: $19.95. "The natural force within each one of us is ...
www.naturaljourneys.com/items
orientalSecretsChinChing.html

63. **Advanced Fitness - Calisthenics and Weights (optional)**
... fitness? This is a way to learn some new routines... Advanced Fitness- Calisthenics and Weights (optional) 45 dayADVFIT $16.95.
shop.store.yahoo.com/militarycom2003/adficoinau.html

64. **Ridgehaven Calisthenics Club**
... Messenger Editorial about Ridgehaven Calisthenics in 28/1/04 edition. ... Welcome to the new Ridgehaven Calisthenics mascot (available to purchase).
... home.iprimus.com.au/bpneumann/Ridgehaven.htm

65. **Tensing Calisthenics**
... Tensing Calisthenics. Introduction. ... You've been warned. Reference, Tensing Calisthenics
http://sy.cowiki.org/TheSite/TensingCalisthenics. ...
sy.cowiki.org/1988.html

66. **????BLOG www.takezou.com: Calisthenics...**
Calisthenics. I always do calisthenics every morning. But my body isn't pliable. Posted by kawai at 2003?07? ... www.takezou.com/archives/000167.html

67. **Safari Triathlon — Three Days of Mental and Physical Calisthenics...**
Safari Triathlon — Three Days of Mental and Physical Calisthenics — by TRUCKWORLD ONLINE! ¨. SAFARI TRIATHLON Three Days Of Mental And Physical Calisthenics. Photos and information on a three day road competition for 4x4 vehicles.
www.truckworld.com/Travel-Adventure/ 00-safari/safari.html

68. **Calisthenics**
Calisthenics. Cyclists Super-Simple Six-Part Calisthenics Program. Bicycling Magazine, December 2001. SINGLE-LEG SQUAT: Stand about ...
www.bikyle.com/excercise.htm

69. **Calisthenics With Charlotte, One Cat Owner's Story, Humor**
Calisthenics With Charlotte. Cat fitness really can be fun. However, it is important to start any fitness program only when you feel like it. ...
www.nanceestar.com/CalWithChar.html

70. **SFU News - Calisthenics for the mind - Oct 02, 2003**
... Calisthenics for the mind. Roberta Staley. Researcher Sandra Cusack says that everyone can have mental ...
www.sfu.ca/mediapr/sfu_news/archives_2003
sfunews10020306.htm

71. **Caterpillar Calisthenics**
Caterpillar Calisthenics. by Sue McKinnell, 8x32 Reel for 3C. Bars. 1-8. 1W set advancing to 2M while 2M set turning over RS to face out. ...
suem18.home.att.net/instructions/caterpillar.html

72. **Kitty Calisthenics**

... Kitty Calisthenics by Steve Duno. Is your tabby getting thick in the midsection? Are chewing and swallowing her only exercises? If ...

www.petsmart.com/cat/answers/health_and_nutrition/ articles/ article_8068.shtml

73. **calisthenics**

Home. Encyclopeadia. C. C, - Cal. calisthenics. ... Slider Search: The Web, Index. Help. Encyclopaedia. calisthenics. see aerobics....

www.slider.com/enc/9000/calisthenics.htm

74. **Calisthenics**

Calisthenics. Another season of calisthenics has come to an end. ... November 14, 2001. March 11, 2002. See you at calisthenics next year! ...

www.ualberta.ca/~rowing/training/calisthenics.html

75. **Welcome to the Gateless Gate**

... Morning Calisthenics. Morning Calisthenics translation should be finished soon. Copyright © Kwan Um Zen and Gateless Gate, 2003. All rights reserved.

www.gatelessgate.org/prison/spanish
morning_calisthenics_(Spanish).html

76. **Amazon.com: Books: Cultural Calisthenics: Writings on Race...**

www.amazon.com/exec/obidos/tg/ detail/-/156663220X?v=glance

77. **Educational Media Online Catalog: Energizers: Calisthenics for the ...**

Energizers: Calisthenics for the Mind. Quantity in Basket: none Code: ECM Price: $10.95 Shipping Weight: 8.00 oz. Quantity: by Carl Olson...

www.educationalmedia.com Merchant2merchant.mv?
Screen=PRODandStore_Code=EMOCandProduct_Code=ECM

78. **Kinesthetic Calisthenics**

Kinesthetic Calisthenics By Scott Wilkinson Electronic Musician, Feb 1, 2003. ...

emusician.com/ar/emusic_kinesthetic_calisthenics/

79. **The Exercise Room: Writing Calisthenics**

... The Exercise Room: Writing Calisthenics. Welcome to the Exercise Room. On this site you'll find links to many interactive writing ...

www.waldenu.edu/acad-rsrcs/writing-center/ ug
exerciseroom.html

80. **calisthenics.us - gymnastik info. This website is for sale!**

... calisthenics.us. This domain is for sale! More details... ... Search. Search the Web. Buy this domain. The domain calisthenics.us is for sale! More details... ...

www.sedo.de/parken/calisthenics.us/

81. **Mathematical Calisthenics: Healthy for Everyone**

Mathematical Calisthenics: Healthy for Everyone. Mathematics is the language of science. Scientists and engineers need to understand...

www.sci.ccny.cuny.edu/~cleary/edit.html

82. **Dictionary of Difficult Words - callisthenics, calisthenics**

... DIFFICULT WORDS. callisthenics, calisthenics. n. strengthening and beautifying exercises. © From the Hutchinson Encyclopaedia. Helicon Publishing LTD 2000. ...

www.tiscali.co.uk/reference/dictionaries/ difficultwords/data/d0002929.html

83. **Cultural Calisthenics: New and used books: Find the Lowest Price**

Cultural Calisthenics - Compare new and used books prices among 97 book stores in a click. Find the lowest price. ... Searched in Books for Cultural Calisthenics. ...

www.fetchbook.info/Cultural_Calisthenics.html

84. **Safari Triathlon — Three Days Of Mental And Physical Calisthenics ...**

Safari Triathlon — Three Days Of Mental And Physical Calisthenics —by TRUCKWORLD ONLINE! ¨. SAFARI TRIATHLON Three Days Of Mental ...

www.truckworld.com/Travel-Adventure/ 00-safari/safari2.html

85. **Good Old Fashioned Body Weight Exercises And Calisthenics Can Be ...**

I am not saying weight lifting is worse than calisthenics, or vice-versa. ... Not.I'm not saying weight lifting is worse than calisthenics, or vice-versa. ...

www.nutritionalsupplements.com/trainingT16.html

86. **calisthenics**

calisthenics, calisthenics@groups.msn.com, ... SOUTHERN PENINSULA SUBURBS. Aspendale Gardens Calisthenics, Elle Calisthenic College, Carrum Downs/Seaford. ...

groups.msn.com/calisthenics/yourlocalclubcollege.msnw

87. **Japara Neighbourhood House Inc. - Education, Children's Services ...**

    Japara Neighbourhood House - childcare, education and calisthenics in Montrose, Victoria, Australia....

    home.vicnet.net.au/~japara/

88. **Carmine Caruso - Musical Calisthenics for Brass - Carmine Caruso ...**

    Carmine Caruso - Musical Calisthenics for Brass - Carmine Caruso | Books | q-Carmine-Caruso—Musical-Calisthenics-for-BrassCarmine Caruso. ... books.mainseek.com/ 1R0P645100-q-Carmine-Caruso—Musical-Calisthenics-for-Brass.html

89. **Amazon.com: Video: Oriental Secrets: Yi Chin Ching - Ancient...**

    ... Have one to sell? Don't have one? We'll set one up for you. Oriental Secrets: Yi Chin Ching - Ancient Calisthenics For Outer Strength (2001) ...

    www.milkthesystem.com/category/us/B00005B32I.html

90. **BoxingWorkout.net FAQ: Calisthenics**

    FAQ: Calisthenics. Discuss this FAQ in Forums... FAQ | Advanced Techniques| Calisthenics Posted by: Jeremy on Sunday, March 23, 2003. ...

    boxingworkout.net/faq/EpuluZZuuEJWOlZkiR.shtml

91. **Mental and Manual Calisthenics**

    Mental and Manual Calisthenics Buster Bailey. Item# : DPR029. A collection of 249 technique building exercises and 34 special contemporary ...

    www.drumplace.com/PR029.html

92. **Amazon.com: Books: Carmine Caruso - Musical Calisthenics for Brass**

    www.amazon.com/exec/obidos/tg/ detail/-/0634046411?v=glance

93. **CALISTHENICS (Search FastHealth.com) CALISTHENICS**

    ... without apparatus 2 usu sing in constr : the art or practice of calisthenics . Published under license with Merriam-Webster, Incorporated. © 1997-2000. ...

    www.fasthealth.com/dictionary/c/calisthenics.php

94. **Microsoft PowerPoint - calisthenics.ppt**

... Sample Routines Standing Calisthenics 1. Head circles (10x each direction) 2. Face left (30 seconds) 3. Chin down (30 seconds) 4. Face right (30 seconds) 5 ...

www.zajko.org/presentation%20calisthenics.pdf

95. **calisthenics**

Chat and share stories with others from all around Australia who enjoy the wonderful sport of Calisthenics. ... Calisthenics. Calisthenics. *Friendship*Fun*Fitness*. ...

communities.ninemsn.com.au/Calisthenics

96. **Welcome to CAWA - Calisthenics Western Australia**

Applecross Calisthenics Club - Training venues: Coolbellup - Pre-Elementaries North Lake Senior Campus - Sub-Juniors, Juniors, Intermediates, Seniors. ...

www.calisthenicscawa.asn.au/clubdetails/

97. **Canyon Calisthenics**

Canyon Calisthenics Callback, September 1999, Issue # 243, Photo by Jean Bizot, The next incident, recounted by the pilot of a high ...

safecopter.arc.nasa.gov/Pages/Columns/SBrief
SafeBrf1 Articles/10Canyon.html

13

Canoeing, Kayaking and Camping

1. **Australian Canoeing and Kayaking Online**
   Australia's Premier Canoeing and Kayaking Site - Including all aspects of Canoeing and Kayaking - Canoe Polo Wildwater Slalom Sprint Marathon Sailing Freestyle ...
   www.canoe.org.au/
2. **Canadian Recreational Canoeing Association**
   www.crca.ca/
3. **Welsh Canoeing Association**
   The Welsh Canoeing Association manages canoeing in Wales, with 1800 individual members and 2000 members of affiliated clubs and centres.
   www.welsh-canoeing.org.uk/
4. **GORP Paddling: Canoeing, Kayaking and Rafting**
   Couples Canoeing: She rudders, he shudders. Who's right? Check out the previous Expert Answers. ...
   www.gorp.com/gorp/activity/paddle.htm
5. **Canoeing and Kayaking Info - Paddling.Net**
   Canoeing and kayaking information including buyers' guide, product reviews, outfitters and rental,...
   www.paddling.net/
6. **Canoeing: learning, starting, enjoying**
   JoJaffa goes canoeing and Kayaking: learn how to start and get more out of canoeing. because life's an adventure. JoJaffa goes Canoeing. ...
   www.jojaffa.com/guides/canoe.htm
7. **Paddle Manitoba Welcome**
   Membership, routes, events, courses and paddling information.
   www.paddle.mb.ca/

8. **Port of Plymouth Canoeing Assoc (Kayak and Canoe Club)**
Non-profit canoe and kayak club run by its members in Plymouth, Devon, England. Its activities include...
www.ppca-canoe-club.org.uk/

9. **Michigan Canoeing and Kayaking Directory**
A directory of Michigan canoe liveries offering canoe, kayak, raft, and tube rentals.
www.michigancanoe.com/

10. **Tennessee Eastman Hiking and Canoeing Club - Appalachian Trail**
The Tennessee Eastman Hiking and Canoeing Club is an outdoors club, offering a year-round program of hikes and paddling trips in our region. ...
www.tehcc.org/

11. **GO TO Red Canoes**
GO TO Red Canoes Website.
www.wilds.mb.ca/redcanoe/

12. **Kanotguiden har flyttat till www.kanotguiden.com**
biphome.spray.se/kanotguiden/

13. **Champaign Canoeing Ltd. - Home Page**
Champaign Canoeing Ltd. - A whitewater open canoe paddling school located in Ossining, NY, (35 miles from NYC). ... Champaign Canoeing Ltd. ...
users.bestweb.net/~keech/cc.htm

14. **American Canoe Association - canoeing, kayaking and rafting...**
American Canoe Association (ACA) is a canoeing, kayaking and rafting organization to promote paddlesports and river conservation. ...
www.acanet.org/

15. **Canoeing Merit Badge**
Boy Scout Merit Badge Requirements. CANOEING. ... Do the following: Name and point out the major parts of a canoe and paddle. Know canoeing terminology. ...
www.meritbadge.com/bsa/mb/033.htm

16. **Queensland Canoeing - Welcome to Queensland Canoeing**
Queensland Canoeing. ... Queensland Canoeing is the state body responsible for the management, coordination, development and promotion of canoeing in Queensland. ...
www.canoeqld.org.au/

17. **Get Out! Canoeing Community**

    A specialist canoeing shop offering over 800 products for the canoeist. A specialist shop including accessories. Site offers product descriptions, on-line catalogue, informatio...

    www.getoutcanoeing.co.uk/

18. **The Paddling Bares Canoe Club - Serious canoeing for people that ...**

    A naturist paddling club, devoted both to paddling activities and skinny dipping.

    www.canoeing.org/

19. **Canoeing in Western Australia**

    Informative canoeing site with detailed maps and event calendars.

    members.iinet.net.au/~rokhor/canoe/

20. **The Georgia Canoeing Association Web Site !**

    The Georgia Canoeing Association Web Site ! Find out about the Georgia Canoeing Association canoe and kayak club: Provides information about meetings, events, activities, instruction clinics, publications, library...

    www.georgiacanoe.org/

21. **NZRCA**

    The NZRCA represents the interests of recreational kayakers and canoeists in New Zealand. It has over...

    www.rivers.org.nz/

22. **Western Canoeing and Kayaking Clipper Canoes**

    Sales, rentals and paddling equipment and accessories, events and lessons, links, on-line store and

    www.westerncanoekayak.com/

23. **Dave Brown's Canoeing Adventures**

    Offering canoeing instruction, and scenic trips on the Potomac River in Northern Virginia.

    canoeadventures.home.mindspring.com/

24. **COME CANOEING**

    UK's premier internet resource for canoeists.

    www.canoeing.co.uk/

25. **Soomaa**

    The bogs have achieved a mysterious, even dangerous aura in traditional Estonian folklore. Today...

    www.ee/soomaa/eng.htm

26. **Canoeing The Grand Inc.**
Rental of canoes and kayaks at Kitchener, Ontario for outdoor paddling and trips on the Grand River,...
www.canoeingthegrand.com/

27. **CANOEING WEBSITES – Canoeing UK, canoes, canoe trips, kayaking ...**
A great variety of links to UK canoeing sites including canoe clubs and equipment suppliers. uk250.co.uk, A great collection of UK Canoeing websites, ... CANOEING ...
www.uk250.co.uk/Canoeing/

28. **Simondawson.com**
Archive of canoeing publications. Includes magazine articles, Corsica River Guide, canoeist's pathogenic...
www.simondsn.dircon.co.uk/

29. **Canoeing and kayaking and canoe rentals in Sweden**
Canoeing in Sweden. Choose paddling area from the list or the map. ...
www.kanotguiden.com/Canoeing.htm

30. **HOME - ORCA - Ontario Recreational Canoeing Association**
Ontario Recreational Canoeing Association. ... Announcing: abridged ORCA Safe Canoeing Program© Money and Marketing Opportunities. ...
www.orca.on.ca/

31. **Indiana Canoeing Guide**
DNR Outdoor Recreation. The Indiana Canoeing Guide has moved!
www.in.gov/dnr/outdoor/canoewww.in.gov/dnr/outdoor canoegui/

32. **Canoeing South Africa**
Canoeing South Africa! ... Please feel free to contact the Canoeing South Africa office with any questions or comments: info@canoesa.org.za. ...
www.canoesa.org.za/

33. **NZRCA: About the NZ Recreational Canoeing Association**
The NZRCA is the national organisation representing whitewater canoeing and kayaking in New Zealand, and is active in conservation, access, safetyand education ...
www.rivers.org.nz/nzrca/

34. **Canoeing North Dakota's Rivers with USGS streamflow data**
Use US Geological Survey real-time streamflow data to plan canoeing or kayaking trips on North Dakota rivers. Canoeing North Dakota's Rivers. ...
and.water.usgs.gov/canoeing/

35. **Champaign Canoeing Ltd. - Odyssey Adventure Racing - Canoe...**
Champaign Canoeing offers weekend whitewater canoeing instruction/certification courses that conform...
users.bestweb.net/~keech/odyssey.htm

36. **Outdoors in MaineToday.com | Canoeing**
Expert advice, gear lists, resources, news and features about Maine outdoor and recreation activities including: biking, camping, canoeing, fishing, golf ...
outdoors.mainetoday.com/canoeing/

37. **Mississippi River Resource Page**
Mississippi River Resource Page! We've included a wealth of information about the Mississippi River, from photos ...
www.caleuche.com/River/Mississippi.htm

38. **Canoe Florida, kayak Florida - canoeing, kayaking, cabin rentals...**
Canoeing, kayaking, cabins, camping and a high and low ropes course, group retreats in beautiful NW Florida.
www.adventuresunlimited.com/

39. **Kanotleder i Sverige**
World > Svenska > Sport > Vattensport > Kanot och kajak
www.kanotguiden.com/

40. **Gecko Canoeing**
Northern Australia, Outback Wilderness Safaris, Nature Tours and Australian Canoeing. Katherine, just south of Darwin, in the Northern ...
www.geckocanoeing.com.au/

41. **Canoeing For Kids Homepage**
Canoeing for Kids. Celebrating 10 years of Smiling Children's faces. ... Come meet the "Boss" Moose and enjoy a canoe trip with Canoeing for Kids.
www.canoeingforkids.net/

42. **Canoeing Safaris - explore the flow of Africa**

On a canoeing safari, you will look into the past, to the days when the great rivers of Africa were highways and byways, shared mainly by hippos and crocodiles ...

www.cansaf.com/

43. **Canoeing**

Name an point out the major parts of a canoe and paddle. Know canoeing terminology.

www.usscouts.org/mb/mb033.html

44. **Canoeing and Kayaking Clubs**

Canoeing and Kayaking Clubs. ... Here are some links to canoeing, kayaking, and rafting clubs around the US and around the world. US clubs are listed first by state. ...

peteandedbooks.com/cclubs.htm

45. **Canoeing in Colorado, whitewater river rafting, kayaking ...**

White water canoeing, rafting and kayak trips/instruction and certifications, we operate on the Upper...

www.canyonadventures.com/

46. **Canoeing Canada: Wilderness Adventures in Manitoba and Nunavut**

Naturalist guided canoe trips in the Canadian Shield and subarctic regions of Manitoba and arctic...

www.wildernessspirit.com/

47. **Canoeing in Florida with Canoe Outpost**

Canoeing...anyone can do it. Canoe Outpost - Suwannee River. ... All rights reserved. For general canoeing questions or website comments contact "Canoe Central".

www.canoeoutpost.com/

48. **Canoe the Mohican River with Smith's Pleasant Valley**

Canoe. ~Please select a trip from one listed above~. Our canoeing is now closed for the season! We thank you for your business this past summer! ...

www.3smiths.com/canoe.htm

49. **Maine Canoeing Guides - Guided Canoing Trips in Maine**

Listing of Maine Canoeing Guides. Let a Maine Professional Canoeing Guide show you the best Maine has to offer on the Kennbec, Pennobscot, Dead, St.

www.maineguides.com/search_by_sport/canoeing.html

50. **Canoeing in Cornwall**

Information for novices and experts alike on all types of canoeing and kayaking in Cornwall. Welcome to. site hosted and maintained...

www.wildthings-canoes.co.uk/cornwall.htm

51. **JJ Canoeing and Rafting Main Page**

JJ Canoeing and Rafting, Wales' premier site for canoeing, kayak, canoes, rafting, abseil, climbing, quad biking, laser clay shooting, archery, gorge walking ...

www.jjraftcanoe.com/

52. **Canoeing Guide to Western Pennsylvania**

Canoeing Guide to Western Pennsylvania and Northern West Virginia. Roy Weil and Mary Shaw, editors. The Canoeing Guide to Western ...

www.cs.cmu.edu/~shaw/CG.html

53. **Canoeing and Kayaking the Beautiful Suwannee River**

A major resource for information on CANOEING, KAYAKING AND CAMPING, the SUWANNEE RIVER from the Okefenokee Swamp to the Gulf. ... Excellent Canoeing or Kayaking. ...

www.canoe-suwannee.com/

54. **Canoeing and its History**

Canoeing voyages, that I will document in the Chapter V of this website. ...

www.geocities.com/xabier_sanjuan_a/kayaking.html

55. **Clipper Canoes**

Designs and manufactures composite canoes and offers over 40 models.

www.clippercanoes.com/

56. **Canoeing and Kayaking - Texas Fun**

Everything you need to know about canoeing and kayaking in Texas and from Texas! ... Back to Texas Fun Travel Guide

CANOEING AND KAYAKING. ...

www.texasfun.com/txfcanoe.htm

57. **Buffalo Camping and Canoeing on the Buffalo National River**

Buffalo Camping and Canoeing. ... Let Buffalo Camping and Canoeing, located in the historic Gilbert General Store, help you see this natural wonder. ...

gilbertstore.com/

58. **Canoeing in Maine: Maine's Outdoor-Sporting Guide**
Hundreds of miles Maine has to offer for your canoeing pleasure. Maine has a fairly long canoeing season thanks to...
www.maineoutdoors.com/canoeing/

59. **Contact Information**
NSW Canoeing acknowledges the support of the following partners -. Copyright © 2001 New South Wales Canoeing Inc. ...
www.nswcanoe.org.au/

60. **The British Canoe Union**
The governing body for the sport and recreation of canoeing and kayaking in the United Kingdom...
www.bcu.org.uk/

61. **Kayaking, Canoeing and Rafting in New Zealand - the TrueNZ Guide ...**
Listings of operators categorised by region.
www.truenz.co.nz/kayaking/

62. **Canoeing Down Under.......**
Provides canoe and kayak instruction from beginner to instructor in and around Perth WA. Social and...
www.canoeingdownunder.com.au/

63. **Indiana Canoeing Guide**
Common Sense; Indiana Canoeing Trails; Topographic Maps; Canoe Liveries; River Organizations; River Flow Information; Fishing Information. ...
www.in.gov/dnr/outdoor/canoe/

64. **Practical Canoeing - Tiphys: Chapter 1**
PRACTICAL CANOEING;. ... CANOEING is one of the earliest of human inventions, and one of the most simple, inexpensive, and enjoyable amusements of the present time. ...
www.friend.ly.net/~dadadata/tiphys/Practical_1.html

65. **canoeing**
British Canoe Union. This is the official Web site of the governing body for the sport and recreation of canoeing and kayaking in the UK. ...
altis.ac.uk/browse/cabi/detail 3f02ea2dd38e03e1eb8c6652d9d238d3.html

66. **Yahoo! Directory Paddling > Canoeing and Kayaking**
Paddling > Canoeing and Kayaking Directory > Recreation > Outdoors > Paddling > Canoeing and Kayaking, Search the Web just this category. ...
dir.yahoo.com/Recreation/Outdoors/ Paddling
Canoeing_and_Kayaking/

67. **Yahoo! Directory Shopping > Canoeing and Kayaking**
Shopping > Canoeing and Kayaking Directory > Business and Economy > Shopping and Services > Outdoors > Paddling > Canoeing and Kayaking, ...
dir.yahoo.com/Business_and_Economy
Shopping_and_Services/ Outdoors/Paddling
Canoeing_and_Kayaking/

68. **Outdoors in MaineToday.com | Getting Started in Canoeing**
The people in the club knew more about whitewater canoeing than I did. ... I learned a lot from that group. Q. What do you love about canoeing? ...
outdoors.mainetoday.com/canoeing/startcanoe.shtml

69. **Amazon.com: Books: Basic Essentials Canoeing, 2nd (rev)**
www.amazon.com/exec/obidos/tg/ detail/-/0762704845?v=glance

70. **Canoeing and Kayaking in Maine - Northern Maine Recreation...**
They are experts in their respective areas, and are there for your canoeing adventure. Supporting Canoeing and Kayaking Businesses. ...
www.mainerec.com/canoeing.html

71. **BCU World Class Performance**
www.worldclass-canoeing.org.uk/

72. **Ketter Canoeing: Best Place to Try a Canoe Before You Buy**
Ketter Canoeing, located on the Mississippi River, is the best place to try a canoe or kayak before you buy. ... Dealers and Outfitters, About Ketter Canoeing. ...
www.kettercanoeing.com/

73. **Canadian Recreational Canoeing Association**
Learn how You can help support the programs and mandates of the Canadian Recreational Canoeing Association. Have some ...
www.paddlingcanada.com/main.php

74. **The Canadian Canoe Museum - Our Canoeing Heritage**
Our Canoeing Heritage Click for larger version The word "canoa" or "canoe" appeared in the earliest writings about the First Peoples of the New World, and was ...
www.canoemuseum.net/heritage/

75. **Sea kayaking, sea kayak adventure tours, canoe trips soper river ...**
Canoeing For a serious canoeing challenge, you may want to consider a canoe trip along one of the remote rivers of Nunavut...
www.innsnorth.com/html/inns-adv-paddling.htm

76. **The canoeing**
Canoeing. ... The Lakes are actually a chain of seven small, picturesque spring-fed lakes which provide great fishing (everything but walleye) and canoeing...
www.trempealeaucountytours.com/canoeing.htm

77. **Amazon.com: Books: Canoeing the Delaware River**
www.amazon.com/exec/obidos/tg/ detail/-/0813524512?v=glance

78. **Canoeing**
Enjoy hiking, horseback riding, canoeing, skiing, antiquing, wine tours. ...
www.jwpublishing.com/gayscape/canoeing.html

79. **Canoeing WA**
Western Australia's Canoe Association web page to proceed
www.canoewa.asn.au/

80. **Kayaking and Canoeing Instruction - Top Whitewater and Sea Kayak ...**
A kayak school directory of white water and sea kayak schools. Companies are pre-screened for a commitmen...
www.kayakschools.com/

81. **Customized alaska canoeing guide service - Wilkinson Expeditions**
Wilkinson Expeditions offers canoeing trips in the Kenai National Wildlife Refuge, the Wood River area on the Alaskan Peninsula and in interior Alaska. ...
alaskatrips.com/canoeing.html

82. **Google Directory - Sports > Water Sports > Canoeing and Kayaking**
Canoeing and Kayaking, Sports ... kayaking. Simon Dawson's Canoeing Archive
directory.google.com/Top/SportsWater_Sports/ Canoeing_and_Kayaking/

83. **INFOHUB Canoeing/Kayaking Page**

Canoeing/Kayaking. General Information. ... Special Interest Tour Database – look up kayaking tours! List of Tour Operators. Canoeing/ Kayaking Aid and Tips. ...

www.biztravel.com/TRAVEL/ADVENTURE/ RECREATION/ kayaking.html

84. **Rotary Foundation Canoe Club**

MISSION STATEMENT Increase the awareness of all Rotarians of the existence and benefits of Rotarian fellowships to individual members ...

www.rotarystratford.com/canoe/

85. **The ARCADIAN Outdoor Guide to Canoeing, Kayaking and Rafting...**

Arcadian Outdoor Guidebooks LLC is pleased to make available to the general public our online version of The ARCADIAN Outdoor Guide to Canoeing, Kayaking and ...

www.thetent.com/arcadia/

86. **Georgia Canoeing Association**

The Georgia Canoeing Association Web Site Has Moved !

ww.mindspring.com/~gacanoe/

87. **Canoeing in Northern Saskatchewan**

A photo journal of a canoe trip starting at Paull Lake. Over the course of a week, travels over 100...

www.lights.com/~muri/canoe96/indexa.html

88. **Adventure Nova Scotia - Canoeing and Camping**

Canoing and Camping. ...

www.whatasite.com/adventure/canoeing.html

89. **Chicago Area Paddling/Fishing Page**

Indiana side. Wonder Lake (Private). Home, Fishing, Sailing, Canoeing, Rowing, Printing. Please e-mail suggestion/comments to: jwn@ripco.com.

pages.ripco.net/~jwn/canoe.html

90. **Moore Canoeing - Sport Canoeing Specialists**

If you are an experienced canoeist and want to tune your skills or upgrade your equipment, Moore Canoeing has what you are looking for. ...

www.moorecanoeing.com/

91. **canoeing tours, kayaking travel, sea-kayak**
Find a wide selection of travel packages of theme Canoeing/Kayaking from InfoHub.com. ... Canoeing/Kayaking. InfoHub has compiled a list ...
www.biztravel.com/TRAVEL/SIT/sit_pages/
Canoeing_Kayaking.html

92. **GORPtravel Canoeing Trips**
Activity Index Active Resorts Beach Trips Biking Trips Bird Watching Trips Canoeing Trips Cross Country Skiing Trips Culinary Tours Culture Trips Dude Ranches ...
gorptravel.away.com/activity_site_map_Canoeing.html?1

93. **Kayaking and Canoeing in North Wales**
Kayaking and Canoeing in North Wales 21 sites in this category. ... Climbing, canoeing, caving, walking, camping and the rest. Local and national outdoor resources. ...
www.northwalesindex.co.uk/pages/352.html

94. **Yukon Wild Canoeing**
Frances Lake Wilderness Lodge Frances Lake Wilderness Lodge Did you ever dream about canoeing in pristine wilderness? ...
www.yukonwild.com/activityCanoeing/index.php

95. **ForestWolf - High Performance Outdoor Gears**
Seat, Chinook Canoe Seat Out Of Stock Strapping system for standard canoe seat, PE framed support system, lightweight seat with support for long canoeing rtips. ...
www.forestwolf.com/shop/default.php?cPath=58

96. **Kayak, Canoe - Enjoy Kayaking, Canoeing and Kayak Polo on Prauss**
Prauss' staff is available to provide visitors with expert advice - the Prauss Team includes athletes who compete in kayaking and canoeing meets around the ...
www.prauss.no/

97. **Canoeing magazines or magazine links US or worldwide**
Canoeing magazines or magazine links US or worldwide or references to the subject of canoeing ... Canoeing magazines or magazine ...
hopcott.com/ukmagazines/canoeing.html

98. **Canoeing in West Kentucky**
Canoeing. West Kentucky canoeing adventure!...
www.thinkwestkentucky.com/canoeing/

99. **New Mexico Fly Fishing, Hiking, Camping, Kayaking, Canoeing...**
New Mexico Fly Fishing, Hiking, Camping, Kayaking, Canoeing, Skiing, Hunting and Outdoor Vacations. New Mexico Fly Fishing, Hunting ...
www.nmosg.com/

100. **Nova Scotia Sea kayaking, Eco tours, whitewater rafting, canoeing**
Offers guided tours, instruction and rentals.
www.eastcoastoutfitters.net/

101. **Canoeing in the Sea Cadets**
Canoeing Rules and Regulations, Competitions, Updates and Feedback.
www.mackinlay.demon.co.uk/canoeing/

102. **Odonnells Cottages index page**
Four Season of Adventure on the Miramichi....
www.odonnellscottages.com/

103. **Coyote Canoeing**
Coyote Canoeing DBA. Tom and Peggy Jenkins. ... ACA CERTIFIED INSTRUCTION. ACA Course Outlines — We teach both Solo and Tandem Canoeing and SwiftWater Rescue...
paddling.home.att.net/

104. **The Great Zambezi Canoeing Safari**
For the most relaxing and visually stunning vacation, take a canoeing safari down the Zambezi River, teeming with wildlife and birds, excellent fishing and ...
www.zambiatourism.com/travel/greatvac/canosafa.htm

105. **Bowron Lakes Canoe Trip BC, Sea Canoeing in British Columbia ...**
Canoeing the Bowron Lakes and more. We love canoeing. ... Book a custom canoeing vacation on northern wilderness lakes and rivers in Western Canada. ...
www.austeneverest.com/canoe.html

106. **Whitewater Rafting, Canoeing and Instruction with Sheltowee Trace**
Offers rafting trips on the Big South Fork, Cumberland, and Russell Fork rivers for family/beginner...
www.ky-rafting.com/

107. **Koh Lanta, Thailand - hotels, resorts, bungalows, travel ...**
Sea Canoeing/Kayaking. Ko Lanta Canoeing offers daily paddle trips by canoe through the exciting world of the mangrove forest and caves. ...
www.ko-lanta.com/activities/kayaking.htm

108. **Scottish Canoe Association. Inaugurated in 1939**
The governing body for canoeing in Scotland. Includes news, membership information, events, water...
www.scot-canoe.org/index2.htm

14
Carrom

1. **U.S. Carrom Association**
   Combination of pool, marbles, and air hockey.
   www.carrom.org/
2. **Carrom Company**
   Includes a current product catalog.
   www.carrom.com
3. **Karum**
   Designer and makers of carrom games.
   www.carrom.co.uk/
4. **Carrom UK**
   Includes information about the game of carom, equipment needed, rules, laws, and links to related sites.
   www.carromuk.co.uk/
5. **Carrom Australia Pty. Ltd.**
   Distributes the international board game in Australia. Approved by the ICF and ACF.
   www.carrom.com.au/
6. **OK Carrom Shop for Carrom Boards and Carrom Rules in Ireland**
   Welcome to OK CARROM. Carrom is a cross between pool and air hockey. It is a novel and fun family game for 2-4 players, played on...
   www.okcarrom.com/
7. **Carrom Board Centre**
   Carrom Board Centre presents information about the game of carrom, equipment needed, carrom rules, laws of carrom, links to carrom sites worldwide and an ...
   www.carromcentre.co.uk/

8. **Carrom Boards and Accessories**

   Buy from a range of carrom boards and accessories for all ages and levels at Valuezone. Valuezone. Carrom Boards and Accessories. Originated ...

   www.valuezone.co.uk/carrom.htm

9. **Carrom UK**

   Carrom explained,UKCA rules,clubs,tournaments,directory of UK players, improve your game, carrom exercises, edited bulletin board.

   www.carromuk.org.uk/

10. **index FFC**

    Documents Tournois Résultats Les Clubs Contacts Classement National 2003. Sponsor officiel de la FFC.

    www.carrom.net/

11. **Carrom Schweiz**

    Die erste und einzige Homepage über Carrom in der Schweiz !!!

    www.carrom.ch/

12. **Deutscher Carrom Verband**

    Copyright 1999 * DCV - Deutscher Carrom Verband Webdesign by P.Steier,

    www.carrom.de/

13. **International Carrom Federation**

    Federation, International Carrom Federation. ... 2nd US Open International Carrom Championship: October 15-19, 2003 Atlantic City, NJ. Mr ...

    www.internationalcarromfederation.org/

14. **Carrom Shop - Carrom und Zubehoer von Mespi, Surco, Lispo**

    Internetshop und Versandhandel für Carrom - Zubehör, Carromboards und andere Spiele. CARROM ONLINE-SHOP. Wir führen Carrom, Carromzubehör ...

    www.carrom-shop.de/

15. **Carrom - Online Guide**

    Carrom. History and Information. Carrom ... Two young men play Carrom on a home made board with bottle tops for counters, Java, Indonesia. Head ...

    www.tradgames.org.uk/games/Carrom.htm

16. **Carrom - Online Guide**

    Carrom. This site has moved to www.tradgames.org.uk. Please update your website links. The Online Guide to Traditional Games Home, ...
    web.ukonline.co.uk/james.masters/TraditionalGames/Carrom.htm

17. **Good-Choice Carrom Shop**

    Online Shop für Carrom Boards und Zubehör Verkauf. Allgemeine Spielinformationen und Regeln zum beliebten indischen Brettspiel. GOOD-CHOICE Carrom Shop. ...
    www.carrom-online.de/

18. **Carromshop.com**

    Sells carrom boards and organizes events in London.
    www.carromshop.com

19. **carrom**

    Carrom ist ein Geschicklichkeitsspiel das aus Indien stammt und vor ca. 20 Jahren nach Europa gekommen ist. Mann ... bezeichnen. Carrom. ...
    www.cccoma.de/

20. **Carrom Association UK**

    CARROM ASSOCIATION UK - Carrom Information for the UK.....Carrom rules, carrom board specifications, carrom clubs and carrom players. ...
    www.carromassociation.com/

21. **Carrom and harvard foosball tables and accessories**

    Carrom and Harvard foosball Tables. ... Carrom Super Soccer Table. I'm not a fan of having a dome over the table, but if you are then ...
    www.foosball-table.com/

22. **Carrom Boards and Accessories**

    Wholesalers of carom or carrom boards in a variety of sizes and carrom accessories including wooden and acrylic pieces or coins, strikers and powder. ...
    www.vaccreations.co.uk/carrom.html

23. **Toys by Brand Name : Carrom - ToysCamp.com**

    Air Powered Hockey - Tabletop (FREE SHIPPING). Air Powered Hockey - Tabletop (FREE SHIPPING) by Carrom Company. ... Bowl-A-Mania (FREE SHIPPING) by Carrom Company...
    www.toyscamp.com/ShowbyBrand.asp?BrandID=44

24. **Games: InHomeGames: Carrom Company** Carrom Company Inhomegames.com is your online source for Carrom products. We offer top quality products that are delivered directly ...
www.inhomegames.com/store/popular/carrom-company.asp

25. **BumperNets Online Catalog: Carrom Boards**... Signs Newgy Robot Shuffleboard Signs Soccette Specials Stick Hockey Table Tennis. Carrom Boards. Classic Games, Game Boards, Hockey.
www.bumpernetscatalog.com/Merchant2
merchant.mv?Screen=CTGY&Store_Code=BOC&
Category_Code=CB

26. **All India Carrom Federation**
Includes information about the organization and the game.
www.carromindiasite.com/

27. **Carrom Equipment, Carrom Sports Equipment, Carrom Equipment** Exporters and suppliers of carrom equipment, carrom sports equipment, carrom sporting equipment, carrom sports goods, carrom sports products, carrom sports ...
www.sporting-goods-industry.com/carrom-equipment/

28. **Play free Carrom games online,download pc computer game, fun** French Carrom Federation (translate). », International Carrom Federation. ... Contact us. Carrom, Crokinole. Search Amateur - Carrom page - Most Popular. ...
www.searchamateur.com/corkboard/Carrom.html

29. **Carrom Basics**
Anhand vieler flash - animierter Beispiele wird das Brettspiel Carrom umfassend erklärt (Material, Standardschüsse, Übungen, Regeln etc...)...
www.carrombasics.com/

30. **Carrom Games and Products, Carrom 100+ Gameboard, Carrom Balance**
Carrom Games and Products, Carrom Balance Board, Carrom Burr Oak Foosball Table, Carrom Complete Tournament Chess Set, Carrom Foosball & Hockey Sidemount ...
www.c-ion.comCarrom_GamesCarrom_Table_Top_Games.html

31. **Compare Prices and Read Reviews on Carrom Games at Epinions.com**

    Epinions has the best comparison shopping information on Carrom Games. ... Home > Kids & Family > Toys We found 21 results for Carrom Games. Refine these Results, ...

    www.epinions.com/kifm-Toys-All-Games-7544992-Carrom

32. **Carrom**

    Playing Carrom board that standing on a steel frame. Click Item No. CBF101. Imported Carrom frame and stand, made by steel...

    www.rksportsusa.com/Allfiles/Carrom.asp

33. **Whats**

    ?top. What's Carrom? ... Copyright(C)2001-2003 Japan Carrom Federation (Tokyo, Nerima)

    www.carromjapan.com/whats.html

34. **Carrom Veda**

    Page officielle Carrom Veda : tout sur le Carrom ou Billard Indien, description, règles du jeu, vente... LE CARROM : C'EST QUOI ? REGLES DU JEU. ORIGINE. ...

    www.multimania.com/carrom/

35. **United States Carrom Association**

    United States Carrom Association, United States Carrom Association. ... USA team wins 3rd place at the Eurocup! Report on Visakapatnam Carrom Tournament. ...

    www.uscarrom.org/

36. **The Carrom Association International...for all your Carrom needs**

    Carrom Association International...Carrom boards, Carrom competitions, Carrom rules, Information and other Carrom Resources. The ...

    www.carromassociationint.com/

37. **Salam For Carrom**

    By Lavina Melwani, from the Little India web site. Carrom comes to the new world.

    206.20.14.67/achal/archive/Jul96/carrom.htm

38. **SAARC Carrom Bangladesh win gold**

    All Categories Advanced Search. Sports SAARC Carrom ...

    nation.ittefaq.com/artman/publish/article_5166.shtml

39. **Carrom Game Board**
Game -Hungry Hungry Hippos | Board Game -Operation | Boggle Junior game | Bowl-A-Mania (FREE SHIPPING) | Brain Quest Game for Grades 1-6 | Carrom Game Board ...
shop.store.yahoo.com/discounttoys/ccm100.html

40. **Carrom Boards**
Double_dice.jpg Monopoly. double_dice.jpg Carrom. double_dice.jpg Puzzles. ... double_dice.jpg Directions.double_dice.jpg Shipping Info. Carrom Boards. ...
www.gamecenteronline.com/gamecenter/html carrom_boards.html

41. **Carrom Test, Preisvergleich, Shopping, Auktionen**
Bei Yopi finden Sie zahlreiche Erfahrungsberichte, Tests und Preisvergleiche zu Carrom. ... Test und Preisvergleich Carrom. ... Erfahrungsberichte (3) über Carrom. ...
www.yopi.de/Carrom

42. **crrmv1**
MODELLI DI CARROM BOARDS DISPONIBILI. (Non tutti i modelli sono sempre disponibili subito, a volte ci vuole un po' di ... pazienza!); ...
198.173.240.77/crrmv1.html

43. **Google Directory - Games > Hand-Eye Coordination > Carrom**
Carrom, ... Carrom Boards Australia - http://www.carrom-boards-australia.com.au Manufacturer and supplier of hand painted and hand crafted boards. ...
directory.google.com/Top/Games/Hand-Eye_Coordination/Carrom/

44. **Le carrom ou karom**
Découvrez le carrom, ou billard indien. ... Toujours est-il que le carrom connaît depuis plusieurs décennies un engouement qui ne se dément pas. ...
www.chez.com/indereunion/utile/carrom/carrom.htm

45. **Carrom Items**
LOC: Carrom. Carrom Items < PREVIOUS, Showing 1 - 13 of 13, NEXT >>. BRAND / ITEM, GROUP. Carrom 100+ Gameboard, Toys : Indoor Games : Board Games. ...
www.interactile.com/brand/b0_Carrom.htm

46. **Compare Prices at NexTag - Carrom Indoor Games, Sports**
Carrom Indoor Games, Sports, Outdoors, More Categories - The NexTag shopping guide has prices, reviews from stores all over the web....
www.nextag.comCarrom_Indoor_Games~2701002z Carromz0zB36ozmainz5-htm

47. **Carrom**
Le carrom est un jeu ancien d'origine orientale, comparable au billard. Dominique ... décoration... Dimensions 67 cm x 67 cm. Visitez notre site Carrom
www.ardeche.com/carrom/

48. **Carrom foosball tables - Prices and Reviews at DealTime**
Compare shop for Carrom foosball tables at DealTime - read reviews and compare prices from stores all across the Web. ...
att.dealtime.com/xDN-Toys-foosball_tables-ty_brands_carrom

49. **Carrom Items**
LOC: Carrom. Carrom Items < PREVIOUS, Showing 1 - 13 of 13, NEXT >>. BRAND / ITEM, GROUP. Carrom 100+ Gameboard, Board Games. Carrom ...
www.upupon.com/brand/b0_Carrom.htm

50. **Carrom Recreation Room Games Toys - Prices and Reviews at**
Compare shop for Carrom Recreation Room Games Toys at DealTime - read reviews and compare prices from stores all across the Web. ...
www.dealtime.com/xDN-Toys—recreation_room_games-ty_brands_carrom

51. **Carrom Foosball and Air Hockey Tables from BuyChoice**
Shop for foosball tables, soccer, air-hockey tables and more at Buy Choice, an authorized dealer for Carrom Sports. ... world globes. Home: Carrom Game Tables. ...
www.buychoice.com/vendor.cfm 646,Carrom%20Game%20Tables,XX

52. **Open Directory - Games: Hand-Eye Coordination: Carrom**
Billiboards - Offers carrom boards and ICF approved accessories. Carrom Australia Pty. Ltd. - Offers carrom boards and accessories approved by the ICF and ACF. ...
dmoz.org/Games/Hand-Eye_Coordination/Carrom/

53. **Le Carrom - Frame Principal**

Si vous voyez ce message, c'est que votre navigateur ne peut pas afficher de frames. Vous pouvez toutefois accéder au menu en cliquant sur : MENU.

perso.wanadoo.fr/experience.bar/carrom/

54. **Amazon.com: Toys & Games: Carrom Game Board: Large**

Carrom Game Board: Large by Carrom Company ... im 42, me and my older brother played carrom when we were yonger. I bought a carrom board for my 6 year old nephew. ...

www.amazon.com/exec/obidos/tg/detail/B00003G4JR?v=glance

55. **The Sports Authority: Search for "Carrom " Page 1 of 3.**

Carrom Arena Pro Hockey Dome Hockey Table Our Price: $999.99, Carrom Ultimate Super Stick Hockey Our Price: $899.99. Carrom Super ...

www.thesportsauthority.com/searchHandler index.jsp?brandId=786

56. **ROBOT CARROM - RULES**

ROBOT CARROM. OBJECTIVE: Build a robot that will put your own carrom coins into a pocket. COINS: nine white, nine black, and one red. ...

www.iitk.ac.in/robotics/carrom/

57. **Apaseo Viajes**

Travel experiences. 1er Campeonato Carrom APASEO Dónde estamos Financiación Visitas concertadas. Programación 2003. Australia Botswana ...

www.apaseo.net/apaseo/interior.asp?app=42&aps=191

58. **Carrom**

Games Directory, Carrom. US Carrom Association - Promotes the game in America and ensures US participation in international tournaments. ...Carrom Australia Pty. ...

www.buyasundial.com/Games/Hand-EyeCoordination/Carrom/

59. **Carrom Board Game,Volleyball Net,Carrom Boards Exporter**

Lovson Exports - Exporter of carrom board game, volleyball net, carrom boards, basketball net, tennis court net, hockey goal net, carrom board, hockey net ...

www.lovson.com/sports/carrom.html

60. **Uwe Petersen Carrom. Regeln und Training.**
Uwe Petersen Carrom. Regeln und Training. Carrom. Regeln und Training. Spielen Raten Carrom Spiel Brettspiele, Würfelspiele Petersen ...
www.buecher-titel.de/Carrom-Regeln-und-Traini-3880345759.html

61. **Fogdog Sports: Search for "Carrom" Page 1 of 2**
18 ITEMS [1] 2. Carrom Arena Pro Hockey Dome Hockey Table OUR PRICE : $999.99, Carrom Ultimate Super Stick Hockey OUR PRICE : $899.99, ...
www.fogdog.com/searchHandler/index.jsp?brandId=786

62. **Excite UK - Directory - Carrom**
13 sites Carrom. 1. Billiboards, Offers carrom boards and ICF approved accessories. http://www.billiboard.com. 2. Carrom Australia Pty. Ltd. ...
www.excite.co.uk/directory/Games/Hand-Eye_Coordination/Carrom

63. **Dominion Web - Directory - Games: Hand-Eye Coordination: Carrom**
Top: Games: Hand-Eye_Coordination: Carrom: Carrom. Links. » Billiboards - Offers carrom boards and ICF approved accessories....
www.dominion-web.com/directory/Top/Games/Hand Eye_Coordination/Carrom

64. **GI Joe's: Search for "Carrom" Page 1 of 2**
18 ITEMS [1] 2. Carrom Arena Pro Hockey Dome Hockey Table OUR PRICE: $999.99. Carrom Ultimate Super Stick Hockey OUR PRICE: $899.99. ...
www.gijoes.com/searchHandler/index.jsp?brandId=786

65. **Foosball, Foosball Table, Foosball Tables - Garlando, Harvard**
Great selection of soccer and foosball tables featuring Harvard, Carrom, Murrey, Rhino, and Garlando from American Super Sports....
www.americansupersports.com/Foosball.html

66. **Spielhimmel**
Holzspiele, Carrom,Carambole, ... Artikelliste. Gefunden 24 Artikel Artikel wurde gesucht nach Kategorie Holzspiele und Unterkategorie Carrom,Carambole. Seiten: 1 2 3. ...
www.spielhimmel.ch/Default.asp?Ct=12&SCt=151

67. **Sport Chalet: Search for "Carrom"**
Carrom Harley Davidson Foosball Table. Our Price: $1499.99. Carrom Arena Pro Hockey Dome Hockey Table Free Shipping Eligible!**. ...
www.sportchalet.com/searchHandler/index.jsp?brandId=786

68. **Carrom Activity and Sports Toys Toys - Find, Compare, and Buy**
Read Carrom Activity and Sports Toys Toys Reviews and Compare Carrom Activity and Sports Toys Toys Prices. Shopping.com helps shoppers ...
www.shopping.com/xDN-Toys—activity_and_sports_toys ty_brands_carrom

69. **Carrom Tables**
Carrom Tables.
www.edandb.com/carrom_tables.htm

70. **Oshman's Supersports USA**
Carrom® Free Throw Duel Basketball Item no: 149071 OUR PRICE: $299.99. The Free Throw Duel basketball from Carrom® gives you a ...
www.oshmans.com/product/index.jsp?productId=149071

71. **Buy Carrom Pro Stick hockey table Online**
The Carrom® Pro Stick hockey table provides you hours of indoor fun with its masonite coated playing surface and fiberglass rods for durability. ...
www.apollonsports.com/buy/products/sticktablehockey.htm

72. **Dunham's Sports: Search for "Carrom" Page 1 of 2**
buy/more info. Carrom Ultimate Super Stick Hockey. Carrom The Professional Air Hockey Table. ...
www.dunhamssports.com/searchHandler/index.jsp?brandId=786

73. **CARROM - Definition by HyperDictionary.com**
Hyper Dictionary. English Dictionary, Computer Dictionary, Thesaurus, Dream Dictionary, Medical Dictionary. Search Dictionary: CARROM. ...
www.hyperdictionary.com/dictionary/Carrom

74. **Carrom boards, carrom men, carrom rules, carrom**
CARROM' Great fun with family and friends. Carrom is a fun boardgame for everyone. ... Carrom is comparable to billiards and originated in India 200 years ago.
www.easternimporters.co.uk/carrom.htm

75. **Carrom Boards**
Home Latest News What is Carrom? Our Carrom Board Range Our Accessory Range How to Order Feedback About Us Links. Click a Carrom ...
www.carrom-boards-australia.com.au/html/products/boards_home.htm

76 **Carrom Boards - Carrom Board Games - Carrom Board Makers - Cabin**

Designers and makers of carrom boards, rules of carrom, how to play carrom, carrom game laws. ...

www.cabinfever-uk.com/

77. **Modell's: Search for "Carrom" Page 1 of 2**

18 ITEMS [1] 2. Carrom Arena Pro Hockey Dome Hockey Table. Carrom Ultimate Super Stick Hockey.

www.modells.com/searchHandler/index.jsp?brandId=786

78. **Sportmart: Search for "Carrom"**

Carrom Harley Davidson Foosball Table Buy/More Info. Carrom Arena Pro Hockey Dome Hockey Table Buy/More Info.

www.sportmart.com

searchHandler/index.jsp?brandId=786

79. **Carrom Foosball Tables: Air Hockey Table, Carrom Games**

Carrom Foosball Tables at Farm Goods for Kids. Your source for air Carrom hockey sports tables, Carrom air hockey and table hockey games. ...

www.farmgoodsforkids.com/brands/brandcarrom.htm

80. **Carrom Foosball tables and table soccer for home recreation**

Carrom foosball tables for home recreation. Included are the full line of Carrom foosball tables and their accessories. ... CARROM'S Foosball Tables. ...

www.moneymachines.com/carromfoosball.html

81. **Carrom Toys**

Pricetool has the best comparison shopping information on Carrom Toys Costing Over $70. ... We found 12 results for Carrom Toys Costing Over $70. ...

www.pricetool.com/kifm-Toys-All-Price-70_to_100000-7544992-Carrom

82. **Carrom Test und Preisvergleich**

Carrom. 4,92/5,00 (von 98% empfohlen) Schwierigkeitsgrad, 2,8. Präsentation, 4,3. Spielanleitung, 4,0. » Testbericht schreiben. ... Testberichte zu Carrom. ...

www.ciao.com/Carrom__240753

83. **MC Sports: Search for "Carrom"**

20 ITEMS [1] 2. Carrom Harley Davidson Foosball Table. Carrom Arena Pro Hockey Dome Hockey Table.

www.mcsports.com/searchHandler/index.jsp?brandId=786

15
Chess

1. **US Chess Federation**
   Official website and online store for the US Chess Federation. The USCF is the official sanctioning body for tournament chess in ...
   www.uschess.org/
2. **Internet Chess Club**
   THE place to play chess online. Over 25000 members and 110000 games played per day. Beginners ... welcome. The best place to play live online chess! ...
   www.chessclub.com/
3. **chess.net (tm)**
   chess.net: Train with Grandmasters; play with friends. Play live chess on the Internet with players from around the world. Free site with for-pay premium services. Requires client which can be downloaded (Windows only) or...
   www.chess.net/
4. **The Week in Chess**
   WELCOME TO THE WEEK IN CHESS. ... MORE. Second Mystery Consultation game on the NAO Chess Club site finishes in a draw. Players names to be published on Monday. MORE...
   www.chesscenter.com/twic/twic.html
5. **The London Chess Centre**
   Chess and Bridge Limited - Click here to enlarge the image We are outside the Congestion Charge Zone Click here for more information. ... Chess and Bridge Ltd. Includes The Week In Chess, which provides the latest chess news, downloadable games and analysis...
   www.chesscenter.com/

6. **Chess is Fun**
   Clear instructions on how the chess pieces move.
   www.princeton.edu/~jedwards/cif/intro.html
7. **FICS - Free Internet Chess Server**
   A free chess server with players of all levels, with lectures to help you improve your play.
   www.freechess.org/
8. **ChessCafe.com**
   Book reviews, endgame studies, and columns on various chess topics.
   www.chesscafe.com/
9. **New In Chess**
   The Indian men's chess championship. Articles, games, analysis, merchandise and links to Internet-based chess information. www.newinchess.com/
10. **Chess News, Chess Programs, Databases - Play Chess Online**
    Publisher of high quality chess programs and databases. ... Because of this and nothing else he will be remembered as long as there is chess. ...
    www.chessbase.com/
11. **WebChess**
    Become a Preferred Member and you won't see these ads. Welcome to the world of GNU Chess, linked to the Web. ... Pieces: text. Kings, Queens. Chess Links. ...
    chess.delorie.com/
12. **World Chess Federation**
    World Chess Championship Regulations and List of Qualifiers
    www.fide.com/
13. **Play chess, checkers, gin rummy, backgammon and chat. million ...**
    Play Chess real-time online. No downloads needed. Search and analyse over 2 million chess games in...
    www.chesslab.com/
14. **Home page of The Chess Variant Pages**
    Rules, information, and links for games that are a variant of chess: three-dimensional chess games,multiplayer chess variants, historic chess variant...
    www.chessvariants.com/

15. **About Chess**
    Chess site for beginning and intermediate chess players. ... Product reviews (chess books, chess sets, chess clocks, chess software) for more advanced players.
    chess.about.com/mbody.htm
16. **Chess Mentor by Aficionado**
    Home page of Chess Mentor chess learning software application. Chess Mentor is the most effective computer-based method for learning ...
    www.chess.com/
17. **New CHESS Home Page**
    Includes an introduction to the facility and basic experimental design information, information for...
    www.chess.cornell.edu/
18. **Chess Corner - www.chesscorner.com**
    A complete chess resource containing a comprehensive chess tutorial, book and software reviews, find a chess opponent to practise skills, discussion forum and ...
    www.chesscorner.com/
19. **Los Angeles Times - Chess**
    US Championship set for San Diego. By Jack Peters. Position No. ...
    www.latimes.com/features/puzzles/chess/
20. **Russian Chess**
    Russian Chess, the chess site devoted to the main chess events,chess games, chess analyses and chess education. ...
    www.ruschess.com/
21. **Chess Mail 2003 index page**
    ICCF site. Cover7_03Welcome to Chess Mail. Soviet chess secrets revealed! ...
    www.chessmail.com/
22. **Tim Krabbé's Chess Curiosities**
    Chess stories, chess games, chess positions, chess endgames, chess studies, chess problems. Chess problems with narrative about how each came about and what really happened after the position....
    www.xs4all.nl/~timkr/chess/chess.html

23. **British Chess Magazine: The Chess Shop and the Bridge Shop**
British Chess Magazine. World's Oldest Chess Magazine ... org.uk. Published by British Chess Magazine. Features international and British chess news.
www.bcmchess.co.uk/

24. **Internet Chess Radio - Chess.FM**
AMERICA'S FOUNDATION FOR CHESS FINDS CO-SPONSOR FOR 2004 US CHESS CHAMPIONSHIPS San Diego's NTC Foundation's Promenade Centre Is New Home for the 2004 US Chess...
www.chess.fm/

25. **Chess Informant**
www.sahovski.com/default.htm

26. **Java TkChess interface**
Works even with text browsers! Frequently Asked Questions. Read the official FIDE Laws of Chess. Find ...
pine.cs.yale.edu:4201/java/chess.html

27. **chessKIDS academy: learn and play chess online with our free...**
How to play chess: free online chess lessons for kids. Play against the computer. Chess resources for teachers and parents
www.chesskids.com/

28. **Log — David Chess**
Mostly-daily musings on philosophy, culture, technology, the emergence of life from matter, chocolate,...
www.davidchess.com/words/log.html

29. **Yahoo! Directory Board Games > Chess**
Board Games > Chess Directory > Recreation > Games > Board Games > Chess, ... SITE LISTINGS.Most Popular: Chess Radio - offers chess news via streaming broadcast.
www.yahoo.com/Recreation/Games/Board_Games/Chess/

30. **Computer Chess Programming**
Information about computer chess programming, links to chess program sources, computer chess publications, computer chess research. Reference material, programming techniques, endgame databases, and computer game research for chess...
www.xs4all.nl/~verhelst/chess/programming.html

31. **Best Sites on the Web -**
Search through Millions of Computer Sites. Find All the Best Computer Results Here. :: Most Searched. · Auto Insurance. · Auctions. · Autos. ...
www.hydra.com/icc/

32. **www.chess.at**
World > Deutsch > Regional > Europa > Österreich > Freizeit
www.chess.at/

33. **Play chess against tkChess**
Offer/claim a draw. Start over. Try the Java version. FIDE Laws of Chess; Frequently asked questions(including an explanation of the move abbreviations).
pine.cs.yale.edu/cgi-bin/chessplayer

34. **Chess: development of micro-electronics, software and business...**
Chess supplies services, products and solutions on the territory of micro-electronics, embedded software and business-critical software....
www.chess.nl/

35. **ItsYourTurn.com - Play online games: chess, checkers, backgammon ...**
Play online multiplayer Internet games: chess, backgammon, checkers, Battleship, Othello, reversi, Go, Connect4, Stratego, Xiangqi, variations. No downloads, no java, just free turn-based (not live) games with thousands of opponents. Play 30+...
www.itsyourturn.com/

36. **GMChess - Grandmastres site!**
Grandmaster site of 1999 FIDE World Chapmpion Alexander Khalifman and other top Grandmasters. Instruct...
www.gmchess.com/

37. **Chess - GNU Project - Free Software Foundation (FSF)**
Chess. [image of the Head of a GNU] Update ... Introduction to Chess. GNU Chess lets most modern computers play a full game of chess. It ...
www.gnu.org/software/chess/

38. **Chess on Stamps**
Chess on Stamps - the award winning site - featuring the world's first dynamic, zooming online catalogue. ... Abcut Chess on Stamps....
www.tri.org.au/chess/

39. **Chess Federation of Canada**

National Chess Federation Homepage...

www.chess.ca/

40. **Home Page for US Chess Center**

Big Things at the US Chess Center. Excellent site for chess students or teachers. Serves Washington DC, Maryland, and Virginia.

www.chessctr.org/

41. **chess.net**

Home. Sign up and Play Chess, Sign up and Play Chess Meet your match. ... News, News, Events and Tournaments Looking for an update of what's happening on chess.net? ...

www.chess.net/home.html

42. **Exeter Chess Club: Chess Coaching Page**

Exeter Chess Club Coaching Page. ... in teaching and learning about chess [whatever gimmicky proprietary browser they use], [4-star Accessible according to Bobby]. ...

www.ex.ac.uk/~dregis/DR/coaching.html

43. **Convekta Chess Site :**

Chess programs: do you want to learn more? Chess Education Online! Lessons by GMs and IMs. Commented games section. ... Chess University is now open! Includes support, demo download, company information, and prices.

www.chessassistant.com/

44. **Chess Today-the first Net-based daily chess newspaper! Chess...**

learn playing chess, professional chess play, online chess newspaper,chess games analyzed. Chess Today, Try our service, free trial. ...

www.chesstoday.net/

45. **Chess Informant**

Informants are chess books in print and on CD of recent games. Most are annotated by top players.

www.sahovski.com/

46. **World Chess Network**

World Chess Network is for players ranging from novice to Grandmaster.... The World Chess Network is designed for players from novice to Grandmaster. Play online chess with opponents from beginners to grandmasters. World Chess Network providesfree...

www.worldchessnetwork.com/

47. **University of Pittsburgh Chess Club**

    The University of Pittsburgh Chess Page contains information about Chess in Pennsylvania, USCF and FIDE Ratings Lists, access to a large Chess FTP Site, and ...

    www.pitt.edu/~schach/

48. **Caissa's Web Chess Home Page**

    Caissa's Web is a World Wide Web-based chess server that allows members from all over the world to play live, real-time games of chess using an easy-to-use ...

    caissa.com/

49. **nav bar**

    New Products Book News Weekly Specials Chessbase USA Chessbase USA Store Chess Improvement. ... Chess Digest 2002, Home, Site Design by CoolCoyotes. Offers a wide selection of chess books and periodicals.....

    www.chessdigest.com/

50. **Chessmaster 9000**

    Ukrainian Chess Set 11/06/2002 Chessmaster Reviews! 11/05/2002 From the World of Chess 11/05/2002, ... PC IGN The best chess game currently available on the PC... The world's best selling chess program, and one of the very strongest PC/Mac chess programs.

    www.chessmaster.com/

51. **Tim Mann's Chess Pages**

    Tim Mann's Chess Pages. ...

    www.tim-mann.org/chess.html

52. **InstantChess.com - Play Chess Online (Cup of coffeecompatible)**

    Play chess online. InstantChess is one of the most popular places for online chess games. Instant Chess ... players. Play chess online! The computer automatically pairs you up with an opponent from around the world. No registration is...

    www.instantchess.com/

53. **Chess**

    US Chess Live, the official online chess service of the US Chess Federation, has joined with the World Chess Hall of Fame to become Chess Hall of Fame Live. ...

    www.uschesslive.org/

54. **Chess is a scientific game and its literature ought to be placed...**

Chess is a scientific game and its literature ought to be placed on the basis of the strictest truthfulness, which is the foundation of all scientific research ... Includes photos and articles about chess and its history.

www.chessarch.com/arch.shtml

55. **Chess City**

Chess City! Chess City is the new incarnation of Chess City Magazine. We are no longer a magazine on a monthly schedul...

www.chesscity.com/

56. **GameKnot — play chess online! Internet chess games.**

Play chess online! Free online chess, Java games. No additional software to download ... of players of all levels. Play chess game for free! Free online turn-based, multiplayer and Java games, all right from your browser. No additional downloads...

gameknot.com/

57. **Chess World - chess contest, games, software, PGN files and ...**

Play Online, chess contest, news, games, software, PGN files. Determine your rating and play with chess grandmasters! Or play an ...

www.very-best.de/ChessWorld.htm

58. **Net-Chess.com**

NET-CHESS.COM Developed and administered by Greg Miller. Correspondence chess with strict time controls.

www.net-chess.com/

59. **ICCF - The International Correspondence Chess Federation**

Includes ratings, tables, rules, and links.

www.iccf.com/

60. **Chess For Juniors**

Chess For Juniors. Senior Master Robert M. Snyder. National Chess Camps Colorado's Chess Club For Youth National Scholastic Chess Internet Training Center...

www.chessforjuniors.com/

61. **ERIC Clearinghouse for Social Studies/Social Science Education**

About ERIC and ERIC/ChESS, ERIC/ChESS 2805 East Tenth Street, Suite 120 Bloomington,Indiana 47408-2698 Telephone: 812/855-3838 Toll-free/TDD: 800/266-3815

www.indiana.edu/~ssdc/eric-chess.html

62. **www.WorldChessRating.com**

16 World Class GMs among them 11 of the 12 top rated players took part in the World Rapid Chess Championship in Cap d'Agde.

www.clubkasparov.ru/

63. **Shizmoo Games**

Kung Fu Chess Fast and furious chess mayhem in this hilarious hit! ... Click to Play. Chess mayhem where you never wait your turn. Fast paced and hilarious! ...

www.shizmoo.com/

64. **Chess Graphics, a collection devoted to all aspects of chess ...**

chess graphics: These pages are devoted to all aspects of chess graphics.Photographs ... banner. Chess Graphics has moved to it's own domain. A site devoted to all aspects of chess graphics. Photographs, cartoons, ray tracing, paintings, drawings...

www.cowderoy.com/graphics/

65. **Chess Communication**

Chess Move – for deg som er på farten! Les mer..

www.chess.no/

66. **CHESS DOT GR Hellas Chess Club**

Hellas Chess Club - Chess Portal.This section aims to inform you about the current status of the Greek and Worldwide Chess. Informing you about the current status of Greek and worldwide chess. Analysis, gameplays and useful...

www.chess.gr/

67. **Index page of The Chess Variant Pages**

Advertisement. The Chess Variant Pages: Index. ... Recognized chess variants: What are considered to be the 'best chess variants'? ... Hexagonal chess variants. ...

www.chessvariants.com/Gindex.html

68. **Chess is Fun**

Want to learn how to play chess? Want to learn how to play a bit better? Here are some fairly easy "lessons." Offers rules, openings, endgames, tactics, book reviews, and game archive.

www.princeton.edu/~jedwards/cif/chess.html

69. **iChess Home Page**

iChess is a Java based, interactive Internet chess game. Players anywhere on the Internet with a Java enhanced browser can pla...

www.ichess.com/

70. **Australian Chess Federation**
Offers news, links, and ratings
www.auschess.org.au/

71. **Le due Torri | la libreria degli scacchi | Chess Department Store World > Italiano > ... > Bologna > Affari e Economia > Negozi**
www.chess.it/

72. **The Chess Oracle - Chess News from around the World**
The Chess Oracle reporting on International and UK chess news including the German Bundesliga and the UK 4NCL. The Chess Oracle - Chess ...
ourworld.compuserve.com/homepages/John_Katrin_Sharp/

73. **CHESS IRELAND**
CHESS IRELAND. Chess Links. Chess League - LCU results. LCU - results section. Reports the goings on in Irish chess world.
Updated approximately monthly with events, results, and ratings.
www.iol.ie/~jghurley/

74. **RandD Publishing World Wide Chess SuperStore**
The Chess Site for the Twenty-First Century! The Official World Wide Web Site of. USA's Top Woman Chess Player IRINA KRUSH. Offers a selection of books, clocks, software, videos, equipment, magazines and related merchandise.
www.smartchess.com/

75. **Continental Chess Association - tournament information**
CONTINENTAL CHESS ASSOCIATION. Chess tournament information. Organizes chess tournaments throughout the United States. Includes schedules, ratings and online play.
www.chesstour.com/

76. **The Chess Drum**
The site champions the success of Black chess players, or those of African ancestry... includes interviews, playble ... around the world. The purpose of the site is to champion the success of black chess players around the world, to give...
www.thechessdrum.net/

77. **ThinkQuest : Library : Chess for Kids**
Chess for Kids. "Chess for Kids"is an exciting resource for chess players of all skill levels, from beginners to advanced tournament players. ...
tqjunior.thinkquest.org/6290/

78. **Knightmare Chess!**

Chess will never be the same! Knightmare Chess is chess played with cards - and what cards! ... Looking for good retailers? Use the Gamer Finder! Cool Chess Links. Chess played with cards. Each card breaks the rules in a wild and unpredictable way, giving the game...

www.sjgames.com/knightmare/

79. **About Chess.com**A wealth of chess resources.

chess.about.com/games/chess/

80. **Logical Chess, Home of Chess on the Web. Learn, read, and study! ...**

Learn how to play chess well with tactical exercises, strategy and endgame lessons, and example games where every move is explained. ...

www.logicalchess.com/

81. **Exeter Chess Home Page**

Exeter Chess Home Page. “”..so sit back in the chair you like best and get ready for the wacky game of chess..” “ ... and Southampton Chess Club. Includes a collection of coaching notes, recommended books, and membership information.

www.ex.ac.uk/~dregis/DR/chess.html

82. **The Great Pawn Hunter: Chess Tutorial, Books, History of Chess**

The Great Pawn Hunter Chess Tutorial. Learn chess the fun and easy way without memorizing moves! Manus Patrick Fealy. ... Note: I love to learn and play chess. Learn the ideas behind the chess moves without memorizing.

members.aol.com/manusfealy/

83. **Chess Doctor: Free Online Downloads and Battle Strategy for Chess ...**

Free online downloads and battle strategy for chess games, free online newsletter, free chess battle secrets, free master strategy report, and online chess.

chessdoctor.com/

16
Common Wealth Games

1. **www.commonwealthgames.com**
   Official site offers the event schedules, spectator information including tickets and travel, Kids'...
   www.commonwealthgames.com/
2. **www.commonwealthgames.com**
   www.commonwealthgames.com/Home/
3. **Melbourne 2006 Commonwealth Games**
   Official Melbourne 2006 Commonwealth Games Website Official site about the Games in Australia includes details about the sports, venues and host city...
   www.melbourne2006.com.au/
4. **Commonwealth Games Federation**
   Official site offers the history of the Games, the role of the CGF and the nations and territories...
   www.thecgf.com/
5. **Commonwealth Games Federation**
   The Commonwealth Games Federation, Re-live the excitement of the Manchester 2002 Games. XVIII Commonwealth Games Melbourne, Australia. ...
   www.thecgf.com/home.asp
6. **BBC Manchester Commonwealth Games 2002**
   BBC Manchester Commonwealth Games 2002 includes news, venues, ticket information, sports, the Queen's Jubilee Baton Relay and more. ... Commonwealth Games Radio. ...
   www.bbc.co.uk/manchester/2002/index.shtml

7. **Australian Commonwealth Games Association**

   The official site for the Commonwealth Games Team in Australia. Includes general information, history of the games, athletes, past esults, medalists, media releases,...

   www.ausport.gov.au/acga/

8. **Jeux du Commonwealth Games Canada**

   Official Canadian site includes results, news, pictures, voice clips, CBC radio and TV schedules,...

   www.commonwealthgames.ca/

9. **BBC SPORT | Commonwealth Games 2002**

   Fireworks brought the Games to a close Manchester Games hailed a success The Commonwealth Games come to a spectacular conclusion after 11 days of competition. ...

   news.bbc.co.uk/sport3/commonwealthgames2002/ default.stm

10. **XVI Commonwealth Games 98 Kuala Lumpur**

    History, general information and competition results of the 16th Games hosted by Kuala Lumpur in Malaysia...

    www.commonwealthgames98.com/

11. **Commonwealth Games**

    Commonwealth Games. ... The first Commonwealth Games were the product of discussions and ideas shared over a thirty year period of time. A brief history of the games plus news clips. List of all host countries by year.

    www.internationalgames.net/commonwe.htm

12. **Commonwealth Games Medallists**

    United Kingdom Track and Field All-Time Lists - Complete list of Medallists in all sports at Commonwealth Games. A complete list of medallists in athletics plus gold medallists in other sports since 1930. Search-by-nam...

    www.gbrathletics.com/commonwealth/

13. **Commonwealth Games of Virginia**

    Virginia's premier amateur sporting event, a multi-sport festival of Olympic and non-Olympic style events.

    www.commonwealthgames.org/

14. **Commonwealth Games Council for Scotland**

    Latest news, press releases and results of the Games plus team profiles, event details and FAQ. Send...

    www.cgcs.org.uk/

15. **ManchesterOnline - Commonwealth Games**
Commonwealth Games. Final Medal Table. News Archive. Venue Guide. Queen's Baton Relay.
www.manchesteronline.co.uk/m2002/

16. **BBC 2002 Commonwealth Games Radio website**
Commonwealth Games Radio The radio station is now off the air, but here's a chance to find out what it was all about. BBC 2002 TeamA little extra. ...
www.bbc.co.uk/manchester/2002/radio/index.shtml

17. **CBBC Newsround What are the Commonwealth ...**
Commonwealth Games, What are the Commonwealth Games? What is the Commonwealth? ... Which countries are the most successful? What are the Commonwealth Games? ...
news.bbc.co.uk/cbbcnews/hi/find_out/guides/2002/commonwealth_games/newsid_2078000/2078843.stm

18. **allAfrica.com: PanAfrica: Nigeria May Bid for 2014 Commonwealth ...**
Nigeria May Bid for 2014 Commonwealth Games. Email This Page Print This Page Visit The Publisher's Site. This Day (Lagos). December ...
allafrica.com/stories/200312090659.html

19. **AfricaOnline.com - Nigeria will bid for 2010 Commonwealth Games**
Nigeria will bid for 2010 Commonwealth Games. Nigeria flag (detail), (Africa Online Ltd.), PANA LAGOS, 22 June 2002 The Nigeria Olympic ...
www.africaonline.com/site/Articles/1,3,48358.jsp

20. **The Commonwealth Institute**
The Commonwealth Games. History of the Commonwealth Games. ... Previous Commonwealth Games hosts. The British Empire Games, Participating Countries. ...
www.commonwealth.org.uk/aboutCW/commGames.htm

21. **Google Directory - Sports > Events > Commonwealth Games**
Google, Directory Help Search only in Commonwealth Games Search the Web. Commonwealth Games, ...
directory.google.com/Top/Sports/ Events Commonwealth_Games/

22. **AfricaOnline.com - Nigeria names 41 athletes for Commonwealth ...**
    Nigeria names 41 athletes for Commonwealth Games. PANA LAGOS, 23 June 2002 Nigeria Sunday released a list of 41 athletes who will ...
    www.africaonline.com/site/Articles/1,3,48355.jsp
23. **ABC Sport - Netball - Commonwealth Games**
    Australia has recorded one of the most remarkable victories in international netball to win the gold medal at the Commonwealth Games in Manchester. ...
    www.abc.net.au/netball/international/ commgames/default.htm
24. **smh.com.au - The Sydney Morning Herald**
    Commonwealth Games, Schedule | Games guide | Tally.
    www.smh.com.au/specials/commonwealthgames/
25. **Department for Tourism, Sport and the Commonwealth Games...**
    Commonwealth Games ... It is not the intention of the legislation to restrict the use of Commonwealth Games references in normal language. ...
    www.dtscg.vic.gov.au/4A256B7500063206/All/ 2
    097D57E92D8DAD4A256B72001EB81B?OpenDocument
26. **SchlumbergerSema | Major Events Experience | Commonwealth**
    Commonwealth Games '98. Commonwealth Games '98, In November 1996, SchlumbergerSema ...
    www.schlumbergersema.com/majorevents/ experience
    cwealthgames98.htm
27. **Manchester City Council - Commonwealth Games 2002**
    Manchester City Council, find. You are in: Manchester City Council > Council wide information > Commonwealth Games. ...
    The XVII Commonwealth Games 2002. ...
    www.manchester.gov.uk/corporate/games/
28. **Yahooligans! - Sports and Recreation:Events:Commonwealth Games**
    Commonwealth Games Federation - get all the info you want about the next Commonwealth Games, from the official site.
    Commonwealth ...
    www.yahooligans.com/sports_and_recreation/ events
    Commonwealth_Games/

29. **Australian Swimming | Team Details - Commonwealth Games 2002**
Events & Records > Meets & Results > Commonwealth Games 2002 > Team Details. ... Team Details - Commonwealth Games 2002. ...
www.swimming.org.au/meets_and_results
teams.cfm?ObjectID=974

30. **Open Directory - Sports: Events: Commonwealth Games**
Commonwealth Games Federation - Official site offers the history of the Games, the role of the CGF and the nations and territories of the Commonwealth. ...
dmoz.org/Sports/Events/Commonwealth_Games/

31. **Commonwealth Games 2002 - Stockport pages**
The XVII Commonwealth Games 2002 have come and gone with Stockport residents playing a large part in the UK's biggest ever multi-sport event.
www.stockport.gov.uk/borough/2002/

32. **The Sunday Herald - Scotland's award-winning independent newspaper**
Scotland bids for Commonwealth Games. ... A twin-city bid is being considered, but that would require the Commonwealth Games Federation to change its rules. ...
www.sundayherald.com/38364

33. **allAfrica.com: PanAfrica: Nigeria May Bid for 2014 Commonwealth ...**
Nigeria May Bid for 2014 Commonwealth Games. Email This Page Print This Page Visit The Publisher's Site.
allafrica.com/stories/200312090659.html

34. **The Commonwealth Games**
The Commonwealth Games. When the ... The presence of tiny Kirsty underlined one of the key features of the 2002 Commonwealth Games. The organizers ...
www.oup.com/elt/global/products/ oald/newsreader com_game/

35. **Department for Tourism, Sport and the Commonwealth ...**
The Department for Tourism, Sport and the Commonwealth Games has a pivotal role in driving planning and preparations for the 2006 Commonwealth Games and the ...
www.dtscg.vic.gov.au/

36. **India for inclusion of cricket in 2010 Commonwealth Games : Sports ...**

India for inclusion of cricket in 2010 Commonwealth Games : Sports News : IndiaExpress.Com. ... in the Commonwealth Games 2010 but it has not been approved so far. ...

www.indiaexpress.com/news/sports/20031216-0.html

37. **CNN/SI - 1998 Commonwealth Games**

Queen Elizabeth presides over festive closing of Commonwealth Games. With political troubles ...

www.cnnsi.com/olympics/1998/commonwealth/

38. **Amateur Swimming Association**

COMMONWEALTH GAMES 2002 SPECIAL NEWS REPORTS AND MEDIA GUIDE. GAMES PHOTO GALLERY. Day-by-day reports. England ... COMMONWEALTH GAMES RESULTS. ...

www.britishswimming.org/specialevents/ commonwealths/2002 commonwealths.asp

39. **ManchesterOnline - Commonwealth Games Brochure**

Contents. dots Commonwealth Games Brochure. dots News. dots Sport. Dots Football. dots Entertainment. ... home > commonwealth games brochure. ...

www.manchesteronline.co.uk/gamesbrochure/

40. **The Commonwealth Games**

Link to home page The Commonwealth Games. Introduction. State Library of Victoria's Commonwealth Games web site.

www.statelibrary.vic.gov.au/slv/resources/cgames/

41. **Manchester Commonwealth Games 2002 New Zealand nzoom.com Site**

Manchester Commonwealth Games 2002 website, covers all news and information about the New Zealand Games team. Medal tables, TV ONE ...

games2002.nzoom.com/

42. **Microsoft Case Studies: Commonwealth Games, The**

Commonwealth Games, The. Microsoft Services helps design, deliver and support infrastructure for global sports event. ... Company Commonwealth Games, The, ...

www.microsoft.com/resources/casestudies/ CaseStudy.asp? CaseStudyID=13165

43. **Microsoft Case Studies: Commonwealth Games, The**
Commonwealth Games, The. Building an agile enterprise infrastructure. Posted ... version. Solution Overview. Company Commonwealth Games, The, ...
www.microsoft.com/resources/casestudies/
CaseStudy.asp?CaseStudyID=13164

44. **Commonwealth Games**
Commonwealth Games. ... It was also the first time since 1958 that South Africa participated. The 2002 Commonwealth Games were will be held in Manchester, England.
www.dfait-maeci.gc.ca/foreign_policy/ commonwealth/imoc317
en.asp

45. **Manchester 2002 Commonwealth Games**
Spectacular Opening Ceremony of the Manchester 2002 Commonwealth Games. ...
www.learn.co.uk/gmgcomp/

46. **XTRAMSN: Business: Business News: Channels Vie For Commonwealth**
Channels Vie For Commonwealth Games 17/12/2003 10:29 AM - The Independent Sky TV and the free-to-air television networks are battling it out for TV rights to ...
xtramsn.co.nz/business/05189-2618999,00.html

47. **Commonwealth Games the target of Bushman protests 30/7/02**
Commonwealth Games the target of Bushman protests. Pro Bushman sympathisers have targeted the opening ceremony of the Commonwealth Games in Manchester, England...
www.survival-international.org/bushman_020730.htm

48. **Badminton Canada: High Performance Selection Criteria - 2002...**
High Performance SELECTION CRITERIA, High Performance Selection Criteria. 2002 Commonwealth Games. Introduction: ... Selection Priority: 2002 Commonwealth Games:
www.badminton.ca/eng/highperf/2002/cwealthg.shtml

49. **Melbourne 2006 Commonwealth Games**
> Home > International > Melbourne 2006 Commonwealth Games. Printer Friendly Version. Melbourne 2006 Commonwealth Games.
www.dcita.gov.au/Article/ 0,,0_1-2_1-3_209-4_105592,00.html

50. **Guardian Unlimited Sport | Special reports**

Commonwealth Games closing ceremony, A festival ...

sport.guardian.co.uk/commonwealthgames2002 0,12238,753640,00.html

51. **Hamilton 2010 Commonwealth Games Bid Secreteriat - Home**

The Commonwealth Games – A special opportunity for all. ... The Government of Canada is pleased to work closely with Commonwealth Games Canada (CGC). ...

www.pch.gc.ca/special/commonwealth2010/index_e.cfm

52. **The 2002 Commonwealth Games**

Location: Home - Sport Canada - The 2002 Commonwealth Games, 2003/12/15. ... The 2002 Commonwealth Games. ... The Manchester 2002 Commonwealth Games include 17 sports:

www.pch.gc.ca/progs/sc/calen/commonwealth-2002_e.cfm

53. **Commonwealth Games Medallists - Athletics (Men)**

United Kingdom Track and Field All-Time Lists - Commonwealth Games Medallists - Athletics (Men). ... COMMONWEALTH GAMES MEDALLISTS - ATHLETICS (MEN)...

www.gbrathletics.com/ic/cg.htm

54. **Commonwealth Games Athletics Results**

Sporting Heroes Logo, <<return to athletics-heroes.net. Commonwealth Games Athletics Results. 2002 Commonwealth Games Mens Results ...

www.sporting-heroes.net/athletics-heroes/stats_athletics/commonwealth/commonwealth.htm

55. **Department for Victorian Communities: homepage**

Office of Commonwealth Games Coordination (previously located at Level 48, Nauru House, 80 Collins Street, Melbourne). This department brings a range of community and local government based programs together to improve...

www.dvc.vic.gov.au/

56. **Commonwealth Games - Wikipedia**

Printable version. Not logged in Log in | Help. Commonwealth Games. From Wikipedia, the free encyclopedia. ... British Empire and Commonwealth Games. ...

en.wikipedia.org/wiki/Commonwealth_Games

57. **ABC Sport - Netball - Aus v Sth Africa 2003**
The other changes to the Australian 12 since the Commonwealth Games in Manchester last July are inclusion of Natasha Chokljat for Alex Hodge who has been ...
www.abc.net.au/netball/international/ ausvsa2003/default.

58. **Major Projects - Melbourne 2006 Commonwealth Games Athletes' ...**
Melbourne 2006 Commonwealth Games Athletes' Village, ww.majorprojects.vic.gov.au/web3/majorproj.nsf/allDocs/ WPCFAA7E0ACB7957D2CA256C24001A6450?OpenDocument

59. **British Commonwealth Paraplegic Games**
Brief history of the games.
www.internationalgames.net/britishCommParGames.htm

60. **Google Directory - Sports > Events > Commonwealth Games > 2002 ...**
Manchester 2002 Commonwealth Games - http:/ www.commonwealthgames.com/ Official site offers the event schedules, spectator information including tickets and ... directory.google.com/Top/Sports/Events Commonwealth_Games/ 2002_Manchester/

61. **idaho technology**
COMMONWEALTH GAMES BUSINESS CLUB http:/ www.nwbusinessclub.com/ Launched ... dramatically. Commonwealth Games Business Club. Commonwealth Connect...
www.idaho.uk.net/portfolio.asp?ID=8&Sector=9

62. **$6.5 million Commonwealth Games deficit - Business - www.theage**
Commonwealth Games budget was approved by the auditor general.
www.theage.com.au/articles/2003/11/06/ 1068013306360.html? from=storyrhs

63. **theage.com.au - The Age**
Commonwealth Games, Schedule | Medal Tally. ...
www.theage.com.au/sport/commonwealthgames/

64. **Australian Commonwealth Games Association (ACGA): Website Detail ...**
The website of the Australian Commonwealth Games Association (ACGA) - the official source for information regarding Australia's participation in past and ...
www.acn.net.au/website/info/827.htm

65. **www.triathlon.org**

Bronze Medal: Nicole Hackett (AUS). Double Gold for Canada at Commonwealth Game Montgomery and Whitfield wins Games titles (August 4th, 2002 - Manchester, ENG).

www.triathlon.org/multi-games/mg-2002/events commonwealth2002/ news/post-race-story-results.htm

66. **This is Bolton | Commonwealth Games**

Commonwealth Games 2002 powered by the Bolton Evening News. Bolton news, Bolton sport and so much more from This Is Bolton. ... Commonwealth Games. ...

www.thisisbolton.co.uk/lancashire/ bolton/sport/games2002/

67. **Scotsman.com News - Commonwealth Games**

Commonwealth Games, 2006 Games team bank ... one high to another. The incredible Commonwealth Games is over and already I'm just a day... ...

www.news.scotsman.com/topics.cfm?tid=418

68. **Games Relay**

Commonwealth Games Relay. About | The Reading Relay Instant story games Links Write a story about the Games Commonwealth Rela Homepage.

kotn.ntu.ac.uk/commonwealth/

69. **XVI Commonwealth Games Kuala Lumpur 98 from Sadec Online**

The XVI Commonwealth Games 98 (aka Kuala Lumpur 98) coverage. Latest Games and Sports information online. ... The XVI Commonwealth Games (KL 98 Games) Archives. Archive site includes games and sports information, medal tally, photo gallery, and results.

www.sadec.com/KL98/Pages/Index.htm

70. **Prairie Gold Saskatchewan Sports - Commonwealth Games**

Commonwealth Games. BIOGRAPHY-Adams, Robert BIOGRAPHY-Beerling, Dennis BIOGRAPHY-Garvie, Gordon BIOGRAPHY-Mitchelmore, Harold BIOGRAPHY ...

www.publib.saskatoon.sk.ca/sports/pages/cwealth.html

71. **Major Projects - Melbourne 2006 Commonwealth Games Athletes'**

Melbourne 2006 Commonwealth Games Athletes' Village. Melbourne Sports and Aquatic Centre (Stage 2). ... Melbourne 2006 Commonwealth Games Athletes' Village, ...

www.majorprojects.vic.gov.au/Web3%5Cmajorproj.nsf headingpagesdisplay/ ProjectsSports+and+recreationMelbou...

72. **Commonwealth Secretariat - Links**

Commonwealth Games Federation. ... Aims: Activities: The federation promotes the Commonwealth Games, held every four years, midway between the Olympic Games. ...

www.thecommonwealth.org/dynamic chooseCatResDet.asp?OrgID=73

73. **Unveiling of the Commonwealth Games Clock Marble Foyer, Parliament**

Speeches. 19 June 2003. TRANSCRIPT OF THE PRIME MINISTER THE HON JOHN HOWARD MP UNVEILING OF THE COMMONWEALTH GAMES CLOCK, MARBLE FOYER, PARLIAMENT HOUSE. E&OE.......

www.pm.gov.au/news/speeches/speech110.html

74. **Yahoo! Directory International Games > Commonwealth Games**

International Games > Commonwealth Games Directory > Recreation > Sports > Events > International Games > Commonwealth Games, Search the Web just this category. ...

dir.yahoo.com/Recreation/Sports/Events/International_Games/ Commonwealth_Games/

75. **Commonwealth Games Trivia and Quizzes**

Special Lists: Newest Quizzes Options: Create a Commonwealth Games Quiz [Special Instructions: READ ME] - Show Ranks Gold Member Stats: Highest 'Commonwealth ...

www.funtrivia.com/quizlistgold.cfm?cat=5775

76. **allAfrica.com: PanAfrica: Four Commonwealth Games Officials Arrive ...**

Four Commonwealth Games Officials Arrive Today for CHOGM. Email This Page Print This Page Visit The Publisher's Site. Daily Trust (Abuja). ...

allafrica.com/stories/200312030370.html

77. **XTRA: National Video: Another Commonwealth Games ...**

Another Commonwealth Games Possible? The possibility of NZ hosting another Commonwealth Games isn't out of the question. 56k 125k 300k. ...

www.xtra.co.nz/broadband/0,10979-2939610-300,00.html

17
Cricket

1. **Wisden CricInfo**
   The world's largest cricket site, CricInfo.com contains live scores, the latest cricket news, features, player columns and profiles, audio and video, shopping ...
   www.cricinfo.com/
2. **Cricket news, fun, scorecards, live coverage and features from...**
   Latest cricket news, results, scorecards, live coverage, statistics, team updates and comment from the world of cricket.
   www.cricket365.com/
3. **Cricket Home**
   Cricket Home. About Cricket. Cricket is a high performance, extremely flexible system for monitoring trends in time-series data. Cricket ...
   cricket.sourceforge.net/
4. **Cricketworld**
   Headlines, links to club and school news, postcards, shop, games, and forum.
   www.cricketworld.com/
5. **Cricket-Online: LIVE scores, stats, news and more!**
   Includes scores, articles, software, emerging players, information on international cricket, events...
   www.cricket-online.org/
6. **Lord's - The Home of Cricket**
   Barbara Cassani confirms key role for Lord's in London's Olympic bid. Lord's will play a key role in London's bid to stage the 2012 Olympic Games, according to ...
   www.lords.org/

7. **Guardian Unlimited Sport | Cricket**

   Offers news and features about test, county and league cricket with live match coverage, interviews...

   sport.guardian.co.uk/cricket/

8. **Cricket news, reports and statistics from Channel 4**

   Cricket site run by English host TV broadcaster Channel 4 overing English and World test cricket, includes comprehensive all-time international test cricket ...

   www.cricket4.com/

9. **Sify.com - India's premier sports portal**

   In Sports. Cricket. Tennis. Motor Sport. Football. Hockey. Others. More Links. Columns New. Discussions. Desktop Scores. Cricket Alerts. Wallpapers. Screensavers. Slideshows ...

   www.khel.com/

10. **ecb.co.uk - the official site of the England and Wales Cricket ...**

    Nottinghamshire's director of cricket Mick Newell has vowed he will fight to keep Kevin Pietersen at Trent Bridge despite the fact that Pietersen wants to be ...

    www.ecb.co.uk/

11. **BBC SPORT | Cricket**

    Sport Homepage. Cricket. Results/Scores. More Statistics. — Aus v Ind. Counties. ... Our resident Aussie has his own ideas on how to jazz up cricket. ...

    news.bbc.co.uk/sport/hi/english/cricket/default.stm

12. **BBC SPORT | Cricket**

    Offers news and results for all levels of cricket with interviews, video and audio clips.

    news.bbc.co.uk/sport1/hi/cricket/default.stm

13. **Indiatimes - Cricket**

    Live cricket scores, updates for all matches, cricket match schedules, news related to cricket world...

    cricket.indiatimes.com/

14. **Australian Cricket**

    Baggy Green - the home of Australian cricket. The very latest news from Cricket Australia, live scores from around the world and much more. ...

    www.baggygreen.com.au/

15. **rediff.com: The Cricket section home page**
    Statistical highlights: Aus vs Ind Nel enjoys dream honeymoon The SA paceman enjoyed what cricket fans might see as the dream ... Advertisement. Cricket Archive. ...
    www.rediff.com/cricket/
16. **Cricketnext.com - For Passionate Cricket Lovers Only**
    The most action packed Cricket site of them all, CricketNext.com's informative resources, interactive elements and on-the-ball news and match coverage makes ...
    www.cricketnext.com/
17. **Thatscricket: Cricket, the way you want it!**
    Indian cricket site providing news, statistics, results, player profiles and regulations for internationa...
    www.thatscricket.com/
18. **123India Cricket**
    World's best cricket site, Cricket.123india.com contains audio and text Commentary, desktop scorecard, the latest cricket news, features, player profiles ...
    cricket.123india.com/
19. **Abc of Cricket - Cricket News - Cricket Scores - Live Cricket...**
    Includes information, resources, live scores, match schedules, news, feature stories, tips, and statistics.
    www.abcofcricket.com/
20. **Wisden CricInfo**
    Contains history of women's cricket, news, English domestic cricket schedule, details of development...
    www.cricket.org/link_to_database/NATIONAL/ENG/
21. **About Cricket**
    Results Australia Bangladesh England India Kenya New Zealand Pakistan South Africa Sri Lanka West Indies Zimbabwe Other Countries Women's Cricket ICC Stats ...
    www.cricket.org/link_to_database/ABOUT_CRICKET/
22. **Cricket Betting - Bet On Cricket At Select Online Sportsbooks**
    Recommended Sportsbooks To Bet On Cricket! Click to Visit. CRICKET BETTING. Find The Best Sportsbooks Online To Bet On Cricket And The World Cup! ...
    www.cricketbetting.ws/

23. **Play-Cricket the ECB Cricket Network**
Officially endorsed by the ECB and MCC, Play-Cricket provides powerful, interactive web sites that...
www.play-cricket.com/

24. **Cricket the Robot**
Cricket is an autonomous robot that walks around by moving all six legs using three motors. He avoids ... batteries. Cricket Features. 6 ...
home.earthlink.net/~henryarnold/

25. **Yahoo! Sport - Cricket**
South Africa, Monday, Jan. More Photos - Cricket. ... Yahoo! Mobile. Mobile Games Cricket Play Cricket on your phone! plus. Keep up with this ...
uk.sports.yahoo.com/cr/

26. **Yorkshire County Cricket Club**
AOL Users Please Click Here to open the Site. Official County Cricket Club web site
www.yorkshireccc.org.uk/

27. **HTCricket.com - India's favourite sport, 24 hours**
Provides news articles and commentary concerning the sport and its players in India. Also contains...
www.htcricket.com/ - 64k - 19 Jan 2004

28. **New Zealand Cricket**
www.nzcricket.co.nz/

29. **United States of America Cricket Association**
The United States of America Cricket Association. ... Official Website of the United States of America Cricket Association.
Official governing body for US cricket.
www.usaca.org/

30. **MCG - Home**
MCG Trust, seating, policies, how to get there and more! Cricket Seating Plan. ... Great for school projects! Go to the official site of the Melbourne Cricket Club. ...
www.mcg.org.au/

31. **Sporting Life - Cricket**
The latest news and live updates about international and county cricket. UK.
www.sportinglife.com/cricket/news/

32. **Lancashire County Cricket Club - for cricket, corporate ...**
    Official website for Lancashire County Cricket Club and its 68 bedroom hotel, the Old Trafford Lodge. In ... hire. ...
    www.lccc.co.uk/

33. **Cricket News, Live cricket, Indian Cricket, live scores**
    A devoted website on cricket covering Live Scores with statistics, rankings, online polls, schedules, contests, Cricket World Cup 2003 and more. CRICKET NEWS. ...
    www.thisiscricket.com/

34. **Sky Sports - The Best Sport Coverage From Around The World**
    Latest cricket news, fixtures, tables, rankings and player photos, plus cricket forum and statistics...
    msn.skysports.com/skysports/cricket

35. **Lord's - Laws of Cricket**
    Laws of Cricket.
    www.lords.org/cricket/laws.asp

36. **West Indies Cricket Board**
    Official home of the West Indies Cricket Board (WICB), the governing body of West Indian cricket....
    www.windiescricket.com/

37. **USCricket.com - Your guide to CRICKET in the United States**
    The complete source of cricket in the USA, USCricket.com contains detailed News, Scores, Leagues, Teams, Players, Tournaments, Grounds and other information on ...
    www.uscricket.com/

38. **Amul - The Taste of India - ISO Certification of the ...**
    How the Rankings are calculated, the Vision behind the Rankings, how they are different, and the team. Cricket as seen through the World of Amul's Topicals. ...
    www.cricket.amul.com/

39. **Sport**
    News and commentary. UK.
    sport.independent.co.uk/cricket/

40. **Cricket Supplies - Cricket Equipment Store and Oakley Sunglasses ...**
    Cricket Equipment Shop - One of the largest selections of adult cricket bats, junior cricket bats, cricket equipment and cricket oakley sunglasses on the ...
    www.cricketsupplies.com/

41. **Cricket Victoria**
... KEITH BURNHAM DIES. Monday, 19 January 2004. Cricket Victoria was saddened to learn of the passing of Footscray Cricket Club stalwart, Keith Burnham early this ...
www.viccricket.asn.au/

42. **BBC SPORT | Cricket**
Low Graphics version | Change Edition. | Help. Sport Homepage. Cricket. Results/Scores. More Statistics. ——. Aus v Ind. Counties. ...
www.bbc.co.uk/go/homepage/int/idx/spo/cric/-/cricket/

43. **Cricket Web**
Cricket Web is dedicated to International and Domestic cricket but we also cover cricket games, cricket downloads, cricket photos, cricket autographs, live ...
www.cricketweb.net/

44. **Dansk Cricket Forbund**
Official site with tour information and other aspects of cricket in Denmark. Some portions of this...
www.cricket.dk/

45. **Salute to Women's Cricket : Home Page**
Women's Cricket : International, Statistics, Players Profiles, and UK Domestic Matches. ... Profile. [Cricket Statz details]. Cricket Statz ...
www.webbsoc.demon.co.uk/

46. **QCA - Queensland Cricket**
Official Home of Queensland Cricket.Official QCA site providing access to resources and information for all participants. Includes fixtures...
www.qldcricket.com.au/

47. **ABC Sport - Cricket**
David Hookes dies aged 48 [RealMedia 28k+] [WinMedia 28k+]. Cricket Essentials. ... Cricket legend who called Tasmania home. j darling ...
www.abc.net.au/cricket/default.htm

48. **ABC Sport - Cricket**
Contains up to date cricket information, photos, scorecards, profiles, news, forum and interviews...
www.abc.net.au/cricket/

49. **intro2**

20,000 seat outdoor concert ampitheatre showcasing top artists and musicians. Located at 2121 North 83rd Avenue, Phoenix Arizona 85035 or call (602)-254-7200.

cricket-pavilion.com/

50. **Cricket news, views and controversies**

News, views and controversies regarding cricket around the world, tributes to masters of the past....

www.gnubies.com/cricket.htm .

51. **The Cricket Indoor Location System: An NMS Project @ MIT LCS**

The Cricket Indoor Location System. overview, -, cricket project description. ... Cricket people. Faculty: Hari Balakrishnan; Seth Teller; Erik Demaine. ...

nms.lcs.mit.edu/projects/cricket/

52. **Sri Lanka Web Server-Cricket**

The official site with current and future competitions, player profiles, scoreboards, and press reports.

www.lanka.net/cricket/

53. **CaribbeanCricket.com**

Includes news, commentary and discussion for cricket in the West Indies and the Caribbean.

www.caribbeancricket.com/

54. **Deutscher Cricket Bund**

World > Deutsch > Sport > Ballsport > Cricket

www.dcb-cricket.de/

55. **Cricket Statistics and Ratings for Test Cricket and one Day ...**

A range of computer ratings of players, teams and performances from Test Cricket and One Day Internation...

www.cricketworld.com.au/

56. **The Cricket**

World > Svenska > Kultur > Musik > Recensioner

www.thecricket.nu/

57. **CricketZone.Com**

Tune in to cricketzone.com for Live Coverage of all cricket matches round the world round the clock Current Series: India in Australia click here for live ...

www.cricketzone.com/

58. **Cricket!**

World > Français > Sports > Balles et ballons

www.eleves.ens.fr/home/mlnguyen/divers/cricket/

59. **Warwickshire County Cricket Club**

Official website of the county cricket club.

www.warwickccc.org.uk/

60. **Federazione Cricket Italiana**

Information and history, championships and tournaments, the team Italia and the clubs. Archive, download...

www.crickitalia.org/

61. **Supersportzone**

www.supercricket.co.za/

62. **An Explanation of Cricket**

An Explanation of Cricket. Contents. ... together again. The Two Forms of Cricket. Cricket is played in two very distinct forms. Covers both the basics and specialised aspects of this sport.

www.cs.purdue.edu/homes/hosking/ cricket/explanation.htm

63. **David Dyte's Zimbabwean Cricket Page**

Zimbabwean Cricket Page. Well, now. ... In the meantime, try The Official ZCU Site for up to date information. What's on the Zimbabwe Cricket Page? ...

zikzak.zikzak.net/~ddyte/

64. **dreamcricket.com**

Create dream selections by choosing players from any of the participating teams. Stock market style game.

www.dreamcricket.com/

65. **United Cricket Board of South Africa**

Names of 14 players to represent South Africa in the 2004 ICC Under-19 Cricket World Cup ...

www.cricket.co.za/

66. **Cricket Direct**

The home of the best cricket equipment in Great Britain. We tock a wide range of world-class brands, at...

www.cricketdirect.co.uk/acatalog/

67. **Ananova - Sport - Cricket**

Latest news and scores from football, cricket, rugby, motorsport and horse racing, plus updates on other sports from athletics to yachting. Ball-by-ball scores, latest news and match reports, fixtures, tables and batting and bowling averages.
www.ananova.com/sport/cricket/

68. **SLAM! Sports - Cricket**

West Indies hopes remain alive in cricket Test versus South Africa CENTURION, South Africa (AP) - Ramnaresh Sarwan and Chris Gayle each scored centuries Monday ...
www.canoe.ca/SlamCricket/home.html

69. **Cricket Canyon, Jewelry and Beaded Gifts**

Personalized Jewelry Watches Beaded Gifts Shopping Cart Wholesale Links.
www.cricketcanyon.com/

70. **Women's Cricket (formerly Women's Cricket Association) merged with ...**

To provide local club, regional and national information about Women's Cricket in the United Kingdom. Providing links to other cricket and related sites. ...
users.ox.ac.uk/~beth/wca.htm

71. **Cricket Heroes - A Photographic encyclopaedia of International...**

Information, athletics heroes, cricket heroes, football heroes, golf heroes, rugby heroes, tennis heroes. about us. ... statistics and results. Cricket Test Match Results. ...
www.sporting-heroes.net/cricket-heroes/default.asp

72. **The Handy Cricket Home Page**

The Handy Cricket is a Microchip PIC-based microcontroller system that lets you build mobile robots, kinetic artworks, and other programmable interactive ...
handyboard.com/cricket/

73. **About Search - Find it now!**

Cricket Displaying results 1 to 10 of 727 Cricket Betting - Cricket Betting and Wagering Find cricket betting resources. ...
search.about.com
fullsearch.htm?terms=cricketandIAM=URL_cricket

74. **Women's Cricket Australia Website**

National organisation that co-ordinates and promotes women's cricket in Australia. Home of the 1998...

www.ausport.gov.au/wca/

75. **NepalCricket : Anything/Everything About Nepal's Cricket**

Features cricket related information, news, player biographies and pictures, and a newsletter.

www.cricket.com.np/

76. **World Cup Cricket 2003 Schedule and Predictions**

Africa and Zimbabwe.Forecast World Cup 2003 in South Africa and Zimbabwe.Betting World Cup 2003 in South Africa and Zimbabwem Performers World Cup Cricket 2003, Who ...

www.cricketastrology.com/

77. **Nottinghamshire County Cricket Club - Trent Bridge**

Official Site. Includes up-to-date news concerning the club and forthcoming international fixtures....

www.nottsccc.co.uk/

78. **Cricket Index**

Cricket Index Cricket Index lists cricket websites from all over the world. ... There are currently 287 links for you to choose from at Cricket Index. Cricket. ...

www.cricketindex.com/

79. **ESSEX COUNTY CRICKET**

Live scores, photos, action shots, news, statistics, and results.

www.essexcricket.org.uk/

80. **World Cricket Store UK - Cricket Merchandise, Cricket Shirts...**

World Cricket Store, ... Version 3.0 © Copyright 2001-2003 by World Cricket Store Ltd. Web / E-Commerce Development by Webcogs, Webcogs - Software Engineers.

www.worldcricketstore.com/default.asp?portalid=41

81. **ScottishCricket Limited**

Online home of the bi-monthly Scottish Cricketeer offers news, results and features including youth...

www.cricketeurope.org/SCOTLAND/

82. **ACT Cricket: Home -> Latest News**

The win places the Comets in equal 1st place on the Cricket Australia Cup ladder at this point, with one match against Western Australia remaining. ...

www.cricketact.com/

83. **Cricket Statz**

Cricket statistics software for individuals, clubs and associations to generate web pages, professional charts and reports. ...

www.cricketstatz.com/

84. **Cricket Science**

Offers educational products that range from a video about the butterflies of Yellowstone to living...

www.cricketscience.com/

85. **EA SPORTS | Product Description - Cricket 2002**

Cricket 2002. Rated: G. ... Description: "EA SPORTS Cricket 2002 will truly be a hallmark game, not only for Cricket, but also for all sport simulations.".

www.easportscricket.com/

86. **Cricket-Hockey.com - Shop online for UK Cricket and Field Hockey ...**

Shop online for uk cricket and field hockey equipment such as cricket bats, field hockey sticks, clothing, helmets, junior and childrens equipment etc. ...

www.cricket-hockey.co.uk/

87. **cricmania - Cricket and only cricket**

Breaking news from AFP, live scorecards and searchable statistics for players and teams.

www.cricmania.com/

88. **Indoor Cricket World - Front Page**

Includes a description of the game, rules, photos, and news. Also features results and schedules of...

www.indoorcricketworld.com/

89. **Learn Cricket. Introduction to the sport!**

If you are clueless about cricket, then this is the ideal place to know more about the sport. This site aims to instruct readers who are new to the sport. ...

cricketlearn.tripod.com/

90. **Northern California Cricket Association (NCCA, Inc.)**
One of California's top cricket clubs, situated in the Bay Area, with information on local leagues, and international news. NCCA,Inc. ... THE SPIRIT OF CRICKET. ...
www.ncalcricket.org/

91. **Cricket Graphics**
Geocities Banner Exchange. Welcome..To..Cricket..Graphics. Best Viewed With. Site Created 3-14-98.
www.geocities.com/Heartland/Pointe/8758/

92. **Berkshire Cricket League.**
Berkshire Cricket League - Official Website. Containing latest news, results, discussions and club information! Testing.
www.berkshirecricketleague.org.uk/

93. **International Cricket Council Official Website**
The International Cricket Council (ICC) website
www.icc.cricket.org/

94. **Manitoba Cricket Association Inc.**
Manitoba Cricket Association. Damian Mills Junior Cricket Trust Fund. ... Contact US General Inquiries: MCA@cricket.mb.ca Webmaster: Ray.Ramrattan@cricket.mb.ca.
www.cricket.mb.ca/

95. **Cricket Press, Website design, maintenance and promotion**
Offers design maintenance, and promotion services.
www.crickpress.com/

96. **Fiddling Cricket Music: home page**
Fiddling Cricket Music home page
www.fiddlingcricket.com/

97. **Cricket - the sport - cricket matches - cricket fans**
The sport of cricket is popular throughout the world (except in the US – where bowlers and wickets are essentially unknown). ... Cricket - the Sport. ...
www.cricket-news.com/

98. **The Cricket Cage**
Arts > Visual Arts > Computer Graphics > 3D > Bryce and Poser
www.thecricketcage.com/

99. **ANTS - Cricket Clubs**

ANTS Cricket Clubs and Associations. ... 3D Animated Flags by Crames Studios, We Are 3D TM. Australia, Vic NSW Qld WA Tas NT ACT SA, Cricket Australia. ...

www.ants.com.au/cricket_clubs.htm

100. **espnstar.com - powered by ESPN STAR Sports: Cricket**

Brings you the best in Cricket coverage from around the world, with News, Stats, Results, Fantasy Games, Competitions, Multimedia and much more ...

www.espnstar.com/jsp/cda/cricket/cricket_index.html

101. **Cricket at Tiscali**

TODAY IN CRICKET. ... Get up to 50% off all your gym gear in the Tiscali sports shop. Plus there's an extra 10% off everything for Tiscali customers. CRICKET NEWS. ...

www.tiscali.co.uk/sport/cricket/

102. **WCCC - Worcestershire County Cricket Club**

Official web-site of the Worcestershire County Cricket Club.

www.wccc.co.uk/

103. **Tree Peony - Chinese Tree Peonies - Peony Nursery**

The Garden Gate - Peony Heaven. Specializing in Chinese Tree Peonies. Provides useful information...

www.treepeony.com/

104. **cricket centre online**

Stocking a wide assortment of high quality cricket equipment including bats and accessories, apparel,...

www.cricketcentre.com.au/

105. **Test Cricket Ratings Service: Home Page**

Ratings updated after each test series. Historical ratings available back to 1877. Free e-mail update...

www.geocities.com/Colosseum/Stands/8832/

106. **SACA - Home**

Program. The following PDF file has the latest 2003-04 cricket program for Adelaide Oval. ... website. 2003-04 Adelaide Oval Cricket Program (PDF). ...

www.cricketsa.com.au/

107. **ANTS - Cricket Sites**
ANTS Cricket Sites. The Summer Game we think about all year long. ... Cricket Clubs and Associations, Cricket Software : Statistics Scoring. ...
www.ants.com.au/sitescricket.htm

108. **Swiss Cricket Association**
The Swiss Cricket Association is the internationally recognized body responsible for cricket in Switzerland. These pages ... this country.
www.swisscricket.ch/

109. **Australian Indoor Cricket Federation**
Focuses on Indoor Cricket in Australia, with news, schedules and results of National and International...
www.aicf.com.au/

110. **Backyard cricket.**
The rules and fools of the game of backyard cricket, with side notes on beach cricket and the Australian way of life. ... BACKYARD and BEACH CRICKET. ...
www.freelance.primetap.com/backyard.htm

111. **All Coupons**
Home All Sports Antepost Dogs Baseball Basketball Boxing Cricket Darts Football Golf Greyhounds Horse Racing Ice Hockey Motor Racing Politics Rugby Union ...
www.willhill.com/iibs/EN/ allsportsandcoupons.asp?sport=CR

112. **Action Packed Cricket Video Tapes: Action Packed Cricket**
DVDs, video and audio tapes featuring the greatest names in the game of cricket from the past and...
www.cricketvideo.com/

113. **Scoreboards, Bats and Equipment - Welcome to SLR cricket, UK**
Scoreboards, bats, practice nets, gloves, stumps, pads, clothing, sightscreens, line markers and all other cricket equipment are supplied by UK specialist ...
www.slrcricket.co.uk/

114. **Hampshire County Cricket Club, Official Website**
Old Hampshire photos required for Web Site The popular Hampshire Cricket website continues to be one of the countries leading club sites going with an average ...
www.hampshire.cricinfo.com/

115. **Kent County Cricket Club - Official Website containing Latest Club**

The official website of Kent County Cricket Club containing latest news,clubmrchandise, player information, playing records, marketing, membership, fixtures ...
www.kentcountycricket.co.uk/

116. **Durham County Cricket Club**

Recreation cameron diaz nude and carmen electra nude free sports cul video sports cricket competitions county championship clubs filmati di rotte in culo ...
www.durham-ccc.org.uk/

117. **Cricket UK, News results, fixtures features from Cricket.co.uk**

Cricket.co.uk has the all the latest UK Cricket, International and worldwide news plus features and results comment on all things about cricket. ...
www.cricket.co.uk/

118. **The CC Morris Cricket Library and Collection**

The CC Morris Cricket Library and Collection website has been moved to http://www.haverford.edu/library/cricket/.
www.haverford.edu/library/cricket/CCMORRIS.HTM

119. **Virtual Cricket**

Virtual Cricket - cricket simulation software for predicting match results based upon players career data.
www.jcole.freeserve.co.uk/vc/

120. **Ajax - Home World > Nederlands > Sport > Cricket**

www.ajax-sc.nl/cricket/

121. **Sports Star**

Players from Australia, New Zealand, India, and Pakistan.
www.koolcelebrities.com/sports/cricket/

122. **MCC - Home**

The official site includes news, member services, clubs, online publications and shop plus details...
www.mcc.org.au/

123. **MagicCricket- Ball-by-ball simulated audio-visual cricket coverage**

Live Cricket- Near-television multimedia webcast, ball-by- ball simulated audio-visual coverage and cricketing action like never before from the award-winning ...
www.magiccricket.com/

124. **Sydney Cricket and Sports Ground Trust**
Sydney Aquatic Centre, Sydney Cricket Ground, Sydney Athletic Centre. Details of membership services, corporate sales, corporate relations, functions, event operations,...
www.scgt.nsw.gov.au/

125. **Open Directory - Sports: Cricket**
Open Directory Project, about dmoz | help. the entire directory. Top: Sports: Cricket (1,207), Description. By ...
dmoz.org/Sports/Cricket/

126. **This is Cricket**
An in-depth links based site dedicated to fullfilling all your cricket requirements, with over 800 links to cricket-related sites.
www.thisis-cricket.com/

127. **cricket.rickeyre.com**
The personal cricket website of Rick Eyre. Established in December 1994, it is one of the oldest cricket websites still in existence. ...
www.rickeyre.com/cricket/

128. **CricketCoachMaster Home Page**
... ATTENTION !!! Highly specialist Cricket Coaching for Schools, Clubs, Counties, National Teams and Individuals delivered by Highly Specialist Coaches. ...
www.cricketcoachmaster.co.uk/

129. **Hong Kong Cricket Association**
Hong Kong Cricket Association
www.hkca.cricket.org/

130. **The Cricket Gear — Home Page**
Quality cricket equipment including bats, protective gear, balls and clothing. USA.
www.cricketgear.com/

131. **Flash detection**
www.pwcratings.com/

132. **SPORT - Cricket Frontpage**
Includes County Cricket, Internationals, One Day Series, Tests, the Ashes, the World Cup. Plus live...
www.compuserve.co.uk/channels/sport/ cricket
cricket_home.asp

133. **Click To Enter MCC**

Includes all the latest news, schedules and cricket information. Illinois.

www.midwestcricket.org/

134. **Cable and Wireless 2002 West Indies Cricket Series...**

Official hosts of West Indies cricket home series.

www.candw.cricket.bb/

135. **Wisden CricInfo**

... Best of 2003 - a look back at the cricket year that was January issue OUT NOW, cricshop.com, ... Buy "Ground Rules" Acclaimed cricket hardback, ...

usa.cricinfo.com/db/NATIONAL/RSA/

136. **The Queensland Blind Cricket Association Inc Homepage**

The Home of Queensland Blind Cricket. Are you interested in umpiring or scoring? ... Graphics Version. you are blind cricket fan at our new homepage.

www.qbca.freeservers.com/

137. **Welcome to - Test Cricket Online**

Test reports from around the world, comment, scores and links. Articles on issues affecting world...

cricketonline.20m.com/

138. **gameofcricket.com - Index**

Buy and Sell Shares of your Favorite Cricket Players, Get Live Match Scores and the Latest Cricket News Updated by the Second, Play the Interactive Quiz, Win ...

www.gameofcricket.com/

139. **HowSTAT! The Cricket Statisticians - Home Page**

HowSTAT is a website providing access to hundreds of cricket records, statistics and graphs of all kinds. ... News. Cricket News and Stories. ...

www.howstat.com.au/

140. **The Swing of a Cricket Ball**

The Swing of a Cricket Ball. Since ... StudyWeb. References. Here is an incomplete list of references related to cricket ball swing. If ...

orca.rsmas.miami.edu/~majumdar/cricket.html

141. **Spicy Cricket Animation!—"3D Computer Character Design and...**

3D Computer Character Animation for Film, TV, Multimedia and Games. Character Animator. Provides work samples, bio, and resources.

www.spicycricket.com/

142. **WACA - Home of The Retravision Warriors - CATCHTHESPIRIT**

Includes details of local teams, news, results, profiles and upcoming events. Western Australia.

www.waca.com.au/

143. **Canada Cricket Online**

www.canadacricket.com/

144. **UK Blind Cricket Home Page**

Official site of blind cricket in the UK. Includes league rules, results, averages and other information.

members.aol.com/bbscricket/

18
Diving

1. **PADI - The way the world learns to dive**
   The largest and most recognized diving organization around the world with courses ranging from Snorkeling...
   www.padi.com/
2. **Scuba Diving Magazine**
   RSD has objective equipment evaluations, information on dive sites the world over and dive medicine answers.
   www.scubadiving.com/
3. **USA Diving**
   WORLD CUP DIVING TRIALS - World Cup Diving Trials, Huntersville, NC More. USA DIVING PRODUCTS - Hoodies, shorts, t-shirts and more. ...
   www.usdiving.org/
4. **Scubadoc (Diving Medicine Online)**
   Updated information about diving and undersea medicine for the diver, the medical professional and an excellent reference source for the medical specialist. ...
   www.scuba-doc.com/
5. **ukdiving-homepage**
   Diving and Scuba resource UK, used kit wanted and for sale sections, UK Wreck Database, find a buddy,...
   www.ukdiving.co.uk/
6. **The Cave Diving Website**
   Your questions about cave diving…answered (including how to learn to cave dive). ... What is it? Cave Diving's Most Important Safety Rules. ...
   www.cavediving.com/

7. **Diving Unlimited International / drysuit manufacture**
Dedicated to developing innovative diving equipment, Diving Unlimited International's ultimate purpose is to provide the diver with superior comfort and ...
www.dui-online.com/

8. **US Masters Diving Home Page**
US Masters Diving Web Page provides information on Masters Diving Events and Other Items of Interest. Provides information on Masters diving events, editorials, articles, message board, and FINA.
www.n2.net/diving/

9. **Peter Hughes Diving | World Class Live Aboard Scuba Diving**
Dancer fleet live-aboards dive the Bahamas, Bali, Palau, Papua New Guinea, Turks and Caicos, Belize,...
www.peterhughes.com/

10. **Great White Shark Diving South Africa**
Great white shark cage diving and viewing at Dyer Island, South Africa by White Shark Ecoventures, Cape Town. ... WHITE SHARK DIVING. ...
www.white-shark-diving.com/

11. **Doc's Diving Medicine Home Page**
Original articles, ongoing research and useful links related to Diving and Undersea Medicine from the University of Washington and Dr Edmond Kay. ...
faculty.washington.edu/ekay/

12. **contents.htm**
SCUBA DIVING EXPLAINED. Cover Illustration. Questions and Answers on Physiology and Medical Aspects of Scuba Diving. Lawrence Martin, MD. ...
www.mtsinai.org/pulmonary/books/scuba/contents.htm

13. **Diving Plongeon Canada**
Diving Plongeon Canada 703-2197 Prom. Riverside Drive, Ottawa, Ontario K1H 7X3 Telephone : 613-736-5238 Fax : 613-736-0409 E-mail: cada@diving.ca.
www.diving.ca/

14. **Poseidon Diving Systems**
Full line manufacturer of scuba diving equipment, including drysuits and the Cyklon and Odin regulators.
www.poseidon.se/

15. **Diving Network Nippon!!**
The summary for this Japanese page contains characters that cannot be correctly displayed in this language/character set.
www.dnn.co.jp/

16. **Abysmal Scuba**
Technical dive planning and hyperbaric simulation software available in multiple languages; supports...
www.abysmal.com/

17. **Phuket scuba diving, Thailand liveaboards and scuba clubs ...**
Information on diving in Phuket, live-aboard cruises, scuba clubs and dive sites in Thailand.
www.diving.phuket.com/

18. **Diving, Scuba, California Diving News**
SCUBA Show 2004 May 22 and 23, 2004 THE Diving Event of the Year!™. California Diving Books: Published By Saint Brendan. Southern ...
www.saintbrendan.com/

19. **Association of Diving Contractors International**
Association of Diving Contractors International, ... Archived News. Entire contents © Association of Diving Contractors International.
www.adc-usa.org/

20. **National Association for Cave Diving**
The NACD was established in 1969 for the purpose of achieving safer cave diving through training and education. ... (c)2003 National Association for Cave Diving.
www.safecavediving.com/

21. **Historical Diving Society | Home Page**
Historical Diving Society USA - an organization dedicated to preserving, and recording diving history. ...
www.hds.org/

22. **The Historical Diving Society**
The Historical Diving Society aims to protect and preserve diving heritage. Everything about historical divers, diving history, underwater ...
www.thehds.com/

23. **California Liveaboard Scuba Diving - Dive Boat Sand Dollar**
California Scuba Diving - Liveaboard Boat Diving Trips on the Sand Dollar Dive Boat. Liveaboard Scuba Diving Trips To California ...
www.diving.net/

24. **Discovery Diving Co., Inc. - Wreck Diving the Graveyard of the ...**
Discovery Diving Co., a Five Star PADI Facility providing the best possible ways to experience the Joy and Adventure of Wreck Diving in the Graveyard of the ...
www.discoverydiving.com/

25. **ProDiving Croatia - Tourist Diving Association. How to dive in ..**
Complete guide about dive in Croatia. Interactive map for destination of diving centers, school, wrecks.
www.diving.hr/

26. **Scuba Diving - What You Need to Know About Scuba Diving**
At About Scuba Diving you'll find original informative SCUBA content, diving links, how-to scuba dive articles, a scuba diving chat room and a scuba diving ...
scuba.about.com/mbody.htm

27. **3Routes Worldwide Scuba Diving Directory**
The 3 Routes Worldwide Scuba diving directory contains web pages, links and contact information on over 5000 Scuba operators, resorts and live-aboards around ...
www.3routes.com/

28. **Aloha from Maui with Maui Scuba Diving and Ed Robinson's Diving ...**
MAUI SCUBA DIVING is your link to scuba information from Maui, Hawaii - Scuba operations, scuba dive sites, whale, dolphin and Hawaiian marine life, Maui ...
www.mauiscuba.com/

29. **DIVING IN NEW ZEALAND**
Diving in New Zealand - Aotearoa THE WEB SPOT to come for a DIVE without getting your feet wet. ... SAFE DIVING, OCEAN 98 OCEAN98 Creating awarenes on oceans. ...
www.marrserv.com/dinzhome.htm

30. **Bali Diving, SCUBA Dive Bali Indonesia with AquaMarine Diving Bali**
Bali Diving. Dive Bali Indonesia with AquaMarine Diving - Bali. Indonesia Diving,Dive ... Juniors 10-14yrs. SCUBA dive in Bali. SCUBA Diving Bali. ... British owned and managed dive shop. Introductory program, day trips, PADI courses up to divemaster...
www.aquamarinediving.com/

31. **Diving Diseases Research Centre Plymouth UK providing hyperbaric ...**
Diving Diseases Research Centre Plymouth UK providing hyperbaric chamber oxygen treatment facilities and medical training for divers, technicians, nurses and ...
www.ddrc.org/

32. **Cave Diving Group**
This is the official Web Site of the Cave Diving Group of Great Britain. ... Thanks. Page Updated Wednesday, 2nd July, 2003 © Cave Diving Group. Valid HTML 4.01!
www.cavedivinggroup.org.uk/

33. **HRS Online**
Krovna organizacija za ronjenje u Hrvatskoj. Croatian Diving Federation – The organisation for diving in Croatia. ... Ronilacki turizam: Pro Diving Croatia. ...
www.diving-hrs.hr/

34. **Diversion II / NJScuba.com**
Join us as we explore and discover the history and excitement of diving the hundreds of shipwrecks of New Jersey coastal waters! ...
www.njscuba.com/

35. **Toucan Diving Bonaire Scuba Diving and Snorkeling**
Toucan Diving Bonaire is a 5-star PADI dive center providing a fully-equipped dive shop, scuba and snorkeling instruction and rentals. ...
www.toucandiving.com/

36. **Scuba Diving Explained - Lawrence Martin, MD**
Hyperlink to full size Cover Illustration. SCUBA DIVING EXPLAINED. Questions and Answers on Physiology and Medical Aspects of Scuba Diving. ...
www.mtsinai.org/pulmonary/books/scuba/welcome.htm

37. **Nekton Diving Cruises, Live-Aboard, Belize, Bahamas, Scuba, Diving ...**

    Nekton Diving Cruises, Diving, Bahamas, Belize, Caribbean, Liveaboard Dive Cruises, Scuba, Diving, Blue Hole, Dolphins, Travel....

    www.nektoncruises.com/

38. **GAS Diving UK Home page**

    Learn more about us OUR DIVING Scapa Flow. EQUIPMENT CONFIGURATION Equipment Configuration Sourcing Equipment. ... Welcome to the Gas Diving UK web page. ...

    www.gasdiving.co.uk/

39. **Bonaire / Diving Guide**

    Diving Bonaire, ... Remember the old diver's saying: "Take only pictures, leave only bubbles." Happy diving and snorkeling in the Marine Park. PARK RULES: ...

    www.geographia.com/bonaire/bondiv01.htm

40. **Diving Cairns - Great Barrier Reef Scuba Diving Holiday Guide ...**

    Cairns and the Great Barrier Reef represents some of the finest and most exotic scuba diving and snorkelling in the world. Whether ...

    www.divingcairns.com.au/

41. **Diving under Antarctic Ice**

    DIVING UNDER ANTARCTIC ICE presents photos and impressions of Antarctica on a National Science Foundation sponsored underwater photography expedition led by ...

    scilib.ucsd.edu/sio/nsf/

42. **Bahamas Diving Association: It just keeps getting better.**

    The official website of The Bahamas Diving Association -a complete scuba diving guide to The Islands of The Bahamas. Nassau, Freeport, Abaco and Bimini.

    www.bahamasdiving.com/

43. **Costa Rica Scuba Diving Resort and Hotel, Ocotal**

    Ocotal Scuba Diving Resort and Hotel, a leader among Costa Rica Hotels and Resorts, located in Ocotal Beach, Guanacaste Costa Rica. ...

    www.ocotaldiving.com/

44. **Diving Into the Gene Pool**

    The Diving Into the Gene Pool exhibition covers five broad areas: ... Sponsors. Diving Into the Gene Pool is made possible in part by the generous support of: ...

    www.exploratorium.edu/genepool/genepool_home.html

45. **DivingHeritage - the worlds largest virtual diving museum**

    DivingHeritage brings a tribute to all involved in the development of professional diving. The museum has over 300 diving helmets and much more on display! ...

    www.divingheritage.com/

46. **Ibiza Diving**

    Ibiza Diving On line is the official web site of the dive centre Ibiza Diving (Baleares / Spain), we are certified PADI Dive Center 5 Star. ...

    www.ibiza-diving.com/

47. **CHEAP Bali Golf- Spa-Cruise-Diving-Rafting Package and More Kecak. ...**

    Fun, attractive and adventurous activities such as romantic cruise, dolphin tour, diving, fishing and snorkeling, wind-surfing, jet ski, or surf the wild wave ...

    www.kecak.com/travel/

48. **Regaldive**

    Regaldive is the UK's number one dive tour operator, sharing your passion for diving. Discover our exciting range of destinations ...

    www.regaldive.co.uk/

49. **ADN Diving, agence de voyages, magasin et école de plongée**

    ADN Diving, agence de voyages, magasin et école de plongée, nombreuses destinations, voyages et croisières.

    www.adn-diving.ch/

50. **Scuba Diving in Bali, Tulamben, Nusa Penida, Menjangan Island**

    Diving in Bali Scuba with its warm water, extensive coral reefs and abundant marine life. Diving in Bali. Bali Forum and News : Diving in Bali. Bali diving. ...

    www.diving-in-bali.com/

51. **Diving Concepts Main Page**

    You are the person to visit this site since 09-18-2000. Makes drysuits for scuba diving. Technical information, product catalog, and form for requesting a...

    www.divingconcepts.com/

52. **Harvard Swimming and Diving**

Friends of Harvard Swimming and Diving The most important fund-raising body for the teams, Technique Swim Camp 2003 Summer swim camp at Blodgett Pool. ...

hcs.harvard.edu/~swim/

53. **Diving Cellar Charters, Scapa Flow, Orkney**

Dive Scapa Flow. Accommodation, minibus, onboard nitrox, shop, souvenirs, and mail order.

www.divescapaflow.co.uk/

54. **DEMA**

Represents companies whose mission is to promote and help provide growth within recreational diving.

www.dema.org/

55. **Cabo San Lucas Diving, near Los Cabos Hotels with Snorkeling and ...**

Los Cabos hotels and Cabo San Lucas diving, snorkeling and scuba sites in Los Cabos, Baja, Mexico. ...

www.cabo-san-lucas-diving.com/

56. **DiveWeb: Commercial Diving, ROVs, Marine Technology, Offshore ...**

Commercial Diving, ROVs, Marine Technology and Construction: Up-to-date Information about Commercial Diving, ROV's, and Marine Technology. ...

www.diveweb.com/

57. **Dive Cayman! Cayman Diving Lodge - All-inclusive dive resort**

Cayman Diving Lodge is an all-inclusive Dive Lodge, with the best scuba diving, the best accomodations and the best food in the Cayman Islands. ...

www.divelodge.com/

58. **Perth Diving Academy - Australia's leading dive store.**

Perth Diving Academy is Australia's leading dive store. Two purpose built facilities provide divers with retail sales, boat charters ...

www.perthdiving.com.au/

59. **Egypt: Red Sea Virtual Diving Center**

The Red Sea Virtual Scuba Diving Center by Tour Egypt: Official Internet Site of the Ministry of Tourism, Egypt is the best resource about Red Sea Scuba Diving ...

www.redseavdc.com/

60. **Scuba Diving, Island Vacations, Diving Packages, Live-Aboards ...**
Specializing in Scuba Diving, Snorkeling, kayaking, Fishing, golfing and ecotourism, World of Diving can customize an adventure travel package to almost ...
www.worldofdiving.com/

61. **Abyss Scuba Diving Sydney - Padi Dive Centre**
Central to Sydney's best diving sites, Abyss Scuba Diving is the ideal place to undertake a PADI scuba diving lessons. ... Scuba Diving in Sydney. ...
www.abyss.com.au/

62. **Bali Diving with Bali International Diving Professionals**
Bali International Diving Professionals. Special offer - don't miss out! ... The Scuba Diving specialists in Bali, Indonesia!
www.bidp-balidiving.com/

63. **Alaska Mining and Diving Supply - ATV's, boats, outboards ...**
Alaska Mining and Diving Supply 2002 and 2003 Ski-Doo National Dealer of the Year! Alaska Mining and Diving Supply, Inc. (AMDS) was founded ...
www.akmining.com/

64. **Phi Phi diving - Thailand liveaboards: Moskito Dive PADI IDC ...**
Phi Phi diving and Thailand liveaboards: Moskito PADI IDC Dive Center, similan cruises and boat charters. ... Phi Phi diving and Thailand liveaboards. ...
www.moskitodiving.com/

65. **SmutFantasies!!!!**
NEXUS VIDEO Only quality porn ... Direct Porn's Movie Post 500+ Daily Porn Movies!
www.bitchpornos.com/videos/ppo/tm.html

19
Equestrian

1. **USA EQUESTRIAN**
   USA Equestrian, as the national equestrian federation of the US, is the regulatory body for the Olympic and World Championship equestrian sports - Dressage ...
   www.equestrian.org/
2. **USET**
   Pan American Games Click Here For The Latest News From The Pan American Games. Some Files require Adobe Reader. USET Pottersville ...
   www.uset.com/
3. **Horse Links Search Engine by Equiworld - Horse Equiworld Horse...**
   Equiworld Horse Links provides a wide range of equestrian information, horse links, equine chat, horse sales, riding schools, and lots more horse, pony, equine ...
   www.equiworld.net/horselinks/
4. **The Bay Area Equestrian Network - Regional directory for equine ...**
   ... California Directory WELCOME to the Bay Area Equestrian Network, serving thousands of horse enthusiasts and equine businesses statewide across California. ...
   www.bayequest.com/
5. **eQUESTRIAN**
   eQUESTRIAN News and Information since 1996, Click to learn more... ... Powered by CityDesk The eQUESTRIAN is Â© 1996-2002 REMUS Group.
   equest.remus.com/

6. **IENN**

International Equestrian News Network Provides news and information for the international equestrian arena.

www.horsenews.com/

7. **Equestrian Connection Keeping Canadian Equestrians Connected...**

Equestrian Connection Contest! Two ... age. Video tapes donated generously by International Equestrian Services. find out how to enter.

www.equestrian-connection.com/

8. **Equine Canada**

Official homepage on the CEF offering information on Young Riders program, awards, and calendar of...

www.equestrian.ca/

9. **British Equestrian Federation**

www.bef.co.uk/

10. **Equestrian**

Basketball Equestrian Soccer Golf Baseball Cycling Martial Arts Motorsports Wrestling Water Sports Football Gymnastics Fishing Winter Sports. ... Equestrian Links. ...

www.equestrian-toplinks.com/

11. **QNET - Coming Soon**

The Difference Is Service. Established as a non-profit corporation dedicated to the acquisition and preservation of trails, promotin...

www.eti.av.org/

12. **Mr Horse: The World Equestrian Site / Il Sito Equestre ...**

Directory of news, results, and additional racing information.

www.mrhorse.com/

13. **Equestrian Land Conservation Resource**

Equestrian Land Conservation Resource Dedicated to promoting access to and conservation of land for equestrian use. Non-profit organization founded to promote national awareness of the importance of land conservation...

www.elcr.org/

14. **BCM**

In more than twenty years Best Communication and Management (BCM) has become a leading international company, specializing in equestrian sport, events and ...

www.bcm.nl/

15. **News by Equiworld Horse Magazine December 2003 - World Wide Horses**
    US Equestrian Accepting Bids To Host FEI World Children's Jumping Final US Equestrian has received notification from the FEI to request bids to host the 2004 ...
    www.equiworld.net/
16. **EquiSearch - In-depth resources for horse owners and enthusiasts**
    Plus many more great stocking stuffers for under $20. Visit Equestrian Collections, the holiday superstore. ... No rain checks. At Equestrian Collections! ...
    www.equisearch.com/
17. **Equestrian Trail Rider**
    Trail riding is my greatest joy, and we have a group of friends who are trying to cover every trail possible! So come in and learn ...
    www.qtm.net/~mitchj/
18. **Meredith Manor - Equestrian trade school preparing students for...**
    An equestrian trade school preparing students for careers in the horse industry. ... Meredith Manor International Equestrian Centre....
    www.meredithmanor.com/
19. **AuburnTigers.com - The Official Website of Auburn Tiger Athletics**
    Auburn Equestrian Falls to Defending National Champion Georgia. November 10, 2003. Kelly Gottfried. ... Full Story. Equestrian rules have many fans curious ... ...
    www.auburntigers.com/equestrian/
20. **Equestrian Holidays Ireland, Irish horseback riding vacation ...**
    equestrian holidays ireland, irish horseback riding holidays, horse back riding holiday in ireland, horseback riding vacation,horse picture, horse riding ...
    www.ehi.ie/
21. **Horseback Riding Vacations, Equestrian Tours from Cross Country ...**
    Before selecting a horseback riding vacation, we've researched and visited most, if not all, of the equestrian facilities in a country or province. ...
    www.equestrianvacations.com/

22. **Google Directory - Sports > Equestrian**
Google, Directory Help Search only in Equestrian Search the Web. Equestrian, Sports > Equestrian, Go to Directory Home. Categories. Art ...
directory.google.com/Top/Sports/Equestrian/

23. **Equestrian Resources**
Groups. equestrianfriends(185) - Equestrian friends meeting to discuss get togethers and other stuff ... Ansteorra-Equestrian(102)
www.utyx.com/equestrian/

24. **American Medical Equestrian Association**
American Medical Equestrian Assoc. News. ... [Questions and Answers] [Attributions for Equestrian Accidents] [AMEA News Items]. June 2000 (Volume XI, No. 2). ...
www.law.utexas.edu/dawson/amea/amea.htm

25. **Equestrian Dreams horse gifts**
Equestrian gifts for Horse Lovers, custom artwork, limited edition artwork,sculptures and Carousel Horses. ... Metal Sculptures. Equestrian Bronzes. ...
www.equestriandreams.com/

26. **Horse.com - The World's Largest Online Equestrian Store**
Horse, Horses, Tack, Riding Equipment, Polo, Breeders, Stables - The World's Largest Online Equestrian Store Distributors, breeders, suppliers, resource and ...
www.equestrianmall.com/

27. **eQUESTRIAN.COM.MY**
South East Asia's first Equestrian Website. ... horses, equestrian, riding, polo, dressage. SEARCH. Coming soon... MAILING LIST. ...
equestrian.com.my/

28. **Equestrian Education Center, Equine Courses, Training school for ...**
Equestrian education and courses. We offer equine studies applied certified programs for preperation to be applied for future coaches, trainers, stable managers ...
equinecenter.homestead.com/

29. **Free Equestrian Web graphics from JFF Miniature Horses**
Free Equestrian, horse web page graphics, backgrounds, clip art, animated gifs, buttons, bars and more. ... Welcome to our Equestrian Graphics site. ...
www.fortunecity.com/meltingpot/thurlow/41/

30. **Horsetalk — Horse news, horse advice, world equestrian news and...**
Comprehensive online magazine with news, information, and features including a chatroom, discussion...
www.horsetalk.co.nz/

31. **Alberta Equestrian Federation**
The AEF is the provincial counterpart of the Canadian equestrian Federation (CEF) and is the organizing, coordinating, sanctioning and administering body for ...
www.equestrian.ab.ca/

32. **Equestrian Federation of Ireland**
Official website of the Equestrian Federation of Ireland, governing body for the sport. The website of the Equestrian Federation ...
www.horsesport.ie/

33. **British Equestrian Vaulting**
BRITISH EQUESTRIAN VAULTING LTD. Future Events. BRITISH CHAMPIONSHIP RESULTS.
www.vaulting.org.uk/

34. **EquestrianLinks.com - your portal to the equestrian world**
Equestrian links portal offering a route into the best of the equine related web. EquestrianLinks.com - your portal to the equestrian world.
www.equestrianlinks.com/

35. **Spruce Meadows Official Website**
Southwest "Community A" and Employment Centre Area Structure Plan. SPRUCE MEADOWS POSITION. ...
www.sprucemeadows.com/

36. **Horses - Forest Ranch Equestrian Center**
Browse the Forest Ranch Equestrian Center classified ads. ... Forest Ranch Equestrian Center is an Internet-based, worldwide equestrian location service. ...
www.horsesense.com/

37. **Dealer in quality recast bronze sculptures (including Frederic ...**
Bronze sculptures, collectible and historical photographs, limited edition prints, sports and horse...
www.eccnet.com/fourwinds/

38. **Washington State Equestrian Network....**

Horseman's internet sevice for the Washington State equestrian. Information management for the local equestrian community. Database about the equine industry and equestrian sports, including shows, events, clincs, breeders,...

www.raineyvalleyfarm.com/wshis/

39. **Equestrian Education WebRing**

Homepage of the Equestrian Education WebRing. ... Equestrian Education WebRing. Welcome to the home page of the Equestrian Education WebRing!

www.geocities.com/Heartland/Valley/1633/eqedring.html

40. **International Equestrian Education Services**

International Equestrian Education Services... (Robert O. Mayer, FN, BHSI). International Equestrian Education Services (IEES) ABN 99309338751....

www.nex.net.au/users/camilu/

41. **Amherst Equestrian Team Home Page**

Offering schedule of shows and events, team roster, and team information. Massachusetts

www.amherst.edu/~riding/

42. **Australian Equestrian Information Service**

Australian equestrian information service providing extensive results, event calendars, photos, classified ads, news and other information for all horse ... Providing a directory and keyword search for Australian equestrian sites.

www.ausvinyl.com.au/aushorse/

43. **Equestrian Artist**

Equestrian artist Katy Sodeau paints watercolours of horse racing scenes, landscapes and animal portraits. Katy became interested ...

www.katy.ndirect.co.uk/

44. **BitsAndBridles.com Equestrian Equipment Forum**

Equestrians create and view ads of Used Tack Horse/Equestrian Equipment. ... Welcome To BitsAndBridles.com Equestrian Equipment Forum. A used equestrian tack directory of classified advertising for all types of equipment.

www.bitsandbridles.com/

45. **Equestrian Federation of Australia :: Home**
There are stories being peddled in some parts of equestrian media and in The Horse Magazine in particular, that need to be put straight. More ....
www.efanational.com/

46. **Lehigh University Equestrian**
The Lehigh Equestrian Club participates in Intercollegiate horse shows,arranges trail rides and riding lessons, and other activities. ...
www.lehigh.edu/~inequest/

47. **Equestrian in Ireland**
Equestrian holidays in Ireland. Whether your interests lie in trail riding, cross-country riding, show jumping, dressage ...
www.equestrian.travel.ie/

48. **Cornell University - Women's Equestrian - Official Athletic Site**
Cornell Athletics, Cornell Athletics. Cornell Women's Equestrian, Cornell
www.fansonly.com/schools/corn/sports/ w-equest/corn-w-equest-body.html

49. **The official website of the Ontario Equestrian ...**
Official website of the Ontario Equestrian Federation! PLEASE NOTE. ... Copyright © 2002 Ontario Equestrian Federation. ...
www.horse.on.ca/

50. **The Harvard Equestrian Team**
Our former captain, Anna Fishko '02, winning the blue ribbon at an IHSA show. For more pictures, see our photo section. News.
hcs.harvard.edu/~horses/

51. **Equestrian Team Homepage!**
Competing in Zone 3, Region 2. Team roster and photos, calendar of events and show information, FAQ,...
www.princeton.edu/~puet/

52. **The Virtual Equestrian**
The Virtual Equestrian - Home. Welcome to the new look Virtual Equestrian!Cyberhorse ... section. The Virtual Equestrian - News Headlines. ...
www.cyberhorse.net.au/tve/

53. **SET- Stanford Equestrian Team (main page)**
Information on the horses and riders, team news and photos. Located in Stanford, CA.
www.stanford.edu/group/set/

54. **California State University, Fresno - <<Dept Name>>**
Official website of the Equine Sciences department. Information on IHSA and NCAA team membership,...
www.csufresno.edu/equestrian/

55. **The Southern California Equestrian Directory**
A Guide to Equestrian marketplace. Horseback riding lessons, training, boarding, services, products,...
www.socalequine.com/

56. **SCA Inc. - Chivalrous Arts**
Arts of Combat and Chivalry. SCA participants engage in armored combat, rapier combat,archery, thrown weapons, and equestrian activities. ... Equestrian Activities. ...
www.sca.org/chivarts.html

57. **The Order of the Holy Sepulcher**
The origins of the Order of the Holy Sepulcher have been disputed for centuries. ...
www.chivalricorders.org/vatican/holysep.htm

58. **sport horses for sale uk / classifieds / pictures of horses ...**
Pictures of horses - dressage horses for sale - showjumping horses for sale - eventing horses for sale - sport horse news - horse sales - equestrian news. ...
www.sport-horses.org/

59. **Horses, Horse Riding, Horses For Sale, UK**
About equestrianism in the UK. Horses for sale, equestrian sports, equine care and health, riding...
www.equine-world.co.uk/

60. **Colby-Sawyer Equestrian**
Event schedule, history of the club, roster, season preview and summary. New London, New Hampshire, USA.
www.colby-sawyer.edu/athletics/equestrian/

61. **Horsearama.com, Horse Rescue Sites - horse, pony, horses, equine...**
Horsearama.com A Equestrian Community. ...
www.snowcrest.net/hawkeye2/whsidx.htm

62. **horse and equestrian discussion forums and chatrooms for dressage ...**

    A range of equestrian forums that cover all aspects of equestrian sports, equestrian breeding and...

    www.sport-horses.org/cgi-bin/yabb/YaBB.pl

63. **UO Equestrian Team**

    UO Equestrian Team. ... Welcome to the University of Oregon Equestrian Team's Web site! If you are interested in the team we will be ...

    uoeq.tripod.com/

64. **Bucknell Equestrian Team**

    For the past 30 years Bucknell Equestrian Team has always being the University's official representative on the intercollegiate equestrian circuit. ...

    www.orgs.bucknell.edu/equestrian_team/

65. **Equestrian Club**

    Directions, team overview, membership details, past highlights, and contacts.

    www.fairfield.edu/athletics/equestrian.htm

66. **RIT Equestrian Team website!**

    Offering a variety of equestrian competition to students. History of team, upcoming shows, results,...

    www.rit.edu/~ihsa2www/

67. **Smith College Equestrian**

    The equestrian program at Smith has much to offer you, whether you're just beginning or are already an advanced rider. Intercollegiate ...

    www.smith.edu/athletics/sports/equestrian/home.html

68. **Bed and Breakfast Inns ONLINE - Missing Page**

    Bed and Breakfast Inns ONLINE. The bbonline web site address that you were trying to view is not available. Either you entered an incorrect ...

    www.bbonline.com/bbci/

20
Fencing

1. **Fencing - Complete Guide to the Sport of Fencing. Olympic Fencing...**
   World-Wide fencing community site featuring online training resources for competing in foil, epee, and sabre, chats, discussions, and a search engine of ... Includes club listings, training drills (footwork and blade work), and general information about the...
   www.fencing.net/
2. **US Fencing**
   Official website for the United States Fencing Association.
   www.usfencing.org/
3. **British Fencing**
   Official website for organization governing Olympic fencing in Britain.
   www.britishfencing.com/
4. **Canadian Fencing Federation / Federation d'escrime canadienne**
   Tournament schedules and results for fencing in Canada at the national level; site is in French and English.
   www.fencing.ca/
5. **Blade Fencing Online**
   Blade Fencing, Inc. The online catalog and information site for an international Fencing Equipment supplier. Supplier for the 1996 United States Fencing team. This New York fencing equipment supplier offers online ordering of Allstar, Russian and Blade equipment.
   www.blade-fencing.com/
6. **INDEX.HTM**
   View products and place orders online for Olympic fencing equipment with this California supplier.
   www.thefencingpost.com/

7. **Elizabethan Fencing**
   This site is dedicated to Historical Fencing. This includes fencing during the Elizabethan Period, the early 16th and 17th Centuries. ...
   jan.ucc.nau.edu/~wew/fencing.html
8. **Fencing Sucks**
   A humorous bulletin board for posting rants and raves about the world of fencing.
   www.fencingsucks.com/
9. **Sports/fencing FAQ Index**
   Archive of USENET FAQs, providing an overview of the sport.
   www.faqs.org/faqs/sports/fencing-faq/
10. **Fencing Footage**
    Videos of various fencing competitions available via on-line catalog.
    www.fencingfootage.com/
11. **Harvard University Varsity Fencing Team**
    The Harvard Fencing Team is an undergraduate team with about 30 members. We fence in the NCAA division I league. We practice 5 days ...
    hcs.harvard.edu/~fencing/
12. **Association for Historical Fencing (AHF)**
    The Association for Historical Fencing (AHF) is a nonprofit corporation that organizes seminars, lectures, workshops, exhibitions, demonstrations and similar ...
    www.ahfi.org/
13. **Howstuffworks "How Fencing Equipment Works"**
    If you have been watching competitive fencing at the Olympics or in a college match, you know that fencing is an unusual sport, and it uses some very ...
    www.howstuffworks.com/fencing-equipment.htm
14. **Blue-Gauntlet Fencing**
    Blue-Gauntlet Fencing offers the most robust products and best service available for fencers of all age groups! Visit our website ...
    www.blue-gauntlet.com/
15. **Southampton University Fencing Club**
    Practise times, location, news, photographs and links.
    www.soton.ac.uk/~fencing/

16. **Frequently asked questions in Rsf**
    Archive of the rec.sports.fencing usenet FAQ.
    www.ii.uib.no/~arild/fencing/faq/faq.html
17. **FRITZ on FENCING**
    A collection of reviews for books and videos about fencing or with a fencing theme.
    members.aol.com/BookKritik/fencing.html
18. **Liste Inverse anglaise**
    Description of actions and items used in fencing with equivalents in French.
    www.synec-doc.be/escrime/dico/engl.htm
19. **Fencing New Zealand - Home**
    Information on fencing in New Zealand.
    www.fencing.org.nz/
20. **Martinez Academy of Arms - Classical Fencing lessons in New York ...**
    A school where the arts of classical fencing and historical swordsmanship are taught.
    www.martinez-destreza.com/
21. **Leon Paul Fencing Equipment, Fencing equipment delivered worldwide ...**
    Fencing Equipment from Leon Paul, The Largest Manufacturer of Fencing Equipment. Delivering fencing equipment worldwide direct from the manufacturer. ...
    www.leonpaul.com/
22. **Classical Fencing: the Martial Art of Incurable Romantics**
    Articles on classical and historical fencing, as well as In Ferro Veritas methods and rankings and...
    www.classicalfencing.com/
23. **Frequently asked questions**
    Faq. for rec.sport.fencing. Top level. PART I: General General: 1.1 What sports and martial arts comprise fencing? 1.2 How did fencing originate? ...
    www.ii.uib.no/~arild/fencing/faq/Top-view.html
24. **George Santelli Inc - Fencing Equipment**
    This is the website for the George Santelli Inc, Fencing Equipment manufacturer Offers Olympic fencing equipment that may be ordered online or via fax or phone; located in New Jersey.
    www.santelli.com/

25. **The Brown University Fencing Team Website**
The Brown University Fencing Team Website! ... Click the top image to return to this page. Both Mens' and Womens' Fencing are currently in season. ...
www.brown.edu/Athletics/Fencing/

26. **Monash Fencing Club Home Page**
The Monash Fencing Club home page! ... TRAINING TIMES. Tuesday,Fencing Area, 6:00pm, Dinner, Games Hall (map), 7:00pm, Warm-up and games, ...
yoyo.cc.monash.edu.au/groups/MUFC/

27. **Negrini Fencing Line Home Page**
Manufacturer and retailer of fencing equipment, clothing and scoring machines.
www.negrini.com/

28. **Fencing Online**
Fencing - Fencing.Net is the premier online resource for training and competing in foil, epee, and sabre. Your online guide to the sport of fencing. ...
www.fencing.net/ring.html

29. **fencing.start4all.com**
International listing of clubs, organizations and vendors.
fencing.start4all.com/

30. **Historical Fencing Manuals Online — Swords and Swordsmanship**
THE ARMARIUM Online Historical Fencing Manuals and Texts. One of the major fencing texts of the period. p071 ... www.thehaca.com/manuals.htm

31. **Zivkovic Modern Fencing Equipment, Inc.**
Online catalog, and order placement facility for this Massachusetts dealer of Olympic fencing equipment.
www.zivkovic.com/

32. **University of Bath Fencing Club**
University of Bath. Fencing Club. [welcome ... Welcome one and all to Bath University Fencing Club's (BUFC) web pages. Hopefully you're ...
students.bath.ac.uk/su4fc/

33. **HMS**
Hrvatski macevalacki savez Federation Croate d'Escrime Croatian Fencing Federation hms@net.hr. ...
public.srce.hr/fencing/hms.htm

34. **Malaysian Fencing Federation**
Contact and tournament information for amateur fencing in Malaysia.
members.tripod.com/~leongpc/fencing/Mff.html

35. **UMass Fencing, Official Home Page**
News, schedule, results, team profiles and club history.
www.umass.edu/rso/fencing/

36. **FENFOOL's FENCING PAGE**
Fencing reference site with news, links, vendors and a list of colleges with fencing teams or clubs. FENFOOL's FENCING PAGE.
members.tripod.com/~fenfool/

37. **Irish Amateur Fencing Federation Index**
The Irish Amateur Fencing Federation (IAFF) is the governing body of the sport of fencing in Ireland. Its aims are to promote fencing ...
homepage.tinet.ie/~iaff/

38. **The Fencing Center of San Jose**
Location, classes, competitive results for club members and related fencing links.
www.fencing.com/

39. **United States Fencing Coaches Association**
International Fencing speeds up its modernisation process with important changes During its congress, held last weekend in Leipzig (Germany), the International ...
www.usfca.org/

40. **American Fencers Supply Co**
Located in San Francisco, California, this supplier offers fencing equipment and stage combat weapons...
www.amfence.com/

41. **Historic Fencing Manuals**
Listing of Historical Fencing Manuals purchasable from Patri J. Pugliese.
www.latourdulac.com/fencing/patri.html

42. **Merlin 3W Fencing Equipment - epee, foil and sabre**
Merlin Fencing Equipment - online catalogue offering the full product range, for one of the leading suppliers of quality fencing equipment at competitive prices ...
www.konect.mcmail.com/merlin/

43. **Brock University Varsity Fencing Team and the Niagara ...**
The Brock University Varsity Fencing Team Niagara Swordsmen Fencing club is a medium sized fencing club located in the Niagara Peninsula of Ontario Canada. ...
fencing.niagara.com/

44. **Carolingian Fencing Page**
The Carolingian Fencing Page. Welcome! Renaissance-style SCA fencing has had a long and active history here in the Barony of Carolingia. Resource for renaissance-style fencers in the Society of Creative Anachronisms located in Boston,...
www.latourdulac.com/fencing/

45. **University of Minnesota Fencing Club!**
This web site courtesy of Black Gryphon Graphics for the University of Minnesota Fencing Club. The views and opinions expressed ...
www.tc.umn.edu/~fencing/

46. **Purdue Fencing Club - Ready? Fence!**
The Purdue Fencing Club is deticated to the teaching and expansion of the sport of fencing. ... Welcome Message. Welcome to the home page of the Purdue Fencing Club!
expert.cc.purdue.edu/~fencing/

47. **University Of Toronto Fencing Club**
University Of Toronto Fencing Club Newsboard. Practice and tournament schedules, results, photos and contacts.
www.utoronto.ca/fencing/

48. **Gauteng Fencing Asscociation**
Information on the administrative body for fencing in the province of Gauteng, South Africa.
www.icon.co.za/~cbkohler/gfa.htm

49. **Rice Fencing Club**
Information on a club operating out of Rice University, in Houston, Texas.
www.ruf.rice.edu/~rfc/

50. **Fencing**
Location, practise times, contacts, results and event information.
www.hull.ac.uk/php/fencing/

51. **Cornell Women's Fencing**
Team profiles, schedule and competition results for this team in Ithaca, New York.
www.ccmr.cornell.edu/~sachse/cu_fencing.html

52. **British Wheelchair Sports Foundation - Stoke Mandeville, the ...**
Sport background and contacts for the organization which manages wheelchair fencing in the United Kingdom.
www.britishwheelchairsports.org/associate/fencing.htm

53. **The Nick Evangelista Fencing Homepage**
Author's page with a number of current and historical of photos.
users.townsqr.com/ale/

54. **Top Class Epee Fencing Clubs in London**
Some of Great Britain's best Epee fencing clubs. Competition, ranking information, times and contacts for this competitive London based epee club.
freespace.virgin.net/peter.hfc/

55. **FANS - Fencing Association of Nova Scotia**
Contact details, competition information, and rankings.
www.chebucto.ns.ca/SportFit/Fencing/

56. **Fencing club**
Fencing Club. Officers. What is Fencing? Latest News and Results. Club Constitution. How do I Join? (Email The Officers). Links.
www.colby.edu/fencing/

57. **Classical Fencing and Historical Swordsmanship Resources**
Resources for studying, practicing, and learning more about classical fencing and historical swordsmanship.
www.kmoser.com/classicalfencing.htm

58. **Classical Fencing Mailing List**
An email list (listserv) for discussing classical fencing and historical swordsmanship, including...
www.kmoser.com/cflist.htm

59. **Victorian Amateur Fencing Association**
Governing organization for fencing in the state of Victoria.
home.vicnet.net.au/~vafa/

60. **Dublin University Fencing Club**
Practise times, location and fixture list and club members' biographies for this club based at Trinity...
www.tcd.ie/Clubs/Fencing/

61. **What Is Fencing**
The sport of fencing is fast and athletic, a far cry from the choreographed bouts you see on film or on the stage. ... What Is Fencing? ...
www.usfencing.org/Welcome/WhatIsFencing.asp

21
Football

1. **NFL.com -**
   The official site of the National Football League, including stats, scores, standings,fantasy football, transactions, injury reports, schedules, team and ...
   www.nfl.com/
2. **FIFA.COM The Official web site of the Fédération Internationale ...**
   FIFA.com is the official web site of the Fédération Internationale de Football Association.
   www.fifa.com/
3. **Football.com**
   If it's football, we got it! NFL, NCAA, CFL, AFL, NFLe, XFL, Prep, Fantasy, and more! Free Newsletter: ... Steve Lassan, NCAA Football. Mike Beacom, Fantasy GMs. ...
   www.football.com/
4. **Football news, fun, results, fixtures and features from ...**
   Latest Premiership, Champions League and Uefa Cup news plus fun features, free downloads, results and comment on all things football.
   www.football365.com/
5. **uefa.com**
   The official site of the European governing body with results from the UEFA Champions League, and...
   www.uefa.com/
6. **TheFA.com**
   The Football Association, All Rights Reserved.
   www.thefa.com/

7. **ESPN Soccernet.com: Home: Football News, Live Scores, Stats and ...**

ESPN Soccernet.com brings you the best football coverage from the English Premiership and around the world. Latest news and statistics from England, Scotland and the rest of Europe. Also includes Euro 2000 pages.

www.soccernet.com/

8. **CFL**

Official website. Provides statistics, cybercasts, player of the week/ month and sections pertaining...

www.cfl.ca/

9. **Fédération française**

World > Français > ... > Sports et loisirs > Sports > Football

www.fff.fr/

10. **ncaafootball - Welcome**

Official home of NCAA Football.

www.ncaafootball.net/

11. **Guardian Unlimited Football**

Coverage includes breaking news, live match reports and latest scores backed up by columnists, club...

football.guardian.co.uk/

12. **Arsenal.com - The Official Arsenal Website**

Arsenal.com. Members Login Lost Password? Join Now. Search Net: - Site Map -.

www.arsenal.co.uk/

13. **Pro Football Hall of Fame**

Honoring the great players of the professional football world since 1920. Located in Canton, Ohio.

www.profootballhof.com/

14. **footballasia.com - All Football All Asia**

Download Media Accreditation. President's Vision. AFC President's vision for Asian football. ... FootballAsia – All Football, All Asia Full Story. FootballAsia TV, ...

www.asian-football.com/

15. **Dream of an Arsenal Christmas**

    Entry button. Enter button. Leather jotter pad. £6.50 Info. AA maglite set The official site with fixtures, league table, reserves, youths, ladies, and forums.

    www.arsenal.com/

16. **Official Website of the Australian Football League**

    Off-field review. As another event-filled football year draws to a close, afl.com.au's Paul Gough looks back at the major off-field happenings

    afl.com.au/

17. **ESPN.com**

    ESPN Web. ESPN Intelligence. NFL Scores | GameCast. College Football Bowls Scores. NBA Scores | GameCast. ... Fantasy Football Playoff Challenge. Fantasy. ...

    msn.espn.go.com/

18. **AFL - Arena Football League**

    Designed and Hosted by. AFL Headlines. New AFL football to debut at All-American Bowl. NEW YORK – The Arena Football League's new ...

    www.arenafootball.com/

19. **Rugby Football Union - Home**

    Contains information about all facets of English rugby and merchandising. The Rugby Football Union...

    www.rfu.com/

20. **FOOTBALL365 accès illimité au football - La Une**

    Kids and Teens > International > ... > Sports et loisirs > Sports

    www.football365.fr/

21. **DenverBroncos.com — Official Web Site of the Denver Broncos**

    KEEPING IT REAL, A rematch means dealing with a foe who knows you well ... and vice versa. "Each team knows what each other's doing," Trevor Pryce said. Official team site with audio and video clips, team news, depth charts, transactions, statistics,...

    www.denverbroncos.com/

22. **CAF Homepage**

    Coverage of the most important club sport competition for Africa.

    www.cafonline.com/

23. **The official Scottish Football Association Website**
Scottish Football Association Official Website. For the latest news on Scotland's national teams, match reports, statistics database ...
www.scottishfa.co.uk/

24. **Liverpoolfc.tv: Home Page**
Club Credit Card. Personalised Cards. Ladbrokes Home. Football Betting. Racing Betting. Greyhounds Betting. Online Casino. The official web site with exhaustive archive, also includes the Hillsborough Memorial. Formerly,...
www.liverpoolfc.tv/

25. **Play Football the Official NFL Site for Kids**
Play Football, the NFL site for kids. Games, fun facts about NFL players and football strategy and positions.
www.playfootball.com/

26. **Dallas Cowboys Official Website**
Official team site with audio and video clips, team news, depth charts, transactions, statistics,...
www.dallascowboys.com/

27. **Funbrain.com Power Football**
Football plus brains equals power. Improve your math skills with a fun game. ... Power Football, How to Play: FUNBRAIN will give you a math problem. ...
www.funbrain.com/football/

28. **Online Gambling at Sports.com: Sports Betting, Online Betting ...**
.... Loading Sports.com ..... sportsbook.
www.sports.com/

29. **ESPN.com: NFL**
Standard | Cable Modem. More Videos. Hershey's Quarterback Challenge Sweepstakes Enter for a chance to win a trip to watch a Sunday football game at ESPN's ...
sports.espn.go.com/nfl/index

30. **FAI!**
Football Association of Ireland, Ireland's Official Football Website. Covers all levels from national team and league to youth and school teams.
www.fai.ie/

31. **Fantasy Football Cafe 2003**
A free cafe site catering to the fantasy football community with news, cheat sheets, sleepers, NFL player rankings, strategy tips and advice, predictions and ...
www.fantasyfootballcafe.com/

32. **evertonfc.com**
The official site with news, results, fixtures, tables, live commentary, statistics, players, and...
www.evertonfc.com/

33. **ESPN.com: College Football**
Daily NCAA news from ESPN Sports Zone television.
college.espn.go.com/ncf/index

34. **Henrik book**
Sports > Soccer > UEFA > Scotland > Clubs > C > Celtic F.C.
www.celticfc.co.uk/

35. **The official site of the St. Louis Rams - Home Page**
Official website. Pre-season and regular season schedules, news, And cheerleader information.
www.stlouisrams.com/

36. **Seahawks**
Official team site with audio and video clips, team news, depth charts, transactions, statistics,...
www.seahawks.com/

37. **ProFootballWeekly.com**
Online version of the venerable NFL paper. Rumors, previews, articles.
www.profootballweekly.com/

38. **SI.com - NCAA Football**
Online version of college football by Sports Illustrated Magazine.
www.cnnsi.com/football/college/

39. **BBC SPORT | Football**
Low Graphics version | Change Edition. | Help. Sport Homepage. Football. Live Videprinter. Results. Fixtures. Tables. My Club.
news.bbc.co.uk/sport/hi/english/football/default.stm

40. **Minnesota Vikings: The Official Team Web Site**
Official team site. News, player and team information, statistics, online ticket purchasing, team...
www.vikings.com/

41. **The Football League**

    The Football League Championship is the world's original league football competition and has provided...

    www.football-league.co.uk/

42. **Football Transfers Information - Index**

    The most comprehensive and accurate guide to football/ soccer transfers on the internet. News on all the latest transfers from around the World. Plus predictions of future players moves.

    www.footballtransfers.co.uk/

43. **ITV Football**

    | LATEST. Struggling Spurs Chase Moreira And Reid. Lens' French international striker Daniel Moreira says Tottenham Hotspur are one ...

    www.itv-football.co.uk/

44. **TEAMtalk Football - Football News Service - Top Stories**

    News updated daily, league tables, fixtures, radio, celebrity columnists, and your say.

    www.teamtalk.com/

45. **USA Football - Galvanizing Amateur Football**

    USA Football will provide you with email updates about the organization and various amateur football topics if you sign up here. Jump To... ...

    www.usafootball.com/

46. **Football at Nationwide - Football News**

    UK football scene indepth with Nationwide football. Coverage of the Premiership, Nationwide League and England team plus an in depth focus on the womens game.

    www.nationwide.co.uk/football/

47. **Football on the Net has Moved**

    Football on the Net has moved to a new and easy-to-remember web domain. Football on the Net wishes to thank NetHut for its support during the past two years.

    www.football.nethut.no/

48. **The Official Site of the Buffalo Bills**

    Official team site with audio and video clips, team news, depth charts, transactions, statistics,...

    www.buffalobills.com/

49. **American Football Coaches Association**

The American Football Coaches Association is the oldest coaching association in the US This is the website for informaton on the football coaching profession. ...

www.afca.com/

50. **Arizona Cardinals Football**

Official team site with audio and video clips, team news, depth charts, transactions, statistics,...

www.azcardinals.com/

51. **Football Culture - Home page**

Football site featuring football culture, football fans, football teams,football players, football trivia, football stats, and footy history. ...

www.footballculture.net/

52. **Southampton Football Club**

The official site with news, fixtures, match reports, club information, live match commentary, a forum,...

www.saintsfc.co.uk/

53. **Football Results, Statistics and Football Betting Odds Data**

Football-Data provides soccer results and football fixed odds + Asian Handicap betting odds data for the development of football betting systems. ...

www.football-data.co.uk/

54. **Collegefootballnews.com**

News and analysis of college football action and recruiting including latest updates and editorials.

www.collegefootballnews.com/

55. **World Football Organization - your source for association football...**

World Football Foundation is a specialised information source focusing on football (soccer, association football). ... World Football Organization, ...

www.worldfootball.org/

56. **High Quality Football Logos :.**

First class football logos from all over the world created using vector graphics making them fully scalable! Ever searched the web ...

www.hqfl.dk/

57. **Football on the Net**

A directory containing more than 15000 links from around the world.
www.footballonthenet.com/

58. **Eurobet Sports Betting - Online Sports Betting. Bet on a wide ...**

Eurobet Sports Betting - Online sports betting owned by Coral (UK), tax-free sports betting operation, offering football odds, betting on asian handicap ...
www.eurobet.com/

59. **Sky Sports - The Best Sport Coverage From Around The World**

News and features about Cup competitions and Premier, Nationwide, Scottish and European Leagues.
msn.skysports.com/skysports/football

60. **Fantasy Football Cheat Sheets and more at 4for4.com**

The Authoritative Fantasy Football Web Site providing Cheat Sheets,Rankings, NFL and Injury Report Information. ... Fantasy Football. Features NFL player rankings, statistics and information.
www.4for4.com/

61. **Colours Of Football**

Quality, soccer, premiership,gif,champions league,european football, strip, football, uniform, images,picture,seria a,football, uniform kit, jersey, calcio ...
www.colours-of-football.com/

62. **Scottish Football - all the soccer from Scotland**

ScottishFootball.com is now closed Please visit one of our other websites to enjoy top quality content and design from Scotland On Line Year Round Sites ...
www.scottishfootball.com/

63. **Google Directory - Sports > Football**

Google, Directory Help Search only in Football Search the Web. Football, ...
directory.google.com/Top/Sports/Football/

64. **This is football**

An in depth links based site dedicated to fullfill all your football requirements, with over 1000 links to football related sites. A portal site with an average of ten links to every UK professional football club.
www.thisis-football.com/

65. **Persian Football Dot Com: Your Source for Iranian Football News**
Covers the Iranian A-League and national team. News, rumors, message board, photos, audio and video clips.
www.persianfootball.com/

66. **About Football - National Football League - NFL News Rumors and...**
About Football provides nfl news and rumors along with offbeat tidbits about the National Football League. Also includes ... football fan! Football. ...
football.about.com/

67. **NIKEFOOTBALL**
Chat with the coolest football players, challenge a friend and win prizes in the game or check out the great football wear.
www.nikefootball.com/

68. **Yahoo! Sports**
Texas hopes to hook another Holiday Bowl win. Unlike many Longhorns, Vince Young hasn't yet played in a Holiday Bowl. Unlike many ...
sports.yahoo.com/ncaaf

69. **USATODAY.com**
Top Stories. A hit on TV, in stands. Games topped ratings in 30 markets; attendance record set. Full coverage. Dolphins eye Wolf....
www.usatoday.com/sports/nfl.htm

70. **Aberdeen Football Club**
Official Aberdeen Football Club site.
www.afc.co.uk/

71. **Irish Rugby**
Irish Rugby : Rugby world cup 2003. Official IRFU rugby site. About irfu, news, contacts. Irish rugby, 5 nations, RWC99, and international...
www.irfu.ie/

72. **Français**
Photo News (click logo's or click here for other partners : Coca-Cola, Sport Foot Magazine, Le Soir, Het Laatste Nieuws, Konica, Sun, Bianca Services, Well ... Official site [English/Nederlands/French]
www.footbel.com/

73. **HNS**

Official site with league and national team results and information.

www.hns-cff.hr/

74. **Football-linX - World of Soccer Links**

Soccer-Drill.com. 100 computer animated drills. Bob's 70-71 Footballers. Football Dome. ... Football Masçot Scrapbook. Worldwide Mascots. ...

www.football-linx.com/

75. **World Stadiums**

Home, STADIUM LIST, |, TOURNAMENTS, |, PAST and FUTURE, |, ARCHITECTURE,|, ABOUT, |. You are here: HOME Add this Site to your Favourites! Mainly soccer stadiums all over the world with pictures and links.

www.worldstadiums.com/

76. **FOOTBALL OUTSIDERS**

Making Football Outsiders the most original football site on the Web takes hard work — and a lot of nights and weekends. Visiting...

www.footballoutsiders.com/

77. **The Football Foundation**

The Football Foundation. Enter the Flash version of our site. ... The Football Foundation 25 Soho Square London W1D 4FF. Telephone 020 7534 4210 Fax 020 7287 0459. ...

www.footballfoundation.org.uk/

78. **RUSSIAN FOOTBALL**

News, results and standings for league, cup and national team play. Archives of past Russian and USSR...

www.quark.lu.se/~oxana/football.html

79. **The Dick Butkus Football Network**

A comprehensive football site that covers NFL, CFL, Arena, College, High School and Youth Leagues.

www.dickbutkus.com/

80. **footpro.fr - Site officiel de la Ligue de Football Professionnel**

World > Français > ... > Sports et loisirs > Sports > Football

www.lnf.fr/

81. **Yahoo! Sports Fantasy Football**

Sports Fantasy Football, or signing up for any of the Fantasy Football Premium Services, you agree to the Additional Terms of Service. ...

football.fantasysports.yahoo.com/f1

82. **The RFL Website**

Official website of the Rugby Football League. The site offers a diverse range of information, including ...

www.rfl.uk.com/

83. **Football in Austria**

World > Deutsch > ... > Verzeichnisse und Portale

www.football.at/

84. **D3football.com: The best source for Division III football ...**

Division III football information, with regional columnists, surveys, message boards and all the scores...

www.d3football.com/

85. **Irish Football Association**

Official governing body of soccer in Northern Ireland. National team roster, Irish Cup and international...

www.irishfa.com/

86. **Home of Football**

Football | Rugby | Formula One | Tennis | Snooker. Results Leagues World Cup Forum Clubs History Quiz, ... See the latest football leagues on your WAP phone. All the latest football news, results and information.

www.homeoffootball.com/

87. **FAM Online**

Official site, includes news, history, and fixtures and results for the national leagues and Malaysia Cup.

www.fam.org.my/

88. **Football Poets - football poetry, poems written by football fans.**

Football Poets - the world's leading collection of football poems. A poetic celebration of the beautiful game. Poetry and Prose for every football fan. A collection of football poems. Poetry and prose for every football fan.

www.footballpoets.org/

89. **Don Hansen's National Weekly Football Gazette - Small College ...**

News articles covering NCAA, NAIA and NCCAA divisions with related links, a chat room, message forum...

www.donhansen.com/

90. **Official AFL Website of the Collingwood Football Club**

Purchase your 2004 membership NOW! What makes Collingwood the biggest national sporting club in Australia? The commitment, passion and pride of its members. Official website for the team includes club history, news, coach information, player profiles, training...

collingwoodfc.com.au/

91. **Football Connect**

The ultimate directory for links to clubs, news, tournaments and any sites related to gloabl junior football / youth Soccer. A searchable global directory of links related to junior football / youth soccer.

www.footballconnect.co.uk/

92. **ladies football league directory UK**

Ladies football league directory an index of clubs in the UK. Ladies and girls who play football. The ladies Football League Directory ...

www.ladies-football.co.uk/

93. **Football Canada**

ENGLISH, FRANÇAIS.

www.footballcanada.com/

94. **United Arab Emirates Football Association**

Official site with national team and league information.

ww.uae-football.org.ae/

95. **www.MackBrown-TexasFootball.com**

News and information from The University of Texas Athletic Department. Lists roster and game schedule.

www.mackbrown-texasfootball.com/

96. **Fantasy Football Mastermind Information Services**

The Definitive Fantasy Football Information Service providing comprehensive fantasy coverage throughout the year since 1996. FANTASY ...

www.ffmastermind.com/

97. **tribalfootball.com**

English Football, 31-12-03. Chairman slams Newcastle performance. ... Australian Football. Providing a comprehensive and entertaining analysis of soccer around the world. Includes news, interviews...

www.tribalfootball.com/

98. **Official AFL Website of the Geelong Football Club**
Visit the AFL Geelong Football Club site for the latest news,stats, results, photos, audio, video and opinion. Official website. Multimedia, player profiles, image gallery, club history, current news and membership...
gfc.com.au/

99. **Weekend Football: UK fixed odds football betting**
Weekend Football: UK football betting information providing online fixed odds coupons, predictions and team form comment. best pricing...
www.weekendfootball.co.uk/

100. **Football Unites, Racism Divides**
An anti-racist project, supported by Sheffield United Football Club, to rid football of racism and to increase the participation of ethnic minority groups in ...
www.furd.org/

101. **Sporting Life - Football**
Latest news, columns, results, statistics, betting prices and online betting.
www.sportinglife.com/football/news/

102. **European Football Statistics**
The target of this site is to collect football statistics which are not easily found on internet. It isn't our target to have the ...
www.european-football-statistics.co.uk/

103. **Fantasy Baseball Leagues - HeySportsFans**
Classic and High Stakes fantasy football, baseball, and basketball leagues with unlimited free trades....
www.heysportsfans.com/

104. **All soccer For You - Online Soccer source -**
soccer, football, fußball, fútbol, soccer, football, fußball, fútbol,soccer, football, fußball, [Homepage] - [Photos] - [Videos ...
www.foot4u.com/english.asp

105. **Malta Football Association**
Our new e-mail address - info@mfa.com.mt. MIA Premier League 2003-2004 Marsaxlokk Pieta Hotspurs 1-0, Msida St Joseph Hamrun Spartans To promote and develop the game of football in the Republic of Malta.
www.mfa.com.mt/

106. **Football Betting Online**
FOOTBALL BETTING. Football-Betting-Links.com brings you the BEST football betting information available on the internet!
www.football-betting-links.com/

107. **The National Football Museum**
Offers the FIFA football collection, interactive, art, club and history galleries. Contains news,...
www.nationalfootballmuseum.com/

108. **BBC Fantasy Football Monthly 2003-04**
Free to enter monthly fantasy football game based on the English Premiership, with prizes available...
bbcfootball.fantasyleague.co.uk/

109. **Gator Football @ Gatorzone.com**
Official web site of Gator football.
www.gatorzone.com/football/

110. **Fantasy Football - Footballguys.com Main Page**
Fantasy football cheatsheets, articles, rankings, advice, VBD tools,and fantasy football links. Fantasy football articles, cheatsheets.
www.footballguys.com/

111. **Pro Football Betting Online - Pro Football Betting Online**
Pro Football Betting Online brings you in-depth sports information so you can keep up-to-date on the sports you love.
www.pro-football-betting-online.com/

112. **ohiostatebuckeyes.com - Ohio State University Official Athletic ...**
Ohio State University Official Athletic Site: complete coverage of all Buckeye NCAA sports including basketball, football, baseball, soccer, volleyball, and ...
ohiostatebuckeyes.ocsn.com/sports/ m-footbl/osu-m-footbl-body.html

113. **Index of /fpage**
A look at the history of soccer in Ireland from its modest beginnings in 1878 through to the golden...
www.clubi.ie/fpage/

114. **Football Transfer Rumours Football Transfer News**
Offers the latest rumours and predictions.
www.football-rumours.com/

115. **FootballCamps.com - The Best Football Camps in the USA!**
Football Camps - The best football camps in America to learn individual and team techniques from Top NFL Players. ... The Best Football Camps in the USA! Youth football camps for ages 8 - 18, each led by a current or former NFL player. Guest appearances...
www.footballcamps.com/

116. **AFL - Arena Football League**
Official site. News and information.
www.af2.com/

117. **American Football Association's Website**
Dave Burch, Ron Real,minor league,AFA, Minor League Football,Semi Pro Football, Arena League, Minor League Professional Football, Semi Pro football, Sports ...
members.aol.com/amerfoot/afa.htm

118. **bomberland :: The Official Website of the Essendon Football Club**
The Official web site of the Essendon Football Club
www.essendonfc.com.au/

119. **Football picture archive by Stuart Clarke - The Homes of Football**
A collection of over 2500 photographs taken by the official Football Foundation photographer Stuart Clarke.
www.homesoffootball.co.uk/

120. **Football LIVE**
Follow all European football-matches live with over 400 direc links with livescores, audiolinks and...
www.footballlive.dk/

121. **indianfootball.com | indianfootball.de - India's Premier Football ...**
Includes articles, interviews, the national team, historical database, hall of fame, news and results.
www.indianfootball.com/

122. **Football Physics has moved!**
Football Physics has moved! If you are not redirected in 5 seconds, please click the link below. http://physics.unl.edu/outreach/football.html. physics.unl.edu/football.html

123. **Sport**
Premiership, World Cup and international coverage, plus news, match reports and comment by team. Extensiv...
sport.independent.co.uk/football/

124. **pro-football-reference.com**
Quick Index: About | Players | Teams | Years | Raw Data | Articles, Support pro-football-reference.com.
www.pro-football-reference.com/

125. **RSSSF Norwegian football server**
News, updated results and tables, Norwegian soccer archive, links and mailing lists.
www.unik.no/~larsa/football.html

126. **youth football directory an index of youth teams in the uk**
youth football directory an index of youth teams in the uk. If your youth team is not listed please click add your team. ... Football Auction.
www.schoolfootball.net/

127. **Professional Football Researchers Association- Pro Football ...**
The Professional Football Researchers Association (PFRA) is dedicated to preserving the complete history of professional football, including the players, teams ...
www.footballresearch.com/

128. **Pure Fantasy Football - The Soccer Management Game**
Fantasy soccer management with UK and European teams. Includes forums.
www.purefantasyfootball.com/

129. **Sports : Football**
Introduction to the game, rules, and fixtures.
www.gaa.ie/sports/football/

130. **Football Prospects College Sports Scholarships And Athletic ...**
Football recruiting service for college bound football prospects.
www.footballprospects.com/

131. **Football Alberta's Home Page**
To regulate and foster the growth of all aspects of amateur football in Alberta.
www.footballalberta.ab.ca/

132. **Dave Campbell's Texas Football**
Includes current schedules, football camps, and information on Texas football from high school to...
www.texasfootball.com/

133. **Fantasy Football Index Home Page**

Contains analysis including advice, rankings, updates, injury reports, columns, depth charts. Pay...

www.fantasyindex.com/

134. **The Official Website of the Women's Professional Football League**

Official league site has league news, schedule, and statistics.

www.womensprofootball.com/

135. **Football America**

Supplier of football equipment to teams and individuals.

www.footballamerica.com/

136. **International Australian Football Confederation**

The role of the International Australian Football Confederation (IAFC) is to coordinate and develop Australian Rules football internationally. Official site of the International Australian Football Council, with links to worldwide Aussie Rules...

www.iafc.org.au/

137. **International Football Results 1872-present**

Results indexed by major and minor championships. Includes latest updates, sitemap, calendar, rumours,...

www.rdasilva.demon.co.uk/football.html

138. **football web rings - soccer web rings**

Football web ring. Soccer web ring. A directory of soccer web sites in the world.

www.footballwebring.co.uk/

139. **D2Football.com**

D2Football.com is the definitive source for Division II Football information on the Internet. From player profiles to up-to-the-minute.

www.d2football.com/

140. **Football BC : Amateur Football in British Columbia**

Looking for Amateur Football Information in BC? Congratulations, you ... below. Check out new Football Clinic and Camp Information. Who ...

www.footballbc.org/

141. **GoPSUsports.com - Official Home of Penn State Athletics**

Includes game schedules, news items, pictures, a roster, and statistics.

www.gopsusports.com/Football/home.cfm

142. **channel4.com - Football Italia**
The best and the rest. Football Italia highlights which individuals are on a high and a low after the Week 14 games. More. ...
www.channel4.com/sport/football_italia/

143. **Sir Norman Chester Centre for Football Research, University of...**
Research. Situated in the Sociology Department at the University. Funded by Football Trust. Leading football research centre. Some results are available online, including...
www.le.ac.uk/snccfr/

144. **FLAG FOOTBALL MAGAZINE WEBSITE**
News, Tournaments, World Cup, Photos, Message board, Chat room.
www.flagmag.com/

145. **The Ultimate Football Page**
One of the biggest soccer sites with over 160 player profiles. Includes player profiles, mailing lists and chat.
www.isfa.com/server/web/uf/

146. **Football Victoria**
Aims to provide Victorians with opportunity to be involved in Australian Rules Football. Includes...
www.footballvic.com.au/

147. **Football Kingz**
The official web site with news, multimedia, team information, results and fixtures.
www.footballkingz.co.nz/

148. **SLAM! Sports - CFL Football**
Delivers news, scores, statistics and features.
www.canoe.ca/Football/home.html

149. **American Youth Football Home**
American Youth Football is a national organization that sanctions local youth footballorganizations and provides leadership, support services, and safety to ...
www.americanyouthfootball.com/

150. **Footballnepal - Home**
Association promoting Nepalese football. Includes association news, membership information, and national...
www.bhakundo.org.np/

151. **The Football Archive**
The Football Archive. This page uses a custom made CGI ... Football Simulator. ThinkQuest Homepage. This page has been optimized ...
library.thinkquest.org/12590/

152. **The Ladies Gaelic Football Association of Ireland - Home page**
History, pictures, and leagues.
www.ladiesgaelic.ie/

153. **Canadian Football Hall of Fame and Museum - Official Website**
Celebrates the Canadian version of gridiron football, featuring the Grey Cup, CFL and CIAU clubs....
www.footballhof.com/

154. **All Football - Best Online Guide To Soccer Shops, Soccer Services**
Guide to soccer shops and services.
www.all-football.com/

155. **Football Anorak - Comprehensive UK Football statistics for ...**
Statistics and tips for English/Scottish matches.
www.footballanorak.com/

156. **Maximum Football**
Links, forums, FAQs, and screenshots.
www.maximum-football.com/

157. **Yahooligans! - Sports and Recreation:Football (American)**
Football (American). All of Yahooligans! just this category. Inside Yahooligans! Big Picture: check out football and other sports news on Yahooligans! ...
yahooligans.com/sports_and_recreation/ Football__American_/

158. **non league football directory an index of clubs in the UK. We have**
Non league football directory an index of clubs in the UK. We have clubs from theconference down to village sides. Please add your team. ... Football Auction.
www.nonleaguefootball.co.uk/

159. **The Football Quotes Page**
The Internet's largest (known) compendium of comedy football (soccer) related quotes.
www.geocities.com/SouthBeach/Palms/6687/quotes.html

160. **CBS.SportsLine.com - NCAA Football**

College Football coverage including NCAA news, scores, standings, schedules, injuries, stats, poll, team and player news, Division I and II, and bowl games. ...

cbs.sportsline.com/collegefootball/

161. **Gee's Football Links - The Worldwide Football/Soccer Club ...**

Worldwide football/soccer club links directory with links to clubs sites on the net from around the world. Menu. A guide to club football around the world.

www.geesfootballlinks.com/

162. **Football HawkeyeSports.com - University of Iowa Official Athletic...**

University of Iowa Official Athletic Site: complete coverage of all Hawkeye NCAA sports including basketball, football, baseball, soccer, volleyball, and swimming ...

www.hawkeyefootball.com/

163. **Football Girls UK - the womens football site**

A fun site about womens football, with songs, games, photos, opinion and an index of clubs in the UK. ..

footballgirls.freeservers.com/

164. **The Football Forum — More Than Just A Game**

Discuss everything and anything football related throughout our World Forums. Also offering a Weekly Quiz, and Prediction League.

www.thefootballforum.com/

165. **InfoSports - Youth Football on the Web**

Youth Football on the Web. InfoSports is a nice resource for youth football. On this youth sports site you will find football tournments.

infosports.net/football/

166. **UK Football Guide**

UK Football Guide - news and results from all the Football Clubs, English and Scottish Premierships, Leagues, Cups and Competitions. ... UK Football Guide. ...

www.ukfootballguide.co.uk/

167. **Paper Football Zone - All About Paper Football**

Paper Football Zone All About Paper Football. ... The football slides to the edge of the table, drawing suddenly to a stop. It doesn't look good. Includes rules of the game, how to fold a football and pictures.www.paperfootballzone.com/

168. **Gateway Football Conference**

A football conference of eight state institutions in the Midwest. Site includes weekly news and statistic...

www.gatewayfootball.org/

169. **Philosophy Football**

Philosophy Football - T-Shirts from the sporting outfitters of intellectual distinction. Order online from the UK here. ... New to the Philosophy Football Range. ...

www.philosophy-football.co.uk/

170. **NFL.com Fantasy**

Fantasy football, Free Fantasy Football, fantasy football commissioner, fantasy football challenge game, fantasy football scout. ...

fantasy.nfl.com/

171. **SportsLists.net Football Finder**

Tiger Tech's site is an alpha index for finding football pages. Formerly Football Crazy.

www.sportslists.net/football/

172. **Asean Football Federation**

Promoting international soccer in Southeast Asia. Includes information about AFF membership and tourname...

www.aseanfootball.com/

173. **Football: PointMe.To it**

Provides link to various leagues and types of football around the world. ... Also includes links to news sources dedicated to American football. ...

pointme.to/football/

174. **East Midlands Football - Leicester City, Derby County, Forest ...**

Includes a free to enter prediction league for East Midlands supporters, test your skills against...

www.emfootball.co.uk/

175. **Football**

Football Links. Sub Categories. ... Websites. Football: Point Me To it - Provides links to football leagues, including American, Canadian and Australian Rules. ...

www.football-toplinks.com/

22
Golf

1. **PGATOUR.COM**
   Providing scores, news, schedules, tickets, and live chat related to all US tours.
   www.golfweb.com/
2. **GolfServ**
   Tournament golf coverage plus sections for courses and travel, instruction, site membership services...
   www.golf.com/
3. **GOLFONLINE**
   Golf, golf, and more golf. If you can't get enough of it, come to GOLFONLINE.com to find the latest golf news, stats, travel guides...
   www.golfonline.com/
4. **PGA.com Home**
   Get golf information, golf tournament updates and golf news from the official site of the PGA of America.
   www.pga.com/
5. **TheGolfChannel.com - Golf's Home Page**
   Golf news, features and commentary, tournament coverage, statistics and schedules, video clips, televisio...
   www.thegolfchannel.com/
6. **GolfDigest.com | How to Play, What to Play, Where to Play**
   Central hub including archived content and information for the magazines Golf Digest, Golf for Women,...
   www.golfdigest.com/
7. **United States Golf Association**
   About the organization, staff, functions, activites and location.
   www.usga.org/

8. **World Golf: Golf courses from around the world**
   Golf course listings, travel, golf links, great golf humor, tour information, golf tips and more. Golf courses from around the world plus course reviews, golf travel, articles and reference pages.
   www.worldgolf.com/

9. **LPGA Official Website**
   Features results of LPGA, womens golf, player interviews, golf merchandise, youth golf programs, a...
   www.lpga.com/

10. **GOLFLINK.com - Web Guide to Golf Courses, Resorts, Schools**
    A resource for golfers featuring info on golf associations, courses, manufacturers, merchandise, pro shops, real estate, golf resorts, schools, services, golf ... An online directory of golf information. Including resorts, courses, tips, equipment and travel.
    www.golflink.com/

11. **clubs/gbbII.asp**
    Manufactures golf balls and the Big Bertha line of clubs. Site includes virtual tours of the company's...
    www.callawaygolf.com/

12. **ESPN.com - Golf Index**
    Five stories from a strange season in golf made The ESPN 100, headed by Annika Sorenstam's groundbreaking foray onto the PGA Tour at No. 12. ...
    sports.espn.go.com/golf/index

13. **GOLFCOURSE.com**
    Data on more than 20000 golf courses. Search the database by course name, city, state, or country.
    www.golfcourse.com/

14. **Golf Today - Europe's Premier Online Golf Magazine**
    Player and tournament news coverage and feature articles, plus a course directory.
    www.golftoday.co.uk/

15. **USGA's Rules of Golf Home Page**
    Rules of Golf— The USGA and The Royal and Ancient Golf Club of St. ... Rules Jurisdiction The USGA and the Royal and Ancient Golf Club of St. ...
    www.usga.org/rules/

16. **National Golf Foundation - Information and Insights on the ...**
    NGF - Information and Insights on the business of golf, Member ID. Password. Industry News. ... first Internet-based data collection tool for golf facilities. Provides golf business research
    www.ngf.org/
17. **CobraGolf.com**
    Makers of Baffler Multi-Metal irons and Gravity Back metal woods, bags and accessories. Site has...
    www.cobragolf.com/
18. **TaylorMade Golf**
    TaylorMade Golf. Please explore all of our products and services. Features specifications on golf clubs and other products, a demo day and retailer locator, and staff...
    www.taylormadegolf.com/
19. **The Golf Circuit**
    Internet golf magazine since 1994. Enjoy the best golf instruction, equipment,rules, travel and much more. ... INSIDE GOLF CIRCUIT. Daily Instruction. ...
    www.golfcircuit.com/
20. **The Official Site of the Masters Golf Tournament**
    IBM presents The Official Site of The Masters Golf Tournament, played at Augusta National. Learn about golf history, see results.
    www.masters.org/
21. **PDGA**
    Includes rules, a world-wide directory of courses, bulletin boards to find partners, a FAQ, membership...
    www.pdga.com/
22. **Golf Course, Golf Resort and Golf Club Links - Linkaway Golf**
    Directory containing over 4000 links to sites of golfing interest around the world.
    www.linkaway.com/
23. **The Royal and Ancient Golf Club of St Andrews**
    The Royal and Ancient Golf Club of St Andrews is the governing authority for the rules of the game in more than 100 affiliated nations and is responsible for ...
    www.randa.org/

24. **PINGGOLF.com**
Makers of PING golf equipment from drivers to putters, with information regarding clubs, apparel,...
www.pinggolf.com/

25. **Plug In to Your Profession - GCSAA Online**
Golf course management information, member areas, and a research section which covers requests for...
www.gcsaa.org/

26. **Cleveland Golf**
Cleveland Golf, preferred golf clubs, irons, wedges of PGA Tour professionals like Vijay Singh, David Toms, and more. Offering a full line of clubs with a classic look and technology. Site provides information on Cleveland...
www.clevelandgolf.com/

27. **GOLFSEARCH.com — From the Editors of GOLFONLINE.com**
PGA, USGA, LPGA - GOLFSearch.com - Everything and anything you wanted to know about golf can be found here on GOLFSearch.com, the world's best golf search ...
www.golfsearch.com/

28. **scottish golf - scotland courses - clubs equipment - golf news ...**
scottish golf clubs courses and equipment with golf news from courses across Scotland from scottishgolf.com. ...
www.scottishgolf.com/

29. **Golf.at - Österreichischer Golf-Verband**
World > Deutsch > Sport > Ballsport > Golf
www.golf.at/

30. **SI.com - Golf**
It was a breakthrough year for Mike Weir and Davis Love, but SI.com's Gary Van Sickle says that Annika Sorenstam was golf's top performer in 2003.
www.cnnsi.com/golf/

31. **Electrotank Online gaming at its best**
Learn more... Email this to a friend! New Game!
www.electrotank.com/games/playGames.asp?gameID=31

32. **Golf Europe: Golf Courses in Ireland, Scotland, England and more**
Golf in Europe with details and reviews of golf clubs in Ireland, UK, Scotland, Portugal, Spain and more. Also golf history, golfer ...
www.golfeurope.com/

33. **Titleist.com**

    Official site for branded golf clubs and golf balls, and includes dealer locations, media center,...

    www.titleist.com/

34. **Golf Illustrated**

    Trial Subscription Free Titleist Driver Paid Subscription Free Titleist Pro V1 Balls Golfer's Shop Incredible Savings On Golf Equipment Advertising Rates ...

    www.golfillustrated.com/

35. **American Golf clubs. California, Texas courses. 18 US states, UK**

    Events planning, golf lessons, corporate services, Nike Junior Golf School,charity events, fundraisers, tournaments. ... AGC THE Golf Resource. ...

    www.americangolf.com/

36. **Golfweek.com | Read It. Live It.**

    Go deep into golf news, golf scores and golf information gathered by the award-winning golf newspaper, Golfweek. Search PGA Tour...

    www.golfweek.com/

37. **World Golf Village, Home of the World Golf Hall of Fame**

    Information on new homes and condominiums available in this golf community.

    www.wgv.com/

38. **About Golf: Golf Club Reviews, Golf Tips, Golf Info**

    Find links, tips, lessons, product reviews and much more information about golf from your About Golf Guide. ... know about Golf. Golf. A compendium of information and resources on golf, including an extensive directory of recommended links.

    golf.about.com/

39. **USATODAY.com**

    Breaking golf news from the main professional tours, including live scoring, results, commentary and...

    www.usatoday.com/sports/golf/sg.htm

40. **GOLF.BE - the nr 1 golfsite in Belgium ! - including hotels, clubs**

    Portal including clubs, organizations, schools, teetime reservations, hotels, news, equipment, travel,...

    www.golf.be/

41. **Global Golf Home Page**
Global Golf contains a comprehensive list of golf courses, hotels etc. from around the world. Users can search for courses in specific ...
www.globalgolf.com/

42. **Golf Tips Magazine is golf's most in-depth instruction and ...**
Golf Tips Magazine is the avid golfer's complete source for golf instruction and equipment reviews. Focusing on user-friendly information ...
www.golftipsmag.com/

43. **Golf Guide - Your complete Golf Course Guide!**
Comprehensive guide to golf information throughout the United States.Search our huge database of courses, pros, retailers, and practice ranges. A comprehensive, state by state, zoned golf course locating system listing over 8000 golf courses....
www.golfguide.com/

44. **ESPN.com - Golf Index**
Standard | Cable Modem Mike McGetrick, landing-area drill ESPN Golf Schools' McGetrick on how to consistently hit your landing area. ...
espn.go.com/golfonline/

45. **Golf in Europe-Europa: European Golf Club Directory and Travel.**
Your guide to almost every golf course in Europe and travel destinations around the world. A directory ... related links. Golf in Europe, ...
www.pmfgolfguide.com/

46. **#1 Golf Search Engine - Find golf equipment, golf links, courses**
Golf's largest search engine! This site has the largest database of golf tips, golf equipment, golf stores, golf manufacturers, golf links, courses and more. ...
www.golfhelp.com/

47. **Nike Golf**
Nike Golf, shoes, footwear, Nike Golf apparel, bags, courses, Nike Golf equipment, products, gloves, players, pros, screen savers, contests, tips, advice ...
www.nikegolf.com/

48. **Golf Online Danmark**

Golf Online Danmark - Golf Online Denmark - Golf in Denmark, 136 Danish Golf Clubs - where to play and where to stay. European Tour...

www.golfonline.dk/

49. **Golfsmith.com**

Offers proline equipment, apparel and shoes, balls, accessories, videos, and training aids, plus...

www.golfsmith.com/

50. **The Original UK-GOLF Home Page**

The old established UK-Golf.com site has moved onwards and upwards to greater things!! Since its creation in 1995 it 'just ...

www.uk-golf.com/

51. **E*GOLF**

The summary for this Japanese page contains characters that cannot be correctly displayed in this language/character set.

www.e-golf.co.jp/

52. **Golf at Cincinnati.Com - Your Key to the City**

Cincinnati Golf Courses and news coverage from The Cincinnati Enquirer, The Cincinnati Post and Cincinnati.Com. ...

www.cincinnati.com/golf/

53. **RCGA**

Association governs Canadian amateur golf, including Rules of Golf, Canadian amateur and junior championships, Future Links, Canadian Golf Hall of Fame, Bell ...

www.rcga.org/

54. **American Junior Golf Association**

Provides information, schedule of tournaments and results, information about volunteering.

www.ajga.org/

55. **GOLF (SOHO) Home page**

The GOLF experiment on the SOHO mission aims to study the internal structure of the sun by measuring the spectrum of global oscillations in the frequency range ...

www.medoc-ias.u-psud.fr/golf/

56. **BBC SPORT | Golf**

Sport Homepage. Golf. World Results. UK Results. Calendar. Men's Rankings. US Tour. European Tour. ... Find out why golf's all in the mind! ...

news.bbc.co.uk/sport/hi/english/golf/default.stm

57. **Golf.no - Møteplassen for norske golfspillere - Golf i Norge ...**

Enter valid description

www.golf.no/

58. **World Golf Championships**

Events co-sanctioned by the European Tour, the Japan Golf Tour, the PGA TOUR, the PGA Tour of Australasia...

www.worldgolfchampionships.com/

59. **Mr. Golf Etiquette**

Visit The Golf Etiquette Confessional. Confess your golf etiquette infractions and become a better golfer! Order The GolfBook For Kids by Mr. Golf Etiquette. ...

www.mrgolf.com/

60. **GOLFSPAIN**

Golfspain is the leading Spanish golf web offering all golf tourism services. These include tee time bookings, golf packages with ...

www.golfspain.com/

61. **Golf Trainer**

Internets Premier Online Golf Fitness Program providing golf-specific workouts, stretches, tips and training programs. ... Golf Fitness Products. Exercise, fitness, training aids, equipment, lessons, swing tips and conditioning advice to improve...

www.golf-trainer.com/

62. **OPENGOLF**

Information on the revised Rules of Golf. Story of the Championship. more. more. ... Coltart and Frost enter international qualifying. World Golf Ranking, The official Web site of the Open Championship in St. Andrews, Scotland.

www.opengolf.com/

63. **golf bc courses - BCgolfguide.com - Free Golf Handicap Tracker**

BCgolfguide.com - features a free golf Handicap Tracker - a complete guide to all golf courses in BC, free contests, video clips, classified ads, course ... Guide to golf courses in BC plus buy and sell ads, reviews, video clips and links.

www.bcgolfguide.com/

64. **Robert Trent Jones Golf Trail**

Nine Robert Trent Jones designed courses throughout Alabama. Course descriptions, rates, and locations...

www.rtjgolf.com/

65. **OttawaGolf - The Internet Resource For Golf In Canada's Capital**

Online tee-time booking and course profiles with detailed maps. Discount Golf Club. OttawaGolf Tour and Open events, supporting Junior golf. ...

www.ottawagolf.com/

66. **The Golf Warehouse - The Net's Premier Online Golf Superstore**

The Golf Warehouse - Golf Clubs, Balls, Bags, Shoes, Apparel, and Equipment - Largest Selection of Golf Items Online. ... 1. Titleist Personalized Golf Balls. ...

www.tgw.com/

67. **Golfballs.com - Golf Balls, Golf Shoes, Golf Bags, Golf Club, Used...**

Offering golf equipment, golf gifts, and golf accessories including personalized golf balls, used golfballs, logo golf balls, golf shoes, golf bags, and golf ...

www.golfball.com/

68. **The San Diego Golf Pages**

The best guide to golf facilities in San Diego: golf courses, driving ranges / practice centers, pro-shops / golf stores, golf manufacturers, local golf ...

www.golfsd.com/

69. **Online golf stores - clubs, gifts, books, videos, training-aids**

Online golf stores with golf clubs, gifts, accessories, books, training aids, videos. Compare our golf club prices to anyone's! Offers books, videos, aids, gifts, art, and accessories.

www.golfprecinct.com/

70. **Golf101: Learn to Golf**

Golf tips, lessons, techniques, news, equipment, handicap calculator, directory of schools, instructors...

www.golf101.com/

71. **The St Andrews Links - The Official Website of The "Home of Golf"**

Home of the Old Course and the rich history of the game which has evolved over 600 years. Royal and...

www.standrews.org.uk/

72. **GolfUS.com**

What's New, New Ohio Regional Golf Site! Through ... packages. Midwest Golf Auctions Thank you for making 2003 another great success! General directory of golf courses,driving ranges, and golf resorts.

www.golfus.com/

73. **Golf Scotland Tailor Made Golfing Holidays**

Golf Scotland are specialists in individually tailored golfing holidays in Scotland. ...

www.golfscotland.co.uk/

74. **www.golf.fi**

World > Suomi > Urheilu > Golf

www.golf.fi/

75. **Golf Stars Online**

Golf tour professionals: find their sites, statistics, photos, interviews and more. Welcome to Golf Stars Online, where you can ...

www.golfstarsonline.com/

76. **GolfColorado.com - Colorado Golf Courses, Golf Resorts Vacations**

Colorado Golf Courses, Golf Resorts and Colorado Golf Tournaments Colorado PGA CGA CWGA CJGA Colorado Golf tee times. ResortQuest.

www.golfcolorado.com/

77. **United States Golf Teachers Federation: Golf Teaching**

United States Golf Teachers Federation: Learn to teach golf. ... United States Golf Teachers Federation®. Leader In The Field of Golf Instruction. Has over 10000 members representing every state in the US.

www.usgtf.com/

78. **GolfBC | British Columbia's Finest Golf Courses | Whistler ...**

The GolfBC Group: the name linked with exceptional golfing, brings you a unique collection of British Columbia's finest golf courses. ...

www.golfbc.com/

79. **Golf holidays, golf breaks, 2-Fore!-1, golf news**

Golf holidays, golf weekends, golf course finder, golf breaks, Ryder Cup feature, and golf travel from ifyougolf.com. View 360° course panoramas, find your favorite course and book a golf weekend; latest golf news.

www.ifyougolf.com/

80. **Southern California Golf Association**

Southern California Golf Association's home page. For more than a century, the SCGA has worked to preserve, protect. Official home of the SCGA. Provides tournament results, golf expo information, membership, courses,...

www.scga.org/

81. **Rockies Golf: Colorado Golf Course Guide**

RockiesGolf.com: The Rocky Mountains' definitive golf course guide! Discover ... TRAVEL FEATURE Calgary has gone crazy for golf. Located ...

www.rockiesgolf.com/

82. **Yahoo! Sports - Golf**

THOUSAND OAKS, Calif. (AP) — Ben Curtis is full of surprises. First, he stunned the golf world by winning the British Open in his first major. ...

sports.yahoo.golfserv.com/

83. **Northern California Golf Association**

NCGA Board Members. Rules of Golf. Handicap and Rating. ... NCGA News and Information.

www.ncga.org/

84. **Golf Club Exchange.com**

Get Help! Browse For Golf Clubs. Sell Your Golf Clubs, Upgrade To Newer Clubs, Request Golf Clubs At your Price. Already know the club you want? Advanced Search. ...

www.golfclubexchange.com/

85. **Arizona Golf Courses, Phoenix, Scottsdale golf packages, tee times**

Arizona's Daily Golf News Authority! Complete golf Arizona course guide, golf club and resort reviews, travel features.

www.scottsdale-golf-resorts.com/

86. **thewgm.com**

PHILADELPHIA GOLF Monthly Free 2-year subscription. News, schedules, tournaments, courses, information in the Washington, DC area

www.thewgm.com/

87. **Golf Equipment - Golf Clubs**

GolfStockpile.com Shop Our Huge Selection of Great Golf Values! Adidas Shoes. Special, Iron Sale. >Just Arrived! >Just a Few Left! ...

www.golfuniverse.com/

88. **Kids Golf "Drive, Pitch and Putt"**

Kids Golf DRIVE, PITCH and PUTT ™ Junior Golf Skills Challenge May 1 - November 30, 2003. The only junior golf skills challenge free to every kid on the planet. Jack Nicklaus, Honorary Chairman....

www.kidsgolf.com/

89. **Maxfli Golf**

Maxfli Golf home page. Product information and specifications for Maxfli clubs and balls, with accessories and information...

www.maxfli.com/

90. **Dansk Golf Union**

World > Dansk > Sport > Golf

www.dgu-golf.dk/

91. **British Golf Museum Official Website**

The official website for the British Golf Museum. ... Enter, Welcome to the British Golf Museum Official Website! Where better to find out about golf than in St. The British Golf Museum tells the fascinating story of British golf from the middle ages through to...

www.britishgolfmuseum.co.uk/

92. **golf.is**

Golfsamband Íslands

www.golf.is/

93. **mizunousa.com**

All contents © 2003 MIZUNO USA Inc. All rights reserved. Legal Notice and Privacy Policy, Business Partners Only. Manufactures and distributes baseball, golf, softball, running, track and field, volleyball equipment,...

www.mizunousa.com/

94. **MacGregor Golf**

Makers of Tourney irons and metalwoods, as well as accessories and men's clothing.

www.macgregorgolf.com/

95. **Golf Vacation Packages.**

Golf Vacation Packages to Scotland Ireland The Masters Tournament Spain Pebble Beach Ryder Cup. ... memories!! © 2003 SGH Golf Inc. ...

www.sghgolf.com/

96. **Golf Network**
The summary for this Japanese page contains characters that cannot be correctly displayed in this language/character set.
www.golfnetwork.co.jp/

97. **Thor's Golf Links**
Links to golf related sites
www.ttsoft.com/thor/golflinks.html

98. **American Society of Golf Course Architects golf course design**
North America professional association. Includes member list, news, directory of suppliers, developer's...
www.golfdesign.org/

99. **Browser Sniffik**
World > Czech > Sporty > Golf
www.golf.cz/

100. **Federgolf**
World > Italiano > Sport > Golf
www.federgolf.it/

101. **GolfReview.com - Golf Equipment Reviews**
Read reviews, write reviews. Buy golf gear. ... more... Discuss everything golf in The 19th Hole Messageboard now powered by VBulletin! ...
www.golfreview.com/

102. **EGA - European Golf Association**
Show more News... Download latest Bulletin with many interesting informations, actual News and lots of happening Reports.
www.ega-golf.ch/

103. **en/default.asp**
/en/default.asp /en/beginning.asp /en/home.asp /en/index.asp /en/linking.asp /en/privacy.asp /en/promise.asp /en/proof.asp /en/putters.asp /en/signup.asp /en ...
www.odysseygolf.com/

104. **Carbite Golf**
Manufactures Polar Balanced putters, and distributes Daiwa golf equipment in North America.
www.carbitegolf.com/

105. **Onlinegolf.co.uk - Europe's No.1 online golf store, golf equipment...**
On-Line Golf UK - Pro Shop, golf store, selling top brand golf equipment at great prices, irons, woods, bags, balls from Taylor Made. Offers equipment, accessories, apparel, shoes, balls, and gifts.
www.onlinegolf.co.uk/

106. **Doral® Golf Resorts | Home**
Luxury accommodations and facilities convenient to the airport. Online availability, tee times and...
www.doralresort.com/

107. **The Official Website of the Australian Golf Union**
Link to Australian Golf Union Homepage. ... Copyright © 2001 Australian Golf Union and TWI Interactive Pty Limited ("TWIi") All Rights Reserved. ...
www.agu.org.au/

108. **amateur-golf.com the Web's leading Amateur Golf Site**
amateur-golf.Com - amateur golf news, information,schedules from the UK, Europe and the World. Covers related golf news and events, with a focus on the United Kingdom.
www.amateur-golf.com/

109. **Troon Golf**
Leading the world in upscale golf management, development, and marketing, Troon Golf proudly represents more than one hundred golf courses located in 20 ...
www.troongolf.com/

110. **Canada golf courses - GolfCanada.com**
CanadaGolfer.com is your source for golf, accommodations, tee times in Canada. Course guides, features and information on Canadian top golf destinations.
www.golfcanada.com/

111. **Orlimar Golf Company : Welcome**
Makes and markets equipment; online sales offered.
www.orlimar.com/

112. **Volkswagen: Golf**
Base MSRP for US 2004 models, excluding taxes, title, options, dealer, emissions, and registration charges. See dealer for details.
www.vw.com/golf/

113. **FOXSports.com :: Golf**

Images of 2003. Surprises dominate year in golf. Tiger Woods didn't win a major. ... More News. Fantasy Golf Season 1 — Dollar Values. ...

www.foxsports.com/named/FS/Golf

114. **Edwin Watts Golf | online golf retailer**

Edwin Watts Golf shop carries all the top brands including Callaway golf, Nike golf, Titleist, Scotty Cameron, Odysseygolf, Ashworth and Taylor Made. ...

www.edwinwatts.com/

115. **New Zealand Golf**

Photo supplied by Wairakei Inernational Golf Club. ... Welcome to NZ Golf. NZ Golf is the governing body for golf in NZ. Throughout our ...

www.nzga.co.nz/

116. **Golf and Travel.com**

GolfandTravel.com is a comprehensive guide to the world's great golf destinations. Enjoy remarkable photography and travel information ...

www.golfandtravel.com/

117. **Australian Golf Courses - AUSGOLF features every one of ...**

Australian Golf Courses - AUSGOLF features every one of Australia's 1500 golf courses plus golf travel information, the latest golf news, golf clubs, courses ...

www.ausgolf.com.au/

118. **Texas - Golf in the SouthWest**

Golf in the SouthWest - Highlighting Golf in the Great State of Texas. New Golf in the SouthWest Features. ... Golf Auctions Looking for a slightly-used golf bag?

www.golfsw.com/

23
Gymnastics

1. **USA Gymnastics Online**
   The official web site of USA Gymnastics. Live events, athlete biographies, member services, and games.
   www.usa-gymnastics.org/
2. **British Gymnastics**
   Detailed information about the BAGA and all the services it offers to Gymnastics. Also the latest...
   www.baga.co.uk/
3. **Gymnastics Canada Home Page - gymnastic sports in canada**
   The Gymnastics Canada Gymnastique home page. Offering news, program updates, event information and more. ...
   www.gymcan.org/
4. **Inside Gymnastics Magazine**
   Inside Gymnastics is the all-new magazine for the sport of gymnastics with stunning photography, athlete profiles, and event coverage. ...
   www.insidegymnastics.com/
5. **Gymnastics Australia WebSite**
   Events, results, news and clubs in Australia.
   www.gymnastics.org.au/
6. **House Gymnastics**
   Harrison and Ford House Gymnastics. A cross breed of yoga, breakdancing,climbing and gymnastics in a domestic setting. Do try this at home. ...
   www.housegymnastics.com/
7. **Non-Traditional Gymnastics**
   Call it educational, developmental, creative, informal or any other kind of gymnastics you want to. But, whatever you call it there ...
   www.geocities.com/Colosseum/Stadium/7261/

8. **Rhythmic Gymnastics**

   Rhythmic Gymnastics (former RSG) in the internet with results, profiles and pictures. ... Gymnastik in Deutsch Deutsch. Rhythmic Gymnastics.

   rsg.net/

9. **British Gymnastics**

   www.british-gymnastics.org/

10. **Gymnastics BC**

    News, newsletter, results, information on recreational and competitive gymnastics in BC, clubs, links.

    www.gymnastics.bc.ca/

11. **The Collegiate Gymnastics Information Center**

    Provides the official NCAA National Rankings for collegiate men's and women's gymnastics.

    www.troester.com/gym/

12. **International Gymnastics Hall of Fame**

    One of the oldest sports in the Olympic Games has one of the newest sites for honoring the world's...

    www.ighof.com/

13. **International GYMNAST Online**

    A magazine dedicated to gymnastics, covering the sport since 1956. Check out the current issue, latest...

    www.intlgymnast.com/

14. **FIG - Fédération Internationale de Gymnastique**

    FÉDÉRATION INTERNATIONALE DE GYMNASTIQUE, GENERAL, CALENDARS, RULES, MEDIA ONLY, FIG SHOP, WRITE US.

    www.fig-gymnastics.com/

15. **UEG: European Union of Gymnastics**

    www.ueg-gymnastics.com/

16. **Gymn, an electronic forum for gymnastics!**

    One of the oldest gymnastics sites on the internet, Gymn Forum has a huge results section, plus articles,...

    www.gymn-forum.com/

17. **Congratulations**

    Events, clubs, member services, job opportunities, resource library, links.

    www.gymsask.com/

18. **The World's Gymnastics Information Center**
    Your personal guide to the exciting world of gymnastics. VIETNAM Sea Games/Gymnastics: Shu Wai finishes credible fourth in ... ...
    www.gymnastics.net/

19. **National Gymnastics Judges Association, Inc.**
    Judging materials, rules, course calendar, photo gallery, international material, NCAA rules, junior...
    www.ngja.org/

20. **Excalibur Gymnastics - Experience the Excellence**
    Parent newsletter, competitive teams, recreational programs, birthday parties, scholarship winners,...
    www.excalibur-gymnastics.com/

21. **AGA - Home**
    Philosophy: The American Gymnastics Association is dedicated to the development of artistic optional gymnastics for girls. Includes events schedule, meet results, team information for all AGA members.
    www.tumble.org/

22. **Alberta Gymnastics Federation**
    Program information for men's, women's, trampoline and tumbling. Events schedule, meets, links.
    www.abgym.ab.ca/

23. **GYMNASTICS LAND**
    A gym library, chat room, floor exercise music, injuries, awards and gymnast birthdays.
    members.tripod.com/~Ma_ayan/

24. **Gymnastics Slovakia**
    News, information, and results from gymnastics in the USA, Slovakia, Iceland and all around the world.
    www.gymnastics-slovakia.com/

25. **Worldwide Gymnastics.com**
    A gymnastics magazine based in Ukraine covering gymnastics around the globe with photography, profiles,...
    www.worldwidegymn.com/

26. **Milton Keynes School of Gymnastics**
    Gymnastics club with classes for artistic gymnastics, sports acro, tumbling and team gym. International...
    www.mksog.org.uk/

27. **Gymnastics QLD WebSite**
www.gymqld.org.au/

28. **Scottish Gymnastics Official Web Site - Main Index**
www.scottishgymnastics.com/

29. **Flash Test**
www.girlsgymnastics.com/

30. **Gymnastics Station**
The summary for this Japanese page contains characters that cannot be correctly displayed in this language/character set.
www3.starcat.ne.jp/~komo/

31. **IGLGU Homepage**
IGLGU Homepage. International Gay and Lesbian Gymnastics Union. ... IGLGU welcomes gymnastics fans as well even if they are not presently doing gymnastics. ...
www.geocities.com/iglgu/

32. **Brown's Gymnastics**
Class schedule and fees. Two locations: Winter Park and Sanford.
www.brownsgym.com/

33. **gymnastics olympica usa**
SiteMap. Copyright © 2002 Gymnastics Olympica USA.All rights reserved. rasc WebTracker"Hit" Details.
www.gousa.org/

34. **Gymnastics Ontario**
About GO, Event Guide, Club Mailing, NCCP, Official Hotel Supplier. GO Clubs, Job Opportunities, Resources, Other Links. Trampoline. Women's. ...
www.ogf.com/

35. **WWW.GYMNASTICS.CA**
A home for Canadian Gymnastics Websites. ... New/updated in December 2003: International Rhythmic Gymnastics Academy of Vancouver, mainland British Columbia.
www.gymnastics.ca/

36. **Region VII Gymnastics**
Region 7 gymnastics information. Calendar, forum, links, news.
www.region7gymnastics.com/

37. **US Gym.Net — The Gym and Gymnastics Sports Resource Center—** The largest database of gymnastics gyms in the United States (including links to websites), coaching...
www.usgyms.net/

38. **Ukrainian Rhythmic Gymnastics**
Personal site features profiles of local gymnasts, photos, results, interviews, articles, and links.
ukrsg.tripod.com/

39. **This page uses frames, but your browser doesn't support them.** Take a tour of the gym, learn about the different programs, view photographs and read tumble talk.
www.cincinnatigymnastics.com/

40. **Gymnastics Today is an online gymnastics community that was ...** Gymnastics Today is an online gymnastics community. Web site design, hosting, secure site design.
www.gymnasticstoday.com/

41. **Rhythmic Gymnastics, by the RhythmicMom**
Photos, news, gymnast profiles, a lively discussion forum. For rhythmic gymnastic fans, parents, and...
www.rhythmicmom.com/

42. **Gymnastics Etc.**
Instruction facility that features a team area, staff biographies, classes, contact information and map.
www.gymetc.com

43. **NCWGA Home Page**
USAG Women's JO state board covering northern California. Rosters, ranking, meet schedule, membership,...
www.norcal-gymnastics.org/

44. **OutofBoundsNess Gymnastics**
Features a chat room, message board, photo gallery, links, trivia, and official gymnast sites.
www.gymn.com/

45. **Academy of Gymnastics**
Teaching gymnastics at recreational and competitive levels. Programs, events, about us. Located in...
www.gymnastics-dance.com/

46. **Gmnastics Mississauga**
Club news, registration, map and history.
www.gymmississauga.org/

47. **Gymnastics Fan Club in Japan**
The summary for this Japanese page contains characters that cannot be correctly displayed in this language/character set.
village.infoweb.ne.jp/~fwhd4064/

48. **Seattle Gymnastics Academy, Inc.**
Dance and gymnastics programs at all levels with competition teams in Seattle WA. ... Offers gymnastics instruction for children and adults. Includes information on classes, schedules,...
www.seattlegymnastics.com/

49. **Best view**
Offering instruction for children 1-18. Class schedule, birthday parties, competitive program, ncaa...
www.airborne-gymnastics.com/

50. **Acrobatics Homepage - Gymnastics Dance Circus , etc.**
Acrobatics , Rhythmic Gymnastics, Dance, Circus, Ballet, Yoga, Fitness, Aerobics, Trapeze. Acrobatics, Rhythmic Gymnastics, Dance, Circus, Ballet, Yoga, Fitness, Aerobics, Trapeze and all similar...
meltingpot.fortunecity.com/belgium/256/

51. **Paragon Gymnastics, Fredericksburg, Virginia**
Paragon Gymnastics, located in Fredericksburg, Virginia, offers gymnastics classes for girls and boys from tots to teens, competitive teams, cheerleading ...
www.paragongymnastics.com/

52. **Gymnastics**
Of all the areas to teach this is my favorite. If I could just teach one thing all year gymnastics would be it. ... Traditional Gymnastics Lessons and Assessments. ...
schools.eastnet.ecu.edu/pitt/ayden/PHYSED3.HTM

53. **gymnastique**
Providing an online resource for gymnastics fans with emphasis on UK and European aspects of the sport including the following
www.gym-media.co.uk/

54. **Website of Auburn Tiger Athletics**
NCAA Division 1, region 4. Tigers latest news, schedule, statistics, roster.
www.auburntigers.com/gymnastics/

55. **Bruins Women's Gymnastics**
UCLA Gymnastics Outlook Winners of four NCAA Championships, including three of the last four, UCLA looks poised to add to its 21st century dynasty.
www.fansonly.com/schools/ucla/sports/ w-gym/ucla-w-gym-body.html

56. **Columbia Gymnastics**
Competitive and recreational programs for boys and girls. Features information on programs and services,...
www.columbiagymnastics.com/

57. **Gymnastics World**
Class descriptions and schedules, fees, happenings, Gym World facts, policies and staff feature. Located...
www.gymworldohio.com/

58. **Croydon School of Gymnastics**
Information on one of the leading gymnastics clubs in London, England.
www.croyschgym.fsnet.co.uk/

59. **Love for Rhythmic Gymnastics**
Pictures of international gymnasts, links, competition results.
www.angelfire.com/mi/rsgkb/

60. **RollTide.com | University of Alabama Official Athletic Site**
Alabama Gymnastics Season's Start is Around the Corner.
www.rolltide.com/Gymnastics/default.asp

61. **Redirecting to new Gymnastic Pages**
The website has been redesigned and simplified, most of the content is the same minus the personal athlete pages You will be redirected shortly or you can go to ...
www.thewere.com/gymnastics/gym.html

62. **Delta Gymnastics | About Us**
Program information, competitions, registration contacts and map.
www.deltagymnastics.com/

63. **Women's Gymnastics — University of Maryland**
Schedule, statistics, season outlook, prospective student-athlete questionnaire, and meet the coach.
umterps.ocsn.com/sports/w-gym/md-w-gym-body.html

64. **Rhythmic Gymnastics Canada Gymnastique Rythmique**
The official web site of the Canadian Rhythmic Gymnastics Federation. Event calendar, results, news...
www.rgc.ca/

65. **International Gymnastics Camp**
Contains pictures, camp information, a chat room and staff information.
www.international-gym-camp.com/

66. **The New Brunswick Gymnastics Association**
A non profit provincial sport organization for artistic gymnastics, trampoline and tumbling.
user.fundy.net/nbga/

67. **Technique Gymnastics - Home**
Boys and girls recreational gymnastics, kindergym, adult classes, tumbling, cheerleading, sports acrobati...
www.techniquegym.com/

68. **Clarington Gymnastics Academy - Fun - Fitness - Fundamentals**
Privately operated gymnastics facility offering competitive and recreational gymnastics programs.
www.clargym.com/

69. **Instructional Gymnastics Videos**
A Great selection of instructional Gymnastics videos! ... Gymnastics Videos. ... Balance beam is the "make it or break it" event in gymnastics competition. ...
www.activevideos.com/gymnastics.htm

70. **Southern Indiana Gymnastics School Cheerleading and Dance**
Programs include cheerleading, general gymnastics, martial arts, men's recreational, parent/child,...
www.sigsgym.com/

71. **Illinois Gymnastics Institute**
An Illinois Gymnastics Club offering training starting with recreational gymnastics up to Olympic Level - boys and girls.
www.region5.com/igi-gymnastics/

72. **Portsmouth School Of Gymnastics**
Facility and coaching information, parties, exchanges, technical information, links. Located in Portsmouth.
www.portsmouth-gymnastics.com/

73. **Gymnastics Saskatchewan**
The sport-governing body for artistic gymnastics and trampoline and tumbling in Saskatchewan.
www3.sk.sympatico.ca/sgym/

74. **Aiken Gymnastics Online**
Newsletters, meet results, Boosters, clip art and links.
www.groupz.net/aiken_gymnastics/

75. **Airborne Gymnastics and Dance**
Gymnastics, Dance, Climbing, and Power Tumbling Instruction in Longmont Colorado. Airborne Gymnastics and Dance. Longmont, Colorado. ...
www.airbornegym.com/

76. **Halifax ALTA Gymnastics**
News, meet results, calendar of events, contact information, chat. Halifax, Nova Scotia.
www.halifaxaltagymnasticsclub.ns.ca/

77. **Men Rhythmic Gymnastics**
This is intended to be the hub for the development of men / boys rhythmic gymnastics. It contains ... Men's Rhythmic Gymnastics. I was ...
www.eliterg.com/eliterg/menrg/

78. **Manx Gymnastics**
Manx Gymnastics Centre of Excellence. ...
homepages.enterprise.net/manxgymnastics/

79. **usolympicteam.com**
USA Gymnastics is the sole National Governing Body (NGB) for the sport of gymnastics in the United States. It gets this designation ...
www.olympic-usa.org/sports2/gy/az_over.html

80. **South African Gymnastics Federation**
www.gymnastics.co.za/

81. **Relocate**
Links, events, facts.
www.gym-wheel.com/

82. **Perfect Grace Gymnastics Products**
Gymnastics gift ideas including, Varsity Practice Balance Beams that look and feel like competition balance beams and a line of Gymnastics jewelry that is sure ...
www.perfectgrace.com/

83. **Providing Youth Fitness Through Gymnasics Instruction for Over 20 ...**
News, programs, team competition, staff, schedules, gym history, facility, registration, directions,...
www.gymnasticsvillage.com/

84. **World of Gymnastics Online!!**
News, registration information, and contacts. Located in Woodstock.
www.worldofgymnastics.com/

85. **Springboard Gymnastics Academy**
members.tripod.com/sga9/sgahome/

86. **Interactive Academy Gymnastics - Where Gymnastics is Fun**
Offers recreational gymnastics classes for preschoolers, girls, and boys, cheerleading, and physical...
www.interactivegym.com/

87. **you are dreaming**
you are dreaming. Forum, photos, a gymnastics TV guide.
www.angelfire.com/mo3/monica917/

88. **Champion Gymnastics Louisville Kentucky**
Champion Gymnastics Louisville, Kentucky At Champion, gymnastics is our business. ... And CHAMPION GYMNASTICS is where you can find them. ...
www.aaksports.com/Champion_Gymnastics/

89. **MoceanuGymnastics.com**
A fan site for Dominique Moceanu including videos and pictures.
www.moceanugymnastics.com/

90. **Tri-Valley Gymnastics - Serving Livermore, Pleasanton, Dublin, San ...**
Gymnastics fitness and recreational center located in Livermore.
www.tvgymnastics.com/

91. **Bobbie's Gymnastics Drawings**
Drawings of famous gymnasts like, Nadia Comaneci, Kim Zmeskal, Svetlana Boginskaya, and others.
bcole9894.freeservers.com/

92. **Phoenix Gymnastics Club**

Team photos, club information, coaches biographies, programs and news. Located in Windsor.

www.phoenixgym.co.uk/

93. **Amazon.com: Video: Gymnastics: Tumbling: How to do a Better Back**

Gymnastics: Tumbling: How to do a Better Back-Handspring, Coach Wayne, Whitestock Productions. ... Gymnastics: Tumbling: How to do a Better Back-Handspring () ...

www.amazon.com/exec/obidos/tg/ detail/-/0965286819?v=glance

94. **Karon Gymnastics**

Karon Gymnastics and Kidsports offering competitive and recreational gymnastics. Karon Gymnastics and Kidsport, www.karongymnastics.com/

95. **Gymnastics Books**

A book of the most frequently asked questions about gymnastics by athletes, parents, and coaches....

hometown.aol.com/gymcoach1966/AskingBook.html

24
Handball

1. **European Handball Federation**
   Official site of EHF. News, event calendar, member federations, national teams, club teams, photo gallery.
   www.eurohandball.com/
2. **Handball-World**
   www.handball-world.com/
3. **USA Team Handball**
   USA Team Handball is the national governing body for the Olympic Sport of Team Handball. THE OFFICIAL SITE OF USA TEAM HANDBALL. ... Team Handball News. Official site of USA Team Handball the American national governing body of the sports. Programs, calendar...
   www.usateamhandball.org/
4. **United States Handball Association**
   The United States Handball Association seeks to promote the game of handball and to foster goodwill and friendship among members. Details of results, fixtures, rules of wall-handball in the USA with pictures of players, on-line...
   ushandball.org/
5. **International Handball Federation | Welcome to the new IHF Web ...**
   Official Site of the IHF. Contains rules and regulations of the sport, competition results and contacts...
   www.ihf.info/
6. **Handball in Southern California**
   Southern California Handball News, Tournaments, League, Clubs where you can play handball, Player List and Links to other handball sites. Includes all the fixtures and results as well as news items.
   www.handball.org/

7. **Bienvenue sur le site de la Fédération Française de Handball]**
   World > Français > ... > Sports et loisirs > Sports > Handball
   www.ff-handball.org/
8. **The Irish Handball Homepage**
   News and results from Ireland including Sligo Handball Club.
   homepage.tinet.ie/~sligohandball/
9. **my team handball page**
   Training, tactics, officiating, and playing rules.
   mitglied.lycos.de/harueckner/handball/
10. **Deutscher Handball-Bund**
    World > Deutsch > ... > Handball > Verbände > Deutschland
    www.dhb.de/
11. **Fédération Canadienne de Handball - Canadian Team Handball**
    Governing body of team handball in Canada. Coaches, calendar, directory, hsitory, news, officiating,...
    www.handball.ca/
12. **Portal Handball Schweiz-Suisse**
    Morld > Deutsch > ... > Ballsport > Handball > Verbände > Schweiz
    www.handball.ch/
13. **Die Handball Bundesliga**
    www.handball-bundesliga.de/
14. **SIS-Handball**
    www.sis-handball.de/
15. **WorldWide Handball Hand-BalLoRg]**
    Includes biographies of the world's best players, history of the sport, links of interest, games,...
    handball.enourense.net/
16. **Australian Handball Web**
    The Australian Handball Web hopes to promote the sport of Handball in
    www-personal.monash.edu.au/~lipcsey/handball/
17. **League Handball Manager Game 2.3x for IBM PC - Freeware Handball...**
    A team handball coach game. Manage a Danish, German, Spanish, or Swedish team.
    snow.prohosting.com/skarp/

18. **Colorado Handball Association Home Page**
Handball fixtures and results from Colorado.
www.cohandball.com/

19. **Handball City**
Information, photographs, discussion, chat room, and links.
www.handballcity.com/

20. **Ballymacelligott Handball Club Homepage**
Handball news, results, fixtures and pictures from Irish Handball Club at Ballymacelligott near Tralee,...
www.ballymachandball.com/

21. **Willkommen bei TEAM Sport-Service**
www.handball.de/

22. **Norges Håndballforbund**
World > Norsk > Sport > Håndball
www.handball.no/

23. **Mehr TV-Präsenz für den deutschen Handball]**
www.handballimfernsehen.de/

24. **Chino Sport Handball**
Big blue, one wall handball tournament in Philadelphia, PA. Information, schedule, and photographs.
chinosport64.tripod.com/handball.html

25. **Oregon Handball**
Contains club and player registries, tournament calendar,entry forms, and results. Additional player...
www.oregonhandball.org/

26. **Handball-sh - Die offizielle Handballseite SCHLESWIG**
World > Deutsch > Sport > Ballsport > Handball
www.handball-sh.de/

27. **Sport1 - Handball**
www.sport1.de/coremedia/generator/www.sport1.de/ Sportarten/ Handball/Main.html

28. **Finland's page for team handball**
Finland's team handball clubs, players, links.
www.abo.fi/~jbacklun/handbeng.htm

29. **ICHA: Inner City Handball Association: Home**

ICHA: Inner City Handball Association, ... I began playing handball in mid 1993, in Brooklyn New York's very own Highland Park handball courts. ...

www.icha.org/

30. **Pallamano veneta, HANDBALL.IT**

World > Italiano > Sport > Pallamano

www.handball.it/

31. **Our Mission**

Wallsports was started by a handball player who got tired of searching the sporting goods stores for handball equipment, only to find that most sporting goods ...

www.wallsports.com/

32. **Atlanta Team Handball**

A site of Georgia's league with merchandise shopping and some more links.

www.teamhandball.org/

33. **New South Wales Handball Association.**

New South Wales Handball Association. Australian team handball clubs. NSW handball competition results, contact details, Australian handball news. Resource for players in Australia. Current competition results, rules, mailing lists and links are...

www.nswhandball.com.au/

34. **Oskaloosa Handball Club**

What is Handball? Handball is a game very similar to racquetball, except that you hit the ball with your hands instead of a racquet. ... Handball Court. Introduction to handball and contact information for the club in Oskaloosa, Kansas.

www.geocities.com/oskyhandball/

35. **Englandhandball**

www.englandhandball.com/

36. **Handball-Verband Niedersachsen eV**

World > Deutsch > ... > Handball > Verbände > Deutschland

www.hvn-online.de/

37. **Handball Ireland Website**

Handball Ireland website is dedicated to all those who play and follow handball - the Perfect Game. It is intended as a starting ...

www.handball.ie/

38. **Japan Handball League**
Site of Japanese Handball League, with information about championships and other information also.
www.jhl.handball.jp/eng/

39. **This page uses frames, but your browser doesn't support them**
The council is the principle body promoting 1-wall, 3-wall and 4 wall handball within the country.
www.aussiehandball.org/

40. **Handball-Praxis**
www.handball-praxis.de/

41. **Andebol Portugal 2003 Official Site**
The official site with news, information, calendar, and results.
www.handballwc2003.com/

42. **Monash University Handball Club**
Includes news, results, photos, and training schedule.
www.geocities.com/monashhandball/

43. **Handball Dossobuono]**
World > Italiano > Sport > Pallamano
www.handballdossobuono.com/

44. **NCHA: Northern California Handball Association Home**
The NCHA promotes and supports handball in Northern California. Listings of three and four-wall handball courts, tournaments and players, with information on supporting...
norcalhandball.org/

45. **Ashandball.com**
The goal is to encourage and support the growth and development for handball throughout the Alaskan...
www.ashandball.com/

46. **rafton Team Handball Club**
General information, rules, map, and contacts. Located in Auckland, New Zealand.
www.graftonteamhandball.org.nz/

47. **The University of Kentucky HandBall Club**
Pictures, contact information, description of the sport and related links.
www.uky.edu/StudentOrgs/Handball/

48. **Minnesota State Handball Association**
The Minnesota State Handball Association. Welcome to the MSHA Web Site The second USA Web site on handball. ... News and info from Minnesota handball. ...
home.comcast.net/~mnhandball/

49. **Irish Olympic Handball Association**
Official site with news, events calendar, information, rules, services, and support for all levels...
www.olympichandball.org/

50. **Handball-World**
www.handball-world.de/

51. **Stord Handbal**
World > Norsk > Regionalt > Europa > Norge > Hordaland > Stord
www.stordhandball.no/

52. **SMSU Handball**
News items, staff, alumni listing, message board, related links and upcoming events.
studentorganizations.smsu.edu/handball/

53. **ACT Handball Association**
To receive a sponsorship package.. Handball Association, Jacob Krog. All Rights Reserved | Top ·Home.
members.iinet.net.au/~jkrog/

54. **iSportsDigest.com/Team Handball**
TEAM HANDBALL - GENERAL, Alabama Team Handball; Atlanta Team Handball; Australian Handball Web; Austrian Handball Federation (German); ... Worldwide Handball....
isportsdigest.tripod.com/teamhandball/main.html

55. **Laureus World Sports Awards - WORLD SPORT AWARDS**
Founding Sponsors, |, Mercedes, |, Cartier. > WORLD SPORTS AWARDSWORLD SPORT AWARDS. View printable format, Send this page to a friend. ...
www.worldsport.com/sports/handball/home.html

56. **Handball help 2003**
hhelp.hbnet.cz/

57. **Handball.net**
Handball Net
www.handball.net/

58. **Queensland Team Handball Association - Home**

Queensland Team Handball Association. Australian team handball clubs. Qld handball competition results, contact details, Australian handball news. Includes news, events, results, club contacts, competition summary, and related links.

www.qldhandball.com.au/

59. **Saskatchewan Team Handball**

News, rules, calendar of events, links.

www.saskteamhandball.com/

60. **HANDBALL**

The summary for this Japanese page contains characters that cannot be correctly displayed in this language/character set.

www.handball.jp/

61. **IHF Beach Handball Rules**

Detailed rules of the sport from the International Handball Federation.

www-personal.monash.edu.au/~lipcsey/ handball/rules/IHF-beach.html

62. **Selects Team Handball**

Player profiles and news.

www.mts.net/~bcrocket/selects.html

63. **Johann and Sandra's Team Handball Message Board**

Find and share information about team handball, including clubs, teams, and events.

pub50.ezboard.com/fjswebfrm28

64. **To view this page, you need a browser that supports frames.**

News, photos, results, fixtures, and contact details of one of the South England's most successful...

www.soton.ac.uk/~handball/

65. **Handball links around the world**

Team handball links around the world. Take your byte. journeys to this page since 17 Oct. ... Yhdysvallat. Österrike. International Handball Federation (IHF). ...

www.abo.fi/~jbacklun/space.htm

66. **Open Directory - Sports: Handball**

See also: Sports: Team Handball (60). ... Kerry, Ireland; Chino Sport Handball - Big blue, one wall handball tournament in Philadelphia, PA. ...

dmoz.org/Sports/Handball/

67. **International Handball Tournament - Schmelz**

Official Site of a Large Junior Tournament in Vienna, Austria

www.eichler.co.at/schmelz/

68. **Sport - Team Handball**

Directory of Team Handball clubs, events and tournaments sorted by location.

www.sportisgood.com/sp/servlet/com.sportisgood.web.SportView?sportID=11

69. **handball.start4all.com**

handball.start4all.com: The handball page of Start4all.com - here you can find the most complete collection of links about handball handball, Start4all, add ...

handball.start4all.com/

70. **Sports**

Team Handball In team handball competition, the women's squad has also earned three African Championships for Angola. In team handball competition, the women's squad has earned three African Championships for Angola.

www.angola.org/culture/sports/hand.htm

71. **The International Handball Page**

International handball site with results, tables, news, EC, WC, cups, links, and much more from all over the world! Info about Kristians and ...

home.online.no/~akvanes/handball/

72. **FTC Handball**

On this site you can find informations about the Women's Handball Team of FTC and the Women's National Handball Team of Hungary. ...

ftc.handball.hu/?lang=eng

73. **Weymouth 2003 - Beach Handball**

The official website of Weymouth 2003, International Beach Handball Championship. 2nd International Beach Handball Championships ...

www.beachhandball.org.uk/

74. **Jughead's WEB Pages**

Promotes handball as a sport in the province. Offers links to provincial, Canadian and World handball...

www.dal.ca/~jughead/

75. **Handball Communication Web**

The summary for this Japanese page contains characters that cannot be correctly displayed in this language/character set.

www.bekkoame.ne.jp/~khc/

76. **DC Diplomats Handball Club**

Includes events, FAQs, news, links, and information about team handball.

www.dcdiplomats.com/

77. **Open Directory - Sports: Team Handball**

the entire directory. Top: Sports: Team Handball (69), Description. Beach Handball (1); Wheelchair Handball (1). ...

dmoz.org/Sports/Team_Handball/

78. **LA Team Handball :: Los Angeles :: California**

Official Website of the LA Team Handball Club

www.lateamhandball.com/

25
Hiking

1. **American Hiking Society**
   American Hiking Society: the only national organization dedicated to serving hikers and protecting hiking trails. National nonprofit organization dedicated to promoting hiking and to establishing, protecting and...
   www.americanhiking.org/
2. **GORP - Hiking Home**
   [Hiking/Trekking Trips, Africa. Asia. ... Southeast. Southwest. BUY RELATED GEAR. Hiking Gear from REI.com. Cycling Gear from REI.com. ...
   www.gorp.com/gorp/activity/hiking.htm
3. **Hiking and Walking Homepage**
   Hiking and walking index to organizations, trails, places to hike and walk, events, gear, tours and treks, clubs. Hike with Bill Russell's Mountain Tours. ... Hiking. ...
   www.webwalking.com/hiking.html
4. **Walking and hiking - World's largest trail database**
   Searchable database of more than 2000 hikes, walks, and trails all over the globe. Includes current...
   www.hejoly.demon.nl/
5. **Superior Hiking Trail Association**
   Superior Hiking Trail Association. The purpose of this web site is to provide information about the Trail and the Superior Hiking Trail Association (SHTA).
   www.shta.org/

6. **Hiking and Backpacking - Hiking and Backpacking.com**
Hiking and Backpacking Hiking and Backpacking.com is your quick and easy way to find info on hiking and backpacking. Provides resources and information on hiking and backpacking.
www.hikingandbackpacking.com/

7. **AZventure in Hiking - Arizona Related Hiking Links, Including A**
The most complete listing of Arizona-related hiking links available on the Web. ... WARNING! Hiking in Arizona is highly addictive. ...
www.swlink.net/~ttidyman/hiking/

8. **Hiking Web Site - Home Page**
Providing information for hikers on day hiking, backpacking, camping, gear, trails,and has forums for the exchange of hiking information. ... The Hiking Web Site.
www.hikingwebsite.com/

9. **HEALTH SPA VACATIONS Weight Loss Spa Vacation Programs Fitness**
A favorite of single travelers as well as couples, Mountain Trek caters to only 14 guests per week, and offers hiking, kayaking, biking, yoga, massage and spa ...
www.hiking.com/

10. **Hiking in Colorado - www.hikingincolorado.org**
Hiking in Colorado contains more than thirty trip reports, more than 500 of photos, and a hike difficulty calculator - all of which can assist in planning your ...
www.hikingincolorado.org/

11. **HIKING THE CAROLINAS**
Hiking the Carolinas is an online guide for hikers of the Southern Appalachians. Extensive resource for hikers in the Southern Appalachians including the Smokies, and the Blue Ridge...
hikingthecarolinas.com/

12. **Outdoors in MaineToday.com | Hiking**
Lists, resources, news and features about Maine outdoor and recreation activities including: biking, camping, canoeing, fishing, golf, hiking, hunting, kayaking ...
outdoors.mainetoday.com/hiking/

13. **Hiking Las Vegas: Hiking information for southern Nevada**
Hiking information about Red Rock Canyon, Mt. ... All rights reserved. Information about Red Rock Canyon, Mt. Charleston, and Lake Mead National Recreation Area.
www.hikinglasvegas.com/

14. **hiking-site.nl, de site voor de actieve buitensporter! Hiking-site ...**
World > Nederlands > Recreatie > Openlucht > Wandelen
www.hiking-site.nl/

15. **Hiking.be - The Belgian Hiking Website**
World > Nederlands > Recreatie > Openlucht > Wandelen
www.hiking.be/

16. **Texas Hiking**
Texas Hiking is your guide to the many opportunities to experience the wonder of the state of Texas as it was meant to be,
on horseback excluded of course. ...
www.texashiking.com/

17. **Yahoo! Directory Outdoors > Hiking**
Outdoors > Hiking Directory > Recreation > Outdoors > Hiking, Search the Web just this category. ...
www.evranch.com. Alaska's Hiking Adventure Denali Trekking Co. ...
dir.yahoo.com/Recreation/Outdoors/Hiking/

18. **Hiking in China — China Hiking Adventures Inc. — Hiking and ...**
China Hiking Adventures Inc. Hiking and Cultural Tours of China. 2003 Hiking Group Diary click here. ... 15 days of Tibet Nomad hiking experience click here. ...
www.china-hiking.com/

19. **Ton de Maagt Hiking Page**
List of links related to travel in Europe, with hiking links listed for most western European countries.
home.planet.nl/~marlaine/ton.htm

20. **Hiking in the Smokies- Win a Free llama trek Hiking Vacation in**
Win a free llama trekking and hiking trip in the smokies and experience mountains close up.
www.hikinginthesmokies.com/

21. **Chattanooga Hiking Club**
The Chattanooga Hiking Club is a non-profit member-supported organization that promotes a program of hiking adventures to outdoor enthusiasts of all social and ...
hiking.chattanooga.net/

22. **Tennessee Eastman Hiking and Canoeing Club - Appalachian Trail**
The Tennessee Eastman Hiking and Canoeing Club is an outdoors club, offering a year-round program of hikes and paddling trips in our region.
www.tehcc.org/

23. **Boston Hiking Guide (with MBTA info)**
Boston Hiking Guide Hiking areas near Boston Massachusetts with distance (if any) from: 1. T stations (color-coded) 2. bus routes Unwanted popup window? ...
www.geocities.com/Yosemite/Trails/1171/

24. **Jackson Hole, Wyoming: Snowshoeing, Hiking and Backpacking Trips**
Subscribe to NATURE NEWS for a bi-monthly update from the Hole Hiking Experience! ... Year-round resident. Welcome to the Hole Hiking Experience! ...
www.holehike.com/

25. **REI.com: For camping, hiking, cycling, climbing, snow sports**
REI offers quality gear, clothing and footwear for muscle-powered outdoor recreation, including hiking, climbing, camping, bicycling, paddling and winter sports ...
www.rei.com/

26. **Guided Hiking, Hikesand Walking Tours - New England Hiking**
New England Hiking Holidays: Offering guided hiking tours of North America, Europe, and the Pacific Rim. Country Inn, Guided Hiking and Walking Holidays. ...
www.nehikingholidays.com/

27. **Hiking on Maui, Hawaii - tours by Maui Hiking Safaris**
Maui hiking tours with Maui Hiking Safaris. We give full and half-day guided Maui Hawaii wilderness hikes. ... Form. HIKING TOURS. Haleakala ...
www.maui.net/~mhs/

28. **Biking in France, Biking and Hiking, Bike Tours in Norway Italy by...**

    Offers guided biking and hiking tours in France, Norway, Italy, Austria and Spain. Company based in Canada.

    www.brindisi.ca/

29. **Vancouver Hiking**

    Vancouver Hiking offers trail descriptions, photos, backpacking tips, wildlife info and more . ... The Link is below. Vancouver Hiking's Wallpaper Page. ...

    vancouverhiking.tripod.com/

30. **GORP.com-adventure travel-hiking, national parks, travel ...**

    Attractions: national parks, wilderness, wildlife. Activities: hiking, biking, canoeing, kayaking, rafting, climbing, skiing, camping, more....

    www.gorp.com/

31. **Northern Virginia Hiking Club**

    Hiking in northern Virginia.

    members.aol.com/nvhc/

32. **Catskill Hiking Shack**

    Specialty shop and resource for backpacking, hiking in the Catskills and beyond. Local backpacking information for the Catskill Mountains as well as pictures, tips, hints, equipment,...

    www.catskillhikes.com/

33. **Allentown Hiking Club**

    The Allentown Hiking Club new member brochure is available to download online. ... About Us. Activities include hiking, walking, backpacking, climbing, cycling, and canoeing. Site features membersh...

    www.allentownhikingclub.org/

34. **Footprint Hiking Club**

    Hiking and backpacking club in South Africa. Plenty of photos and useful African links

    www.footprint.co.za/

35. **Hiking and Trekking in Thailand, Vietnam, Myanmar, Laos, Malaysia ...**

    The best of hiking and trekking tour packages to the countries of Thailand, Vietnam, Myanmar, Laos, Malaysia and Bali; Indonesia. ...

    www.asia-hiking.com/

36. **Hiking Merit Badge**
Boy Scout Merit Badge Requirements. HIKING. Show that you know first ... care of feet and footwear. Explain how hiking is an aerobic activity. ...
www.meritbadge.com/bsa/mb/061.htm

37. **Lets Start Hiking ! StartHiking.com**
Offers safety tips, general tips, and a database of hiking trails.
www.starthiking.com/

38. **Winter Hiking and Backpacking!**
Tips, techniques, and gear advice.
www.backpacking.net/winter.html

39. **Hiking Alabama**
Guide to backpacking trials through the mountains of Alabama.
www.alabamatrail.org/hikingAL/

40. **Arizona Hiking Trails**
Provides descriptions, reviews, and ratings of Arizona's hiking trails.
www.arizonahikingtrails.com/

41. **Hiking Long Island**
A resource for both the new or experienced hiker. Information on trails, events and membership.
www.hike-li.com/

42. **YORK HIKING CLUB**
This web page is about the York Hiking Club of PA. and the hiking Trails in this area of Pennsylvania. Central Area. ... YORK HIKING CLUB. ...
www.angelfire.com/pa2/yorkhikingclub/

43. **Cal Hiking and Outdoor Society**
Membership information, pictures, related links, and contact information.
www.emf.net/~chaos/

44. **Arizona Hiking Shack**
Backpacking, camping, hiking, climbing, and whitewater equipment. Lots of action photos.
www.hikingshack.com/

45. **The California Hiking Page**

Book Reviews, The California Hiking Page Hiking in the "Range of Light" ... Cyberhikes Award For Outstanding Hiking Web Site, This Webring is managed by Bill Finch. ...

www.employees.org/~ciwata/

46. **Hiking in Western New York**

Descriptions and photos of about 30 hiking and walking spots in Western New York. Most are in Erie County.

www.wnyhikes.com/

47. **Backpacking and Hiking TrailHead**

Variety of backpacking and hiking links: Backpacking and hiking pages, lightweight backpacking, navigation, leave no trace, low-impact, online recreation ...

www.geocities.com/Yosemite/Falls/ 9200
backpacking_and_hiking.html

48. **Bay Area Hiker: Home page**

Information about hiking trails in the San Francisco bay area, including photos of wildflowers, animals, trees, plants, and butterflies. ...

www.bahiker.com/

49. **Ultralight hiking, ultralite backpacking, lightweight long ...**

Ultralight hiking, ultralite, Ultra-Light, ultra-lite, Backpacking, lightweight hiking, tramping, long distance hiking, liteweight, camping, gear lists ...

www.ultralight-hiking.com/

50. **Lambda Hiking Club**

Gay/Lesbian Hiking Club of Salt Lake City. Outdoors activities for everyone! We meet on the 1st and...

www.gayhike.org/

51. **Hiking - Kayaking Kauai, Hawaii - Princeville Ranch Hike and Kayak**

Guided hiking and kayak tours on 2500 acres of private lands on Kauai's North Shore that are otherwise inaccessible. Informative

www.kauai-hiking.com/

52. **Alaska Mountaineering and Hiking**

Mountaineering supplies including snow and ice protection, crampons, axes, altimeters, boots, skis,...

www.alaskan.com/amh/

53. **Hiking in Lake Tahoe**
Hiking in Lake Tahoe, the nets best resource for hiking information in the Tahoe Basin. ... URL: http://www.tahoesbest.com/Hiking/index.html. ...
www.tahoesbest.com/Hiking/

54. **HikingNewZealand.com : New Zealand Hiking**
HikingNewZealand.com is brought to you by New Zealand Nature Safaris. We take people hiking / trekking New Zealand style (Kiwi's call it tramping). ...
www.hikingnewzealand.com/

55. **Hiking Forum Frigate**
Forum, and live chat devoted to hiking.
carolinanavy.com/fleet2/f2/zoutdoors/ Hikinghall/shakespeare1.html

56. **American Hiking Society: Hiker's Info Center**
The following agency partners for their leadership in and support of American Hiking Society's trail stewardship and educational programs. ...
www.americanhiking.org/infocenter/

57. **Metsähallitus - Hiking Pages Provide Information on Hiking on ...**
The Hiking Pages of Metsähallitus, earlier known as the Forest and Park Service, provide information on hiking on state-owned lands: hiking and wilderness ...
www.metsa.fi/hiking/

58. **The Manchester University Hiking Club - comprehensive club**
FAQs about the club and suggested equipment for walking.
www.umu.man.ac.uk/hiking/

59. **Romania Hiking Old Page**
Hiking in Romania. This page has moved! The new link is: http:/www.bio.miami.edu/tom/personal/romania/romhike.html.
fig.cox.miami.edu/Faculty/Tom/ personal/romania/romhike.html

60. **Smoky Mountains Hiking Club**
A group of people of all ages who enjoy the outdoors together. Conducts frequent group hikes, maintains...

26
Hockey

1. **NHL.com - The National Hockey League Web Site**
   The official National Hockey League web site includes features, news, rosters, statistics, schedules,...
   www.nhl.com/
2. **USA Hockey**
   Player information, coaches, officials, national teams, inline hockey, new, rinks, fan forum, merchandise...
   www.usahockey.com/
3. **Official Website of the Hockey Hall of Fame**
   Official Hockey Hall of Fame website. Home to hockey's greatest players. Home to hockey's greatest players. Unrivaled collection of photos, statistics, profiles, global coverage,...
   www.hhof.com/
4. **Science of Hockey**
   The Science of Hockey takes you inside sport and explains the worlds fastest game. Why ice is slippery to what high-tech materials are used in the game.
   www.exploratorium.edu/hockey/
5. **thehockeynews.com**
   On-line edition of the Toronto hockey newspaper contains news and editorial content.
   www.thn.com/
6. **Hockey Canada**
   The CHA is the sole governing body for amateur hockey in Canada following the merger in July 1994...
   www.canadianhockey.ca/

7. **The Internet Hockey Database — Hockey Statistics, Logos**
The Internet Hockey database is an archive for hockey statistics,hockey logos, and hockey cards. You will find more information ...
www.hockeydb.com/

8. **www.nhlpa.com - The Official Website of the National Hockey League**
The National Hockey League Players' Association. All rights reserved. Official site offering video clips, player of the day, roster and injury information, and a trivia game.
www.nhlpa.com/

9. **The Home of Hockey on the Internet.**
The most visited field hockey resource on the web. Daily news, information on coaching and rules,...
www.fieldhockey.com/

10. **International Hockey Federation : Homepage**
Works in co-operation with both the national and continental organisations; site features news, regulatio...
www.fihockey.org/

11. **IIHF - INTERNATIONALICE HOCKEY FEDERATION**
Sports > Hockey > Ice Hockey > Regional
www.iihf.com/

12. **ESPN.com: NHL**
This web site produced by the NHL's TV partner contains news and expansive editorial content. [Membership...
sports.espn.go.com/nhl/index

13. **The Official Site of the Colorado Avalanche (flash and browser**
Official team site with news, ticket sales, and information about team members.
www.coloradoavalanche.com/

14. **Dallas Stars**
Official site. Features team information, news, a schedule, message boards, and ticket information.
www.dallasstars.com/

15. **SLAM! Sports - Hockey**
NHL live score-updates, news, features, comment and team pages produced by the Canada Sun newspapers.
www.canoe.ca/Hockey/home.html

16. **St. Louis Blues Online**
Official site includes information on team, statistics, schedule, history, live scoreboard, press...
www.stlouisblues.com/

17. **US Field Hockey Association: Official Site for Field Hockey in the...**
National governing body. National teams, club hockey section and league information, tournaments,...
www.usfieldhockey.com/

18. **A to Z Encyclopaedia of Ice Hockey**
Everything one might want to know about ice hockey, arranged alphabetically.
www.azhockey.com/

19. **England Hockey :: Welcome**
The National Hockey Stadium Silbury Boulevard Milton Keynes MK9 1HA. ... Company registration number: 4623333 England Hockey is a company limited by guarantee. Official site features news of the National Leagues, competitions, and clubs.
www.hockeyonline.co.uk/

20. **The Women's Hockey Web**
Playing and skating tips, pictures, tournament results, US and Canada hockey camp information, and...
www.whockey.com/

21. **Carolina Hurricanes Web Site**
Official site includes news, team, schedule, tickets, arena, merchandise, and hockey 101.
www.caneshockey.com/

22. **European Hockey.Net - Ice Hockey News and Stats for Europe**
Information about European hockey players, leagues, and teams, as well as speak to fans from all over...
www.eurohockey.net/

23. **Minnesota Wild - Official Web Site**
Official site featuring news, a schedule, tickets, merchandise and team information.
www.wild.com/

24. **Hockey East Online**
The official web site of the Hockey East Association - the nation's premier college hockey conference. Hockey East Online provides ...
www.hockeyeastonline.com/

25. **ECHL, America's Premier AA Hockey League**
Official ECHL website has press releases, statistics, schedules, standings, rosters, and other league...
www.echl.com/

26. **Hockey Australia**
National governing body; features includes information on men's and women's national teams, schedule...
www.hockey.org.au/

27. **Hockey's Future: The Hockey Prospects Resource (Covering the WHL**
Coverage of NHL player prospects in Europe, junior leagues, and minor pro leagues, as well as the NHL draft.
www.hockeysfuture.com/

28. **Central Hockey League**
Official league site includes news, schedules, teams, statistics, store, and league information.
www.centralhockeyleague.com/

29. **Western Hockey League**
Official site of the WHL includes league information, news, statistics, teams, player profiles and...
www.whl.ca/

30. **Hockey Betting Lines, Odds, And Recommended Sportsbooks**
HOCKEY BETTING. Click to Visit. Hockey Betting Lines, Odds, Futures And Recommended Sportsbooks To Bet On Hockey! Featured Hockey Sportsbooks. ...
www.hockeybetting.ws/

31. **Hockey Player® announces the most comprehensive, searchable**
Hockey tips, drills, instruction and interviews for ice, roller and inline players, coaches and parents. The most comprehensive, searchable ...
www.hockeyplayer.com/

32. **Hockey Injuries**
To educate people about the understanding, management, prevention and rehabilitation of hockey injuries. NHL.com ...
www.hockeyinjuries.com/

33. **The UHL**
Official site includes teams, news, statistics, scores, standings, history, and merchandise,
www.theuhl.com/

34. **MODO Hockey**
World > Svenska > Sport > Hockey > Ishockey > Elitserieklubbar
www.modohockey.se/

35. **Planet Field Hockey.com - International**
Connecting the field hockey world. News, Updates, Discussion from the latest games and tournaments. Resource for scores, statistics, and coaching materials. ...
www.planetfieldhockey.com/

36. **Hockeyweb - The Field Hockey Community**
Clicking Here at any time throughout the site will bring you back to this page, The Field-Hockey Community. Site Updated: This years ...
www.hockeyweb.co.uk/

37. **Roller Hockey**
Roller Hockey Books and Videos Check out the collection of books and videos about the fastest sport on wheels! ...
www.rhockey.com/

38. **USATODAY.com**
Contains news, statistics, and analysis.
www.usatoday.com/sports/nhl.htm

39. **HOCKEY.COM | Hockey Equipment | Ice Hockey Equipment Online Store**
Hockey Equipment from Hockey.Com, the best name in Hockey! Online Store features huge selection of Ice Hockey Equipment and Inline ...
www.hockey.com/

40. **CBS SportsLine: NHL**
Expansive coverage of the NHL, including news and feature articles.
cbs.sportsline.com/u/hockey/

41. **MASSACHUSETTS HOCKEY ON-LINE**
The mission is to introduce children to the game of ice hockey.
www.masshockey.com/

42. **United States Hockey League - USHL.com**
Official site features news, alumni, links, personnel, schedule, scores, statistics, and standings.
www.ushl.com/

43. **Ice Hockey Glossary**

Interactive Ice Hockey Glossary: terms and phrases with definitions for Ice Hockey, as they appear in Ice Hockey Made Simple: A Spectator's Guide.

www.firstbasesports.com/hockey_glossary.html

44. **www.theihl.com**

Consolidate Debt, Credit Counseling, Debt Free. Popular Searches. Ihl hockey, Ihl, Solar bears. Colorado, Wolves, Manitoba.

www.theihl.com/

45. **Central Collegiate Hockey Association**

Contains press releases, current standings, player highlights, history, records, merchandise, and...

www.ccha.com/

46. **Inline Hockey Central, your source for inline hockey ...**

Inline Hockey Central provides the latest roller hockey and inline hockey news. Source for inline hockey (amateur, pro, scholastic and women's) news and information.

www.inlinehockeycentral.com/

47. **Hockey Lines and Betting Odds - Bet on hockey on the internet**

Hockey Lines .net, The Latest NHL Hockey Betting Lines. Be sure to check back here often for the latest hockey betting lines. ... Hockey Lines World Wager. ...

www.hockeylines.net/

48. **Electrotank Online gaming at its best**

Click to learn more... Email this to a friend! New Game!

www.electrotank.com/games/playGames.asp?gameID=34

49. **Koninklijke Belgische Hockey Bond - Association Royale Belge de ...**

World > Français > ... > Sports et loisirs > Sports > Hockey

www.hockey.be/

50. **ACHA - Main**

Official ACHA page includes news, team lists, and tourney information.

www.achahockey.org/

51. **Latvijas Hokeja majas lapa**

World > Latvian > Sports

www.hockey.lv/

52. **Minnesota Hockey**
Minnesota Hockey would like to thank all of those association presidents and board members that attended the recent series of meetings held in Mankato ...
www.minnesotahockey.org/

53. **DHB - Deutscher Hockey-Bund**
World > Deutsch > Sport > Ballsport > Hockey
www.deutscher-hockey-bund.de/

54. **TSN.ca - NHL - Canada's Sports Leader**
News, editorial content, statistics and team schedules.
www.tsn.ca/nhl/

55. **Just Hockey**
A magazine devoted to covering the minor leagues in North America.
www.justhockey.com/

56. **The Hockey Phreak**
A general resource for hockey players, card collectors, and fans.
www.hockeyphreak.com/

57. **HockeyResearch.com - Home page**
An Internet-based society dedicated to the preservation of hockey history. View member projects,...
www.hockeyresearch.com/

58. **Hockey Giant**
Ice and inline equipment from Mission, Bauer, and CCM, Tour, Easton, and V-Form.
www.hockeygiant.com/

59. **Norges Ishockeyforbund**
World > Norsk > Sport > Ishockey
www.hockey.no/

60. **Hockey Alberta ... Challenge the Future**
The governing body for amateur hockey in Alberta, a province wide volunteer organization. Site includes...
www.hockey-alberta.ca/

61. **Let's Play Hockey.com – Online version of hockey's favorite**
Hockey publication featuring youth and amateur hockey news and information from Minnesota and the...
www.letsplayhockey.com/

62. **Welsh Hockey / Hoci Cymru, Hockey Links**
Welsh Hockey. Links to every hockey related Web Site in the World. Hockey in Wales. WELSH HOCKEY (40). Home About the Web Site News ...
www.welsh-hockey.co.uk/

63. **OHF Home**
Site includes news, championships, tournaments, clinics, schedule, standings, and links.
www.ohf.on.ca/

64. **Pelland's Hockey Emporium**
Contains links to many hockey related sites.
www.cyberbeach.net/~pelland/

65. **Joy of Hockey/NHL Teams and Player Statistics**
NHL Teams and Player statistics updated daily (unofficial). A web page for every current player and...
www.joyofhockey.com/

66. **Ice Hockey UK**
Official Ice Hockey UK website Our new website is still under construction, so some areas are not yet active. ... Ice Hockey UK. ...
www.icehockeyuk.co.uk/

67. **Austrian Hockey Federation**
World > Deutsch > Sport > Ballsport > Hockey
www.hockey.at/

68. **Log in**
World > Nederlands > Sport > Hockey
www.knhb.nl/

69. **No matter how you SAY it, no matter how you PLAY it, it's HOCKEY!**
National organization that coordinates, develops and facilitates the promotion of the sport of sledge...
www.shoc.ca/

70. **"Home of our Hockey Legends"**
The United States Hockey Hall of Fame is America's hockey designated shrine and showcase to all levels of the sport. Profiles for enshrinees, US Olympic hockey teams, events, mission, and online gift shop.
www.ushockeyhall.com/

71. **SLEDHOCKEY.ORG**
USSHA promotes the sport of sled hockey nationally and internationally for athletes with disabilities....
www.sledhockey.org/

72. **Roller Hockey Equipment and inline hockey skates**
Hockey Equipment - ALL Hockey, Giant Selection hockey product closeouts from Mission Bauer CCM Easton Ice Inline Skates Gloves Pants wheels jerseys. ...
www.rollerhockey.com/

73. **MCQ : Facts about society : Mad about hockey**
Includes a history of the game, information about the Stanley Cup, and hockey superstitions.
www.mcq.org/hockey/aaindex.html

74. **IndianHockey.com**
Provides hockey fans with top stories, guestbook, results, events calendar and scoreboard for men's...
www.indianhockey.com/

75. **North American Hockey League Official Web Site**
About the NAHL, team USA, awards, news, schedule, scores, statistics, standings, alumni report and playoffs.
www.nahl.com/

76. **EHF European hockey Federation**
News of international tournaments and national teams throughout Europe. Contact details for national...
www.eurohockey.org/

77. **Scottish Hockey Union - The official site of the SHU**
Scottish Hockey's new home on the web Our site will be completed over the coming weeks and months. ...
www.scottish-hockey.org.uk/

78. **Ontario Hockey Association**
The OHA has 136 teams in 12 leagues. Official site includes league pages with schedule, standings,...
www.ohahockey.org/

79. **Hockey Trade Rumors - Hockey Information and Rumors**
Providing the latest hockey trade rumors and speculation regarding player transactions in the NHL.
www.hockeytraderumors.com/

80. **BharatiyaHockey.org - Internet Home of Indian Hockey**
A comprehensive resource on Indian field hockey.
www.bharatiyahockey.org/

81. **Hockey History Inc. - Photographs, Photos, Statistics ...**
Publisher of hockey yearbook and CD-ROMs, including many historical photos of players and teams.
www.hockeyonline.com/

82. **Hockey Manitoba**
A voluntary association of members and individuals designed to promote and develop amateur hockey...
www.hockeymanitoba.mb.ca/

83. **TPS Louisville Hockey - World Leader In Custom Goalie and player**
Official website for TPS Louisville Hockey.
www.louisville-hockey.com/

84. **USA Hockey**
USA Hockey InLine.com. Welcome to USA Hockey InLine! USA ... Association. USA Hockey InLine Announces '04 Championships Slate. ...
www.usahockey.com/inline/

85. **Field Hockey Canada - redirect**
National governing body of this men's and women's team sport; site features include information on...
www.fieldhockey.ca/

86. **EIHA Home Page**
EIHA has administered ice hockey in England since 1983 providing news, fixtures/schedules, game reports...
www.eiha.co.uk/

87. **Planet Hockey - Hockey Camps - Hockey Schools - Hockey Tours**
The Ultimate Resident Hockey Camp. Train with Planet Hockey while enjoying the thrills of the Rocky...
www.planethockey.com/

88. **Hockeynet.com**
Hockeynet.com is junior hockey's place on the web. Hockeynet.com sells premier hockey apparel and equipment.
www.hockeynet.com/

89. **Official site of the AHL powered by SLAM! Sports**

AHL grads prevalent on NHL benches. Former Calder Cup-winning head coach Peter Laviolette returned to the National Hockey League last Monday as the bench boss ...

www.canoe.com/AHL/home.html

90. **New Zealand Hockey Federation**

Aims to offer the widest possible opportunities for all persons through participation and achievement...

www.nzhockey.org.nz/

91. **The Hockey Depot hockey equipment skates**

The best on the net for hockey equipment and skates - Black Biscuit, CCM, Jofa, Itech, Koho, Mission, Tour and more. ... Welcome The Hockey Depot. ...

www.thehockeydepot.com/

92. **Hoofdklasse Hockey (Rabobankcompetitie) De hockey portal in de ...**

World > Nederlands > Sport > Hockey

www.hoofdklassehockey.nl/

93. **Official site of the AHL powered by SLAM! Sports**

All-Star fan balloting begins Friday. The American Hockey League announced today that fan balloting for the 2004 Pepsi AHL All-Star Classic will begin Friday ...

www.canoe.ca/AHL/home.html

94. **infoHOCKEY.com**

World > Español > Deportes > Hockey > Patines

www.infohockey.com/

95. **Hockey Made Easy**

This is Canada's best hockey instruction manual for youth and minor coaches, parents, boys, girls, men, and women players who are involved with youth and minor ...

www.hockeymadeeasy.com/

96. **The Hockey Shop - A huge selection of player ice hockey equipment...**

Our store is renowned for the very best selection of player ice hockey equipment and goalie equipment at the GUARANTEED lowest prices. ...

www.thehockeyshop.com/

97. **Mission Hockey**

Official site for Mission Ice and Roller Hockey.

www.missionhockey.com/

98. **WCHA Athletics**

To permanently bypass this page Click Here.

www.wcha.com/

99. **Hockey Equipment Sports Store Outlet Shop**

Hockey equipment for ice hockey and roller hockey. Accessories and gear for all your hockey needs. Were not just the regular hockey store. ...

www.apihockey.com/

100. **home1**

Dedicated to coaching and teaching ice hockey. Offers tips and suggestions, bulletin board, and links.

www.hockeycoach.com/

101. **International Unicycle Hockey Homepage**

A good general page on unicycle hockey that includes rules for playiny hockey, team information, and...

www.unicycling.org/hockey

102. **BCAHAflash**

Amateur hockey for youths, juniors, men and women. Information, hockey resources and links for hockey...

www.bcaha.org/

103. **Field hockey in Vancouver at the Hockey Net**

Field hockey website for Vancouver, British Columbia. You'll find the following information and resources: ...

www.fieldhockey.org/

104. **Ice Hockey in Greece**

Scan history, players, statistics, photos, and information for Greek ice hockey.

www.icehockey.gr/

105. **Dansk Hockey Union : Alt om Landhockey i Danmar**
World > Dansk > Sport > Hockey > Landhockey

www.dk-hockey.dk/

106. **MAXIMONLINE**

Hockey is known for speed, intensity, and a long tradition of silly,tongue-abusing names. From Dave Andreychuk to Dimitry Afanasenkov ...

www.maximonline.com/sports/hockey_name/

107. **Hockey Nova Scotia**

Dedicated to the advancement of amateur hockey for all individuals by ensuring participants opportunities...

www.nshockey.org/

108. **New York FireFighters Hockey Team**

An organization comprised of firefighters, officers and members who donate their time and efforts...

www.fdnyhockey.com/

109. **Underwater Hockey in Australia**

Underwater Hockey in Australia. This is Australian web site for the exciting sport of Underwater Hockey underwater, underwater hockey ...

www.underwater-hockey.com/

110. **THE HOCKEY COACHING RESOURCE**

Features (shockwave required for some animations), articles, and information for hockey coaches, players...

www.geocities.com/Colosseum/1571/

111. **INSIDE HOCKEY - Inside Hockey is the ultimate ice hockey site**

Editorial content, regularly updated hockey news, fantasy hockey resources and a portal to local content...

www.insidehockey.com/

112. **England Hockey**

Back, Page Not Found, England Hockey - Home. You have tried to reach a page which no longer exists, either because of an old link within ...

www.hockeyonline.co.uk/neweha/news
news_list.php?section=homeandtype=all

113. **Information About Women's Hockey**

General Women's Hockey Information. Team Sweden vs Team Canada, at 1994 World Championships. ... Information Available on the Net. (1) women-in-hockey mailing list. ...

www.cs.toronto.edu/~andria/general/

114. **Inline Hockey Network : Inline/Roller Hockey News**

Source for inline hockey news and information. Features product reviews, bulletin boards, event listings,...

www.inlinehockey.net/

115. **Better Hockey**
Information for players to improve their game, computer games, coaches forum, newsletter, and advice...
www.betterhockey.com/

116. **amateurhockey.com Search Page**
Amateurhockey.com, | Online Casino | Cellular.com | Homes for Sale | Health | Cars | Printers | Doctors | Marketing | Loans | Tickets | Music|. ...
www.amateurhockey.com/

117. **The Official Site of the LA Kings**
Official site. Includes team information, a schedule, statistics, and ticket information.
www.lakings.com/

118. **CBS.SportsLine.com - NHL Home**
NHL and pro hockey coverage including scores, stats, Fantasy Hockey, standings, schedules, transactions, team and player news, NHL playoffs, NHL Championship ...
cbs.sportsline.com/nhl/

119. **HOCKEYnet - the hockey network for field hockey**
HOCKEYnet - a network for field hockey - providing a source for information on clubs, fixtures and results throughout the uk and ireland. ...
www.hockey-net.co.uk/

120. **Official Website of the Ottawa Senators Hockey Club**
Welcome to the Official Website of the Ottawa Senators Hockey Club - National Hockey League (NHL) - Ottawa Senators Hockey Club (NHL). ...
www.ottawasenators.com/

121. **FANTASY HOCKEY JOURNAL-All your tools for your hockey pools**
News, information and links to help participants in hockey pools and fantasy leagues.
www2.ebtech.net/~randyd/

122. **Sports | Hockey | canada.com**
News and editorial coverage of the NHL, minors, juniors, European and college leagues.
www.faceoff.com/

123. **hotHOCKEY: The Hockey Global Arena**

A hockey portal incorporating a directory/search engine, free members section, and giveaways.

www.hothockey.com/

124. **Houston Aeros**

Official site includes merchandise, tickets, team information, booster club, hockey information, fan...

www.aeros.com/

125. **Boston Bruins Official Web Site**

Official site includes team history, players, schedule, statistics, tickets, arena, multimedia, news,...

www.bostonbruins.com/

126. **Phoenix Coyotes**

Official site of the Phoenix Coyotes Hockey Club. Members of the National Hockey League's Western Conference, Pacific Division. Includes news, game day information, ticket information, statistics, schedule, fan...

www.phoenixcoyotes.com/

127. **Lifetime Hockey Home**

Lifetime Hockey is devoted to the advancement of adult no-check ice and in-line hockey.

www.lifetimehockey.com/

128. **Atlanta Thrashers**

Official site. Includes player information, team statistics, tickets, and message boards.

www.atlantathrashers.com/

129. **Professional Hockey Newspaper and Media Source**

Guide to newspapers, online media, team sites, statistics, scores, transactions, and hockey information for all levels of professional hockey — NHL, all minor ...

www.allsports.com/nhl/media/

130. **USATODAY.com**

Player news, interactive stats, advice and games; projections. USATODAY.com extras. Weekly hockey chat. Ted Montgomery, 1 pm ET Wed.; previous weeks. ...
www.usatoday.com/sports/hockey/front.htm

131. **The Birthplace of Hockey, Windsor, Nova Scotia, Canada**
The definitive guide to the origins of the game of ice hockey and the Birthplace of Hockey, Windsor, Nova Scotia, Canada. ... Hockey Windsor, Nova Scotia, Canada. A guide to the origin of ice hockey as the game took form in the early 1800s: the early game, photos...
www.birthplaceofhockey.com/

132. **About Hockey - Stanley Cup - NHL - fantasy hockey - NHL trade**
All the hockey you need. Stanley Cup ... Ice Hockey. I can help you find what you need to know about Pro Ice Hockey. Pro Ice Hockey....
proicehockey.about.com/

133. **Hockey North America**
Beginner hockey for adults.
www.hna.com/

134. **All Hockey Links**
Fill out this form and your site will be added ASAP! This page has had about visitors since 5/21/96. Long Island High School Hockey. Ice and inline hockey links, classifieds, business directory and hockey shop.
www.hockeylinks.com/

135. **American Hockey Equipment Center**
Offers hockey equipment, skates, t-shirts, and listings of hockey schools,hockey tournaments, and ice arenas. ... Free Hockey Services.
www.americanhockeycenter.com/

136. **Hockey: Cincinnati.Com**
Cyclones Season complete. Advertiser Spotlight. Columbus Hockey. Follow Ohio's first NHL team, the Columbus Blue Jackets. Offical Blue Jackets Site NHL News. ...
www.cincinnati.com/sports/hockey/

137. **Hockey**
Offers a complete online store with everything for the hockey player and fan.
www.oceanhockey.com/

138. **Planet Hockey - Premier South African Field Hockey Shop**
Specialist retail shop that features news, photos, player interviews, and resources on South Africian...
www.planethockey.co.za/

139. **Women's In-Line Hockey**

Women's In-Line Hockey. ... Women's In-Line Roller Hockey. This version of roller hockey uses regular ice hockey sticks and a hard plastic puck. Information about the sport in both its quad and inline forms.

www.whockey.com/inline/

140. **American Hockey Coaches Association**

The association includes professional, collegiate, junior, high school, and youth hockey coaches,...

www.ahcahockey.com/

141. **Hockey-Stats.com - NHL Stats, Scores and News Archive**

Online archive of National Hockey League statistics includes player statistics and top statistical leaders.

www.hockey-stats.com/

142. **Hockey101**

What is Hockey 101? Hockey101.com is a community site for players,fans, and coaches of non-varsity college ice hockey programs. ...

www.hockey101.com/

143. **Field Hockey West - Welcome**

Field Hockey West: Resource for field hockey in the Western United States and Canada. Field Hockey West: A Chapter of USField Hockey. ...

www.fieldhockeywest.org/

144. **Peliplaneetta.net Tervetuloa**

Free ice hockey simulator for PC.

eastside.peliplaneetta.net/

145. **CAN/AM Hockey**

CAN/AM Hockey has been organizing hockey camps and tournaments for youth and adult recreational ice hockey players for over 30 years. International adult and youth ice hockey tournaments.

www.canamhockey.com/

146. **Cricket-Hockey.com - Shop online for UK Cricket and Field Hockey...**

Secure online shopping for all cricket and hockey equipment and accessories. Worldwide delivery, based...

www.cricket-hockey.co.uk/

147. **Legends of Hockey Net - An official web channel of the Hockey Hall**

Legends Of Hockey Net is an extensive website offering in-depth information about hockey's greatest players, including statistics, photos, and merchandise. ...

www.legendsofhockey.net/html/home.htm

148. **Pakistan Field Hockey**

pin.net.pk/hockey/

149. **Official Home of the Pittsburgh Penguins**

Official site. Includes team information, statistics, a schedule, multimedia, and ticket information.

www.pittsburghpenguins.com/

150. **Le Journal du hockey**

World > Français > Sports > Hiver > Hockey

www.ljdh.com/

151. **Calgary Flames Hockey - NHL**

Official site. Includes team information, video highlights, statistics, history of the team, and tickets.

www.calgaryflames.com/

152. **RDS - Hockey**

RDS.CA offre une couverture complète du hockey, incluant la

World > Français > ... > Sports et loisirs > Sports > Hockey

www.rds.ca/hockey/

153. **NWHL**

Statistics, schedule, rosters, fan registry, interactive, arena and ticket information, player of...

www.nwhlhockey.com/

154. **Women's University Hockey**

Information and links for college women's hockey in the United States and Canada.

www.cs.toronto.edu/~andria/University_Hockey.html

155. **Tamp A Ba Y Lightning**

Official site includes players, coaches, news, schedules, statistics, history, multimedia, merchandise...

www.tampabaylightning.com/

SPORTS WEB ENCYCLOPEDIA

SPORTS WEB ENCYCLOPEDIA

(In Two Volumes)
(Volume - 2)

Dr. C. Ashok

KALPAZ PUBLICATIONS
Delhi-110052

Spo[illegible]eb Encyclopedia

Rs. [illegible]

ISBN: 81-7835-335-0 (set)
ISBN: 81-7835-337-7 (Vol. 2)

Published in 2005 in India by
Kalpaz Publications,
C-30, Satyawati Nagar, Delhi-110052
E-mail : Kalpaz@hotmail.com

Laser Typesetting at : Shiva Infosystem, Delhi
Printed at : Salasar Imaging Systems, Delhi

Contents

27. Human Resource Development 347
28. Indian National Flag 361
29. Indian Olympic Asssociation 373
30. International Olympic Committee 383
31. Journals 399
32. Karate 411
33. Kho-kho 417
34. Kabaddi 421
35. Korfball 445
36. Marathon 453
37. Olympics 457
38. Modern Pentathlon 471
39. National games 477
40. Netball 483
41. Parasailing 495
42. Physical education colleges 505
43. Pinball 517
44. Polo 527
45. Rugby 531
46. Skating 537
47. Skiing 547
48. Snooker 553
49. Sports authority of india 563
50. Squash 571
51. Swimming 583
52. Table tennis 599
53. Tennis 603
54. Tennikoit 621
55. Trekking 623
56. Volleyball 631
57. World cup 647
58. Wrestling 653
59. Yatching 661
60. Yoga 667

27
Human Resource Development

1. **SHRM Online**

   Home page for the Society for Human Resources Management.
   www.shrm.org/

2. **Admission Procedure...**

   Scholarships for outstanding Sports Men/Women ... Pradesh University Shimla - 171 005 (India). ... Public Administration, Diploma in Human Resourse Development, Chairman ...
   hpuniv.nic.in/adproc.htm

3. **The Tribune, Chandigarh, India - Sport**

   A voluntary oranisation, has been sponsored by the Ministry of Human Resourse Development, Depatment of Youth Affairs and Sports, Government of India. Top. ...
   www.tribuneindia.com/2001/20010204/sports.htm

4. **The Times of India - Reader's.**

   ... is the only region having promise to excell in development of human ... only tool required is 'effective management of all human and natural resourse.'SAARC is ...
   timesofindia.indiatimes.com/opinions/411472.cms

5. **OurKarnataka.com : Mangalore this week**

   ... Manohar Joshi Union Minister for Human resourse development and Ms ... Union Minister of state for sports and youth ... diverse cultural heritage of India is protecting ...
   www.ourkarnataka.com/Mang_This_Week/3week.htm

6. **PIB India fact sheet**

   ... 1999 - Press Information Bureau, Government of India. ...
   pib.myiris.com/pq/

7. **ArabSites Search Engine for the Middle East: Business and Economy...**

   ... Consultants, Employee Training and Development, Negotiation Tactics and ... Contact us for your Human Resourse Challange. ... online placement agency of India: we fix ...

   www.arabsites.com/links/Business_and_Economy/ Employment/

8. **Feedback**

   ... in pointing out certain wrong practices to the relatively younger Resourse Persons helping ... Human Development : Concept and Reality. ... 10. Why NE India is backward

   www.assamgov.org

   edu_assam/universities/ Gauhati/UGC_ASC1.htm

9. **OMC**

   ... human resource developement and human resourse planning have ... for complete development of human resources, organized ... to the industrial development of the State. ...

   www.orissamining.com/oldnewletter.asp

10. **Grant Aid**

    ... The Project For Human Resourse Development Scholarship. 2.66. ... The Project for Human Resource Development ... The Project for Groundwater Development and Sanitation ...

    www.mofa.go.jp/policy/oda/note/grant-2.html

11. **PIB Ministries and Departments**

    ... The business of the Government of India is transacted by the ...

    pib.myiris.com/ministry/

12. **BEAR/HUMAN INTERACTIONS: ASPECTS OF FOOD-CONDITIONING IN PRUDHOE...**

    ... generaly corn), the bear prefers to operate this resourse. ... 368, Hoopa, CA 95546, USA Abstract: Development of a ... found high levels of bear-human interaction on ...

    www.dfg.ca.gov/ hunting/bear/iba

    bearhumaninteractionsposters.pdf

13. **BENGAL Engg. College Profile**

    ... The new syllabus covers latest development in the field ... Planning 25 9: Mathematics 10: Human Resourse and Management ... a branch of United Bank of India inside the ...

    www.becs.ac.in/bec/bec1.htm

14. **The Tribune, Chandigarh, India - Punjab**
    ... January 10 Under its community development programme, the ... the new building of the Block Resourse Centre constructed ... Bail denied in human trafficking case Our ...
    www.tribuneindia.com/2004/20040111/punjab1.htm
15. **LIST OF ON-LINE RESOURCES**
    ... AND INFORMATION (An excellent resourse for answers to ... IWGIA supports indigenous peoples' human rights, self ... cultural integrity, and the right to development.
    www.geocities.com/angryindian/links.html
16. **Search4i.com - Health and Medicine**
    ... Site of formation and information on human african sleeping ... organisation of Qualified Allopathic Doctors in India. ... Forum : Discussion forum, resourse site for ...
    www.search4i.com/directory/cat/1005/
17. **Business**
    ... you will learn about the development of accounting. ... Human Resourse Management By: Eric Scioscia There are many ... india and ebiz By: tunna INDIAN OVERVIEW The ...
    www.midtermpapers.com/TermPapers/Business/index4.shtml
18. **Iraq Reconstruction - Your One Stop Manpower Shop**
    ... Lalwani General Manager Santini Human Solutions PO ... implement the ERP (Enterprise Resourse Planning Software ... 3. Development of Road Connectivity to Jawaharlal ...
    www.alicp.com/forums/topic.asp?TOPIC_ID=352
19. **Excelsior... Nation**
    ... human interaction, many importers may shun East Asia and come to India. ... the survey - to which 108 companies in it, human resourse development, textiles, food ...
    www.dailyexcelsior.com/web1/03may03/national.htm
20. **»»Reviews for Associations««**
    ... and will serve as a major resourse for clinicians ... researchers, scholars and students of human development in the ... articles by Monica Melanchton, India; Lily Kuo ...
    www.booksunderreview.com/Sports/Badminton/ Associations/ Associations_55.html

21. **AFFILIATES-DIRECT for International Business Opportunities and...**
... Spiritual Greeting cards Digital resourse allocation recording ... information with a human face. ...
affiliates-direct.com/

22. **CEMCA : News Letter Sep - 1997**
... In India, there are plans to extend ... vocabulary and dimensions of human movement, health ... expressive movement, affective development, learning, reinforcement of ...
www.cemca.org/newsletter/sep1997/sep1997.htm

23. **Roster of Instructional Staff - Spring 2003**
... 530 (U) Computer User Interface Development; CSC 540 (U ... MS Statistics, Osmania University, India, CIS 200 ... University Georgia, MS Human Resourse; BS Rehabilitation
campus.murraystate.edu/sacs/reference/
roster_inst_staff_sp03.htm

24. **»»Reviews for Schools««**
... An Important Resourse. This book helped me a great ... Champions. Published in Paperback by Human Kinetics (T ... Excellent Source for Youth Development and Training. It's ...
www.booksunderreview.com/Arts/Animation/ Training/Schools
Schools_11.html

25. **Education Link Directory**
... class, college, program or resourse that I ... undergraduate, graduate and professional development courses ... structured classes focusing on human capital development ...
www.superperformance.com/educationlinks.html

26. **Retired and Supply Teachers List**
... Qualifications : Field placements in resourse room, kindergarten ... I hold a Bachelor of Human Kinetics in ... I am a former Canadian National Development Team Member ...
www.pedagonet.com/other/hireliste.htm

27. **BizWiz Experts for Publishing**
... Compensation Law; Employment Law and Human Resourse Management. ... up Hewlett-Packard's human resources program ... Windows Programming, Web development - Java, HTML ...
www.bizwiz.com/ cgi-bin
corrsam.pl?publish=yesandsearchterms=Publishing

28. **Mumfordbooks Book Catalogue**
... Chapter 13 The long childhood, development of the brain ... A most valuable visual resourse (if anyone has the ... SECTION 1. The Religious Emotions purely Human, 275; 2 ...
www.mumfordbooks.co.uk/CAT.asp?CatID=8

29. **Timorese NGOs**
... Education (formal and non formal); Human Development, Community Development, Health, Emergency Relief. 26, 25. Clinic St Antonio Motael (CSt.AM). ...
www.geocities.com/etngoforum/Dili.xls

30. **Ewebeye.com sites list page 61**
... Market Analisys Business Consultancy Human Resource Management HRM ... looking to outsource software development of their ... business This web resourse represents the
www.b2bmine.com/lists/ewall61.html

31. **Kandungan muka surat Prakata :- i. Naib Canselor Universiti ...**
... Site and its impact on human health 1 ... dan Herba Processing and product development technology Agronomic ... perbandingan Melayu-Inggeris-Cina- India 4. Pengembangan ...
ppp.upsi.edu.my/img/hala.pdf

32. **INSTITUTIONS AND COLLEGES IN AHMEDABAD AND GANDHINAGAR**
File Format: PDF/Adobe Acrobat ... Working for Children, Adolsent and Women's Health and Development, Training. ... O)6854248 Librarian : Ms Hetal Bhatt Activities : Courses on human Right Enrichment. ...
www.alibnet.org/Istitute-Dir.pdf

33. **Education [Science: Social Sciences: Geography: Geographic ...**
... fifth framework project aiming at the development of a ... Russia. Moscow 18:02 (January 24), India. New Delhi 21 ... Help build the largest human-edited directory on the
www.worldsearch.com/science/social_sciences/geography/geographic_information_systems/education/

34. **Ewebeye.com sites list page 6**
... co.at Summary: AMST Systemtechnik Human Centrifuge AIRFOX ... B An Australian music resourse listing bands ... Specialising in the research development and manufacture ...
www.b2bmine.com/lists/ewall6.html

35. **URL-Album**
... of Paleontology USGS by Theme Virtual Hospital: The Human Brain Volcano ... SOHO America Taxes - Twelve Myths Women's Business Development Center. ... Oracle Resourse ...
nv-study.intramail.ru/links/links_urlalbum.html

36. **WAPA member directory, 11-2002**
... Geographic areas: natural resourse-dependent US communities; E ... to Health Services; Access to Human Services; Systems ... Topical Areas: Aging; Applied; Development. ...
www.smcm.edu/wapa/password/directory11-02.html

37. **Rajasthaninfoline>Business and Economy>Companies>Software**
... And new, human-determined values are in ... database application development, website development, Multimedia presentation ... specialize in Enterprise resourse planning ...
www.rajasthaninfoline.com/be/com/soft.htm

38. **Holistic Health Centers Information**
... Disease, and Health, Long Life of Human Being—Jin Tong ... Submitted on 8/23/2000; Natural Resourse 95% effective ... Therapist certification and career development. ...
www.naturalhealthweb.com/topics/subtopics/
holistic_health_centers.html

39. **Nonviolence International - Direct Action Training Resources**
... Handbook Resourse and Teaching Material in Conflict Resolution, Education for Human Rights, Peace ... on Peace Research, Education and Development and the ...
www.nonviolenceinternational.net/datr.htm

40. **factsheetdiesel**
... include building smaller vehicles, developing advanced technologies ... Website of the Natural Resourse Defence Council ... is detrimental to human health." "The ...
www.cseindia.org/campaign/apc/pdf/factdies.pdf

41. **Classifile - Index By Name**
... NASA Human Space Flight Category: Technology; Space. ... Research and Development; Canada. ... Native Online: The Resourse Center for Native Art Category: Humanities ... ...
www.classifile.com/ index_results.asp?alpha=Nandtype=Name

42. **final teledir**

    ... and Rand D libraries requires skilled human resources to ... ERNET India will provide backbone and host 16 ... PHARMACEUTICAL EDUCATION and RESEARCH DEVELOPMENT(PERD) CENTRE ...
    www.alibnet.org/DIRECTORY.pdf

43. **AGNET APRIL 22, 1999 EU biotech storm plants few seeds of ... ...**

    ... of the biotech tools from the human genome project ... The Institute for Food and Development Policy, 398 ... having resources listed in the PANUPS Resourse Pointer to
    131.104.232.9/agnet/1999/4-1999/ag-04-22-99-01.txt

44. **Iraq Reconstruction - HR solutions from sub continent**

    ... Dear Sir Human Resource to rebuild Iraq is ... implement the ERP (Enterprise Resourse Planning Software ... 3. Development of Road Connectivity to Jawaharlal Nehru Port ...
    www.alicp.com/forums/topic.asp?TOPIC_ID=480

45. **Geometry.Net - Basic_I: Ijo Indigenous Peoples Africa**

    ... Untitled Human Rights news service stories about ... of Parliamentarians on Population and Development Association for ... Ijaw Resourse Center The Ijaws are the most ...
    www.geometry.net/ basic_i
    ijo_indigenous_peoples_africa_page_no_2.php

46. **Daily Excelsior... Editorial**

    ... is the bottom of the middle human development category, way ... says that the Western path of development, brings at ... poor, and the damage to the resourse base of
    www.dailyexcelsior.com/02apr07/edit.htm

47. **The Deaf Resource Library**

    ... and provides information on test development and testing ... Maharashtra Deaf Fellowship of India; Japan: Japanese ... deaf medical professionals (human medicine, dental ...
    www.deaflibrary.org/

48. **STUDENT AFFAIRS and STUDENT SERVICES**

    ... responsibility for enhancing the human condition. ... Resume Referral, the Career Resourse Center also ... environment conducive to student development and academic
    www.ugs.usf.edu/pdf/cat9798/studaff.pdf

49. **Seeing The Forest**

... we need is to pursue economic development, but not ... blackcranein: one which sees nature as resourse and exploits ... The natural human condition, they held, is not ...

seetheforest.blogspot.com/
2003_10_01_seetheforest_archive.html

50. **Kum Kum Tandon - Chat Interviews - Indiatimes**

... a lawyer or police officer in india because I ... and the electronic(TV and Radio) developing activities rapidly. ... cultures and there impact on Human resourse is used ...

chatinterviews.indiatimes.com/articleshow/13563569.cms - 41k - **Cached - Similar pages**

51. **M_TRANSFER_EVALUATION.htm**

... RS 501 Neuroscience ELECTIVE RS 505 Motor Development PEES 226 ... Media MEDA 201 CMN 111 Speech: Human Commun SPCH ... Mgmt MGMT 301 MGMT 306 Hum Resourse Mgmt MGMT ...

www.lander.edu/admissions/transfer_evals/
M_TRANSFER_EVALUATION.HTM

52. **The RSS Weblog - rss.weblogsinc.com**

... is: the human brain (ok, the human brain if ... a contributor to Lockergone's RSS Resourse (as well ... Anil Dash Vice President, Business Development, Six Apart; Jon ...

rss.weblogsinc.com/

53. **FACULTY**

... Professor Management/Human Resources Management BS, University of ... Director Student Life and Development BA, Scripps College ... MA, University of Bombay, India; Ph.D ...

www.csulb.edu/~janicej/catalog-01-02/faculty.pdf

54. **NANET GLOBAL - ALPHABETICAL MEMBER LIST**

... This site is still developing, but honors the ancient ... Links to resourse dealing with Wicca, New Age ... Tools for Activating memories, healing, human potential, and ...

www.v-j-enterprises.com/nanlista.html

55. **Insight May 03 base**

... the community to this higher level in its development. ... combat three great evils of human society, namely ... over the world include Bangladesh, India, Pakistan, Iran ...

www.world-federation.org/NR/rdonlyres/E6CD6645-88DD-43D6-A470-536CD7B02E08/0/InsightMay03.pdf

56. **Online Degree Travel**

... Dua, a secluded yet luxurious resort development in the ... A helpful directory resourse for the City of Berkley ... the UK's web award winning human logistics service ...

www.online-degree-information.com/Travel.html

57. **Recent Australian Publications September 2003 - Alphabetic**

... Planned communities Australia, Housing development Economic aspects ... of Human Services. ... for the Australian environment [electronic resourse] : proceedings of ...

www.nla.gov.au/kinetica/rap/sep03alp.html

58. **List of top 100,000 most searched search engine optimization ...**

... loan rate homemade ice cream human growth hormone ... magazine students tap the sims resourse the thing ... cow pics currency conversions dead development diode dirt ...

www.hostrich.com/search-engine-optimization/ most-searched-popular-keywords-011.html

59. **People:Personal Home Pages:S**

... links to information about the third world, human rights, aid to development, data konsult ... Samuel, James - chat resourse, music resourses, and just cool ...

netlec.com/host/pages.html

60. **DATE RUN 07/01/03 The University of Toledo REPORT PAGE 1 TIME RUN ...**

... ELECTIVE 400 LEVEL ANTH421.10 INDIA 5.00 964 ... LEVEL ANTH640.02 GROWTH AND DEVELOPMENT 5.00 964 ... CONFLICT RESOLUTN and NEGOTIATIONS BUSH651 HUMAN RESOURSE POLICY:CO ...

registrar.utoledo.edu/tca/osu.pdf

61. **People**

... Campaign The three words - human, rights, campaign ... Amreican Sportsman Page Outdoors resourse page; Free ... Contract game and tool development; Vinton Enterprises ...

www.ntgi.net/ntg/mall/people.htm

62. **DX LISTENING DIGEST 3-158, September 2, 2003 edited by Glenn...**

... term blueprint for the development of digital ... 73s, (Swopan Chakroborty, Kolkata, India, DX LISTENING ... journalism to increase the human resourse capability in ...

www.worldofradio.com/dxld3158.

63. **Inside front cover**

... from low-income homes - participate in sports programs, which ... Psychology of Women and the Development of Girls ... the Maryland Department of Human Resources, the ...

www.marylandwomen.org/pdf/girltowomen.pdf

64. **Massachusetts Dedicated Domain Hosting Services Directory - MA ...**

... Support Technology Web Design Resourse Group Softlockcom Inc ... Web Solutions Pagination Web Development P Zazz ... Giga Information Group Human Capital Interactive ...

www.dedicated-domain-hosting-services.com/ MA Massachusetts-Domain-Hosting.htm

65. **Partners in Print 2002 Art and Politics Portfolio**

... fix-it-mentality" without thought to the human beings who ... be the next stage in their nation's development. ... add comment MEDIUM/RESOURSE CHAT: On a visit to ...

www.pnp.org.au/pics/2002ap/2002Page3.asp

66. **International Ichthyoparasitology Newsletter No. 10 January 2003**

... net/ AquaVetMed Information and Resourse Database For ... o interest to ichthyoparsitologists (development, phylogeny, molecular ... Risk of transmission – Human cases ...

www.diplectanum.dsl.pipex.com/newsletter/newsl10.pdf

67. **International Ichthyoparasitology**

... Information and Resourse Database. ... fish parasitology but also veterinary parasitology, human parasitology and ... we are examining the development, early pathogenesis ...

www.diplectanum.dsl.pipex.com/newsletter/newsl10.doc

68. **Poker - Video Online Poker Game - Carribbean Pai Gow Stud Internet ...**

... gambler going grand human inc jsp ... designs detailseite deuceswildvideopoker deutscher developing devices df ... res reservation resortsac resourse response ressort

poker.w3onlinecasino.com/

69. **Bulletin 17.pmd**

... its highlights is the sharing of human resources and ... in the WWF Kikori Intergrated Conservation Development Project Area ... dull green on top but sports bright red ...

www.wwfpacific.org.fj/pdfs/spc_17.pdf

70. **Graduate Student Information Package**
... Ofc. Canadian Paraplegic Association (Alberta) Central Park Lodge Cross Cancer Institute Elves Memorial Child Development Centre East Good Samaritan Auxiliary ...
www.uofaweb.ualberta.ca/ rehabmed/pdf
Grad%20handbook%202003-2004%20MSc.pdf

71. **ScotsGay Magazine - 25**
... will range from activism to personal development to just ... visit http://www.bi.org for a fantastic bisexual resourse. ... of the Universal Declaration of Human Rights ...
www.scotsgay.co.uk/sg25/sg.html

72. **<html> <head> </head><body><pre>andlt;htmlandgt; andlt;headandgt; andlt ...**
... Australia, Planned communities Australia, Housing development Economic Added ... of Human Services ... the Australian environment [electronic resourse] : proceedings of ...
www.nla.gov.au/kinetica/rap/sep03alp.txt

73. **2002-2003 Heidelberg College Catalog: Courses of Study (EF)**
... for young children, and use the Internet as a resourse for locating ... Foundation Courses: 14 semester hours EDU 503
Human Growth and Development 3 hrs. ...
www.heidelberg.edu/registrar/past-catalogs/ catalog02-03/courses-e-f.html

74. **Poker - Video Online Poker Game - Carribbean Pai Gow Stud Internet ...**
... developed developer developers developing development devices devoted ... hu huge hugh hughes human humor hundred ... resource resources resourse respected respective ...
poker.w3onlinecasino.com
Index_al_Poker_Video_Online_Poker_Game_Carribbean_Pai_Gow_Stud_Internet_Poker_On...

75. **[Spearfishing: Good or Bad?] - DeeperBlue.net Forums**
... way you choose, do it w/ respect for the resourse. ... it's a lot more difficult to minimize human impact on ... With the rapid development of the apnea diving during ...
forums.deeperblue.net/archive/topic/18128-1.html

76. **Finding aid**

... Education Fund, Lawyers Committee for Human Rights, and ... support or for the development and implementation ... and abroad especially in Europe, Africa, and India....

www.nypl.org/research/chss/spe/rbk/faids/aarondia.pdf

77. **jan1994**

... The latter is the cumulative effect of human cave visitation. ... Roswell Resourse Area. ... cave and karst features within the Barren River Area Development District....

oldsci.eiu.edu/physics/len/grotto/jan1995.htm

78. **Report**

... facility includes a world-class human movement laboratory ... Report -6- British Journal of Sports Medicine. ... La Trobe University Research and Development Park The

www.latrobe.edu.au/rgso/dvcr/info/01resrep.pdf

79. **DC Indymedia: feature/87517**

... afford to loss such a precious resourse for lack ... the community development corporations supposedly fail on this ... rethink failed approaches to meeting human need

dc.indymedia.org/feature/display/87517/index.php

80. **Ma, P. and D. Armstrong (1984). The Acquired Immune Deficiency ...**

... Sexual diversity and Catholicism : toward the development of moral ... Kaapstad, Human and Rousseau en Tafelberg. ... in numbers : a lesbian, gay, and bisexual resourse.

membres.lycos.fr/jgir/biblio/congres.txt

81. **Accreditation Disclaimer**

... Intellectual advancement of the graduate student, development of initiative, research technique, advanced skill and proficiency, and designing enthusiasm are ...

www.uog.edu/gsr/GradBulletin2003-2004.pdf

82. **Duke University Office of the University Registrar**

Page 1. Page 2. 0 Duke University Academic Calendar* Trinity College of Arts and Sciences; The Pratt School of Engineering; The Nicholas...

registrar.duke.edu/webpage/acesfall2003.pdf

83. **EFFECT OF HABITAT ALTERATION ON HERPETOFAUNAL ASSEMBLAGES OF ...**
... yet the frogs do not die in sport but in ... and in the existing situation in Northeast India both are ... ecologically sound as long as the human population density ...
www.bio.utexas.edu/grad/sp/Miz_herp.pdf

84. **Schengen – consequences for national migration Policy**
... of legislative, financial and human resourse problems ... of the United Nations Development Program, starting ... incapacity and corruption facilitate human traffic and ...
www.ipp.md/projects/Ch.1~integral.doc

85. **Annual Reports**
... pilot countries for GEMS, Russia, India, Argentina, Macedonia ... in the field of professional development and conduct ... and learning and making a human difference at
www.iearn.org.au/international/re2001.pdf

86. **Ukraine.com Discussion Forum - Ukrainians**
... Here is a quote from an American: In developing a policy ... Do you happen to know a good online resourse? ... what we do not know about the laws of human life." p1440 ...
www.ukraine.com/forums/printthread.php3?threadid=5181

87. **(JICA) ACTIVITIES OF JICA**
... Center of the Ministry of Coal Industry INDIA The Sanjay ... Development to Support Poverty Alleviation Programs The Human Resource Development in the ...
iggi.unesco.or.kr/web/iggi_docs/05/952411672.pdf

88. **ORDINANCE NO**
... and all the articles and uniform issued to him for sports or NCC ... of candidates so disqualified shall be circulated to all Universities in India requesting them ...
www.itcenter.dauniv.ac.in/rules/ordinance.doc

89. **2002-2003 Heidelberg College Undergraduate Catalog**
... rooms, a weight room and a sports medicine facility. ... Founders Hall, The Guest House, The Development House (now ... who can act effectively with human values in a
www.heidelberg.edu/registrar/ 0203-undergrad-catalog.pdf

90. **ACCENT ON LEARNING**

... 974-2125 Bachelor of Independent Studies Program External Degree Program, HMS 443 974-4058 Career Development Counseling Center for Human Development, SVC 2124 ...
www.ugs.usf.edu/pdf/cat9798/cat9798.pdf

91. **Vimukt Shiksha**

... as the primary means of nurturing human learning and ... existing models of education and development, and (2 ... Shikshantar is based in Udaipur (Rajasthan, India). ...
www.swaraj.org/shikshantar/ls1.pdf

92. **Sea Man Ship guestbook**

... that our cooperation is going very well and developing. ... a Master's Degree in Supervision and Human Relatios from ... managed to establish a useful resourse for the
www.sms.lv/gbview.sql

93. **JOINT STANDING COMMITTEE**

... Jacqueline QUINN, Ms Rapin, Department of Human Geography, ANU ... unlike some of the problems of development of a small Pacific island, but in India the whole ...
www.aph.gov.au/hansard/joint/commttee/j7026764.pdf

94. **WSG MaryJune 03**

Page 1. Let our adorable stork, carriage, sailboat or moon signs announce your little one in a big way. Each rental includes a personalized
www.dy-dee.com/Wsgmayjune03.pdf

95. **SITES**

... Recreation and Sports .... Facility Human Resource ...
www.photomann.com/misawainfo/site2575.pdf

96. **Installation**

... Things To Do - Clubs and Social 54. Things To Do - Recreation and Sports 55. Schools 55. ... Photo Developing..... 222-5898. ... 222-5111. Human Resources..... ...
www.dmdc.osd.mil/sites/books/site2575.rtf

97. **John Mark Ministries Guestbook Archive (1999)**

... Wonderful resourse right at my keyboard and fingertips. ... Bible has nothing good to say about the human race ... in talking with anyone who is developing ministries to ...
www.pastornet.net.au/jmm/guestbook/gba1999.htm

28

Indian National Flag

1. **Flag of India - Indian flag history, pictures, history, facts ...**
   Flag of India, indian flag, the Tiranga, with pictures, amendmends to Indian Flag code etc. cheap web hosting provided by Directi. FLAG OF INDIA - Indian Flag. Features description and pictures of the Indian flag, flag code of India, flag trivia and flag sites.
   www.indianchild.com/flag_of_india.htm
2. **Indian flag code india image picture facts**
   Amendmends to the flag code of India in 2002, Indian flag pictures and decription etc. cheap web hosting provided by Directi. Indian flag code amendment. ...
   www.indianchild.com/indian_flag_code.htm
3. **Indian Flag Tiranga**
   Indian Flag Tiranga. Mrs. Sarojini ... it. Some Indian flag staffs were surmounted by a figure similar to that displayed on the flag itself. An autobiographical narration of the flag and information about the amendment to the flag code on...
   www.liveindia.com/tiranga/
4. **Flags of India - geography; Indian Flags, India Map, India Economy ...**
   Flag of India; small, medium and large Flag of Indian; Interactive Factbook: India GEOGRAPHY, Flag, India's Map, Geography, People, India Government, Economy ...
   www.theodora.com/wfb/india/india_flags.html
5. **Tiranga**
   ... Indian National TRI- COLOUR , the pride of India. TIRANGA. Thus ! I Was Born. Genesis of Tiranga. Evolution of Tiranga. Birth of Tiranga. The Ancient Dhvaja (Flags). On the national flag, its evolution, the history of flags and other emblems in history in India.
   www.tiranga.net/

6. **Indian Flag**

   Culture of India. | About me | Hindu Religion | Bollywood | India | Planets |. | Desi Jokes | Hindi Songs | Games | Search |. | Sign Guestbook | View Guestbook |. A small description of the flag and the significance of its tricolor.

   jayhind.tripod.com/Iindiaflag.html

7. **India**

   ... Note: we have found it almost impossible to represent the shade of saffron on the Indian flag adequately for all monitors - some show it too yellow, other too ...

   flagspot.net/flags/in.html

8. **Gorshkov will fly Indian flag by 2008**

   ... Gorshkov will fly Indian flag by 2008 By: MK Tayal January 21, 2004 New Delhi: India and Russia yesterday ended a decade of negotiations ...

   ww1.mid-day.com/news/nation/2004/january/74452.htm

9. **Biographies of Great Indians**

   Biographies of Great Indians. We present here, biographies of great men and women from India (Bharat). This list is by no means complete. ...

   www.freeindia.org/biographies/

10. **Indian Flag - AllYouCanRead.com**

    AllYouCanRead.com, Indian Flag. ... Home / Flags of the World / Indian Flag. Indian Flag. Indian Flag Click to enlarge, India Facts. Capital ...

    www.allyoucanread.com/flag.asp?id=76

11. **"The Flags of the Native Peoples of the United States"**

    ... The Citizen Band Potawatomi; The Colorado River Indian Tribes; The Colville Confederated ... The Wichita; The Yakima or Yakama(note this flag recently corrected the ...

    users.aol.com/Donh523/navapage/

12. **Indian Flag**

    ... For a brief history of the origins of the Indian flag we have to go back to August 1, 1906 to the Parsee Bagan Square (Green Park) at Calcutta where the first ...

    india.punjabilit.com/national/flag.htm

13. **AllRefer Countries - India: Flag (Indian Flag)**

    ... T U V W X Y Z. World. Countries. Flags. Maps. You are here : AllRefer.com > Reference > World > Countries > India > India - Flag. India: Flag (Indian Flag). Also See:
    reference.allrefer.com/world/countries/india/flag.html

14. **National Flag of India, flag of India, Indian flag, India national ...**

    National Flag of India, flag of India, Indian flag, India national flag, national flag, flag, nation. ...
    www.mapsofindia.com/maps/india/national-flag.htm

15. **Indian Flag Tiranga**

    Indian Flag Tiranga. Jana gana mana adhinayaka, jaya he Bharata bhagya vidhata. Punjab Sindhu Gujarata Maratha. Dravida Utkala Banga. ...
    www.liveindia.com/tiranga/NationalAnthem.html

16. **Indian Flag Proposals**

    This page is part of © FOTW Flags Of The World website Indian Flag Proposals. ... Musings on Indian flags (some mild political commentary follows): ...
    flagspot.net/flags/in!.html

17. **Flag of India | Indian Flag.**

    ... You are here > 1Up Travel > National Flags > Flag of India | Indian Flag. ... white band. More On the Indian Flags. Reveals every detailed ...
    www.1uptravel.com/flags/largeflags/india.html

18. **Indian Flag - Tricolour (Tiranga Jhanda)**

    The Indian Flag. The Indian Flag is called the Tiranga or the Tricolour. The reason for this is apparent. It has three strips of ...
    www.geocities.com/Paris/2583/indiaflag.html

19. **CIA - The World Factbook — British Indian Ocean Territory**

    ... name: Definition Field Listing conventional long form: British Indian Ocean Territory ... Flag description: Definition Field Listing white with six blue wavy ...
    www.cia.gov/cia/publications/factbook/geos/io.html

20. **Plan to carry LNG thro Indian flag vessels**

    ... Plan to carry LNG thro Indian flag vessels. Manoj. NEW DELHI, Dec. 17. AFTER lobbying strongly for a buy free-on-board (fob) policy ...
    www.thehindubusinessline.com/businessline/ logistic/2001/12/18/ stories/0918f051.htm

21. **India's Flag Quiz/Printout - EnchantedLearning.com**
... The Indian flag has three equal horizontal bars (saffron, white and green) with a blue Dharma Chakra (the wheel of law) in the center. ...
www.enchantedlearning.com/asia/ india/flag/flagquizbw.shtml

22. **The Flag Code**
... A foreigner or a foreign firm/institution may fly the National-Flag of India along with the flag of his/its country on the Indian National days or his/its own ...
www.tiranga.net/flagcode.htm

23. **The Indian flag and national anthem**
... the world. The Indian Flag and National Anthem. Indian Flag. A larger Indian flag. The Indian National Anthem. Thou art ...
www.abacci.com/atlas/anthem.asp?countryID=222

24. **Flags of the Native American Peoples of the US**
... I do not sell any of these flags see Item 5 off the main menu!! The Abenaki (VT); The Absentee Shawnee (OK); The Affiliated Tribes of Northwest Indians (ID,MT,OR ...
users.aol.com/donh523/navapage/indexdbs.htm

25. **World Flag Database: British Indian Ocean Territory**
... Languages: English British Indian Ocean Territory [Ratio 1:2]. Index | What's New | Flag Shop | Contact Us | About Flags | Help. Flag image and general country facts.
www.flags.net/BRIN.htm

26. **CIA - The World Factbook — Flag of British Indian Ocean Territory**
... Flag of British Indian Ocean Territory. ...
www.cia.gov/cia/publications/ factbook/flags/io-flag.html

27. **the Flag**
... days. "The Indian flag does not just belong to the government or the bureaucracy, it belongs to every Indian," says Naveen Jindal. ...
www.the-south-asian.com/April2002/Naveen_Jindal.htm

28. **The Hindu Business Line : New norms on right of first refusal on...**
... The difference in the bid price between the Indian flag vessel exercising the right of first refusal and the lowest rate quoted by the foreign flag vessel will ...
www.thehindubusinessline.com/2004/01/ 15/stories
2004011502030500.htm

29. **Flag**

    ... An Indian Flag To Tell Our Nation's Story The Colours The white represents the purity of our land base where equality and respect for all life forms exists. ...

    www.ubcic.bc.ca/flag.htm

30. **Melting Pot Math**

    ... The Indian flag was designed as a sign of freedom. It is a horizontal tricolor in equal proportions. ... Indian Flag Solutions. Back to Melting Pot Math.

    sln.fi.edu/school/math3/india_flag.html

31. **Indian Flag**

    INDIAN TRICOLOUR FLAG. ... Its use and display are regulated by the Indian Flag Code. To learn more about the Tiranga and the Amended Indian flag code. ...

    www.bsu.edu/web/immadisetty/INDIA/Flag.htm

32. **L³ - The Lewis And Clark Rediscovery Project**

    ... You can listen to this flag song sung recently at the Big Hole Memorial in ... 40 miles from the Canadian border, ; a bitter battle ensued and the Indian camp was ...

    www.l3-lewisandclark.com/
    ShowOneObject.asp?SiteID=34andObjectID=99

33. **Study on status of and challenges before the Indian Shipping ...**

    ... Energy and national security The protection of Indian flag vessels carrying imported crude from other locations to Indian ports, strategic port locations in ...

    www.teriin.org/reports/rep26/rep26.htm

34. **National Heritage**

    National Flag. The Indian flag is horizontal tricolor with equal proportion of deep saffron on the top, white in the middle and dark green at the bottom. ...

    www.geocities.com/Tokyo/Shrine/4287/flag.htm

35. **Indian maestros make British Indians proud : HindustanTimes.com/UK ...**

    ... The concert aptly titled Tiranga, meaning Three Colours, is a celebration of the Indian flag. The concert began with a short documentary ...

    www.hindustantimes.com/news/5983_549977,00430005.htm

36. **Children's House International Adoptions - India**
... NRI (Non-Resident Indian) ADOPTION: ... Nepal Adoptions: Please see our Nepal page for information on adoption from Nepal. INDIAN GOVERNMENT REQUIREMENTS.
www.adopting.com/chi/india.html

37. **The Native Flags of Florida History**
... Florida Kids. The Flags of Florida History. Indian Tribal Flags. Miccosukee Flag 1962-Present. It is a Miccosukee belief that life spins ...
dhr.dos.state.fl.us/flafacts/peo_flag.html

38. **Maps of India - Indian Flags, Maps, Economy, Geography, Climate...**
India Maps of the World - Interactive World Fact Book - Indian Flags, Maps, Economy, Geography, Climate, Natural Resources, Current Issues, International ... Contains a few maps of India made available for use on personal websites.
www.geographic.org/maps/india_maps.html

39. **Diego Garcia - ABC Maps of British Indian Ocean Territory; Flag...**
Map of Diego Garcia British Indian Ocean Territory; Interactive Factbook: GEOGRAPHY, Flag, Map,Geography, People, Government, Economy, Transportation ...
www.theodora.com/ maps/new
british_indian_ocean_territory_maps.html

40. **List of keywords beginning with I**
... india company (united kingdom) | finials and fringe | flags for components of the indian army | india - construction details of the indian flag | india - index'...
www.allstates-flag.com/fotw/flags/keywordi.html

41. **India**
... It was this flag that was first hoisted as the "official" Indian flag in Berlin on 3 December 1941. The spoked Ashoka Chakra (the ...
www.1uptravel.com/flag/flags/in.html

42. **HindustanTimes.com**
... tricolour enjoying a purple patch The Indian flag, restricted to "official" use till it was virtually unfettered two years ago, is enjoying its best spell. ...
www.hindustantimes.com/news/specials/ iday2003/feature
tri.shtml

43. **Mardi Gras Indians of Mardi Gras, New Orleans — their parade ...**
... the Indians were violent; Indians would meet on Mardi Gras, it was a day to settle scores." - Larry Bannock, President, New Orleans Mardi Gras Indian Council. A brief history and exposition of Mardi Gras Indian customs, interview with Larry Bannock, Chief of...
www.mardigrasneworleans.com/mardigrasindians/

44. **Indian King Tavern News: Francis Hopkinson Visits**
... Hopkinson explained how he came to design the first US flag (above, left ... by the state's revolutionary legislature at a meeting in the same Indian King Tavern ...
www.levins.com/iknews11.html

45. **WORLD FOOD SUMMIT: Five Years Later**
... Anwar. 379. Indian flag. 60,53 tons of milking 154,695 tons of clover 99,760 tons of Indian pea. 4/10/1999. 12. ... 494 sheep. 25/6/2000. 27. Nour Al-Husseini. -. Indian flag.
www.fao.org/DOCREP/005/Y4172M/rep2/reply2.htm

46. **Yahoo! Directory India > National Symbols and Songs**
... SPONSOR RESULTS. Indian Flags on Sale Indian flags on sale from $1.60. ... www.usflags.com. "Indian Flag" on eBay Find matches for "indian flag" on eBay. ...
dir.yahoo.com/Regional/Countries/India/ Government/National_Symbols_and_Songs/

47. **Flag**
... Later, Choctaw and Chickasaw Indian lands were added to the territory. This US flag also waved in 1817, as Mississippi was admitted as the 20th US state. Pictures and descriptions of eight flags that have flown over the state as well as the text of the...
www.its.state.ms.us/et/portal/MSFlags/flags.html

48. **British Indian Ocean Territory**
... Names: conventional long form: British Indian Ocean Territory conventional short form: none. ... Flag: white with the flag of the UK in the upper hoist-side ...
www.ems.psu.edu/~williams/states/io.htm

49. **Indiafocus -Society and Culture-Indian History**
... My Indian Flag My Indian Flag projects significant information about indian flag which include valuable information about the independence and its History ...
indiafocus.indiainfo.com/society_and_culture/history/

50. **India's Flag - EnchantedLearning.com**
... The flag was based upon the design of the flag of the Indian National Congress. ... Answers, Indian flag Indian Flag Quiz/Printout A flag quiz/coloring printout. ...
www.enchantedlearning.com/asia/india/flag/index.shtml

51. **udupipages-Philatelic**
... showing the stamp issued by USSR which shows Indian flag hoisted on theRed Fort in Delhi. ... This is how the Indian flag is being prepared. ...
www.udupipages.com/postal/kayya.html

52. **Google Directory - Reference > Flags > Regional > India**
... Indian Flag - http://www.indianchild.com/flag_of_india.htm Features description and pictures of the Indian flag, flag code of India, flag trivia and flag sites ...
directory.google.com/Top/Reference/ Flags/Regional/India/

53. **India Travel Guide @ TravelNotes.org**
... Indian Flag Flag of India. Local Currency Convert your currency into Indian rupees. Taj Mahal, India. Viewing the Taj Mahal © Travel Notes. ...
www.travelnotes.org/Asia/india.htm

54. **Indian flag-hoisting ceremony**
... Indian flag-hoisting ceremony. By Azaraimy HH. Indian nationals as well as friends of India in Brunei have been invited to attend ...
www.brunet.bn/news/bb/sunday/news/jan25h9.htm

55. **Geographica Indica: The Indian National Flag**
Kamat's Potpourri. The Indian National Flag. . kamat . com, New Contents. ... Arts of India. Natives of India. Indian Mythologies. © KL Kamat India's National Flag. ...
www.kamat.com/indica/763094.htm

56. **The Sault Ste. Marie Tribe of Chippewa Indians**
... and we will enter you into a drawing to win a 3' x 5' Sault Tribe Flag! Sault Tribe Members Only. ... Marie Tribe of Chippewa Indians 523 Ashmun, Sault Ste. ...
www.sootribe.org/

57. **Tribal Flag and Symbolism: Southern Ute Indian Tribe**
Tribal Flag and Symbolism. ... Indian Head - Represents the tribe as a person, a very "Colorful Man" with the colors of red, yellow, black, blue and white ...
www.southern-ute.nsn.us/seal.html

58. **Buy British Indian Ocean Territory flags, British Indian Ocean ...**
... 3' x 5' Polyester Flag $30.00 Qty: More British Indian Ocean Territory items Click for more information. 2.5" x 2.75" Shield Patch ...
flagline.com/id01A3235

59. **AllRefer Countries - British Indian Ocean Territory: Flag (British...**
... British Indian Ocean Territory - Flag. British Indian Ocean Territory: Flag (British Indian Ocean Territory Flag). Also See: • Background...
reference.allrefer.com/world/countries/british-indian-ocean territory/ flag.html

60. **Indian Flag....Indian Culture at CuisineCuisine.com**
... The Indian Flag. The Indian flag was designed as a symbol of freedom. The late Prime Minister Nehru called it a flag not only of ...
www.cuisinecuisine.com/IndianFlag.htm

61. **Indian artistes salute Tiranga in UK R-Day fete**
... on Monday night gave a standing ovation to five of India's top artistes who participated in a unique concert Tiranga, a salute to the Indian flag, at the 55th ...
www.rediff.com/news/2004/jan/27rday.htm

62. **rediff.com Special: Naveen Jindal battles for his right to fly the ...**
... Unfortunately, as time passed, the use of the Indian flag became limited to a privileged few. ... No Indian law, he added, prohibited him from flying the flag. ...
www.rediff.com/news/2001/jun/13spec.htm

63. **Indian High Commision holds flag raising ceremony**
... The High Commissioner of India to Brunei Darussalam officially hoisted the Indian national flag followed by the country's national anthem. ...
www.brunei-online.com/bb/tue/jan27h14.htm

64. **Flag-hoisting ceremony at Indian High Commission**
... Flag-hoisting ceremony at Indian High Commission. By Azaraimy HH. Indian nationals as weil as friends of India in Brunei have been...
www.brunei-online.com/sunday/news/jan18h8.htm

65. **The Indian National Flag**
Home >> India Fact File, The Indian National Flag, The ... 1947. The Indian Flag Code regulates the use and display of the National Flag....
stweb.ait.ac.th/aitia/factfile/nat_flag.html

66. **American Indian Heritage Month**

... letters. And people would drive through the reservation, walk up to me and ask, 'Are you the Indian who raised the flag on Iwo Jima"....

www.defenselink.mil/specials/americanindian/flag.html

67. **India (British Empire and Commonwealth Land Forces)**

... the World); Flags of the Princely States, by Ed Haynes. Military Flags: Indian Military Flags (Flags of the World). Music: Indian Military ...

www.regiments.org/milhist/southasia/india.htm

68. **Mardi Gras Indians of Mardi Gras, New Orleans — their parade ...**

... invisibly watermarked, Mardi Gras Indians Spy Boy, Flag Boy, and Big Chiefs! ... Bannock. The Flag Boy is the next ranking Indian. It ...

www.mardigrasindians.com/indirank.html

69. **British Indian Ocean Territory, Map and Flag**

... Country name: conventional long form: British Indian Ocean Territory conventional short ... Flag description: white with six blue wavy horizontal stripes; the flag ...

www.greatestcities.com/ Asia British_Indian_Ocean_Territory.html

70. **British Indian Ocean Territory Flag - AllYouCanRead.com**

AllYouCanRead.com, British Indian Ocean Territory Flag. ... British Indian Ocean Territory Flag. British Indian Ocean Territory Flag Click to enlarge, ...

www.allyoucanread.com/flag.asp?id=254

71. **American Indian Heritage Month**

... echoed through the school's gym, the grand entry ceremony was led by Doug Hall, who was carrying the eagle staff, the traditional American Indian flag. ...

www.defenselink.mil/specials/americanindian/

72. **BBC - Kent - Message Board Index**

... Should speed limits be raised? Indian flag. Call centres Should local companies be allowed to relocate their call centres abroad? Trolley. ...

www.bbc.co.uk/kent/have_your_say/index.shtml

73. **Fenimore Art Museum - The Flag in American Indian Art**
The Flag in American Indian Art. "The flag enjoys widespread utilization as a symbol to show beauty and attractiveness, lend meaning ...
www.fenimoreartmuseum.org/exhibitions/usaflag.htm

74. **22-2-601. American Indian monument and tribal flag circle ...**
22-2-601. American Indian monument and tribal flag circle — competition for design. ... American Indian monument and tribal flag circle — competition for design. ...
data.opi.state.mt.us/bills/mca/22/2/22-2-601.htm

75. **Manas: History and Politics, Cultural Politics of the National ...**
... and indeed the observance of January 26th as Republic Day goes back to 31 December 1929, when Jawaharlal Nehru hoisted the flag of the Indian National Congress www.sscnet.ucla.edu southasia/ History/Independent/flag.html

76. **Oklahoma State Flag Facts Map and Symbols**
... Oklahoma State Flag adopted by the State Legislature in 1925, is Oklahoma's 14th flag. This shows a sky blue field with a central device: an Indian war shield ...
www.imagesoft.net/flags/i-flag/usa-ok.html

77. **Dubai, Indian Postal Stationery Errors, Bangladesh Stamps**
DUBAI - INDIAN POSTAL STATIONERY - BANGLADESH - US "FLAG OVER..." EFO'S. R. Howard Courtney. Chicago, IL. Please note that I am NOT ...
friends.peoria.lib.il.us/community/howardcourtney/

78. **The Indian National Anthem and Flag**
The Indian National Anthem and Flag. The creators of this page are: Shashi Mohan and Navulur Kumar
pasture.ecn.purdue.edu/~agenhtml/ agenmc/india/gaana.html

79. **BIG Cleveland Indians Product List (84 Items)**
... Indians (84) Accessories. AAS USA American Car Flag, Hal Cleveland Indians Pewter Hitchcover, Hal Hitch Cover Lock Pin. SK Cleveland ...
www.footballfanatics.com/pages/ClevelandIndians.html

80. **Flag Officer Sea Training — Indian Navy**
... The Flag Officer Sea Training conducts operational sea training through three teams ... and Visakhapatnam covering the three major naval bases of the Indian Navy. ...
www.indiannavy.nic.in/fost_main.htm

29

Indian Olympic Association

1. **IOA**

   Provides an overview of the Indian committee.
   indianolympic.hypermart.net/

2. **Indian Olympic Assocation : Directory : State Olympic Associations**

   ... 1. Andhra Pradesh Olympic Association, Olympic Bhawan, Fateh Maidan, Hyderabad 500 001, Fax : +91-40-23243692. ... 2. Assam Olympic Association, ...
   indianolympic.hypermart.net/html/member-state-olympic-association/ main.htm

3. **Indian Olympic Association : Site Map**

   ... Competitions, National, International, Directory, Indian Olympic Association, National Sports Federation, State Olympic Association, International Olympic Committee, ...
   www.nocindia.nic.in/sitemap.html

4. **Indian Olympic Association : Homepage**

   ... Sitemap Contact Us. This site is Designed, Developed and Hosted by NICSI, NIC Information is provided and updated by : Indian Olympic Association.
   www.nocindia.nic.in/

5. **Search4i.com - Indian Olympic Association**

   ... Site Title : Indian Olympic Association. Site Description : information about member associations and sports federations in India, forthcoming events, and more. ...
   www.search4i.com/directory/link/24741/

6. **SAMSUNG's Digital World - Press Release**

   ... Mr. Suresh Kalmadi, President of the Indian Olympic Association signed the Memorandum of Understanding at a joint Press Conference held in the Capital today. ...
   www.samsung.com/in/presscenter/pressrelease/corporatenews_20030923_0000021693.asp

7. **Indian Olympic body to bid for Olympic Games : HindustanTimes.com ...**

   Indian Olympic Association has unanimously decided to project Delhi as 2016 Olympics venue. ...

   www.hindustantimes.com/2004/Jan/ 12 5983_529945,00430001.htm

8. **Google Directory - Sports > Events > Olympics > National Olympic ...**

   ... Official site. Indian Olympic Association - http:// indianolympic.hypermart.net/ Provides an overview of the Indian committee. San ...

   directory.google.com/Top/Sports/Events/ Olympics National_Olympic_Committees/

9. **INTERNATIONALOLYMPIC COMMITTEE - ORGANISATION - STRUCTURES**

   ... Olympic Games in 1964 and 1968; President of the Indian Hockey Federation for 16 years; former Secretary General of the Indian Olympic Association; member of ...

   www.olympic.org/uk/organisation/ ioc/members bio_uk.asp?id=142

10. **Yahoo! Directory Olympic Games Organizations > National Olympic ...**

    ... Indian Olympic Association - information about member associations and sports federations in India, forthcoming events, and more. ...

    dir.yahoo.com/.../Sports/Events/International_Games Olympic_Games/ Organizations/National_Olympic_Committees/

11. **Greater Kashmir**

    ... Hosted by JandK Tourism department and JandK Olympic Association under the auspices of the Indian Olympic Association, the games would give fillip to winter sports ...
    www.greaterkashmir.com/news6.htm

12. **Sports to heal rift: Indian Olympic chief -DAWN - Sport; 31 March ...**

    ... political tension exists between Pakistan and India and whatever be the political scenario, sports should go on," Indian Olympic Association (IOA) President ...

    www.dawn.com/2002/03/31/spt3.htm

13. **IOA LOGO**

    ... the Seoul Olympics. The two stamps depict the Glory of Sport and the lago of the Indian Olympic Association. The first stamp embraces ...

    www.indianpost.com/viewstamp.php/Print%20Size/3.75%20X%201.9/I.O.A.%20LOGO

14. **ACROPOLIS and OLYMPIC EMPLEM**

    ... The Indian Olympic Association, which is the National Olympic Committee of India is very old member of the IOC. Indian Olympic Association ...

    www.indianpost.com/viewstamp.php/Alpha/ A ACROPOLIS%20and%20OLYMPIC%20EMPLEM

15. **Sri Lanka International Games News**

    ... Initial reports said that meetings would be held April 1. A report from Pakistan on March 29th stated the "Indian Olympic Association had assured its ...

    www.internationalgames.net/newssrilanka.htm

16. **kuknalim.co**

    ... | 1608 bytes more | comments? | Score: 3.5), News Nagaland Olympic Association gets affiliated to the Indian Olympic Association KOHIMA, Feb. ...

    www.kuknalim.com/modules.php?name=Newsandnew_topic=1

17. **Government Agencies**

    ... Indian Olympic Association Mr. Suresh Kalmadi (President) Jawahar Lal Nehru Stadium, New Delhi-110003, India. Tel: 011-24366950, 24366951, 24366952. ...

    www.ispsquash.com/SportsDept_IOA_PRESS_EMAIL.htm

18. **Cricket news, views and controversies**

    ... But from the perspective of the Indian Olympic Association, which claims to have fought for the inclusion of cricket in the Commonwealth Games, this will not do ...

    www.gnubies.com/india/india49.htm

19. **rediff.com: Indian Olympic hockey team on expected lines**

    ... Indian Olympic Association had asked for the pruned list of 16 players and four officials as the August 25 deadline of sending entries to the Sydney Olympic ...

    www.rediff.com/sports/2000/aug/22hock1.htm

20. **SuperLinks Directory**

... the team and committee. Indian Olympic Association - Provides an overview of the Indian committee. Ireland Olympic Council - Official ...

www.superlinksdirectory.com/xq/asp category.sports:olympics:committees/ qx/

21. **SI.com - More Sports - India to bid for 2016 Games in New Delhi ...**

... NEW DELHI (AP) — The Indian Olympic Association said Monday it has unanimously decided to bid for the 2016 Olympic Games to be held in the capital, New Delhi. ...

www.cnnsi.com/2004/more/01/12/ bc.as.spt.oly.india2016.ap/

22. **The Hindu Business Line : Samsung sets up Olympic Fund**

... Samsung also signed a memorandum of understanding with the Indian Olympic Association to become the official sponsor of the Indian team to the Athens Olympics ...

www.thehindubusinessline.com/2003/09/ 24/stories 2003092401150600.htm

23. **rediff.com: The Rediff Sports Interview / Randhir Singh**

... The Government of India's decision to allow the staging of the Afro-Asian Games in November has come as a shot in the arm for the Indian Olympic Association. ...

www.rediff.com/sports/2001/apr/26rand.htm

24. **Commonwealth Games: DELHI 2010**

... The Government of India has accorded its approval to the proposal of the Indian Olympic Association to bid for 2010 Commonwealth Games to be hosted by the city ...

www.cwgdelhi2010.com/html/FULL-GOVT-SUPPORT-FOR-CWG/ main.htm

25. **Business Wire: Satyam Infoway Sponsors the Indian Olympic Team to ...**

... the Sydney Games 2000. And www.IOA.Khel.com will be the official website of the Indian Olympic Association for the Sydney Games. ...

www.findarticles.com/cf_dls/m0EIN/2000_August_22/ 64453298 p1/article.jhtml

26. **International Olympic Committee - Organisation - Structures**
Home, ORGANISATION, NOC > INDIAN OLYMPIC ASSOCIATION, ... Indian Olympic Association indianolympic. hypermart.net. PRESIDENT Mr Suresh Kalmadi.
www.olympic.org/uk/organisation/ noc
noc_uk.asp?noc_initials=IND

27. **IOA to bid for Olympic Games : HindustanTimes.com**
... Indian Olympic Association decides to bid for 2016 Games for New Delhi Associated Press New Delhi, January 12 The Indian Olympic ...
www.hindustantimes.com/2004/Jan/ 12/181_529809,00070007.htm

28. **Raja Bhalindra Singh (1919-1992)**
... At that time his own brother, both were born of different Ranis, Maharaja Yadvindra Singh, was President of the Indian Olympic Association. ...
www.punjabilok.com/misc/sports/bhalindra_singh.htm

29. **Indian delegation due today -DAWN - Sport; 30 January, 2004**
... LAHORE, Jan 29: An eight-member Indian Olympic Association (IOA) delegation will reach here on Friday to attend a South Asian Sports Federation (SASF) meeting ...
www.dawn.com/2004/01/30/spt12.htm

30. **Olympics**
... Hungarians in the Olympics. Indian Olympic Association - information about member associations and sports federations in India, forthcoming events, and more. ...
sportsweb.home.att.net/olympics.htm

31. **Bangladesh Sport**
... contingent of around 400 athletes to Pakistan next month for the South Asian Federation Games, the president of the Indian Olympic Association said yesterday. ...
bangladeshsport.com/

32. **SLAM! Sports - Olympics News - Twenty-one Indian athletes in ...**
... NEW DELHI (AP) - The Indian Olympic Association found 21 athletes guilty of doping offences during last year's National Games and said Wednesday they should ...
slam.canoe.ca/Slam/Olympics/News/ 2003/04/30/76375-ap.html

33. **India to Bid for 2012 Olympic Games**
PDO — Indian Youth Affairs and Sports Minister Uma Baharti asked the Indian Olympic Association here on Wednesday to Bid for the 2012 Olympic Games, saying ...
fpeng.peopledaily.com.cn/200204/ 25/eng20020425_94677.shtml

34. **GamesBids.com - Olympic Bid News and Information Website**
... Reuters reports that that the Indian Olympic Association (IOA) will bid to host the 2012 Olympic Summer Games with full support from the government. ...
www.gamesbids.com/ cgi-bin/news
viewnews.cgi?category=1andid=1019663174

35. **Indo-Pak Punjab Games in Nov - The Times of India**
... A four-member team of the Indian Olympic Association (IOA), led by its president Suresh Kalmadi, is leaving for Rawalpindi on January 30 to take part in a ...
timesofindia.indiatimes.com/articleshow/447969.cms

36. **IOA to bid for 2016 Olympic Games - The Times of India**
... NEW DELHI: Having realised its 2010 Commonwealth Games bid dream, the Indian Olympic Association (IOA) has jumped into the fray for the 2016 Olympic Games. ...
timesofindia.indiatimes.com/articleshow/ msid-418435,prtpage-1.

37. **There is a genuine concern now**
... The fact that Suresh Kalmadi, President, Indian Olympic Association, prescribes a time frame of 2005 to make sport free of doping is in itself an admission of ...
www.sportstaronnet.com/tss2620/ stories
20030517005700600.htm

38. **Indiainfo.com - Olympics - India - Pritchard - First Indian to win...**
... Olympics at Paris. India's participation in the Games became more organized with formation of the Indian Olympic Association in 1927.
www.thatscricket.com/olympics/ 2000/india/athletics.html

39. **pictures of olympic**
... Indian Olympic Association ... Contact information : Indian Olympic Association. NB Singh,. Indian Olympic Association, Jawahar Lal Nehru Stadium,. ...
words.elf.cz/2001_52_385/olympic.html

40. **Cricket news, views and controversies**

    ... The climbdown has come, as expected, but the board, it would appear, still wants to thumb its nose at the Indian Olympic Association. ...

    www.gnubies.com/india/india50.htm

41. **Sports - National Sports Federations of India**

    ... Indian Olympic Association Jawaharlal Nehru Stadium, Lodi Road, New Delhi-110003 Tel: (091) (011) 4636952, 4636950; Fax - 4636953. Top. ...

    www.meadev.nic.in/sports/addresses1.htm

42. **Direito do Desporto - ESTIG/IPBeja**

    ... National Alliance For Youth Sports (NAYS - EUA), Comités Olímpicos. Saudi Arabian Olympic Committee (SAOC), Indian Olympic Association (IOA). ...

    www.estig.ipbeja.pt/~ac_direito/ ddesportoinstitutestrpriv.html

43. **Indian Squash Professional**

    ... Email, Add of Press / Ministry of Sports / Indian Olympic Association / ASF and WSF. Rankings : Indian/ World Feb 2004 Top Players ...

    www.ispsquash.com/

44. **BBC SPORT | Commonwealth Games 2002 | Other Sports | Weightlifting**

    ... positive test. But Indian Olympic Association director AVS Prasad confirmed Rai's positive test on Monday. Fellow Indian lifter ...

    news.bbc.co.uk/sport3/commonwealthgames2002/hi
    other_sports/ weightlifting/newsid_2170000/2170918.stm

45. **First Preemnient Sports Law India Conference of the Millennium...**

    ... of Shri VC Shukla Vs. Indian Olympic Association and the International Charter of Physical Education and Sports of UNESCO-1978. ...

    www.sportslawindia.org/conference/

46. **London Web Guide including London Congestion Charge and London ...**

    ... olympc olympcs olimpics NYC 2012.com Madrid 2012.es Olympic Moscow.ru lympia-Leipzig-2012.de Olympist.org Indian Olympic Association. Italian Olympic Committee. ...

    www.thebigproject.co.uk/london/

47. **BSNL Portal || Sports News**

... NEW DELHI: Buoyed by its recent success in getting the hosting rights for the 2010 Commonwealth Games, the Indian Olympic Association (IOA) has decided to bid ...

www.bsnl.in/
Sports.asp?intNewsId=27137andstrDisplayStyle=blockandintDays Before=4

48. **Commonwealth Games: DELHI 2010: Delhi is delighted by the 2010 ...**

... The offices of the Indian Olympic Association and the Delhi bid team for the 2010 Commonwealth Games were celebrating and exuding optimism today after ...

www.cwgdelhi2010.com/html/bid-news/main.htm

49. **Interference of politics in sport**

... Suresh Kalmadi, President, Indian Olympic Association, calls the decision as needless interference of politics in sport, and this can affect the image of the ...

www.sportstaronnet.com/tss2610/ stories
20030308004900600.htm

50. **[goawebnews] New Delhi to host 2010 Commomwealth Games-beats...**

... The people felt it was high time India got the Games," Indian Olympic Association president Suresh Kalmadi told reporters. "It means a lot to us. ...

www.goacom.com/news/news2003/nov/msg00065.html

51. **1 - Number One News Resource of Pakistan - The News - Jang Group**

... The President of Indian Olympic Association, Suresh Kalmadi, will lead the Indian delegation which also includes IOA Secretary, Randhir Singh, who is also the ...

www.jang.com.pk/thenews/jan2004-daily/ 30-01-2004/sports/s16.htm

52. **NDTV.com - For the latest news from India**

... begun in India. A five company mission from UK is in India sharing their expertise with the Indian Olympic Association ... more....

www.ndtv.com/sports/default.asp?sportname=Report

53. **Zeal.com - United States - New - Sports - All Sports - Sports ...**
... 4. Indian Olympic Association | http:/
indianolympic.hypermart.net/ Find contacts for this New Delhi organization, plus member directories, publications and a ...
zeal.com/category/preview.jhtml?cid=554306

54. **News**
... The sources said that, irrespective of the Indian Olympic Association's official stance on the matter, it is in no hurry to accommodate cricket "after what ...
www.cricket.com.np/news/news51.htm

55. **Wauu.DE: Sports: Events: Olympics: National Olympic Committees**
... en.asp. Indian Olympic Association Official site. http://
indianolympic.hypermart.net/. Ireland Olympic Council Official site. http ...
www.wauu.de/Sports/Events/Olympics
National_Olympic_Committees/

56. **The Hindu : Indian women grab four Olympic quota places**
... winning aggregate compiled by Chinese Sheng Shichun, must be causing concern to the Indian Weightlifting Federation (IWF) and Indian Olympic Association (IOA). ...
www.hindu.com/2003/11/25/stories/2003112501951900.htm

57. **Google Directory - Regional > Asia > India > Recreation and Sports**
... game. Indian Olympic Association - http:
indianolympic.hypermart.net/ Official site with information on its activities and members. ...
directory.google.com/Top/Regional/ Asia/India
Recreation_and_Sports/

58. **Barbados Olympic Association**
... Barbados became part of the West Indian team, which competed at the Olympic Games in Rome in 1960. Copyright @ 2000 - 2001 by the Barbados Olympic Association.
www.olympic.org.bb/home/boa.html

59. **Olympia-Lexikon | Links**
... Guam National Olympic Committee. Hungarian Olympic Committee. Indian Olympic Association. Japanese Olympic Committee. Korean Olympic Committee. ...
www.olympia-lexikon.de/
index.php?c=linksandcat=Olympische+Komitees

60. **Open Directory - Sports: Events: Olympics: National Olympic**
... progress of the Games. Indian Olympic Association - Provides an overview of the Indian committee. Ireland Olympic Council - Official...
dmoz.org/Sports/Events/Olympics/
National_Olympic_Committees/

30

International Olympic Committee

1. **The Official Website of the Olympic Movement**
   International Olympic Committee - Discover the organisation, the heroes, the past Games, the news of the Olympic movement, Live sports news, the Olympic Museum ...
   www.olympic.org/
2. **International Olympic Committee - Organisation - Structures**
   ... Movement groups together all those who agree to be guided by the Olympic Charter and who recognise the authority of the International Olympic Committee (IOC). ...
   www.olympic.org/uk/organisation/ioc/index_uk.asp
3. **International Olympic Committee - Wikipedia**
   International Olympic Committee. From Wikipedia, the free encyclopedia. The International Olympic Committee is an organization created ...
   en.wikipedia.org/wiki/International_Olympic_Committee
4. **@International Olympic Committee / Comité International Olympique**
   This page is part of © FOTW Flags Of The World website @International Olympic Committee / Comité International Olympique. Last ...
   www.allstates-flag.com/fotw/flags/olympic.html
5. **Pravda.RU International Olympic Committee attaches special ...**
   The representatives of the International Olympic Committee attach special importance to the International Youth Games in Moscow, said mayor Yuri Luzhkov. ...
   english.pravda.ru/sport/2002/06/14/30387.html

6. **ScienceDaily Magazine: Your Source For The Latest Research News**

   ... International Olympic Committee. From Wikipedia, the free encyclopedia. The International Olympic Committee is an organization created ...

   www.sciencedaily.com/encyclopedia/ International_Olympic_Committee

7. **Mount St. Mary's College: College News**

   International Olympic Committee Lecture on November 5 - November 3, 2003. Dr. John A. Lucas, Official Lecturer of the International ...

   www.msmary.edu/ college/html collegenews.htm?article=1689andarchive=1

8. **Encyclopedia4U - International Olympic Committee - Encyclopedia...**

   International Olympic Committee. The International ... Documentation License. It uses material from the Wikipedia article "International Olympic Committee".

   www.encyclopedia4u.com/ i/international-olympic committee.html

9. **INTERNATIONAL OLYMPIC COMMITTEE - PASSION - THE OLYMPIC MUSEUM ...**

   Français. WWW.MUSEUM.OLYMPIC.ORG, OLYMPIC MUSEUM LAUSANNE. The symbol of the union of sport, art and culture - exhibitions, events ...

   www.museum.olympic.org/

10. **Yahoo! News Full Coverage - Sports - Olympics and the IOC**

    ... Yahoo! News (Jan 20, 2004). more. Related Web Sites. -, International Olympic Committee - official site of the Olympic movement. -, Athens ...

    fullcoverage.yahoo.com/Full_Coverage/Sports/ International_ Olympic_Committee/

11. **Dr. Jacques Rogge, President, International Olympic Committee...**

    st11-connectlive.com/drjacrogpres.html - 3k - **Cached** - **Similar pages**

12. **International Olympic Committee - ezResult.com**

    ... International Olympic Committee. The International Olympic Committee is an organization created by Pierre de Coubertin in 1894 to...

    www.ezresult.com/ article/International_Olympic_Committee

13. **Yahoo! News Full Coverage - Sports - Olympics and the IOC**
... Yahoo! News (Jan 20, 2004). more. Related Web Sites. International Olympic Committee - official site of the Olympic movement. -, Athens ...
fullcoverage.yahoo.com/Full_Coverage/Sports/International_Olympic_Committee/

14. **2002 International Olympic Committee Women and Sports Trophy**
2002 International Olympic Committee Women and Sports Trophy. Daw Nu Nu Yee receiving the trophy from the Chairman of the IOC at ...
www.myanmar.com/Women/MWSF/Trophy.html

15. **International Olympic Committee / Comité International Olympique**
International Olympic Committee / Comité International Olympique. IOC / CIO ; Olympic Games / Jeux Olympiques. ... International Olympic Committee Website. ...
flagspot.net/flags/oly@ioc.html

16. **United States Olympic Committee**
index.
www.usolympicteam.com/

17. **The Sport Journal: Volume 5, Number 3, Special Edition 2002 ...**
In light of the International Olympic Committee's recent discussion to drop the Modern Pentathlon from the Olympic Games, the President of the United States ...
www.thesportjournal.org/2002Journal/ Vol5-No3 Special_Edition/drop.asp

18. **The Sport Journal: Volume 3, Number 1, Winter 2000: International ...**
International Olympic Committee Commission for Culture and Olympic Education. FORUM. ... Juan Antonia Samaranc President of the International Olympic Committee.
www.thesportjournal.org/2000Journal/ Vol3-No1/winter2000.asp

19. **A Message of the President of the International Olympic Committee...**
A Message of the President of the International Olympic Committee (October 2, 1989). A Message of the President of ...
www2.arnes.si/~jsater/message.html

20. **international olympic committee and drug testing**
Offers international olympic committee and drug testing urine and time and ethanol and marijuana and detection and home remedies for passing a drug urinalysis. ...
www.beat-your-drug-test.com/ drug/international-olympic committee-and-drug-testing.html

21. **The Sport Journal: Volume 3, Number 1, Winter 2000: International...**
International Olympic Committee Commission for Culture and Olympic Education. FORUM. ... Juan Antonia Samaranch President of the International Olympic Committee.
www.thesportjournal.org/2000Journal/ Vol3-No1/winter2000.asp

22. **international olympic committee and drug testing**
Offers international olympic committee and drug testing urin and time and ethanol and marijuana and detection and home remedies for passing a drug urinalysis. ...
www.beat-your-drug-test.com/drug/international-olympic committee-and-drug-testing.html

23. **International Olympic Committee**
International Olympic Committee. Vi anbefaler disse siter forstavn information angående International Olympic Committee Andre informationssiter: ...
www.etraffik.com/international-olympic-committee.html

24. **Geneva Briefing Book: International Olympic Committee**
The International Olympic Committee (IOC) is the international non-governmental organization which conducts, promotes and regulates the modern Olympic Games. ...
www.genevabriefingbook.com/chapters/ioc.html

25. **UNESCO and the International Olympic Committee discuss an**
UNESCO and the International Olympic Committee discuss an international convention against doping in sport 12-12-2003 - Today in Lausanne, Switzerland, at the ...
portal.unesco.org/ en/ev.php@URL_ID=17591andURL_DO=DO_TOPICandURL_SECTION=201.html

26. **UNESCO and the International Olympic Committee discuss an**
UNESCO and the International Olympic Committee discuss an international convention against doping in sport Pas disponible en Français.Disponible en Anglais. ...
portal.unesco.org/ fr

27. **4th International Olympic Committee Main Page**
... Unlike previous occasions, this time the venue was not the Olympic Museum in Lausanne but the Hilton Salt Lake City Center in Utah, USA. ...
www.worldbridge.org/tourn/Salt%20Lake.02/ Salt%20Lake.htm

28. **List of Presidents of the International Olympic Committee ...**
List of Presidents of the International Olympic Committee. (Redirected from International Olympic Committee Presidents). REDIRECTInternational Olympic Committee. ...
en.wikipedia.org/ wiki
International_Olympic_Committee_Presidents

29. **The International Olympic Committee - www.ezboard.com**
Support our community, visit one of our sponsors... Author, Comment. freebird Moderator Posts: 58 (2/25/02 9:13 am) Reply, The International Olympic Committee ...
pub79.ezboard.com/ fpositivelivingfrm8.showMessage?topicID =31.topic

30. **LookSmart - International Olympic Committee Scandal News**
... International Olympic Committee Scandal News - 2002 Olympics in Salt Lake City have been tainted by a bribery scandal. Read news and editorials about it. ...
search.looksmart.com/p/browse/us1/us317902/ us575637 us954049/us290352/

31. **Australian Olympic Committee**
Olympic Highlights Highlights are published by weekly by the International Olympic Committee (IOC). Click here to search the IOC Highlights archive. ...
www.olympics.com.au/

32. **International World Games Association : transparent news**
... sports governing body's Ethics Committee to investigate ... one following the Summer Olympics, they jointly ... of the respective sport's International Federations for ...
www.worldgames-iwga.org/.../ 0,10869,1044-127176-19728-4769-113393-4299-889-layout03-128483-news-item,00.html

33. **International World Games Association : transparent news**
... Under the Patronage of the IOC. The International Olympic Committee. © 2004 International World Games Association. All Rights Reserved. powered by sportcentric.
www.worldgames-iwga.org/.../ 0,10869,1044-17298-19728-4769 113393-4299-889-layout03-18448-news-item,00.html

34. **Pravda.RU IOC tries to block appeal from Russian women skiers**
The International Olympic Committee /IOC/ is trying to block examination of an appeal from Russian skiers Larisa Lazutina and Olga Danilova in the arbitration ...
english.pravda.ru/sport/2002/07/02/31632.html

35. **International Olympic Committee awards Beijing 2008 Games**
World Tibet Network News. Published by the Canada Tibet Committee. Saturday, July 14, 2001. 2. International Olympic Committee awards Beijing 2008 Games. ...
www.tibet.ca/wtnarchive/2001/7/14_2.html

36. **International Olympic Committee backs IYV 2001**
International Olympic Committee backs IYV 2001. LAUSANNE/ BONN, 2 February 2001 — National Olympic Committees worldwide...
www.unv.org/infobase/news_releases/ 2001.
01_02_02USA_olympic.htm

37. **BBC News | World | Timeline: Olympics corruption scandal**
... Analysis: Putting the Olympic house in order Members of the International Olympic Committee (IOC) are considering their position following the publication of ...
news.bbc.co.uk/hi/english/world/ newsid_297000/297030.stm

38. **Mailing List ENVCEE-L: Appeal to the International Olympic ...**
Appeal to the International Olympic Committee. Ildiko Takacsova (TAKACSOVA@fns.uniba.sk) 20 Oct 98 14:55:44: ... APPEAL to the International Olympic Committee. ...
ecolu-info.unige.ch/archives/envcee98/0378.html

39. **International Olympic Committee**
This page is part of © FOTW Flags Of The World website International Olympic Committee. Olympic Games. ...
www.flags-by-swi.com/fotw/flags/olimpics.html

40. **Olympic history of Prague recalled at the International Olympic...**
... Olympic history of Prague recalled at the International Olympic Committee session, [02-07-2003] By Mirna Solic. The Czech capital...
www.radio.cz/en/article/42987

41. **Geneva International Forum**
International Olympic Committee (IOC). Name: Mr. Juan Antonio Samaranch. Position: President. Address: Château de Vidy, CH-1007 Lausanne. Phone: +41-21-621 61 11. ...
geneva.intl.ch/gi/egi/egi272.htm

42. **International Olympic Committee - anagrams**
Rearranging the letters of international olympic committee gives 'Nicely maim tolerant competition'! ... International Olympic Committee anagrams. ...
www.anagramgenius.com/archive/intern5.html

43. **Mailing List ENVCEE-L: Appeal to the International Olympic ...**
Appeal to the International Olympic Committee. Ildiko Takacsova (TAKACSOVA@fns.uniba.sk) 20 Oct 98 14:55:44: ... APPEAL to the International Olympic Committee. ...
ecolu-info.unige.ch/archives/envcee98/0378.html

44. **International World Games Association : transparent news**
... Under the Patronage of the IOC. The International Olympic Committee. powered by sportcentric.
www.worldgames-iwga.org/.../0,10869,1044-17298-19728-4769 113393-4299-889-layout03-18448-news-item,00.html

45. **International Olympic Committee**
This page is part of © FOTW Flags Of The World website International Olympic Committee. Olympic Games. ...
www.flags-by-swi.com/fotw/flags/olimpics.html

46. **International Olympic Committee Grand Prix**
... one of the most dramatic finals in the history of bridge, Brazil and China tied in the Grand Prix competition organised by the International Olympic Committee. ...
www.bridge.gr/tourn/Lausanne.98/IOC.htm

47. **Olympic history of Prague recalled at the International Olympic**
... Olympic history of Prague recalled at the International Olympic Committee session, [02-07-2003] By Mirna Solic. The Czech capital
www.radio.cz/en/article/42987

48. **INTERNATIONALOLYMPICCOMMITTEE - NEWS**
... The Constituent General Assembly of the Iraqi National Olympic Committee (NOC) will be held under the auspices of the International Ol Committee
(IOC) on ...
www.asoif.org/index.php4?coe_i_id=1869

49. **allAfrica.com: PanAfrica [press release]: International Olympic...**
International Olympic Committee to Donate $100,000 to UN for Aids Fight. Email This Page Print This Page Visit The Publisher's Site. United Nations (New York). ...
allafrica.com/stories/200105080264.html

50. **Statement of Anita DeFrantz Vice President International Olympic...**
Statement of Anita DeFrantz Vice President International Olympic Committee Before the Senate Committee on Commerce, Science, and Transportation April 14, 1999...
www.senate.gov/~commerce/hearings/0414def.pdf

51. **THE FIRST INTERNATIONALOLYMPIC COMMITTEE**
THE FIRST INTERNATIONAL OLYMPIC COMMITTEE. The members of the first International Olympic Committee. Colonel Victor Balk (Sweden), Dr ...
www.forthnet.gr/olympics/athens1896/ pictures/docs ioc1896.html

52. **About Andrew Jennings and the International Olympic Committee**
... his favorite is the 1994 jail sentence he received in Switzerland at the International Olympic Committee's request for alleging that IOC members took bribes. ...
www.ajennings.8m.com/about.htm

53. **International Olympic Committee - IOC members' support**
... Reedie, who is also member of the International Olympic Committee... Reedie, member of the IOC's evaluation commission for the 2008 Olympics, had been in a ...
www.websitesaboutchina.com/main/2008_olym/part2 olympic_1.htm

54. **Selling the Five Rings: The International Olympic Committee and...**
Selling the Five Rings: The International Olympic Committee and the Rise of Olympic Commercialism. Selling the Five Rings: The International ...
www.historyamericas.com/Selling_the_Five_Rings_The_International_Olympic_Committee_and_the_Rise_of_Olympi...

55. **International Olympic Committee Corruption**
... Terry Hall on Sep 23, 2000. Australian Olympic committee scared to act on drugs. Justin on Jul 15, 2000. Phil Coles safe, but blacks and women gone!. ...
www.network54.com/Hide/Forum/12581

56. **Bulgarian Olympic Committee - the Official Site**
... The Olympic day, organized in honour of the anniversary of the foundation of the International Olympic Committee by baron Pier du Cuberten on 23 June 1894 in ... Bulgarian Olympic Committee official page.
www.bgolympic.org/index.php?lang=en

57. **The International Olympic Committee - www.ezboard.com**
Support our community, visit one of our sponsors... Author, Comment. freebird Moderator Posts: 58 (2/25/02 9:13 am) Reply, The International Olympic Committee ...
pub79.ezboard.com/
fpositivelivingfrm8.showMessage?topicID=31.topic

58. **International Olympic Committee Ignores China's Rights Abuses...**
World Tibet Network News. Friday, February 22, 2001. 2. International Olympic Committee Ignores China's Rights Abuses Students For A Free Tibet Targets IOC. ...
www.tibet.ca/wtnarchive/2001/2/22_2.html

59. **NZOC Public Site**
... Nine applicant cities have met the deadline for submitting preliminary documents to the International Olympic Committee to host the 2012 Olympic Games. ...
www.olympic.org.nz/

60. **International Olympic Committee and International Paralympic...**
Press Release 05 March 2001 International Olympic Committee and International Paralympic Committee Meetings in Salt Lake City Games ...
www.paralympics2002.com/press/press_030501_2.html

61. **111TH SESSION OF THE INTERNATIONAL OLYMPIC COMMITTEE**
... 111TH SESSION OF THE INTERNATIONAL OLYMPIC COMMITTEE. SYDNEY. SUNDAY, 10 SEPTEMBER 2000. ... I declare open the 111th Session of the International Olympic Committee.
www.gg.gov.au/speeches/rtf/2000/sp000910.rtf

62. **Radio Australia News - 25/01/01: International Olympic Committee ...**

    An International Olympic Committee delegation has completed a seven-day visit to East Timor with a view to helping them create a national Olympic committee The ...

    www.abc.net.au/ra/newsdaily/s237653.htm

63. **An Open Letter Regarding China to the International Olympic...**

    Capitalism Magazine: In Defense of Individual Rights. An Open Letter Regarding China to the International Olympic Committee by Andrew Bernstein (July 9, 2001) ...

    www.capmag.com/article.asp?ID=956

64. **Usefull addresses - International Olympic Committee**

    ... IOC. International Olympic Committee Château de Vidy CP 356 CH - 1007 Lausanne Tel: (41.21) 621 61 11 Fax: (41.21) 621 62 16. Top....

    europa.eu.int/comm/sport/info/ usefull_add/c_ioc_en.html

65. **8741. Avery Brundage, President, International Olympic Committee. ...**

    8741. Avery Brundage, President, International Olympic Committee. ... 1988. NUMBER: 8741. AUTHOR: Avery Brundage, President, International Olympic Committee. ...

    www.bartleby.com/63/41/8741.html

66. **Association of Summer Olympic International Federations (ASOIF)**

    ... GAISF), in partnership with the Association of Summer Olympic International Federations (ASOIF) and the Association of International Olympic Winter Sports ...

    www.asoif.org/

67. **Amazon.com: Books: Selling the Five Rings: The International**

    www.amazon.com/exec/obidos/tg/ detail/-/0874807131?v=glance

68. **1 Women's International/Olympic Committee Policy and Procedure**

    Women's International/Olympic Committee I. Purpose a. To win gold medals in the sport

    www.usawaterpolo.com/...

    Women's%20International%20Olympic%20Committee/ WIOC 2004-PnP.pdf

69. **The First International Olympic Committee**
The First International Olympic Committee. (Center: Demetrios Bikelas, President. On his right is Baron Pierre de Coubertin, Secretary.). ...
www.thegreekinstitute.org/bikelas/page7.htm

70. **HRIC Issues Open Letter to International Olympic Committee**
HRIC ISSUES OPEN LETTER TO INTERNATIONAL OLYMPIC COMMITTEE. - Hong Kong Voice of Democracy
www.democracy.org.hk/EN/2001/feb/mainland_06.htm

71. **An Open Letter Regarding China to the International Olympic...**
An Open Letter Regarding China to the International Olympic Committee By Andrew Bernstein July 9, 2001 Dear International Olympic ...
www.andrewbernstein.net/articles/10_openletter.htm

72. **Spokesperson on The Evaluation Commission of the International...**
Spokesperson on The Evaluation Commission of the International Olympic Committee (IOC) 's inspection in Beijing. 2001/02/21. Q: The ...
www.fmprc.gov.cn/eng/gjhdq/dqzzywt/ 2633/2637/2638t15577.htm

73. **International Olympic Committee threatens to "close down" Internet ...**
Enforcing its billion dollar media deals. International Olympic Committee threatens to "close down" Internet sites. By Richard Phillips 5 September 2000. ...
www.wsws.org/articles/2000/sep2000/ioc-s05.shtml

74. **A Message of the President of the International Olympic Committee...**
A Message of the President of the International Olympic Committee to the 30 Anniversay of the International Children's Games. ...
www2.arnes.si/~jsater/message3.html

75. **International Olympic Committee**
... Webmaster Public Forums ***** Advertise Here. International Olympic Committee. GoGuides > Sports and Recreation > Olympics > International Olympic Committee. ...
www.goguides.org/DIR/index.php?c=2449

76. **International Olympic Committee**
Virtual Reference Desk Abstract. International Olympic Committee. Home page of the International Olympic Committee. Go to this Site NOW. Subjects for this Item: ...
www.virtualref.com/abs/46.htm

77. **8765. Richard W Pound, International Olympic Committee. Simpson'_...**
Richard W Pound, International Olympic Committee. Simpson's Contemporary Quotations. ... NUMBER: 8765. AUTHOR: Richard W Pound, International Olympic Committee. ...
www.bartleby.com/63/65/8765.html

78. **Home : Rate International Olympic Committee (IOC)**
Home : >Rate International Olympic Committee (IOC). Rate International Olympic Committee (IOC). Language: Albanian ...
www.slavophilia.com/cgi-bin/links/rate.cgi?ID=566

79. **CNN - International Olympic Committee bans visits to bid cities...**
... International Olympic Committee bans visits to bid cities. December ... change. The new millennium will see a new international Olympic Committee.". ...
www.cnn.com/1999/WORLD/europe/12/12/ioc.reforms/

80. **INTERNATIONALOLYMPICCOMMITTEE**
CITIUS - ALTIUS - FORTIUS. INTERNATIONAL OLYMPIC COMMITTEE. THE PRESIDENT. The programme of the Games of the I Olympiad in 1896 in ...
home.lynx.net/bactau/listy.htm

81. **A Message of the President of the International Olympic Committee ...**
A Message of the President of the International Olympic Committee (October 2, 1989). A Message of the President of ...
www2.arnes.si/~jsater/message.html

82. **International Olympic Committee Presidential Candidate Anita ...**
January 29, 2001. International Olympic Committee Presidential Candidate Anita DeFrantz to Speak at Occidental College Speakers Forum Feb. 27. ...
www.oxy.edu/news/articles/010129-defrantz.html

83. **The International Olympic Committee and Site Decisions: The Case ...**
The International Olympic Committee and Site Decisions: The Case of the 2002 Winter Olympics. - From Event Management, Vol. 6 By ...
www.etour.mh.se/5.d09ad3f53ee3ea197fff2313.html

84. **Youth Concern: International Olympic Committee and the Doping...**
International Olympic Committee and the Doping issue. By Spiros Tzelepis, Greece. The IOC's official position and some research on the subject. ...
users.otenet.gr/~tzelepisk/yc/dop.htm

85. **Run-Down Running Portal: Rate International Olympic Committee (IOC ...**
Rate International Olympic Committee (IOC). Please rate the link International Olympic Committee (IOC) between one and ten, with ten being the highest. ...
run-down.com/index.php?do=rateandlink_id=364

86. **international olympic committee**
international olympic committee The International Olympic Committee (IOC) was founded on June 23, 1894 by the French educator Baron Pierre de Coubertin who was ... usocpressbox.org/.../(staticreports)/USOC'02.OlympicFamily/
$File/USOC'02.OlympicFamily.pdf

87. **Dr. Jacques Rogge, President, International Olympic Committee ...**
st11-connectlive.com/drjacrogpres.html

88. **United States Olympic Committee (AUSOC@), International Olympic ...**
... 1-OLYMPIC.COM is an unauthorized domain name and, upon information and belief, was registered by a cybersquatter, and is listed on the Whois Data Sheet as. ...
www.sgbdc.com/exhibit10.htm

89. **Encyclopedia4U - International Olympic Committee Presidents ...**
International Olympic Committee Presidents. International Olympic Committee Presidents, listed with years of service and nation of origin: ...
www.encyclopedia4u.com/ i/international-olympic-committee presidents.html]

90. **Why International Olympic Committee Picks Beijing ±±·½Íø>**
...... Why International Olympic Committee Picks Beijing. ¡¡¡ ¡MOSCOW — Front-runner didn't stumble this time. The International Olympic ...
english.enorth.com.cn/system/ 2001/07/16/000093352.shtml

91. **Green Games Watch 2000: Does the International Olympic Committee ...**
NCC Index, Area : Frequently Asked Questions. Does the International Olympic Committee (IOC) regard the environment as an important issue? Date: 12 July 2000. ...
www.nccnsw.org.au/member/ggw/projects/ FrequentlyAsked Questions/faq10.html

92. **Selling the Five Rings: The International Olympic Committee and ...**
Booksearch Selling the Five Rings: The International Olympic Committee and the Rise of Olympic Commercialism. Author: Robert Knight ...
www.booksearch.nu/0874807131

93. **Selling the Five Rings: The International Olympic Committee and ...**
... Selling the Five Rings: The International Olympic Committee and the Rise of Olympic Commercialism. Selling the Five Rings: The International ...
www.liftthis.com/shopping/0874807131.htm

94. **NEWLY INSTALLED MICROS OPERA ENTERPRIS SOLUTION SERVES ...**
NEWLY INSTALLED MICROS OPERA ENTERPRISE SOLUTION SERVES INTERNATIONAL OLYMPIC COMMITTEE AND NBC ...
www.micros.com/press_room/press_releases/ pdf sinclair_oil.pdf

95. **International Olympic Committee - Wikipedia**
... Back to Encyclopedia Main Page Printable Version of this Page Encyclopedia help PhatNav's Encyclopedia - A "Wikipedia". International Olympic Committee. ...
www.phatnav.com/wiki/wiki.phtml?title=IOC

96. **The International Olympic Committee — nice work if you can get it ...**

... So let's have a bit of sympathy for the International Olympic Committee, shall we? Spare a little compassion for those courageous...

yesrick.com/012299.htm

97. **International Olympic Committee Grand Prix 2000**

... The 3rd Grand Prix was organized by the World Bridge Federation under the auspices of the International Olympic Committee. It took...

www.bridge.gr/tourn/Lausanne.00/IOC_00.htm

31
Journals

1. **Sports Journals**
   Sports Journals and Diaries for secure online purchase at great prices in association with Amazon.com! ... Sports Journals. Writing Journals and Diaries! ...
   www.journaldepot.com/sportsjournals.html
2. **Sports Journals, Magazines, Periodicals and Publications ...**
   Enjoy your favorites sports magazines, journals, periodicals and newspapers. ... Enjoy your favorite sports magazines, journals, periodicals and publications. ...
   newspaper-world.com/magazines/sports.asp
3. **The Physician and Sportsmedicine Online**
   The Physician and Sportsmedicine is the most widely-read clinical sports medicine journal in the world. Find articles on exercise, nutrition, injury prevention, personal fitness, and rehabilitation written...
   www.physsportsmed.com/
4. **Sports Journals**
   Sports Journals. Thousands of full text journals are available to members of the Emory community*. ... Also included are different ways of locating sports journals. ...
   business.library.emory.edu/researchaids/ courserelated/sports publications.html
5. **Olympic Information Center Sports Journals**
   The AAF is a private non-profit foundation dedicated to the development of youth sport. The AAF provides several online sports journals in its digital archive. ...
   www.aafla.org/6oic/journal.htm

6. **PPPS: NC Sports Journals and Periodicals**

   ACC Area Sports Journal. Publisher: Dennis Wuycik. Editor: Dave Glenn. ...

   www.unc.edu/depts/ppps/journals/

7. **UT Library Online - PCL Periodicals and Microforms Unit - Sports ...**

   Sports Journals Unless noted otherwise, the current loose unbound issues of the following titles are all located in the PCL Periodicals Room. ...

   www.lib.utexas.edu/pcl/per_micro/subjects/sports.html

8. **Multimedia Year Books Sports Journals Home and School Web Learning ...**

   Multimedia Year Books Sports Journals Home & School Web Learning Tools English Español Français MacOS X, Windows, Linux, Solaris, UNIX www.10Min.com

   www.leboe-grice.com/IMAGES/10Min_info.pdf

9. **Sports Journals**

   Senior Basketball Players. Raul Cedeno and Tori Brown. LaVergne's Lady Wolverines have had a great start winning five of our first six games. ...

   www.lhs.rcs.k12.tn.us/Sports%20Journals.htm

10. **British Journal of Sports Medicine**

    Get BJSM and other journals on your handheld. Developing-world FREE Access. BMJ Publishing Group Ltd HighWire Press. British Association of Sport and Exercise ...

    bjsm.bmjjournals.com/

11. **Sports Journals**

    Sports Journals. One of the genres of writing that I read the most is sports writing - mostly hockey, baseball and CFL football. ...

    home.ican.net/~clarkent/ted/sports_journals.htm

12. **SpringerLink - Publication**

    Publication, Knee Surgery, Sports Traumatology, Arthroscopy. Publisher: Springer-Verlag Heidelberg. ... Linking Options. About this Journal. Editorial Board. ...

    link.springer.de/link/service/journals/00167/

13. **Electronic Journals in Physical and Health Education**
Links to Recreation and Leisure Studies Journals
http:/www.lin.ca/contents.htm;
Sports Journals http://www.sportsjournal.com/temp.htm. General Sports Journals. ... stauffer.queensu.ca/inforef/physed/elec.htm

14. **Sports Links Central.com: Sports Ecducation: Academic Journals**
Academic Sports Journals. JOURNAL PUBLISHERS. Human Kinetics. Sage Publications. ... Aethlon - The Journal of Sport Literature. The Sport Journal. SPORTS LAW JOURNALS. ...
www.sportslinkscentral.com/Sports_Education/
academic_journals.htm

15. **Edinburgh University Press Journals - Sports Biomechanics**
ISBS Coaches' Information Service website: www.sportscoach-sci.com Find out more about the journal Sports Biomechanics. ...
www.eup.ed.ac.uk/newweb/journals/Sports/

16. **Medbioworld: Orthopaedics and Sports Medicine Journals**
Search millions of documents at elibrary! Orthopaedics and Sports Medicine Journals. Search Orthopaedics and Sports Medicine in the media from eLibrary. ...
www.sciencekomm.at/journals/medicine/ortho.html

17. **Dr.Tarek Said's Homepage - Zamalek's Links**
NEW Egyptian Sports Journals. General. Al-Kora Al-Masreya (Egyptian Soccer) Official Magazine of The Egyptian Football Association ...
www.angelfire.com/ak/EgyptianSports/ZamalekLinks.html

18. **NSIC - Products and Services**
Sports Journal Update Database ... Find what journals we hold (indexed in Sport Discus), Australian Sports Journals and Sports Journals with a web presence. ...
www.ausport.gov.au/nsic/nsicpans.html

19. **A Taylor and Francis Health Sciences Journal: Journal of Sports...**
Journal of Sports Sciences. ... The Journal presents research findings in the growing area of exercise and sports sciences to an international audience. ...
www.tandf.co.uk/journals/titles/02640414.html

20. **Human Kinetics - Journals**
Books. Journals. Software. Videos. Distance Education. Sport Sciences. Fitness & Health. Sports. Sports Medicine. Physical Education. Dance. Recreation. Aquatics. ...
www.humankinetics.com/products/journals/index.cfm

21. **A Taylor and Francis Health Sciences Journal: Research in Sports ...**
Aims and Scope: Research in Sports Medicine is a broad journal that aims to bridgethe gap between all professionals in the fields of sports medicine. ...
www.tandf.co.uk/journals/titles/10578315.html

22. **Browse Health, Fitness and Sports Journals**
Browsing Selected Health, Fitness & Sports Journals. (350 ... current. International sports journal, Academic Search Premier, Jan 2002, current.
www6.wittenberg.edu/lib/research/ejournals/browse.php?url_subj=hfs&all=all

23. **FindLaw for Students: Academic Law Journals and Law Reviews...**
Entertainment and Sports Law Journals. ... Marquette Sports Law Journal Marquette University. ...
stu.findlaw.com/journals/art_sports.html

24. **Physical Therapy in Sport**
Home > Journals > Physical Therapy in Sport
www.harcourt-international.com/journals/ptsp/

25. **ASEP—Exercise Physiology Journals**
Biomedical Databases British Journal of Sports Medicine. British Medical Journal. ... (Q) (R) (S) Science & Sport. Sociology of Sport Journal. Sport History Review. ...
www.css.edu/users/tboone2/asep/journals.htm

26. **Scandinavian Journal of Medicine and Science in Sports Aims and ...**
Scandinavian Journal of Medicine and Science in Sports: journal information, contents lists and abstracts on the Blackwell Publishing website. ...
www.blackwellpublishing.com/journal.asp?ref=0905-7188

27. **ePodiatry**
    Books. Learning resources. Sports Medicine Journals. Sports Medicine Organisations. Sports Medicine Websites. Contact us | Privacy statement | Advertise with us.
    www.epodiatry.com/
    education_sub1.asp?Topic=Sports%20Medicine
28. **UltraGlyph Adventure Journals - Outdoor Sports Logbooks and Travel ...**
    UltraGlyph journals are specifically designed for travel and outdoor sports. Our journals are built on a binder system so the pages ...
    www.ohjoesports.com/
29. **JSSM - JOURNAL OF SPORTS SCIENCE and MEDICINE**
    JOURNAL OF SPORTS SCIENCE and MEDICINE. ... findings to members of JSSM. The Journal of Sports Science and Medicine is indexed/listed in....
    jssm.uludag.edu.tr/
30. **Psychwatch - Sport Psychology Page**
    United States Olympic Committee. Sport Psychology Journals: ...British Journal of Sports Medicine; Journal of Excellence - focus is on the mental side of sports. ...
    www.psychwatch.com/sport_psychology.htm
31. **Australian Sports Commission**
    The Australian Sports Commission (ASC) produces journals to meet the information needs of the wide range of ASC target audiences, and to provide a mechanism ...
    www.ausport.gov.au/asc/journals/
32. **Villanova University School of Law - Current Students - Journals and ...**
    Sports and Entertainment Law Journal, ... copies are distributed at or below cost,; the author and the Villanova Sports and Entertainment Law Journal are identified ...
    www.law.vill.edu/currentstudents/journalsandmootcourt/
    sportsandentlj/sportsandentlj.asp
33. **Sport and Exercise Psychology**
    American Alliance for Health, Physical Education, Recreation and Dance (AAHPERD) Journals: Research Quarterly for Exercise and Sport, Strategies, JOHE, JOPERD. ...
    spot.colorado.edu/~collinsj/

34. **Sports, Leisure and Tourism Journals**
Sports, Leisure Management and Tourism Journals. ... American Journal of Sports Medicine. From 1976, access to table of contents, abstracts and search facility. ...
www.bell.ac.uk/libraries/JNL/Leisurej.htm

35. **JournalDepot.com Journals and Diaries**
Relationship Journals. ; Religious Journals. ; Solid Color Journals.Sports Journals. ; Travel Journals. ; Wedding Journals.; Wildlife and Nature Journals. ...
www.journaldepot.com/

36. **UVa Education Library: Collections - Sports Psychology and ...**
Sports Psychology and Physical Education Journals. ... Journal of Sports Sciences - Refereed (Online coverage: not yet available, coming soon). ...
www.lib.virginia.edu/education/collections/ journals physicaleducation.htm

37. **Sports and Leisure Studies Arena - Journals**
The Journal of Sports Sciences The Journal of Sports ... Research in Sports Medicine: An International Journal Research in Sports Medicine ...
www.leisurestudiesarena.com/leisurestudiesarena/ journals.html

38. **Reference journals and Research**
Sports Medicine Journal Listings A directory listing of all the best sports medicine journals available online. If you are looking...
sportsmedicine.about.com/cs/reference/

39. **Adis**
Sports Medicine.The world's premier sports medicine review journal, relied upon by leading international medical and academic institutions and libraries. ...
www.adis.com/page.asp?ObjectID=35

40. **Sports Science Directory of open access journals**
Journal of Sports Science and Medicine - [Full record]. Sociology of Sport online - [Full record]. The Sport Journal - [Full record]. ...
www.doaj.org/links/term1870/term1871/

41. **OrthoLinx - Orthopedic Medical News Journals Daily**
A peer-reviewed monthly journal serving the practicing physician's professional and personal interests in the medical aspects of exercise, sports, and fitness. ...
www.mdlinx.com/OrthoLinx/ index.cfm?go=portal&dir_id=27

42. **Rider Journals :: Echelon Sports Performance**
Echelon Sports Performance has several dedicated riders who will be glad to share their ... Select the journal of the rider you'd like to know more about and enjoy ...
www.espcycling.com/journals/index.asp

43. **EJMAS Electronic Journals of Martial Arts and Sciences splashpage**
Journal of Combative Sport ISSN 1492-1650 Journal of Non-lethal Combatives ISSN 1492-1634 Journal of Theatrical Combatives ISSN
ejmas.com/

44. **Medical Texts, Journals, Medical School, Research**
Testing and Prescription ACSM's Guidelines for Exercise Testing and Prescription by: American College of Sports Medicine, American...
www.medical-school-books.com/ store-mode-books-node-14411 locale-us.html

45. **Sports Medicine**
Publishers of books and journals in sports medicine for professionals, lecturers, and students. Home, Your essential information ...
www.harcourt-international.com/ sportsmedicine/journals.cfm

46. **Australian Society for Sports History Bulletin**
BSSH Index to Current Contents of Sports History Journals: (AZ). ... Japanese Journal of History of Physical Education. Japanese Journal of Sports History. ...
www.umist.ac.uk/sport/ccontent.html

47. **Sports Resources : Electronic Sports Magazines**
The following is a compilation of sports journals (kinesiology, sports medicine, physical therapy, physical education, exercise science, recreation, leisure ...
www.lib.msu.edu/bryants/sports/mag.htm

48. **UTLOL - Journals - Sports and Recreation**
UTLOL - Resources - Journals - Sports and Recreation. Journals Sports and Recreation. All. Journals 1 to 19 of 19. ...
www.lib.utexas.edu/journals/s-sportsandrecreation.html

49. **BMJ Publishing Group - Products - British Journal of Sports ...**
British Journal of Sports Medicine is an international journal featuring the latest advances in research and clinical practice. ...
www.bmjpg.com/template.cfm?name=specjou_sm

50. **ABE Marketing >> JOURNALS >> SUBJECT >> medicine >> sports med.**

The Journal for Sports Health Care Professionals. ...
www.abe.pl/html/english/searchj.php?grid=82

51. **Thieme Medical Publishers : Journals : Author Instructions ...**

Thieme Medical Publishers Homepage, International Journal of Sports Medicine - Author Instructions, Scope of the Journal. The International ...
www.thieme.com/SID2005632764890/journals/ ita pubid926886473.html

52. **Sports Medicine Links to articles, journals, associations for ...**

Sports medicine care you provide but we find the following journals to carry high proportions of material ...
www.clinicalsportsmedicine.com/links.htm

53. **Physical Education and Sports: Free-Access Journal**

A| N | O | P | Q | R | S | T | U | V | W | X | Y | Z | RUSS |. American Journal of Sports Medicine. ... Biomedical Databases. British Journal of Sports Medicine. ...
n-online.jp/FreeJ/PhysicalEducation.html

54. **LookSmart - Search results for "American Journal of Sports ...**

American Journal of Sports Medicine - Find Articles View this journal about athletic ...
search.looksmart.com/p/
search?qt=American+Journal+of+Sports+Medicine+subscription

55. **Sports Medicine Journals**

M ost popular sports medicine journals. Find your favorite and scan the headlines to get the latest news.... ... Sports Medicine Journals. ...
sportsmedicine.about.com/b/a/050612.htm

56. **Medbioworld: Physical Medicine and Rehabilitation Journals**

Therapeutics Journal of Musculoskeletal Research Journal of Occupational Rehabilitation Journal of Orthopaedic and Sports hysical Therapy Journal of Prosthetics ...
www.sciencekomm.at/journals/medicine/physi.html

57. **Napier University Learning Information Services**

Sports Journals. Top. ... psychology; British journal of sports medicine; British journal of sports medicine (on campus access only);...
nulis.napier.ac.uk/SubjectGuides/Spo/SpoJnlList.htm

58. **PEC: Health and Physical Education Journals**

Research Quarterly for Exercise and Sport, American Journal of Health Education, The Pulse Online (A newsletter from AAHPERD keeping ...

www.pecentral.org/professional/pejournals.html

59. **Entertainment & Sports Law Journals**

Resource Center » Online Publications » Professional Publications » Entertainment & Sports Law Journals. Entertainment & Sports Law Journals. ...

resource.lawlinks.com/Content/Online_Publications/entertainment_&_sports_law_journals.htm

60. **Academic Journals**

Biomechanics/Sport Science Journals. ... Author guidelines. Journal of Science & Medicine in Sports; Journal of Sports Science and Medicine, J SPORTS SCI MED: ...

www.health.uottawa.ca/biomech/journals.htm

61. **UVa Education Library: Collections - Sports Medicine and Athletic ...**

Sports Medicine and Athletic Training Journals. ... Journal of Sports Sciences - Refereed (Online coverage: not yet available, coming soon). ...

www.lib.virginia.edu/education/collections/ journals sportsmedicine.htm

62. **SCI-BITES: Journals Ranked by Impact: Sport Sciences**

Sport Sciences. Rank, ... 8, Int. J. Sports Medicine (1.43), Journal of Motor Behavior (2.61), Euro. J. Appl. Physiol. (10.23). 9, J. Orthop. ...

www.in-cites.com/research/2002/june_10_2002-1.html

63. **Exercise, Sport, and Health Studies Journals**

Following is a list of selected journals in the area of Kinesiology and Sports Medicine. All journals in the Central Library are now housed on the third floor. ...

www.uta.edu/library/guides/exer_spt.html

64. **National Institute for Sports Reform**

return to our home page. NISR Journal of Sports Reform. ... The Journal of Sports Reform is the official journal of the National Institute for Sports Reform (NISR). ...

www.nisr.org/top/journal.html

65. **Sports Science Journals - Leeds University Library**

They are shelved in alphabetical order at Sports Science A-0.01. Older journals may be in Stack eg Psychology A-0.01 or General Biology A-0.01 on Level 8 ...

www.leeds.ac.uk/library/subjects/sportsci/journals.htm

66. **Online Library of the United States Sports Academy**

The Sport Journal, an electronic publication of the United States Sports Academy, Accreditation Information, Current Job Opportunities with the Academy ...

www.ussa.edu/online-library.htm

67. **Sports Studies journals, newspapers**

Sports Studies Information Access Guide - Journals, Newspapers, etc. ... American journal of sports medicine (via Health Reference Center). ...

www.canberra.edu.au/library/iag/scides/sports_db.htm

68. **ACSM Journals**

Articles report on new educational developments as well as sound physical fitness practices and the treatment of sports injuries. The journal helps readers ...

www.lww.com/acsmcrc/fitjour.html

69. **BMJ Publishing Group - Products - Specialist Journals**

British Journal of Sports Medicine - (full text) British Journal of Sports Medicine is an international journal featuring the latest advances in research and ...

www.bmjpg.com/template.cfm?name=specjou

70. **WSSU Library Services - Periodicals: D:\InetPub\wwwroot\library ...**

THE AMERICAN JOURNAL OF SPORTS MEDICINE. 1987-. ATHLETIC JOURNAL. ... JOURNAL OF SPORTS MEDICINE AND PHYSICAL FITNESS. 1997-. JOURNAL OF SPORTS SCIENCES. 1985-. ...

www.wssu.edu/library/journals/journal.asp?jrnl=educ %5CPhysical +Education.htm

71. **e-journals**

American journal of sports medicine (Abstracts only). American scientist. American track and field. ... British journal of sports medicine. British runners. ...

www.hksdb.org.hk/hksdb/html/front/e_e-journals1.html

72. **His Majesty's Government of Nepal >> Ministry of Education and...**
Reports / Documents/ Journals
www.moe.gov.np/comm/index.php

73. **pantheon E-Sports**
Recent journals. li0n, .wma windows media thingi, 13/12. Hankz, Home, 12/12. kommando, Watercooling,
www.auspantheon.com/journals.x

74. **Google Directory - Shopping > Sports > Fitness > Books and Videos**
Google, Directory Help Search only in Fitness Journals Search the Web. Fitness Journals, ...
directory.google.com/Top/Shopping/Sports/Fitness/Books_and_Videos/Fitness_Journals/

75. **SOSIG: Sociology of Sport**
Sociology of Sport Journal, Bibliographic Databases, Up. ... Browse this resource, Villanova Sports and Entertainment Law Journal, ...
www.sosig.ac.uk/roads/subject-listing/ World-cat/socsport.html

76. **Library Ejournals: Subject Title List**
American Journal of Sports Medicine. International Journal of Sports Medicine, Thieme Journals, V.20 N.7 1999 -, ...
toby.library.ubc.ca/ejournals/ subjectlist4.cfm?facultyid=12

77. **Gateway: Sports Studies**
Journal of Sport and Social Issues Type: eJournals. Coverage: v.23:issue 1(1999:Feb.)-. Catalog Record. ...
lib.nd.edu/eresources/gateway/subjects/ sports_studies Journals.html

78. **Thieme Medical Publishers: Journals: International Journal of ...**
International Journal of Sports Medicine.
www.thieme.com/SID2144438416131/journals pubid926886473.html

79. **Carnegie Mellon Libraries: History: Sports History**
Journals Below are major journals in sports history. ... Sporting Traditions: Journal of the Australian Society for Sports History Full text
www.library.cmu.edu/Research/Humanities/ History/sports.html

80. **Journals & Research Reports: Links: Centre for Research into Sport ...**

Sport Specific Journals & Reports - Free Full Text Articles. One of the ... them. Sport Specific Journals - Limited Access. The following...
www.le.ac.uk/crss/resources/links/journals.html

81. **Electronic journals: Sports: Oxford Brookes University Library**

Electronic journals for Sports and Coaching. ... The Library also subscribes to many other journals in the field of Sports and Coaching in printed format. ...
www.brookes.ac.uk/services/library/ sport
scelectronicjournals.html

82. **Edinburgh University Press Journals - Sports Biomechanics**

For publication in any of the following sections of Sports Biomechanics: Original ... referenced in keeping with the requirements of other scientific journals. ...
www.eup.ed.ac.uk/newweb/journals/ Sports/submission.html

83. **The North Carolina Sports Literature Newsletter | Sports Business ...**

North Carolina has several major sports business journals published in our state. ... The ACC Area Sports Journal. The ACC Area Sports Journal. ...
www.unc.edu/depts/ppps/NCSLNews/business/business.

84. **Electronic Journals - Physical Education and Sports Sciences**

Physical Education & Sports Sciences - Electronic Journals. < Back. ... Journal of Sport and Social Issues, Athens, Yes, Yes. Journal of Sports Sciences, Athens, Yes, Yes. ...
www.marjon.ac.uk/library/electronic_resources/
electronic_journals/pe_sportsci.asp history. ...
members.fortunecity.com/korfball/

32
Karate

1. **Shotokan Karate of America**
   Non-profit organization headed by Tsutomu Ohshima. Pages include world wide SKA dojo directory, contact...
   www.ska.org/
2. **KARATE NET HOME PAGE**
   Kickboxing Karate Martial Arts Aerobic Kickboxing
   karatenet.com/
3. **WKF**
   IWGA International World Games Assosiation. |EKF European Karate Federation. FISU International University Sports Federation. ...
   www.wkf.net/
4. **SOUTHERN | karate**
   southern records. news; tours; labels; gallery; contact. karate home | biography | discography | contact | catalog. ... Read Gavin's Karate European tour diary.
   www.southern.com/southern/band/KARAT/
5. **USA Karate home**
   The USA Karate Federation is a tax exempt nonprofit corporation. ... The USA Karate Federation is the premier federation of the United States of America. A non-profit organization dedicated to promoting karate within the USA. Includes information on the...
   www.usakarate.org/
6. **Shotokan Karate Magazine**
   Magazine featuring the most senior and famous Shotokan Sensei in an apolitical manner.
   www.zee.com/skm/

7. **ISKF - International Shotokan Karate Federation**

   The ISKF is headquartered at: the Philadelphia Shotokan Karate Club Headquarters in Philadelphia, Pennsylvania. Pages include world club listing, and events posting.

   www.iskf.com/

8. **Martial Arts Supplies karate equipment uniform supply**

   Martial arts supplies including martial arts uniforms, karate equipment, sparring gear. Offering brand name Martial Arts equipment, uniforms, weapons and accessories.

   www.karatedepot.com/

9. **Karate BC**

   The Governing Body for Karate in British Columbia, Canada.

   www.karatebc.org/

10. **Karate on the Web - websites and books**

    WWW Karate directory contains an extensive list of karate and other martial arts-related resources. Self-Defence products. Karate on the Web. ...

    www.ethologic.com/sasha/karate.html

11. **Karate 1: Listings of Dojo's in the US and World Wide and Largest ...**

    ... Links. WELCOME TO THE HOME PAGE. OF. KARATE ONE. ... On these pages you will find the most concise listings of. Karate Schools and Dojo's.

    www.karate1.com/

12. **The Karate Kid Movie WebSite**

    The definitive source of information on The Karate Kid Movie on the internet. ... Hello and welcome to the Karate Kid Website. We're pleased you stopped by. ...

    www.fast-rewind.com/kkid/

13. **Karate the Japanese Way**

    Karate in Japan, the training, the teachers, the experience.

    aratethejapaneseway.com/

14. **Karate-Online Homepage**

    World > Deutsch > ... > Karate > Verbände > Deutschland

    www.karate-online.de/

15. **Homepage des DKV \ World > Deutsch > ... > Karate > Verbände > Deutschland**

    www.karate-dkv.de/

16. **USA National Karate-do Federation**
    The National Governing Body for Karate in the United States, under the auspices of the US Olympic Committee. A representative body governing national competitions and operating as a member of the US Olympic...
    www.usankf.org/
17. **The Karate World**
    Access count.
    www.karatedo.co.jp/
18. **International Traditional Karate Federation**
    International Traditional Karate Federation. Traditional Karate > Traditional Karate: Home. Welcome to www.ITKF.org. Search our Database ...
    www.itkf.org/
19. **THE KARATE WORLD**
    Head in Tokyo, Japan. Includes history, master's biographies, news, videos, and contact information.
    www.jka.or.jp/english/e_index.htm
20. **KARATE FOR CHRIST**
    KARATE FOR CHRIST INTERNATIONAL is a world wide outreach teaching Christian martial arts, Karate, judo, jujitsu, aikido, kido, hapkido, shotokan, Yoshikai ...
    www.karateforchrist.com/
21. **English Karate Governing Body EKGB**
    The governing body for Karate in England recognized and supported by the national sports council,...\
    www.ekgb.org.uk/
22. **Audio Karate**
    Official home page of the band Audio Karate.
    www.audiokarate.com/
23. **Dillman Karate International**
    George A. Dillman's Dillman Karate International pressure point karate and self-defense based on Ryukyu Kempo Karate is world famous for it's martial arts ...
    www.dillman.com/

24. **EKF - European Karate Federation**

European Karate Federation Karate Man copyright © 1999 ScandNet AB. The official body representing Karate in Europe. A member of the World Karate Federation. Includes...

www.eku.com/

25. **Karate Website Portal: News**

Italian Internet Karate Website, Italian Official Karate Website

www.karate.it/

26. **Ashihara Karate International - Kaicho Hoosain Narker**

Ashihara Karate is considered to be one of the most practicalkarate systems today. It is a system based on Sabaki..... An organization headquartered in South Africa teaching a style based on Sabaki. Site features curriculum...

users.iafrica.com/a/as/ashihara/

27. **SKV - FSK**

World > Deutsch > ... > Karate > Verbände > Schweiz

www.karate.ch/

28. **KarateBushido.com**

Includes current issue articles and related information.

www.karatebushido.com/

29. **Karate Angels**

Karate Angels a kids-only web site with chats, art and creative writing contests, games, an adventure story room, writers heaven, kids hall of fame, teen ...

www.karateangels.com/

30. **Australian Kyokushin Karate**

Events, FAQs, photos, articles, and related information on Kyokushin Karate.

www.safesci.unsw.edu.au/karate/

31. **Martial Arts Supplies, Karate Equipment, Martial Arts Supplies**

Arts Supplies. Karate Equipment, Boxing Equipment, Ninja Gear, Punching Bags, Weapons, Sparring Gear, and Martial Arts Supplies....

www.karate-mart.com/

32. **KARATE JOE REC**

ww.karate-joe.at/

33. **Shotokai Karate Budo Encyclopedia Chile Sports > Martial Arts > Karate > Shotokan**
www.shotokai.cl/

34. **Shotokai Karate Encyclopedia of Budo, Karate-do, Japanese Martial**
A complete site on Shotokai Karate Budo, Karate-do and Japanese Traditional martial arts, includes more than 200 megabytes of information. History, interviews, philosophy, technical essays, photos, and videos on Shotokai Karate-do and Budo...
www.shotokai.com/

35. **Karate-karate**
World > Nederlands > Sport > Vechtsport > Karate
members.chello.nl/~c.koops1/

36. **Karate High School - Arcade Rock For the New Millenium**
Official site of the five-piece rock/hip-hop band. Includes news, gig schedule, biographies, MP3 files,...
www.karatehighschool.com/

37. **Bikini Karate Babes**
A special thanks and Happy holidays to all of our loyal Bikini Karate Babes fans! 12/18/03 Collector Sets gone! ...
www.bikinikaratebabes.com/

38. **Karate Union of Great Britain**
The Official website for KUGB Shotokan Karate in the UK.
www.kugb.org/

39. **Karate Tournament Central Martial Art Tournament Listings**
Karate Tournament Central is the Ultimate Competitors Guide to Martial Arts Tournaments. ... Karate Tournament Central Message Board, Message Board. Provides the an index of martial arts tournaments available on the web as well as a bulletin board,...
www.karatetournaments.com/

40. **"Adidas,Kamikaze,Kid,Shureido,Karate,judo Martialarts wear"**
Suppliers of martial arts clothing, martial art shoes, tkd shoes, karate suits, karate gi's, judo suits, black belts, black belt embroidery, training equipment ...
www.karate-kid.co.uk/

41. **Isshinryu Karate**
Isshinryu Karate - Including History, Technique, Kata, Belt Requirements and more. Isshinryu Karate. Includes history, techniques, kata and belt requirements.
w3.trib.com/~smammon/isshin.html

42. **Theoretische Grundlagen zum Shotokan Karate-Do World > Deutsch > ... > Japan und Okinawa > Karate**
www.karate-do.de/

43. **World Seido Karate**
Community information, schedule, calendar, meditation, philosophy, programs, videos and world wide dojos.
www.seido.com/

44. **Shotokan Karate of America**
What Is Karate? "True karate ... Karate practice is divided into three aspects: kihon (basics), kata (forms), and kumite (sparring). The word ...
www.ska.org/karate.shtml

45. **Polski Zwiazek Karate**
World > Polska > Sport > Sztuki walki > Karate
www.karate.org.pl/

46. **Japan Karate-Do Ryobu-Kai**
Japan Karate-Do Ryobu-Kai is an international traditional Japanese martial arts organization. The ... Kai. JAPAN KARATE DO RYOBU-KAI. ...
www.jkr.com/

47. **Black Belt Magazine Martial Arts Dictionary**
New Buzzline Events Books CD-Roms Videos Subscriptions Pro ...
www.blackbeltmag.com/dictionary/

48. **Karate; the knockout band, with biography - discography - real...**
karate. site contains; .biography.pics.interviews.
.contributions.real audio. .discography.song tabs. .lyrics.live shows. .links. and more.
home.hetnet.nl/~unsolved/
history. ...
members.fortunecity.com/korfball/

33
Kho-Kho

1. **Sports - Traditional Games - Kho-Kho**
   Kho-Kho. Kho-Kho ranks as one of the most popular traditional sports in India. ... The first ever rules on Kho-Kho were published from Gymkhana Baroda, in 1924. ...
   www.meadev.nic.in/sports/tr_games/kho-kho1.htm
2. **Kho Kho**
   About Kho-Kho: Kho-Kho ranks as one of the most popular traditional sports in India. ... Kho-Kho can be played by men, women, and children of all ages. ...
   www.geocities.com/jasleen_m/kho.html
3. **KHO KHO**
   KHO KHO. Kho- Kho is an Indian game. It is popular in the whole of India. ... Its team in India is called Kho- Kho Federation of India (KKFI). ...
   www.webindia123.com/Sports/khokho/
4. **Khoj - Directory for khokho**
   Kho-Kho A site that give more details of the game like the evolution, how it is played, the different organisations and much more. KhoKho Site provides general ...
   www.khoj.com/Sports_and_Games/Sports/KhoKho/
5. **Kho-Kho**
   Kho-Kho. Kho-Kho. Kho-Kho Coaches. Kho-Kho Players. Kho Kho Teams. Mysore District Kho-Kho Association. About, Contact, Service, Advertisement, Feedback, Home.
   www.mysoresports.com/pages/KhoKho/Index.htm
6. **Search4i.com - Kho-Kho**
   One of the most popular traditional sports in India. ...
   www.search4i.com/directory/link/24726/

7. **khokho . com**
   www.khokho.com/
8. **Information on Kabaddi Cricket Golf Snooker Tennis Kho-Kho**
   Kabaddi Cricket Chess Badminton Tennis Table Tennies Formula I Golf Hockey Kho-Kho Football Derby Snooker Pool Billiards.
   www.gamestosports.com/
9. **Kho-Kho Players**
   KHO - KHO. Players. Chennabasaviah - Employed in Karnataka State Police. Represented the country in SAF games. Captained Indian Kho-Kho team in the SAF games. ...
   www.mysoresports.com/pages/khokho/Html/KKPlayers.htm
10. **Angel Island Picnic / KhoKho.jpg**
    Angel Island Picnic/KhoKho.jpg. Previous | Home | Next.
    www.netip-sfba.org/Events/2002/Angelisland/ pages KhoKho_jpg.htm
11. **Kho Kho**
    Know India in a better way. Search Web Webindia123.com. ...
    www.webindia123.com/Sports/khokho/terms.htm
12. **Administrative - Sports**
    1. Football (Men). 8. Kabaddi (Women). 2. Cricket (Men). 9. Kho - Kho (Men). 3. Athletics (Men & Women). 10. Kho - Kho (Women). 4. Aquatics (Men & Women). 11. ...
    www.caluniv.ac.in/admin/sports.htm
13. **Sports**
    Football (boys). Kabaddi(boys&Girls). Kho-Kho(Boys & Girls). ... Kabaddi (girls under 17)- State Runner-up. Kho-Kho (girls under 17)- State Runner-up.
    dhenkanal.nic.in/SchoolSports.HTM
14. **Traditional Sports of India**
    Kho Kho: Kho-Kho ranks as one of the most popular traditional sports in India. ... The first ever rules on Kho-Kho were published from Gymkhana Baroda, in 1924. ...
    www.nriofindia.com/Sports/various_sports1.htm

15. **THE BANGLADESH OBSERVER - Net Edition**

    National Kho Kho begins. The Second Pepsi National Women Kho Kho Championship, organised by Bangladesh Kho Kho Federation (BKKF), began ...

    www.bangladeshobserveronline.com/ new/2003/09/19/sports.htm

16. **India Sports links**

    Associations / Federations. Indigenous Games. Chess; Kabaddi; Kho-Kho;Malla-Khamb; Indian Martail Arts; Otherb IndigenousIndian Games. Cricket: ...

    members.tripod.com/HebbarU/sports.html

17. **The Official Web site of Government of Kerala**

    The sports and game which regularly practiced in this college are Athletics, cross country, Football, Kabaddi, Kho-kho, Handball, Softball, cricket, Table ...

    www.kerala.gov.in/dept_colligiate/achievement.htm

34
Kabaddi

1. **All Desi Kabaddi**
   Kabaddi. ... Kabaddi is played all over Asia with minor variations. A Kabaddi match in progress. Kabaddi is also known by various names viz. ...
   www.alldesi.net/fun/sports/kabaddi.htm
2. **Kabaddi**
   Kabaddi. Though kabaddi is primarily an Indian game, not much is known about the origin of this game. ... Kabaddi is played all over Asia with minor variations.
   www.goindiago.com/sports/kabaddi/kabaddi1.htm
3. **Kabaddi**
   A brief introduction.
   www.hiroshima-cu.ac.jp/C/ASIA/Sports/kabaddi.html
   Category: **Sports > Kabaddi**
4. **Kabaddi**
   "Kabaddi, Kabaddi, Kabaddi, Kabaddi....". Got a bunch of people, a big open space and nothing else? How about a round of Kabaddi? ...
   www.angelfire.com/wrestling3/kabaddi/
5. **Kabaddi in the UK**
   Promtoes the development of kabaddi in the U.K. as well as providing coaches and workshops.
   www.southampton-kabaddi-association.co.uk/
6. **Kabaddi Site**
   Kabaddi. Kabaddi is primarily an Indian game. ... The game is very popular and regular Kabaddi Tournaments are held now. Its rules have been formulated and refined. ...
   www.geocities.com/kennykabb/

7. **Games**

Access Database: GAMES IN INDIA. As in most other countries, games are also very popular in India. Some of the most popular games ...

cs.art.rmit.edu.au/projects/media/elephants/draupadi/story gamesdat.html

8. **Yahoo! Directory Sports > Kabaddi**

Sports > Kabaddi Directory > Recreation > Sports > Kabaddi, Search the Web just this category. ... SITE LISTINGS. Kabaddi [hiroshima-cu.ac.jp] - a brief introduction. ...

dir.yahoo.com/Recreation/Sports/Kabaddi/

9. **Google Directory - Sports > Kabbadi**

Kabaddi Association of Malaysia - http://geocities.com kabaddimalaysia/ Governing body for the sport of kabaddi. Kabaddi - http://www ...

directory.google.com/Top/Sports/Kabbadi/

10. **Search4i.com - Kabaddi**

No sub categories found in this category. ... , Kabaddi : About the game and types of kabaddi played. Jump. Other Categories....

www.search4i.com/directory/cat/2638/

11. **?ESPLANADE KABADDI CLUB?...**

The summary for this Japanese page contains characters that cannot be correctly displayed in this language/character set.

www.geocities.co.jp/Athlete/8886/

12. **Asian Kabaddi**

Kabaddi. Kabaddi was one of the first indigenous games that came to the UK with Punjabis. ... The England Kabaddi Federation was formed in November 1969. ...

www.historytalking.com/Kabaddi.htm

13. **XIII Asian Games, Bangkok (ASIAD 98) from Sadec Online**

Kabaddi. ...

www.sadec.com/Asiad98/Pages/Event20.htm

14. **BBC - CBBC - Sport - Get A Sport - Kabaddi**

How do you prove you haven't run out of breath? By repeating 'kabaddi, kabaddi, kabaddi' of course! There are two ...

www.bbc.co.uk/cbbc/sport/getasport/combat/combat kabaddi.shtml

15. **Kabaddi Literature**

    A Complete Handbook of Kabaddi written by AAKF Technical Director E Prasad Rao is perhaps the authorative book on the subject now. ...

    uk.geocities.com/asiankabaddi/page9.html

16. **Hambleton District Council - Kabaddi**

    Sports Clubs - Kabaddi National Kabaddi Association UK Mr Taj Butt C/o Recreation Service Ground Floor, Jacob's Well Bradford, BD1 5RW Tel: 01274 752654 Click ...

    www.hambleton.gov.uk/hambleton%5Cleisure.nsf/webpages sportsclubskabaddi.html?OpenDocument&Start=1&Count=1000&ExpandView

17. **Khojhyderabad.com > Entertainment**

    Kabaddi Kabaddi Cast :Jagapati Babu , Kalyani , Tanikella Bharani, Surya, Preeti Nigam, Featured Links: Listen to Music of Kabaddi Kabaddi Stills of the movie

    www.khojhyderabad.com/ent/movies/Display.asp?q=327&H=2

18. **Kabaddi - Wikipedia**

    Kabaddi. From Wikipedia, the free encyclopedia. Kabaddi is team pursuit sport, primarily played in India. Kabaddi is known by various ...

    www.wikipedia.org/wiki/Kabaddi

19. **Kabaddi**

    Home:: Games:: Kabaddi, Kabaddi. The origin of the Kabaddi is not much known. However, the game is about 4,000 years old. It is a ...

    www.safgames2003.com/Uploadedsite/Games/DetailGames Kabadi.htm

20. **Yahoo! Recreation>Sport>Kabaddi**

    Sport > Kabaddi Directory > Recreation > Sport > Kabaddi, ... Kabaddi [hiroshima-cu.ac.jp] open this site in another window - a brief introduction. ...

    www.yahoo.co.uk/recreation/sport/Kabaddi/

21. **S1NGH.com - Kabaddi History**

    NAVIGATION, ::KABADDI, >>Though kabaddi is primarily an Indian game, not much is known about the origin of this game. ... >FOLKLORE. >>PUNJABI FOOD. >>KABADDI. ...

    www.amozaghi.fsnet.co.uk/virsa1/kabbadi.htm

22. **Virtual Bangladesh : Sports: Kabaddi**
Sports: Kabaddi. Kabaddi is the national sport of Bangladesh. ... The kabaddi playing area is 12.50mx 10m, divided by a line into two halves. ...
www.virtualbangladesh.com/sports/kabaddi.php

23. **KABADDI**
KABADDI. Kabaddi is an Indian game which requires both power and skill for its play. ... Regular Kabaddi tournaments are held throughout the country. Field of play. ...
www.webindia123.com/Sports/kabaddi/

24. **Kabaddi Classifieds Free at Hoobly**
Kabaddi Classified Ads from Everywhere (0 ads). No ads found.
www.hoobly.com/listings/browse/0/1994/0/

25. **123India.com Kabaddi : Sports**
Search all of 123India.com Search only in Kabaddi. Kabaddi - Sites. Kabaddi - about the game and types of kabaddi played. Click here ...
dir.123india.com/sports/kabaddi/

26. **?????(kabaddi)?**
The summary for this Japanese page contains characters that cannot be correctly displayed in this language/character set.
www.lifecity.ne.jp/genesis/marina/west3/marcoola_beach page8.html

27. **Kabaddi**
Kabaddi Though kabaddi is primarily an Indian game, not much is known about the origin of this game. ... Kabaddi is played all over Asia with minor variations.
www.jatt.com/pdf/kabaddi.PDF

28. **Yahoo! e???? : Hiroshima-kabaddi**
Hiroshima-kabaddi. ... ??????: Hiroshima kabaddi@egroups.co.jp; ? ???????(????): Hiroshima-kabaddi-subscribe@egroups.co.jp; ...
www.egroups.co.jp/group/Hiroshima-kabaddi

29. **rediff.com: Sports: The Asian Games 2002: Games: Kabaddi**
Technology About the Game, Kabaddi is a team sport. Two ... points. The radar must keep calling, "kabaddi, kabaddi" during the offense. If ...
www.rediff.com/sports/ag/kaba.htm

30. **Indiafocus -Sports-Kabaddi**
Home > Sports Kabaddi. Brief Intro about Kabaddi - a teaching site how to play kabaddi. SUGGEST A SITE. Online Florist. Home | About ...
indiafocus.indiainfo.com/sports/kabaddi/

31. **Kabaddi - Web World**
All Desi Kabaddi Kabaddi is one of the popular game among the peoples of Asia, especially in the villigers of India, Pakistan, Bangladesh, Sri Lanka, Nepal ...
www.webworldindex.com/phtml/Recreation_and_Sports/Sports/Kabaddi/

32. **Image Gallery - Kabaddi Kabbadi**
Album list Last uploads :: Last comments :: Most viewed :: Top rated :: Search. Home > Film Gallery > Telugu > K. Kabaddi Kabbadi. NAME, +, -. DATE, +, -. 1.jpg. 2.jpg.
gallery.musicindiaonline.com/thumbnails.php?album=755

33. **Punjab Online:Punjab Web Guide**
Links: Rules of Kabaddi Page of illustrated rules of Kabaddi/ URL: http://www.lancs.ac.uk/ug/morrisj/rules.htm. ... URL: http:/ /www.kabaddi.ca/. ...
www.punjabonline.com/servlet
directories.searchEngine?Action=Category&Id=49

34. **Kabaddi**
KABADDI. Though kabaddi is primarily an Pakistani game, not much is known about the origin of this game. ... How to Play Kabaddi is a team sport. ...
www.pakwatan.com/main/sports/kabaddi.php3

35. **Recreation: Sports: Kabaddi**
Qango Directory Kabaddi all of Qango only this category Options Help. Home > Recreation > Sports > Kabaddi, Suggest a Site. Recreation, etc. ...
www.qango.com/dir/Recreation/Sports/Kabaddi/

36. **Medal Tally Kabaddi in SAF Games**
Medal Tally of Kabaddi in SAF Games. Game, Year, Venue, Gold, Silver, Bronze, Total. 2nd, 1985, Dhaka, -, -, 1, 1. 3rd, 1987, Calcutta, -, -, 1, 1. 4th, 1989, Islamabad, -, 1, -, 1. ...
www.sports.gov.pk/html/medal_tally_kabaddi_saf_games.htm

37. **Kabaddi**

Modify a Link. Search India, ===>>. Home : Indian Sports » Kabaddi >> Add Url. Kabaddi. Kabaddi. Votes: 0 | Rating: N/A, Rate it | Comments.

www.thefamousindia.com/html/Indian_Sports/Kabaddi/

38. **Music India OnLine - Kabaddi Kabaddi**

Punjabi - Rajasthani - Sindhi - Tamil - Telugu. Privacy Policy. Kabaddi Kabaddi (2003) Cast: Jagapati Babu, Kalyani. Review. Songs: ...

www.musicindiaonline.com/music/l/XY00000A1O

39. **REQUEST : Looking for rules etc for kabaddi**

Info. about the ancient hindu sport of kabaddi. ...

www.hindunet.org/srh_home/1996_7/msg00324.html

40. **Kabaddi - BritishSports.com: the OFFICIAL sports sites directory** Kabaddi This site is best viewed using Microsoft Internet Explorer. Southampton Kabaddi Association. Kabaddi Association of Malaysia (KAM). ...

www.britishsports.com/kabaddi.htm

41. **ChitraSeema Audio — Kabaddi Kabaddi**

Kabaddi Kabaddi, ... Kabaddi Kabaddi Music Composed by : Chakri Audio Released by : Aditya. Goruvanka..Godarivanka... Singer(s) : Ravivarma ...

www.chitraseema.com/chitraseema/album.jsp?aid=49

42. **Asian Underground - Kabaddi Master Foils Armed Robbery**

KABADDI MASTER FOILS ARMED ROBBERY. ... I cannot tolerate impoliteness so decided to teach them a lesson kabaddi style.". A trained killer. ...

www.asianunderground.co.uk/articles/sport/kabaddi.asp

43. **Kabaddi**

Kabaddi. Though kabaddi is primarily an Indian game, not much is known about the origin of this game. ... A Kabaddi match in progress. ...

www.punjabilok.com/misc/sports/spo_trad_kabd.htm

44. **Kabaddi - Wikipedia**

Kabaddi. From Wikipedia, the free encyclopedia. Kabaddi is team pursuit sport, primarily played in India. Kabaddi is known ...

www.wikipedia.com/wiki/Kabaddi

45. **www.kabaddi.org Finally a website for those kabaddi fanatic**
JaTT INC Board > News & Sport > www.kabaddi.org Finally a website for those kabaddi fanatic, pub49.ezboard.com fjattincboard30296frm9.showMessage?topicID=46.topic

46. **Index of /activity/k/kabaddi**
Index of /activity/k/kabaddi. Name Last modified Size Description Parent Directory 17-Oct-2002 11:07 - ASA/ 13-Nov-2000 16:47 - Budget ...
web.mit.edu/activity/k/kabaddi/

47. **Forum-Search: Sports/Kabaddi**
Forum-Search.com - Home, Search our forums directory for: the entire directory only this category, More search options. Home : Sports : Kabaddi. ...
www.forum-search.com/Sports/Kabaddi/

48. **Indias.com Your Gateway into INDIA**
Country Sites Category Sites ...
www.indias.com/Sports/Kabaddi.htm

49. **S1NGH.com - .amo_'s Dreambook**
Comments: i really like this web site i think please put more kabaddi pic in this web..cuz ima kabaddi player too..i play under 21..but im only 17 year old ...
books.dreambook.com/amozaghi/book.html

50. **Chutki.com**
Though kabaddi is primarily a Pakistani game, not much is known about the origin of this game. There is, however, concrete evidence ...
www.alephinc.net/chutkinew/html/kabaddi.asp

51. **KABADDI World Cup 2003 Chicago**
DIWALI 2003. Photos courtesy of RANJIT SINGH AHLUWALIA. GIDHA. BHANGRA. CROWD. GIDHA. BHANGRA. CROWD. PHOTOS TAKEN BY. RANJIT SINGH AHLUWALIA. Email you comments.
www.punjabi.co.nz/diwalli2003page.htm

52. **Indiainfo.com -> News -> Spotlight -> Busan Asian Games -> India**
Busan: India maintained its stranglehold on Kabaddi and won its fourth successive Asian Games gold medal with a 37-7 drubbing of Pakistan on Monday in the last ...
newsarchives.indiainfo.com/spotlight/asiad/07kabaddi.html

53. **TeluguCinema.Com - Kabaddi.. Kabaddi... - Audio Review**
Kabaddi.. Kabaddi... - Audio Review - by NaChaKi. Maharshi Cinema. Kabaddi.. Kabaddi... Lead Pair: Jagapathi Babu, Kalyani. Producer: Valluripalli Ramesh. ...
www.telugufilmserver.com/kabaddikabaddi_audio.shtml

54. **Kabaddi squad**
Kabaddi squad. ... OCTOBER 21: The Mumbai University men's kabaddi team will leave for the West Zone inter-university tournament, at Rahuri from October 24. ...
www.indianexpress.com/ie/daily/19991022/isp22072.html

55. **kabaddi**
The summary for this Japanese page contains characters that cannot be correctly displayed in this language/character set.
northfront.lifecity.jp/verdandi/bastion/sherry_beach/page7.html

56. **Kabaddi Kabaddi - movie review - jagapathi babu, kalyani**
Kabaddi Kabaddi. Review by Jessica Vergheeze. Clash between two neighbouring village teams in a kabaddi match, to unite two lovers, forms the story. ...
www.megafans.com/chiru/others/kabaddi.html

57. **Kabaddi**
Kabaddi. Kabaddi is team pursuit sport, primarily played in India. Kabaddi is known by various names in India - chedugudu in the ...
www.4reference.net/encyclopedias/wikipedia/Kabaddi.html

58. **Open Directory - Sports: Kabbadi**
Brief Intro about Kabaddi - A teaching site how to play Kabaddi, includes game schedule with results. ... Kabaddi - Descriptions of the various forms of kabbadi.
dmoz.org/Sports/Kabbadi/

59. **Kabbadi**

Brief Intro about Kabaddi — http://www.hiroshima-cu.ac.jp/c/asia/sports/kabaddi.html A teaching site how to play Kabaddi, includes game schedule with results. ...

www.directory.net/Sports/Kabbadi/

60. **Kabbadi**

Do you know "Kabaddi"? ... Kabaddi ! Kabaddi !Kabaddi ! Kabaddi ! can be heard during the game. ...

www.tokyo-japan-guide.com/weekly-tokyo6-eng.htm

61. **urdustan.com :: View topic - Kabaddi?**

Kabaddi? ... *SilverZ*~ urdustan dost Joined: 23 May 2002 Posts: 1154 Location: USA, PostPosted: Tue Feb 18, 2003 4:31 am Post subject: Kabaddi? Reply with quote. ...

mehfil.urdustan.net/viewtopic.php?t=2613

62. **Kabaddi Link Navigators**

The summary for this Japanese page contains characters that cannot be correctly displayed in this language/character set.

www1.linkclub.or.jp/~t-kikuti/cgi/link/linkv.html

63. **AnySearchInfo Directory - Sports Kabbadi**

Brief Intro about Kabaddi A teaching site how to play Kabaddi, includes game schedule with results. ... Kabaddi Descriptions of the various forms of kabbadi. ...

search-info.com/search/engine/index/Sports/Kabbadi/

64. **Kabaddi Kabaddi @ TeluguPeople.com**

Reviews -> Kabaddi Kabaddi. Title: Kabaddi Kabaddi = Rhythm of an Indian sport Theme: Rambabu (Jagapathi Babu) is a jolly go around ...

www.telugupeople.com/cinema/content.asp?contentId=984

65. **Bangladesh will play in Asian Kabaddi - www.ezboard.com**

ashiq2k Marshal of the Air Force Administrator BMF Website CEO & Webmaster Posts: 15546 (23/9/03 11:09 pm) Reply, Bangladesh will play in Asian Kabaddi ...

pub38.ezboard.com

fbanglatopicsfrm36.showMessage?topicID=160.topic

66. **Excite UK - Directory - Kabbadi**
Brief Intro about Kabaddi, A teaching site how to play Kabaddi, includes game schedule with results. ... 7. Kabaddi Association of Malaysia, ...
www.excite.co.uk/directory/Sports/Kabbadi

67. **Indiaglance.com - Sports - Kabaddi**
Kabaddi. Introduction. History. How To Play. Photo Gallery. Home. 1. TC.
www.investmentmap.com/IG/Kabaddi.htm

68. **kabaddi season**
www.khabarnama.com { Punjabi Newspaper Khabarnama } afpxI mF boll 'pMjfbI' ilKx, pVHn aqy bolx ivwc iJjk mıhsUs nf kro sgoN mfx aqy PKr nfl afpxy bwicaF nUM vI ...
www.khabarnama.com/kabaddi_season.htm

69. **AJE Dir / Sports / Kabbadi /**
Brief Intro about Kabaddi A teaching site how to play Kabaddi, includes game schedule with results. www.hiroshima-cu.ac.jp/C/ASIA/Sports/kabaddi.html. ...
www.ajemalaga.org/web.directory/Sports/Kabbadi/

70. **Download Games Free Game Downloads: Sports : Kabbadi**
Brief Intro about Kabaddi - A teaching site how to play Kabaddi, includes game schedule with results. ... History, rules, and adaptability of kabaddi. ...
www.download-games-and-free-game-downloads.com/directory Sports/Kabbadi/

71. **Review On Kabaddi by jimmy — MouthShut.com**
Review On Kabaddi by jimmy, read consumer reviews on thousands of products and services - MouthShut.com. ... Kabaddi, Kabaddi. Average Product Rating. ...
www.mouthshut.com/readreview/1991-1.html

72. **Bangladeshinfo.com : The Leading Portal of Bangladesh**
BDD clinches Kabaddi championship title. Bangladesh Rifles clinched the title of the 25th National Kabaddi Championship beating Bangladesh ...
www.bangladeshinfo.com/sports other_head.php?head=head7&desc=desc7

73. **Angel Island Picnic / Kabaddi.jpg**
Angel Island Picnic/Kabaddi.jpg. Previous | Home | Next.
www.netip-sfba.org/Events/2002/Angelisland/pages
Kabaddi_jpg.htm

74. **Log in ....Tribune—The world of dot.com**
THE origin of Kabaddi can be traced to pre-historic times when man learnt how to defend in groups to ward off animal attack for survival and food. ...
www.tribuneindia.com/2002/20020520/login/dot.htm

75. **metaEUREKA Sports/Kabbadi/**
A teaching site how to play Kabaddi, includes game schedule with results. http://www.hiroshima-cu.ac.jp/C/ASIA/Sports/kabaddi.html, ...
www.metaeureka.com/cgi-bin/odp2.pl?dir=Sports/Kabbadi/

76. **Kabbadi**
Brief Intro about Kabaddi - A teaching site how to play Kabaddi, includes game schedule with results. Kabaddi - Descriptions of the various forms of kabbadi. ...
www.findsports.net/Sports/Kabbadi/

77. **Walhello**
Related Categories regional>asia>india>recreation_and_sports Web pages 1. brief intro about kabaddi - a teaching site how to play kabaddi, includes game ...
www.walhello.info/top/sports/kabbadi

78. **Kabaddi? Kabaddi? movie review**
Kabaddi? Kabaddi?,wallpapers,screensavers,trailers, ... Movie: Kabaddi? Kabaddi?. Kabaddi? Kabaddi? is a film is clearly influenced ...
movies.usaindians.com/movies/reviews/KabaddiKabaddi.htm

79. **Telugu Cinema - Review - Kabaddi Kabaddi - Thatstelugu.com**
Search Telugu. ...
www.thatstelugu.com/cinema/sameeksha/kabaddikabaddi.html

80. **The Wolverhampton Kabaddi Tournament2003**
Sikhnet Event Calendar THE WOLVERHAMPTON KABADDI TOURNAMENT2003. Event Posted by: JN Dairies. ... Brief Description: THE WOLVERHAMPTON KABADDI TOURNAMENT2003. ...
www.sikhnet.com/sikhnet/events.nsf091918f46a4364af287256d4300460927? OpenDocument&Date=200306-15

81. **Sports: Kabbadi**
Brief Intro about Kabaddi: A teaching site how to play Kabaddi, includes game schedule with results..
http://www.hiroshima
cu.ac.jp/C/ASIA/Sports/kabaddi.html. ...
https://slider-secure.vendercom.com/Sports/Kabbadi.htm

82. **Kabbadi - Sports - kevinbinder.net**
Brief Intro about Kabaddi A teaching site how to play Kabaddi, includes game schedule with results. ... Kabaddi Descriptions of the various forms of kabbadi. ...
www.kevinbinder.net/Sports/Kabbadi/

83. **Sports/Kabbadi**
Brief Intro about Kabaddi pop A teaching site how to play Kabaddi, includes game schedule with results. http:/
www.hiroshima-cu.ac.jp/C/ASIA/Sports/kabadd... ...
bn23.com/portal/Sports/Kabbadi/

84. **Wauu.DE: Sports: Kabbadi**
Brief Intro about Kabaddi A teaching site how to play Kabaddi, includes game schedule with results. ... History, rules, and adaptability of kabaddi. ...
www.wauu.de/Sports/Kabbadi/

85. **Dominion Web - Directory - Sports: Kabbadi**
Kabbadi. See also: Top/Sports/K. Links. » Brief Intro about Kabaddi - A teaching site how to play Kabaddi, includes game schedule with results. ...
www.dominion-web.com/directory/Top/Sports/Kabbadi

86. **Inicio Sports Kabbadi :: tematics.net**
Brief Intro about Kabaddi A teaching site how to play Kabaddi, includes game schedule with results.
[http://www.hiroshima cu.ac.jp/C/ASIA/Sports/kabaddi.html]. ...
ingles.tematics.net/index.php/Top/Sports/Kabbadi

87. **Golf | Hockey | Soccer | Kabaddi | Badminton | Sports2002 Home**
15th Australian Sikh Sports Carnival - Perth 2002. KABADDI. Matches will start at the designated times. Failure of a team to appear ...
www.multicultural.online.wa.gov.au/wppuser/sawa/games
Kabaddi.html

88. **Kabbadi - Sports LoCuaL.com**
Brief Intro about Kabaddi · Sports Kabbadi URL: http:/ www.hiroshima-cu.ac.jp/C/ASIA/Sports/kabaddi.html A teaching site how to play Kabaddi, includes game ...
locual.com/D/Sports/Kabbadi/

89. **Welcome to kabaddi.com**
Welcome to kabaddi.com We apoligize for the delay in makig this a real kabaddi site but something will be happening soon. ... email to photos@kabaddi.com. ...
kabaddi.com/

90. **AnsMe Directory - Sports > Kabbadi**
Kabaddi is a popular game among the people of Asia, especially in the villiges of India, Pakistan, Bangladesh, Sri Lanka, Nepal, and Japan. ...
dir.ansme.com/sports/84296.html

91. **Searchpixie.com: Sports : Kabbadi**
LINKS: Brief Intro about Kabaddi A teaching site how to play Kabaddi, includes game schedule with results. ... History, rules, and adaptability of kabaddi. ...
www.searchpixie.com/Sports/Kabbadi/

92. **kabaddi**
Kabaddi. Kabaddi, 12-a-side field pursuit game (only 7 players on each side may take the field at once) very common in India, and also played in Pakistan, Burma
lovepk.freeyellow.com/kabaddi.htm

93. **info services by mainseek.com**
Brief Intro about Kabaddi A teaching site how to play Kabaddi, includes game schedule with results. jp/ C/ ASIA/ Sports/ kabaddi. ...
www.mainseek.com/ca/84296/Sports/Kabbadi/

94. **Kabbadi Rules**
The Game and its Rules. In Kabaddi, two teams compete with each other for higher scores, by touching or capturing the players of the opponent team. ...
punjabsportsclub.com/kabbadi_rules.htm

95. **KABADDI**

The summary for this Japanese page contains characters that cannot be correctly displayed in this language/character set.

ww4.tiki.ne.jp/~keguri/KABADDI/KABADDI.html

96. **Excite Italia - Directory - Kabbadi**

Brief Intro about Kabaddi, A teaching site how to play Kabaddi, includes game schedule with results. ... 2. Kabaddi Association of Malaysia, ...

www.excite.it/directory/Sports/Kabbadi

97. **Webschooling**

Kabaddi. Kabaddi is primarily an Indian game. ... The game is very popular and regular Kabaddi Tournaments are held now. Its rules have been formulated and refined. ...

www.webschooling.com/sports6.html

98. **Directory :: Look.com**

Brief Intro about Kabaddi A teaching site how to play Kabaddi, includes game schedule with results. Kabaddi Descriptions of the various forms of kabbadi. ...

www.look.com/searchroute/directorysearch.asp?p=84296

99. **uk.searchengine.com - Kabbadi info**

Kabbadi Description. A teaching site how to play Kabaddi, includes game schedule with results. ... . Governing body for the sport of kabaddi. ... ...

uk.searchengine.com/Top/Sports/Kabbadi/

100. **Peel Regional Police - Peel Police forms Kabaddi team to compete**

Attention News Editors: Peel Regional Police - Peel Police forms Kabaddi team to compete. ... The sport of Kabaddi is a very challenging and physical game. ...

www.newswire.ca/releases/July2003/12/c1962.html

101. **Kabaddi**

Kabaddi. Punch. Head Butt, 1 pt. Strike of Sleep, 5 pt. Kick. Slidekick, 2 pts. Block. Energy Reflection, 3 pts. San He, 3 pts. Grab. Air Suplex, 2 pts. ...

www.pvv.ntnu.no/~leirbakk/rpg/streetfighter/styles
kabaddi_tbl.html

102. **DINO - Language: Englisch - Sports - Kabbadi**

Dieser 'externe' Link öffnet sich in einem neuen Fenster Brief Intro about Kabaddi - A teaching site how to play Kabaddi, includes game schedule with ...

www.branchendino.de

dino_page_fe4f8f56f3c7e8ab47ef9fe8729adae0.html

103. **kangaroolinks.com: Sports/Kabbadi**

Brief Intro about Kabaddi A teaching site how to play Kabaddi, includes game schedule with results. ... Kabaddi A short description of how Kabaddi is played. ...

www.kangaroo-links.com/Sports/Kabbadi/

104. **MetaXearch > Sports Kabbadi**

Brief Intro about Kabaddi A teaching site how to play Kabaddi, includes game schedule with results. Kabaddi Descriptions of the various forms of kabbadi. ...

www.metaxearch.com/en/odp_84296/Sports/Kabbadi/

105. **Martial Arts**

Index. Kabaddi ????? A game that teaches defence. ... Cheibi Gad-Ga. Kalari Payattu. Silambam. Thang-ta. Thoda. Kabaddi. ...

www3.sympatico.ca/sandyxavier/emirates/gatka.htm

106. **Kabbadi : Top : Sports : Kabbadi**

Sites. Brief Intro about Kabaddi: A teaching site how to play Kabaddi, includes game schedule with results. ... History, rules, and adaptability of kabaddi. ...

www.theolympicsite.org/Top/Sports/Kabbadi/

107. **Kabbadi**

Brief Intro about Kabaddi A teaching site how to play Kabaddi, includes game schedule with results.

http://www.hiroshima cu.ac.jp/C/ASIA/Sports/kabaddi.html. ...

www.checkburst.com/Sports/Kabbadi

108. **Sportingtimes Online Magazine: SportsPlus/Kabbadi**

Brief Intro about Kabaddi pop A teaching site how to play Kabaddi, includes game schedule with results. ... Kabaddi Descriptions of the various forms of kabbadi. ...

www.sportingtimes.com/SportsPlus/Kabbadi/

109. **Sports Kabbadi Polish Yellow Pages - Polska - Poland - Polen**
Brief Intro about Kabaddi- A teaching site how to play Kabaddi, includes game schedule with results. Kabaddi- Descriptions of the various forms of kabbadi. ...
www.yellowpages.pl/ca/84296/Sports/Kabbadi/

110. **Findtarget.com - Internet Search Engine**
Brief Intro about Kabaddi A teaching site how to play Kabaddi, includes game schedule with results. ? Kabaddi Information ...
www.findtarget.com/ODP/Top/Sports/Kabbadi

111. **Geometry.Net - Sports: Kabbadi**
Directory :: Look.com s of the various forms of kabbadi.Kabaddi Association of Malaysia Governing body for the sport of kabaddi. kabbadi (7) Featured Sites. ...
www.geometry.net/sports/kabbadi_page_no_5.html

112. **India Day Activity Reports**
We did lots of Indian activities like tie-dye and went to the gym to do drama and Kabaddi. ... Kabaddi is a game where you get people out. ...
www.kingspark.bournemouth.sch.uk
india_day_activity_reports.htm

113. **Sports: Kabbadi - WorldSearch.com**
Kabaddi Descriptions of the various forms of kabbadi. ... 2. Kabaddi Association of Malaysia Governing body for the sport of kabaddi. ...
www.worldsearch.com/dp.lisa/en/Sports/Kabbadi

114. **Tiscali - Search**
Brief Intro about Kabaddi A teaching site how to play Kabaddi, includes game schedule with results. 2.Kabaddi Descriptions of the various forms of kabbadi. ...
directory.tiscali.it/Sports/Kabbadi

115. **Kabbadi**
KABADDI. Kabaddi - Descriptions of the various forms of kabbadi. Kabaddi - A short description of how Kabaddi is played. Kabaddi ...
www.sportsfansofamerica.com/Links/Other/Kabbadi1.htm

116. **Kabbadi**
Brief Intro about Kabaddi - A teaching site how to play Kabaddi, includes game schedule with results. ...
www.linkspider.org/index.cgi/Sports/Kabbadi/index.shtml

117. **Kabbadi**
Brief Intro about Kabaddi A teaching site how to play Kabaddi, includes game schedule with results. Kabaddi Descriptions of the various forms of kabbadi. ...
portal.redbox.cz/portal/directory/Sports/Kabbadi

118. **Websoochi-Marathi World**
MarathiWorld-Home. About Us, About Marathi World, Suggest a site, Feedback, Contact, Site Map. Sports > KABADDI, Home. KABADDI - . Write ...
www.marathiworld.com/websoochi/subcate.php?v=14&v1=154

119. **Kabbadi - web directory**
Kabaddi Descriptions of the various forms of kabbadi. url: www.goindiago.com/sports/kabaddi/kabaddi1.htm. ...
bestofthenet.tv/Sports/Kabbadi/

120. **India a2z Your Comprehensive guide to Indian Web**
Your, Sports : Kabaddi. Personalize Your Page, ... Kabaddi — About the game and types of kabaddi played —
http:/www.indiagov.org/sports/tr_games/kabaddi1.htm. ...
www.indiaa2z.com/htmlPages/Sports/Kabaddi/Default.htm

121. **Kabbadi**
The summary for this Japanese page contains characters that cannot be correctly displayed in this language/character set.
homepage2.nifty.com/kabaddi-nippon/

122. **Sports Kabbadi**
Kabbadi. Top Web Sites: Brief Intro about Kabaddi - A teaching site how to play Kabaddi, includes game schedule with results....
www.pastconnect.com/odp/index.cgi/Sports/Kabbadi/

123. **News Behind the News**
Kabaddi Discovery India - History of Kabaddi and the rules of the game Brief Intro about Kabaddi - Rules on Kabaddi. ...
www.india-newsbehindnews.com/kabbadi.html

124. **Sports: Kabbadi**

Websites on Kabbadi: Brief Intro about Kabaddi A teaching site how to play Kabaddi, includes game schedule with results. Kabaddi ...

cheap-holidays-flights.co.uk/dir.cgi/Sports/Kabbadi/

125. **SPORTS PROMOTION TEAM - IGTF**

Inter District Kabaddi Tournament A1 Super Veeron-ke-Veer 2002....

www.sptindia.com/kabaddi.htm

126. **Detailed Article Title Here] - [News] - CRI Online**

India wins its third gold in Asiad Kabaddi. India won the gold medal in Kabaddi in the 14th Asian Games, beating Pakistan 37 7 in the last game on Monday. ...

web12.cri.com.cn/english/2002/Oct/73790.htm

127. **AlMisbar Home Online translation AlMisbar E-mail Search the web**

AlMisbar>>Sport>Sports List>More Sprots>Kabaddi. Illustrated Rules of Kabaddi; Kabaddi. Kabaddi in India; Sports fan's whole kit and kabaddi. ...

www.almisbar.com/sport/Kabaddi.html

128. **News**

Grand welcome for Kumble?s Kabaddi star. DH News Service MANGALORE, Nov 1. Kabaddi star Jagadish Kumble, member of the winning Kabaddi ...

www.deccanherald.com/deccanherald/nov02/d3.asp

129. **The Hindu : A star without stardom**

But International Ramesh's achievements on the kabaddi court will continue to inspire those who follow a sport that has a thriving rural base and appeal. ...

www.hinduonnet.com/thehindu/mp/2002/11/14/stories 2002111400430400.htm

130. **Betting Links: SportsPlus/Kabbadi**

Kabaddi, includes game schedule with results. Bookmark Review It Visit Site. Kabaddi - Descriptions of the various forms of kabbadi....

www.bettinglinks.com/SportsPlus/Kabbadi/

131. **News India-Times.com, Online Edition**
Manhattan on Oct. 8. More... Kabaddi team wins fourth successive gold medal By V. KRISHNASWAMY Unbeaten team demolishes Pakistan ...
www.newsindia-times.com/2002/10/18/sports-b-40-top.html

132. **Channelnewsasia.com: Asian Games**
Kabaddi Medal Standing. Kabaddi, Medal, Country, Name. ? Men's Team, Gold, India, SINGH Shamsher with 11 players. Silver, Bangladesh, AHAMMAD Md. Bashir with 11 players. ...
www.channelnewsasia.com/cna/asiangames/mkabaddi.htm

133. **freenet.De Webkatalog - Language: Englisch - Sports - Kabbadi**
Sports. Websites 1. Brief Intro about Kabaddi - A teaching site how to play Kabaddi, includes game schedule with results. 2. Kabaddi ...
webkatalog.freenet.de
freenet_page_fe4f8f56f3c7e8ab47ef9fe8729adae0.html

134. **Daily Mirror Online**
Sports. From track and field to kabaddi By Bruce Maurice A sportsman par excellence who proved himself as an athlete, soccerite and spiker at Central College
www.dailymirror.lk/2002 08/30/sports/4.html

135. **Gogog Directory**
Brief Intro About Kabaddi - **http://www.hiroshima-cu.ac.jp/C/ASIA/Sports/kabaddi.html A teaching** site how to play Kabaddi, includes game schedule with results. ...
gogog.com/directory/Top/Sports/Kabbadi/84296

136. **WATCHED IT! - Classic Kids TV**
And Darrel - KABADDI was not a childrens' show, but C4's televising of an Indian(?) national sport. ... ...kabaddi, kabaddi, kabaddi, kabaddi...KABADDI").
www3.shellnet.co.uk/gmc gbview.php?gbnum=16&page=245

137. **PusanWeb Writings - Essays, Fiction, and Poetry from Busan, Korea**
Kabaddi Fever. October 8, 2002. by Patrick Carle. Some friends of mine and I got up early last Saturday morning to go see Kabaddi. It was totally worth it. ...
www.pusanweb.com/writings/essays/kabaddi.htm

138. **Bernie DeKoven's Fun Findings**

Kabaddi, Dho-Dho-Dho: New Games Revealed. ... The side winning the toss sends a 'raider', who enters the opponents' court chanting, 'kabaddi-kabaddi'. ...

www.deepfun.com/weblog/2002_12_13_blogger.html

139. **Nettlinx**

Kabaddi... Maharshi Cinema' Kabaddi.. Kabaddi... ... Rambabu challenges to defeat the Kabaddi team of Sakhinetipally and asks marriage with Kaveri as the prize. ...

www.nettlinx.com/Entertainment

Tollywood_desc.asp?Id=E11_181

140. **Ipswich Summer Activities Survey Winner**

54%. Horse Riding. 36%. Kabaddi (See Explanation to the right). 11%. Fishing. 24%. ... Male. Female. What gender are you? 40%. 60%. what is kabaddi? Kabaddi is a team sport. ...

www.thesource.me.uk/news/sa_winner.htm

141. **DATABARN**

websites. (1) Brief Intro about Kabaddi. A teaching site how to play Kabaddi, includes game schedule with results. http ... html (2) Kabaddi. ...

www.databarn.com/dmoz/Top/Sports/Kabbadi/

142. **India Directory > Sports & Games > Local Games Directory**

History Of Kabaddi - Game of Kabaddi involves skill, stamina and teamwork. An essay describing nuances of kabaddi, its development and future. ...

directory.indbazaar.com/director.asp?catID=293&linkseries=13

143. **Kabbadi**

See also: Regional/Asia/India/Recreation and Sports. Sites: Brief Intro about Kabaddi - A teaching site how to play Kabaddi, includes game schedule with results ...

directory.webguest.com/index.cgi/Sports/Kabbadi/

144. **Traditional Sports of India**

Kabaddi: Though kabaddi is primarily an Indian game, not much is known about the origin of this game. ... Kabaddi is played all over Asia with minor variations.

www.nriofindia.com/Sports/various_sports.htm

145. **Cultural Heritage**

Among indigenous games perhaps the best known is kabaddi. It involves two teams standing across a line on the ground. By ...
www.journeymart.com/Dexplorer/AsiaIS/India/culturalheritage sports.asp

146. **Pakistan News Service**

India to hold Kabaddi World Cup. ISLAMABAD (APP) - The inaugural World Cup kabaddi tournament
paknews.com/1999/mar/spt1mar-22.html

147. **Chembur Marathi Madhyamik Shala**

Playground: The institution has a big playground and special coaching is given to the students in Handball, Volleyball, Kabaddi and Kho-kho by expert coaches. ...
www.vpillaiscampus.ac.in
chembur_marathi_madhyamik_shala.htm

148. **Kabaddi Originating in India, somewhat resembles the ...**

Kabaddi Originating in India, Kabaddi somewhat resembles the moves made in both wrestling and rugby and the game is always played in teams, usually consisting ...
for.yna.co.kr/Agame/E/event/event_3.asp

149. **Pursuit games**

Who step outside the area will be out of the game. Kabaddi Choo. Name, Kabaddi Choo, Hindi, Area, Rectangle, ü, Square, ü, Circle, ü. ...
www.hssworld.org/all/sharirik/pursuit_games.html

150. **Materiaali: national sport**

Kabaddi is another popular game. It ... The kabaddi playing area is 12.50mx 10m, divided by a line into two halves. The side winning
.totyx.joensuu.fi/thule/eno2000/materiaali.nsf/0
800a5fd2ab18d2aec2256d220029ac8c?OpenDocument

151. **Zeal.com - Sports AZ**

Alldesi - Kabaddi | http://www.alldesi.net/fun/sports/kabaddi.htm Features rules of Kabaddi, its brief history, federations, and pictures. ...
www.zeal.com/category/preview.jhtml?cid=10091957

152. **DirZilla - Powered by the Open Directory Project**
ODP: Sports: Kabbadi: Kabaddi - A short description of how Kabaddi is played. Kabaddi - Descriptions of the various forms of kabbadi. ...
dirzilla.com/ODP/Sports/Kabbadi

153. **Kabaddi has bright future, say stars**
Kabaddi has bright future, say stars Ajai Masand New Delhi, October 11 They have always played the humble sport of kabaddi and humility is their virtue. ...
www.hindustantimes.com/news/5830_82647,00340007.htm

154. **Kabbadi**
Intro ... how to play Kabaddi, includes game schedule with results ... Kabaddi.ca - Information on Canadian tournaments ... related links. Kabaddi ...
www.topiasearch.com/topia/Kabbadi

155. **Sports News The Kathmandu Post (Nepal)**
No good omen for kabaddi team as SAF Games near. By Somesh Verma. ... No Kabaddi tournament has been held in the country after the 4th National Games, two years ago.
www.nepalnews.com.np/contents/englishdaily/ktmpost/2001 aug/aug23/sports.htm

156. **Taksvärkki 2002**
Den bangladeshiska nationalsporten är kabaddi. ... I kabaddi tävlar vå lag om poäng genom att beröra eller ta fast spelare i motståndarlaget. ...
www.taksvarkki.fi/bangladesh/ruotsi/ru312.html

157. **Millennibrum Video Shorts**
Munier a Kabaddi coach in Birmingham talks about the game, its history, rules and its future. ...
www.millennibrum.org/videoshort/videoshort_02.html

158. **The Probert Encyclopaedia - Sport (AM)**
Kabaddi is a traditional team pursuit game played in India and requiring players to run and hold their breath for a long time. ...
www.fas.org/news/reference/probert/O1.HTM

159. **CMU Libraries — Stump the Librarian**
Kabaddi is an ancient Indian game and its origin and founder are not known. ... The Amateur Kabaddi Federation of India (AKFI) was founded in 1973. ...
www.lib.cmich.edu/libraryweek/answers.htm

160. **Sports**

Football (boys). Kabaddi(boys&Girls). Kho-Kho(Boys & Girls). ... f) Mini Games & Sports . Kabaddi (boys & girls under 14). Athletics (boys & girls under 14). ...

dhenkanal.nic.in/SchoolSports.HTM

161. **Newsletter July 2002**

Kabaddi, Soccer and Volleyball teams' tournament will start early due to a packed schedule of juniors, adults and women's teams.

www.pcschicago.org/news/letter/july2002.htm

162. **Kabbadi Alternative Sports Sports Leisure UK**

Mirago : Sports: Kabbadi Search for ... Brief Intro about Kabaddi - A teaching site how to play Kabaddi, includes game schedule with results. ...

www.v8go.co.uk/leisure/sports/alternative-sports/kabbadi.asp

163. **Khoj - Directory for Kabbadi**

Websites Kabaddi A site that explains how the game is played, different types of the game and much more. Kabaddi Kabaddi is a team sport. ...

www.khoj.com/Sports_and_Games/Sports/Kabbadi/

164. **Global Citizens News Vol.59**

He introduced his own country, the language and then a game called "kabaddi". ... Mr.Milan then introduced them to "kabaddi". Kabaddi ...

www1.city.nagasaki.nagasaki.jp/kokusai/gcnews/200308 index_e.html

165. **1 - Number One News Resource of Pakistan Jang Group**

Pakistan meet India in crunch kabaddi encounter. ... One of the three matches on Monday, the last day of the kabaddi competition, is between Japan and Malaysia.

www.jang.com.pk/thenews/oct2002-daily/07-10-2002/sports/ s14.htm

166. **Sports Round-Up**

The team from Central Zone won the championship. North Zone Kabaddi Tournament. The Instruments ... DRDO Central Zone Kabaddi Tournament. The Proof ...

www.drdo.org/pub/nl/june2002/sports.htm

167. **Indbazaar Sports**

India Golf Watch Sports Club Your Golf Guru Bharatiya Hockey Hockey Indian Hockey Indian Polo Polo Clubs in India, Chess Mate History of Kabaddi Kabaddi Rules ...

www.indbazaar.com/services/sports/index.asp

168. **HOINA: Dan Fuchs**

Back to Top. Story. Kabaddi- Sport Unites. During our stay at the boys? home in Bapatla, our group had the privilege of learning the game of kabaddi. ...

web.shc.psu.edu/~hoina/fuchs.htm

35
Korfball

1. **Korfball.com - Korfball's home on the web**
   Information about the game internationally and world championships.
   www.korfball.com/
2. **International Korfball Federation Site**
   Official site with results, rules, addresses, clubs, photos, news, information, and links.
   www.ikf.org/
3. **KorfballNet - the number one Korfball news site from AFM Sports**
   Korfball news. Contact us. Crucial NL clash this weekend Full round up | Premier fixtures, Fortuna win Korfball challenge final Full details | Final results. Includes results for leagues in Great Britain, Netherlands, Belgium, the Czech Republic and Catalonia.
   www.btinternet.com/~afm.sports/
4. **Korfball World - International korfball resource**
   Korfball international resource site, giving news, information and background about this challenging, fast paced, mixed team sport. Includes a chat room, news and photos from around the world, message boards and links to global Korfball...
   www.korfballworld.com/
5. **The British Korfball Association**
   The British Korfball Association, Korfball the fast and exciting mixed team sport. The BKA Website has moved. Click here to go to korfball.co.uk.
   www.british-korfball.org.uk/bka.htm
6. **Korfball New Zealand**
   News, contacts, equipment, links and photos for korfball as it is happening in New Zealand.
   www.korfball.org.nz/

7. **WebRing: hub**

   University Of Wales Korfball club Official homepage of Cardiff University Korfball club. Includes information about Korfball, photos ...

   f.webring.com/hub?ring=korfball

8. **Cambridgeshire Korfball Association**

   Information about Korfball in Cambridgeshire, including news, fixtures and results

   www.cambskorfball.co.uk/

9. **iSportsDigest.com/Basketball**

   KORFBALL - GENERAL, British Korfball Association; British Korfball Association Competitions; British Student Korfball Association; ... Visit Korfball Ring home. ...

   isportsdigest.tripod.com/korfball/main.html

10. **Kent Korfball Association**

    Kent Korfball Association, KKA, playing Korfball the mixed team sport and associated social activities. Includes news, events, contact information, competitions, referees, rules and related links. www.kentkorfball.co.uk/

11. **Korfball Victoria**

    Hosted By VICNET. Information about Korfball in Victoria and Bacchus-Marsh/Melton, Australia, including news, fixtures,...

    home.vicnet.net.au/~korfball/

12. **British Korfball Association**

    The British Korfball Association, governing body of Korfball in Great Britain

    www.korfball.co.uk/

13. **The Scottish Korfball Homepage**

    scottish-korfball.org.uk Your browser does not support frames. To ... SKAwebpage. For more information contact webmaster@scottish-korfball.org.uk.

    www.scottish-korfball.org.uk/

14. **! Korfball Die einzige gemischte Mannschaftssportart der Welt World > Deutsch > Sport > Ballsport > Korfball**

    www.korfball.de/

15. **Croydon Korfball Club**

    Includes news, photographs, match reports, and statistics.
    www.croydonkorfball.com/

16. **Woking Korfball Club**

    Information, fixtures, maps, photographs, and links. Members of the London league based in Surrey.

    www.korfball.com/woking/

17. **The University of Bristol Korfball Club**

    Includes news, club information, fixtures, photos, and alumni.

    www.bris.ac.uk/Depts/Union/Korfball/

18. **LANCASTER UNIVERSITY KORFBALL CLUB**

    Site contains information on the sport, a diary, a reports page and the training schedule, information...

    www.lancs.ac.uk/socs/lukc/

19. **Tottenham Korfball Club**

    Features reports, results, player statistics, photos, related links, and general information about...

    www.tottenhamkc.ndirect.co.uk/

20. **Oxford University Korfball Club - Welcome to OUKoC!**

    All about Oxford University Korfball Club, including fixtures and results.

    users.ox.ac.uk/~korfball/

21. **Cardiff University Korfball**

    The homepage of the University of Wales Cardiff Korfbal Features history, results, player profiles, related links, and games including drinking games and...

    www.cf.ac.uk/suon/korfball/

22. **Dragons korfball club**

    General information, events, training details, fixtures, results and a photo gallery.

    www.nukorfball.org.uk/

23. **Pelham Korfball Club Index**

    Club info, fixtures, results, related links and contact details.

    website.lineone.net/~pelhamkc/

24. **Korfball Australia website**

    PO Box 498 Blackwood SA 5051 Email:info@korfballaustralia.com.au.

    korfballaustralia.com.au/

25. **KorFeD.co.uk - Korfball Coaching:.**

    Includes player information, teams, calendar, tournaments, photos, and related links. Also features...

    www.nottingham.freewebspace.com/

26. **Stingers Korfball Club**

This website should hopefully show you everything you ever wanted to know about Stingers Korfball Club. Upcoming events, league information, a picture gallery, news items and training details.

www.stingers.co.uk/

27. **UEA Korfball**

Info about the club, committee and korfball.

www.uea.ac.uk/~gs644/

28. **Oxford City Korfball Club Home Page**

Information, diary, directions, results, statistics, match reports, players, and photographs. England.

www.oxfordcitykorfballclub.co.uk/

29. **Abingdon Korfball Club**

Features club information including an event calendar, results, match reports, photo gallery and related...

www.abingdonkorfball.co.uk/

30. **Yahoo! Directory Sports > Korfball**

Sports > Korfball Directory > Recreation > Sports > Korfball, Search the Web just this category. ... Korfball on eBay Find korfball items at low prices. ...

dir.yahoo.com/Recreation/Sports/Korfball/

31. **St. Andrews Korfball Club**

St Andrews Korfball Club website. Recent News. 1st/2nd March : 10th in the Student Nationals. 25th/26th January : 12th in Edinburgh Tournament. ...

www.st-and.ac.uk/~korfball/

32. **SUKC**

Club info, news, photos and fixtures.

www.shef.ac.uk/korfball/

33. **Open Directory - Sports: Korfball**

British Korfball Association - Includes description of korfball, competitions, rules and regulations, bulletins, notice board, and related links. ...

dmoz.org/Sports/Korfball/

34. **Kwiek Korfball Club**

Based in Rochester, Kent. Events, news and results for Kwiek Korfball Club. Also includes links to...

www.kwiek.co.uk/

35. **North Downs Korfball Club**

North Downs Korfball Club website. If you have any comments about the site, additions you'd like to see on it etc ...
www.geocities.com/ndkcuk/

36. **main**

Information on the club and the sport in general. Includes fixtures, results and some photos.
www.cam.ac.uk/societies/korfball/

37. **Edinburgh University Korfball Club**

Home of the Infamous Millennium Calendar.
homepages.ed.ac.uk/korfball/

38. **The Official UNU Korfball Web Site**

The official korfball site from Nottingham University bringing you the MaD SkillZ of Korfball to your screens.
www.students-union.nottingham.ac.uk/~korf/

39. **Lancaster University Korfball Club**

LANCASTER UNIVERSITY KORFBALL CLUB. SO WHAT IS KORFBALL? Korfball ... wins. History of Korfball. Korfball Terminology. Official Rules of Korfball.
www.lancs.ac.uk/socs/lukc/korfballexpl.htm

40. **ANTiHACKeRLiNK**

News items, upcoming events, contact information, a newsletter and related links.
www.nckc.co.uk/

41. **Edinburgh University Korfball Club**

Edinburgh University Korfball Club. President Vanessa Humphrey Secretary Laura Wilson Treasurer Nick Jellema. Contact The Club...
www.eusu.ed.ac.uk/clubs/korfball/korfball/

42. **Korfball im TV Ensen-Westhoven 07**

World > Deutsch > Sport > Ballsport > Korfball
www.tv-ensen-westhoven.de/NeueSeiten/ frame_korfball.html

43. **SuperNova Korfball Club**

The Only Mixed Team Sport. SuperNova Korfball Club was formed in 1996, and fields teams in the National League and the LDKA London league. ...
www.supernova.org.uk/

44. **What is Korfball**
British Korfball Association. What is KORFBALL????? ... Playing Korfball. Action consists almost entirely of passing the ball by hand from person to person. ...
www.british-korfball.org.uk/whatiskorfball.htm

45. **Korfball**
Home of South Australian Korfball on the web. If you're here to find out about Korfball, this is the place to be. ...
www.korfballsa.asn.au/

46. **Worldchampionship korfball 2003**
www.wkkorfbal.nl/index_e.html

47. **Google Directory - Sports > Korfball**
Korfball, ... Korfball New Zealand - http://www.korfball.org.nz/ News, contacts, equipment, links and photos for korfball as it is happening in New Zealand. ...
directory.google.com/Top/Sports/Korfball/

48. **International World Games Association : Korfball**
Korfball - 1 of 30+ sports of The World Games! Korfball. Korfball is ... sports. But in that respect too, korfball is truly unique. Devised ...
www.worldgames-iwga.org/vsite/vcontent/page/custom/0,8510,1044-127188-128495-18064-62415-custom-item,00.html

49. **CASTLE KORFBALL CLUB**
Castle Korfball's web site. We ...
www.keele.ac.uk/depts/as/korfball/korfball.htm

50. **What Is Korfball**
What Is Korfball? Korfball is a mixed team sport, that combines the best of basketball and netball. ... This doesn't have much to do with Korfball realy: ...
www.cf.ac.uk/suon/korfball/rules/whatis.html

51. **Cambridge Kites Korfball Club: Korfball FAQ**
Korfball FAQ. The material on this page is not unique to this site History of korfball. 1903: Foundation of Dutch Korfball Association.
www.cambridgekites.co.uk/faq.html

52. **University Of Bristol Korfball Club**
Welcome to the University of Bristol Korfball Club. The club's website is currently undergoing a heavy session of plastic surgery
www.korf.pwp.blueyonder.co.uk/

53. **So what exactly is Korfball ?**

So what exactly is Korfball ? Korfball is the exciting mixed teamsport that is increasing in popularity throughout the world. ... Not so in Korfball. ...

www.btinternet.com/~afm.sports/ korfball/whatiskorfball.htm

54. **Reviews for Korfball**

Korfball Reviews. ... Book reviews for "Korfball" sorted by average review score: The Glory of Their Times: The Story of the Early Days

www.booksunderreview.com/Sports/Korfball/

55. **Oxford University Korfball Club**

Oxford University Korfball Club, ... Quick Guide to Korfball. ... We will also be sending a team to the International Student Korfball Tournament in Groningen in March. ...

users.ox.ac.uk/~korfball/whatthe.html

56. **Korfball**

IAS group, UvA Web. UvA | Fac. Science | IAS | Jelle Kok | Sport Results | Korfball, 3 hits in December 2003. Publications. RoboCup. ... Snooker. Soccer. Tennis. Korfball. ...

carol.wins.uva.nl/~jellekok/sports/ korfball/index_en.html

57. **NDKC - About Korfball**

About Korfball Korfball, invented in 1901 by an Amsterdam schoolmaster Nico Broekhuysen, is a game comparable to netball and basketball with one major ...

ndkcuk.tripod.com/aboutkb.htm

58. **Korfball Movie Reviews**

Korfball Movie Reviews. ... Family movie reviews for "Korfball" sorted by average review score: On Any Sunday. Released in DVD by Monterey ...

www.family-movie-review.com/Sports/Korfball/

59. **Korfball site KCC Sokol Ceske Budejovice**

Information about our korfball club in three languages, results, programme, photos and more.... ... Korfball site KCC Sokol Ceske Budejovice. ...

go.to/korfballCB

60. **VL of Sport - Korfball**

Korfball is a mixed team sport, that combines the best of basketball and netball. ... More from The Cardiff University Korfball Club. The Game. ...

sportsvl.com/ball/korfball.htm

61. **Korfball Club - korfball, europe, uk, england, britain, club ...**
Korfball Club. The ultimate web resource for Korfball clubs in Europe. Team biographies and information on techniques, Match schedules, Submit Your Site! ...
www.beckc.com/

62. **Sport Clubs**
Home: Sport Clubs: Korfball. Korfball. Training Times: Mondays: 19:00 Thursdays: 19:00. Venue: Groenkloof Campus outside courts. Sport Manager:
www.up.ac.za/sport/sportclubs/korfball/

63. **Korfball - Intro**
Korfball, da game. Its not barfball, thats certain. This is a website about Korfball ... gaining new admirers by the hour! Korfball history.
members.fortunecity.com/korfball/

64. **Hambleton District Council - Korfball**
Sports Clubs - Korfball British Korfball Association Mr Chris Neasham 39 Wheeldale Close Darlington DL1 2TL Click here to return to Sports Club Listings Launch ...
www.hambleton.gov.uk/.../
sportsclubskorfball.html?OpenDocument&Start=1&Count=1000&ExpandView

65. **Korfball Community > Game > Training & Coaching**
Korfball Community The place for korfball fanatics around the world to meet,» back to Korfball World. ... Korfball Community Training & Coaching. ...
www.korfballworld.com/cgi-bin/ ikonboard/forums.cgi?forum=3

36
Marathon

1. **Boston Athletic Association**
   Past marathon results and champions, photo gallery, qualifying times, application, information about...
   www.bostonmarathon.org/
2. **Marathon Oil Corporation**
   Integrated company including transportation, refining and product sales. Includes product and service...
   www.marathon.com/
3. **The Official Flora London Marathon Website**
   Official site for the Flora London Marathon, which is an annual festivity showcasing the world's premiere distance runners and state of the art technology. History of the event, charity details, merchandise, past results, news articles, registration and...
   www.london-marathon.co.uk/
4. **The LaSalle Bank Chicago Marathon**
   Chicago, marathon, marahton, Pinkowski, Carey, Nishi, LaSalle Marathon, chicago marathon, The LaSalle Bank, LaSalle, LaSalle Banks, The LaSalle Bank Chicago ...
   www.chicagomarathon.com/
5. **ING New York City Marathon**
   New York City Marathon, New York Marathon, NYC Marathon, NY Marathon, New York Road Runners Club, New York.
   www.nycmarathon.org/
6. **The Honolulu Marathon**
   Official Website of the Honolulu Marathon
   www.honolulumarathon.org/
7. **LA1**
   Results, photos, articles, archives, training, and FAQ. Online registration for marathon, bike tour,...
   www.lamarathon.com/

8. **MarathonGuide.com - Marathons, Running Directory and Community**
MarathonGuide.com - the complete marathon resource and community. Complete marathon race directory, results, athlete and race news, results, history, training schedules,...
www.marathonguide.com/

9. **Portland Marathon**
The Portland Marathon and related events History of the event, contacts, registration, exposition events, results, lodging details and results.
www.portlandmarathon.org/

10. **New York Road Runners**
The official web site of the world's largest marathon. Contest and hotel information. Course map,...
www.nyrrc.org/

11. **Site officiel du Marathon de Paris 2004**
English Version. **World > Français > ... > Sports > Course à pied**
www.parismarathon.com/

12. **Marathon-Veranstaltungen in Deutschland**
World > Deutsch > Sport > Laufen > Marathon > Veranstaltungen
www.marathon.de/

13. **Citizens Bank Philadelphia Marathon**
Description: Results, photo gallery, application, information and course maps, accommodations and FAQs.
www.philadelphiamarathon.com/

14. **OLYMPUS MARATHON HAMBURG**
World > Deutsch > Sport > Laufen > Marathon > Veranstaltungen
www.marathon-hamburg.de/

15. **Marathon and Beyond — The web site for marathoners and ultrarunners**
Published six times a year - website contains tables of content, sneak previews and ordering information.
www.marathonandbeyond.com/

16. **Twin Cities Marathon - Index**
Registration, organization, results, special events, sponsors and a message board.
www.twincitiesmarathon.org/

17. **ING Amsterdam Marathon**
World > Nederlands > Sport > Atletiek > Weg > Marathon
www.amsterdammarathon.nl/

18. **Grandma's Marathon**
News/Updates. Registration Information. Results. Women's National Half Marathon Championships. Located in Duluth with information about the race, videos and photos, results, entry form, history.
www.grandmasmarathon.com/

19. **HP Houston Marathon**
Greek Trip Awards. Marathon Registration. Travel Info. ... the HP Houston Marathon invites you to be a part of Houston's largest single-day sporting event. ...
www.hphoustonmarathon.com/

20. **San Diego Marathon - Index**
Race information, event schedule, course, entry form, training and results.
www.sdmarathon.com/

21. **AIDS Marathon**
1,700 AIDS Marathoners completed the Honolulu Marathon on Dec 8 raising $6 million for the fight to end AIDS. Click here to view a webcast of the event. ...
www.aidsmarathon.com,/

22. **Columbia Marathon Association- HOME**
A non-profit volunteer organization committed to providing exceptional running and walking events.
www.carolinamarathon.org/

23. **2004 Nokia Sugar Bowl Mardi Gras Marathon**
2004 Nokia Sugar Bowl Mardi Gras Marathon. 7:00AM Sunday, February 29, 2004 New Orleans, Louisiana. Marathon, Hal Marathon, and 5K. Located in New Orleans with event description, course map, merchandise, past results and contacts.
www.mardigrasmarathon.com/

37
Olympics

1. **The Official Website of the Olympic Movement**
   WWW.OLYMPIC.ORG ...
   www.olympic.org/
2. **Special Olympics Public Website**
   An international program of year-round sports training and athletic competition for more than one...
   www.specialolympics.org/
3. **Salt Lake 2002 - Official Site of the Olympics 2002**
   Official site of the 2002 Winter Olympics in Salt Lake City, Utah. Includes current news, pictures and highlights, competition results ...
   www.saltlake2002.com/
4. **Perseus FAQ**
   The Perseus WWW Frequently Asked Questions List. This list is a summary of the most frequently asked questions received by the Perseus webmaster. ...
   www.perseus.tufts.edu/Help/faq.html
5. **Perseus Update in Progress**
   The Perseus Digital Library is Being Updated. Notice. The main Perseus web site (at Tufts) is unavailable from 5:00 to 7:00, US Eastern ...
   www.perseus.tufts.edu/cgi-bin/papybrowse
6. **ATHENS 2004 Olympics**
   The official website of the ATHENS 2004 Olympic and Paralympic Games, ...
   www.2004.gr/

7. **Ancient Olympics @ University of Pennsylvania Museum of ...**
For more information regarding the Ancient Olympics, check out these sites outside the Museum (will open in a new browser window): Were the ancient games better than ours? More fair and square? More about sports and less about money?...
www.upenn.edu/museum/Olympics/olympicintro.html

8. **Olympics Through Time**
Historical profile from prehistory through revival. Contains glossary, links and a comprehensive bibliogr...
www.fhw.gr/projects/olympics/

9. **British Olympic Association**
Official site with updated team news and other information with related links.
www.olympics.org.uk/

10. **Special Olympics**
What is Special Olympics Special Olympics is a yeaı round sports training and competition programme for children and adults with a learning/intellectual ...
www.2003specialolympics.com/

11. **Index of /~tpayne/lingolym**
An educational problem-solving site where students compete by solving puzzles based on real languages...
www.uoregon.edu/~tpayne/lingolym/

12. **Australian Olympic Committee**
Playing in the big time motivates Baseball team. Two key factors have boosted Australia's chances in Baseball at the Athens Olympics.
www.olympics.com.au/

13. **Utah Education Network: 2002 Olympics Education**
Learn about Olympic and Paralympic sporting events, participating countries, the torch relay, and...
www.uen.org/2002/

14. **Special Olympics Canada - Home**
Canadian Special Olympics - providing sports training and competition for people with a mental disability. A national not for-profit grassroots organization that provides sport training and competition opportunit...
slam.canoe.ca/CanadianSpecialOlympics/home.html

15. **Special Olympics Massachusetts**

    Special Olympics Massachusetts Night at the Boston Celtics on Friday, December 19th! Click here for more information. SOMA provides year-round sports training and athletic competition in a variety of well-coached Olympic-ty...

    www.specialolympicsma.org/

16. **CNNSI.com - Olympic Sports**

    Olympics organizers want to forget about scandals and court cases and start having fun. ...

    www.cnnsi.com/olympics/

17. **CNNSI.com - 2002 Winter Olympics**

    CNNMoney.com Olympics Inc: The Bottom Line. ... CNNSI.com's Leigh Montville: Give it away now North America has seen enough of the Olympics. Latest news, athlete biographies, and features by CNN/SI columnists.

    www.cnnsi.com/olympics/2002/

18. **Science & the Olympics**

    Sport science meets the Olympics 1996 marks the Centennial of the modern Olympics. ... Imagine an Olympics without that newfangled stuff. ...

    whyfiles.org/019olympic/

19. **Gateway Computers - Olympic Sponsorship**

    Following the Games, Gateway donated more than 4,000 of the systems used to power the Olympics to nonprofit organizations across the United States. ...

    www.gateway.com/olympics/donations.shtml

20. **Special Olympics Northern California**

    Information on Special Olympics and the activities at the Chapter (state) level.

    www.sonc.org/

21. **Wisconsin Special Olympics**

    The Special Olympics has been a source of pride to participants and an inspiration to supporters for millions of individuals with cognitive disabilites. Providing year-round sports training and athletic competition in a variety of Olympic-type sports...

    www.wiso.org/

22. **ESPN.com - Olympics**

Games. Phelps' weighty problem Michael Phelps' biggest problem on his path to the Athens Olympics is keeping the pounds on. Hollobaugh ...

espn.go.com/oly/

23. **2003 Special Olympics**

The Official Website of the 2003 Special Olympics World Games, Ireland. This ... Special Olympics World Summer Games 2003. ...

www.2003specialolympics.com/en/default1.asp

24. **audi olympics**

Audi olympics. 'funny, and not a little bit strange' - the guardian; 'an offbeat treat' - web user. Tuesday, December 30, 2003. A daily journal of life as a copywriter, editor, corporate commentator and tennis player

audiolympics.blogspot.com/

25. **Especial Bruno Bozzetto**

"Olympics". Especial Bruno Bozzetto. Europe and Italy; Yes & No; Adam. xeron.org.

www.infonegocio.com/xeron/bruno/olympics.html

26. **Special Olympics Missouri**

Special Olympics, Get Into It! Be A Part of the Team! Shop & Support Special Olympics, Official site. Year-round athletics helping children and adults with developmental disabilities.

www.somo.org/

27. **ATHENS 2004 - Welcome to the Official Site**

www.athens.olympics.org/en/

28. **The Salt Lake Tribune - 2002 Winter Olympic Games**

The 2002 Winter Games should produce lasting benefits for the economy, but it is too early to speculate on just how far-reaching the Olympics' financial ripple Ongoing coverage including news, commentary and events.

www.sltrib2002.com/

29. **The Olympic Games in the Ancient Hellenic World: A Virtual Museum**

New site collecting thoughts and concerns about the modern Olympic Games, and would value your input. The Ancient Olympic Games Virtual Museum with a plethora of information about the games that are the...

minbar.cs.dartmouth.edu/greecom/olympics/

30. **Special Olympics VA -Home Page**

Virginia Beach's Corprew named SOVA Athlete of the Year Special Olympics Virginia announce top awards at Fall Championships Special ...

www.specialolympicsva.com/

31. **Special Olympics Illinois**

Special Olympics Illinois "Let me win. ... Find out how you can get involved in the Special Olympics Illinois Tribute Park! Breaking News: Providing year-round sports training and athletic competition in a variety of Olympic-type sports...

www.ilso.org/

32. **Olympics**

Olympic sportsSports Olympics. Salt Lake City: 2002 Winter Olympics. A complete review ... events. Nagano: 1998 Winter Olympics. A complete ...

www.infoplease.com/cgi-bin/id/A0114094.html

33. **Women in the Olympics**

Feminist Majority's Women in the Olympics section commemorating 96 years of womens participation in the Olympic games. This section...

www.feminist.org/fmf/graphics/intro.html

34. **Special Olympics Maryland - Inspire Greatness**

Special Olympics Maryland, Provides year-round sports training and athletic competition in a variety of Olympic-type sports for...

www.somd.org/

35. **Olympics 2000**

We've Redesigned Infoplease.com. To view Infoplease.com properly you'll need to upgrade to a standards-compliant web browser. Home: Infoplease.com, ...

www.infoplease.com/00olympics1.html

36. **Winter Olympics: Sport and Science**

The enormous appeal of the Winter Olympic Games creates several teachable moments for showing how science illuminates human activity. ...

btc.montana.edu/olympics/

37. **Special Olympics Southern California**

Worth magazine cover, December/January 2003 issue. For the second consecutive year Special Olympics was named by Worth magazine as one of the 100 Best Charities ...

www.sosc.org/

38. **donate**

Special Olympics Oregon is a year-round program offering 14 different Olympic-style sports to athletes with mental retardation....

www.soor.org/

39. **ABC Online News - Latest Olympics News Bulletin**

Association warns Olympics may hurt self-esteem The Sydney Olympics could be contributing to falling self-esteem among people at risk of eating or exercise ...

www.abc.net.au/news/olympics/

40. **Special Olympics Indiana Home Page**

New Year's Day Dip on the Agenda? The year 2004 will start with a Polar Bear Plunge in Muncie to raise money for Special Olympics Indiana. ...

www.specialolympicsindiana.org/

41. **Special Olympics Michigan**

A year-round program of sports training and competition for individuals with mental retardation.

www.somi.org/

42. **Special Olympics Connecticut!**

Special Olympics Connecticut (SOCT) is a non-profit, charitable organization which contributes to the lifelong physical, social and personal development of ...

www.soct.org/

43. **sunspot.net | olympics**

A skater speeds toward Olympics Speed skating: A win in the 1,500 meters at the US Long Track Olympic Trials gives Dulaney grad JP Shilling a spot ...

www.sunspot.net/sports/olympics/

44. **allAfrica.com: Olympics**

Africans Get The Last Word. Gezahagne Abera of Ethiopia crosses the finish line to claim gold in the final event of the Olympics - the men's marathon. ...

allafrica.com/olympics/

45. **Michigan Senior Olympics**

Michigan Senior Olympics promotes healthy lifestyles by organizing state games, sports competitions, and health, fitness, and wellness programs for active ...

michigansenniorolympics.com/

46. **Special Olympics Colorado**

For the Love of the Game, For the Love of the Athletes...Show your love for Special Olympics Colorado's athletes at the 2004 Hall of Fame Gala, January 24 at ...

www.specialolympicsco.org/

47. **Special Olympics Italia**

World > Italiano > Sport > Disabili

www.specialolympics.it/

48. **Special Olympics Italia**

World > Italiano > Sport > Disabili

www.specialolympics.it/

49. **Special Olympics Minnesota**

Special Olympics Minnesota proudly announces that Matt Blair, former All-Pro of the Minnesota Vikings, having earned six consecutive Pro Bowl appearances, has ...

www.somn.org/

50. **Special Olympics of North Carolina**

Special Olympics North Carolina provides year-round sports training and competition for more than 32,000 children and adults with mental retardation in nearly www.sonc.net/

51. **Special Olympics New Hampshire!**

Special Olympics NH, Welcome to Special Olympics New Hampshire Special Olympics New Hampshire (SONH) is a non profit organization providing sports training and ...

www.sonh.org/

52. **Olympics - EnchantedLearning.com**

Olympics: Salt Lake City, Utah, USA, is where the year 2002 Winter Olympics were held. ... Olympics-Related Printouts and Activities: www.enchantedlearning.com/olympics/

53. **Michigan Senior Olympics**

Michigan Senior Olympics promotes healthy lifestyles by organizing state games, sports competitions, and health, fitness, and wellness programs for active ...

michiganseniorolympics.com/

54. **Special Olympics Alaska**

Special Olympics Alaska provides year-round sports training and athletic competition in a variety of Olympic-type sports for people eight years of age and ...

www.specialolympicsalaska.org/

55. **SOWA**

SOWA provides a year-round program of sports training and competition for children and adults with...

www.sowa.org/

56. **BBC SPORT | Winter Olympics 2002 | Front Page**

A firework display over the Olympic flame Games end under a cloud More doping offences overshadow the 2002 Winter Olympics closing ceremony in ...

news.bbc.co.uk/winterolympics2002/default.stm

57. **Special Olympics Georgia**

Special Olympics Night at the Atlanta Hawks! ... 2003 World Games. Mission of Special Olympics Georgia....

www.specialolympicsga.org/

58. **Unusual Sports in the Olympics**

What sport do you think should be added to the next Olympics? Enter your vote by clicking here! Sports | Athletes | Links | Activities library.thinkquest.org/J002862/

59. **Special Olympics Kentucky Home Page**

Provides year-round training and athletic competition for individuals with mental retardation.

www.soky.org/

60. **Special Olympics**

New Website Special Olympics New York has created a new website to better serve our volunteers, athletes, families, and sponsors. ...

www.nyso.org/

61. **Special Olympics Ohio Home**

The mission of Special Olympics Ohio is to provide year-round sports training and athletic competition in a variety of Olympic type sports for children and ...

www.ohiospoly.org/

62. **Special Olympics Iowa Front Page**

SPECIAL OLYMPICS IOWA BREAKS GROUND ON THE RICHARD O. JACOBSON SPECIAL OLYMPICS IOWA HEADQUARTERS AND TRAINING CENTER. Provides year-round sports training and competition for children and adults with mental retardation.

www.soiowa.org/

63. **The Olympics**

THE OLYMPICS. ... World War I and World War II forced cancellation of the Olympics in 1916, 1940, and 1944, but they resumed in 1948 and are held every 4 years. ...

www.umkc.edu/imc/olympics.htm

64. **Special Olympics Manitoba**

Special Olympics Manitoba (SOM) is the provincial sport governing body responsiblefor the delivery of sport for people with a mental disability in the ...

www.specialolympics.mb.ca/

65. **SPECIAL OLYMPICS SLOVAKIA**

Regional_>_Europe_>_Slovakia_>_Recreation_and_Sports

www.shso.sk/

66. **Special Olympics Texas (SOTX)**

Special Olympics Texas Is A Privately-funded Non-profit ThatProvides Year Round Sports Training And Competitions For Children And Adults With Mental ...

www.sotx.org/

67. **ACT-SO**

ACT-SO. ACT-SO Participants at the annual conference. Today's Youth....Tomorrow's Legend. 4805 Mt. Hope Drive Baltimore, MD 21215 ...

www.naacp.org/work/actso/act-so.shtml

68. **Special Olympics Oklahoma**

Special Olympics Oklahoma. ... 8th Annual Special Olympics Oklahoma 2004 Winter Games. January 16-18, 2004 Norman, Oklahoma. ...

www.sook.org/

69. **Special Olympics _ Kansas**

Year-round athletics helping children and adults with developmental disabilities.

www.ksso.org/

70. **New Mexico Senior Olympics**

Information on their annual state games and events held throughout the year. Includes a quarterly...

www.nmseniorolympics.org/

71. **Special Olympics Delaware — www.sode.org**

Special Olympics Delaware, SPECIAL OLYMPICS DELAWARE ... 2002 Special Olympics Delaware 619 South College Avenue Newark, DE 19716-1901 302-831-4653 sode@sode.org.

www.sode.org/

72. **MENU**

Special Olympics Louisiana. Site provides history of organization, a calendar and descriptions of events, fund raising activities...

www.laso.org/

73. **Special Olympics Arizona**

Special Olympics Arizona. ... For the second consecutive year Special Olympics was named by Worth magazine as one of the 100 Best Charities in America. ...

www.specialolympicsarizona.org/

74. **"Faces of the Olympics" Collaborative Project**

A collaborative Internet project enabling submission of Olympic reports by anyone involved.

www.mtpleasps.vic.edu.au/olympics

75. **Olympics!**

Cartoons about Olympics, and bribery scandals.

cagle.slate.msn.com/olympics/

76. **Special Olympics New Jersey**

Special Olympics New Jersey is a non-profit organization that provides athleti training and competition for children and adults with mental retardation. ...

www.sonj.org/

77. **Special Olympics Pennsylvania**

The 2003 Special Olympics World Summer Games, took place from June 20- 29 in Dublin, Ireland, and was the largest sporting event in the world this year. ...

www.specialolympicspa.org/

78. **Winter Olympics Worksheets and Puzzles**

Winter Olympics Critical Thinking Logic Worksheets Bobsled Competition Figure Skating Gold Medals Medal Totals Winter Olympic Events Olympics: Countries Word ...

www.edhelper.com/olympics.htm

79. **Winter Olympics 2002: Ready Reference Resources**
Compilation of links to Winter Olympics coverage includes team member biographies, statistics, and...
www.freepint.com/gary/olympicreference.html

80. **Special Olympics Nederland**
World > Nederlands > Sport > Olympische Spelen
www.specialolympics.nl/

81. **British Columbia Special Olympics : sports : olympics : special...**
British Columbia Special Olympics is a non-profit sport organization for individuals with a mental disability. Special ...
www.bcso.bc.ca/

82. **Nutrition Science & the Winter Olympics**
Nutrition Science & the Olympics. ... One of these sports, women's ice hockey, has its debut as a medal sport in the 1998 Winter Olympics! ...
btc.montana.edu/olympics/nutrition/default.htm

83. **Special Olympics Hawaii**
Providing year-round sports training and athletic competition in a variety of Olympic-type sports...
www.specialolympicshawaii.org/

84. **Australian Olympics, 2000**
Meet Olympic mascots Millie, Olly, and Syd as they help provide kids with some facts on the history...
www.gigglepotz.com/ausolympics.htm

85. **Anti-Olypmic Alliance**
For every positive optimistic person there has to be someone who doesn't agree.
www.cat.org.au/aoa/

86. **Youths Urged To Join Miniolympics (from Staines Guardian)**
Youths urged to join mini-Olympics. By Emily Manson. A SPORTS event that is bigger than the Olympics is about to ...
www.stainesguardian.co.uk/news/olympics/
display.var.298051.0.youths_urged_to_join_miniolympics.php

87. **TAMU_CBC**
Mini Olympics, 1, MSN Nickname Yu_Tao, 10/18/2003 4:26 AM. ... play game this Friday and miniOlympics, 1, MSN Nickname Yu_Tao, 10/8/2003 7:03 PM. ...
groups.msn.com/TAMUCBC/messages.msnw

88. **SC Shack - Mini Olympics**
http:/schools.tdsb.on.ca/riverdale/events/miniolympics miniolympics.html. ...
schools.tdsb.on.ca/riverdale/sc/miniolympics.html

89. **miniolymp1**
Miniolympics: Fördern Sie doch wieder einmal den Spieltrieb! Ob Sommer oder Winter, ob Fun Games oder trickreiche Spiele, wir bringen ...
www.funtimepark.ch/miniolymp1.htm

90. **Dolomiti.org - Services - Dynamic Tour Travel Agency**
MINIOLYMPICS This is the funniest activity to be organised for a group. It consists of a race, of individual people or teams, in various sports. ...
www.dolomiti.org/dengl/Cortina/ cser/dynamictour/groups.html

91. **Jaworski at the ARCSO Mini-Olympics**
Mikee Cojuangco-Jaworski highlighted the 2nd Mindanao State University-Association of Registered Campus Student Organization (MSU-ARCSO) Miniolympics held on...
www.msumain.edu.ph/news/2002/dec/week3-1.html

92. **News :: News Article**
City of Port Adelaide Enfield Community Development Department. Files for Download. MiniOlympics planned for young athletes - 0Kb. Return to Top. ...
www.portenf.sa.gov.au/news/ news_article.asp?article=761

93. **DCS Newsletter**
Dubbo Christian School. Take a Tour around our Community. CLICK THE ARROW TO GO BACK TO SEE MORE NEWS. The Miniolympics and the Miniolympics Torch. ...
www.dubbocs.com.au/News/Sports.html

94. **FIRE Gallery**
Friends In Reaching Eternity - My Awesome Family Group! Enjoy these pics for now! =). Mini Olympics Team Picture: February 4, 2003: ...
students.wharton.upenn.edu/~parkdani/photo_fire.htm

95. **ISA**
ISA Mini Olympics. Every year the International Student Association hosts an event known as the Mini Olympics. This is a chance for ...
www.tamu.edu/isa/miniolympics.htm

96. **Spring Harvest Holidays - Programme - Children**

... Urchins programmes are packed with 'get stuck in' art and craft activities, water games, drama, parachute games, scavenger hunts, miniolympics, quizzes and ...

www.springharvestholidays.com/programme/children.html

97. **sommer**

Sommer. Bogenschiessen, Brückenbau, Catering, Fun am Seil, Miniolympics, Mountain Biking, Seminare, Treasure Hunt, Trottinett, Wandern,

www.funtimepark.ch/sommer.htm

98. **Corporate Meetings and Incentives Activities Information**

Relax yourself practising aquatic sports or let us arrange miniolympics, where competition will be a stimulus encouraging the spirit of bettering oneself ...

www.marbellatop100.com/
corporate_meetings_incentives_activities.htm

99. **World Wide Web Access Statistics for watserv1.uwaterloo.ca**

Program/miniOlympics watserv1.uwaterloo.ca/stats-2003
Jan.wwwstats.html

100. **World Wide Web Access Statistics for watserv1.uwaterloo.ca**

Program/miniOlympics
watserv1.uwaterloo.ca/stats-2003/Feb.wwwstats.html

101. **The Crusader Publication Online**

The Inter-Ateneo MiniOlympics might finally be held this year, pitting the teams of the five Ateneos – Manila, Naga, Zamboanga, Davao, and XU – against

webserver.cc.xu.edu.ph/~webgrp/crusader/2001-07/ Columns
column03%20-%20CrunchTime.html

102. **TURISMO**

The program of the "European Culture Week" in the ambit of which the 2001 Miniolympics will be held, will be presented on July 30th in Florence at the seat of

www.adnkronos.com/news/prod/bolletti/ history/2001/luglio/
tuilug4.htm

103. **Pictures 2003 - 2004**

Member of acts ministries international. Pictures 2003 - 2004. Mini Olympics 2003 (Sort of) - October 4, 2003. What Happened After the Rain. ...

www.gracecovenant.net/pictures/2003-2004/ miniolympics/ miniolympics.php

104. **Scrapbook - gracecovenant.NET**

Member of acts ministries international. Picture List. The Fourth Annual Mini Olympics. annette.jpg annette.jpg, banana01.jpg banana01 ...

www.gracecovenant.net/pictures/ picture-miniolympics.php

105. **2003 Mini Olympics Results**

For Immediate Release. 2003 MINI OLYMPICS RESULTS (December 3, 2003) Corona, www.answerracing.com/company/newspages/ 120303-miniolympics.html

106. **Mini Olympics**

Here's our Mini Olympics Team. This was my first major GCC event, and my these guys were hardcore. They had Pastor Young, the senior ...

www.sas.upenn.edu/~abrahaml/church/miniolympics.htm

107. **WSAHS - Mini Olympics**

www.wsahs.nsw.gov.au/events/miniolympics/

108. **table.htm**

Men's Long-jump final at the Hull Mini-Olympics for people with a learning disability.

www.jjphoto.karoo.net/sport/miniolympics.htm

38
Modern Pentathlon

1. **Union Internationale de Pentathlon Moderne**
   Union International de Pentathlon Moderne has the object to promote the development of the Modern...
   www.pentathlon.org/
2. **United States Modern Pentathlon Association**
   Extensive information about the Modern Pentathlon and the US team.
   usmpa.home.texas.net/
3. **Modern Pentathlon Australia**
   Official homepage for Modern Pentathlon Australia - Pistol Shooting, Fencing, Swimming, Showjumping and Running: the 5 sports that consist a ...
   www.pentathlon.org.au/
4. **Modern Pentathlon**
   Guide to this Olympic sport features its history, disciplines, competitions, scoring, and calendar of modern pentathlon events. ... What is Modern Pentathlon? ...
   www.modern-pentathlon.com/
5. **Alberta_Pentathlon**
   Alberta Modern Pentathlon Association. Dedicated to promoting the sport of Modern Pentathlon in Alberta. We're based in...Alberta, Canada. Provincial governing body promoting the sport in Alberta, Canada. News, rules, forms, links, events...
   www.alberta_pentathlon.homestead.com/
6. **What is OUMPA?**
   Offers information on the sport, and the organization's training and competition schedule, along with...
   users.ox.ac.uk/~oumpa/

7. **British Columbia Modern Pentathlon Association**
British Columbia Modern Pentathlon Association. ... Copyright © 2001 British Columbia Modern Pentathlon Association.
www.bcmpa.bc.ca/

8. **HickokSports.com - History - Modern Pentathlon**
This document is a history of modern pentathlon, with a list of all Olympic champions in the sport. It is ... Modern Pentathlon. A history of modern pentathlon, with a list of all Olympic champions in the sport.
www.hickoksports.com/history/modpent.shtml

9. **Modern_Pentathlon_Association_of_Great_Britain**
Description of the five sports involved, calendar of events, news and results service.
www.mpagb.org.uk/

10. **Cambridge University Modern Pentathlon Club**
Offers details on training, social and competitive events calendar, news, photo gallery and links.
www.srcf.ucam.org/cumpc/

11. **NW Pentathlon**
The NWMPA provides this information space for northwest pentathletes, their families, friends and...
www.nwmpa.org/

12. **Modern Pentathlon**
The Official Homepage of the Sport Modern Pentathlon in Sweden. Everything you need to know about the sport modern pentathlon! Modern Pentathlon. ...
home.swipnet.se/modernfemkamp/eng/

13. **Helsingin Nykyaikaiset 5-ottelijat Ry:n kotisivut**
Provides information on practices and training, events calendar, guestbook and links.
personal.inet.fi/urheilu/silvergym/hn5o/

14. **All Olympic Sports - Modern Pentathlon**
Modern Pentathlon. Parts. The modern pentathlon has 5 parts: 800 meters horse-riding, swordfencing, pistole-shooting 25 meters, 300
library.thinkquest.org/25114/eng/sporten/vijfkamp.html

15. **ABC Online News - Sports: Modern Pentathlon**
History of Modern Pentathlon and results of Australian pentathletes in Olympic Games.
www.abc.net.au/news/olympics/sports/pentathlon.htm

16. **Olympics 2000: Modern Pentathlon**
News, photos, results, rules, venues, athletes, history, and medals.
cbs.sportsline.com/u/olympics/2000/pentathlon/

17. **Modern Penthathlon (Jang Group on Line, Olympics2000)**
Modern Pentathlon
www.jang.com.pk/thenews/spedition/ olympics200 modernpen.htm

18. **Google Directory - Sports > Multi-Sports > Modern Pentathlon**
Modern Pentathlon, ... United States Modern Pentathlon Association - http://usmpa.home.texas.net/Extensive information about the Modern Pentathlon and the US team. ...
directory.google.com/Top/Sports/ Multi-Sports Modern_Pentathlon/

19. **Armed Forces Sports Modern Pentathlon**
CISM Championship, WORLD GAMES, Italy. Armed Forces Modern Pentathlon Team Places 5th In Relay At World Military Championship
www.dod.mil/armedforcessports/zmod.html

20. **OMPA - Ontario Modern Pentathlon Association**
Ontario Modern Pentathlon . . . Modern Pentathlon ... for equipment? Ontario Modern Pentathlon Association Shirley White 519-833-9449.
www.ompa.ca/

21. **Know Your Sport**
An event combining completely different sports, the modern pentathlon was by the adventure of one Napoleonic officer, who had to cross enemy lines with a ...
www.woaolympians.com/modern_pentathlon.html

22. **Union Internationale de Pentathlon Moderne**
What is Modern Pentathlon? ... Education Modern Pentathlon is an educational sport. This was the primary wish of its creator, Pierre de Coubertin. ...
www.pentathlon.org/what_is.cfm

23. **youth 2004**
The Games: The sports: Modern pentathlon, ... Modern pentathlon. ... on a team. The modern pentathlon is made up of the following 5 events: ...
www.olympiceducation.gr/pub/
docLocator.asp?docId=1957&lang=en

24. **pentathlon-scotland**
A site for the Scottish Modern Pentathlon Association an Olympic sport of five diverse and unrelated events - shooting, fencing, swimming, riding and running. ...
www.pentathlon-scotland.co.uk/
1154.html?*session*id*key*=*session*id*val*

25. **Open Directory - Sports: Multi-Sports: Modern Pentathlon**
Alberta Modern Pentathlon Association - Provincial governing body promotin the sport in Alberta, Canada. ... General information on modern pentathlon. ...
dmoz.org/Sports/Multi-Sports/Modern_Pentathlon/

26. **Modern Pentathlon**
Australian Sports Commision Logo, Modern Pentathlon. Australian Sports Commision Logo, ... Modern Pentathlon Australia. International Modern Pentathlon Union. ...
www.ausport.gov.au/info/modernpentathlon.htm

27. **Army Modern Pentathlon and Tetrathlon**
Army Modern Pentathlon and Tetrathlon Adventurous Training Army Sports Lottery Army Sports News Clubs and Associations. Army ...
www.army.mod.uk/sportandadventure/clubs/
army_modern_pentathlon_and_tetrathlon/

28. **Sydney 2000 Post Games Report**
Cycling. Equestrian. Fencing. Football. Gymnastics. Handball. Hockey. Judo. Modern Pentathlon. Page 1. Page 2. Page 3. Rowing. Sailing. Shooting. Softball. Table Tennis. ...
www.gamesinfo.com.au/postgames/en/pg000079.htm

29. **Pravda.RU Russia Second in the World Cup Modern Pentathlon**
Russian Andrei Moiseev won the silver medal in the World Cup modern pentathlon finals.
english.pravda.ru/sport/2001/08/13/

30. **International Olympic Committee-Sports**
Home, SPORTS, MODERN PENTATHLON, ... Modern Pentathlon Olympic sport since 1912, ABOUT ... So, legend has it, was born the modern pentathlon. The ...
www.olympic.org/uk/sports/programme/
index_uk.asp?SportCode=MP

31. **EIS SUPPORTING MODERN PENTATHLON HOPEFUL**
Great Britain Modern Pentathlon squad that trains at the University of Bath. ...
www.eis2win.co.uk/tex/news_harland170503.aspx

32. **Team Bath Performance Sport**
Performance Sport. Modern Pentathlon. Britain's Modern Pentathlon World Class Performance Athletes have made TeamBath their UK training base since October 1999.
www.teambath.com/sport/3_3_9.cfm

33. **Modern Pentathlon in Athens 2004 Olympic Games Accommodation**
Modern Pentathlon in Athens 2004 Olympic Games Accommodation - Residences, lodgings, Apartments, Houses, Rooms, Villas, Hotels, residence, apartment, room, villa
www.hotels-in-athens.org/olympic-games-in-Athens-Greece-2004/
modern-pentathlon.htm

34. **Modern Pentathlon World Championships 2001**
The official web site of the 2001 Modern Pentathlon World Championships
www.mpwc.co.uk/

35. **Modern Pentathlon Resources**
Fencing Swimming Riding Running Pentathlon Scoring Team Relay Competitions Calendar of Events Resources Pentathlon News Contact, Modern Pentathlon Resources
www.modern pentathlon.com/links.html

36. **Modern Pentathlon history**
The Modern Pentathlon, introduced at the 5th Olympiad in Stockholm (SWE) 1912, comprised of the contemporary sports of pistol shooting fencing, swimming ...
mujweb.atlas.cz/sport/petiboj/Historie/Historie-MP.htm

37. **HickokSports.com - History - Modern Pentathlon Medalists**
This document lists all Olympic modern pentathlon medalists. It is a page in the History section ... Olympic Modern Pentathlon Medalists.
www.hickoksports.com/history/olmodpent.shtml

38. **Modern Pentathlon - BritishSports.com: the OFFICIAL sports sites**
Modern Pentathlon.
www.britishsports.com/modernpentathlon.htm

39. **Multi-Sports : Modern Pentathlon**
Modern Pentathlon. ... Sites: Alberta Modern Pentathlon Association - Provincial governing body promoting the sport in Alberta, Canada.
directory.webguest.com/Sports/Multi-Sports/Modern_Pentathlon

40. **Modern Pentathlon**
Modern Pentathlon (15). Websites on Modern Pentathlon: Alberta Modern Pentathlon Association Provincial governing body promoting the sport in Alberta ...
www.sweden.org/Sports/Multi-Sports/Modern_Pentathlon/

41. **Modern Pentathlon Australia**
Modern pentathlon is an exciting diverse sport, steeped in history dating back to the ancient Olympic Games in Greece. The ancient...
vic.pentathlon.org.au/history.htm

39
National Games

1. **National and regional card games: India**
   Card games in India. This page is part of the National and Regional Card Games Index of the Card Games Web Site. There are probabl...
   www.pagat.com/national/india.html
2. **The Tribune, Chandigarh, India - LUDHIANA**
   XXXI National Games, Punjab-2001. Arrangements for ... closing ceremony of National Games Ludhiana.
   www.tribuneindia.com/2001/20011129/ldh.htm
3. **32nd National Games wows everyone.**
   The 32nd National Games that was rung down today at Hyderabad has been acclaimed the best ever organised in India.
   www.goodnewsindia.com/Pages/content/ newsclip/story 32_0_2_0_C/
4. **Taekwondo Federation of India - Championship Results**
   ... 13 - 22 Dec 2002, 32nd National Games - Hyderabad, Vishakapatnam ... Boys & 20th Girls National Junior Taekwondo ... Copyright © Taekwondo Federation of India 2003
   www.tfiindia.com/html/results/results_home.asp - 24k - **Cached - Similar pages**
5. **results of 31st National Games of India - Judo competitions**
   31st National Games of India - Judo Competitions. Venue: Anandpur Sahib, Punjab.
   www.geocities.com/podarjudo/competitions/national/ 200102/ results31nationalgames.htm
6. **National Games of India**
   XXXI National Games of INDIA. 31st National Games of India - www.geocities.com/podarjudo/competitions/ national/200102/ nationalgamesofindia.htm

7. **President of India**
Our young sportspersons returned with 69 medals, India securing 4th position in these games. ... all assembled here to make this National Game truly memorable ...
presidentofindia.nic.in/S/html/speeches/ others dec13_2002_1.htm

8. **The Hindu : SAF games: India confirms participation**
Online edition of India's National Newspaper International | Previous | Next SAF games: India
www.hindu.com/thehindu/2001/09/02/stories/03020002.htm

9. **The Courier-Mail: Doping scandal rocks India (archived)**
... medal winning rower has been banned for life by the Rowing Federation of India following a positive test at the multi-discipline National Games, but Singh said ...
www.couriermail.news.com.au/common/story_page/
0,5936,6257651%255E23218,00.html

10. **Rediff On The NeT: IOC takes note of India_'s National Games**
IOC takes note of India's National Games. From today, May 31, all roads in Bangalore lead to the Kanteerava Stadium, where President
www.rediff.com/sports/may/31b.htm

11. **rediff.com Olympics Special: PT Usha, India_'s golden girl**
XXV National Games, February 17 to 22, Hyderabad: 100m - 12.5s, New Meet Record (NMR) - I; 200m - 26.1s - II; 80m hurdles - 12.2s, NMR - I; 4 x 100m ...
www.rediff.com/sports/2000/sep/11usha3.htm

12. **The Hindu : India to host World championships**
So I am very confident the sport will make its debut in this year's National Games itself would be another big boost to the development of chess in India.". ...
www.hinduonnet.com/thehindu/2002/03/ 11/stories
2002031106291700.htm

13. **SCFI - Soft Ball Cricket Federation of India - Article**
National Championships in India. ... to promote interest therein, particularly in connection with the National games and other ...
www.softballcricket.com/scfi/article.php

14. **Indiainfo.com -> News -> India ->**
Kalam in Hyderabad inaugurated National Games Hyderabad: President APJ Abdul Kalam
news.indiainfo.com/2002/12/13/13kalam1.html

15. **Zimbabwe National Team Competitions 2003**
20 December 2003. Zimbabwe Soccer National Team Competitions 2003. SportScheduler.gif
www.sportscheduler.co.sz/zimbabwe_national.htm

16. **Statistics Data about fairs and festivals, monuments, sports ...**
Membership category. How To Become A Member? Membersh...
www.indiastat.com/india/Sports/Sports.asp?secid=6356

17. **Hockey**
Achievements. Hockey is the National Game of India. Unmatched excellence and incomparable virtuosity brought India a string of Olympic gold medals. ...
www.goindiago.com/sports/hockey/hockey1.htm

18. **NDTV.com - For the latest news from India**
Assam gears up to host 2005 National Games Assam is the host for the 33rd National Games in 2005 and is now ... Is India headed for a washout in the VB Series ...
www.ndtv.com/sports/default.asp?sportname=Report

19. **Afro-Asian Games: India clinch women_s hockey gold : Sports News ...**
Afro Asian Games 2003 > Afro-Asian Games: India clinch women's hockey gold
www.indiaexpress.com/news/sports 20031030-1.html

20. **Special Olympics Bharat - Home**
Special Olympics Bharat, a National Sports Program for the ... training in 26 Olympic-type sports and games.
www.specialolympicsbharat.org/

21. **The Hindu : Senthil picks up bronze**
Richa Misra who failed to match her stunning National Games performance ... By all means, it was a disappointing day for India on the whole ...
www.hindu.com/2003/10/30/stories/2003103005901800.htm

22. **ALL INDIA CHESS FEDERATION**
Kozhikode by winning 15 out of the 17 games she played. ... OILUM National Women 'A' Chess Championship. ... the qualifiers to the Indian team to represent India in the ...
www.chessindia.org/

23. **IOA promises dope free India by 2005**

Report IOA promises dope free India by 2005 May 07, 2003 19:33 IST Days after stripping the dope-tainted athletes of the 32nd National Games of their ...

ushome.rediff.com/sports/2003/may/07ioa.htm

24. **IOA: India to bid for 2010 C'_wealth Games**

Jamaica to bid for the 2010 Commonwealth Games. ... delegation as he has a special attachment with India. ...

indian olympic.hypermart.net/html/Current-News/ India-to-bid-for-2010-Cwealth-Games.htm

40
Netball

1. **IFNA International Netball**
   About IFNA and the sports of netball, news, future events, netball links, archives.
   www.netball.org/
2. **IFNA International Netball - About Netball**
   About Netball. Netball is a fast, skillful team game based on running, jumping, throwing and catching. Teams may include up to 12 ...
   www.netball.org/thesport.htm
3. **Netball Australia**
   Official site of Australian Netball.
   www.netball.asn.au/
4. **All England Netball Association (AENA) Ltd**
   All England Netball Association site featuring the latest news and press releases, advice, England...
   www.england-netball.co.uk/
5. **Netball New Zealand**
   Home of New Zealand Netball. News, player profiles, competitions.
   netballnz.co.nz/
6. **Netball Resources home page - compliled by Andy Dawson**
   Links to netball resources: basic resources, organisations, associations, clubs, descriptions of the...
   www.ucl.ac.uk/~uczcw11/netball.htm
7. **Sport - Netball**
   Netball club, event, team or reservation information.
   www.sportisgood.com/netball.html

8. **Netball Victoria**

   Netball Victoria is responsible for the management and development of the sport across The official site for the Victorian Netball Association.

   www.netballvic.com.au/

9. **Netball Singapore**

   Official site of Singapore netball. News, national squad, results and awards, coaches and umpires,...

   www.netball.org.sg/

10. **netball in sussex [Index Page]**

    A site with information about netball in the English county of sussex. ... Tracey Neville in action at CWG 2002. Welcome to Gordon's Netball in Sussex Website. Coaching, umpiring, tournaments, news and views, East Grinstead Netball Association and East Grinstead...

    homepages.which.net/~gordon.dudman/

11. **Netball Game**

    Basic guide for playing netball.Netball for starters. Rules, positions, general information, history, skills, how to play, photographs, and related links.

    www.playingnetball.plus.com/

12. **LATEST NEWS**

    Netball news in Scotland, youth development programs, international matches, national teams.

    www.netballscotland.freeserve.co.uk/

13. **Just Netball**

    Provides Netball uniforms, jackets, bodysuites, and accessories.

    www.justnetball.com.au/

14. **The Welsh Netball Association Web-Site**

    National governing body; offers tournaments and events, national squads, coaching tips, news and press...

    www.welshnetball.co.uk/

15. **Nevis Netball**

    2000 Caribbean Netball Championships. Also sections on netball history and regulations.

    www.nevisculturama.net/nevisnetball/

16. **California Netball Association**

    Information about netball clubs in California as well as other United States locations. Includes photos,...

    www.californianetball.com/

17. **WA Netball**

    Governing body for netball in Western Australia. Also home of the Perth Orioles Netball Team. Includes...

    www.wanetball.com.au/

18. **Netball SA**

    Information regarding playing and watching Netball in South Australia, Coaching, Umpiring, Commonwealth Bank Trophy, Dairy Farmers Cup, other competitions ...

    www.netballsa.asn.au/

19. **Netball UK – buy netball kit, netball posts, netball skirts ...**

    Netball UK – your one-stop shop for netball kit, netball posts, netball skirts, netball tops, netball balls, fitness & sports equipment in the UK. ...

    www.netballuk.co.uk/

20. **British Columbia Netball Association**

    BCNA is a non-profit organisation run by a group of volunteers whose sole purpose is to finance, organise and train athletic members in the game of Netball. ...

    www.bcnetball.com/

21. **netball.html**

    Netball is a team sport adapted from the game of basketball. ... In 1970 the name of the game was changed from basketball to netball....

    www.cybersydney.com.au/kids/sar/netball.html

22. **Netball NSW Home Page**

    Contains state league and interdistrict information. Also contains associations in New South Wales.

    www.isport.com.au/netball/netnsw/

23. **Netball QLD - No longer at this address**

    Netball Queensland. >> No longer resides at this address <<. Click HERE for the iSport iNetball website. Contains information on team, events, links, sponsors and contact information.

    www.isport.com.au/netball/qld/

24. **Netball NSW - Official Site**

    About Netball NSW. Netball Match Results - State Comps, Netball NSW State Teams, Netball Associations, Netball Umpiring, Netball Coaching, ...

    www.netballnsw.com/

25. **Netball**

    Origins of the Great Girlie Game. Netball derived from basketball and in fact it used to be called women's basketball when I was a pup. Provides information on the history and rules of Netball. Also includes links to other sites.

    warriordoc.com/netball.htm

26. **Netball Queensland**

    Netball Queensland, Look who's new?

    www.netballq.org.au/

27. **Apex Netball Home Page**

    1st recreational Vancouver Netball club (b division) a sport play by women in Vancouver British ColumbiaBC Canada by a netball club called Apex Netball Club ...

    www.members.shaw.ca/rhallqui/netball.html

28. **Georgia Netball Association**

    Contains information on events, committee, goals and a history of netball in the Atlanta area.

    www.geocities.com/georgianetballassoc/

29. **GRASSHOPPERS NETBALL CLUB**

    Netball club in Dorset, England. freespace.virgin.net keith.hensby/ Grasshoppers%20web%20page.html

30. **Website**

    Netball association promoting netball in West London. Many teams.

    www.millennia-netball.co.uk/

31. **STORM NETBALL CLUB**

    Organising a netball tour abroad Try

    www.netballtour.co.uk

    a new website dedicate to everything you need to know about organising a netball tour abroad. ...

    www.stormnetball.co.uk/

32. **ABC Sport - Netball**

    Netball Essentials. Photo Galleries. Netball in pictures... including Phoenix's win in this year's Grand Final. ...

    www.abc.net.au/netball/default.htm

33. **NIKE NEtball CLub Singapore**

    Official website for nike Netball Club Singapore. Nike Netball Club is one of the top netball clubs in Singapore. ...

    www.nikenetball.xudio.net/

34. **TNC home page - Taywood Netball Club**

    The home page of the TNC - Taywood Netball Club, with contact information and data on its teams (Women's, Men's and Mixed), players, achievements, history etc. ...

    www.ucl.ac.uk/~uczcw11/taywood/taywood.htm

35. **Redwood Netball Club**

    Two adult teams playing in the Basildon League and four youth teams playing in the Thurrock Sunday League.

    www.redwoodnetballclub.co.uk/

36. **Netball**

    Ants Netball Club Basingstoke Netball League Chamberlayne Netball Club East Hampshire Netball Association Hampshire North County Netball Association Mid ...

    www.hants.gov.uk/istcclr/ixx198.html

37. **BBC Sport Academy | Netball**

    Rules. Features. Latest Sports News CBBC Around the BBC Get the newsletter. Netball, Around the Academy: GIVE IT A GO :: This is the place to talk about netball! ...

    news.bbc.co.uk/sportacademy/hi/sa/netball/default.stm

38. **Netball coaching resources from Network Coaching International**

    Network Coaching International - for the very best netball coaching resources for players of all standards: coaching manuals, videos, CD ROMs, umpiring and more ...

    www.netballcoaching.com/

39. **Coogee Netball Club**

    Netball Season to commence. Be there! ... for the meat raffle! Coogee is a family netball club. ...

    www.geocities.com/coogeenetball/

40. **nynetball**

    The weekend was a resounding success for the Manhattan International Netball Club, with the Twisters, Lightning and Hurricanes all playing to their full ...

    www.nynetball.homestead.com

41. **Yahoo! Directory Sports > Netball**

    Sports > Netball Directory > Recreation > Sports > Netball, Search the Web just this category. ... SPONSOR RESULTS. Netball on Bay Find netball items at low prices. ...

    dir.yahoo.com/Recreation/Sports/Netball/

42. **Netball Scotland**

    European Netball Championships. Match and ticket information now available from the Welsh Netball Association in Cardiff...

    www.netballscotland.com/

43. **Birmingham Netball for All Ages**

    Birmingham Netball: The official site for news, courses and league information with contributions from all of Birminghams leading netball organisations. ...

    www.birmingham-netball.co.uk/

44. **University of Warwick Mixed Netball**

    University of Warwick Mixed Netball

    www.mixednetball.co.uk/

45. **XTRAMSN: Sport: Netball**

    Netballers Top Sporting Honours List Netball has been the big sporting winner in the New Year Honours list. more... ...

    xtramsn.co.nz/sport/0,,3823,00.html

46. **Stellenbosch Netball Institute**

    SNI aims to present an unique scientifically based opportunity for South Africa's talented netball players and officials to become experts. ...

    www.snetballi.co.za/

47. **SIM Netball Club**

    Website of Team Alantis, the Singapore Institute of Management Netball Club.

    simnetball.tripod.com/

48. **Orroroo Netball Club**

Contains information on club events, officers and contact information.

www.orroroo.com/netball/

49. **<<<cumberland netball team>>>**

A young, developing netball club, part of a larger sports club with excellent facilities and a thriving social network. ...

turbo10.com/cumberlandnetball/

50. **World Netball Championships 2003 Website**

Want to cover the event? Media persons, download the Accreditation Form. View the overall standings of the 11th World Netball Championships 2003. HIGHLIGHTS. ...

www.worldnetball2003.org/

51. **Matrics Netball Club**

Latest News, News. Newsletter. History. Board. Sponsors. Teams. Match Results. Player Registration. Policies. Matrics mail list! Join Now for the latest matrics news. ...

www.matricsnetball.com.au/

52. **SAS Netball Club**

SAS Netball club are based in St Albans for training and matches.

freespace.virgin.net/mick.warnes/sas/

53. **Netball ACT**

Netball ACT is dedicated to promoting and assisting the growth of Netball in the ACT and surrounding region. Netball ACT. Netball ...

www.netballact.com.au/

54. **Mopage**

Coach information, the team, performance, and goals.

members.shaw.ca/mo-ronni/mopage.html

55. **Google Directory - Sports > Netball**

Web. Netball, ... interest. Netball is good - http:/
www.sportisgood.com/netball.html

Netball club, event, team or reservation information. ...

directory.google.com/Top/Sports/Netball/

56. **Open Directory - Sports: Netball**

Andy Dawson's Netball Resources - Links to netball resources: basic resources, organisations, associations, clubs, descriptions of the game, and netball ...

dmoz.org/Sports/Netball/

57. **Indoor Netball Australia - The Home of Indoor Netball - ©2004**
Indoor Netball Australia - Home In sporting circles Indoor Netball is basically a new sport. The National Body was formed in 199...
www.indoornetball.org.au/

58. **Sport Netball Shop**
www.sportnetballshop.com.au/

59. **Netball : UK category on LimeySearch.co.uk**
Listing all UK websites in the category: UK > Recreation and Sports > Sports > Netball. ... Buy netball equipment at Racquet Zone.co.uk ...
www.limeysearch.co.uk/Recreation_and_Sports/ Sports/Netball/

60. **LCNC**
Club news, calendar, training, club shop, history, age groups, tournaments, awards, links.
www.lincolncitynetball.co.uk/

61. **Dominoes Netball**
Dominoes Netball Club! We are a Manchester netball club who train each Thursday evening at Manchester's Leisure & Sports Development Centre. ...
www.dominoes-netball.co.uk/

62. **Camelot Netball Club Home Page**
Knight, Camelot Netball Club Hertfordshire, United Kingdom. Provides details of teams, leagues, fixtures, contact information and latest gossip for this Hertfordshir...
www.members.aol.com/erikavincent/camelot/home.htm

63. **Panther Netball Club - Index**
The Panthers Netball Club. We are a small but expanding club located in the Medway Towns. On these pages you will be able...
www.panthersnetballclub.org.uk/

64. **Wasaaabi! - Home of Indoor Netball**
Interested in Indoor Netball? Team Wasaaabi will teach you all you need to know to get into this fast growing sport. ...
planet.wasaaabi.tripod.com/

65. **Netball**
Loughborough Students' Netball Club. The Netball Club has four teams as well as a recreational section.
www-lsu.lboro.ac.uk/au/clubs/netball/own/

66. **SANZA Netball**

Competitions : Netball. SANZA Netball. INTO SPORT? WANT TO MEET NEW PEOPLE, KEEP FIT AND HAVE A GOOD TIME? THEN JOIN SANZA NETBALL'S ...

www.sanza.co.uk/pub/1145.asp

67. **Poynton Netball Club**

Home, Poynton Netball Club was established in 1975. There are 4 teams currently registered with the Manchester Evening Netball League ...

homepages.tesco.net/~poynton.netball/

68. **Bradley Stoke Netball Club**

Contains details about Bradley Stoke Netball Club, South Gloucestershire, UK Fixtures, Umpiring, Coaching, Club History, General Netball Information. ...

homepages.tesco.net/~bradleystoke.netball/INDEX.HTM

69. **Lakers Netball Club**

Contains information on club officials, history and photographs.

lakersnetballclub.freeservers.com/

70. **Netball Message Board**

Netball Message Board.

www.sportingimages.com.au/wwwboard/netball/

71. **Trevor.Net.Ball**

Trevor- The last bastion of social netball

www.relax.com.au/~parris/

72. **All England Netball Association (AENA) Ltd**

Latest Headlines. New Netball Magazine Finally on the Way! ... Following the recent launch of the England Netball squad's sexy, state of t.... ...

www.england-netball.co.uk/index.cfm

73. **ANU Netball Club**

clubs.anu.edu.au/clubs/netball/

74. **Leapoole Netball Club: Home Page**

Leapoole Netball Club. Welcome to our website! Leapoole Netball Club has been up and running since May 2001. We are a friendly ...

beehive.thisisnottingham.co.uk/leapoolenetballclub/

75. **Netball**

Netball. The standard of ... in 1999. For this reason Netball has come back to Blandford and all Corps training now takes place there. It ...

www.army.mod.uk/royalsignals/netball.html

76. **Harlequin Netball Club - Home**

The Central District Harlequin Netball Club has bolstered its State League squad for the 2004 Dairy Farmers Cup season, with three players returning to the ...

www.grit.net.au/harlequin/index.asp

77. **University of New South Wales Netball Club**

Organises competitive, social, State League, beginners, mixed, women and men's netball. Includes gallery,...

www.unswnetball.org.au/

78. **WEST DORSET COUNTY NETBALL (homepage)**

West Dorset County Netball Team Homepage, Join the teams and coaches for information on the Notice Board, Fixtures, Tournament Photo's, Events, etc... ...

www.westdorsetnetball.com/

79. **The Home Page of UNP Netball**

Homepage of netball club situated in Pietermaritzburg, Kwazulu Natal, South Africa.

www.netball.unp.ac.za/

80. **CANCoach Netskills - netball coaching resources, multimedia CDs**

Interactive Multimedia Netball Coaching CD Titles - all drills with video clips and much more. ... Available NOW NETBALL TRAINING GAMES Available as CD or Manual. ...

www.cancoach.com.au/netball/

81. **Australian Sports Gallery :. Memorabilia Store Netball**

... 15) Cricket (33) Custom Framing (6) General (4) Golf (13) Hockey (5) Horse Racing (19) Military (14) Motor Sports (47) Movie Stars (14) Netball (3) Olympics (32 ...

memorabiliastore.com/catalog/default.php?cPath=30

82. **Netball New Zealand: The Game**

A brief summary of the basic rules of netball. Click here for the IFNA Revised Rules for 2002. Netball was very different to the game we play now. ...

netballnz.co.nz/thegame/thegame_subcategory/0,1471,,00.html

83. **What is Netball**

What Is Netball? Netball is a particularly fast and highly skilled sport. ... Some of these teachers travelled the world teaching Netball in other countries. ...

www.nevisculturama.net/nevisnetball/whatis.htm

84. **Netball Southland - Welcome to all**

What's On | News | Our Sponsors | Competitions | The Teams | Netball Centres Netball NZ | Umpires | Coaching | Associate Groups | Resources ...

www.netballsouthland.org.nz/

85. **Netball rules**

Netball is growing in popularity, and may well become the next soccer phenomenon to hit the US. Here's an intro to the rules of the game. Netball rules. ...

www.allsands.com/Sports/HowTo/netballrules_wdi_gn.htm

86. **Netball - Wikipedia**

Netball. ... Later, the name "netball" was adopted as women were beginning to play basketball proper, and netball started to attract male players. ...

en.wikipedia.org/wiki/Netball

87. **Bangor Netball Club - We have moved**

BANGOR NETBALL CLUB. We have moved. You will be redirected to the new site in 5 seconds or click here to access the new website.

www.ee.qub.ac.uk/dsp/staff/Dougherty/Netball/

88. **Comberton: Netball Club**

Comberton Netball Club. Comberton Netball Club is an excellent friendly club for netballers of all standards and all ages. We ru...

www.comberton.org.uk/netball.htm

89. **Cardiff University Netball Homepage**

This is Cardiff University's Netball Website! (Although still a work in progress so please bear with us!). We ... NETBALL TOURNAMENTS. ** Warwick ..

www.cf.ac.uk/suon/au/netball/

90. **UK Netball**

UK Netball Given that i-sport and All England fell out over the original England Netball website.

www.network54.com/Forum/185483

91. **Netball NSW - Regional News**

The Hunter office for Netball NSW.

www.netballnsw.com/netball-nsw-regional-news/

92. **Holdall - Netball**

Boxing Clearance Items Cricket Croquet Fitness Football Footwear Garden Games Golf Gifts Handball Hockey Indoor Games Medical Items Netball Netballs Replica ...

www.holdall.co.uk/section.php?xSec=29

93. **StudentZone - Sport - Netball**

City of Edinburgh Netball Association; England Netball; Hampshire County Council Netball Clubs; ... University Netball Clubs. ...

www.studentzone.org.uk/sport/netball.html

94. **BBC - Jersey - Sport - Netball - Fixtures**

You are in: Jersey » Sport. Deutsche Bank Offshore Netball League. Action from the first day of the local netball season. ...

www.bbc.co.uk/jersey/sport/netball/fixtures.shtml

95. **Oxford Science Park Netball Team**

Oxford Science Park Netball Team. ... The Oxford Science Park Netball Team is a newly established club based at the Oxford Science Park, Oxford. ...

www.ospnetball.org.uk/

96. **Sports Books Direct - Netball**

... United books, cricket books, boxing books, rugby books, golf books, books on fitness, tennis books, general sports, soccer books netball, skiing, squash ...

www.sportsbooksdirect.co.uk/sport.asp?SportID=17

97. **Ledbury Magpies Netball Club**

Official site of the Ledbury Magpies Netball Club, featuring the latest news, information, results, match reports, tournaments, player profiles and much more. ...

www.ledburymagpies.co.uk/

98. **Malta Netball Association**

Netball has been played in Malta ever since it was introduced to the Island by the wives of members of the British Services serving in Malta. ...

sites.waldonet.net.mt/pcuta/mna/Default.htm

99. **St Cuthberts Society JCR**

Sports Sites. badminton basketball cricket croquet darts football golf gym hockey netball pool rowing rugby rugby squash/ tennis Quick Links. ...

www.dur.ac.uk/st-cuthberts.jcr/ activities/sports/netball/

100. **cardiff : Netball**

CARDIFF UNIVERSITY NETBALL CLUB. Cardiff Uni's netball club is one of the largest in the Athletic Union and is as active off the court as it is on!! ...

www.cardiffstudents.com/main/au/netball

101. **International World Games Association : Netball**

... Netball - 1 of 30+ sports of The World Games! Netball. ... Netball is a fast, skillful team game based on running, jumping, throwing and catching. ...

www.worldgames-iwga.org/vsite/vcontent/page/custom/ 0,8510,1044-127190-128497-18066-62417-custom-item,00.html

102. **Oxford Sports Network**

NETBALL NEWS, TUE JANUARY 20 2004. Summer Netball Season Stays Close to the End. ... Full Story. Tight At the Top of Summer Netball League. ...

www.oxfordsportsnetwork.com/sport.cfm?TopID=24

103. **Flava Netball Club**

www.flavanetball.co.uk/

104. **Netball**

Australian Sports Commision Logo, Netball. Australian Sports Commision Logo, ... Netball at the Australian Institute of Sport. Netball Australia. ...

www.ausport.gov.au/info/netball.htm

105. **Uniservity: Netball Homepage**

Netball. So you want to play netball? ... We have a structured training season, with a brand new coach, who has coached the Australian Netball team! ...

www.uniservity.net/club_homepage.asp?clubid=1098

106. **NETBALL TRAINING DRILLS**

NETBALL TRAINING DRILLS.

homepages.which.net/~gordon.dudman/netball_skill/

107. **Netball**

Netball. An independent sport, although has a lot in common with basketball. International Federation of Netball Associations (IFNA). ...

www.internationalbasketball.com/netball.html

108. **Netball - Open Site**

The entire directory. Top: Sports: Netball (228): World Netball Championship (0). Australia (228); New Zealand ...

open-site.org/Sports/Netball/

109. **HAZLEHEAD NETBALL CLUB**

Netball club in Aberdeen, Scotland. Schedules, teams, tournaments.

www.netballscotland.freeserve.co.uk/hazlehead.html

110. **Netball Equipment,Netball Equipment Manufacturers,Netball ...**

Manufacturers, exporter of netball equipment, wholesale netball equipment, netball sports equipment, netball sporting equipment, netball accessory, netball ...

www.sporting-goods-industry.com/netball-equipment/

111. **Netball Victoria - Shop Resources**

Netball Victoria sells a range of resources to help people involved with Netball. ... Netball Victoria resources order form File size:65K...

www.netballvic.com.au/shop.htm

112. **Oxford University Netball Club**

OXFORD UNIVERSITY NETBALL CLUB.

users.ox.ac.uk/~netball/

41
Parasailing

1. **Parasailing USA - The Complete Parasail Information**
   Parasailing rides in USA, parasail history, articles, terms, faq's and weather check. ... Parasailing. Parasail is a parachute attached...
   www.parasailing.com/
2. **Mackinaw Parasailing**
   Mackinaw Parasailing.
   www.mackinawparasailing.com/
3. **San Diego Parasail. Go Parasailing while vacationing in San Diego ...**
   Offers winch-direct parasailing excursions leaving from Mission Bay. Hours, prices, directions, policies,...
   www.goparasailing.com/
4. **parasailing**
   These are the most popular parasailing related searches. Click on a link below to see the full results of each search Home | parasailing ...
   www.places-to-go-things-to-do.com/parasailing/
5. **Lake Tahoe parasailing- Williams Sports, Lake Tahoe**
   Come enjoy breathtaking views while parasailing over Lake Tahoe. It's fun! It's Safe! It's Addicting! USCG Approved. Parasail Rides, 400' Ride, $48.50. ...
   www.tahoesports.com/parasailing.htm
6. **Parasailing in Big Bear!**
   PARASAILING — Note: Unless otherwise noted use (909) area code for all phone numbers.
   www.bigbearinfo.com/parasail.html

7. **PERU - Hang Gliding and Parasailing in Peru.**
   PERU - Hang Gliding and Parasailing in Peru. Peru - Hang gliding Ala Delta Parasailing in Peru, Information, photos and hang gliding, ala delta and parasailing ...
   www.enjoyperu.com/peru_travel_tours_information peru_adventure_sports/ peru_hang_gliding_parasailing.html
8. **Aquaskier - Water Sports Resources - Parasailing**
   Surfrider International Parasailing Boats. Designers and original manufacturers ...
   www.aquaskier.com/parasailing.htm
9. **Parasailing ebooks (e-books) links**
   Parasailing ebooks (e-books) links with ebook (e-book) references to the subject of parasailing ... Parasailing ebooks (e-books) links...
   www.hopcott.plus.com/ebooks/parasailing.html
10. **UFO Parasailing, Maui and Kona Hawaii**
    Get out of this world... Above, Below, Beyond, with UFO Parasailing. ... Parasailing on Maui from May 16 to December 14. Kailua-Kona Parasailing, all year 'round.
    www.ufoparasailing.com/
11. **Parasailing**
    Santiagos Ocean Services offers Charter Fishing services, Parasailing, Bird Island Tours. #1 For Fun in Rocky Point. ...
    www.santiagosoceanservices.com/parasail.html
12. **Parasailing in the Bahamas**
    For those unfamiliar with it, parasailing turns you into a human kite suspended hundreds of feet above the emerald green waters of the Gulf Stream. ...
    www.geographia.com/bahamas/parasailing.htm
13. **Blue Edge Para-Sailing**
    Blue Edge Para-Sailing. Santa Barbara, California. Santa ...
    www.spiderside.com/blueedge/
14. **Polterabend Sønderborg Parasailing Faldskærm Vandski World_>_Dansk_>_Fritid_>_Flyvning**
    www.parasailing.dk/
15. **Peru - Parapente Ala Delta En Peru**
    www.enjoyperu.com/deporte-avent/parapente/index2.htm

16. **Your Guide To Parasailing At Lake Tahoe Tahoe Keys Resort Lake ...**

    Parasailing and other watersports at Lake Tahoe! Lake Tahoe Vacation Guide—Where To Stay & Where To Play. ... Parasailing is safe, fun and easy. ...

    www.tahoevacationguide.com/Activities/parasailing.html

17. **Bermuda Parasailing**

    The most comprehensive listings of Bermuda related information including watersports,parasailing, sailing, business, travel, Bermuda tourism. ... Parasailing. ...

    www.bermuda.com/categories/watersports/parasailing.htm

18. **Parasailing, California**

    PARASAILING.

    www.caoutdoors.com/Parasailing_MP.htm

19. **Walt Disney World Recreation Information - Parasailing / Water...**

    Carriage Rides Fishing Excursions Golf Courses Miniature Golf Parasailing/Skiing Richard Petty Spa Services Specialty Cruises Surfing Lessons. ... Parasailing. ...

    www.wdwinfo.com/recreation/parasail.htm

20. **Parasailing and Paragliding in Barbados!**

    Imagine Paragliding and Parasailing in beautiful Barbados - click here to find out how! Barbados: Parasailing and Paragliding. ... Parasailing: The Falcon Ltd. ...

    www.barbados.org/parastuff.htm

21. **Myrtle Beach, Captain Dicks water sports Murrells Inlet**

    ParaSailing 2004. Fly Solo (Single) Or Double (Two Together). It's the GREATEST THRILL! Nothing else compares to the thrill and exhilaration ...

    www.captdicks.com/para.htm

22. **Cozumel -Cozumel Tours/ Parasailing**

    Cozumel. Parasailing Glide on a parachute while safely admiring the island from 400 feet up on the air. The spectacular aerial views ...

    www.cozumel.net/tours/parasail.htm

23. **SkyTribe - Parasailing**

    PARASAILING. ... Exhilarating, yet tranquil is the paradox world of ascending canopies, or what is more commonly refered to as

    www.skytribe.co.za/Parasailing/parasail.htm

24. **Virginia Beach, Va. - Parasailing**
Parasailing. Until ... Va. Beach parasailing business here, please contact Virginia Beach Net: Adventure Parasail: 200 Wonston Salem Ave. ...
www.vabeach.com/sun/parasail.htm

25. **dekust.org - Parasailing**
... Zeilen. Zeilwagen. Kitesurfen. Wavecarting. Surfen. Zwemmen.Parasailing. Duiken. Hengelen. ... Parasailing. Bij het parasailen hang je aan een parachute boven het water.
www.dekust.org/NL/bezoeker/ontspanning_uitgaan/ zeesporten parasailing/

26. **Hawks Cay Resort, The Heart of the Florida Keys!**
Experience the thrill of flying as you get a bird's eye view of waters around Hawks Cay, the Atlantic Ocean, and the Florida Bay! ...
www.hawkscay.com/pop-ups/Parasailing.asp

27. **Tidal Wave Water Sports—Parasailing Fun**
Tidal Wave Water Sports offers the finest parasailing experience in Charleston, SC. Choose to fly at 600 or 1200 feet elevation ...
www.tidalwavewatersports.com/html/parasail.html

28. **Maui Discount Activities – Mauii Hawaii Parasailing Hawaii ...**
Enjoy a breathtaking parasailing ride above Maui's scenic coastline. Anyone can do it! ... Parasailing. Enjoy a breathtaking ride above Maui's scenic coastline. ...
hawaiiactivityworld.com/maui/parasailing/

29. **Parasailing**
Parasailing. ... Water-skiing and Parasailing Seven days a week 8 am-5:30 pm (Hours vary according to season) (407) 939-0754. **Prices as of September 2003**. ...
allearsnet.com/btp/parasail.htm

30. **Grand Bahama Island — Parasailing**
Not only is parasailing a thrilling experience, it is probably the best way to get an unobstructed view of Grand Bahama Island. ...
www.grand-bahama.com/parasailing.htm

31. **Florida Keys and Key West parasailing**
PARASAILING. P. PARASAILING. Water Sports at Hawks Cay Resort - MM 61, Duck Key Drive - Duck Key
www.floridakeysbest.com/families/ florida_keys_parasailing.htm

32. **Parasailing in Vanuatu**
Vanuatu - Scuba diving, parasailing, fishing, extreme tours and scooter hire in Vanuatu.
www.nautilus.com.vu/parasailing.asp

33. **Parasailing at Lake Tahoe**
Parasailing at Lake Tahoe. ... Rentals - Parasailing - Jet Skis-Sportfishing. PARASAILING. ©2000-2003 Alpine Marketing.
www.laketahoeconcierge.com/parasail.html

34. **Parasailing**
Woohoo...Go Parasailing. ... A few years ago, my older sister and I decided to indulge ourselves in this "exciting adventure" of parasailing over Maui. ...
atdpweb.soe.berkeley.edu/2130/vchan/parasail.html

35. **Breakaway Cruises Parasailing on the Kelley Rhea**
Fly with the Island's Only Coast Guard Certified Parasail Boat! Join Breakaway Cruises for your parasail adventure. Your professional ...
www.breakawaycruises.com/html/
parasailing_on_the_kelley_rhea.html - 25k

36. **Aruba Activities - Parasailing, Beaches, Sea, Carnival, Cruises...**
Aruba Activities - parasailing, beaches, aruba sea, swimming, tours events, carnival, watersports, restaurants, sightseeing, shopping ...
www.enjoyaruba.com/parasailing/

37. **dekust.org - Parasailing**
Wavekarting. Surf. Natation. Parasailing. Plongée. Pêche à la ligne. Ports de plaisance. Ski nautique. Bateaux à moteur. Clubs de Plage ...
www.dekust.org/FR/visiteur/detente_sortie/ sports_nautiques Parasailing/

38. **Big Island Parasailing - Discounted Hawaii Vacations Hawaii ...**
Big Island Parasailing. Fly high above Kona's scenic coastline! ... Regular Price $42.82 per person. Big Island Parasailing. Fly high above Kona's scenic coastline! ...
hawaiiactivityworld.com/bigisland/parasailing/

39. Snorkeling, Helicopter Tours, Luaus, Dinner Cruises, Bike Tours, Land Tours, Scuba Diving, Deep Sea Fishing, Entertainment & Shows,Parasailingand Kayaking ...
mauisightstreasures.com/activities/parasailing/

40. **Cyprus Holiday Guide- Welcome to your adventure holiday ...**
CYPRUS HOLIDAY GUIDE. Holiday in Cyprus for 340 Days in the Sun, Our role is finding and looking after your Cyprus Holiday Requirements. ...
www.cyprus-holiday-guide.com/cyprus-holiday/ parasailing.htm

41. **Parasailing On Maui Hawaii - Play Maui Hawaii**
Maui Hawaii Parasailing Information Resource. Bookings for all Maui Parasailing Activities. ... West Maui Parasailing. Maui Hawaii Parasailing. ...
www.playmaui.com/parasailing.html

42. **Parasailing Lawsuit Overview - Find Trial Lawyers and Attorneys ...**
Parasailing Overview - Parasailing: Overview - Find Trial Lawyers and Attorneys with Experience in Parasailing Personal Injury Law. ... Parasailing: Overview. ...
www.injuryboard.com/view.cfm/Topic=518

43. **Parasailing**
PARASAILING Parasailing by ParaliteUSA has the number 1 selling parasailing, Sky-Cruiser. ... Powered Paraglider. PARASAILING. Parasailing. parasailing. para sailing.
...www.paraglidingusa.us/parasailing.html

44. **BVI Welcome On-line: Parasailing in Paradise**
Huge, billowing chute of the new parasailing operation undulating across the afternoon sky. ...
www.bviwelcome.com/articles/parasail/para.html

45. **Sint Maarten**
Orient Beach is the place for parasailing. ... Strap yourself into the parasailing rig and soar 30-50 ft above the ground - taking in the spectacular view.... ...
www.st-maarten.com/parasailing.htm

46. **Travel -> Parasailing: Trade and Industry Business Directory...**
Hotel Consultants Hunting Guides and/or Tours Jet Boat Tours Lake and River Tours Motor Camps Motorhomes and Campervans Rental Parasailing Photographers Passport and ...
www.ubd.co.nz/all-categories/Travel/Parasailing/

47. **Negril Parasailing**

Negril Parasailing - Come Visit the Island and Stay in a Villa with More Comforts Than Your Own Home - Only With a Pristine Beach in Your Backyard! ...

www.jamaicanegril.com/Keywords/Negril_parasailing.html

48. **Jamaica Parasailing**

Jamaica Parasailing - Come Visit the Island and Stay in a Villa with More Comforts Than Your Own Home - Only With a Pristine Beach in Your Backyard! ...

www.jamaicanegril.com/Keywords/ Jamaica_parasailing.html

49. **Parasailing, Cairns, Australia - Cairns Attractions - Cairns, Far ...**

Parasailing Cairns, Australia. ... Parasailing operators in Tropical North Queensland include: Cairns Watersport Adventures – The Pier Marketplace,

www.cairnsattractions.com/a_parasailing.html

50. **Cyprus in a wheelchair at C & A Tourist Apartments in Polis. ...**

Whether you are able-bodied or a wheelchair user, male or female, young or old we are all one and the same!! PARASAILING IS DONE AT YOUR OWN RISK!! ...

www.evas-apartments.com/Parasailing.htm

51. **Groovy Adventures: Parasailing_Hang_Gliding**

Groovy Adventures : Parasailing Hang Gliding. By: Gossamer Threads Inc. ...

groovyadventures.com/Parasailing_Hang_Gliding/

52. **Parasailing**

Parasailing. The Fantasea Flyer ... Bermuda's natural high is a safe,fun experience for everyone. Coming soon - Night Parasailing! ...

www.fantasea.bm/watersports/parasail.htm

53. **Rum Cay Bahamas:Moonlit Cove Lagoon at Munroe Beach on the Island**

For those unfamiliar with it, parasailing turns you into a human kite suspended hundreds of feet above the emerald green waters of the Caribbean. ...

www.rumcaybahamas.com/parasailing.htm

54. **Parasailing**

Macro Island's largest waterports concessionate - Parasailing, Waverunners, Beach services. Please visit our links. ... Para/Pictures PARASAILING ...

www.marcoislandwatersports.com/para.html

55. **Parasail**

Parasail. Parasailing has really taken off in Key West. Soar above the sights and see the town and all the treasures of the sea. ...

www.islandconcierge.com/activities/ parasail/parasail.htm

56. **Aquarius Parasailing and Tours Siesta Key**

Sightseeing tours and excursions. Information on activities offered, maps, photos and contacts.

www.aquariusparasail.com/

57. **Frommers.com : Destinations : Maui : Active Pursuits : ...**

Active Pursuits | Parasailing. ... Keep in mind, though, that parasailing tours don't run during whale season, which is roughly December through May. ...

www.frommers.com/destinations/maui/0015020653.html

58. **parasail parasailing para-sail water sports ride Miami Beach**

All para-sail water sports parasailing parasail waverunners jetskis rental,Miami Beach, Florida.Tour Miami:ride sailboats kayaks charters windsurfing. ...

www.boucherbrothers.com/Parasail.htm

59. **Parasailing and Jetski - Cairns, Australia**

Parasailing and other Watersports 1 of 1. North Queensland Watersports. Parasail, Jetski and Bumper Tube Rides. For all your watersport ...

www.barrier-reef-holidays.com/actparasail.htm

60. **Parasailing - Wild Thing Water Sports - Norman Manley Boulevard ...**

... to offer several fun-filled party cruise options [Rhodes Hall Plantation Cruise,Half Moon Bay Cruise, Negril's West End Sunset Cruise] and parasailing for the ..

www.wildthingwatersportsnegril.com/Parasail_1.shtml

61. **Key West Sebago Watersports**
Parasailing. Experience Key West from the air! ... Truly an unforgettale experience! All ages can enjoy parasailing, flying solo or tandem.*. ...
www.keywestsebago.com/parasailing.php

62. **Parasailing on Maui**
Kayaking. Whale Watching. Parasailing. ATV Tours. Van Tours/ Guides. ... Parasailing in Paradise. UFO Parasail. Kaanapali Beach. List Price, Our price, 800' line. $57.
adventuremaui.com/parasailing.htm

63. **Menorca-Info.de - Parasailing auf Menorca**
Parasailing.
www.menorca-info.de/parasailing.htm

64. **HAWAII PARASAILING - Maui Parasailing near Kaanapali Beach, west ...**
Maui Hawaii Parasailing Information Resource only available when no Whale season and Dolphin near Kaanapali and Lahaina maui hawaii beach activity in the ...
www.mauigateway.com/~uofh/mauiparasailing.html

65. **Travel Hawaii/Activity Warehouse**
Maui: Parasailing. All of the boats are referred to as "winch boats". ... West Maui Parasail (400 ft). ACTIVITY CATEGORY: Parasailing Island: Maui. ...
www.travelhawaii.com/maui_parasailing.php

66. **Outdoor Resources Online: Parasailing**
Outdoor Resources Online: Parasailing, General Information; Parasailing Products; Travel/Trips. Recommended Reading: Sky Adventures
www.outdoor-resources.com/Parasailing/

67. **Garden Gate Bed and Breakfast Inn - Maui Parasailing - Hawaii**
Parasailing is one of Maui's most popular activities. There is not a better place in the world to parasail than Maui during the whale season. Maui Parasailing. ...
www.gardengatebb.com/pages/air_activities/ parasailing.html

68. **Travel to the Bahamas - Nassau, Atlantis, Freeport, Vacation**
Travel to the Bahamas What To Do - Parasailing. ... Parasailing is readily available on Nassau/Paradise Island and Grand Bahama Island....
www.traveltothebahamas.com/what_parasailing.htm

42
Physical Education Colleges

1. **Physical Education — College Catalog — Drew University**
   Quick links: Drew University > Catalog > College > Course Listings > Physical Education. Drew University, College Catalog, Tools *SEARCH ...
   www.drew.edu/catalog/cla/courses/pe/index.php
2. **Australian College of Physical Education - Home**
   Training Australian professionals in Sports Studies, Physical Education, and Teaching, the Australian College of Physical Education provides flexible degree ...
   www.acpe.edu.au/
3. **Physical Education Colleges**
   Vasantrao Naik Physical Education college, Nandanvan, Trimurti Square, 1992, 742965. Bapurao Deshmukh Physical Education College, Vanadongri Hingna rd, 1990, ...
   www.nagpuronline.com/academic/phyed.htm
4. **Pat Keiffner, Lecturer in Physical Education - College of ...**
   Physical Education for Elementary Teachers; HPES 320 - Motor Skills and Development;
   www.louisville.edu/edu/hpes/facandstaff/ pe/keiffner.html
5. **Taipei Physical Education College**
   Taipei Physical Education College ... College, Department, Bachelor's Program Established. Physical Education, Athletics Sports, 1996. Recreational Sports
   www.edu.tw/bicer/english/cphysicaledu.htm

6. **August 2002 Physical Education Teaching Major School of Education**

   Physical Education Teaching Major School of Education College of Human Development and Education North Dakota State University Name ...

   www.ndsu.nodak.edu/teachered/Curriculum_Guides/Phy_Ed_Major.pdf

7. **Bachelor of Arts in Education College of Education, ASU Secondary ...**

   For students entering the major Fall 2003-04 catalogs BAE Bachelor of Arts in Education College of Education, ASU Secondary/Physical Education (K-12 ...

   www.asu.edu/provost/articulation/ chksheets/03-04/03ckl knsbae.pdf

8. **online physical education college courses**

   online physical education college courses. BEST Search the Web. Here you can get lot of interesting info about online education! Click ...

   www.abrp.net/online-physical-education-college-courses/online-physical-education-college-courses.html

9. **Pomona College : Athletics**

   Pomona College Home Page, Pomona College Home Page. The Daily Hen Sports

   www.physical-education.pomona.edu/

10. **St. Mary's University College - Physical Education**

    Teaching is undertaken by the College's Physical Education Department supplemented in part from other college departments There ...

    www.stmarys-belfast.ac.uk/acad/prosp/depts/pe.html

11. **Chosun University**

    College of Physical Education. The College of Physical Education aims to teach the theories and practices of physical education and ...

    www.chosun.ac.kr/eng/academics/page2_8.html

12. **Lekshmibai National College Of Physical Education**

    www.lncpe.org/

13. **Columbia College Bulletin**
Asian Languages and Cultures Music Philosophy Physical Education Physics Political ... Programs Academic Advising Admissions Columbia College Bulletin Center ...
www.college.columbia.edu/students/ academics/depts/pe.php

14. **College of Physical Education**
The summary for this Chinese (Traditional) page contains characters that cannot be correctly displayed in this language character set.
www.ntcpe.edu.tw/

15. **College of Physical Education**
Official site of the Blue with news items, facilities details, scores, game schedules and rosters.
www.wellesley.edu/Athletics/main.html

16. **De Anza College Physical Education and Athletics**
Physical Education and Athletics. About. Staff. ...
www.deanza.fhda.edu/pe/

17. **Physical Education teacher vacancies - Secondary Comprehensive...**
Physical Education Teacher Vacancies Ref p1002 - Teacher Physical Education jobs Comprehensive Technology College UK part time Secondary School Sixth Form ...
www.physical-education-teacher-vacancies.co.uk/

18. **Idrottshögskolan - in English**
It is the task of the University College of Physical Education and Sports to provide advanced education for those who are going to fulfil those needs. ...
www.ihs.se/english.htm

19. **Hudson Valley Community College - Physical Education Studies**
Adapted physical education teacher, athletic trainer or an athletic administrator, Hudson Valley Community College's Physical Education Studies program may be ...
www.hvcc.edu/academ/schools/las/ped/

20. **Macalester College Catalog: Physical Education**
Macalester College Catalog 2003-2004. Program Description. Physical Education. Full Time Staff: Irv Cross (Director), Vanessa Seljeskog ...
www.macalester.edu/academic/catalog/program/phs_m.html

21. **Washington College | Catalog**
Washington College Catalog, Washington College Catalog ... Science Economics Education Engineering English ... Pharmacy Philosophy Physical Education Physics Political ...
www.washcoll.edu/wc/prospective/ academic/catalog_phy1.html

22. **Pierce College Catalog Course listing**
Physical Education courses offered at Pierce College. ...
www.pierce.ctc.edu/programs/courselist/PE.php3

23. **Undergraduate Record, Chapter 6: College of Arts and Sciences**
Only courses numbered 320 or higher in the Department of Health and Physical Education of the Curry School of Education are accepted for College credit. ...
www.virginia.edu/registrar/records/98ugradrec/ chapter6 uchap6-3.35.html

24. **Physical Education - Athletics**
RMC programme are academics, military training, physical education and second ... of each cadet's education, a process ... the basis for the College motto - Truth ...
www.rmc.ca/academic/registrar/programme/cal-phys_e.htm

25. **Colby College: Catalogue: Physical Education**
The Department of Physical Education and Athletics offers workshops and clinics ... The New England Small College Conference Mission Statement The New ...
www.colby.edu/catalogue/9900/physed.shtml

26. **Saddleback College, Mission Viejo - California**
For those whom participation in a regular Physical Education setting would appropriate assistance, and knowledgeable staff, the Saddleback College APE Program ...
www.saddleback.cc.ca.us/SS/couns/dsps/pe.html

27. **Oxford College Physical Education and Dance Division**
Oxford College Emory University For more information
www.emory.edu/OXFORD/PEDance/

28. **Albion College Physical Education Department**
The Department of Physical Education is located in the Dow Recreation and Wellness Center ... Albion College 517/629 - 1000 Albion A to Z | People Directory | Site ...
www.albion.edu/physed/default.asp

29. **New Mexico Junior College - Physical Education**
    Physical Education. ... Richard Morris – Director of Athletics New Mexico Junior College
    www.nmjc.edu/academics/programs/pe.asp
30. **Health & Physical Education - Monroe Community College Web Site**
    Health and Physical Education 585-292-2840. ... Our Department of Health and Physical Education prepares you for many and varied career opportunities...
    www.monroecc.edu/depts/pe/
31. **Academics at Alfred State College**
    Philosophical aspects of physical education and athletics. ... Variable Credit Hours HPED 3061 - Physical Fitness 1 ... and the Alfred State College Super Circuit. ...
    www.alfredstate.edu/academics/ course_descriptions/hped.html
32. **Physical Education and Dance Department :: Vassar College ...**
    Physical Education and Dance Department. Office: Athletics and Fitness Center. Phone (845) 437-7470. e-mail: pe@vassar.edu. ... Physical Education. I. Introductory. Top. ...
    departments.vassar.edu/~register/catalogue/physEd.html
33. **Wellesley College Physical Education**
    ... Archives | Administration | Friends of Wellesley College Athletics. Alison DiTomaso aditomaso@wellesley.edu; Department of Physical Education, Recreation and ...
    www.wellesley.edu/Athletics/pe/new/
34. **College of Health, Physical Education, Recreation and Teache...**
    For more than 75 years, the College of Health, Physical Education, Recreation, and Teacher Education (HPERTE) has prepared thousands of individuals for careers ...
    www.uwlax.edu/hperte/
35. **Davidson College Physical Education**
    More than 50 courses offered in the physical education curriculum range ... sports to develop skills to aid in physical well-being after college years; and ...
    www.davidson.edu/administrative/athletics/physed.html

36. **College Programs in Health and Physical Education - Health and ...**
University/College Programs by State College Programs in Health and Physical Education Health and Physical Education Programs. Arkansas ...
www.campusprogram.com/programs/subjects
Health_and_Physical_Education.html

37. **Physical Education - Pasadena City College**
Physical Education Activity Open/Closed Class List: [Fall] [Winter] [Spring] [Summer] Schedule of Classes: [Fall] [Winter] [Spring] [Summer] College Catalog. ...
www.pasadena.edu/divisions/physical-ed/

38. **Accounting, Accounting Other, Accounting Technician, Acting and ...**
Communications Technology and-or Technicians Other, Community And Junior College Administration, ... Health And Physical Education and-or Fitness Other, ...
www.universities.com/Search/Degrees/Masters_degree/

39. **KANGNUNG National University**
College of Arts & Physical Education The college consists of music, fine arts, industrial craft arts, and physical education. It ...
www.kangnung.ac.kr/english_home/ college
index.php?temp=arts

40. **Western Society for Physical Education of College Women, WSPECW**
Western Society for Physical Education. of College Women.
www.angelfire.com/ca/wsociety/

41. **Collingwood College - Physical Education**
Head of Department: Mrs H Avoth Introduction: Physical Education encourages pupils to learn about ... During the College day the college has the use of Camberley ...
www.collingwoodcollege.com/pages.php?fid=93

42. **Columbia College Academics > Core Curriculum > Physical Eduation**
Physical Education Requirement. General Information: Physical Education Department Dodge Physical Fitness Center Phone: 212-854-3439. ...
www.college.columbia.edu/students/ academics/core/pe.php

43. **Hugh Christie Technology College > Select Section**
Hugh Christie Technology College >. Physical Education. The PE Department. AS Level.
www.hughchristie.kent.sch.uk.
www.secondaryschoolsonline.co.uk
clubs_list.asp?groupid=1527&unionid=92

44. **Mission College Physical Education**
The Mission College Physical Education Program includes a variety of physical education activities, including Fitness, Dance, Individual Sports, Team Sports ...
www.missioncollege.org/depts/pe/

45. **Shepherd College Catalog 2001-03**
An introduction to teaching health and physical education. ... principles of sport and physical activity, as ... procedures, the Shepherd College Teaching Model for ...
www.shepherd.edu/pub_info/catalog/ courses
physical_education.html

46. **Locate an Advisor - Montgomery College, MD**
Academic Disciplines/Programs at Montgomery College. ... Menu, Exercise Science, Health Enhancement, and Physical Education (Rockville) Advisors,
www.montgomerycollege.edu/Departments/ studevgt/Advisors.htm

47. **Pierce College Catalog**
Physical Education. Faculty, (Fort Steilacoom): Steve Crain. Degree: Associate in Arts and Sciences. Pierce College offers a variety of activities to meet students ...
www.pierce.ctc.edu/programs/programlist/pe.php3

48. **Auckland College of Education | Programmes | Bachelor of Physical ...**
Auckland College of Education is a leading provider of specialist professional education and related training in New Zealand. Bachelor of Physical Education. ...
www.ace.ac.nz/progs/teacher/bpe/index.asp

49. **Grinnell College - Department of Physical Education**
American Sport Education Program (ASEP). ... Grinnell College, Grinnell, IA ...
www.grinnell.edu/academic/pe/

50. **Physical Education - Curriculum - Merici College - Canberra**
Physical Education at Merici College is designed to help the students develop a positive attitude towards physical activity...
www.merici.act.edu.au/curriculum/physical_ed.htm

51. **Hesston College Physical Education Department**
Physical Education Department. At Hesston College Fall Sports, Winter Sports, Spring Sports. Soccer-Men, Basketball-Men, Baseball. ...
www.hesston.edu/academic/depts/physed/physed.htm

52. **Northern Oklahoma College - Faculty :: Health Physical Division**
Fine Arts. :: Roustabouts. Health, Physical Education & Recreation. :: Cheerleading Tryouts. Northern Oklahoma College.
www.north-ok.edu/2002/faculty/health_physical_main.htm

53. **Academic Programs : Physical Education Studies - AS Degree...**
Genesee Community College offers an outstanding physical education curriculum, a knowledgeable faculty, and outstanding facilities and resources. ...
www.genesee.edu/programs/PhysEd.cfm

54. **The Official Site of MWC Athletics**
Education and Athletics is seeking applicants for a Physical Education Instructor/Head ... was drawn at halftime of the men's basketball game against York College.Official site of the Eagles with news items, rosters, statistics, pictures, and past results.
www.mwc.edu/hepe/

55. **Chaffey College Athletics and Physical Education**
The Chaffey College athletic and physical education programs serve a wide range of student needs and interests, as well as providing strong links with other ...
www.chaffey.cc.ca.us/ath-pe/index.shtml

56. **JCC Jamestown Community College**
Physical Education Internship Students receive on-the-job experience consisting of ... All guidelines in the original college internship policy will be ...
www.sunyjcc.edu/college-wide/offerings/phe.html

57. **Physical Education**
Physical Education University College Chichester Bishop Otter Campus College ...
www.ucc.ac.uk/physed/

58. **Morehouse College**

The Department of Health and Physical Education at Morehouse College stands prepared to ensure that every student who has chosen Health and Physical Education as ...

www.morehouse.edu/academics/humsocsci/healthphysed/

59. **Ottawa University - The College - Academics - BA Physical ...**

An official transcript from an accredited college or university ... concerning additional requirements inquire at the Physical Education Department Office. ..

www.ottawa.edu/TheCollege/Academics/BA_PhysEd.html

60. **The Official Columbia University Athletics Website**

Bernstein, a member of the Columbia College Class of 1954, was 70 years old. ... me to begin to make room for someone else to lead physical education and athletics ...

www.columbia.edu/cu/athletics/

61. **Albertson College of Idaho Catalog 2001-2002**

A course designed to acquaint the student with the concept of physical education as a profession and to orient the student to the College program. ...

www.albertson.edu/academics/catalogarchive/catalog0 physeduc.htm

62. **College of Education and Human Services**

Health, Physical Education, and Recreation Wright State University Copyright © 2003 College of Education and Human ...

www.ed.wright.edu/

63. **Physical Education - Royal Military College of Canada**

Physical Education. RMC's physical education programme enables you to achieve a high level of physical fitness. It emphasizes conditioning ...

www.rmc.ca/admission/options/ugrad_physed_e.html

64. **Purchase College - Physical Education**

www.purchase.edu/studaff/physicaleducation/default.asp

65. **majors\physed**

This means that college graduates use their education in a ... list contains a representative sample of current job titles of former Physical Education majors. ...

www.uncwil.edu/stuaff/career/Majors/physed.htm

66. **Pepperdine University - Seaver College - Natural Science Division**
Seaver College home page. Natural Science Division. ... Physical Education. The physical education major is designed for ...
seaver.pepperdine.edu/naturalscience/
academics physicaleducation.htm

67. **Associate of Science - Health and Physical Education, Georgia...**
Associate of Science Degree - Health and Physical Education class requirements for Georgia Perimeter College. ...
www.gpc.peachnet.edu/~acadaff/cat/ programs
AS_HealthPhysicalEd.html

68. **Physical Education (M.Ed./initial licensure) - College of ...**
Physical education students enter a 12-month program integrating educational theory with ... is offered by the School of Kinesiology at the College of Education ...
education.umn.edu/SPS/programs/lic/PhyE-home.htm

69. **Ridley College**
The physical and health education department of Ridley College provides a quality program of instruction and activity for students choosing physical education ...
www.ridley.on.ca/departments/ academics/physed/index.php

70. **Saddleback College, Mission Viejo - California**
Physical Education activity skills ... 60 units including the general education requirements with ... 12 units must be completed at Saddleback College. ...
www.saddleback.cc.ca.us/CC/PAGES/CERT/CERT75.html

71. **Jamestown College - Jamestown, North Dakota**
Physical Education Major. Physical Education Minor.
www.jc.edu/scripts/home/academics/pe.php

72. **Cardinal Newman College**
How physical education, leisure and ... The role of sport within the education system; the ... their academic study and sport performance at Cardinal Newman College. ...
www.cardinalnewman.org.uk/sportandpysicaled.php

73. **GASHE - Gallery - Dunfermline College of Physical Education**
This collection of images are representative of the types of records held by Dunfermline College of Physical Education. [Back to ...
www.gashe.archives.gla.ac.uk/gallery/ ue/dcpe/dcpepics.html

74. **Saddleback College, Mission Viejo - California**
Saddleback College Logo, You can click here anytime to return to...
www.saddleback.edu/CC/PAGES/CUR/CUR74.HTML

75. **Health Promotion, Physical Education & Sport Studies - College of...**
Health Promotion, Physical Education and Sport Studies. ...
www.louisville.edu/edu/hpes/

76. **Bryn Mawr College Athletics**
Students may also take physical education courses at Haverford College and have the option of taking two self-designed courses or courses outside the College ...
www.brynmawr.edu/athletics/physical-education/

77. **Shepherd College Catalog**
GENERAL STUDIES PHYSICAL EDUCATION (GSPE). The general studies physical education program is part of the College wide program of general studies. ...
www.shepherd.edu/pub_info/catalog/courses/general_studies_physed.html

78. **University of Idaho, College of Education: HPERD**
Physical Education, Recreation and Dance is "the place" to study, appreciate, understand, and experience movement. One of three divisions in the College of ...
www.uidaho.edu/ed/hperd/

79. **Amherst College Physical Education and Athletics**
Physical Education and Athletics. ... Contact. Physical Education and Athletics main
www.amherst.edu/~athletic/

43
Pinball

1. **The Pinball Pasture**

   Pinball Pasture. News, Work and ... future. The Internet Pinball Database now has photos of over 2000 machines! Contents, The...

   www.lysator.liu.se/pinball/

2. **The Internet Pinball Database**

   Welcome to the Internet Pinball Database. The Internet Pinball Database is the most comprehensive list of pinball machines that have been manufactured. ...

   www.lysator.liu.se/pinball/IPD/

3. **Pinball.org**

   Pinball.org is for all pinball enthusiasts looking for Publications, Designers, rulesheets on your favorite game and much more. ... Pinball-related images. ...

   www.pinball.org/

4. **Pinball Machines from Stern Pinball Inc.**

   The only company presently making pinball machines. The official company site. Download game ROMs...

   www.sternpinball.com/

5. **Pinball**

   Pinball in a Browser by Burkhard Ratheiser. Press Space to start. Press down to eject ball. Press left and right to move flippers.

   www.uni-mainz.de/~rathb000/Pinball/Game.html

6. **Visual Pinball News**

   A PC pinball emulator where you can more or less faithfully reproduce the gameplay of most tables...

   www.randydavis.com/vp/

7. **Mr. Pinball Home Page**

   The largest pinball classifieds on the Net. They specialize in EM (pre 1978) machines and sell a price...

   www.xmission.com/~daina/pinball.html

8. **Williams Electronic Games, Inc.**

   Made pinball machines under the Williams and Bally labels. No longer producing pinball machines, site...

   www.pinball.wms.com/

9. **Pinball Owners Association**

   Information about the Pinball Owners Association and their magazine, Pinball Player, together with news and features about pinball.

   dspace.dial.pipex.com/poa/

10. **The Internet Pinball Machine Database**

    The Internet Pinball Machine Database; over 9000 images of over 4500 pinball machines. Pictures, technical documentation, production counts, links, historical info and other data for every...

    www.ipdb.org/

11. **PINBALL: Pinball Repair Guides. Collector buys pinball, coin...**

    Offers repair and restoration information on 1940's to current day games. Information on game modification.

    marvin3m.com/fix.htm

12. **Pinball Links — Pinball Game Web Index Site**

    Pinball Links is a WWW links index site for pinball and games pages on the Internet. pinlinks.org Pinball Links Pinball Game Web Index Site ...

    homepages.paradise.net.nz/~frenzy/pinlinks/

13. **World Pinball Directory**

    The ultimate guide to pinball around the world. Includes places to play pinball around the world, info. on upcoming pinball machines ...

    www.daveland.com/pinball/

14. **Pinball Heaven, the best pinball machine site in the UK, new and...**

    The Pinball Heaven is a company dedicated to supplying the finest pinball machines in the country. Come and visit this excellent ...

    www.pinballheaven.co.uk/

15. **VPForums - Complete Pinball Discussion**

    A moderated discussion forum about Visual Pinball, Visual PinMAME, other computer pinball simulations,...

    www.vpforums.com/

16. **Pinball News - First and Free**

    Also inside this edition of Pinball News: Latest industry news. What's new in Pinball News. Reports from around the world. See the latest games on site. ...

    www.pinballnews.com/

17. **Mr. Pinball Classifieds**

    Brought to you by. Silver Ball Amusement—Pinball Circuit Board Repair Mr.Pinball Classifieds. ... Copyright Mr. Pinball 2003. All Rights Reserved.

    www.xmission.com/~daina/classified/

18. **Pinball Expo**

    Pinball Expo Web Site! Keep posted ... info. Pinball Expo Tournament Winners. Special Events. A yearly pinball event (October) in Chicago, IL. Website has information on dates, tournaments, and...

    www.pinballexpo.net/

19. **Pinball Nostalgia**

    PINBALL NOSTALGIA [Flipperspel] Hundreds of pictures of pinball, arcade and slot machines! ... Pinball flyers, a collecting guide,...

    hem.passagen.se/ergu6021/

20. **Free Shockwave Pinball - Candystand.com**

    Free shockwave pinball, Water Park Pinball, at Candystand. Play kids pinball game and arcade, sports, card, multiplayer and extreme sports games. ...

    www.candystand.com/games/ls_shock_lspb.htm

21. **The Pinball Resource**

    The Pinball Resource - Pinball Parts. Questions about this old VirtualAve Web site? Contact the Webmaster.

    pinballresource.virtualave.net/

22. **Bookmark Tail Gunner Page**

    The pinball is basically under normal physical laws and it is especially designed when it is near the flippers so that accurate bouncing and slipping can be ...

    www.start4all.com/pinball/pinball.htm

23. **Pinball World ha cambiado de direccisn**
World_>_Español_>_Juegos_>_Con_moneda
www.arrakis.es/~pinball/

24. **LittleWing PINBALL Official Website**
Official site including Angel Egg, Crystal Caliburn, Golden Logres, Jinni Zeala, Loony Labyrinth and...
www.littlewingpinball.com/html/eng/

25. **Pinball Publishing**
Independent press focusing on the creative production of fine printed material.
www.pinballpublishing.com/

26. **PinballMachines.Com - Pinball News, Pinball Chat, Pinball Auctions**
Includes live auctions, pinball repair, and art.
www.pinballmachines.com/

27. **Arcade Pinball Game - Creme Savers**
Play the arcade pinball game, Creme Savers Pinball, at Candystand. Free pinball games, sports, card, trivia, and multiplayer games. Arcade Pinball Game, ...
www.candystand.com/games/cs_shock_cspb.htm

28. **Microsoft Pinball Arcade**
Pinball Arcade is a collection of seven licensed tables that represent the evolution of pinball in America. A state of ... on the PC. ...
www.microsoft.com/games/pinball/

29. **3D Realms Site**
Mailing List. Join the 3D Realms Mailing List and be kept up to date via email - FREE! August 21, 2003. MORE MAX COVERS 5:15 PM [Discuss this news story]. ...
www.pinballwizards.com/

30. **Pinball Games Online Directory**
Snowball Pinball 2, www.gamerival.com. Snowball pinball is back again! Use the z and m keys to control the arrows and try to Ring...
www.thepinballzone.coolfreepages.com/onlinepinball.htm

31. **Pinball Paradise**
Epic Pinball. Extreme Pinball. Offers pinball demos for PC and Macintosh, also hosts the Original 'Epic Pinball' and 'Extreme Pinball'...
www.dmwright.com/pinball/

32. **Rulesheets**

    Pinball.org is for all pinball enthusiasts looking for Publications, Designers, rulesheets on your favorite game and much more. Rulesheets, ...

    www.pinball.org/rules.htm

33. **Visual Pinball Introduction**

    Visual Pinball is a new tool that allows users to create and play their own pinball tables. ... plot. All the pinball parts are here. ...

    www.randydavis.com/vp/intro.htm

34. **Classic Pinball Corporation Home Page**

    Details of machine sales and service.

    www.classicpinball.com/

35. **rec.games.pinball**

    A FAQ for the newsgroup.

    cascade.mit.edu/pins/faq.html

36. **Pinball 80 World_>_Español_>_Juegos_>_Con_moneda**

    www.geocities.com/pinballhome/2enter.html

37. **The Pinball Resource**

    THE PINBALL RESOURCE WEBPAGE, we offering a unique blend of Pinball parts, manuals, schematics, and accessories.

    www.pbresource.com/

38. **Flash Pinball**

    www.media-division.com/flashgames/pinball/pinball.htm

39. **Goodbye**

    Site dedicated to the collection, restoration, preservation and enjoyment of pinball machines. Features...

    www.pinball.nu/

40. **Stockholm Pinball Locator**

    A database of all pinball machines available for playing in the inner city of Stockholm, Sweden.

    stockholm.pinball.org/

41. **Pinball 2000**

    It is unique, it is revolutionary, it is the future of pinball. Introducing Pinball 2000, the most TECHNOLOGICALLY ADVANCED pin the world has ever seen. ...

    www.pinball.wms.com/pinball2000/home.html

42. **Unique Development Studios**
The official site, including a demo and screenshots.
www.uds.se/games/?iId=31

43. **Russ Jensen_s Pinball History Page**
RUSS JENSEN'S PINBALL HISTORY PAGE! Genco's METRO (1940). This "city of the future" artwork was done by famous pinball artist ROY PARKER. Contains great information on how pinball has developed over the years.
members.aol.com/rusjensen/

44. **Adventure Pinball**
Journey through a series of linked pinball tables, each one more difficult to master than the last, to survive the perils of Forgotten Island. ...
www.pinball.ea.com/

45. **TecnoPinball World_>_Español_>_Juegos_>_Con_moneda**
www.tecnopinball.com/

46. **Martin_s Pinball Simulation Reviews**
Reviews of pinball simulation games for Windows and DOS with ratings and high scores.
www.lastbandit.com/pinrevue.html

47. **The Pinball Wizard**
Contains "Cows & Easter Eggs", owner lists for The Addams Family Gold and Earthshaker, sounds, pictures...
w1.853.telia.com/~u85304218/Pinball.htm

48. **QuadGames - play free online games**
A Shockwave pinball game.
www.quadgames.com/games/highgear.html

49. **Amusement Video Pinball_s Home Page - Balto, Md**
Amusement Video Pinball. ... Occasionally pinball machines up to 15 years old and video games over 20 years old are available....
pettitcompany.com/pinbuoy/

50. **Doctor Who Pinball: Time Streams**
Doctor Who Pinball: Time Streams. Which version of this site do you want? Please choose one now. Attractively Framed Site - Recommended for 800x600 or greater.
www.missingpiece.com/pinball/drwho/

51. **Howstuffworks "How Pinball Machines Work"**
The pinball machine is an arcade standard, and there are those who have truly mastered its secrets.
www.howstuffworks.com/pinball-machine.htm

52. **RapidMotion**
www.secretlevel.de/RapidMotion.html

53. **Play pinball, win geld met het spelen van de game pinball**
Pinball the online game, speel het online spel pinball en win geld prijzen met pinball.
www.playpinball.nl/?user=7

54. **Star wars Pinball 2000**
www.pinball2000.com/

55. **gameroom, pinball, jukebox, slot machines, video arcade, soda...**
Free online classified ads for buying and selling pinball machine and parts.
www.gameroommagazine.com/

56. **World Pinball Directory**
The ultimate guide to pinball around the world. Includes places to play around the world, info. on upcoming machines, and pinball links/tournament info. ...
www.daveland.com/pinball/index2.html

57. **Action Pinball and Amusement- Home Page**
A dealer in authentic arcade game equipment for use in the home. They buy, sell, and service most...
www.aros.net/~rayj/action/

58. **PINBALL PERFECTION**
Pinball machine restoration and home sales.
members.aol.com/pindan/

59. **Pinball**
Home page for Pinball, a MECA (Museum of Ephemeral Cultural Artifacts) exhibit that features pinball art. MECA MECA. Pinball Art Kiss. ...
www.edgechaos.com/MECA/PINBALL/pinball.html

60. **Official home of VocaTest**
Official home of VocaTest. General information (FAQ). What is VocaTest? VocaTest is a small and simple vocabulary tester written in Java.
www.cyd.liu.se/~oloho217/

61. **ROBO Pinball | Home**
Pinball game using Shockwave 3D and the Havok Xtra programmed with Macromedia
www.cerberos.de/pinball/home.php

62. **Magic Pinball**
Play some pinball online! Includes a feature to save high scores.
www.bonus.com/bonus/card/raster_magic.html

63. **Pinball Heaven. Quality sales service and repairs**
The Pinball Heaven is a company dedicated to supplying the finest pinball machines in the country. Come ... facility! Pinball Dealers, ...
www.pinballheaven.com/

64. **Free State Pinball Association (FSPA)**
How to join the association, stats, groupings, rules and a photo gallery. For those in Maryland,...
www.fspazone.org/

65. **PINBALL RESCUE - Playfield Plastics and Back Glasses**
Reproduction playfield plastics, backglasses, decals, game room clocks and novelty items.
www.pinballrescue.com/

66. **Rising: The Tower of Pin**
Pinball simulation reviews, demo, news, and tips.
www.pcpinball.com/

67. **Pinball Inc.!**
Your source for high quality replacement pinball ramps. NEW !!! NEW !!! Information on the best ramps for pinball machines. ...
www.pinballinc.com/

68. **the pinball ark**
THE PINBALL ARK Flipperspel Indiana Jones, Eartshaker, Funhouse, Star Trek.TNG och Twilight zone. Arken är stängd för gott. Det ...
www.pinballark.com/

69. **IRPinball**
Downloads of Visual Pinball recreations of classic pinball tables (1920-1980). New tables continually...
irpinball.ztnet.com/

70. **Ken's Pinball Pages at www.pinballrebel.com**
Specific game pages, videos, and some free custom instruction and score cards for your own machine.
www.pinballrebel.com/game/pins/pins.htm

71. **ROBO Pinball**
Pinball game using Shockwave 3D and the Havok Xtra programmed with Macromedia Direcctor 8.5.
www.cerberos.de/pinball/popup.php?js=1

72. **Latest site update**
Presents the top 100 games, a pinball quiz, and an archive with information on hundreds of different pins.
www.arkadia.nl/

73. **Wakefield Pinball**
Details of pinball machines in Wakefield and the rest of West Yorkshire, UK.
www.wakey.com/pinball/

74. **Stand Alone, Inc. - Handheld Software**
A shareware pinball game for Palm OS organizers.
www.standalone.com/palmos/dragon_hunter_pinball/

75. **Empire Interactive**
Empire Interactive's website featuring their pinball simulation series.
www.propinball.com/

76. **Absolute Pinball - Review**
A review and overview of its tables. Features screenshots.
www.gamesdomain.com/gdreview/zones/ reviews/pc/oct96 absolute.html

77. **Addiction Pinball - Review**
A review, including an overview of the tables. Also features screenshots.
www.gamesdomain.com/gdreview/zones/ reviews/pc/jun98/ apinball.html

78. **We buy and sell pinball machines**
Buys, sells and trades pins. Based in Colorado, USA.
www.pinballuniverse.com/

79. **Pinburgh 2003**
Contains information about Pittsburgh's three-day "premier pinball event."
www.pinburgh.com/

80. **Pinball Location**
The summary for this Japanese page contains characters that cannot be correctly displayed in this language/character set.
www.tea-works.com/pl/

81. **Pinball Simulations Portal Site by Digital Playfield**
Provides links to Visual Pinball sites along with free VP front-end interface to manage VP and VPMame.
www.digitalplayfield.com/

82. **The Tower of Pin - Reviews (Absolute Pinball)**
A review, including system requirements and screenshots.
www.pcpinball.com/reviews/english/ sims/absolute_pinball.html

83. **Video Game, Pinball Machine, Foosball, Air Hockey, Dart and ...**
Listing of available pinball and arcade machine parts for the collector and operator of these machines.
www.moneymachines.com/parts.html

84. **This Old Pinball, pinball restoration and pinball repair video ...**
"Incredible! The best 'This Old Pinball' video yet. Shaggy ... Pinball. Click Here for Pinball Information & Repair Guides. Site...
marvin3m.com/top/

85. **Pinball Repair and Maintenance Books at Bell Springs Alley**
Pinball Repair and Maintenance Books by Bell Springs Pinball Alley. ... Pinball Machines. Buy - Maintain - Adjust - Repair. Animated Pinball Bumper. ...
www.saber.net/~bellsprings/

86. **Pinball Pleasure - supplier of quality second-hand and new pinball ...**
Supplies restored pintables in the UK.
www.pinball-pleasure.co.uk/

44
Polo

1. **Polo.com**
   Polo.com offers the world of Ralph Lauren online including clothing for men, women and children, bedding and bath luxuries, gifts and much more. Clothing and accessories for men, women, and children. Includes travel service and Polo store locator.
   www.polo.com/
2. **MarcoPolo - Internet Content for the Classroom**
   Access lesson plans, student activities, reviewed
   marcopolo.worldcom.com/
3. **United States Polo Association - Home Page**
   The United States Polo Association (USPA) was organized in 1890 to promote the game of polo, coordinate the activities of its member clubs and individuals and ...
   www.uspolo.org/
4. **United States Water Polo Home Page**
   WATER POLO NEWS Water Polo Trivial Pursuit Contest (Win Prizes from the 2004 Aquatics Grand Prix @ Long Beach!...click here). ... Official USA Water Polo Partners: ... Description: Resource for water polo news and information.
   www.usawaterpolo.com/
5. **H2O Polo - An Interactive Community for Water Polo Players**
   H2O Polo is a real-time interactive site for the sport of water polo with daily news, scores and schedules posted by the water polo players, coaches and fans! ...
   www.h2opolo.com/

6. **Polonews.com / Polo-Player.com / Poloplayer.org**
   Provides information about the sport. Includes a forum, bulletin boards, directories, events and tourname...
   www.polonews.com/
7. **Polo Towers Home Page**
   Polo Towers is the first and only purpose-built vacation ownership resort on the Las Vegas Strip. Located right in the heart of ...
   www.polotowers.com/
8. **The Federation of International Polo - FIP**
   FIP - Federation of International Polo Official Web Site. The world governing body to the sport. Includes history, rules, news, membership information, links,...
   www.fippolo.com/
9. **Water Polo Canada - Gloucester Ontario Canada**
   Water Polo Canada. Official page of the Water Polo Canada. Merchandise, national programs, competitions, job opportunities,...
   www.waterpolo.ca/
10. **Ascot Park Polo Club - Polo Tuition, Corporate Hospitality and...**
    Ascot Park Polo Club - Polo Tuition, Corporate Hospitality and Events, Polo Sponsorship, Teambuilding Days: have an exciting Day Out with our Unique Learn to ...
    www.polo.co.uk/
11. **Hurlingham Polo Association**
    Hurlingham Polo Associaton (HPA) web site. The governing body for polo in the UK. Includes a club directory.
    www.hpa-polo.co.uk/
12. **Bicycle Polo - US Bicycle Polo Association, Inc.**
    Ride into the fastest growing sport on the edges of the mountain biking world...bike polo! Rules, strategies, history, photos, video, school program specials, how to get started and information...
    www.bikepolo.com/
13. **The World Elephant Polo Association**
    The 22nd World Elephant Polo Championship - Tiger Tops Tuskers from Nepal are the new World Elephant Polo Champions .....more. ...
    www.elephantpolo.com/

14. **Collegiate Water Polo Association**
Latest News, Schedules & Results, School Profiles, Coaching Resource Information, General Information, Officiating Information, Frequently Asked Questions, ...
www.collegiatewaterpolo.org/

15. **POLO Players' Edition: Online**
POLO Players' Edition is a sports magazine that offers profiles of polo's personalities, professional advice on everything from care to polo playing ...
www.poloplayersedition.com/

16. **ICF Canoe Polo Committee**
ICF Canoe Polo Committee. ... site. Copyright © 2002 International Canoe Federation Canoe Polo Committee Official site of the International Canoe Federation Canoe Polo Committee. Includes schedules, rules,...
www.canoe-polo.com/

17. **USWP.ORG (USA WATER POLO, INC)**
The information from USWP Online has moved. Go to the newest and most complete website devoted to water polo at www.usawaterpolo.com. ...
www.uswp.org/

18. **San Diego Polo Club**
Hosts polo matches and events at grounds in Rancho Santa Fe. Season schedule, special events, polo...
www.sandiegopolo.com/

19. **A World Wide Web of Polo**
Extensive club listings and links. Web design services also offered.
www.polo.org/

20. **Polo Associations, Organizations, Clubs, Players, News, equipment ...**
A directory of over 30000 horse polo and other equestrian links and listings for you and your horses categorized by Country, State and City. Horse coach, box, float, trailer and van manufacturers worldwide indexed by country.
www.polocenter.com/

21. **Polo Gear USA**
    Manufactures, distributes and sells polo products to players, teams and polo events worldwide.
    www.pologearusa.com/
22. **Coaching Water Polo**
    Coaching Water Polo Email to paulw01@msn.com.au, This is a hobby. There is ... Conundrum! This site is a forum for water polo coaches. Finding ...
    www.users.bigpond.com/MSN/paulw01/
23. **Australian Water Polo Home Page**
    AUSTRALIAN WATER POLO Inc. The official website of Australian Water Polo Inc. This site updated daily. Maintained by Russell ...
    www.waterpoloaus.asn.au/
24. **Home - Polo Wicklow**
    This club boasts Ireland's only all weather polo arena in Kilpoole Hill, Wicklow. Season reports and...
    www.herbstgroup.com/polo/
25. **FINA Water Polo Rules and Regulations**
    FINA WATER POLO RULES, FINA HANDBOOK. . CONSTITUTION. ... FACILITY RULES. DOPING RULES. MEDICAL RULES. FINA WATER POLO RULES NEW RULES
    www.fina.org/waterpolorules.html
26. **Polo Times**
    Features Feature Nora Heguy St Tropez Polo Masters Elephant Polo Thailand News from the USA Kenya Open. Regular Articles HPA Newsletter ...
    www.polotimes.co.uk/
27. **New Zealand Water Polo Home**
    The New Zealand Water Polo Association website encourages the growth of waterpolo at all levels. The official site of the New Zealand Water Polo Association and your one-stop-shop for the sport that...
    www.waterpolo.org.nz/
28. **Palm Beach Polo Golf and Country Club, Wellington, FL**
    Home Members Calendar Golf Tennis Facilitics Polo Equestrian Real Estate Contact, Description: Includes a Country Club and offers 13 fields and a polo stadium. Tournament schedule, player roster,...
    www.palmbeachpolo.com/

45

Rugby

1. **Rugby World Cup news, fun, results, fixtures and features fro...**
   With international rugby rankings and an archive going back to 1871.
   www.planet-rugby.com/
2. **Rugby.com.au | Rugby.com.au**
   Rugby union news, fixtures results and articles.
   www.rugby.com.au/
3. **Rugby Football Union - Home**
   Home, News and Contents, The Rugby Store, Results, Fixtures, Forums/Chat, Tickets.Community Rugby, England Rugby, Zurich Premiership, Women's Rugby, Sevens, Twickenham. Contains information about all facets of English rugby and merchandising. The Rugby Football Union...
   www.rfu.com/
4. **USA Rugby**
   Lists players, coaches, referees, administrators and national teams; also includes calendar and youth...
   www.usarugby.org/
5. **Scrum.com - Rugby News, Rugby Results, Rugby Action from Scrum ...**
   World rugby news, results, leagues, reports on all major internationals and European club matches, regular...
   www.scrum.com/
6. **Rugby World Cup 2003 - RugbyHeaven**
   Coverage on the Super 12 series, Tri-Nations series, the Bledisloe Cup and the Rugby World Cup, along...
   rugbyheaven.smh.com.au/

7. **Scottish Rugby**
Scotland | Edinburgh | Glasgow | The Borders | Club Rugby | Shop | Tickets | My Setting | Login. ... SRU, Sponsors, Get Active in Rugby. :: Who's Who. :: Rules & Regs.
www.sru.org.uk/

8. **National Rugby League Season 2003**
News, information, season draw, video replays, and multimedia.
www.nrl.com.au/

9. **Rugby news, results and features from RugbyRugby**
News, tournaments, columnists, fixtures, results, laws, referees, photographs, and a message board.
www.rugbyrugby.com/

10. **Rugby World Cup 2003**
Official site with news, schedule and ticket information.
www.rugby2003.com.au/

11. **Rugby Canada**
Information on Canada' national teams, super league, and national championships. Refereeing, coaching...
www.rugbycanada.ca/

12. **Welsh Rugby Union : WRU Home Page**
Includes information, fixture lists, league tables, results and merchandise.
www.wru.co.uk/

13. **Irish Rugby**
Best news source for Irish Rugby, with news on the Six Nations, Munster rugby, the IRFU, and Ireland's friendlies. Buy rugby shirts and jerseys online. ...
www.irfu.ie/

14. **World of Rugby League - rleague.com**
With the latest news, results and information.
www.rleague.com/

15. **nzrugby.com**
The official site of the New Zealand Rugby Union.
www.nzrugby.co.nz/

16. **Web Rugby - Rugby Union Index**
Find official Rugby Union web sites in this directory.
webrugby.com/

17. **Rugby Imports Online Catalog**
    Store specializes in rugby clothing and equipment.
    www.rugbyimports.com/

18. **SA Rugby**
    The President of the South African Rugby Football Union, Brian Van Rooyen, has expressed his deep sympathy to the family and friends of Jomo King, following ...
    www.sarugby.net/

19. **LE SITE RUGBY**
    World_>_Français_>_..._>_Rugby_>_Actualité_et_médias
    www.lesiterugby.com/

20. **Rugby news,fun and features from Rugby365.com**
    Premiership, Heineken Cup, Six Nations, Tri Nations, Super 12 and World Cup 2003 news plus features, fixtures, results and comment from the world of rugby union ...
    www.rugby365.com/

21. **IRB RWC 2003**
    OFFICIAL WEBSITE OF THE IRB RUGBY WORLD CUP 2003, ... 2003 RUGBY WORLD CUP LTD,
    www.rugbyworldcup.com/RugbyWorldCup/

22. **Zurich Premiership rugby news, results, fixtures and clubs**
    The Rugby Club is the official rugby website of the Zurich Premiership. Latest news, results, stats, live scores, team and player...
    www.zurichrugby.co.uk/

23. **Home@Rugby**
    RBC Home Tourist information, leisure, business, transport, education and training, local services and local...
    www.rugby.gov.uk/

24. **Rugby Magazine: the journal of record for the sport of rugby i...**
    The journal of record for the sport in the US Every US championship is covered, as well as all...
    www.rugbymag.com/

25. **RUGBY NEWS - Welcome to Rugby News**
    New Zealand Rugby News, the only WEEKLY Magazine providing full coverage of our national sport from the home country of the mighty All Blacks. ...
    www.rugby.co.nz/

26. **FIR - Federazione Italiana Rubg**
World_>_Italiano_>_Sport_>_Rugby
www.federugby.it/

27. **RFL Website**
The official website of the Rugby Football League. The site offers a diverse range of information, including ...
www.rfl.uk.com/

28. **World of Rugby**
News from the world of rugby, updated during the day. Also offering rugby talk, results and reports.
www.worldofrugby.com/

29. **TOTALRL.COM - Total Rugby League Online**
The official website of Rugby Leaguer & League Express and Rugby League World Magazine. ... Official site of Rugby Leaguer & League Express, and Rugby League World, ...
www.rugbyleaguer.co.uk/

30. **Supersportzone**
Krige's future in the balance Corné Krige's days at the helm of the Springbok rugby team may be numbered. ... A/Attractions home; Full Rugby Schedule; Live Scores. ...
www.superrugby.co.za/

31. **Super 12 Rugby**
Tables, squads, fixtures, news, reviews and links to all the Super 12 team sites.
www.super12rugby.com/

32. **Rugby Song Links from around the World**
The most complete and up to date index of RUGBY SONGS from web sites around the world. A MUST to ... Rugby Songs. | traduisez ce site ...
www.fhrugby.org/songs.html

33. **RugbyInfo**
Unofficial repository of rugby information. Information on all significant data on the game of rugby union to be found on the Internet.
www.uidaho.edu/clubs/womens_rugby/RugbyRoot/

34. **Bath Rugby Club**

The official Bath Rugby Club website for all the latest match reports,player profiles and official merchandise. ... Bath Rugby Homepage. ...

www.bathrugby.com/

35. **Rugby School**

Co-educational boarding school. Details of school life, admissions, business & tourism, development...

www.rugbyschool.net/

36. **Quad Rugby - Wheelchair Rugby - Home of the United States Quad ...**

Includes all the latest news, information and rules.

www.quadrugby.com/

37. **SourceNom.com**

SourceNom.com sells domain name registrations including a premium service set all included in the discount price of the ...

www.rwc99.com/

38. **Welcome Page**

Online shopping for rugby needs. The site includes equipment, clubs and links.

www.rugbystore.com/

39. **CNNSI.com - Rugby**

Sports News from Cable News Network(CNN) and Sports Illustrated Magazine.

www.cnnsi.com/rugby/

40. **Rugby World Magazine Online**

Rugby World. As the world's biggest selling rugby magazine we thought it was time to take the Internet by storm. We hope ...

www.rugbyworld.com/

41. **RugbyGuide.com :: Your Link to the World of Rugby**

A in-depth listing of rugby related links, everything from news, teams, coaching, and even humor.

www.rugbyguide.com/

42. **www.rugby.ro World > Română > Sport > Rugby**

www.rugby.ro/

43. **Hong Kong Rugby Football Union**
Official site includes news, fixtures, member clubs, photos, and related links. Also provides information...
www.hkrfu.com/

44. **Ontario Rugby Union**
The official website of Rugby Ontario the largest rugby union in Canada
www.rugbyontario.com/

45. **This is Rugby**
A rugby guide site with links to all the top teams also includes information on rugby league/union, international teams, national teams, super league ...
www.thisis-rugby.com/

46. **BALL'S OUT! Rugby**
Rugby is a full service rugby supply company featuring the highest quality jerseys, shorts, cleats, individual and team apparel and gear, field equipment ...
www.ballsout.com/

47. **Laws of Rugby**
The Laws of the Game of Rugby Football. with Instructions and Notes on the Laws as framed by the International Rugby Football Board. About these on-line laws. ...
www.uidaho.edu/clubs/womens_rugby/RugbyRoot/ rugby Rules/LawBook/contents.html

48. **Rugby Museum of New Zealand**
The New Zealand Rugby Museum holds the complete history of the game in NZ, plus hosts the most comprehens...
www.rugbymuseum.co.nz/

49. **AmericanRugby.com**
Rugby jersey and rugby gear supplier.
www.americanrugby.com/

50. **The British Amateur Rugby League Association**
The official site covering Open-Agc, Youth, Junior and Women and Girls Rugby League.
www.barla.org.uk/

46
Skating

1. **US Figure Skating Online!**
   The USFSA is the national governing body of the sport of figure skating in the United States and has...
   www.usfsa.org/
2. **ISU : Home**
   The ISU's speed skating page, including schedules, records, official communiques and results.
   www.isu.org/
3. **www.skating.com**
   Equipment reviews, skater profiles, and a large database of links to related Web sites. Also includes...
   www.skating.com/
4. **Inline Skating Resource Center : International Inline Skating...**
   Inline skating resources for new and experienced skaters, media, and the inline skating industry. Trade organization of industry suppliers formed in 1990. Includes instructor certification program...
   www.iisa.org/
5. **SkateWeb: The Figure Skating Page**
   Index which includes links to current news items, fan and/or official webpages, related businesses,...
   www.frogsonice.com/skateweb/
6. **Skate Canada - Patinage Canada**
   An association dedicated to the principles of enabling every Canadian to participate in skating through
   www.skatecanada.ca/

7. **Ice Skating Institute**
   "Dedicated to providing leadership, education, and services to the ice skating industry." Focuses...
   www.skateisi.com/
8. **International Figure Skating**
   Redirecting to the new IFSmagazine.com. If the page does not change in 10 seconds, click the button below. Newsmagazine for the sport and art of figure skating. Based in the US with correspondents in Canada,...
   www.ifsmagazine.com/
9. **Skating the Infobahn — Inline Skating Web Links**
   Comprehensive directory with more than 2000 links to inline, quad, artistic, aggressive, speed, and...
   www.skatecity.com/links/
10. **About Inline Skating**
   Articles and information about inline skating and quad roller skating, including aggressive skating, artistic skating, fitness skating, roller hockey ...
   inlineskating.about.com/mbody.htm
11. **Skate FAQs**
   Anthony Chen's comprehensive general skating reference answers frequently asked questions about buying...
   www.skatefaq.com/

12 **Speed Skating Canada - Patinage de Vitesse Canada**
   Contains details of events and results.
   www.speedskating.ca/

13. **Top20Skating.com - Your Top20 Guide for Skating!**
   List of 20 links to skating sites.
   www.top20skating.com/
14. **Aggressive.com - Aggressive Skating, Inline Skating**
   This web site is hands down the most comprehensive inline skating page on the web. It ... Aggressive skating is all about fun. It's ...
   www.aggressive.com/
15. **Figure Skating**
   Figure Skating Internet Portal - the starting place for exploring Figure Skating and staying updated with weekly features, interviews, fan pages, and much more ...
   figureskating.about.com/

16. **SKATING.CH - The Swiss Skating Website**
    The website for ice skating in Switzerland and around the world. Unofficial website of Swiss Skating...
    www.skating.ch/
17. **SLAM! Sports - Figure Skating**
    Figure skating news from Canadian Online Explorer (Canoe).
    www.canoe.ca/SlamSkating/home.html
18. **Harlick Skating Boots**
    Boots for ice and roller skaters. Includes photo gallery of skaters who use Harlicks.
    www.harlick.com/
19. **SABAH Home**
    Events, volunteering information and contacts for this not-for profit company that provides skating...
    www.sabahinc.org/
20. **Roller-Skating > Home**
    World > Français > ... > Patins > Patin à roulettes > Vitesse
    www.roller-skating.com/
21. **Ice Skating Clipart Galore - Over 450 Ice Skating Images**
    Over 325 free clipart images including figure skaters, hockey, speedskating, precision, cartoons,...
    www.icesk8.com/clipart.htm
22. **Figure Skating WebRing**
    This is the place to link all the skating pages on the 'net! To join the Figure Skating WebRing, fill out the simple form below. ALL fields must be completed!
    www.geocities.com/Colosseum/Field/6193/skatering.html
23. **National Ice Skating Association of the UK**
    Features news, information and events surrounding the sport in the United Kingdom, including links...
    www.iceskating.org.uk/
24. **US Figure Skating Association - About the USFSA - Jobs**
    The United Stated Figure Skating Association (USFSA) is the national governing body of the sport of figure skating in the United States and has a membership of ...
    www.worldskatingmuseum.org/

25. **Ice Speed Skating Home-page**
Ice Speed Skating Home-page. This Winter 2002-2003: All events. ... Big events. Calender by ISU. Ice Skating Pages in the world. ...
www.dsdelft.nl/~skate

26. **Ice Skating Australia**
Ice Skating Australia. Sun Skate 2003. Australian Figure Skating Championships. 29 November 2003 to 6 December 2003. ...
www.isa.org.au/

27. **Hamburger Inline-Skating Club**
World_>_Deutsch_>_Sport_>_Rollsport_>_Inline-Skating
www.skating-hamburg.de/

28. **Home - NMRS**
National Museum of Roller Skating! Located in Lincoln, Nebraska ... Copyright © 2003 National Museum of Roller Skating. Images and articles about the history of roller skating, along with a store.
www.rollerskatingmuseum.com//

29. **Recreational Figure Skating FAQ**
The Ancient But Honourable Recreational Figure Skating FAQ ... Please follow This Link to view the new and improved Recreational Figure Skating FAQ. ...
www.cyberus.ca/~karen/recskate/

30. **ITALIANSKATING FORUM CENTER PRE-HOME**
World_>_Italiano_>_Sport_>_Pattinaggio_>_A_Rotelle
www.italianskating.com/

31. **www.icesk8.com - An Ice Skating Super Site!**
Includes ice skating in the desert, clipart, accessories, services, and links.
www.icesk8.com/

32. **Figure Skating Journal, Reflections of an Adult Figure Skater**
Weekly journal of an adult figure skater. Includes skating novel, glossary of figure skating terminology...
www.skatejournal.com/

33. **Fitness and SpeedSkating Times Online**
Cover of This Issue of Fitness and Speed Skating Times Magazine.
www.fasst.com/

34. **Hockey Skating Tips**

Hockey Skating Tips. This page is under construction. So far I have ... skating stride. These are called "toe starts" 4. Forward skating. o stay ...

www.cs.toronto.edu/~andria/tip/skating/

35. **SkatingMunich.de**

Kids_and_Teens_>_International_>_Deutsch_>_Sport_und_Hobby

www.skatingmunich.de/

36. **Ice Skating International: Online**

Online magazine by George Rossano.

www.iceskatingintnl.com/

37. **Sports/skating Index**

Usenet FAQs for ice, roller, inline, and racing newsgroups.

www.faqs.org/faqs/sports/skating/

38. **British Artistic Roller Skating**

British artistic roller skating: where you can do it, who governs it, what tests you can do, championship results, calender of events, club and rink directory ...

www.british-roller-skating.org.uk/

39. **Barry Mittan .:. Skating Calendar**

2004 Art of Figure Skating Calendar. The 2003 Art of Figure Skating Calendar with text and photos by Barry Mittan is sold out.

www.jbmittan.com/calendar.htm

40. **BC/YT Section Skate Canada Skating In BC - The Information Source ...**

Skatinginbc.com is the web site used by the british columbia/Yukon section to communicate with its skating members. The site offers News, information, competition results, talk forums, and skating links. Based in British Columbia...

www.skatinginbc.com/

41. **Fleet Skating Center - Phone (401) 331-5544**

Outdoor ice skating rink open during the winter at Kennedy Plaza. Includes general information about...

www.fleetskating.com/

42. **New York City Inline Skating Guide —**

Detailed information on where to skate, clubs and leagues, skate shops, safety, and the law.

www.skatecity.com/nyc/

43. **synchroskating.com**
Forums, links, team profiles, and information about the sport. Includes both English and French sections.
www.synchroskating.com/

44. **Official Site For US Speedskating**
The official website of the National Governing Board for speedskating in the United States.
www.usspeedskating.org/

45. **Skating, Inc. - Skating, Inc. - Figure Skating_s Most Popular ...**
The largest site on the Internet devoted to figure skating, with official sites,fan pages, chat room, message board, and interactive features. ...
skatinginc.com/

46. **Indiana/World Skating Academy**
INDIANA/WORLD SKATING ACADEMY (I/WSA) provides for the physical and educational needs of both amateur and professional athletes in figure skating, hockey and ...
www.iwsa.org/

47. **Lovena_s Ice Skating Page! - ©1996-2003 by Lovena Harwood**
Figure skating page with general information for the Massachusetts/ New Hampshire area. Offers ice...
lovenaonline.com/

48. **Lovena_s Ice Skating Page! - ©1996-2001 by Lovena Harwood**
General figure skating and ice skating information for the ice skating fan, Iceskating information in the state of Massachusetts USA. Lovena's Skating Page! ...
www.netway.com/~lovena/graphics.htm

49. **Ice Skating World . com - The Internet_s most comprehensive ice ...**
A one-stop shop for all your skating needs. ... FREE Ice Skating World monthly newsletter. Enter your e-mail address and click subscribe! Buy and sell anything skating. Free monthly newsletter, ask the Pros section, links, library, and lounge.
www.iceskatingworld.com/

50. **Speed Skating Results**
Historical results of major speed skating championships, including Olympic results. Viewable by event...
weasel.student.utwente.nl/~speedskating/

51. **Figure Skating Universe**

Supplies a forum where users can chat about figure skating and life in general.

www.fsuniverse.net/

52. **Blading Central: In-line Skating with Your Dog**

Tips and equipment required to skate with a dog on a leash. Includes links to other sites.

www.caryn.com/francis/francis-blade.html

53. **The Physics of Ice Skating - Main Page**

How does ice skating work? This site uses (and explains!) simple physics to explain ice skating. The Physics of Ice Skating - Main Page. ...

satchmo.as.arizona.edu/~jrigby/skating/main.html

54. **FFRS World_>_Français_>_..._>_Sports_>_Patin_à_roulettes**

www.ffrs.asso.fr/

55. **Ice Skating Blades supplied by Skating World**

Skating World - Suppliers of quality ice skating equipment including blades, ice skates and dresses. ...

www.skating-world.com/

56. **Articles and News About Skating - SkateLog.com - Inline Skating ...**

A collection of articles, photos, and news about inline skating and quad roller skating all over the world. ... Skating T-Shirts. Skating T-Shirts. ...

www.skatelog.com/

57. **Skating Club of Wilmington_'s Home Page**

Ice skating, including hockey. Lessons available.

www.wilmicesk8.com/

58. **World Skating Federation**

The World Skating Federation is a new international skating organization that has been formed with the purpose of becoming the new IOC-recognized international ...

www.worldskating.org/

59. **The Figure Skating Calendar**

The greatest skating stars at Worlds, the Olympics, the Grand Prix events and other prestigious competitions, superb quality and large images, this is the ...

www.figureskatingcalendar.ca/

60. **Die Eiskunstlauf-Ecke/The Figure Skating Corner**

The Figure Skating Corner: Results, reports, biographies, figure skating history and figure skating related links to personal home pages, fan pages and ...

home.snafu.de/eberl/english/

61. **Figure skating and related issues**

About the various issues related to the sport of figure skating, including sports psychology, nutrition, eating disorders, off-ice training, and more.

www.angelfire.com/il2/figskating/

62. **Website Not Found**

SelectNet Internet Services. Web hosting and Internet services for the business community. This 75 year-old roller skating great grandmother won a gold medal in artistic roller skating at the...

www.hotskatinggrandma.com/

63. **NIISA Homepage**

2002 Northern Ireland Open Championships. NISA bulletins, info on local skaters, history of ice skating in NI, competition results, Roll of Honour.

www.niceweb.demon.co.uk/

64. **Portland 2005**

Experience the athletic excellence and spirited competition of the 2005 State Farm US Figure Skating Championships and the Chevy Skating Spectacular in Portland ...

www.portland2005.com/

65. **Amazon.com: Books: Figure Skating For Dummies®**

Figure Skating For Dummies®, Kristi Yamaguchi, Christy Ness,Jody Meacham, Christy Kjarsgaard-Ness, Jody Meachem....

www.amazon.com/exec/obidos/tg/ detail/-/0764550845?v=glance

66. **Skating Plus Main**

www.skatingplus.com/

67. **Figure Skating Fan Listing**

Official Figure Skating Fanlisting! Are you a figure skating fan? If you know what a salchow is.... If you love artistry ...

heatherw.com/fsfan/

68. **2004 State Farm US Figure Skating Championships: Atlanta, Georgia**
Official home of the 2004 State Farm US Figure Skating Championships at Philips Arena in Atlanta, Ga. ... 2004 US Figure Skating Championships, Inc. Features news, schedules, event history and information\ about tickets and accommodation.
www.atlanta2004.org/

69. **Robby Glantz International Power Skating**
Skating coach of LA Kings and his staff hold three day clinics and weeklong schools nationwide....
www.robbyglantz.com/

70. **International Skating Center of Connecticut - Home Page**
The International Skating Center of Connecticut is a world classtwin rink facility designed to meet needs first time competitors and Olympic Champions alike. ...
www.isccskate.com/

71. **CHRISTIANSKATING.NET**
Starting place on the web for Christian skaters.
www.christianskating.net/

72. **www.figureskatingdivas.com**
Features articles, news headlines, and information about the top eligible competitors in Ladies' Figure...
www.figureskatingdivas.com/

73. **Calgary Speed Skating Association**
The official website of the Calgary Speed Skating Association, about joining, ice times and equipment.
www.calgaryspeedskating.com/

74. **Doomwheels Kite Skating, Kite Surfing, Kite Buggying, Kite Skiing ...**
Off-road, in-line kite skating with lessons and building instructions by Bob Childs plus kite traction...
www.doomwheels.com/

75. **Tuesday Night Skating 2003**
World_>_Deutsch_>_Sport_>_Rollsport_>_Inline-Skating
www.t-n-s.de/

76. **The Skating Beauty and... Beast**
The summary for this Japanese page contains characters that cannot be correctly displayed in this language/character set.
member.nifty.ne.jp/~cross/

77. **usolympicteam.com**
A brief history of roller skating from the US Olympic Committee site.
www.olympic-usa.org/sports2/ro/az_hist.html

78. **The Home of Romanian Skating**
Everything about Romanian skating, results, athletes, clubs, and future events.
internettrash.com/users/roskate/

79. **skating boots and blades hockey equipment in-line skates an...**
skating supplies from world leading suppliers and quality sharpening from specialist skating services at
www.iceskate.co.uk. Specialist ...
www.iceskate.co.uk/

80. **Speed Skating Pictures**
The latest happenings and information concerning speed skating in Southern California.
www.socalspeedskating.org/

81. **WILSA Home**
Resource for skaters in Washington State, with articles, reviews, places to skate, and message boards.
www.wilsa.org/

82. **Dynamic Skating**
Dynamic skating programs designed by Paul Vincent to emphasize technique and speed. Individual drills...
www.dynamicskating.com/

83. **FIGURE SKATING TAPES**
My Figure Skating Page! Before you email mail me about trading, please read my Conditions for trading. If you do not ...
www.geocities.com/colosseum/court/6845

47
Skiing

1. **SkiNet.com | The skiing resource for ski gear, travel, resorts and ...**
   Skiing resource for gear, travel, resorts, snow conditions, ski instruction, news, and racing results.
   www.skinet.com/
2. **GoSki.com - The worldwide guide to ski resorts and mountain sports ...**
   Worldwide skiing and snowboarding guide. Provides resort and area information by region and by type...
   www.goski.com/
3. **SkiingMag.com**
   Skiing/content/images/indexpagephotos2004
   ResortFinder2004m.jpg, Resort Finder 2004
   www.skiingmag.com/
4. **About Skiing | Ski Vacations and Ski Resort Guides, Skiing Gear**
   Find ski resorts and reviews of mountain destinations, get ski vacation ideas for alpine skiing, backcountry, telemark and cross-country skiing.
   skiing.about.com/mbody.htm
5. **US Ski Team**
   US Ski Team. US Snowboarding. USSA Members. US Ski Team Home. About USSA. Major Events/TV Schedules.
   www.usskiteam.com/
6. **SkiCentral - The #1 Search Site for Skiing and Snowboarding**
   SkiCentral is the #1 index and search engine for skiing and snowboarding, featurin more than 8300 snow sport sites, ski reports, resorts, snowcams, travel ...
   skicentral.com/

7. **Skiing, Snowboarding, Dogsledding, and Snowshoeing**
Downhill Skiing & Snowboarding US Guide • International •Gear • Family •Clubs • Trips • Forum More Dogsledding • Snowshoeing • Other • Gear ...
www.gorp.com/gorp/activity/skiing.htm

8. **Skiing.com - Your Site for Skiing**
Skiing.com, Your Site for Skiing. Skiing | Ski Gear | Ski Resorts |Ski Vacation | Lake Tahoe Skiing | Colorado Skiing | Water Skiing ...
www.skiing.com/

9. **Ski Utah - Your information source for skiing, snowboarding ...**
Great resource for ski information around the state, also updated for summer activities as well.
www.skiutah.com/

10. **Skiing the Net - Jobs for skiers and snowboarders**
Snow sports employment opportunities with ski resorts, hotels, restaurants, ski shops. Professional...
www.skiingthenet.com/

11. **SnoWeb - Lake Tahoe Skiing and Snowboarding!**
Guide for Tahoe-area cross-country, backcountry and downhill skiing and snowboarding. Includes weather,...
www.snoweb.com/

12. **AspenSnowmass.com : Skiing, Snowboarding & MORE in Aspen and ...**
www.aspensnowmass.com/

13. **XC Skiing Information from Cross Country Ski Areas Association**
National resort guide, industry demographics, events listings and CCSAA logo clothing.
www.xcski.org/

14. **American Skiing Company**
Welcome to American Skiing Company web site. Here you'll find everything need know about our company and resorts, from conditions ...
www.peaks.com/

15. **Speed Skiing Extreme Ski Snow Sport - Speedski Racing**
Speed Skiing, Ski de Vitesse, Extreme Speedski Racing, Fastest non-Motorized Sport on Earth. Speed Skiing nearly past fear and terminal...
www.speedski.com/

16. **Skiing.NL - Welkom**
World_>_Nederlands_>_Sport_>_Wintersport_>_Skiën
www.skiing.nl/

17. **SLAM! Sports - Skiing**
Louise More Skiing News ...
www.canoe.ca/SlamSkiing/home.html

18. **Madnordski Skiing Page**
Sponsored by the Madison Nordic Ski Club. Includes stories, snow conditions, events, discussion forum,...
www.madnorski.org/

19. **Skiing in Canada**
The Comprehensive Canadian Skiing Guide. Skiing in Canada has moved. You will be automagically redirected in 10 seconds to the new address. ...
grover.educ.ualberta.ca/skican.html

20. **SAL Home**
Governing body, supports and promotes snow sports. Includes recent results and links to resorts and...
www.skiingaustralia.org.au/

21. **West Virginia Skiing**
Discover West Virginia skiing and you will ski some of the finest resorts in the Eastern US. WV Bookmarks, ...
www.skiwv.com/

22. **Canadian Mountain Holidays**
Offers heliskiing and snowboarding packages for guided powder tours of Canada. Provides prices, photo...
www.cmhski.com/

23. **Maine Handicapped Skiing - Headquartered at Sunday ...**
Information about Maine Handicapped Skiing, Ski-A-Thon schedules, the Ski-A-Thon team, and ways to...
www.skimhs.org/

24. **CDAST Home Page**
Information on Alpine skiing programs for the disabled.
www.canuck.com/cads/

25. **Ski Packages and Ski Vacations, Jackson Hole Skiing, Lodging, Hotels ...**
Complete guide to skiing and winter recreation in Jackson Hole, Wyoming
www.jacksonhole-skiing.com/

26. **Ski Area Resort and Lodging Guide**
    Skiing on Top of the World - Utah Some of the country's top resorts lie within an hour or less of downtown Salt Lake City. ...
    www.travelbase.com/activities/skiing/
27. **US Skiing**
    Ski ResortGuide.com. Home. Click here for more information. US Skiing is the most comprehensive guide to ski and snowboard areas in the United States. ...
    www.usskiing.com/
28. **Outdoors in MaineToday.com | Downhill Skiing**
    Camping, canoeing, fishing, golf, hiking, hunting, kayaking, nature, wildlife, rafting, sailing, downhill and cross-country skiing,v snowboarding, snowmobiling ...
    outdoors.mainetoday.com/downhillskiing/
29. **Ski Vacation - Skiing Package Vacations to Ski Resorts - Ski.com**
    Ski Vacation Packages to over thirty ski resorts. Aspen Ski Tours offers skiing vacations, snow reports, ski equipment shopping and more. ...
    www.ski.com/
30. **Snow co : New Zealand Ski and Snowboard info at all NZ skiing and ...**
    New Zealand skiing and snowboarding resort, snow reports and webcams all ski and snowboard areas in New Zealand. ...
    www.snow.co.nz/
31. **FIS Next FIS World Cup Events**
    Official snowboarding website of the Fédération Internationale de Ski with details of competitions,...
    www.fis-ski.com/
32. **SKILEB.com - Skiing and Snowboarding in Lebanon**
    Skiing in Lebanon. Ski Resorts including Faraya-Mzaar, the Cedars (al Arz), Laqlouq, Qanat Bakish,...
    www.skileb.com/
33. **Ski History**
    Skiing History and Skiing Heritage are published by the International Skiing History Association, the world's leading organization dedicated to the history of ...
    www.skiinghistory.org/

34. **Traditional Skiing in Finland**

    An overview of cross country skiing in Finland including historical background and pictures

    virtual.finland.fi/finfo/english/skiing.html

35. **Cross Country Skiing Online - Cross Country Skis and Gear**

    Cross-Country Skiing Online is a quick and easy way to find cross country ski, skis and skiing info. Skis and Equipment, ...

    www.cross-countryski.com/

36. **Travel**

    Skiing. Make ... appeal. Resort Report: Val d'Isère,France

    travel.independent.co.uk/themes/skiing/

37. **Leavenworth Snowcat Skiing**

    Guided backcountry snowcat skiing and snowboarding in the Cascade Mountains near Leavenworth, Washington....

    www.leavenworthsnowcat.com/

38. **rec.skiing FAQ**

    The rec.skiing Frequently Asked Questions List. -or- Everything you always wanted to know about skiing and were *just* about to ask by posting. ...

    www.darryl.com/skiing/

39. **Purcell Helicopter Skiing Ltd. in the Canadian Rocky Mountains...**

    Offer heliskiing, boarding and hiking. Based in Golden, British Columbia, Canada.

    www.purcellhelicopterskiing.com/

40. **Whistler Heli Skiing**

    Whistler Heli-Skiing takes groups of skiers and riders into the mountain terrain that surrounds the...

    www.heliskiwhistler.com/

41. **Rocky Mountain Skiing- Ski New Mexico**

    Official web site for all ski resorts in New Mexico, with information on snow conditions, cross-country...

    www.skinewmexico.com/

42. **Ski Vacations**

    Ski - Vacations .com. 8th Ski Season Online - Presented by. International Translation. Ski Vacations arrange ski trips for you, your ...

    www.usa-skiing.com/

43. **USA Water Ski**
    Competitions, other events. Latest news. Lists and links for member schools, dealers, clubs, and camps....
    www.usawaterski.org/

44. **Snow Skiing Forum Frigate**
    Forum and live chat devoted to skiing.
    jollyroger.com/zz/youtdoord/SnowSkiinghall/ shakespeare1.html

48
Snooker

1. **World Snooker Association**
The official website of the world governing body featuring the latest snooker news and results, plus...
www.worldsnooker.com/
2. **Embassy World Snooker**
The Embassy World Championship was first staged at the Crucible in 1977 and is now as famous for snooker...
www.embassysnooker.com/
3. **WWW Snooker**
An comprehensive index of snooker on the world wide web, with over 1000 links registered.
www.laboremus.no/snooker/
4. **Snooker**
The site includes news, latest results and an online shop for the snooker community. Chat with 110...
www.110sport.com/snooker/
5. **Snooker Images - Welcome**
A collection of snooker photography, daily results, photographs, news, rankings and information.
www.snookerimages.co.uk/
6. **BBC SPORT | Other Sport | Snooker**
Low Graphics version | Change Edition. | Help. Sport Homepage. Snooker. Results. Calendar. World Champs 2003. Grandstand: Have Your Say. ...
news.bbc.co.uk/sport1/hi/other_sports/ snooker/default.stm

7. **SnookerUSA.com - The Official Website of the United States Snooker ...**

   The official web site of the United States Snooker Association, with the latest snooker news, results...

   www.snookerusa.com/

8. **Snooker News**

   Worldwide coverage of events, news, and scores.

   www.snookernews.com/

9. **Snooker Games - Forget virtual, discover the reality.**

   The site covers tuition, book reviews, clip art, queries, rules, and history.

   www.snookergames.co.uk/

10. **Picasso_s Belgian Snooker Page**

    Everything about snooker in Belgium, Tournament results, competition results, calendars, rankings and links.

    www.snooker.org/

11. **Global Snooker Centre**

    The site provides information for and by contributors worldwide including players, coaching, ladies...

    www.globalsnookercentre.co.uk/

12. **worldofsnooker.co.uk | snooker on the web - Betfair Premier ...**

    The latest news and results.

    www.worldofsnooker.co.uk/

13. **CBSA - The Canadian Billiards & Snooker Association**

    The official web site with news, results and statistics from the world of Canadian cue sports.

    www.cbsa.ca/

14. **Sporting Life - Snooker**

    ... Home, Snooker, News, Betting News, Calendar, Draws, Results, Rankings, Form Guide, Fanzine, Competitions, Diary, Calendar, Results, About Us, Contact Us, SNOOKER NEWS. ...

    www.sportinglife.com/snooker/news/

15. **Aussie Snooker (plus Billiards and Pool (8-ball & 9-ball)) Home...**

    Australian Cue Sports site with focus on Snooker, Billiards, Pool (8-Ball and 9-Ball) and Carom (3 Cushion). ... November Snooker at Mounties. ...

    www.billsnook.com.au/

16. **Ananova - Sport - Snooker**
Latest breaking snooker news, with email updates
www.ananova.com/sport/
?keywords=Snooker&menu=sport.snooker

17. **FantasySnookerLeague.com Fantasy Snooker League Competition**
Fantasy snooker league competition. Select players and score points throughout the snooker season. League tables, your own team ...
www.fantasysnookerleague.com/

18. **fcsnooker - snooker and pool coaching, information, products and ...**
Includes scores of world championship matches from 1927 to present, Flash presentations of trick shots,...
www.fcsnooker.co.uk/

19. **Billiards - Pool - Snooker - Links - A categorised directory of ...**
The following links will take you deep into the world of Billiards, Pool and Snooker across the continents in the following categories, and will be updated on ...
www.blackball.org.uk/

20. **Snooker Hangout - snooker, snooker table, snooker game, snooker ...**
Snooker. Welcome to snooker-hangout.com, the place to come for all your information on the game of snooker. ... Playing snooker is easier than you think. ...
www.snooker-hangout.com/

21. **EASB | English Association for Snooker and Billiards**
The official website of the governing body for snooker and Billiards in England, providing tournaments,...
www.easb.co.uk/

22. **Cookstown Snooker League**
Includes a rundown of snooker league activities, player profiles, sponsorship opportunities, challenge...
website.lineone.net/~cdsl/

23. **Austrian Snooker Homepage World_>_Deutsch_>_..._>_Kegel _und_Kugelsport_>_Billard_>_Snooker**
www.snooker.co.at/

24. **Photos from California, San F, USA**
California USA. ...
www.esatclear.ie/~irish-snooker/

25. **Snooker**
The site is not being updated but it has good information about Clubs.
www.geocities.com/Colosseum/1283/snooker.html

26. **Snooker.net :: Snooker News Headlines.**
Home. Baseball. Basketball. Boxing. Golf. Snooker. Soccer. Soccer UK. Soccer US. Tennis. Sports Tickets. Links. Soccer.net. Baseball.us.com.Basketball.us.com.Boxing.net. ...
www.snooker.net/

27. **Snooker-Manager - computer controlled snooker/pool price ...**
Computerised price monitoring system for snooker clubs/pool balls which includes reporting, digital...
www.servcare.demon.co.uk/snookwin/

28. **Cornwall Billiards & Snooker Association_'s Home Page**
All the latest news of Billiards and Snooker.
www.cornwallbilliardssnooker.fsnet.co.uk/

29. **Swiss Snooker. Wir heissen Sie herzlich Willkommen World_>_Deutsch_>_..._>_Kegel _und_Kugelsport_>_Billard_>_Snooker**
www.snooker.ch/

30. **Pool Tables from Tim Franklins**
Local supplier: catalogue, FAQ, contact details, ordering form and map.
www.pool-and-snooker.com/

31. **Snooker**
Embassy World Snooker Championship. Snooker sites I found a number of sites about snooker. ...
www.euronet.nl/users/cor/snooker.html

32. **Snooker Rules**
Rules of Snooker. Type of Game: International or "English" snooker is the most widely played form of snooker around the world. ... h) a snooker with free ball. ...
www.billiardworld.com/snooker.html

33. **Home Page 1**

This site is designed by a snooker player for snooker players. Information and news for fans and players.
clarky81.tripod.com/

34. **The Snooker Room**

Worldwide dealers in quality antique and new snooker tables. Secure online ordering of tables, accessories and prints. The Snooker Room, Home Page, About, Store, ...
www.snookerroom.com/

35. **First Snooker Experience**

.. Version (????). Let's enjoy your snooker time! This page is written in purpose for spreading snooker culture in Japan. ...
www.st.rim.or.jp/~tomio/Snooker/

36. **Northern Ireland Billiards and Snooker Association**

The latest news, results, rankings and competitions from the Northern Ireland Billiards and Snooker Association.
homepage.ntlworld.com/snooker.nibsa/

37. **snookerscene.com**

www.snookerscene.com/

38. **TV Programs - EuroTV : Snooker**

Program schedules for snooker on European television.
www.eurotv.com/snooker.htm

39. **ibsf.org - The International Billiards & Snooker Federation (IBSF)**

The official site of the world governing body for snooker and English billiards. News, organisation,...
www.ibsf.org/

40. **Professional Snooker**

How to play snooker, different types of accessories, top tips, world rankings, and theatres.
www.professionalsnooker.co.uk/

41. **CueSport - Snooker Pool & Billiards Magazine**

Coaching, referees, mail order, and tournament diaries based in the UK.
www.cuesport.org/

42. **Queen's University Belfast Snooker, Billiards and Pool Club**
The site includes information on the latest competitions. Belfast, Northern Ireland.
quis.qub.ac.uk/snooker/welcome.htm

43. **Cleveland Billiards & Snooker League**
The league run ten KO competitions with awards or trophies provided for winners and runners-up in...
homepage.ntlworld.com/ian.whittle/cbsl1.htm

44. **Thje Vic Harris Snooker League**
The web site includes league tables, forthcoming events and news. Essex, England.
www.seves.pwp.blueyonder.co.uk/

45. **SS & A Snooker**
Shirley, Samantha and Adrian's page with photographs of Australian and UK players.
home.iprimus.com.au/maskdesigns/

46. **Snooker Loopy**
www.snookerloopy.com/

47. **Home of Snooker**
Football | Rugby | Formula One | Tennis | Snooker. Players History Quiz, News Headlines. You must have a JavaScript enabled browser ...
www.homeofsnooker.com/

48. **Droitwich Snooker Centre**
The site includes rules, tips, tricks, links and a virtual bar.
www.droitwichsnooker.co.uk/

49. **Free Online Games**
Developer of online 3d multi-player web games
www.flyordie.com/

50. **Snooker en Pool Centrum Heerenveen**
World_>_Nederlands_>_..._>_Friesland_>_Gemeenten_>_Heerenveen
www.spcheerenveen.nl/

51. **andrew gibbs snooker cue, andrew gibbs snooker cues, pool cue, www....**
The site offers snooker cues and cases.
www.smartsnooker.com/

52. **snooker.startkabel.nl**

World_>_Nederlands_>_Sport_>_Biljart_>_Snooker

snooker.startkabel.nl/

53. **index.html**

Details on regional Canadian tournaments, member news, Seniors snooker activities, membership information...

www.obsa.on.ca/

54. **Bebington & District Snooker League**

Official site with a listing of officials, area clubs, history of the league, and upcoming events.

www.snookeronline.net/Beb/intro.htm

55. **147 Snooker Billiards Pool**

coname=147 Snooker Billiards Pool snooker billiards pool biljart billard Belgium europe europa hasselt limburg sport peradon bce cuecraft craftsman boxxer ...

www.freewebs.com/147mjm/

56. **Snooker Coaching**

Hints, tips, and coaching, provided by Anthony Wonnacott.

anthonywonnacott.mysite.freeserve.com/

57. **Snooker.com.hk**

www.snooker.com.hk/

58. **Live Snooker Scores - Websites Providing Snooker Live Scores and ...**

Snooker Live Score - Websites Providing Live Snooker Scores & Tennis Results,as well as Scores for Other Sports. ... Live Snooker Scores. ...

www.tennismaster.co.uk/tennis/ live-snooker-scores.shtml

59. **Pool, Billiards and Snooker: Rules, tips, tutorials**

Links to a wide variety of how-to guides covering topics from rules to form.

www.knowledgehound.com/topics/pool.htm

60. **Cornwall Snooker Scene and Cornish Mining Videos**

General snooker site for the enthusiast, tips, questions, books, tournament reports and local snooker. Nearly 50 pages of snooker plus Cornish mining videos. ...

hometown.aol.com/snookermag/

61. **Sky Sports - The Best Sport Coverage From Around The World**
Snooker. more sports: More sports - Sky Sports Shows Sky Sports Experts Football Cricket Rugby Union Rugby League Golf Tennis Boxing Formula One Speedway ...
www.skysports.com/skysports/snooker

62. **Neptune Snooker Club Home Page**
Snooker club overlooking Neptune Marina. Ipswich, England.
www.neptunes.demon.co.uk/neptune.htm

63. **snooker-square**
World_>_Nederlands_>_Sport_>_Biljart_>_Snooker
web.wanadoo.be/snooker/

64. **Wirral Amateur Billiards and Snooker League**
Offering information on officials, fixtures, snooker division, and tournaments.
wirral.snookeronline.net/

65. **Westerham Snooker League**
Add Me! Westerham Snooker League. Welcome to the 'Official' web-site for the Westerham Snooker League created and designed by Robin Lawes of Westerham RBL. Official site with fixtures and tables. Photo gallery and directory of member clubs.
uk.geocities.com/robin123uk/welcome.html

66. **Snooker Store: Snooker and pool and billiard tables, football tables...**
Supplier of Snooker tables, Billiards tables, Pool tables, football tables, cues, darts, dartboards and accessories. Also offering snooker table restoration. ...
www.snookerstore-pooltables.co.uk/

67. **6ft Pool Tables Snooker Table Football, Air hockey low prices.UK ...**
A retailer of snooker, pool and table football tables. Also specialises in excess stock, cancelled...
www.4onemonthonly.co.uk/

68. **SnookerSports Ltd** - snooker tables
Supply and manufacturer of small home tables to professional full size tables.
www.snookersports.com/

69. **Snookerclub - Snooker & Pool Tournament Diary**
International snooker and pool news, United Kingdom competitions and leagues, and discusson forums...
www.snookerclub.com/

70. **RIBSA MEMBERS DRAW**
The official web site with news rankings and coaching.
www.ribsa.net/

71. **Cue & Case Man: For Snooker, Billiard, Pool Cues and Cue Cases.**
A large selection of snooker, billiards, pool cues, cue cases, tables, accessories and equipment. ...
www.snooker-cues-cuecases.co.uk/

72. **Alliance Snooker**
Snooker, pool and billiad tables manufactured to the highest quality by Alliance snooker based in Liverpool UK. ...
www.alliancesnooker.com/main.html

73. **BB Billiards - The Best for Pool and Snooker Accessories u...**
FREE Delivery in UK, a range of over 25 Pool; Snooker; Table Football and Air Hockey tables, over 150 different cues available, over 200 supporting accessories ...
www.bbbilliards.co.uk/

74. **The Skipton Snooker League Website**
All the news on the competitions, players and activities. Contact information and diary.
www.skiptonsnooker.org.uk/

75. **TopCue - Shop online for snooker cues, billiard cues, pool cues...**
Shop online for snooker cues, billiard cues, pool cues, cases and accessories.
www.topcue.co.uk/

76. **Snooker, Pool and 9 ball game**
Snooker, Pool and 9 ball for your windows desktop. Fast fun internet enabled multiplayer snooker game, shareware snooker game. Play ...
www.quickgames.co.uk/

77. **Index of /snooker.nu**
World_>_Nederlands_>_Sport_>_Biljart_>_Snooker
users.telenet.be/snooker.nu/

78. **Cardiff University Snooker Club**

The club are current British Champions, the third time this has been achieved in the past six years.

www.cf.ac.uk/suon/au/snooker/

79. **Thurston - The Home of Snooker**

Supplying all services in connection with snooker tables and equipment since 1799.

www.thurston-games.co.uk/

80. **Crosby Snooker Services - For Value, Quality and Customer Service**

Provide renovations and repairs of snooker and pool tables.

www.crosbysnooker.co.uk/

81. **Snooker Tables**

Shopmole brings you Snooker Tables deals and makes finding Snooker Tables deals so easy that it has caused a revolution in internet shopping. ... Snooker Tables. ...

www.shopmole.co.uk/result/keyword/Snooker-Tables.xhtml

82. **WWW Snooker**

www.laboremus.no/Snooker/

83. **The Mad Snooker - Capt. Dave Pomerleau**

"The Mad Snooker" Capt. Dave Pomerleau The West Coasts Nocturnal Fishing Guide Extraordinaire. ... Weather. You have found the website of the "MAD SNOOKER", Capt.

www.madsnooker.com/

84. **Snooker in UK Sports Guide**

Snooker. Rack 'em up. Our selection of Snooker sites will have you on cue for a wealth of information covering the snooker world. ...

www.uksportsguide.co.uk/netguide/PPF/UK_Sports_Guide/Snooker/GCID/845/Guide.asp

85. **VBSA Home Page**

This Australian association lists bylaws, tournament results, affiliated clubs, links, events, and...

www.vbsa.org.au/

86. **the snooker room at the Langstone Cliff Hotel, Dawlish, Devon**

... Snooker Room... Opened in ... airy room. There is a selection of snooker cues available in the room and billiard chalk is also\ provided. ...

www.langstone-hotel.co.uk/Leisure/Snooker-Room.htm

49
Sports Authority of India

1. **Sports Authority of India**
   www.sportsauthorityofindia.com/
2. **Sports Authority of India - Netaji Subhas National Institute of ...**
   ... in India. On behalf of Sports Authority of India I would also welcome your personal visit to this Sports Institute. Through this ...
   www.nsnis.org/
3. **SPORTS AUTHORITY OF INDIA**
   SPORTS AUTHORITY OF INDIA Office of Executive Director (Teams), JN Stadium, New Delhi. Sports Science Research Fellowship. Sports ...
   www.themedicaljobs.com/sai.htm
4. **TheSportsAuthority online coupon, the sports authority, ww...**
   ... online coupon, plano sports authority , sports authority , sports authority coupon online coupon, sports authority of india , sports authority com , sports ...
   www.online—coupon.com/TheSportsAuthoritycoupon/
   TheSportsAuthoritycoupon.asp
5. **Sports - Development of Sports in India**
   ... The Sports Authority of India (SAI) was established in 1984 as a registered society in pursuance of a Government of India resolution. ...
   www.meadev.nic.in/sports/develop/feature.htm
6. **The Sports Authority Free Coupons - authority sports tampa ...**
   ... authority coupon printable sports , authority plano sports Free Coupons, sports authority coupon , sports authority of india, sports authority Free Coupons ...
   www.1-free-coupons.com/The_Sports_Authority_coupons/

7. **IMPACT OF NATIONAL COACHING SCHEME OF SPORTS AUTHORITY OF INDIA**

Impact of national coaching scheme of sports authority of india : a study on sports promotion in the eastern region sponsored by planning commission new ... planningcommission.nic.in/reports/sereport/ser
stdy_ncsprts.pdf

8. **Sports Authority Deals & Coupons - authority coupon printabl...**

... deals, sports authority store coupons, sports authority coupon, sports authority com coupons, sports authority of india, sports authority coupons coupons ...
www.deals-coupons.com/Sports_Authority_coupons/

9. **TheSportsAuthority Deals & Coupons - authority sports tampa...**

... coupons, authority plano sports, sports authority store coupons, sports authority coupon, sports authority com coupons, sports authority of india deals, sports ...
www.deals-coupons.com/TheSportsAuthority_coupons/

10. **Sports Authority Coupons - the sports authority, www ...**

... military hwy Coupons, plano sports authority, sports authority, sports authority coupons Coupons, sports authority of india , sports authority com, sports ...
www.online-coupon-code.com/Sports_Authority_coupon.asp

11. **Sports**

... Public-Private Partnership : Road Map to Excellence in Sports in India" was organised by FICCI in Association with Sports Authority of India (SAI), Ministry of ...
www.ficci.com/ficci/BUSINESS/sports.htm

12. **Policy Note - Youth Welfare and Sports Development Dept.**

... tournaments and competitions for all age groups are being conducted by the Sports Development Authority of Tamil Nadu as well as the Sports Authority of India. ...
www.tn.gov.in/policynotes/ywsd2003-04-4.htm

13. **AIBA**

Sports Authority of India, invites technical and financial offers in separate sealed cover from the foreign / Indian manufacturers or their authorized dealers ...
www.aiba.net/pressreleases/federationreleases/
federation_releases5.html

14. **Sports Authority coupons - the sports authority, www ...**
... military hwy coupon, plano sports authority, sports authority, sports authority coupons coupon, sports authority of india , sports authority com, sports ...
www.promotion—code.com/Sports_Authority_coupon/

15. **SurfWax — News Articles Mentioning Sports Authority**
uck of the sports authority called it "What we believe is the ...
brands.surfwax.com/files/Sports_Authority.html

16. **Sports Activities of Department of Youth Affairs and Sports ...**
... The selected players are sent for participation in the All India Women Sports Championship organized by Sports Authority of India. ...
manipur.nic.in/sports/sports.htm

17. **AIC - Annual Report 1998-99**
... coaches in three selected sports, and four-week placements at Australian Institute of Sport facilities in Australia by Sports Authority of India officials. ...
www.dfat.gov.au/aic/aic_annual_report/ 98_99/activities10.html

18. **sports authority**
... Hind authority corporate sports steady should along. Being authority india sports noisiest vicinity did. Shall being eaten authority liquid sports shut lacked. ...
search.nola.info/?t=sports%20authority

19. **Directory of official web sites of Government of India**
... Association (MRA); Sports Authority of India (SAI) Related Links. Sports Centres: Netaji Subhas National Institute of Sports (NSNIS); Syama ...
goidirectory.nic.in/sports.htm

20. **the sports authority**
... sports authority com; authority nj sports; authority canada sports; authority india sports; authority new sports york; authority job ...
www.sbsdc.com/the-sports-authority.shtml

21. **HARYANA URBAN DEVELOPMENT AUTHORITY**
... Rules/instructions. QUALIFICATIONS. 1. Jr. Coach (Boxing). Graduate of recognized University and; Diploma in Coaching from Sports Authority of India/NIS. ...
web1.hry.nic.in/jobs/jobs/huda-4.htm

22. **When You Gotta Know...AskCandy.com Pay Per Click Search Engine**

    ... Sports Authority coupons - best the sports authority Coupons & ... .. Codes, sports authority of india coupons, sports authority com Coupons & Online Coupon ...

    www.askcandy.com/search.php?keywords=sports%20authority%20coupon

23. **District Sports Authority Stadium, Kakinada**

    ... Name: District Sports Authority Stadium End names: Home Team: Andhra. ... Australia v India South Africa v West Indies Queensland v NSW S Australia v Victoria, ...

    usa.cricinfo.com/db/GROUNDS/IND/KAKINADA/DISTRICT_SPORTS_AUTHORITY_STADIUM_01041/

24. **Netaji Subhas National Institute of Sports Patiala - The Institute**

    ... Palace of Maharaja (King) of Patiala (Punjab), National Institute of Sports, which is now the Academic Wing of the Sports Authority of India was established by ...

    www.nsnis.org/institute.html

25. **Indian Minister again mentions 2012 bid from India**

    ... Last month the Federation of Indian Chambers of Commerce and Industry (FICCI) and the Sports Authority of India (SAI) signed a Memorandum of Understanding to ...

    www.internationalgames.net/news/0502/005.htm

26. **Drugs in Sport: Websites**

    ... The Director General of the Sports Authority of India says of this site: This site would be highly informative in the general understanding of drug taking ...

    www.drugsinsport.net/websites.htm

27. **Dope-tainted athletes to be heard**

    ... of the IOA, along with a representative of the IOA, a sports scientist and the in-charge of the dope control lab of the SAI [Sports Authority of India]. ...

    www.rediff.com/sports/2003/apr/23dope.htm

28. **selection enquiry for UK club — UK Sports Directory - Clubs ...**

    ... member of my School team and, during that period, worked on my game at the National Stadium, New Delhi, under the auspices of the Sports Authority of India. ...

    www.voy.com/135083/70.html

29. **The Tribune, Chandigarh, India - Sports Tribune**
... He should be replaced and Virender Nanavati should be 'kicked up' to become president while KV Sharma, now out of Sports Authority of India (SAI), to ...
www.tribuneindia.com/2003/20030614/spr-trib.htm

30. **Sports - Development - Incentives for promotion of sports ...**
... The scholarships are also not available to those who are enrolled in the residential sports coaching programmes of Sports Authority of India, State Governments ...
www.meadev.nic.in/sports/develop/incentives.htm

31. **www.EducationBangalore.com**
Sports Authority of India. Admission - 2000-2001 ... Write to Executive Director, Sports Authority of India, NS South Centre, University Campus, Bangalore 560 056. ...
www.educationbangalore.com/pages/16_admission_notices
sportsauthorityofindia.html

32. **Retail Projects Re-engineering networking solutions management ...**
... Client, Sports Authority, FL, USA. Technology, ... Description, Lawson is a retail package on the AS/400 used by Sports Authority in USA, Canada and Japan. ...
www.magnai.com/casestudies/retail.htm

33. **The Sports Authority - More Sports: Climbing**
... The North Face Expeditions Himalaya, Descending India Free Shipping Eligible!**. Videos/DVDs < view ... com may vary from those appearing in Sports Authority stores ...
www.thesportsauthority.com/ category
index.jsp?categoryId=713071&cp=717754

34. **Telecom Regulatory Authority of India**
... a similar portion of the time during an important sports event; (f ... CAS areas, until a final determination by the Telecom Regulatory Authority of India on the ...
www.trai.gov.in/
Press%20Release%2014th%20January%202004.pdf

35. **Re: selection enquiry for UK club — UK Sports Directory - Clubs ...**

... of my School team and, during >>that period, worked on my game at the National >>Stadium, New Delhi, under the auspices of the Sports >>Authority of India. ...

www.voy.com/135083/129.html

36. **Citizens Charter of Sports Development Authority of Tamil Nadu**

... The State has currently go the training centres run by the Sports Authority of India at Chennai and Salem. Plans are afoot to construct ...

www.tn.gov.in/citizen/sdat.htm

37. **sports authority**

... fastener. Those that following authority india sports would should sell. Miscast did strewed sports authority discount slamming engages. ...

search.nola.info/search2.php?t=sports%20authority

38. **Goacom: Goanow November 2001 - Tribute**

... She firmed up into a very fine athlete. Her track performance fetched her a place at the Sports Authority of India (SAI) in Mapusa in July 2000. ...

www.goacom.com/goanow/2001/nov/tribute.html

39. **blank**

... Accreditation of Dope Control Centre Under Sports Authority of India, New Delhi. The Dope Control Centre under the Sports Authority ...

www.compad.com.au/ cms/ilac/articleDisplay.php?artId=190

40. **Sunita Sharma-India's first woman cricket coach**

... coach has been training many India team probables for the last 21 years at Delhi's National Stadium Cricket Academy run by the Sports Authority of India (SAI ...

www.the-south-asian.com/ February2002/Sunita%20Sharma%20 %20first%20woman%20cricket%20coach.htm

41. **Indiantelevision dot com's Special Report on Sportzbiz 2003 ...**

... Sports Authority of India director general Shekhar Dutt justified the government's stand by stating: "The government has to look after 38 Olympian and 30 more ...

www.indiantelevision.com/headlines/y2k3/jan/jan144.htm

42. **UK mission in Capital - The Times of India**

... The visiting group would be meeting senior Indian Olympic Association officials, Sports Authority of India and a Confederation of Indian Industries delegation ...

www1.timesofindia.indiatimes.com/ articleshow/447739.cms

43. **Commonwealth - Wrestling**

... 55 kg category in the Commonwealth Games, was honoured today for his achievement in the presence of senior officers of the Sports Authority of India, host of ...

groups.msn.com/CommonwealthWrestling/ archievesindia.msnw

44. **Sports Dec 22-Jan 6 1999**

... country. She has vowed to reform the Sports Authority of India (SAI) and wants to close down the non-performing centres of the SAI. ...

www.nenanews.com/OT%20Dec22-Jan6,99/SportsC.htm

45. **TheSportsAuthority.com coupons - get the sports authority, www**

www sportsauthority com coupons, the sports authority military hwy, sports authority coupons, sports authority of india, sports authority coupon coupons ...

www.coupons-coupons-codes.com
TheSportsAuthority_com_coupons/

46. **NALCO invests one crore to aid Olympic hopefuls : HindustanTimes. .....**

The government and the Sports Authority of India have finalised Long Term Development Plants (LTDP) for various sports disciplines in consultaion with the ...

www.hindustantimes.com/news/181_551221,00070007.htm

47. **Abilympics: Support Us**

... Council of India; Sports Authority of India; Vocational Rehablitation Centres. Corporates. ABN Amro Bank; Ajant ffset. Ltd. Delhi Blue ...

www.abilympicsindia.org/supporters/Supporters.htm

48. **Sports & Recreation**

Sports & Recreation. Cricket World Cup 2003; National Games 2002; Sports Authority of India (Eastern Centre); Flight 10 Bowling Alley ...
www.pcuf.fi/~tmo/sports.htm

49. **Government Connections - Search by Department**
www.andamantelecom.com/GOVT_QRY_DEPT.asp

50
Squash

1. **www.squash.org**
   www.squash.org/
2. **Squash Player - the World of Squash at your Fingertips**
   UK based squash magazine.
   www.squashplayer.co.uk/
3. **US Squash**
   United States Squash Racquets Association
   www.us-squash.org/squash/
4. **SquashTalk.com The squash information exchange with no barriers**
   A global resource for squash players with news, comment, club directories, camp directories, tournament...
   www.squashtalk.com/
5. **World Squash**
   - Results, calendar, history, contacts, game rules, court specifications and ranking lists. English...
   www.worldsquash.org/
6. **New squash and a guide to squash rules**
   Squash coaching. Squash sport and squash rules (for squash raquet sports) guide by Liz Irving and Alan Murray; the guide to squash ...
   www.guide-to-squash.org/
7. **England Squash**
   Includes news, events calendar, history, rankings, juniors, development, coaching and official's resource...
   www.englandsquash.com/

8. **Squash Canada**

Rankings. National Championships. Calendar. Canadian Circuit. High Performance. Coaching.Officiating. Skill Awards. Marketing. Store. Rules. About Squash Canada. Francais.

www.squash.ca/

9. **Squash BC**

Squash BC Web Site, serving the sport of squash in the province of British Columbia. ... more...Vanlawn's ThunderKnick Squash Camps Spaces are limited. Serving the sport of squash in the province of British Columbia. An organization centered around the...

www.squashbc.com/

10. **Indian Squash Professional**

A Non profit making Organization with the sole aim of promoting Squash in India, Squash Encyclopedia. IST Time :: ... MOTILAL SANGHI INTER-CLUB SQUASH TOURNAMENT. News, results, and lots of information on different aspects of squash.

www.ispsquash.com/

11. **Squash Australia - Home Page**

The Official Website of Squash Australia. ... Squash Australia congratulates Peta on her Scottish victory. Grays Australian Junior Graded Results - Click Here. ...

www.squash.org.au/

12. **Squash On Line World > Español > Deportes > Squash**

www.squash.com.ar/

13. **SquashWeb - Dé internet pagina voor squash in Nederland - Dutch World_>_Nederlands_>_Sport_>_Squash**

www.squashweb.nl/

14. **ffsquash.com**

World_>_Français_>Sports_et_loisirs_>_Sports_>_Squash

www.ffsquash.org/

15. **Dansk Squash Forbund - Her finder du alt om det fremragende World_>_Dansk_>_Sport_>_Squash**

www.dsqf.dk/

16. **Qsquash - Squash in Queensland**

The traditional Calendar displayed at Squash Centres will still be produced BUT a glossy Tournament Booklet is also being prepared. ...

qsquash.com/

17. **Squash Magazine**

    Squashmagazine.com is the website for the sport of squash. Magazine subscriptions, news, tournament calendar and results, rules, drills ...

    www.squashmagazine.com/

18. **Squash Pics - the best Squash Pictures in the World**

    Top Squash Events of 2003 Photographs must not be copied from this site without the permission of Steve Line. Welcome to SquashPics ...

    www.squashpics.com/

19. **Squash New Zealand**

    Includes news items, a calendar of competitions, club listing, rankings, and coaching courses offered.

    www.nzsquash.co.nz/

20. **SQUASHCLUB World_>_Czech_>_Sporty_>_Squash**

    www.czechsquash.cz/

21. **Irish Squash - Your complete resource for Squash in Ireland**

    The Irish Squash web site aims to provide a resource page for Squash in Ireland,with all the information they need to play squash, enter tournaments, meet ...

    www.irishsquash.com/

22. **Squash.it - International Squash Magazine - official WSF PSA WISPA**

    International Squash Magazine, the best squash magazine ever published, official WSF PSA WISPA.

    www.squash.it/

23. **Worldwide Squash Ladder**

    Squash ladder that is now forming. Free for all players and helps find opponents, track results, post/review classifieds, and find quality squash links. ...

    www.sportsladders.com/squash/

24. **SWISS SQUASH**

    World_>_Deutsch_>_Sport_>_Ballsport_>_Squash_>_Verbände

    www.squash.ch/

25. **Squash Ontario On-line**
Squash Ontario, working to promote and develop the sport of squash in the province Ontario. ... canadianjunioropen/. Provincial governing body offering news, an events calendar, championships and tournaments, photo...
www.squashontario.com/

26. **SQUASH FINLAND World_>_Suomi_>_Urheilu_>_Squash**
www.squash.fi/

27. **Prince, Wilson, Head, Dunlop and Slazenger racquets.**
Squash Pro has quality squash and tennis racquets, accessories, squash advice, links and where to get lessons. Join Our Newsletter Specials & News email address. ...
www.squashpro.com/

28. **Bienvenido a la Página de Squash en Español World_>_Español_>_Deportes_>_Squash**
www.squashespanol.com/

29. **Squash Courts**
Comprehensive site with plenty of information regarding squash courts.
mikegreenwood.members.easyspace.com/

30. **Squash Bond Nederland World_>_Nederlands_>_Sport_>_Squash**
www.squash.nl/

31. **Österreichischer Squash Rackets Verband World_>_Deutsch_>_Regional_>_Europa_>_Österreich_>_Wien_>_Sport**
www.squash.or.at/

32. **squash.FreshAddress.com**
Squash Enthusiast! ... Wish you could find the current email addresses of former, current, or potential squash partners? Email address registry for registered users.
squash.freshaddress.com/

33. **The Squash Rules as Sonnets Project**
Do you play Squash? Do you like Poetry? Do you write Poetry? Is your knowledge weak about The Rules of Squash? Project for writing the rules of squash as sonnets.
www.geocities.com/Colosseum/Bench/7571/

34. **Squash Leagues - worldwide squash competition**

The Squash Leagues Management System. Join a squash club near you, or run your own squash league. Free to join, all ages and squash ...

www.squashleagues.com/

35. **The Guide-to-Squash**

The 'original' guide-to-squash. Your own personal squash lesson with Liz Irving on the web. ... or go straight to NEW Intermediate drill section, ...

www.guide-to-squash.org/pages/front/index2.html

36. **Página oficial de SQUASH en Venezuela**

World_>_Español_>_Deportes_>_Squash

members.tripod.com/~squash1998/

37. **Squash Photos - a gallery of squash photos**

Squash Desktop Themes (Includes wallpaper, cursors, icons, and sounds), Moving Squash Pictures - animated GIF files (Be prepared to wait for download). ...

www.squashphotos.com/

38. **Herts Squash County Association England UK of GB Great Britain ...**

Everything on Squash in Hertfordshire, England GB UK. Herts Squash promotes squash at all levels throughout Hertfordshire. A voluntary organisation whose aim is to promote squash at all levels throughout Herts, England. League,...

www.herts-squash.org.uk/

39. **Squash Almere World_>_Nederlands_>_Sport_>_Squash**

www.squash-almere.nl/

40. **Stanford Squash**

Home of the West Coast's fastest rising squash program, the Stanford University men's and women's intercollegiate teams and recreational club. ...

www.stanford.edu/group/squash/

41. **This page uses frames, but your browser doesn't support them**

Information on clubs in Somerset, County competitions, Winter League, Junior Squash, and World Squash news.

www.btinternet.com/~doverhay/

42. **Universal Squash Camps**

Bryan Patterson squash camps have now been running for 14 years and well over 1000 junior players have attended these camps. ... 2004. ...

www.microsec.co.uk/unisquash/

43. **Squash Scotland - Scottish, clubs, rackets, rules, links, clubs**

Buy titan squash rackets online. Can't find what you are looking for? Search here. All of ScottishSport.co.uk ...

www.scottishsport.co.uk/squash/

44. **ABIDJAN SQUASH LADDER**

Abidjan Squash Ladder. www.geocities.com/abidjansquash.

www.geocities.com/abidjansquash/

45. **South Australian Masters Squash**

Sam Wombat The Complete Scaffold Contracting Australian Masters Squash Championships. Fun and Compeditive Squash for men over 35 and women over 30. All Rankings catered for.

www.sams.asn.au/

46. **Dartmouth Squash**

Photo Gallery. The Dartmouth Squash website is undergoing some changes and will be moving to a new site. Please be patient and stay tuned for changes. ...

www.dartmouth.edu/~squash/

47. **SQUASH :: Home**

Complete squash information - covering rules, history, equipment, tips (squash.sports-resource.com). ... Squash - Sports Resource. Information on the game of squash, its history and rules, including tips on selecting the right equipment...

squash.sports-resource.com/

48. **FIGS - Federazione Italiana Giuoco Squash**
World_>_Italiano_>_Sport_>_Squash

www.figs.it/

49. **Squash Unlimited**

Squash racquets, shoes, DVDs, and more. ... Squash Unlimited is proud to have been the Official Stringer for the 2003 Pace Canadian Squash Classic. ...

www.squashunlimited.com/

50. **squash.start4all.com**

squash.start4all.com: squash, competition, ranking, yellow, ball, play, psa, wispa, magazines The Squash Start page Our quality partner sites: Submit4all ...

squash.start4all.com/

51. **Luxembourg Squash (FSL)**

List of clubs, details on the national federation and committee, calendar and championship results.

www.flsr.lu/

52. **Squash in Japan(Unofficial) - Since 1996**

The summary for this Japanese page contains characters that cannot be correctly displayed in this language/character set.

www.bekkoame.ne.jp/~nomurate/

53. **Dural Squash & Fitness**

Dural Squash and Fitness in North-West Sydney, Australia. Facilities include Squash (12 courts), gym,...

www.users.bigpond.com/duralsquash/

54. **Prince Squash Home**

www.princesquash.com/

55. **Are You Squash Mad....**

Are You Squash Mad.... Because We Are. ... Tell me how to improve my site. Or just post a genral discussion about Squash and Im sure someone could help!!! ...

www.angelfire.com/co3/ozzy1/

56. **Squashclub Blaricum World_>_Nederlands_>_..._>_Noord Holland_>_Gemeenten_>_Blaricum**

www.squashblaricum.nl/

57. **Cornwall Squash Home Page**

Includes information about local results and the different leagues.

www.cornwall-squash.co.uk/

58. **Squash**

2003-04 Wellesley Squash. ... Wellesley College squash posted an impressive 15-9 record in 2002-03, for its most wins in a season since the 1984 season. Information and pictures on the Wellesley College (MA USA) team.

www.wellesley.edu/Athletics/athletics/squash.html

59. **Munster Squash**

    Organisation for players in Munster, Ireland. Contains a list of area clubs, upcoming events, league...

    www.munstersquash.com/

60. **Suffolk Squash Homepage**

    Suffolk Squash - which must be viewed using a Browser which supports Frames. Site courtesy of. Suffolk leagues, championships, rankings, news and list of Suffolk clubs.

    www.suffolksquash.co.uk/

61. **Super Squash - direct access to the top squash sites**

    Quick access to the best of Squash on the Web. SQUASH NEWSFEED. ... Top Squash, Squash Player. World Squash. Squash Pics. Squash Now. Squash NEWS.

    www.supersquash.com/

62. **Federación madrileña de squash**

    World > Español > Deportes > Squash > España

    www.fms.es/

63. **ut squash :: home**

    UT Squash. This is the home page for UT Squash, the squash club at the University of Texas-Austin. ... Texas Squash Dallas Squash, Houston Squash. ...

    studentorgs.utexas.edu/utsquash/

64. **Tynemouth Squash**

    Tynemouth Squash - the North-East's top squash Club. Lists membership fees, pictures, details of their teams, a facilities description, and a hall of fame...

    www.tynemouthsquash.com/

65. **Squash Design: Moisture Managed Sports Apparel & Footwear for ...**

    World-class squash players rely on Squash Design to meet their training and competition demands. Squash Design offers squash players ...

    www.squashdesignusa.com/

66. **Squash New Zealand**

    Squash New Zealand's CEO Peter Fergusson.

    www.squashnz.co.nz/

67. **Hampton-In-Arden Squash and RacketBall Club - Home Page Solihull ...**
News, team updates, and information about the West Midlands UK club.
www.hamptonsquash.org.uk/

68. **PakSquash.com — All About Squash in Pakistan**
The Pakistan Squash Federation's official web site. Includes tournament coverage, live coverage of events in Pakistan, a message ...
www.paksquash.com/

69. **Kolding Squash World_>_Dansk_>_Sport_>_Squash**
www.kolding-squash.dk/

70. **QUB SQUASH**
Queen's University Belfast team. Includes practice schedule, membership details, a roster, and league...
uis.qub.ac.uk/ssc/

71. **Le Squash Web World_>_Français_>_Sports_>_Raquettes_>_Squash**
cedric.brehaut.chez.tiscali.fr/squash.html

72. **squash**
squash contemporary. garden. design. and. creation. ... example garden one. services what squash gardens do, how, and where we do it. the victorian jungle ...
www.squashgardens.com/

73. **SquashNow!**
Latest news from the international circuit.
www.squashnow.com/

74. **Wiltshire Squash Rackets Association - Home Page**
Everything related to the playing and organisation of the game of squash in the County of Wiltshire. Club details, summer and winter leagues, cup competition and player rankings. Includes players gallery,...
personal.rmcs.cranfield.ac.uk/squash/

75. **The Bermuda Squash Racquets Association**
Includes news announcements, a calendar of events, fees, pictures, and the contents of their pro shop.
www.bermudasquash.com/

76. **Premier Online Squash Retailer - Sport Discount.com**
UK based online store specializing in squash.
www.squashdiscount.com/

77. **Squash South Africa - Squash SA**
Squash SA is the official representative sports body for squash in South Africa. ... Read all about international squash news on the SquashNow web site. ...
www.squashsa.co.za/

78. **Searching for plug-in please wait**
Women's Professional Squash tour - World rankings, tour calendar, news, draws and results.
www.wispa.net/

79. **Velkommen til Herlev/Hjorten Squash**
World_>_Dansk_>_Sport_>_Squash
www.herlevhjortensquash.dk/

80. **NavySports.com**
Schedule, roster, results, and news. (Damian Walker, Coach)
www.navysports.com/sports/squash/

81. **Squash Wellington**
Loading site. This site is best viewed at 800x600 or higher.
www.squashwellington.org.nz/

82. **Charlie Johnson_'s Squash Shop**
Charlie Johnson's Squash Shop is America's Best Squash Pro Shop. We mail-order squash racquets, squash equipment, attire and accessories. Charlie Johnson's Tennis and Squash Shop serves the USA by web or phone order. CJ Squash features...
www.cjsquash.com/

83. **Squash in Japan(Unofficial) - Since 1996**
National rankings, regional news, court dimensions (in Japanese), tips on play and list of courts...
www.bekkoame.ne.jp/~nomurate/eindex.html

84. **World Squash Day**
WORLD SQUASH DAY 2004 - Sat 24th April. Our aim is for EVERY SQUASH CLUB ON THE PLANET to get involved in promoting squash. ... World Squash Day Gallery. ...
www.worldsquashday.org/

85. **craig@aldredsquash.freeserve.co.uk**

Professional Squash Coach offering services worldwide to individuals or clubs, Unsquashable racket...

www.aldredsquash.freeserve.co.uk/

86. **Princeton University Squash Team**

Coach Profiles. Squash Parent's Weekend. 2000 Junior Tournament. 2000 Adult Championship.Friends of Princeton Squash. Prospective Athlete Form. 2000 Squash Camp. ...

www.princeton.edu/~mwsquash/

87. **NSW Squash**

News, courts, clubs, results, rankings, events calendar, and player profiles.

www.nswsquash.com.au/

88. **Federación Canaria de Squash**

World > Español > Deportes > Squash > España

www.squashcanarias.com/

89. **Squash**

Offers information on history, clubs, stars and useful links. The summary for this Russian page contains characters that cannot be correctly displayed in this language/character set.

www.squash.com.ua/

90. **Grove Park Squash Club - Cheshire club located in Stockport, South ...**

Grove Park Squash Club, one of the leading and most friendly clubs in the North West of England. Profile, teams, news, competitions, FAQ and information about social activities. Located in Manchester,...

www.groveparksquash.org.uk/

51 Swimming

1. **USA Swimming Home**
   Official website for the national governing body of competitive swimming in the United States. Contains...
   www.usswim.org/
2. **SwimInfo.com Home Page**
   Includes news, swim meet results, work out advice, technique tips, and links. Publishers of Swimming...
   www.swiminfo.com/
3. **United States Masters Swimming**
   The elite athlete. USMS is swimming for life. ... Welcome to United States Masters Swimming! We are swimming for life for all ages. Governing body for adult swimmers in the US. Provides news, forums, information about places to swim,...
   www.usms.org/
4. **SWIMMING SCIENCE JOURNAL**
   Swimming Science Journal. ... Click on an Entry Below to View the Table of Contents of a Particular Feature of the Swimming Science Journal. How Champions Do It. ...
   www-rohan.sdsu.edu/dept/coachsci/swimming/
5. **Amateur Swimming Association**
   The Official web site of the Amateur Swimming Association and Amateur Swimming Federation of Great Britain. ...
   www.britishswimming.org/
6. **Australian Swimming**
   Australian Swimming's official website sponsored by Telstra. ... For all the latest swimming news and updates, subscribe to eSwimmer...
   www.ausswim.telstra.com.au/

7. **Swimming/Natation Canada**
   Official site for the national governing body of swimming in Canada.
   www.swimming.ca/

8. **ISHOF-International Swimming Hall of Fame**
   ISHOF honors and remembers outstanding athletes and contributors in swimming, diving, water polo, synchronized swimming and water safety. ...
   www.ishof.org/

9. **FINA - La Fédération Internationale de Natation**
   www.fina.org/

10. **About Swimming - for fitness competitive swimmers, triathletes**
    Learn about swimming, swimmers, and other swim information, news, links, and ideas about swimming and other water related, aquatic sports for beginners to ...
    swimming.about.com/

11. **Harvard Swimming & Diving**
    Friends of Harvard Swimming & Diving The most important fund-raising body for the teams, Technique Swim Camp 2003 Summer swim camp at Blodgett Pool. Official web site of the Crimson swimming and diving teams—includes news, roster, schedule, and results.
    hcs.harvard.edu/~swim/

12. **SWIMMING HOLES EAST**
    The web site for beautiful, natural swimming places in the Eastern US – swimming holes from Maine to Florida. ... NH KANCAMAGUS AREA Swimming hole heaven. ...
    www.swimmingholes.org/

13. **Swimming Pool (2003)**
    Swimming Pool (2003) - Cast, Crew, Reviews, Plot Summary, Comments, Discussion, Taglines, Trailers, Posters, Photos, Showtimes, Link to Official Site, Fan ...
    www.imdb.com/title/tt0324133/

14. **NSW Swimming**
    The New South Wales Swimming Association, located in Sydney Australia, aims to encourage, establish, foster, promote, develop, extend and control swimming ...
    www.nswswimming.com.au/

15. **Swimming View**

    The summary for this Japanese page contains characters that cannot be correctly displayed in this language/character set.
    swimmingview.org/

16. **Scottish Swimming**

    The definitive internet resource for swimming in Scotland - the home of Scottish Swimming. ...
    www.scottishswimming.com/

17. **Colorado Swimming - CSI Competitive Swimming in Colorado and ...**

    Colorado Swimming, CSI - Governing Body for competitive swimming in Colorado, featuring in depth articles covering the sport of swimming, swimming officiating ...
    www.csi.org/

18. **The Swimming Teachers' Association**

    A registered charity founded in 1932 with the objective of preserving human life by the teaching of...
    www.sta.co.uk/

19. **Swimming Technology Research - advanced technology for swimming ...**

    Products and services for analyzing and improving performance in swimming, aquatic therapy, rowing, and other aquatic activities. Swimming Technology Research. ...
    members.aol.com/swimbetter/

20. **Swimming — Starring Lauren Ambrose of HBO's Six Feet Under**

    Swimming is the breakthrough feature that helped land Lauren Ambrose her role on HBO's Six Feet Under. Includes pictures, audio, bio's ...
    www.swimmingthemovie.com/

21. **Connecticut Swimming**

    Provides swimming information, results, meets, events, records, organization minutes, coaches, officials,...
    ctswim.org/

22. **The Swimming Index - Swimming Sites Portal**

    The Swimming Index Portal comprises the largest automated Index of Swimming Site Links. ... MI Sports The Swimming Index.
    www.lornet.com/swimming/active/swimming.asp

23. **The Swimming Index - Swimming Sites Portal**

    The Swimming Index Portal comprises the largest automated Index of Swimming Site Links. ... Log It Books The Swimming Index. See also The Swimming Index 2. ...

    swimindex.lornet.com/

24. **AUSTIN SWIMMING**

    Austin, Texas, is the home of the University of Texas Longhorn Swim Teams, Texas Aquatics, and the Texas Swimming Center. ... South Texas Swimming, Inc. ...

    www.realtime.net/~dhbrown/

25. **emmet swimming :: Home**

    Emmet swimming (full band) will be playing a special show at our favorite club, The 9:30 CLUB in Washington, DC. ... The band: emmet swimming. ...

    www.emmetswimming.com/

26. **YMCA of the USA National Swimming and Diving Advisory Committee**

    YMCA of the USA National Swimming and Diving Advisory Committee. ...

    www.ymcaswimminganddiving.org/

27. **Swimming Champion**

    Diving Sailboats Swimming Surfing. INDOOR SPORTS. ...

    www.worldswimming.com/

28. **Illinois Swimming, Inc.**

    Includes records, time standards, officials, adaptive swim, age group, and senior information.

    www.ilswim.org/

29. **Swimming Victoria**

    Governing body that features the latest news, results, rankings, photos and profiles in Victorian Swimming.

    www.swimmingvictoria.org.au/

30. **Swimming Pool by Francois Ozon - Trailer**

    Swimming Pool (2003) 35mm, color. Synopsis: Sarah (Charlotte Rampling) is a rigid and conservative, yet successful English mystery writer. ...

    www.francois-ozon.com/anglais/ozon.audiovideo14.html

31. **Southern California Swimming**
    Southern California Swimming, Includes meet results, records, news, calendar, time standards and related links.
    www.socalswim.org/
32. **Oregon Swimming, Inc.**
    Governing body for competitive swimming in Oregon, except Malheur County, and also includes Clark,...
    www.oregonswim.org/
33. **Virginia Swimming**
    Governs competitive swimming in the State of Virginia. Includes regional swimming news and links...
    www.virginiaswimming.com/
34. **Pacific Masters Swimming - Competitive and Fitness Swimming for...**
    Pacific Masters Swimming is the local governing body for organized adult swimmers in the Northern California and Nevada. ...
    www.pacificmasters.org. ...
    www.pacificmasters.org/
35. **Aloha, Swimming In Hawaii !**
    Includes schedules, meets, events, results, records, photos, team directory and related links.
    www.hawaiiswim.org/
36. **WebSwim :: Index**
    Your Internet Swimming Community. A popular swimming forum giving you answers to all your swimming questions. Also has a FAQ section and book reviews. ... Swimming, ...
    www.webswim.com/
37. **Team Map**
    Southeast Texas - Includes a searchable times database, team listing, meet schedules and results,...
    www.gulfswimming.org/
38. **The National Swimming Pool Foundation Official Website**
    National Swimming Pool Foundation
    www.nspf.com/default.htm

39. **Morley Swimming Pools Homepage**

Morley Swimming Pools provides above ground pools, swimming pools, swimming pool accessories, swimming pool enclosures and sand cartridge filters. ...

www.morley-swimming-pools.sagenet.co.uk/

40. **Swimming**

Swim styles, events, photographs, World records, and contacts.

www.swimming.host.sk/

41. **Pacific Northwest Swimming**

Covers the state of Washington west of, but not including, Okanogan, Chelan, Kittitas and Yakima Counties...

www.pns.org/

42. **Queensland Swimming**

Queensland Swimming. KEEPING QUEENSLAND SWIMMING NUMBER ONE. ... To receive the latest information on swimming in Queensland, subscribe to the Queensland Swimming. ...

www.qld.swimming.org.au/

43. **Amateur Swimming Association**

Comprehensive site for learning resources, continuing professional development and introductory teaching...

www.istc.co.uk/

44. **Swimming News - Swimmersworld.com**

FINA World Cup Short-Course Swimming Results. Tuesday (1/13/04) results for both men and women's events [More]. Indiana swimming legend dies. ...

www.swimmersworld.com/

45. **A & P DIY Swimming Pool Kit Specialists**

A&P is proud to bring you the first true heat retaining DIY swimming pool kit, the only turnkey solution for do-it-yourself enthusiasts. ...

www.diyswimmingpools.co.uk/

46. **North Texas Swimming Homepage**

North Texas Swimming, The USA Swimming member Local Swimming Committee and recognized governing body for competitive swimming in North Texas. ...

www.ntswim.org/

47. **USA Swimming Sub Page -Programs and Services**
USA Swimming Logo. USA Swimming Logo, ... Click here to view a site outline map. About adapted swimming: General Information. Information ...
www.usswim.org/programs/template.pl?opt=adapted

48. **Maryland Swimming's "Top 5" for December 2003**
The US local swim committee for the majority of the state of Maryland. Provides news, schedule,...
www.mdswim.org/

49. **Yahoo! Directory Swimming and Diving**
Swimming and Diving Directory > Recreation > Sports > Swimming and Diving, Search the Web just this category. ... Open Water Swimming - tips on open water swimming. ...
www.yahoo.com/Recreation/Sports/Swimming_and_Diving/

50. **Apple - Trailers - Swimming Pool**
... Swimming Pool, Trailer - 2:05 Drama, Mystery Charlotte Rampling Ludivine Sagnier Charles Dance Marc Fayolle Jean Marie Lamour Official Movie Site, ...
www.apple.com/trailers/focus_features/swimming_pool/

51. **USA Swimming Logo**
USA Swimming Logo. USA Swimming Logo. Welcome to Middle Atlantic Swimming Online. Middle Atlantic Swimming, Inc. ... ENTER MA Swimming. Includes general, result and meet information, policy manual, handbook, news, team directory, records...
www.maswim.org/

52. **Alaska Swimming, Inc.**
Alaska - Meet schedules, posting of championship results, club listing and online Swim Guide of ASI's...
www.akswimming.org/

53. **Swimming Merit Badge**
Boy Scout Merit Badge Requirements. SWIMMING. ... Explain why swimming or survival floating will hasten the onset of hypothermia in cold water. ...
www.meritbadge.com/bsa/mb/014.htm

54. **Le Swimming**
www.leswimming.com/

55. **Kalamazoo College Swimming and Diving : Home**
Official web site maintained by the team—includes photos, roster, records, schedule, results, top...
www.k-swimming.org/

56. **Ohio Swimming Incorporated website**
Includes administrative information, meet schedule, time standards, Ohio Top 16, forms, FAQs, downloadabl...
www.ohioswim.org/

57. **Channel Swimming Association**
Governing body of official swim records for swimming the English Channel. Includes records, history,...
www.channelswimmingassociation.com/

58. **Masters Swimming Canada**
Masters Swimming Canada is a national organisation designed to promote adult swimming through organised training programs for the recreational and competitive ...
www.compusmart.ab.ca/masterssc/

59. **Louisiana Swimming**
Louisiana Swimming. Swimming Rules. Louisiana Swimming Office Phone Numbers . Jack L. Jordan. ...
www.louisianaswimming.org/

60. **Baby Swimming~The Gentle Journey**
Baby Swimming The Gentle Approach is designed to support parents and teachers seeking an expanded awareness into the gentle "whole child" approach to teaching ...
www.babyswimming.com/

61. **Western Australian Swimming Association**
The Western Australian Swimming Association on the Web. News, reviews, meet results and personal bests for swimming around Western Australia and Australia. ...
www.wasa.asn.au/

62. **Southeastern Swimming, Inc.**
Southeastern Swimming. IMPORTANT INFORMATION. ... The new Junior Representative for Southeastern Swimming is MITHCELL JOHNSON from BSL. ...
www.seswim.org/

63. **New England Swimming**
Includes club list, news, records, standards, calendar, results, policy and forms.
www.neswim.com/

64. **Infant Swimming Resource - Home Page**
Infant Swimming Resource students can swim... just watch them! Infant ... sequence.
www.infantswim.com/

65. **INDIANA SWIMMING, INC.**
Oversees all competitive age group swimming in the state. Includes news items, workshops, policies...
www.inswimming.org/

66. **Swimming.com -**
Swimming.com, SWIMMING | SWIMMING POOLS | SWIMSUITS | SWIM WEAR | POOL SUPPLIES | SWIM GOGGLES, SWIMMING. SWIMMING POOLS. SWIMSUITS. SWIM WEAR. POOL SUPPLIES. ...
www.swimming.com/

67. **Gay Swimming Netherlands**
Gay Swimming Netherlands is the succesfull cooperation of the Dutch Gay swimteams. Find here ... Welcome to Gay Swimming Netherlands. ...
www.geocities.com/gayswimmingnl/

68. **Minnesota Swimming, Inc.**
Communication and business of Minnesota Swimming, Inc. ... Important Events and National News. Minnesota Swimming News. Minnesota Top 16 Jacket/Patch Order Form.
www.mnswim.org/

69. **New Jersey Swimming - Home**
The Governing Body for Competitive Swimming in New Jersey. ... NJSI Announce, Topical NJSI Announcements. Announcements, No Announcements. New Jersey Swimming, Inc. ...
www.njswim.org/

70. **Canadian Swimming Coaches Association (csca.org)**
Includes information, articles, national standards, Full Speed issues, results, members, forum, and links.
csca.org/

71. **Swimming Coaches Information Service**
Contains the latest findings of many of the leading sport science researchers with implications for...
www.education.ed.ac.uk/swim/

72. **Border Swimming, El Paso, Texas**
Information about Texas swimming. Includes schedules, minutes, events, results, records, coaches and...
www.borderswimming.org/

73. **Sierra Nevada Swimming**
Provides member services, administration, meet information and results, forms, news, club list and...
www.sn-swimming.org/

74. **Owner's Guide to Swimming Pool Water Chemistry**
Swimming pool owners' guide to water chemistry in everyday language - an independent non-commercial site.
www.ftech.net/~jshep/pools.htm

75. **Potomac Valley Swimming (PVS) Homepage**
Governing body for competitive swimming in the metropolitan Washington, DC area. Includes news, forms...
www.pvswim.org/

76. **Georgia Swimming - Official Web Site**
Includes news, events, Georgia swim clubs, articles, calendar, records, facilities, photos, and related...
www.gaswim.org/

77. **SwimmingOnLine.net - The First Italian Portal of Swimming and ...**
Techiques, tips, and workouts.
www.swimmingonline.net/mainmenu/mainmenu_e.htm

78. **Schwimmen Tipps & Ratgeber | Swimming Tips & Advice**
Information about swimming technique and skills, prevention of injury, training aids, apparel, nutrition...
www.svl.ch/svlimmat_ratind.html

79. **Swimming Pool | Kinostart**
www.swimming-pool-film.de/

80. **River and lake swimming**
Has safety advice, essays, reviews of swimming places, a message board and links to clubs. The Associatio...
www.river-swimming.co.uk/

81. **CSCAA - College Swimming Coaches Association of America**
The College Swimming Coaches Association of America (CSCAA) invites you to browse our web page designed to give you a more interactive affiliation with our ...
www.cscaa.org/

82. **Wisconsin Swimming, Inc.**
Governing body for competitive swimming in Wisconsin. Includes news, forms, time standards, teams,...
www.wisconsinswimming.org/

83. **Swimming New Zealand - swim and coach**
Swimming New Zealand provides learn to swim and coach education courses as well as providing national and international swimming competitions. ...
www.swimmingnz.org.nz/

84. **This page uses frames, but your browser doesn't support them.**
Governing body of competitive swimming for the state of Mississippi. Includes standards, records,...
www.msswim.org/

85. **Oklahoma Swimming - Home**
Oklahoma Swimming, Inc. .... . products of Oklahoma Swimming and United States Swimming. Swim Meet Bid Form — see Admin Page. Meet of Champs - Qualifier Info here. ...
www.oks.org/

86. **FINA Swimming Rules and Regulations**
FINA SWIMMING RULES, FINA HANDBOOK. . CONSTITUTION. ... DOPING RULES. MEDICAL RULES.
www.fina.org/swimrules.html

87. **Arizona Swimming**
www.azswim.org/

88. **Southeastern Swim Club**
Information and links, relating to Hamilton Southeastern High School and Junior High School swimming...
www.southeasternswim.org/

89. **American Red Cross - Health, Safety and Community Services**
Includes a water safety quiz, overviews of programs offered for families with children, and information...
www.redcross.org/services/hss/aquatics/

90. **Active.com - Swimming with Active.com : swim training tips ...**
Active.com is your swimming source! We provide swim training tips, swimming drills, and online registration for open water swims and races. ...
www.active.com/swimming/

91. **Legends of the Pool.**
Short biographies and photos of over 30 of the world's best swimmers.
www.geocities.com/Hollywood/Boulevard/ 6152/swimmers.html

92. **OFFICIAL FLORIDA SWIMMING WEBSITE.....**
Florida Swimming, Inc. 297 E. Hwy. ... FS Announces Athlete Rep Elections..... Florida Swimming Releases Senior Championship Information and Entry Forms..... ...
www.floridaswimming.org/

93. **Official site of the Australian Swimming Coaches & Teachers**
News, Swimming In Australia Magazine The Swimming In Australia magazine December 2003 edition is now online. Visit our ...
www.ascta.com/

94. **Beau Sejour Barracudas Swimming Club**
Home of the largest competitive swimming club in Guernsey - one of the Channel Islands.
www.barracudas-sc.org.gg/

95. **Swimming Pool (2003): Charlotte Rampling, Ludivine Sagnier**
SWIMMING POOL (2003) reviews from the nation's top critics and audiences. ...
www.rottentomatoes.com/m/SwimmingPool-1123621/

96. **The Official site of the Welsh Amateur Swimming Association - SWIM ...**
Official site of the Welsh Amateur Swimming Association, the national governing body. Features informatio...
www.welshasa.co.uk/

97. **Pool Etiquette**
"Don't Be a Fool at the Pool". Guidance on how to swim laps, especially in busy pools, without...
www.cartegic.com/pooletiquette.htm

98. **IPC Swimming web site**
The official IPC Swimming web site.
www.ipcswimming.org/

99. **TexasSports**
Official web site of the Longhorns' men's team, includes news, roster, photos, top times, schedule,...
www.texassports.com/mainpages/sw_index.html

100. **Guernsey Swimming Club**
Includes club a calendar, gala reports and Master's Meet. Associated with the Amateur Swimming Association.
swimming.guernsey.net/

101. **The Sport of Masters Swimming**
Website is run by the original webmaster of the Masters Swimming Canada website. The Sport of Masters Swimming. ... Some links for. International Masters swimming. ...
www.unb.ca/web/Masters_swimming/

102. **Central California Swimming**
Includes swim meets, records, results, and National Championships listings.
www.centralcalswim.org/

103. **Swim Link**
The summary for this Japanese page contains characters that cannot be correctly displayed in this language/character set.
www.mazcal-bf.co.jp/link/swimlink.html

104. **Swimming the Tiber**
Swimming the Tiber. ...
swimmingthetiber.blogspot.com/

105. **The Swimming Index - Swimming Sites Portal**
The Swimming Index Portal comprises the largest automated Index of Swimming Site Links. ... Swimmers Guide The Swimming Index 2. See also The Swimming Index. ...
swimindex.usswim.net/

106. **A and P Swimming Pool Design and Installer Specialists**
Offers hot tubs, swimming pools and accessories. Describes its product range and services with price...
www.appools.co.uk/

107. **Brisbane Swimming Association - Main Page**
Swimming club association, providing swimming calendar, list of clubs, record holders, competition...
www.brisswim.org.au/

108. **METROPOLITAN LSC**
Covers the Metropolitan New York area. Includes standards, records, news, calendar, club list, results,...
www.metroswimming.org/

109. **Swimming Pool FAQ**
A swimming pool FAQ with common questions and answers for pool owners and operators. Grown by the FAQ Farm question and answer co-op. ... Swimming Pool FAQ.
www.swimmingpool.info/

110. **Univeristy Of Bristol Swimming and Waterpolo Club**
Offers fixture list, statistics for Water Polo teams, news, training and pool opening times, pictures,...
www.bris.ac.uk/Depts/Union/Swim/

111. **USS Michigan Swimming Website**
www.uss-michigan.com/

112. **Jesus Swimming**
JESUS SWIMMING.
www.jesusswimming.com/

113. **Oxford University Swimming Club**
Oxford University Swimming Club. Welcome to the Oxford University Swimming Club's website! FIRST TIME VISITORS to the site, click ...
users.ox.ac.uk/~swimsoc/

114. **Masters Swimming as Enjoyed in Canada**
No longer affiliated with Masters Swimming in Canada, but represents the continuing efforts of the...
personal.nbnet.nb.ca/ATREE/

115. **The Swimming Pool Operators and Owners Resource Pages Index**
Information about installation, water testing and analysis, and chemical safety.
www.caromal.co.uk/Resource%20Index%20Page.HTM

116. **BBC Sport Academy | Swimming**
Swimming. Skills. Give It A Go. ... Disability. Email a Coach. Latest Sports News CBBC Around the BBC Get the newsletter. Swimming, Around the Academy: ...
news.bbc.co.uk/sportacademy/hi/sa/swimming/default.stm

117. **Singapore Swimming Club**
Milestones | Swimming Achievements | Mission and Management | Club Directory. Facilities Operating Hours and Booking Rates. Social | Sports | Swimming. Home. Sitemap.
www.sswimclub.org.sg/

118. **Impington Swimming Club (Cambridge, England)**
News, swimmer profiles, directions to pool, session time table, competitions and results, fees, club...
www.impingtonswimmingclub.org.uk/

119. **University of South Dakota Swimming and Diving**
Swimming Diving College Water Polo Clinic University South Dakota
ww.usd.edu/sports/swimming/

120. **AAOS Online Service Fact Sheet Tips To Prevent Swimming Injuries**
Tips To Prevent Swimming Injuries. ... The American Academy of Orthopaedic Surgeons offers the following tips to prevent swimming injuries: ...
orthoinfo.aaos.org/fact/
thr_report.cfm?Thread_ID=56&topcategory=Sports

121. **swimming**
Amateur Swimming Association (ASA). This is the home page of the national governing body for swimming, diving, water polo, open water ...
altis.ac.uk/browse/cabi/detail
f853b10af73a04a4c8b35b2ade1f40b9.html

122. **Swimmers Guide**
More in formation about more swimming pools in more places than on any other resource! More swimming links than any of the swimming indexes! ... of swimming pools. ...
www.swimmersguide.com/

123. **The Swimming Pool Operators and Owners Pages**
The Swimming Pool Operators and Owners Resources Pages. The Swimming Pool "Resource on The Web".
ww.caromal.co.uk/Homepage.htm

52
Table Tennis

1. **Table Tennis / Ping-Pong**
   Includes playing tips, weekly features, newsletter, chat and links.
   tabletennis.about.com/
2. **Table Tennis - Miniclip.com**
   www.miniclip.com/tabletennis.htm
3. **Denis' Table Tennis / Ping-Pong World**
   Denis' table tennis / ping-pong world, 27 active users (more stats), Includes rules, tips, exercises and articles for players and coaches of all levels.
   www.tabletennis.gr/
4. **Table Tennis New Zealand**
   Peter Jackson. kli1.jpg (12194 bytes). Barry Wynks. Profiles photos this page. Index - Site Contents. What's New. Includes information on affiliated associations, coaching manual, club help, championships, ratings,...
   www.tabletennis.org.nz/
5. **Tabletennis**
   www.tabletennis.com/
6. **Sweden Table Tennis**
   Welcome to Sweden Table Tennis AB! STIGA tabletennis products are marketed and sold today in over 100 countries. Your browser do not support frames! Manufactures balls, blades, bats, rubbers, tables, nets, and accessories and apparel for table tennis....
   www.tabletennis.se/
7. **PING-PONG**
   TableTennis-OnLine.info :: streda,
   tabletennis-online.info/

8. **Tabletennis**

   The summary for this Russian page contains characters that cannot be correctly displayed in this language/character set.

   tabletennis.hobby.ru/

9. **Tabletennis**

   Super Circuit. Enjoy the real Tabletennis movies!

   www.sc-tabletennis.com/

10. **Tabletennis Club KMIT'L**

    Tabletennis or pingpong club of kmitl ladkrabang,train play tabletennis,join to the thai link website,thaitabletennis.

    www.kmitl.ac.th/tabletennis/

11. **Worldwide TableTennis Links & Information**

    Advanced Topics in TableTennis. USA Table-tennis. ... TableTennis FAQs / Rules / Clubs.

    www.freeyellow.com/members2/qxjanc/page4.html

12. **TableTennis Tips from your LifeTips.com TableTennis Guru**

    Become A Guru Now! Need TableTennis Tips? ...

    tabletennis.lifetips.com/

13. **Tabletennis Super Group**

    Tabletennis Super Group. Costs: Free. Duration: about 4 months/ season (not sure yet).

    www.pbm.com/~lindahl/pbm_list

    descriptions/ table_tennis.html

14. **TableTennis3D by Xavier Martin**

    TableTennis 3D is an addictive Table Tennis simulation. ... TableTennis 3D should also run on most PalmOS 3.x devices. Color screen highly recommended. ...

    www.viex.org/?page=tabletennis3D

15. **Gallery :: Tabletennis & Pizza Borrel !!**

    Tabletennis & Pizza Borrel !! ... What an action! Viewed: 265 times. Some weren't really interested in tabletennis... Viewed: 258 times. ...

    www.catalysis.nl/~photos/tabletennis

16. **Namizni tenis**

    Tennis. Mini golf. Cycling. Tabletennis. Basketball. Volleyball. Badminton. Kayak. ... Excursions. PRICE. RESERVATION. WEATHER. BLUE FLAG. TABLETENNIS. btn-home.gif(2410 bytes).

    www.sobec.si/ang/namizni_tenis.htm

17. **www.suug.co.uk: Tabletennis**
This is the Tabletennis page of the Greenwich Student Union site, hosted by Oncampus. Advert. home. services. activities. barsandents. news. about us. forum. ...
www.suug.co.uk/main/studentactivities/SportSoc/Sports Tabletennis

18. **The International Tabletennis Webring**
The international tabletennis sitering site!
www.geocities.com/ITTsitering/

19. **North Harbour Table Tennis**
This Table Tennis site will try and keep you all up to date on current events in tabletennis, in particular in North Harbour and NZ. ...
www.geocities.com/Colosseum/Stadium/6131/

20. **TableTennis class Reference**
TableTennis Class Reference. Include <TableTennis.h> List of all members. Public Methods. TableTennis (). virtual, ~Table Tennis (). ...
www.csafe.utah.edu/Information/Documentation/ UCF classTableTennis.html

21. **Snooker/football/tabletennis table : Buy at the best price on ...**
Compare prices and buy through Kelkoo at the best shops. search.kelkoo.co.uk/b/a/ss_Snooker/ football tabletennis_table.html -

22. **TableTennis**
The summary for this Chinese (Simplified) page contains characters that cannot be correctly displayed in this language character set.
bbs.njust.edu.cn/cgi-bin/bbs/bbsdoc?board=TableTennis

23. **TableTennis**
The summary for this Japanese page contains characters that cannot be correctly displayed in this language/character set.
www.sc-tabletennis.com/index2.html

24. **Tabletennis**
Tabletennis. Japanese version of this page is here . Women's Singles. Final Standings 1. Koyama, Chire (Japan) 2. Deng, Yaping (China ...
www.hiroshima-cu.ac.jp/C/ASIA/Sports/ Result/eachgame/ tabletennis.html

25. **Tabletennis**
At the sports club Snel en Lenig (SEL) in Wassenaar, many different sports are being practiced intensively by its members. In 1969 ...
www.snelenlenig.nl/tabletennis.htm

26. **Tabletennis**
Tabletennis for Females. This game was admitted to the university since 1994.The university saved the hall and the equipments of
www.aabu.edu.jo/stu_affaires/sport/tabletennis.htm

27. **Coach ed. TableTennis**
Coach ed. TableTennis. Coach ed. Tennis. Coach ed. Swimming. Triathlon. Nice One Coach!
www.northamptonshiresport.org
content-480

28. **www.tabletennis.co.nz**
Enter http://www.nhtta.com/.
www.tabletennis.co.nz/

29. **European YMCA - European YMCA Events 2001 - EAY Events**
European Tabletennis Championship. Date: 10 - 13 May 2001 Place: Germany. Responsible: European Physical Education Group (EPEG). Participants ...
www.eay.org/whatwedo/events/eventsbrochure/ 01/eayevents/tennis.html

30. **Funny.co.uk - tabletennis funny**
See The Following Related Pages On Funny.co.uk: So You Think You're Funny? So You Think You're Funny? THE NEW LOOK FUNNY.CO.UK. ...
www.funny.co.uk/keywords/tabletennis-funny.html

31. **tabletennis.com.sg :-An information advisory on tabletennis in**
"Singapore tabletennis information & services", ...
www.singaporesports.com.sg/tabletennis_com_sg.htm

32. **Worldwide TableTennis Ladder Update Profile**
TableTennis ladder that is now forming. Free for all players and helps find opponents, track results, post/review classifieds, and find quality squash links.
www.sportsladders.com/tabletennis/update.asp

53
Tennis

1. **Tennis Magazine**
   news, instruction, gear, fitness, travel, and more.
   www.tennis.com/
2. **ATP Tour**
   Official site. All the latest results, rankings, and news.
   www.atptour.com/
3. **United States Tennis Association (USTA)**
   Promotes the development of tennis in the United States. Site includes news, tournament results, rankings, schedules, membership information, trivia, fun facts, and more.
   www.usta.com/
4. **The Tennis Server**
   Here are a few things not to miss: TENNIS FEATURES: ... EDITOR'S LETTER: A look at how we got here and our vision for the future. TENNIS COMMUNITY:
   www.tennisserver.com/Tennis.html
5. **International Tennis Federation (ITF)**
   Information for media, enthusiasts and officials involved in tennis.
   www.itftennis.com/
6. **ESPN.com: Tennis**
   Latest news and features from the tennis world.
   espn.go.com/tennis/
7. **Wimbledon Championships**
   Official site of the Wimbledon Championships, with live results, interviews, historical facts, and more.
   www.wimbledon.org/

8. **TennisONE**

Comprehensive tennis site covering the entire United States. Instructional columns, regional listings for clubs, tournaments, stores, school and resorts.

www.tennisone.com/

9. **Tennessee Aquarium**

A freshwater aquarium.

www.tnaqua.org/

10. **CBS Sportsline: Tennis**

Features the latest tennis news.

cbs.sportsline.com/tennis/

11. **Tennis Australia**

Official site. News and information on the Australian tennis scene, including international tournaments.

www.tennisaustralia.com.au/

12. **TennisOnline.com**

TennisOnline.com, TennisOnline.com, TennisOnline keeps track of popular tennis-related Web sites around the Internet. To get a list ...

www.tennisonline.com/

13. **Yahoo! Sports: Tennis**

Match results, news, scores, rankings, schedules, and player information.

sports.yahoo.com/ten

14. **U.S. Open Tennis Championships**

Official site. August 25 to September 7, 2003 at the USTA National Tennis Center in Flushing Meadows, New York.

www.usopen.org/

15. **Canadian Tennis Association**

Helps players and fans stay in touch with the latest happenings in the Canadian tennis scene.

www.tenniscanada.com/

16. **SI.com - Tennis**

On the news. Jon Wertheim TENNIS MAILBAG. Despite similarities to Anna, Maria Sharapova has what it takes on the court. Frank Deford ...

www.cnnsi.com/tennis/

17. **Lawn Tennis Association**
    Governing body for the game of tennis in Great Britain.
    www.lta.org.uk/
18. **Tennis Worldwide Magazine**
    The tennis magazine for and by tennis players around the world.
    www.tennisw.com/
19. **Coudal Partners - Photoshop Tennis**
    An overview of The Third Season of PsT can be found in this open letter from The Royal and Ancient Society For Photoshop Tennis. ...
    coudal.com/tennis.html
20. **US Professional Tennis Association - USPTA Little Tennis,**
    tennis Professional Tennis Association - USPTA, Little Tennis, tennis coaches, certification. HOME . . . SITE MAP . . . ... Sign up here. US Pro Tennis Shop. ...
    www.uspta.org/
21. **Fédération Française de Tennis**
    De l'Alsace aux Yvelines Pour plus d'infos sur tout le tennis dans votre région ou dans votre ville, allez surfer sur le web de votre ligue via notre site ...
    www.fft.fr/
22. **Tennis Warehouse - tennis racquets, tennis shoes, tennis apparel**
    Toll Free in the US 1-800-8-TENNIS | US Customer Email info@tennis-warehouse.com International Email twint@tennis warehouse.com.
    www.tennis-warehouse.com/?from=wta
23. **Deutscher Tennis Bund Homepage**
    Deutscher Tennis Bund Hallerstraße 89 20149 Hamburg Tel.: 040 / 41 17 8 - 0 Fax: 040 / 41 17 8 - 222 dtb@dtb-tennis.de. Deutschland
    www.dtb-tennis.de/
24. **Advantage Tennis Photo site - View and purchase photos of the**
    Advantage Tennis photo site, the photos of tennis players on this site have been taken at Grandslam, ATP and WTA tournaments around the world.
    www.advantage-tennis.com/

25. **Tennis rackets, UK Pro Racket Specialist. Tennis, Squash**
MASSIVE Savings & megadeals all year round on ..... Tennis - Squash - Badminton - rackets, shoes, clothing, equipment ....
www.tennis.net/

26. **Tennis Week**
Site includes updated draws, interviews, and feature articles.
www.tennisweek.com/

27. **ATP Tour**
Official site. All the latest results, rankings, and news.
www.atptennis.com/

28. **WTA Tour**
Official site. All the latest results, rankings, and news.
www.wtatour.com/

29. **tennis.se**
Arkiverade. SÖK. sök. Ny butik på nätet! Den exklusiva Tennis Sweden kollektionen finns ute nu. Läs mer... Prenumerera på Tidningen Tennis! ...
www.tennis.se/

30. **Intercollegiate Tennis Association**
Serves as the governing body of collegiate tennis in the United States.
www.itatennis.com/

31. **Tennessee Aquarium**
A freshwater aquarium.
www.tennis.org/

32. **New Zealand Tennis**
Information on the national and international tennis scenes. Features results for teams from the school to national level, calendar, links, news, rankings and more.
www.tennis.org.nz/

33. **tennis.org.uk - Easyspace Business Card**
Tennis.org.uk. This domain is for sale. Also, the following are available : Cricket.org.uk Snowboarding.org.uk Please email for details. EMAIL. ...
www.tennis.org.uk/

34. **Real Tennis**
    The oldest of all the racket games, and unlike most of the others, such as squash or modern lawn tennis, it is a product of evolution rather than pure invention.
    www.real-tennis.com/

35. **Championship Tennis Tours**
    Full service tennis tour operator. Offers travel to the French Open, Wimbledon, U.S. Open, Australian Open, and more.
    www.tennistours.com/

36. **World Wide Tennis Ladder**
    Free service for tennis players of all levels which helps players find opponents and maintains worldwide, local and personal stats.
    www.sportsladders.com/tennis/

37. **Women of Tennis**
    Including photo galleries, bios, and stats on the major names in women's tennis.
    www.igs.net/~bmitchell/Tennis/tennis.htm

38. **Junior Tennis**
    Features free membership, player profiles, coaching advice and articles, and links.
    www.juniortennis.com/

39. **Tennis at About.com - A comprehensive source of tennis**
    Tennis.about.com covers tennis instruction, the pro tours, tennis history, and how to buy racquets and other equipment. Resources ...
    tennis.about.com/mbody.htm

40. **USA Today: Tennis**
    Talk of tennis on the take, What ... No. 1 ranking in women's tennis Monday, one week after surrendering the spot to Justine Henin-Hardenne. ...
    www.usatoday.com/sports/tennis/tennis.htm

41. **mytennis**
    Official Swiss Tennis Homepage. Allianz Suisse Junior Trophy 2003 European ... Tournament. 01. - 08. 11.2003, Swiss Tennis - Leistungszentrum, Biel. ...
    www.mytennis.ch/

42. **www.Tennis Europetennis.com - The Official Website of Tennis**
To open page of National Association; right click + 'open link in new window'. Copyright © Tennis Europe 2001. All Rights Reserved.
www.etatennis.com/

43. **Tennis Information Home**
We plan on updating our home page each month with the best photos from our tournaments' photo galleries. So encourage your tournament ...
www.tennisinformation.com/

44. **College and Junior Tennis**
Results, standings, and news from college and junior tennis.
www.collegeandjuniortennis.com/

45. **CollegeTennisOnline**
Provides official college tennis rankings, NCAA and ITA results, news, and recruiting information.
www.collegetennisonline.com/

46. **World TeamTennis**
Professional coed team sport. Founded by Billie Jean King.
www.worldteamtennis.com/

47. **Australian Tennis Magazine**
Features rankings, statistics, stories, off and on court photos, and more.
www.tennismag.com.au/

48. **Tennis Masters Series**
Official site of the Tennis Masters Series events which occur around the world.
www.masters-series.com/

49. **Tennis Express - The Ultimate Equipment Site for racquets, shoes**
Tennis Express - The Largest Tennis Resource and Directory. Your online tennis resource for shopping,instruction tips, classifieds ...
www.tennisexpress.com/

50. **TennisLovers.com**
Tennis screensavers,logos and more|TENNISopedia|Tennis News|Tennis Money Leaders|Tennis Gear|Tennis PC Games|New Rankings|Tennis Calendar|Tennis Results|108 ...
www.tennislovers.com/

51. **Tennis Industry Magazine**
Addresses the needs and concerns of professionals in all aspects of the tennis business, from specialty...
www.tennisindustry.com/

52. **Top Tennis**
Le Magazine du tennis sur Internet
www.top-tennis.com/

53. **Shockwave Tennis Game - Tennis Open - Candystand**
Shockwave tennis game Tennis Open at Candystand.com. Play computer tennis games, sports, card, arcade games for free and win prizes. Computer Tennis Games, ...
www.candystand.com/games/cs_shock_cstn.htm

54. **Australian Open**
Official site. Features live results, tennis news, interactive cameras, real-time scoreboard, interviews, player profiles, and more.
www.ausopen.org/

55. **Tennis Ireland**
Organization to promote the development of tennis in Ireland.
www.tennisireland.ie/

56. **Tennis Betting - Tennis Master makes Big Profits from Tennis**
At Tennis Master - We love Tennis Betting ! We have made big profits from Tennis Betting and we will show you how. ... Tennis Betting Advice from Tennis Master. ...
www.tennismaster.co.uk/

57. **Tennis Channel**
Advertiser-supported television network devoted to tennis.
www.thetennischannel.com/

58. **Tennis Company**
Pro shop offering a complete selection of equipment including racquets, shoes, bags, eyeware, accessories, and clothing.
www.tenniscompany.com/

59. **Federazione Italiana Tennis**
ATTENZIONE!!! Per poter accedere al sito occorre avere abilitato JavaScript.
www.federtennis.it/

60. **tennis.pagina.nl**
In samenwerking met www.startpagina.nl. tennis.pagina.nl. ...
tennis.pagina.nl/

61. **BBC Sport: Tennis**
The latest news and features from the tennis world.
news.bbc.co.uk/sport/hi/english/tennis/default.stm

62. **Prince Sports Group**
Designing and manufacturing tennis, squash, badminton, racquetball rackets and other products for players of all skill levels.
www.princetennis.com/

63. **tsn.ca: Tennis**
Tennis on TSN. ... Please enable Javascript to enjoy TSN.ca's features. Next on TSN: Tue Nov 11 @ 1:00 PM et Tennis: Bell Challenge. ...
www.tsn.ca/tennis/

64. **International Tennis Federation: Wheelchair Tennis**
Official site featuring rankings, tournaments, player bios, news, and more.
www.itfwheelchairtennis.com/

65. **Nos estamos mudando. La pagina del Libro de Texto de Aeronautica ...**
Link to access the new site: (http://wings.avkids.com/Tennis/) Nos estamos mudando. La pagina ...
wings.ucdavis.edu/Tennis/

66. **Tennis Warehouse - tennis racquets, tennis shoes, tennis apparel**
Search. Tennis Racquets. ? Babolat Racquets ? Dunlop Racquets ? Estusa ... Finder ? Racquet Categories. Tennis Apparel. ? Men's Apparel ...
www.tenniswarehouse.com/

67. **Tennis Resorts Online**
Directory of tennis resorts and camps.
www.tennisresortsonline.com/

68. **Official Tennis Sites of Japan**
Supported by F-BIT Communications, ...
www.tennis.or.jp/

69. **Home of Tennis**
Football | Rugby | Formula One | Tennis | Snooker. Players Tour Events History Quiz, News Headlines. You must have a JavaScript enabled ...
www.homeoftennis.com/

70. **sunspot.net | tennis**
All-Metro Tennis team. Jun 1, 2003 All-Harford County Tennis team. All-Baltimore City/County Tennis team. Jun 4, 2002 All-Carroll County tennis team.
www.sunspot.net/sports/tennis/

71. **Golf And Your Feet: Information From The APMA**
YOUR PODIATRIC PHYSICIAN TALKS ABOUT TENNIS AND YOUR FEET. Information ... Association. Tennis And Your Feet Advice From The APMA. A Game for Everyone....
www.apma.org/sports/tennis.html

72. **rowztennis.com**
A fan's view of the world of professional tennis, featuring photos of up-and-coming and veteran tennis...
www.rowztennis.com/

73. **Tennis Corner**
Tournament results, rankings and misc info.
www.tenniscorner.net/

74. **Steve G_'s ATP Tour Rankings and Results Page**
The most complete tennis results and rankings archive on the web. Results ... Promotion RadioTennis.com Play French Club Tennis. results ...
www.stevegtennis.com/

75. **Amazon.com: Books: The Inner Game of Tennis**
Video Customers interested in The Inner Game of Tennis may also be interested in: Sponsored Links (What's this?) Feedback: Inner ...
www.amazon.com/exec/obidos/tg/detail/-/0679778314?v=glance

76. **Cross Court Tennis**
News and interviews direct from The Grand Slams, plus events from the ITF, ATP Tour and the Corel WTA Tour.
www.crosscourt.com.au/

77. **Welkom bij de KNLTB**
Actueel, de competitie, nationale teams en verenigingen.
www.knltb.nl/

78. **tennis-center.de >> the vision of tennis**
Tennis-center.de >> the vision of tennis bietet Ihnen topaktuelle Informationen rund ums Tennis. Angefangen bei der ATP Tour über ...
www.tennis-center.de/

79. **j-tennis.com**
The summary for this Japanese page contains characters that cannot be correctly displayed in this language/character set.
www.j-tennis.com/

80. **mytennis**
Official Swiss Tennis Homepage. Nike Junior Tour Nationales Masters im Swiss Tennis Leistungszentrum, Biel.
www.swisstennis.com/

81. **AmericaToday Tennis Coverage**
Globe-trotting AmericaToday tennis editor, Frank Fulton rubs (tennis) elbows with the stars as he follows the tournament around the world.
www.americatoday.com/sports/tennis/

82. **Beach Tennis - Miniclip.com**
Miniclip.com - free online games, multiplayer games and online tournaments.
www.miniclip.com/beachtennis.htm

83. **Tennis de Table.com**
Tennis de Table .com, le premier portail de tennis de table et ping pong, en France. ... Tennis de Table.com, toute l'actualité du ping et du pong ! ...
www.tennis-de-table.com/

84. **Bob Larson's Tennis News**
Offers news coverage and carries news releases from tennis associations and schools.
www.tennisnews.com/

85. **The Tennis Job Line Tennis Professional Employment Service**
Tennis Professional employment service advertising job openings at country clubs, tennis clubs, resorts, tennis camps, public facilities, and college coach ...
www.tennisjobs.com/

86. **Royal Tennis Court - Hampton Court Palace**
Includes history of the courts and palace, club rooms, the history of tennis, and links.
www.realtennis.gbrit.com/

87. **Ontario Tennis Association**
Includes rankings, tournament information, and more.
www.tennisontario.com/

88. **The Tennis Bookshop**

The Tennis Bookshop Web Site. ... Welcome to The Tennis Bookshop Web Site! ... My name is Alan Chalmers and I am the proprietor of The Tennis Bookshop. ...

www.tennisbookshop.com/

89. **Tennis Book Bibliography**

TENNIS BOOK BIBLIOGRAPHY. Welcome to the ... The Latest Tennis Bibliography in HTML. Fed Cup 2003 The Aspen Hill Gang. Read the Offensive

www.tennisbooks.com/

90. **Tennis Victoria**

News and information on the Victorian scene, including coaching services, junior results, and tournaments.

www.tennisvic.com.au/

91. **Colony Beach and Tennis Resort**

On the island of Longboat Key; known world wide for its beautiful accommodations, award winning restaurant, and world class tennis.

www.colonybeachresort.com/

92. **SLAM! Tennis**

Includes a variety of tennis news and information from CANOE's online tennis section.

www.canoe.ca/SlamTennis/home.html

93. **Van Der Meer Tennis**

Offers tennis clinics for adults, juniors, seniors, groups, and ranked juniors.

www.vandermeertennis.com/

94. **Tennisinternet.com is the YAHOO of TENNIS!!!! Voted by Computer ...**

Tennis magazine, online pics, interview, find a tennis partner and streaming media. "Over 800,000 unique tennis viewers since Year 2000 and counting!!!".

www.tennisinternet.com/

95. **Tennis-Statistiken**

Resultate, Ranglisten, Spieler Portraits, Statistiken der deutschen Tennis Herren im Einzel. Tennis-Statistiken http://tennis statistiken.de/.

www.tennis-statistiken.de/

96. **TennisIndia.org**
Includes news, player profiles, and results.
www.tennisindia.org/

97. **Tennis**
TennisSports Tennis. Tennis Summary. Tournament champions. 2002 Season. Major tournament results and schedule. 2001 Tennis Season. ...
www.infoplease.com/ipsa/A0109948.html

98. **Tennis Menace**
Tennis equipment and supplies for both the player and the industry.
www.tennismenace.com/

99. **Site Web FFTT**
Cliquez ici pour entrer dans le site FFTT.
www.fftt.com/

100. **Fédération québécoise de tennis**
NOUVEAU Exposition-photos de la Fédération québécoise de tennis (Cliquez ici). ... Logo TAC. Le numéro d?hiver 2004 du Tennis-mag est maintenant disponible! ...
www.tennis.qc.ca/

101. **GoTennis.com**
Offers pro tour news coverage, event calendar, gear shopping, web pages, and more.
www.gotennis.com/

102. **Supersportzone**
ATP. Henman wins first Masters title Tim Henman capped the finest week of his tennis career by winning the Paris Masters title with a 6-2 7-6 7-6 defeat of
www.supertennis.co.za/

103. **Sport**
Wealth Check Charity worker needs advice on pension. Tennis. ... Henman rolls over exhausted Federer to reach last four 01 November 2003 TENNIS. ...
sport.independent.co.uk/tennis/

104. **Tennis Elbow Central**
Contains an overview of the causes, diagnosis, treatment, and resources available to sufferers.
www.tennis-elbow.net/

105. **Paddle Tennis.biz**

Offers places to play, how to, rules, and more.
www.paddletennis.biz/

106. **TOPDOGTENNIS - Home**

USTA purchases Dynamic Computer Tennis Rating for Tennis in the US · Sportsrating.com (Internet Version) read more about the internet version. ...
www.topdogtennis.com/

107. **World Tennis Ratings**

Global tennis rating system for club, school, college, and professional tennis players throughout the world. WORLD TENNIS RATINGS. HOME. ...
www.worldtennisratings.com/

108. **Info Tennis : Le magazine du tennis sur le web !**

Le magazine du tennis sur le Net: actualité atp et wta, résultats, classements, joueurs, photos. ... La Boutique Info Tennis. Entrez dans la boutique 100% tennis
www.infotennis.com/

109. **Wellington Tennis**

For information on the Wellington, National, and International tennis scenes.
www.wellingtontennis.org.nz/

110. **Joe_'s Tennis String Forum**

Joe's Tennis String Forum, ...
www.stringforum.net/

111. **TENNIS SPORT SCIENCE**

TENNIS SPORT SCIENCE. Congratulations Mark! ... Tennis Guy, TENNIS OVER THE NET Start Here For Information On How To Use This Resource. ...
wings.avkids.com/Tennis/

112. **Tennis.info**

THE tennis site - searchable men's pro-tennis results database and the best pictures of pro tennis players anywhere! ... All content © 2000- 2003 tennis.info.
www.tennis.info/

113. **Wilson Tennis**

Offers tennis rackets, ball, strings, grips, bags, and more.
www.wilsonsports.com/tennis/

114. **Home About Us Contact Info Online Catalog Links**
Search for an item below. Welcome to the Internet home of Rayco Tennis. Bringing tennis equipment bargains to the World since 1969. ...
www.tennisrays.com/

115. **Suomen Tennisliiton Portaali**
... Copyright © 2003 Suomen Tennisliitto, webmaster@tennis.fi, ^ Alkuun ^, << Takaisin.
www.tennis.fi/

116. **Indian Tennis - The Home of Indian Tennis on the Internet**
For a better future for Indian tennis! Run by the lp-mb fanclub (200+ members since 1996) If you would like to be a member of the ...
www.its.uci.edu/~jaykay/indx.html

117. **Please wait while your screen resolution is determined...**
You are being redirected to the our new website. If you are not rediected, please click here. Please wait while your screen resolution is determined...
www.glta.org/

118. **Tennis Software - Free Download - Logiciel Shareware**
Tennis Software for players - Free Download Le logiciel pour votre tennis. ...
tennis3000.free.fr/

119. **Atlanta Team Tennis Association (ATTA)**
Metropolitan Atlanta's gay and lesbian nonprofit tennis organization.
www.atta.org/

120. **projo.com | Providence | Tennis**
Outdoors. Soccer. Tennis. MARKETPLACE. ? Archives. ... Make this your home page. The Providence Journal — Subscribe now. Tennis. Stories | Links | Bulletin board. ...
www.projo.com/tennis/

121. **Tennis Report**
News from current and forthcoming tournaments, results and rankings, and links.
www.tennisreport.com/

122. **Sport1 - Tennis**

Vor knapp einem Jahr stand Tommy Haas zum letzten Mal auf dem Tennis- platz. ... Stellen Sie aus den besten Tennis-Spielern der Welt Ihr eigenes Team zusammen! ...

www.sport1.de/coremedia/generator/www.sport1.de/Sportarten Tennis/Main.html

123. **Players Tennis Page**

Offering equipment, accessories, tournaments, and bulletin board.www.playerstennis.com/

124. **Tennis**

Isn't he cute?! Please check out this great tennis site "CentralFloridaTennis.com": ... Go there NOW...and then come right back here ;-). Manu playing tennis. ...

www.manuela.com/tennis.htm

125. **Fussball**

Link zu Tennis Borussia, Fußball und anderen interessanten Seiten. Links Tennis Borussia Berlin Tennis Borussia, die Männerseite ...

www.tennis-borussia.de/

126. **REVOLUTIONARY tennis instruction, tennis strokes, tennis tips, ...**

Revolutionary tennis instruction, tennis strokes, tennis lessons, tennis tips, tennis advice, tennis secrets, tennis teacher, tennis teaching, tennis skills ...

www.revolutionarytennis.com/

127. **tennis ixxxxi**

Tennis. ixxxxxxxxxxi.net. ... contact serve@ixxxxi.net 805.983.7657. For tennis sites with information on scores, matches, and players, visit the tennis links page.

tennis.ixxxxxi.net/

128. **TennisMundo Search Engine**

TennisMundo Search Engine.

www.tennismundo.com/

129. **Legg Mason Tennis Classic**

Warm up event to U.S. Open.

www.leggmasontennisclassic.com/

130. **Medinfo: Tennis Elbow (Lateral Epicondylitis)**
Medinfo's patient information on Tennis Elbow (Lateral Epicondylitis), a condition when the outer part of the elbow becomes painful and tender, usually as a ...
www.medinfo.co.uk/conditions/tenniselbow.html

131. **Museum of Tennis**
Virtual museum featuring photos of sculptures, paintings, and other historical objects.
www.museumoftennis.com/

132. **TennisWarrior.com**
Offers tips and techniques on how to improve mental toughness. Also offers books and audio tapes.
www.tenniswarrior.com/

133. **Cliff Richard Tennis Foundation**
runs grass-roots tennis schemes across U.K. primary schools.
www.cliffrichardtennis.org/

134. **Tennis4you.com**
News, articles, classifieds, and links galore.
www.tennis4you.com/

135. **Tennis Ministry International**
Tennis Ministry International a christian mission that sends to news to players, fans, touring pro's, tennis coaches, university teams and clubs. ...
www.tennisministry.com/

136. **THE NEUTRAL TENNIS by Giuliano Acierno**
Neutral tennis è un sito in lingua italiana nel quale potrete trovare interessanti informazioni su questo sport. ::. sito ottimizzato ...
home.datacomm.ch/neutraltennis/

137. **Tennis Bahamas!**
Tennis Bahamas! Home Page. http://tennisbahamas.virtualave.net.
tennisbahamas.freeservers.com/

138. **TENNISWIZARD.COM - The best tennis instruction available**
TennisWizard.com educates coaches, parents, children, ATP and WTA tour professionals on tennis fitness, tennis nutrition, opponents tendencies and weaknesses. ...
www.tenniswizard.com/

139. **Professional Tennis Registry**
Founded by Dennis Van der Meer to educate, certify, and service tennis teachers and coaches around the world.
www.ptrtennis.org/

140. **Tennis Forum Frigate**
Tennis Forum Frigate [Post Message][The Jolly Roger][One Page Version]. ... Tennis Forum Frigate. Post yer opinion, a ...
jollyroger.com/zz/youtdoord/Tennishall/shakespeare1.html

141. **Tennis Network: Website Services - Home**
Tennis Network is the only - exclusively tennis - website hosting company offering an easy-to-use WebWriter, Content Management Service, for tennis clubs ...
www.tennisnetwork.com/

142. **Las Vegas Golf & Tennis**
Las Vegas Golf & Tennis has been serving the needs of golf and tennis enthusiasts since 1974. The largest full service retailer in the United States.
www.lvgolf.com/

143. **http://web.tiscali.it/tennisforafrica/**
Charity association for helping African children through the promotion of tennis. Information on...
web.tiscali.it/tennisforafrica/

144. **Engine Tennis: tutto il tennis in italiano**
Portale con calendari, classifiche, immagini e risultati dei tornei ATP e WTA. Biografie dei campioni...
www.engine-net.com/tennis/

145. **Tennis**
Bell Challenge tennis tournament.
www.allsports.com/tennis/

146. **Herald.com - Your Miami Everything Guide**
Motor Sports. ? Outdoors. ? Soccer. ? Tennis. ? Wrestling. ? Youth Sports. Business. ... Back to Home > Sports > Tennis, TOP STORY, ...
www.miami.com/mld/miamiherald/sports/tennis/

54
Tennikoit

1. **Tennikoit Ring(44901) - Gujral Industries**
   Home | Trade Leads | Adv. Sourcing Service | Help. Product Search | Supplier Search. Gujral Industries. Product ID: 44901. Tennikoit Ring....
   www.allproducts.com.tw/india/gujral/18-44901.html
2. **Tennikoit Ring(44901) - Gujral Industries**
   ... Product, Product ID:44901. Tennikoit Ring. Specifications: Sponge rubber filled; Colour: Red, Green, Blue,Yellow and White; 44901: 190-200gms; 44902: 230-240gms.
   www.allproducts.com/india/gujral/18-44901.html
3. **CITY SPORTS**
   National junior tennikoit tourney. ... The 22nd National Junior Tennikoit Championship for boys and girls will begin here ...
   newstodaynet.com/20dcc/cs3.htm
4. **Ringtennis in Indien**
   ringtennis.die-hummels.de/intern/indien/index.php
5. **Ringtennis in Indien**
   ringtennis.die-hummels.de/intern/indien/Regelkunde.php
6. **Ringtennis South Africa - Official homepage of ringtennis ...**
   Official page of the South African Tenniqoits Board. Match results, history, game rules and guestbook.
   www.ringtennis.co.za/
7. **Ringtennis.co.za - Ringtennis in India**
   www.ringtennis.co.za/
   default.asp?page=IndiaArticle1&language=english

8. **2. Fundamentals in Drill and Marching**

... (c) Jumping for distance and height exphasising on basis fundamentals of take off and landing. (d) Throwing cricket ball/ tennikoit etc. 4. Games. (a) Relays. ...

shikshanic.nic.in/cd50years/g/52/4I/524I0402.htm

55
Trekking

1. **Nepal Trekking Tours: Nepal Treks, Camping, Touring (Himalaya)**
   Nepal Trekking by Royal Exclusive Travel. Nepal Trekking. ... Nepal Trekking. Trekking is one long-term activity that draws repeat visitors to the country. ...
   www.nepal-trekking.net/
2. **Asian Trekking**
   Asian Trekking for your expeditions, treks, tours in Nepal, Tibet, Bhutan to Everest, Annapurna, Pumori, Ama Dabla, Makalu, Shisha Pangma, Lhotse, and other ...
   www.asian-trekking.com/
3. **Trekking Hellas**
   Trekking Hellas organises tours in neighboring Bulgaria and Turkey. •. Trekking in Bulgaria. By interest. ...
   www.trekking.gr/
4. **Trekking in Nepal Himalaya**
   Nepal Trekking information including equipment for a trek, trekking agencies, and links to Nepal trek operators. Trekinfo.com. ... Nepal Trekking Specialists. ...
   www.trekinfo.com/
5. **Southwest Trekking -> Home**
   Southwest Trekking features outdoor recreation activities, attractions, gear and active travel opportunities in the south west! Professional guides provide a full range of mountain bike, hiking, trekking, trail running services...
   www.swtrekking.com/

6. **Adventure Travel Vacations-Gunflint Trail Minnesota-Boundary**
Boundary Country Trekking adventure travel vacations (Gunflint Trail Minnesota) offers guided canoeing trips, mountain biking, hiking, snowshoeing, cross ...
www.boundarycountry.com/
7. **HistoricalTrekking.com**
The most comprehensive site online dedicated to Living History, Historical Trekking and Re-enacting within the 1600 to 1840 Time Period. ...
www.historicaltrekking.com/
8. **Nepal Trekking, Tours, Lodge Treks, Rafting, Wildlife Safari,**
Nepal trekking, tours, hiking, lodge treks, river rafting, peak climbing, wildlife safari in Nepal, Tibet, Bhutan, Kailash, Sikkim, Darjeeling and Ladakh. ...
www.trekking-in-nepal.com/
9. **La Rivista del Trekking**
World_>_Italiano_>_Acquisti_>_Editoria_e_Stampa_>_Riviste
www.trekking.it/
10. **Trekking in Austria**
www.Npublish.at/trekking/default.htm
11. **TREKKING - TEAM - Bungy jumping - Caving - Rafting - Climbing**
Trekking Team Schweiz - Das ultimative Team wenn es um Bungy Jumping, Canyoning, Hölloch oder Teambildung geht. ... Tel: +41 (0)848 808 007 email:info@trekking.ch. ...
www.trekking.ch/
12. **Rando-Trekking.com**
World_>_Français_>_..._>_Sports_et_loisirs_>_Sports_>_Randonnée
www.rando-trekking.com/
13. **Trekking**
Trekking Articles
www.trekking.fr/
14. **Nature Trekking?Nature Photo Gallery???Trekking?**
Yoshizumi Suzuki. Information, PhotoGallery, WallPaper, GreetingCard, ...
www.cx.sakura.ne.jp/~nature_t/
15. **Trekking-Mahlzeiten - Homepage**
World_>_Deutsch_>_Sport_>_Klettersport_und_Wandern_>_Firmen
www.trekking-mahlzeiten.de/

16. **Trekking and Kayaking in Chile**
    Hiking and whitewater tours in Chile, photos, accommodation, Adventure Handbook Central Chile
    www.trekkingchile.com/
17. **Amazon.com: Books: Trekking in Nepal: A Traveler_s Guide**
    Trekking in Nepal: A Traveler's Guide, Stephen Bezruchka, Stephen Bezruchka MD, Robert Kunstaetter.
    www.amazon.com/exec/obidos/tg/ detail/-/0898865352?v=glance
18. **Trekking Italia**
    ww.trekkingitalia.com/
19. **MTB Trekking**
    Have a nice Trekking. introduction.
    homepage1.nifty.com/kitot/
20. **Sun Valley Trekking, Idaho, backcountry ski, huts yurts ...**
    Sun Valley Trekking LLC Backcountry Adventure Sports Specialists! Join Sun Valley Trekking for an incredible vacation. Guided ski tours, hikes, and mountaineering in Sun Valley and Yellowstone. Guide profiles and trip...
    www.svtrek.com/
21. **Trekking Parapentes**
    www.trekking.fr/parapente/
22. **Green Lotus Trekking welcomes you in Nepal !**
    Green Lotus Trekking, located in Kathmandu Nepal, organises trekking, rafting, expeditions and mountain biking. Provides trekking, mountaineering, rafting, cultural tours, and internal travel services. Navigation...
    www.green-lotus-trekking.com/
23. **Alaska Hiking, Backpacking, Trekking, Outdoors and Wilderness ...**
    Denali Trekking Company is a Alaska hiking, backpacking, and wilderness tours company dedicated to providing our guests the greatest opportunity for exploring ...
    www.denalitrekking.com/
24. **Nepal - Reisen und Trekking home**
    World_>_Deutsch_>_..._>_Reisen_>_Reiseberichte_>_Asien_>_Nepal
    www.nepal-dia.de/

25. **Amazon.com: Books: Kilimanjaro & Mount Kenya: A Climbing and ...**
30 top climbing and trekking routes on ...
www.amazon.com/exec/obidos/tg/ detail/-/0898865573?v=glance

26. **Travel, climbing, adventure tourism, rafting, wildlife in Central ...**
Web site provides information for adventure travel and tourism in Central Asia and Kyrgyzstan with local travel agency Dostuck Trekking. ...
www.dostuck.com.kg/

27. **Velkommen til Trekking Bureauet**
World_>_Dansk_>_Fritid_>_Rejser_>_Rejsebureauer
www.trekkingbureauet.dk/

28. **NAToUR trekking . Isla de La Palma ... no flash**
Trekking and walking excursions on La Palma, with maps and descriptions of the walks.
www.natour-trekking.com/

29. **Sky Trekking Alaska_'s Trek Adventures**
Designs and hosts custom, comprehensive aerial adventures within and across Alaska.
www.skytrekkingalaska.com/

30. **Trekking in Nepal - trekking, Rafting, Nepal lodge trek, camp trek ...**
Trekking in Nepal - Operating lodge treks, camping trek, expedition climbs and overland journeys exclusively in the majestic Himalayan of Nepal, Tibet, Bhutan ...
www.thamserkutrekking.com/

31. **MOUNTAIN TREKKING & TOURS**
Mountain Trekking & Tours. Summer. Summer Adventures. Winter. Winter Adventures. Mountain Trekking & Tours What is Mountain Trekking & Tours? ...
www.mountaintrekking.com/

32. **Hiking Trekking hillwalking Holidays in Ireland**
Viking trekking company are the premier hillwalking and hiking tour holiday operators in ireland. HIKING, TREKKING & HILLWALKING HOLIDAYS IN IRELAND. Contains travel itineraries for short, moderate, and long distances specialising in Irish culture...
www.vikingtrekking.com/

33. **NOVA Trekking**
Français, Deutsch, English, E-mail TRAVEL AGENCY REISEB Ü RO AGENCE DE VOYAGE, English English Deutsch Deutsch Français Fran ç ais. Web Design by Ing.arch. ...
www.nova-trekking.sk/

34. **NEPAL TREKKING & EXPEDITIONS PVT LTD**
Office Location Map map.jpg (11884 bytes). This site is created and maintained by WebNepal dot com Copyright @ Nepal Trekking and Expeditions Pvt. Ltd. Offers tours and treks in Nepal. Features a profile, services, prices and a photo gallery. Accessible...
www.nepal-trek.com/

35. **TREKKING TRAVEL, Mendoza Turismo & Aventura**
The company TREKKING TRAVEL is located in Mendoza (Argentina). We have broad experiences in horseback riding and trekking in Los Andes Mountain Range... ...
www.trekking-travel.com.ar/

36. **Peter Schneider Sagarmatha Trekking**
www.sagarmatha-trekking.de/

37. **Abode Himalaya Windhorse Trekking - Climbing and Trekking in the ...**
Ang Karma Sherpa, Windhorse Trekkering offers mountaineering, expedition packages and back up service, climbing courses, trekking, white water ...
www.windhorse-trek.com/

38. **Unique Path Trekking and Expedition, Nepal treking, trekking Nepal ...**
Unique Path Trekking and Expedition offers Nepal trekking, trekking in Nepal, Nepal treks, Treks to Nepal, Trek to Nepal, Nepal treking, trekking Nepal, treking ...
www.uniquepath.com/

39. **Alaska Glacier Trekking : Alaska Glaciers : Helicopter Tours**
Alaska Glacier trekking is the best way to see Alaska Glaciers. Helicopter tours and glacier landings...
www.glaciertrekking.com/

40. **Kānguru Trekking Jena**
Trekking | Klettern | Paddeln | Alpin | Eis | Hochtouren | Expedition | Wandern. ...
www.kaenguru.com

41. **Trekking in the Alps and Trekking and Snowshoeing Holidays led by...**
Trekking in the Alps is a small friendly company offering guided walking holidays in Europe, with small groups led by Hilary Sharp, an experienced, qualified ...
www.trekkinginthealps.com/

42. **Horse trekking in New Zealand. TrueNZ Guide to New Zealand**
Guide to horse trekking in New Zealand, with many listings and details of trekking operators across...
www.truenz.co.nz/horsetrekking/

43. **Nature Trail Trekking:Nepal trekking,Nepal tours,Trekking in Nepal...**
Nature Trail Trekking and Expeditions for Nepal for your expeditions, treks, tours and adventure trips in Nepal, Tibet and Bhutan. ...
www.allnepal.com/

44. **Trekking Plan**
Trekking Plan is a highly efficient tourist office specialising in mountain bike tours and trekking. Trekking Plan is based in Chania, Western Crete. ...
www.cycling.gr/

45. **Salta - Argentina Norte Trekking Expeditions**
Salta, guide of adventure travel offer trips over Argentina North West and Atacama Desert in Chile.Private and small groups in 4x4, trekking, horseback riding ...
www.nortetrekking.com/

46. **Yemen Trekking Hiking Walking Paragliding in the Haraz mountains**
A Yemeni guide offering his guiding services for treks through the Haraz mountains, a volcanic region...
yementreks.tripod.com/

47. **Himalaya Trekking Wandelreizen, voor een wandelvakantie met of...**
World_>_Nederlands_>_..._>_Actieve_Vakanties_>_Wandelen
www.htwandelreizen.nl/

48. **Peru BergSport - Huaraz, Peru**
Based in Huaraz, offer llama treks and hiking programs in Cusco and Huaraz.
www.perubergsport.com/

49. **Thailand Trekking - Consolidated Treks in Thailand Adventure**
Thailand Trekking. Destination Guides, Thailand Hotels, Tour Packages, Trekking, Adventure. ... Consolidated Treks in Thailand Trekking in Chiang Mai. ...
www.asia-discovery.com/thailand-trekking.htm

50. **Trekking tours, trekking expeditions, trail treks**
Trekking. InfoHub has compiled a list of trekking tours, trekking expeditions and trail treks around the world. ... Tibet. Activity: Trekking. Duration: 23 days. ...
www.biztravel.com/TRAVEL/SIT/sit_pages/Trekking.html

51. **Trekking in Nepal**
Trekking in Nepal. The Annapurna Circuit. Namaste and Eternal Memories. A travelogue of a visit to Nepal and Thailand. A daily diary which includes a twenty one day trek...
www.geocities.com/Yosemite/Trails/6335/

52. **Trekking Collective.........Alternative Treks, Tours and Travel**
Trekking Collective Co. Provides Alternative Treks, Tours, travel and services in Northern Thailand, Mekong region, SE Asia. trekkingcollective ...
www.trekkingcollective.com/

53. **Trekking in the Faroe Islands - Faroe Trekking**
Faroe Trekking is a faroese trekking tours company, based in the Faroe Islands, dedicated to providing our guests guided tours in small groups exploring the ...
www.trekking.fo/

54. **Uyuni Salt Flat - Bolivia**
Local guide of adventure travel over Argentina North West and Atacama Desert in Chile.Private trips, small groups in 4x4, trekking, horseback riding and rafting ...
www.nortetrekking.com/uyuni1.htm

55. **Stowarzyszenie Turystyczne Trekking Club**
www.trekkingclub.republika.pl/

56. **Everest Trekking Canada Home Page**
Everest Trekking Canada specializes in high quality treks to classic Nepal Himalayan destinations. ... email: Everest Trekking Canada. ...
www.everesttrekking.com/

56
Volleyball

1. **VOLLEYBALL WORLD WIDE, Volleyball.ORG, The oldest and most ...**
   VOLLEYBALL WORLD WIDE.
   http://www.Volleyball.ORG. History, FAQs, rules, organizational contacts, and links for amateur, professional, collegiate, and...
   www.volleyball.org/
2. **Volleyball.ORG, The oldest and most complete internet site on the ...**
   VOLLEYBALL WORLD WIDE.
   http://www.Volleyball.ORG/. Volleyball World Wide, your global source of information on the sport of volleyball. ...
   www.volleyball.org/Index.html
3. **Volleyball.Com — volleyball equipment, clothes, shoes and rules**
   Full equipment line of indoor court volleyball and outdoor beach volleyball, shoes, nets & gear. Coaches corner, active volleyball forums, search for where to play, some information about professional...
   www.volleyball.com/
4. **USA Volleyball**
   The USA men's national volleyball team will start the new year with its second-chance to qualify for the 2004 Olympic Games in Athens, Greece. Official site of the governing organization for volleyball in the US; includes overviews and contacts...
   www.usavolleyball.org/
5. **Fédération Internationale de Volleyball (FIVB)**
   Latest results, news, press releases, player rankings and profiles from this organization which governs...
   www.fivb.ch/

6. **VolleyBallMag.com - The Net and Beyond**
Forums, polls and scores, along with an archive of selected articles from the printer version of this...
www.volleyballmag.com/

7. **Volleyball**
Volleyball is a growing sport and About.com's volleyball site is the place to keep up on all the volleyball happenings around the world. ...
volleyball.about.com/

8. **AVCA - the American Volleyball Coaches Association**
Eastern Mennonite Selected Molten Division III Men's Invitational Volleyball Championship Host. ... A Conversation On Coaching Championship Volleyball-Video Version. ...
www.avca.org/

9. **Volleyball Hall of Fame - Holyoke, Massachusetts**
Volleyball's Birthplace: Holyoke, Massachusetts 1895. History of the game, photo gallery, honorees profiles, and merchandise.
www.volleyhall.org/

10. **AVP PRO BEACH VOLLEYBALL TOUR**
Volleyball fans find exclusive coverage of AVP Pro Beach Volleyball Tour. ... get you everywhere on the pro beach volleyball circuit. Just ask AVP Elaine Youngs. ...
www.avp.com/

11. **Volleyball Canada**
National team news, press releases, and contacts from the association which governs volleyball in Canada.
www.volleyball.ca/

12. **Collegiate Volleyball Update (cvu.com)**
The most comprehensive collection of daily updates and scores from around the USA in mens and womens volleyball. ... Ball State Men's Volleyball Remains Alive. ...
www.cvu.com/

13. **Volleyball in Deutschland: Ergebnisse und Tabellen aus Halle World_>_Deutsch_>_..._>_Volleyball_>_Verzeichnisse_und_Portale**
www.volleyball-online.de/

14. **Volleyball.it - BUON NATALE E FELICE ANNO NUOVO World_>_Italiano_>_Sport_>_Pallavolo_>_Notizie_e_Media**
www.volleyball.it/

15. **VolleyballOne.com has moved to SpikeNashbar.com!**
 Provides equipment, accessories, gear, and training resources, as well as a volleyball discussion...
 www.volleyballone.com/

16. **CEV Home**
 Executive contacts, country-level organization listings, and rankings and results for European cups,...
 www.cev.lu/

17. **Schweizerischer Volleyball-Verband**
 World_>_Français_>_..._>_Sports_et_loisirs_>_Sports_>_Volleyball
 www.volleyball.ch/

18. **English Volleyball Association**
 The Official Home Page of the English Volleyball Association.National Governing Body of Volleyball in England. The Home Page of ...
 www.volleyballengland.org/

19. **Naked Volleyball**
 schedule information. Home, E-mail, Please e-mail us if you play volleyball and live (or vacation) in Southern California. Link to ...
 www.nakedvolleyball.com/

20. **VOLLEYBALLMEMORABILIA.COM**
 Experience the history of volleyball with our collection of international volleyball memorabilia. ... Photograph taken at a Volleyball Memorabilia Roadshow. ...
 www.volleyballmemorabilia.com/

21. **Volleyball Festival**
 Epic Volleyball Club. A volleyball tradition since 1984. Nation's largest girls tournament.
 www.volleyball-festival.com/

22. **Cool Site - VOLLEYBALL ON THE NET**
 THE VOLLEYBALL NET! Volleyball information. Spread the ... to add!! Great deals on Volleyball gear for VballNet.com visitors!! ...
 www.vballnet.com/

23. **Schneid_'s Volleyball Page**
 Instructional site with information about volleyball, exercise and fitness, sports medicine, and nutrition.
 www.volleyweb.com/

24. **Volleyball BC: Adult and Youth leagues, tournaments, training and..**
The BCVA is the provincial sport governing body which actively encourages and provides opportunities...
www.bcva.com/

25. **Norges Volleyballforbund**
World_>_Norsk_>_Sport_>_Volleyball
www.volleyball.no/

26. **Volleyball Forums :: Index Online Volleyball Community**
Online volleyball discussion forums. Volleyball community where all players, coaches, and fans are welcomed. Learn all about the sport of volleyball. ...
www.volleyballforums.com/

27. **drills site**
Volleyball Drill Archive. Thank for the tremendous ... web site. Click on the box of the aspect of volleyball you would like a drill on. Some have ...
www.emporia.edu/vball/drills/

28. **Midwest Volleyball Warehouse**
Offers clothing, shoes, accessories and equipment. Includes specials, volleyball links, event and...
www.midwestvolleyball.com/

29. **Fairway Volleyball (Home)**
FAIRWAY VOLLEYBALL is REAL VOLLEYBALL... offering the largest volleyball selectionat competitive prices. ... Fairway Volleyball is Real Volleyball !! ...
www.fairwayvolleyball.com/

30. **Beach Volleyball Database**
News and database searchable by player, tournament and history.
www.bvbinfo.com/

31. **United States Professional Volleyball**
2003 USPV Season Cancelled. Description: Promotes womens professional indoor volleyball; includes contacts and tournament results.
www.uspv.com/

32. **Volleyball Victoria Home Page**
volleyball Coaching articles, volleyball rules information, updates on Victoria Volleyball, beach volleyball. ...
hypbus.com/vicvball/

33. **Australian Volleyball Home Page**
The official site for the Australian Volleyball Federation. ... Australian Volleyball Federation. Kerri Pottharst - one of her finest moments! ...
www.isport.com.au/volleyball/avf/

34. **The Volley ball Web page**
David Lowthers volleyball web page Thanks for visiting my school project. This page is devoted to the renown sport of Volleyball. Provides a timeline of the history of volleyball, information on scoring systems, and tips on some...
www.davesvolleyball.20m.com/

35. **Volleyball Québec**
World > Français > ... > Sports et loisirs > Sports > Volleyball
www.volleyball.qc.ca/

36. **WOVD Logo**
Competition results and contacts from the governing international organisation of volleyball for disabled...
www.wovd.com/

37. **1-on-1 Volleyball — Bubbletoonia — Free Online Shockwave Flash ...**
Fight for your glory !!! Represent your school to beat your arch-enemy in this fast pace, 1-on-1 VolleyBall game ! You should enable ...
www.bubbletoonia.com/game/volleyball.html

38. **Søger du efter Dansk Volleyball Forbund?**
World > Dansk > Sport > Volleyball
www.volleyball-dvbf.dk/

39. **The Volleyball Newsletter for the UK & Ireland.**
Volleyball News site for Players, Organisers and Club Members in the UK & Ireland. Check out ... The Volleyball Newsletter. An independent ...
www.volleyballnewsletter.com/

40. **NW Volleyball**
Offers junior and adult tournament information, along with club specifics and contact links.
www.volleyballnw.com/

41. **Volleyball Atlanta Contact Information**
Not for Profit Volleyball club serving the Metro Atlanta Area.
www.volleyballatlanta.org/

42. **Volleyball Ventures**
Volleyball Ventures is an organization dedicated to the pursuit of recreational volleyball in the Los Angeles area. ...
www.vbventures.com/

43. **volley.de - Volleyball**
World_>_Deutsch_>_Sport_>_Ballsport_>_Volleyball
www.volley.de/

44. **Alberta Volleyball**
Latest news, results, program, information about indoor and beach, staff overview, shop and link collection.
www.albertavolleyball.com/

45. **Tidewater Volleyball Association**
The Tidewater Volleyball Association is a non-profit charitable organization located in Virginia Beach, Virginia. ... Tidewater Volleyball Association. ...
www.spike.net/

46. **Yankee Volleyball Association**
Tournament schedules, results, and information about regional opportunities for
www.yankee.org/

47. **Volleyball 101**
Articles on the sport of volleyball. Discover and lear more about this sport through tutorials and...
home.earthlink.net/~tfakehany/index2.html

48. **Cobra Volleyball Equipment - Indoor / outdoor Volleyball products**
Cobra Volleyball net system indoor outdoor equipment. Action photos of players and sport net systems. volleyball tournament photo. ...
www.cobravolleyball.com/

49. **Volleyball**

All Volleyball, Inc. Novelties, clothing, training, coaching, and reffing equipment, volleyballs and ball carts.

www.allvolleyball.com/

50. **Volleyball Pictures — Hundreds of indoor and beach volleyball**

Volleyball pictures featuring indoor and beach action shots from national, international, collegiate and junior teams.

www.volleyball-pictures.com/

51. **Volleyball Association of Ireland**

This is the website of the Volleyball Association of Ireland (VAI).

www.clubi.ie/volleyball/home.html

52. **Volleyball Magazine - Instruction Archives**

www.volleyballmag.com

Our online instruction center features articles from past issues of Volleyball, authored by pros to help you get the most out of your game. ...

www.volleyballmag.com/instruct.htm

53. **Boom Boom Volleyball - Miniclip.com**

Boom Boom Volleyball, The aim is to get the bomb on the other players ground, reducing their boom boom resistance. Use ARROW KEYS to MOVE.

www.miniclip.com/boomboom.htm

54. **volleyball**

The summary for this Greek page contains characters that cannot be correctly displayed in this language/character set.

www.volleyball.gr/

55. **Blacklight Volleyball glow-in-the-dark corporate event ...**

Glow necklaces, glow sticks, techno bubbles, glow in the dark volleyballs and blacklight body paint.

www.blacklightvolleyball.com/

56. **Statistik - Rekorde (HV)**

World_>_Deutsch_>_Wissen_>_Weltrekorde_>_Sport

www.smash-hamburg.de/statistik/ deu/statistik-hv-rek.htm

57. **Atlantic Volleyball**

Offers mini-balls and volleyballs for indoor and outdoor.

www.atlanticvolleyball.com/

58. **Volleyball Equipment, Volleyball Shoes, Nets - Shopping Mall**
Volleyball equipment and beach volleyball equipment comparison shopping. Volleyball shoes and volleyball nets. Shop for equipment ...
www.volleyballcommunity.com/

59. **Authoritative Volleyball - Todd_s Volleyball Pages**
Information on volleyball rules, volleyball equipment, and recreational/competitive adult play in Austin, TX, and Chicago, IL USA. Todd's Volleyball Page. ...
www.vbref.org/

60. **NCAA Volleyball**
Polls/rankings; Participation rates; Playing rules (USA Volleyball Web site); ...
www.ncaa.org/sports/volleyball/

61. **nudistvolleyball.com - Tournaments, Events, News and much more...**
Nudistvolleyball.com. We are dedicated to enhancing and promoting volleyball at family nudist resorts, beaches and clubs.
www.nudistvolleyball.com/

62. **World Volleyball**
World Volleyball provides sport World News from the most comprehensive global news network on the internet. ... World Volleyball, Search the World News Network. ...
www.worldvolleyball.com/

63. **Volleyball WORLD Home Page**
Volleyball WORLD Official Site. A FREE WebRing about Volleball. Beacome a menber is EASY ... This is the Volleyball WORLD Official Site. ...
www15.brinkster.com/vwwebring/

64. **Just Volleyball store offers the best in volleyball equipment ...**
As a volleyball player and team sponsor, I pledge that I have practical experience with the products sold here and that they offer the best combination of ...
www.justvolleyballstorc.com/

65. **volleyball.com - volleyball equipment, shoes, clothes & rules for ...**
Full equipment line of indoor court volleyball and outdoor beach volleyball, shoes, nets & gear. ...
www.volleyball.com/home.html

66. **Discount store for volleyball shoes, volleyball equipment ...**
Net systems, shoes, ankle braces, jumpsoles, apparel, uniforms, bags, balls, and accessories from...
www.allstatevolleyball.com/

67. **Rules Information - Volleyball**
Rules listing and interpretation, as well as hand signals, for secondary school volleyball in the...
www.nfhs.org/rules-volleyball.htm

68. **SVA the home of Scottish Volleyball**
Home page of the Scottish Volleyball Association News, league and cup information, club overview, courses and related links.
www.scottishvolleyball.org/

69. **VolleyBall Corner**
Online ordering of equipment, braces, apparel, and net systems, as well as links to Volleyball sites.
www.volleyballcorner.com/

70. **Queensland Volleyball Asscociation - Home Page**
Queensland Volleyball Association, ... Welcome to the official Web Site of the Queensland Volleyball Association. Where can I play? click to find out. Latest News. ...
www.qva.org.au/

71. **V-SPIRIT - World Volleyball Online Magazine**
At V-SPIRIT you could find information of World Volleyball, Photo, Result, Player's information and Special feature. ... 2004 VOLLEYBALL CALENDER. ...
www.v-spirit.com/

72. **Ontario Volleyball Association**
Ontario Volleyball Association.Site production by Sporting Technologies.
www.ontariovolleyball.org/

73. **Yahoo! Directory Volleyball**
Volleyball Gear for Sale on eBay Great deals and amazing selection on volleyball gear.
www.yahoo.com/Recreation/Sports/Volleyball/

74. **Mid-Atlantic Volleyball**
Mid-Atlantic Volleyball (MAV) serves volleyball players and enthusiasts with volleyball clinics, leagues, schedules, tournaments and equipment sources in the ...
www2.ari.net/mavball/

75. **Amazon.com: Books: Beach Volleyball**
Editorial Reviews Ingram Specific to off-court volleyball, this book covers all the important skills, techniques, training exercises, and competitive tips ...
www.amazon.com/exec/obidos/tg/ detail/-/0880118369?v=glance

76. **AggieAthletics.com :: The Official Website of Texas A&M Athletics**
1 USC, 3-0. Laura Jones. (12/12/03)—The 17th-ranked Texas A&M volleyball team played a tough match but fell to No. ... A Class Act: 2003 Volleyball Preview. ...
www.aggieathletics.com/index.php?SID=WVB

77. **Volleyball New Brunswick**
Provincial Champions! Volleyball New Brunswick was very busy this past weekend with 3 Provincial Championships taking place. The ...
www.vnb.nb.ca/

78. **WVV - Westdeutscher Volleyball-Verband - Willkommen**
World_>_Deutsch_>_..._>_Volleyball_>_Verbände_>_Deutschland
www.wvv-volleyball.de/

79. **Nordbadischer Volleyball-Verband**
World_>_Deutsch_>_..._>_Volleyball_>_Verbände_>_Deutschland
nvv.volleyball-online.de/

80. **Gotham Volleyball**
www.gothamvolleyball.org/

81. **Open Directory - Sports: Volleyball**
Volleyball World Wide - History, FAQs, rules, organizational contacts, and links for amateur, professional, collegiate, and Olympic variations of the sport. ...
dmoz.org/Sports/Volleyball/

82. **East End Volleyball**
Hampton Bays beach volleyball organization. Site includes tournament information, standings, general...
www.eevb.net/

83. **NJVB: New Jersey Area Volleyball**
Holmdel Volleyball League! ... The Matawan-Aberdeen Recreation Volleyball League —
www.njvb.com/

84. **Volleyball Equipment Guide: Low Prices, Great Brands, Secure**
Lowest Price Guarantee on a complete selection of Volleyball Machines at Volleyball Equipment Guide.
www.volleyball-machine-guide.com/

85. **Columbia Doubles Volleyball**
COLUMBIA DOUBLES VOLLEYBALL hosts the largest outdoor Doubles Volleyball tournament series in the world. CDVA operates in central ...
www.charm.net/~jedi/

86. **Vancouver Volleyball**
The source of volleyball information for recreational players in Vancouver, BC. Drop in, leagues, tournaments, and more. This page ...
www.vancouvervolleyball.com/

87. **411 Volleyball—Volleyball Southern California Style**
News, scholarship information, links and general training tips; focuses on high school volleyball.
home.earthlink.net/~tfakehany/

88. **Slime Volleyball!**
diddly.com/slime/

89. **NLHI Volleyball**
World_>_Norsk_>_Sport_>_Volleyball_>_Klubber
nlhstud.nlh.no/~nlhi/volley/

90. **Lugi Volleyboll**
World_>_Svenska_>_Sport_>_Volleyboll
www.lugi.se/volleyboll/

91. **Gator Volleyball @ Gatorzone.com**
The University of Florida volleyball team (36-2) fell to Southern California in the national title match
www.gatorzone.com/volleyball/

92. **Vas_s Volleyball Page**

Vas's Volleyball Page. I've been playing volleyball for about ... Likely Injuries To High School Volleyball Players. Common Volleyball Injuries. ...

www.gigaflop.demon.co.uk/volley/

93. **Volleyball Berlin]**

VOLLEYBALL BERLIN:Informationen rund um den Volleyball Sport in Berlin - Indoorvolleyball,Beachvolleyball (Boerse, Volleyball, Berlin, Finanzen, Sport, Magazin ...

www.volleyball-berlin.de/

94. **Vball**

The USA men's national volleyball team began the 2003 season with a 3-2 loss to Korea at Butler-Hancock Hall on the University of ...

www.vball.com/

95. **OSI Volleyball**

World_>_Norsk_>_Sport_>_Volleyball_>_Klubber

www.osi.uio.no/volleyball/

96. **Jersey Shore Volleyball Association - JSVBA**

Jersey Shore Volleyball Association 2003 Miller Lite/JSVBA Pro Beach Volleyball and Amateur VB Tour Entire Contents Copyright © 1996-2003 Jersey Shore ...

members.aol.com/jsvba/

97. **Manitoba Volleyball Association**

The Manitoba Volleyball Association provides quality services and programs to all individuals and groups that will assist in the promotion, development, and ...

www.mts.net/~mbvolley/

98. **Starlings Volleyball**

Home Page to Starlings Volleyball Clubs, USA. ... The intent was to broaden the opportunities for girls to participate in the benefits of Club Volleyball. ...

www.starlings.org/

99. **Velkommen til BSI VOLLEYBALL**

World_>_Norsk_>_Sport_>_Volleyball_>_Klubber

www.bsi.no/volleyball/

100. **Mid-Atlantic Volleyball**
Mid-Atlantic Volleyball (MAV) serves volleyball players and enthusiasts with volleyball clinics, leagues, schedules, tournaments and equipment sources in the ...
www.mavolleyball.org/

101. **Hope Volleyball Tournament**
Annual tournament which raises money for local charities. Features event details, entertainment lineup,...
www.hopehelps.com/

102. **Georgia Volleyball - Main Page**
Georgia Volleyball. Sponsored by the Georgia Volleyball Coaches Association. Dedicated to high school girl's volleyball, this site provides coach contacts and links to teams for...
www.georgiavolleyball.com/

103. **Yahoo! Directory Volleyball**
Rules of Volleyball - contains basic rules for playing the game. ... Volleyball Gear for Sale on eBay Great deals and amazing selection on volleyball gear. ...
dir.yahoo.com/Recreation/Sports/Volleyball/

104. **Volleyball Nova Scotia - English**
Volleyball Nova Scotia —. About us. News. Membership Information. ... Book a Volleyball On Wheels Clinic for your team. VNS introduces Mini Volleyball in Nova Scotia. ...
www.volleyballnovascotia.ca/

105. **Official Beach Volleyball Victoria Web Site**
All the info on Beach Volleyball in Victoria, Australia.... news, results, rankings, calendars, interviews and pictures. ...
www.bvv.asn.au/

106. **Pennsylvania Volleyball Coaches Association**
Pennsylvania Volleyball Coaches Association web site includes volleyball discussion, helpfull volleyball links, statistics, forums and high school volleyball ...
www.pavbca.com/

107. **Midwest Professional Volleyball Association**
WELCOME TO THE MPVA Midwest Professional Volleyball Association Pro Beach Tour! Check out the best beach volleyball players in the Midwest! ...
www.mpva.com/

108. **Westside Volleyball Home Page**
Westside Volleyball, Please Download Adobe Acrobat Reader. Tournament and league schedule and rules for this organization offering adult team play in the Los...
www.westsidevolleyball.com/

109. **Volleyball Plays, Volleyball Drills and Coaching Software**
Online volleyball plays and volleyball drills, in an easy to use plays and drill database. With coaching playbook software to make ...
www.jes-soft.com/volleyball/

110. **AuburnTigers.com - The Official Website of Auburn Tiger Athletics**
Auburn Volleyball Hands Out Awards at Postseason Banquet.
www.auburntigers.com/volleyball/ - 51k - **Cached - Similar pages**

111. **Volleyball Tours**
Goodwill Ambassadors - International Volleyball Tour's for Junior and Senior age players and teams. ... That's what the Goodwill Volleyball Tours is all about. ...
volleyballtours.com/

112. **Volleyball Victoria Home**
www.volleyballvictoria.com.au/

113. **Colorado Volleyball Home**
Official web site for outdoor volleyball events in the Mile High state. Here you will find comprehensive information ...
www.coloradovolleyball.com/

114. **Österreichischer Volleyballverband**
World_>_Deutsch_>_..._>_Volleyball_>_Verbände_>_Österreich
www.volleynet.at/

115. **Stjepanidze_'s Volleyball Hall of Fame**
Women's Volleyball during the 80s & 90s, ... However, most of what is available on-line is only about volleyball since the advent of the internet. ...
volleyperu.webstrikesolutions.com/home.stm

116. **California Beach Volleyball Association - CBVA**
CBVA is a nonprofit California Corporation which promotes fast-growing sport of outdoor beach volleyball at the grassroots level.
www.cbva.com/

117. **Southern California Volleyball Association**
... The Southern California Volleyball Association (SCVA) is a non-profit organization affiliated with USA Volleyball- the national governing body for amateur ...
www.scvavolleyball.org/

118. **NVV-Online**
World_>_Deutsch_>_..._>_Volleyball_>_Verbände_>_Deutschland
www.nvv-online.de/

57
World Cup

1. **1800-Worldcup.com — World Cup Football Coverage**
   1800-Worldcup.com provides World Cup Finals reports from Uruguay 1930 through to Germany 2006 and the applicants for 2010. ...
   1800-worldcup.com/
2. **Worldcup Soccer**
   Contains statistical data of all games played from 1930 to the present.
   www.worldcup-soccer.info/
3. **World cup 2002, The Digital Collection**
   Digital collection of online World Cup coverage, searchable by title, match and language. Includes screen shots from online media sites from all ...
   www.interactivepublishing.net/worldcup/
4. **KOWOC-[Korea Organizing Committee for the 2002 FIFA WorldCup Korea ...**
   Official site. Includes match schedule, ticket and accommodations information, current news, volunteer...
   www.2002worldcupkorea.org/
5. **World Cup History. Every Tournament.Detailed player profiles.Match ...**
   Information available on every tournament. Includes detailed player profiles with birth place and...
   worldcup-history.com/
6. **PWA Windsurf and PKRA Kiteboard Worldcup 2003**
   PWA Windsurf and PKRA Kiteboard Worldcup 2003 http://fuerteventura-worldcup.org/.
   www.fuerteventura-worldcup.org/

7. **IOL: SPORT**
   Resource for Irish fans and those interested in the Irish view of the World Cup.
   www.worldcup.ie/

8. **2002 Fifa World Cup, Japan, Korea.**
   Information including results, teams, history, news, interviews, competitions and squads.
   www.worldcup-2002.co.uk/

9. **WorldCup_s world**
   The summary for this Japanese page contains characters that cannot be correctly displayed in this language/character set.
   members.jcom.home.ne.jp/wcup/

10. **2002 FIFA???(TM) in INCHEON**
    The summary for this Korean page contains characters that cannot be correctly displayed in this language/character set.
    worldcup.inpia.net/

11. **worldcup.seoul.go.kr**
    worldcup.metro.seoul.kr/

12. **Fifa-worldcup**
    ffa-worldcup.cc: Fifa-worldcup bestellen Fifa-worldcup von AZ Infos, News, Produkte:
    www.fifa-worldcup.cc/

13. **2002 worldcup**
    The summary for this Korean page contains characters that cannot be correctly displayed in this language/character set.
    www.worldcup.daegu.kr/

14. **Alpine skiing world cup news, database, results and standings**
    www.irisco.net/ski/Worldcup.htm

15. **ESPNsoccernet.com World Cup 2002: Home**
    ESPNsoccernet.com brings you the best football coverage from the 2002 FIFA World Cup.
    worldcup.espnsoccernet.com/

16. **ESPNsoccernet.com World Cup 2002: Home**
    Heroes' welcome for Brazil. A m5ilitary escort over Brasillia for the victorious national team (Reuters). Escorted by four air force
    worldcup.espnsoccernet.com/index?lang=en

17. **World Cup Shootout - Miniclip.com**
Miniclip.com - free online games, multiplayer games and online tournaments.
www.miniclip.com/football.htm

18. **2002**
The summary for this Chinese (Simplified) page contains characters that cannot be correctly displayed in this language/character set.
cn.worldcup.yahoo.com/

19. **Worldcup 2003**
The summary for this Japanese page contains characters that cannot be correctly displayed in this language/character set.
www.xleague.com/w_cup/

20. **Worldcup 2003**
German Football Partners Rechteverwertungssgesellschaft: Partner des AFVD und der GFL.
www.worldcup2003.info/

21. **The ISST speedskydiving worldcups**
"rage against the machine". Home. Worldcups. WC 2003. WC 2002. WC 2001. WC 2000. The fastest non motorized sport on earth The ISST speedskydiving world cup. ...
www.speedskydiving.net/worldcups/index.php

22. **IOL: SPORT**
Beckham: Butt exit is a mistake David Beckham believes Manchester United manager Alex Ferguson would be making a mistake by letting Nicky Butt leave Old ...
www.worldcup.ie/index.asp

23. **Avaya FIFA Partnership**
Home. You are Here: Home > Corporate Information > Avaya FIFA Partnership. Avaya FIFA Partnership, ...
worldcup.avaya.com/

24. **Mainichi INTERACTIVE**
The summary for this Japanese page contains characters that cannot be correctly displayed in this language/character set.
www.mainichi.co.jp/entertainments/ sports/worldcup/worldcup/

25. **Thomas Pilot Pages**
Worldcup. ... Worldcup is a tool to keep up-to-date with the results and tables of the upcoming FIFA World Cup 2002 in Korea and Japan. ...
www.pundt.de/pilot/worldcup/

26. **Zurimetzgete**
World_>_Deutsch_>_Sport_>_Radsport_>_Rennrad_>_Rennen
www.worldcup-zuerich.ch/

27. **Goedemorgen welkom bij de KNSB**
The official KNSB Live internet website, November 20th and 21st.
www.knsb.nl/wc99/

28. **english 2002 worldcup Incheon**
worldcup.inpia.net/english/

29. **World Cup History. Every Tournament.Detailed player profiles.Match ...**
www.worldcup-history.com/index.php?siden=yearstat

30. **Worldcup.nl, Alle Sportfun op 1 locatie!**
www.worldcup.nl/?user=006

31. **World cup, mundial, coppa del mondo, francia 98, FIFA**
... [Realvideo] [Notizie] [Canali Tv] [Euromoneta] [Worldcup] [Newsgroup] [Ricerca] [Import-Export] [Servizi] [Rubriche] [Arte&Cultura] [Tg Commerciale].
www.agus.it/worldcup/

32. **Kvitfjell 2004**
The races will take place on the Olympic Downhill and Super-G courses on Saturday the 6th and Sunday the 7th of March 2004. read more. ...
worldcup.kvitfjell.no/

33. **MWEB e-Card**
The summary for this Thai page contains characters that cannot be correctly displayed in this language/character set.
ecards.mweb.co.th/worldcup/

34. **Worldcup.nl, Alle Sportfun op 1 locatie!**
www.worldcup.nl/?user=417&pi=humor

35. The summary for this Bulgarian page contains characters that cannot be correctly displayed in this language/character set.
worldcup.dir.bg/

36. **HotlineSoccer.com World Cup**
The summary for this Thai page contains characters that cannot be correctly displayed in this language/character set.
www.hotlinesoccer.com/worldcup/

37. **2003 FIVB World Cup Volleyball For Men And Women Official Website**
The 2003 World Cups represent the most important international competition for men and women in the pre-Olympic year. The world? ...
www.worldcup2003.jp/en/about.html

38. **Bet on Sports Online : The place to bet on Sports**
sports bet online with bet on sports online NBA basketball and NHL hockey preseason betting, bet on superbowl and hockey. Bet on ...
www.soccer-bettingodds.com/

39. **WorldCup 2002**
premiersoccer.com/store/worldcup.html

40. **World Soccer**
www.countrylife.co.uk/worldsoccer/worldcuppage.html

41. **TIME 2002 FIFA World Cup**
www.time.com/time/worldcup2002/

42. **NIKKEI NET SOCCER@Express**
The summary for this Japanese page contains characters that cannot be correctly displayed in this language/character set.
sports.nikkei.co.jp/soccer/wc2002/

43. **WorldCup 2002 T-Shirts**
Please call for team or custom orders ... (818)957-2645 ... we also specialize in authentic name and numbering. WorldCup 2002 T-Shirts. ContactEmail. ...
premiersoccer.com/store/worldcup2.html

44. **WC Berlin 2004**
The ARENA Worldcup Berlin 2004 website. Welcome to the Arena worldcup 2004 in Berlin. Please follow this shortcut to the competition sites. ...
www.arena-worldcup.de/

45. **Cricket Worldcup 2003 Portal**
Australia Wins the Cricket World Cup 2003. Australia won a record third World Cup with an overwhelming display against India in front ...
cricket.indiangroups.com/

58
Wrestling

1. **WWE.com**
   Official site with wrestler information, corporate details, news, merchandise, and a directory of...
   www.wwe.com/
2. **USA Wrestling - The National Governing Body for Olympic Wrestling**
   Youth News. USA Wrestling News. Newsstand. Women's News. Title IX News. ...
   www.usawrestling.org/
3. **WRESTLING USA Magazine, High School Wrestling, College Wrestling ...**
   www.wrestlingusa.com/
4. **Intermat : Amateur Wrestling News, Wrestling Results and Wrestling ...**
   Complete line of wrestling products and gear and national amatuer wrestling news, rankings, and articles.
   www.intermatwrestle.com/
5. **ProWrestling.com - #1 Wrestling Website in the World!**
   The largest, oldest, most updated, most trusted, wrestling news and rumors website on the planet!
   www.prowrestling.com/
6. **wrestling observer - the newsletter by dave meltzer**
   WWE, WCW, ECW, and International wrestling news from Dave Meltzer, Bryan Alvarez, and Alex Marvez.
   www.liveaudiowrestling.com/wo/

7. **1Wrestling.com - Pro Wrestling's Daily News Source**
Pro Wrestling's Daily News Source.
www.1wrestling.com/

8. **TheWrestlingMall.com**
One stop for everything in wrestling. Amateur. and Speakers. Want more Wrestling? ...
www.thewrestlingmall.com/

9. **Amateur Wrestling News**
NCAA Division III Preview NAIA Preview NJCAA Preview High School Insider Dual Meet Schedules Awn Interview with Steve Powell USA Wrestling Wrap Tournaments Mat ...
amateurwrestlingnews.com/

10. **Pro Wrestling Torch - News Leader Since 1987**
Wrestling's online journal of news and opinion.
www.pwtorch.com/

11. **SLAM! Sports - Wrestling**
SLAM! Wrestling 2003 Poll. The good, the bad and the ugly. ... The Year End poll is about you. It is your turn to pass judgment on all things wrestling in 2003. ...
www.canoe.ca/SlamWrestling/home.html

12. **Wrestling Canada Lutte**
The Canadian Amateur Wrestling Association (Wrestling Canada Lutte) is the national sport governing body for Olympic style wrestling in Canada. ...
www.wrestling.ca/

13. **fila-wrestling.org**
The international wrestling governing body.
www.fila-wrestling.org/

14. **Wrestling shoes - wrestling gear and equipment - Dan Gable**
DanGable.com is the source for wrestling information, wrestling shoes, and wrestling gear online. Along with the finest in wrestling
www.dangable.com/

15. **Wrestling-Online.com**
MEGASTORE TOP SALES. WRESTLING-ONLINE NEWSLETTER. Subscribe to the largest and longest running wrestling newsletter on the Internet today! ...
www.wrestling-online.com/

16. **WrestlingReport.com The Heart of Amateur Wrestling**
General Wrestling Links. Gimps Software. Wrestling Champions. Wrestling Camps. ...
www.wrestlingreport.com/
17. **Professional Wrestling news, rumors and information. ...**
The top site for pro wrestling! Read articles from the top wrestling sites on the Internet containing the latest news from the WWE ...
www.wrestlinginc.com/
18. **Professional Wrestling Online Museum**
Read the stories behind the stars of yesterday and today. Hear the sounds of live wrestling action....
www.wrestlingmuseum.com/
19. **National Wrestling Hall of Fame**
The Wrestlers, National Wrestling Hall of Fame and Museum, Search Options
www.wrestlinghalloffame.org/
20. **Pro Wrestling Daily - Your Total Source For Wrestling ...**
News, editorials, images and interviews.
www.prowrestlingdaily.com/
21. **California USA Wrestling: News, tournaments, wrestling links, and ...**
California USA Wrestling, the official state governing body for amateur wrestling. News, tournaments, wrestling links, and more! California USA Wrestling. ...
www.ca-usaw.org/
22. **WrestlingOne - The World's #1 Wrestling Supplier**
Wrestling equipment, books, and shoes
www.wrestlingone.com/
23. **411wrestling.com**
www.411wrestling.com/
24. **PA Wrestling What's New**
Pennsylvania Wrestling has moved to http://pasportsbeat.com. BRUTE.
www.pawrsl.com/pa/
25. **Fila Wrestling : site de la Fédération Internationnal de Lutte**
This Site Tracked by WebTrendsLive. ...

www.fila-wrestling.com/

26. **Live Audio Wrestling**
    Weekly online wrestling radio show
    www.liveaudiowrestling.com/
27. **4w-wrestling.com: Pro Wrestling News & Rumors**
    Pro wrestling news, discussion forum, editorials, images, backstage photos and almanac
    www.4w-wrestling.com/
28. **NCWA**
    Dedicated to Expanding Athletic Opportunity to Tomorrow's Leaders. The NCWA works to provide a spawning ground for new wrestling teams at the college level. ...
    www.ncwa.net/
29. **The Web_s Best of Amateur Wrestling by Tom Fortunato, Rochester ...**
    The Web's Best of Amateur Wrestling. by Tom Fortunato. ... Thanks amateur wrestling fans! Search this site powered by FreeFind. Send an Internet greeting card! ...
    www.geocities.com/colosseum/sideline/9563/
30. **Impact Wrestling.com :: WWE Wrestling News, Video Games**
    WWE wrestling news and rumors, features wrestling alert newsletter, wallpapers, fan forum, video game news, reviews, hints, cheats and original columns. ...
    www.impactwrestlingonline.com/
31. **Pro Wrestling History**
    Includes supercards and tournaments, a video guide, and historical match results for a wide array...
    www.prowrestlinghistory.com/
32. **Wrestling-Edge.com - Wrestling News, Rumors, Info, Women & More**
    News and interviews, photos, merchandise, and interactive features.
    www.wrestling-edge.com/
33. **Total-Wrestling - All Your Pro-Wrestling Needs!**
    Contains original articles and interviews, news, PPV results, forum, contests and other interactive...
    www.total-wrestling.co.uk/

34. **Wrestling**
    Steel Domain Wrestling No more WWE for me, thanks, I'm driving...
    slashwrestling.com/
35. **Herald.com - Your Miami Everything Guide**
    ADVERTISEMENT. MORE WRESTLING NEWS, ...
    www.miami.com/mld/miamiherald/sports/wrestling/
36. **International Wrestling Institute and Museum**
    The mission of the International Wrestling Institute and Museum is to preserve, maintain and promote the long and illustrious heritage of mankind's oldest ...
    www.wrestlingmuseum.org/
37. **Innovators of Wrestling - Your Ultimate Source For Pro Wrestling ...**
    Wrestling news, rumors, and results.
    www.iowrestling.com/
38. **GLORY Wrestling: The Hardest Working Women In Wrestling**
    Includes appearances, news, profiles, and results about a variety of wrestlers and valets.
    www.glorywrestling.com/
39. **All Pro Wrestling**
    APW - Hayward, California - Official site includes events news, photos, profiles, and television schedule.
    www.allprowrestling.com/
40. **Joey_s Wrestling Room**
    Over 600 female wrestling news articles, lots of female wrestling links. History of women's wrestling.
    www.wrestlegirl.com/
41. **SLAM! Sports - Wrestling**
    Canadian site that contains many articles from Canadian newspapers, original columns, and guest articles....
    www.canoe.ca/SlamWrestling/
42. **Wrestling Tournament**
    Nation wide wrestling tournament information.
    www.wrestlingtournaments.com/

43. **Welcome to || Christian Wrestling Federation || ChristianWrestling ...**

- Exciting Church and area wide wrestling events - Cross ... Visitors since April 8, CWF - Rockwall, Texas - Official site includes events, media, profiles, and school.
www.christianwrestling.com/

44. **Amateur Wrestling**

Amateur Wrestling. (Please be patient as the links are updated and current information is added to this old website . . . ... Youth/Age Groups Wrestling. ...
w3.trib.com/~dont/wrestling.html

45. **ACCURATE Wrestling News, No Pop Ads, Theme Music Radio**

Accurate wrestling news, #1 Online Theme Music Radio Station, and lots of Divas! ... If you want to listen to Wrestling Themes right now, Click the "Equalizer". ...
www.wrestling-news.com/

46. **CZWWrestling.com: ULTRAVIOLENT ENTERTAINMENT**

The Internet source for the MOST ULTRAVIOLENT Wrestling pomotion on the planet, Combat Zone Wrestling. Get Ultraviolent and Join the Ultraviolent Revolution!!! ...
www.czwwrestling.com/

47. **OVWrestling.com! Tomorrow_s Superstars Today!**

Ohio Valley Wrestling, a premiere development and training facility for the World Wrestling Federation! This is where ...
www.ovwrestling.com/

48. **TWNP-Wrestling News and Information**

Get wrestling news & rumors, wrestling game hints & cheats, wrestling game reviews; join forums, or obtain specific information about WWE, NWA-TNA and other ...
www.twnpnews.com/

49. **The Official Website of Pennsylvania Junior Wrestling**

Results and news for Pennsylvania wrestlers. Includes a large number of youth wrestling links.
www.pajw.org/

50. **www.wrestling-games.de**

World_>_Deutsch_>_Spiele_>_Computerspiele_>_Newsseiten
www.wrestling-games.de/

51. **Wisconsin Amateur Wrestling Website**
Wisconsin's Premiere Amateur Wrestling Website.
www.wiwrestling.com/

52. **Default HawkeyeSports.com - University of Iowa Official Athletic**
owa Hawkeye Athletics Iowa Hawkeye Athletics Iowa Hawkeye Athletics. ...
www.hawkeyesports.com/news/2002/075.htm

53. **Kansas Wrestling**
Kansas Wrestling. Kids. ... Links. Rules. Wrestling Talk. Search. Folkstyle Nationals. ...
www.usawks.com/

54. **Backyard Wrestling: Don't Try This At Home**
www.bywgame.com/

55. **National Wrestling Coaches Association - Amateur Wrestling**
National Wrestling Coaches Association. Serving, protecting and promoting amateur wrestling since 1928.
www.nwcaonline.com/

56. **Minnesota USA Wrestling**
MNUSA Wrestling Tournament History. ... mnusaw@citilink.com. MN/USA Wrestling is dedicated to Freestyle, Greco-Roman and Folkstyle Wrestling at all levels. ...
www.mnusawrestling.org/

57. **WP 2003**
Enter Wrestling Planet Main Page! AddFreeStats.com Free Web Stats in real-time !
www.wrestlingplanet.com/

58. **The Professional Wrestling Online Museum - The Professional**
www.wrestlingmuseum.com/homeie.html

59. **Wrestling at allsports . com - A complete source for wrestling**
Wrestling at allsports.com provides wrestling news headline reports, message boards, links, and more. ... What does that angle have to do with wrestling anyway? ...
www.allsports.com/prowrestling/

60. **Wrestle World - Your Online Portal to the Professional Wrestling ...**
Searchable directory of professional wrestling related websites.
www.pro-wrestling.com/

59
Yatching

1. **PUPA Yachting - charter company in Bodrum, Marmaris and Göcek ...**
   Bareboat sailing yachts and crewed power or sailing yachts out of Bodrum.
   www.pupa.com.tr/
2. **rediff.com : The Yatching home page**
   rediff.com rediff.com, Sports, HOME | OLYMPICS | YATCHING. ... weightlifting. wrestling. yatching. Yatching. The Dummies' Guide to Yatching Sydney rivals Spanish Armada. ...
   www.rediff.com/sports/yatch.htm
3. **Lets Go Travel Agency**
   Blue Voyage. GO WITH THE RHYTHM OF THE LIGHTS AND WATER. It is no longer just a far off dream to sail on the blue waters of the Mediterranean ...
   www.letsgo-turkey.com/yatching.html
4. **Sailing and Yachting Cruises in Turkey - by PEDINI**
   SAILING IN TURKEY. Turkey is surrounded by four seas; Mediterranean, Aegean, Marmara and Black sea with the total coast line of more than 8,000 km. ...
   www.pedini-tr.com/y/ymain.htm
5. **Andinia.com - yatching**
   Yatching and related topics - specialty search engine for outdoor sports enthusiasts. Ourdoor Gear 468x60. Yatching: Tips ...
   www.andinia.com/nautic_yatchingen.shtml

6. **The Wexford Harbour- Hilton Head Island, South Carolina.**
The Wexford Plantation Hilton Head Island, South Carolina The Wexford Harbour Winding through the center of Wexford is a lock-controlled ...
www.irhhi.com/wexford/yatching.cfm

7. **SWECO**
SWECO FFNS in competition for Olympic Games yatching marina in ...
www.sweco.se/templates/NewsPage____10910.asp

8. **TURKEYGUIDE~YATCHINGINTURKEY**
YATCHING IN TURKEY. The Mediterranean, Aegean, and the Black Seas, as well as the Sea of Marmara, surround Turkey to the north, west and south. ...
www.turkeyguide.com/tourism/yatching.htm

9. **Mexico - Yatching clubs**
The World website Mexico – Yatching clubs. Clubes de Yates. ... Acapulco Yatching Club Club de Yates Acapulco. ...
flagspot.net/flags/mx@yc.html

10. **Voile Abordable / Affordable Yatching**
Rend la voile accessible ! Makes sailing accessible! ...
www.voile.org/

11. **YATCHING CASINO**
www.casinos-jackpots.net/jeux-de-casino/ yatching-casino.htm

12. **regata velica**
World > Italiano > Sport > Acquatici > Vela > Eventi
www.tradecenter.sm/ycsm/

13. **Journaux.fr]**
www.journaux.fr/revue.asp?revue=M4925H

14. **Andinia.com - yatching]**
www.andinia.com/nautic_yatchingsp.shtml

15. **Armada Nacional de Colombia - Yatching**
www.armada.mil.co/index.php?idcategoria=1341

16. **shopborneo.com : Recreation : Yatching**
The Borneo Yatching Challenge could help promote Miri as a ...
www.shopborneo.com/schlcen/pgsen/Recreation/Yatching/

17. **Mexico - Yatching clubs: Zihuatanejo Yatch Club**
This page is part of © FOTW Flags Of The World website Mexico – Yatching clubs: Zihuatanejo Yatch Club. Club de Yates Zihuatanejo.
flagspot.net/flags/mx@zyc.html

18. **Yatching**
Yatching. Sailing Etaps. A Sailing Paradise. The Mediterranean, Aegean, and the Black Seas, as well as the Sea of Marmara ...
www.mfa.gov.tr/grupc/ca/caa/uu/e1012.htm

19. **Mexico - Yatching clubs**
This page is also a part of © FOTW Flags Of The World website Mexico - Yatching clubs. Clubes de Yates. ... Acapulco Yatching Club Club de Yates Acapulco. ...
fotw.unislabs.com/flags/mx@yc.html

20. **Sailing, Adventure Sailing, Surfing in India, Sailing Trip, Surfing**
Offering Sailing, Yatching and Surfing in India, sailing, adventure sailing, surfing in india, sailing trip, surfing vacation in india, boat sailing, yatching in ...
www.indianadventureportal.com/water-sports-india/ boat-sailing-surfing-yatching.html

21. **Yatching**
Yatching.
acrylic.monsite.wanadoo.fr/page1.html

22. **SPORTS: YATCHING NEWS @ NewsZoom**
Business General Science Sports. Home » News Directory » Sports » Sports: Yatching News. Weather Info. United States Canada Europe ...
www.newszoom.com/cat/sub/Sports/
Sports:%20yatching%20news/

23. **Yatching, Sailing & Blue Voyage in Turkey**
"The great mountains and forests trembled Under the feet of the immortal Poseidon. He took three steps, reached Aigia on the fourth. ...
www.melitour.com/yatching.htm

24. **Yatching Casino**
www.annuaire-casinos.com/yatching_casino.htm

25. **blouson microfibre yatching**
Blouson microfibre yatching.
www.cadeaux-hommes.com/catalogue/ blouson-microfibre yatching.htm

26. **Sand-Yatching on St Malo Beach in Brittany**
Previous Photo < Photo Index > Next Photo, Put this Listing in My TravelGuide! Sand-Yatching on St Malo Beach in Brittany Photo from F. de la Mure - MAE. ...
www.brittany.worldweb.com/PhotoGallery/ RecreationalActivities/10-4892.html

27. **Jeff's Site: Archives > Sport > Sailing and Yatching**
Sport > Sailing and Yatching. Cartoons about Sailing and Yachting.
www.geoffhook.com/archive/sport/sailing/

28. **Aries Yachting**
World_>_Italiano_>_..._>_Sport_>_Nautica_>_Charter
www.ariesyachting.it/

29. **Mexico - Yatching clubs # fahnenversand.de - Fahnen Flaggen Fahne ...**
The World website Mexico - Yatching clubs. Clubes de Yates. ... Acapulco Yatching Club Club de Yates Acapulco. [Club de Yates Acapulco ...
www.fahnenversand.de/fotw/flags/mx@yc.html

30. **cowes yatching**
www.iwight.com/council/committees/ Mod-Executive/31-5-01 paper-b.htm

31. **TURKEYGUIDE~YATCHING IN TURKEY**
MARINAS IN TURKEY. Yachting remains a popular activity for residents as well as visitors to Turkey. Over the past 40 years the industry ...
www.turkeyguide.com/tourism/marinas.htm

32. **La Voile Royal Yatching Association Sports Navigation**
La Voile Royal Yatching Association Sports Navigation à voile.
www.france-livreclub.com/ Royal-Yatching-Associatio-La-Voile 2907601628.html

33. **Yatching**

Kalamis Marina Ayvalik Marina Cesme Marina Finike Marina Antalya Marina. Yatching in Turkey. Marinas. Yachting remains a popular activity ...

www.kusadasi.com/yatching2.html

34. **Yatching**

Yatching in Turkey. Welcome To a Sailing Paradise. The Mediterranean, Aegean, and the Black Sea, as well as the Sea of Marmara, sorround ...

www.kusadasi.com/yatching3.html

35. **blowkart**

BloKart - Land Yachting. After discovering the BloKart - the only land yacht steered by hand and folds down into a suitcase - we ...

www.player.pt/player/Pages%20from%20homepage/New%20Projects/blowkart.html

36. **LOTTI YACHTING - Broker and Charter**

if you're looking for the ideal boat. Broker and Charter. Lotti Yachting is the group company specialised in yacht brokerage and charter services. ...

www.portolotti.it/home/eng/l_y_broker_charter.html

37. **Danforth Yatching routes**

The following sailing packages are a guideline, and can be tailored to suit your individual preferences. All packages are flexible ...

www.wildweb.co.za/malawi_destinations/a

nforth%20yachting%20routes.htm

60
Yoga

1. **Yoga Site — yoga mats, yoga clothes, yoga videos, yoga teachers**
Online yoga resource center featuring a free teacher directory, posture info, Yoga Therapy Report, style guide, Q&A, retreats, links and the Shop@ Yoga Site ...
www.yogasite.com/
2. **Yoga Journal Magazine: The Voice of Yoga Online. The trusted**
Introducing Yoga Journal's Yoga Step-by-Step TM The Total Guide to Beginning Your Home Practice, Develop and grow your home yoga ...
www.yogajournal.com/
3. **Yoga Directory: listings and links of yoga resources**
The Yoga Directory contains a list of yoga teachers, yoga centers, organizations, books, music, yoga therapists, health products, yoga retreats, vacations ...
www.yogadirectory.com/
4. **Yoga Yoga Books Yoga Videos Yoga Mats Yoga Clothing**
For all your yoga videos, books, clothing and mats, as well as pilates equipment, Yoga.com is the best source on the web for fitness and wellness products. ...
www.yoga.com/
5. **Sivananda Yoga - Om Page**
Introduction to the Official Web site of the Internationa Sivananda Yoga Vedanta Centers. Lots of information on Jnana Yoga, Bhakti
www.sivananda.org/
6. **YREC - Yoga Research and Education Center - Homepage**
Yoga Research and Education Center (YREC) informs about Yoga — its practice, history and philosophy. ... About Yoga Research and Education Center (YREC). ...
www.yrec.org/

7. **Yoga Anand Ashram**

   A free resource for Yoga information including the philosophy of Yoga, practice and benefits of Yoga postures, meditation, and much more. ...

   www.santosha.com/

8. **Largest Yoga Directory to find a Yoga Class :: Yoga Studios ...**

   Largest yoga directory on the INTERNET with yoga listings for Yoga Classes, Yoga Retreats, Yoga Conferences; Yoga Teacher's training, Yoga workshops,Kirtans ...

   www.yogafinder.com/

9. **YogaClass.com - the YogaChannel**

   Site uses RealAudio to offer yoga teaching experience. Information and walk-throughs for pranayam,...

   yogaclass.com/

10. **Sahaja Yoga Meditation and Self Realization**

    Sahaja Yoga is a unique method of meditation introduced in 1970 by Shri Mataji Nirmala Devi by which Self Realization (Kundalini awakening) is achieved ...

    www.sahajayoga.org/

11. **Yoga retreats, holistic health, mind/body workshops at Kripalu**

    Kripalu is the largest center for yoga and holistic health in the US, serving people of all backgrounds for more than 20 years. ... Yoga and a Whole Lot More... ...

    www.kripalu.org/

12. **Bikram's Yoga College of India**

    A unique yoga series designed by Bikram and proven for over 30 years to do more for your health, body, and general well-being than you ever imagined possible.. Worldwide school locations, books and tapes, teacher training and information on Bikram Choudhury...

    www.bikramyoga.com/

13. **Yoga Basics: online guide to the practice of yoga, pranayama, ...**

    ward winning yoga resource center featuring a yoga teacher directory, yoga pastures, yoga therapy, meditation techniques, discount yoga store offering yoga ...

    www.yogabasics.com/

14. **Desktop Yoga - prevention and healing of RSI and Carpal tunnel**
Animation of Ellen reaching up. Everyday Yoga: Use these exercises at your desk to help alleviate the strain of working at the computer. ...
www.mydailyyoga.com/

15. **The American Yoga Association**
Your Source for Excellence in Yoga Instruction. "Mystical Awareness is a ... Unseen Part of You". "Yoga Makes the Rough Road Smooth". Not-for-profit educational organization. Site includes information on the philosophy and techniques...
www.americanyogaassociation.org/

16. **Yoga Movement = an Index to Yoga Information and Resources**
An online magazine about the practice of yoga and meditation. ... Around Yoga Movement. Yoga Events: A calendar of major yoga events. An exploration of yoga and related subjects such as breathing and meditation.
www.yogamovement.com/

17. **yoga international magazine - honesdale, pennsylvania yoga teachers ...**
Authentic hatha yoga content, sacred link, himalayan institute, swami rama, meditation, and holistic health. asana, yoga community ...
www.yimag.org/

18. **Yoga Vidya - Infos and Kursangebote zu Yoga and Meditation**
World_>_Deutsch_>_..._>_Religion_und_Spiritualität_>_Yoga
www.yoga-vidya.de/

19. **Yoga Oline, online magazine about yoga and meditation**
Yoga Online, online Yoga and meditation magazine. Articles, links and practical advice about ashtanga, Iyengar and other styles. ... One line Yoga magazine. ...
indigo.ie/~cmouze/yoga_online/yoga_online.htm - 8 k

20. **Iyengar Yoga Resources**
Find Information on Iyengar Yoga. - Socialize with other yoga students and teachers in our discussion forum. - Read our articles on Iyengar yoga. This site provides information about Iyengar Yoga.
www.iyengar-yoga.com/

21. **Yoga Alliance Home Page**
International professional organization provides support services and yoga teacher certification....
www.yogaalliance.org/

22. **Yoga Ireland, information about yoga and meditation in Dublin and ...**
Irish Yoga site with list of yoga classes and teachers in Ireland, calendar of yoga seminars and holidays, information about teacher training courses. Providing information about yoga and meditation, particularly Iyengar and Ashtanga Vinyasa yoga.
indigo.ie/~cmouze/yoga.htm

23. **A World of Yoga**
Site by Ramakrishna Ananda (Graham Ledgerwood) provides overviews to many aspects of Yoga and its practice.
www.yogaworld.org/

24. **Ashtanga Yoga - Ashtanga.com**
Ashtanga Yoga is the system of Yoga taught by Sri K. Pattabhi Jois at the Ashtanga Yoga Research Institute in Mysore, India. ... Group Ashtanga Yoga Yahoo! Group. ...
www.ashtanga.com/

25. **Spirituality/Yoga/Hinduism Home page**
Lord Krishna instructing Bhagavad-Gita to Arjuna. Spirituality, Yoga, Hinduism Page. A humble offering at the lotus Feet of the Divine Mother. ... Yoga. Hinduism. ...
www.geocities.com/RodeoDrive/1415/

26. **Welcome to Siddha Yoga meditation - SYDA Foundation**
The Siddha Yoga path leads us to Self-realization - muktananda – bliss of liberation - the unceasing experience of unity with God. Official site of the SYDA foundation, the largest Siddha Yoga group, directed by Gurumayu Chidvilasanan...
www.siddhayoga.org/

27. **Yoga-Age.com - yoga forum/shop/directory/practice**
Good Day Welcome to the Yoga-Age, Resource of classic yoga texts, Directory of Yoga studios and Teachers, Asana Photos and more. ...
www.yoga-age.com/

28. **Power-Yoga.com**

    At power-yoga.com you can find information on The Hard & The Soft Astanga Yoga Institute and our programs (with locations in New York City and East Hampton). ...

    www.power-yoga.com/

29. **Yoga for the Special Child**

    Yoga for babies and children with special needs: Down syndrome, autism, attention deficit disorder, ADHD, cerebral palsy and learning disabilities.

    www.specialyoga.com/

30. **Anusara Yoga & John Friend: yoga positions that open the heart**

    Anusara Yoga, led by yoga teacher John Friend, offers yoga positions that flow from the heart. A system based on Hatha Yoga founded by John Friend. Information on the Yoga, its philosophy, teachers,...

    www.anusara.com/

31. **BKS Iyengar - Home**

    Official website of Yogacharya BKS Iyengar includes biography, overview of Iyengar yoga, articles,...

    www.bksiyengar.com/

32. **Yoga for HIV/AIDS**

    Yoga classes in many cities for people living with HIV/AIDS, list of recommended poses, articles on yoga for HIV/AIDS, and other information about yoga. ...

    www.yogagroup.org/

33. **BDY - Berufsverband der Yogalehrenden in Deutschland Yoga**

    www.yoga.de/

34. **The Diet & Fitness channel at iVillage has been updated!**

    Can't find what you're looking for? Don't worry, it's still here! We are making iVillage easier to navigate, and in the process some links have changed.

    www.ivillage.com/diet/articles/ 0,5050,34_257145,00.html

35. **Amazon.com: Books: Light on Yoga : The Bible of Modern Yoga...**

    Go beyond Yoga, Tai Chi and Qi...: A guide by Robert Wood, A Yoga and Qi Gong practitioner and more... ... Light on Yoga : The Bible of Modern Yoga... ...

    www.amazon.com/exec/obidos/tg/ detail/-/0805210318?v=glance

36. **KUNDALINI YOGA - Try our FREE On-Line Training for Beginners - You**

Our FREE on-line Kundalini Yoga course will help you realize your true potential! ... The world's most popular site for Kundalini Yoga
www.kundaliniyoga.org/

37. **Yoga & health .. naturally**

Learn all about yoga from a beginners perspective including meditation, yoga cleansing methods, pregnancy yoga, pranayama and discover exciting yoga supplies ...
www.healthandyoga.com/

38. **YogaClass.com - YogaCentral**

Asanas (yoga postures) are designed to provide your body with this necessary changing orientation to gravity. In order ...
yogaclass.com/central.html

39. **yoga postures**

The Yoga Site's Yoga Posture Page includes descritpions and simple drawings of the basic oga postures or asanas. ... Be kind to yourself when you practice yoga. ...
www.yogasite.com/postures.html

40. **Yoga, le magazine et la boutique du yoga**

World_>_Français_>_..._>_Religion_et_spiritualité_>_Hindouisme
www.yoga.fr/

41. **YogaKitty Home Page**

Yoga Videos for You & Your Cat. For the ... health. PURR-FECT YOGA Cat and Karl image AN INSTRUCTIONAL YOGA VIDEO SERIES FOR YOU... AND ...
www.yogakitty.com/

42. **Information Yoga New Zealand, Free Yoga Video**

Yoga Online, New Zealand Yoga, Yoga Facts, Stress Management,World Peace, Beginners Yoga, Advanced Yoga. ...
yoga.org.nz/

43. **Yoga at ABC-of-Yoga: Yoga Exercise, Breathing and Meditation**

Yoga at ABC-of-Yoga: Yoga Exercise, Breathing and Meditation. Our practice section has a diverse range of Yoga Pose, Exercise and Position. ...
www.abc-of-yoga.com/

44. **The British Wheel of Yoga (BWY) - The British Wheel of ...**
The British Wheel of Yoga. Registered Charity No. 264993 Patrons:Dr. Rosy Daniel BSc MBBCh, Satish Kumar. ... Latest BWY News. "Yoga Now" - The Video.
www.bwy.org.uk/

45. **Hare Krishna Home Page**
Bhaktivedanta Book Trust. Founder-Acarya His Divine Grace AC Bhaktivedanta Swami Prabhupada. ...
www.webcom.com/~ara/

46. **Look great - Feel great - Be great! Kundalini yoga is fast acting**
Discover the path to personal empowerment. Try our free online yoga sets. Buy Yoga Books, Yoga CDs, Yoga DVDs, Yoga Videos.
www.yogatech.com/

47. **Yoga Postures Step-By-Step - Featured Asanas**
Yoga Postures Step-by-Step is a complete interactive guide to the practice and benefits of Yoga postures featuring animations, photographs, illustrations ...
www.santosha.com/asanas/asana.html

48. **Yoga in Daily Life - Official international homepage**
A holistic system for body, mind, consciousness and soul, based on ancient teaching of yoga and adapted for today. System concerning body, mind, consciousness and soul founded by Paramhans Swami Maheshwarananda. Offers...
www.yoga-in-daily-life.org/

49. **YogaZone — Yoga and Pilates, Mats, Props, Videos, Clothing and ...**
Old Brookville - offers yoga classes and an extensive online store of yoga merchandise.
www.yogazone.com/

50. **Yoga Village UK - information about yoga in the uk**
Information about yoga teachers, events and products in the UK, including Yoga UK online magazine. ... . Information about yoga teachers, centers, events and resources in the UK.
www.yogauk.com/

51. **Byron Bay Yoga Retreat & Yoga Video - Yoga Retreats Yoga Holiday ...**
Describes Hatha Yoga getaways and retreats in New South Wales, Australia.
www.byronbayyoga.com/

52. **All-Embracing Yoga Directory: Your Guide to yoga centers, yoga ...**
All-Embracing Yoga Directory. Your Guide to yoga centers, yoga teachers, yoga studios, yoga ashrams, yoga associations, yoga traditions ...
www.self-realization.com/yoga_directory.htm
53. **Abhidhyan Yoga Institute - Authentic, no-nonsense spiritual ...**
Genuine tantra yoga meditation sorcery teachings from the Western perspective. Abhidhyan Yoga Institute, Inc. ... Our 10th Year on the Web! ...
www.abhidhyan.org/
54. **Yoga Home Page, yoga breathing, yoga postures, Pranayama ...**
yoga, breathing, yoga postures, yoga breathing, yoga home page. Yoga site provides complete information about yoga, yoga breathing ...
www.holistic-online.com/Yoga/hol_yoga_home.htm
55. **YOGADARSHANA**
Theory and practice of classic yoga: asanas, pranayama, meditation and Yogasutras of Patanjali.
usuarios.lycos.es/Offroy/
56. **Yoga**
What is Yoga. Yoga is the GNU replacement for Lotus Notes. ... and contribute your ideas and your time. Yoga Snapshot (Developers Only).
samba.anu.edu.au/gnuotes/
57. **YogaChicago**
Free bimonthly publication devoted to yoga activities and events around Chicago, Illinois, and elsewhere....
www.yogachicago.com/
58. **YOGA**
Yoga. Yoga defined. Yoga is from the Sanskrit word 'Yug' meaning union {with the Divine}. Different types of yoga. There are various types of yoga. ...
www.geocities.com/RodeoDrive/1415/indexc.html

59. **The Integral Yoga of Sri Aurobindo and the Mother**
The Integral Yoga of Sri Aurobindo and the Mother. "This net of sweetness woven of aureate fire." Savitri, p.372. Welcome What is The Integral Yoga? This site includes introductions to Integral Yoga and to the people and centers who aspire to its...
www.miraura.org/

60. **Eco Yoga Mats - Natural - PVC Free - Yoga Mats - shop online**
Yoga Mats: Eco Yoga Mat: shop online for environmentally friendly Yoga mats: The Yoga Directories. ...
www.yoga.co.uk/

61. **Burren Yoga and Meditation Retreat Centre, Co Galway, West of ...**
Beautiful comfortable retreat centre on the West coast of Ireland, offering holidays, evening classes and weekend workshops in hatha yoga (Astanga & Iyengar & ...
www.burrenyoga.com/

62. **Yoga, Online Yoga, Animated Hatha Yoga Postures, Stress and Yoga ...**
Free Online Yoga, Animated Yoga Postures, Stress Relief Exercise & Animated Breathing Techniques. Learn All Aspects Of Yoga Online With Our 75 Free Animations.
www.hathayogalesson.com/

63. **Scandinavian Yoga and Meditation School**
Scandinavian Yoga and Meditation School is the Independent School of yoga, tantra and meditation. ... Twice a year the acknowledge magazine bindu. ...
www.scand-yoga.org/

64. **Jivamukti Yoga Center**
JIVAMUKTI Yoga Center OM—ENTER When the mind and the heart are stretched together in expanding self awareness, I assure you, there is instantaneous self ...
www.jivamuktiyoga.com/

65. **Ashtanga Yoga Research Institute**
The official site of Sri K. Pattabhi Jois and his Ashtanga Yoga school in Mysore, India. ... Tim Miller will represent Guruji at the Krishnamacharya Yoga Festival. ...
www.ayri.org/

66. **Yoga Circle - Yoga in the Iyengar tradition for 19 years!**
Welcome to the website for the Yoga Circle. We are an Iyengar yoga studio located in Chicago's River North area. We offer introductory ...
yogacircle.com/

67. **Keyboard Yoga: Learning to Breathe**
... YOU ARE HERE: iVILLAGE > Keyboard Yoga. [an error occurred while processing this directive].
www.ivillage.com/fitness/tools/yoga/

68. **Focal Point Yoga**
Yoga improves mood and tones the body. ... FEEDBACK - WE'D LOVE TO GET FEEDBACK ON YOUR DREAM YOGA STUDIO... ASK FOR WHAT YOU WANT AND YOU MIGHT JUST GET IT!
www.focalpointyoga.com/

69. **It_s Yoga San Francisco**
Celebrating 13 years It's Yoga was founded in San Francisco by Larry Schultz in 1990. ... Larry's Ashtanga Yoga practice of 23 years has given him a refined style. ...
www.itsyoga.com/

70. **Yoga Tree San Francisco: San Francisco_s Premier Yoga Center**
Yoga Tree: San Francisco's Premier Yoga Center. ... If you are new to yoga, check out our Yoga 101 workshop to help you get started. Take your Yoga to a new level! ...
www.yogatreesf.com/

71. **OM yoga center for vinyasa hatha yoga classes in New York City**
OM yoga center, in New York City's Flatiron district, offers asana yoga classes in the vinyasa or flowing style, a vigorous style of hatha yoga. New York City - Center offers asana classes in the vinyasa style of hatha yoga. Includes schedules,...
www.omyoga.com/

72. **Integral Yoga Institute of New York (Hatha)**
Integral Yoga Institute offers a broad array of classes, courses, and workshops in hatha yoga, stress management, deep relaxation, meditation, and more to ...
www.integralyogany.org/

73. **Yoga Fitness**
Iyengar yoga classes and workshops for all levels. Site includes instructor profiles.
www.iyoga.com/yf/

74. **internetyoga**

A virtual shrine to teachers and teachings of yoga. A cyberspace ashram, a conscious touch point, an electronic ...

www.internetyoga.com/

75. **Bryan Kest_s Power Yoga**

Bryan Kest's Power Yoga specializes in Ashtanga (power) yoga classes workshops, retreats, videos and yoga products.

www.poweryoga.com/

76. **Yoga, INTERNATIONALYOGAFEDERTION, World Union of Yoga**

INTERNATIONAL YOGA FEDERATION. World Governing Body of Yoga. ... Federacion Internacional de Yoga en castellano. International Yoga Federation. Lists the national and continental yoga organizations.

fiy.yoganet.org/

77. **Recovery and ExTension Yoga - A free yoga educational resource by...**

Extension & Recovery Yoga by Sam Dworkis. Free for yoga students and teachers. Yoga for health, fitness, recovery. Safe yoga exercise...

www.extensionyoga.com/

78. **Cardiac Yoga**

What is Cardiac Yoga? The Cardiac Yoga ® Program ... Training Programs. M. Mala Cunningham, Ph.D. Founder & Director of Cardiac Yoga. M. Mala...

www.cardiacyoga.com/

79. **Wai Lana Yoga : Videos - Music - Mats - Asanas - Meditation ...**

Find out why millions of people are raving about the health benefits offered by Wai Lana yoga. Lifestyle. Yoga for beginner, Yoga kid, Yoga Mats. ...

www.wailana.com/

80. **Phoenix Rising Yoga Therapy**

Phoenix Rising School of Yoga and Movement Therapy offers trainings in leading-edge, body-mind healing practice. ... Yoga Teacher Training. ...

www.pryt.com/

81. **The Yoga Vasistha**

The Yoga Vasistha offers clarity to the disallusioned, and reconcilation of spirituality and science for rigorous thinkers. ... An Index. to the Yoga Vasistha. ...

www.yogavasistha.com/

82. **Kriya Yoga Institute**

Articles and information about Kriya, as taught by Paramahamsa Hariharananda and his gurus.

www.kriya.org/

83. **A Yoga Life.. T-Shirts, Jewelry, Maternity products, Yerba Mate**

Yoga & Meditation Tools. Healthy Living Appliances. Framed Yoga Art/Prints.

www.ayogalife.com/

84. **Yoga Oasis, Hawaii Big Island retreat center**

Yoga Oasis on Hawaii's Big Island is a retreat center located in the rainforest. ... Come to Yoga Oasis and experience a paradigm shift of your consciousness. ...

www.yogaoasis.org/

85. **"Yoga Shop" yogamats, yoga mats, yoga props, and more yoga goodies**

Union Yoga Centre UNION YOGA. Click to Listen. Find a Pose. Ask the Expert. New to Yoga?

www.theyogashop.co.uk/

86. **HRIH: Yoga Sutras of Patanjali. International Language**

The Internet archive of the Yoga Sutras of Patanjali, is an all in one page, with different interpretations translated in different languages. ...

hrih.hypermart.net/patanjali/

87. **Yoga Point.com - Online Yoga Resource For Everyone**

Yoga Positions, Meditation, Pranayama, Yoga for treatment of diseases, personality development, stress management, Yoga for Kids, Yoga for women. ...

www.yogavidyadham.org/

88. **Temple of Kriya Yoga!**

The Temple of Kriya Yoga is a center of spiritual study for people of any religion. ... horoscope, Kriology, Seminary. Meditation, om symbol, Yogi. Meditate, Catalog, Yoga.

www.yogakriya.org/

89. **Bread, coffee, chocolate, yoga**
BREADCOFFEECHOCOLATEYOGA.
home.earthlink.net/~frelkins/

90. **Introduction to Yoga - IndiaExpress**
An Introduction to Yoga. The word Yoga automatically calls to mind Sage "Patanjali" the founder and father of Yoga. He ... Hatha Yoga. Overview of the history, origins, benefits and practice of Yoga. From the IndiaExpress newspaper.
indiaexpress.com/mind/yoga/

91. **Satyananda Yoga**
A system of yoga developed by Swami Satyananda Saraswati and his lineage, which incorporates practices...
www.satyananda.net/

92. **yoga vermont**
Astanga yoga studio in Burlington, Vermont USA offering instruction, workshops and yoga clothing (including City Lights), yoga books, ashtanga videos, yoga ...
www.yogavermont.com/

93. **Richard Freeman_'s The Yoga Workshop**
Yoga class and schedule information for Richard Freeman's The Yoga Workshop, as well as a variety of articles by Richard on Ashtanga yoga and yoga philosophy ...
www.yogaworkshop.com/

94. **Yoga Health Secrets: relaxation, stress-relief, health and inner**
Yoga Health Secrets is a comprehensive guide to yogic techniques for happiness and good health, with onsite information and a new eBook. A guide to yoga techniques for happiness, relaxation and good health, with onsite information and...
www.yogahealthsecrets.com/

95. **Texas Yoga**
Discover Texas Yoga. Attend the annual Texas Yoga Retreat, learn about Yoga Teacher Training, and visit our statewide Directory of Yoga Teachers
www.texasyoga.com/

96. **HATHA-YOGA.com.ar**
World_>_Español_>_Sociedad_>_Religión_>_Yoga
www.hatha-yoga.com.ar/

97. **Yoga Clothes and Gear from The Yoga Place**

The Yoga Place - your online source for apparel and supplies including books, DVDs, mats and kits. The Yoga Place. ... Yoga Apparel. Women's. ...

www.the-yoga-place.com/

98. **Yoga for Beginners**

This website provides basic information for beginning yoga practitioners as well as useful books, tapes, and internet websites. Welcome to Yoga for Beginners. ...

www.mv.com/ipusers/howell/ejh/

99. **Yoga - Suite101.com**

Begin to unravel the mystery of yoga here. ... Yoga Note: This topic has been archived and is available for Adoption! Contact Member Sevices for more information. ...

www.suite101.com/welcome.cfm/yoga

100. **RiverMaya**

YOGA -

Everything you have always wanted to know about yoga. A complete online guide to yoga practices, exercises, meditation and more. Guide to yoga practices, including exercises, meditation and breathing.

www.rivermaya.com/

101. **Everyday Yoga**

Tunnel Syndrome. These, and more "Desktop Yoga" exercises are available to license for use within your company Intranet. Contact ...

www.mydailyyoga.com/yoga/everyday_yoga.html

102. **What is meditation**

The Integral yoga approach is simultaneous application of a little of all stages together. ... Hand Woven Yoga Mats. Hand Woven Yoga Mat. Understand the concept and discover methods to make meditation a joyful experience. Explore various...

www.healthandyoga.com/meditation.html

103. **Brefoot yoga co. Yoga Supplies to Inspire the Practice of Yoga**

Offering unique products to inspire the practice of Yoga: yoga mat bags, yoga mats, eye pillows, practice rugs, straps, books, shirts and more. ...

www.barefootyoga.com/

104. **The Yoga Sanctuary, Toronto Yoga Studios in Central Downtown**
The Yoga Sanctuary with two yoga studios in Toronto has beginner, intermediate and advanced ashtanga yoga, hatha yoga, kripalu yoga, kids yoga, pre-natal yoga ...
www.theyogasanctuary.net/

105. **Yoga Works**
Classes in Ashtanga, flow, Iyengar, pre- and post-natal, and yoga for kids. Instructor bios. Workshops...
www.yogaworks.com/

106. **Destiny Yoga Supplies;Yoga Mats: Yoga clothing, yoga clothes**
Destiny Yoga Supplies;Specializing in yoga mats, yoga clothing, yoga pants, equipment and products. ...
www.destiny-yoga-supplies.com/

107. **Yoga is Youthfulness Studio in Mountain View, California**
Yoga is Youthfulness (YiY) in Mountain View, California, offers daily drop-in hatha yoga classes, including Iyengar, Bikram, Ashtanga and Vinyasa flow yoga; we ...
www.yogaisyouth.com/

108. **Yoga Classes - Hatha Yoga, Kundalini Yoga, Ashtanga Yoga**
Yoga Yoga Austin, home | studios | classes | new to yoga?
ww.yogayoga.net/